Guide to Network Security

Michael E. Whitman

Herbert J. Mattord

David Mackey

Andrew Green

COURSE TECHNOLOGY
CENGAGE Learning®

Australia • Brazil • Japan • Korea • Mexico • Singapore • Spain • United Kingdom • United States

COURSE TECHNOLOGY
CENGAGE Learning

Guide to Network Security
**Michael Whitman, Herbert Mattord,
David Mackey, Andrew Green**

Vice President, Careers & Computing:
Dave Garza

Executive Editor: Stephen Helba

Director, Development, Careers &
Computing: Marah Bellegarde

Senior Product Manager: Michelle
Ruelos Cannistraci

Developmental Editor: Kent Williams

Editorial Assistant: Jennifer Wheaton

Director, Market Development:
Lisa Lysne

Market Development Manager:
Mark Linton

Marketing Coordinator:
Benjamin Genise

Director, Brand Management:
Jason Sakos

Brand Manager: Kristin McNary

Production Director: Wendy Troeger

Production Manager: Andrew Crouth

Content Project Manager: Brooke
Greenhouse

Art Director: Jack Pendleton

Cover Image: © iStockphoto

For product information and technology assistance, contact us at
Cengage Learning Customer & Sales Support, 1-800-354-9706

For permission to use material from this text or product,
submit all requests online at **cengage.com/permissions**
Further permissions questions can be emailed to
permissionrequest@cengage.com

Library of Congress Control Number: 2012942876

ISBN-13: 978-0-8400-2422-0

ISBN-10: 0-8400-2422-3

Course Technology
20 Channel Center Street
Boston, MA 02210
USA

Cengage Learning is a leading provider of customized learning
solutions with office locations around the globe, including
Singapore, the United Kingdom, Australia, Mexico, Brazil, and
Japan. Locate your local office at: **international.cengage.com/region**

Cengage Learning products are represented in Canada by Nelson
Education, Ltd.

For your lifelong learning solutions, visit
www.cengage.com/coursetechnology

Purchase any of our products at your local college store or at our
preferred online store **www.cengagebrain.com**

Visit our corporate website at **cengage.com**.

Printed in the United States of America
1 2 3 4 5 6 7 16 15 14 13 12

Brief Contents

Table of Contents

Introduction

This book provides a broad review of the field of network security, background on related elements, and enough detail to facilitate understanding of the topics. It covers the terminology of the field and also provides a guide for hands-on lab education in network security topics.

Approach

To present a textbook that is both current and pedagogically useful, the material has been organized to introduce concepts in a logical sequence and provide learning support elements in each chapter. These include:

Chapter Scenarios Each chapter opens with a short story that follows activities at a fictional company as it encounters some of the issues of network security.

Hands-On Learning At the end of each chapter, students will find a Chapter Summary and Review Questions as well as Hands-On Projects, which allow them to examine the information security arena outside the classroom. Using these projects, students can research, analyze, and write about various topics so as to reinforce learning objectives and deepen their understanding of the text.

Features:

As a new edition, this text contains the best of the previous texts (*Guide to Firewalls and Network Security*, 2nd ed., and *Web Security*) along with a new approach and structure more conducive to the instruction of network and Web security. Specifically, this edition includes:

- **Enhanced Sections on Information, Network, and Web Security**—A large portion of *Guide to Firewalls and Network Security* is dedicated to firewall operations, with a simplified foundation in information and network security. This edition further expands on network theory content, which allows it to be used as a stand-alone text or as a follow-on text to a detailed Introduction to Information Security course that uses a text like *Principles of Information Security*.

- **Reorganized Chapter on Security Policy and Standards**—This version streamlines the coverage of policy as a guide for the use of security technologies; it also revises the discussion of modern security standards by reducing the number being discussed and focusing on those having the most impact on the topic of network security.

- **Improved and Streamlined Section on Network and Web Security Technologies**—This text seeks to provide coverage of firewall material in a coherent approach that provides an overall flow while appropriately integrating VPN and encryption discussions without missing coverage of relevant content.

- **Incorporated Overlapping Material**—The two precursor texts from which this book is drawn, *Guide to Firewalls and Network Security* and *Web Security,* have several chapters in common. By combining the best of each, this text, with enhanced coverage of network security issues, encryption, intrusion detection, standards, and assessment (testing), offers students a comprehensive approach without the redundancy coming from the use of multiple texts in a single course.

Other Improvements Include:

- New chapter on the role of the network security professional
- Enhanced chapter on contingency planning (incident response, disaster recovery, and business continuity)
- Increased material on data communications and networking as the foundation of network security
- New material on wireless security and enhanced integration of Web security
- Organization of material to allow hands-on application in a network security lab environment

Author Team

The established author team of Michael Whitman and Herbert Mattord joined forces with security consulting executive David Mackey and Systems and Web Administrator Andy Green to develop this text. Each has brought his individual experience to bear on the most challenging aspect of information security—protecting networks and Web resources—by merging knowledge gained from the world of academic study with practical experience from the world of business.

Michael Whitman, Ph.D., CISM, CISSP is a professor of information security and assurance in the Information Systems Department, Michael J. Coles College of Business at Kennesaw State University, Kennesaw, Georgia, where he is the director of the KSU Center for Information Security Education (*infosec.kennesaw.edu*). Dr. Whitman is an active researcher in information security, fair and responsible use policies, and computer-use ethics. He currently teaches graduate and undergraduate courses in information security. He has published articles in the top journals in his field, including *Information Systems Research*, the *Communications of the ACM*, *Information and Management*, the *Journal of International Business Studies*, and the *Journal of Computer Information Systems*. He is a member of the Association for Computing Machinery and the Association for Information Systems. Under Dr. Whitman's leadership, Kennesaw State University has been selected by the National Security Agency and the Department of Homeland Security as a National Center of Academic Excellence in Information Assurance Education, with coursework that has been reviewed by national-level information assurance subject matter experts and determined to meet national training standards for information systems security professionals. Dr. Whitman is also the coauthor of *Principles of Information Security*, 4th edition; *Management of Information Security*, 3nd edition; *Readings and Cases in the Management of Information Security*; *Readings and Cases in Information Security: Law and Ethics; The Hands-On Information Security Lab Manual*, 3rd edition; *Roadmap to the Management of Information Security for IT and Information Security Professionals*; *Guide to Firewalls and VPNs*, 3rd edition; *Guide to Firewalls and Network Security*, 2nd edition; and *Principles of Incident Response and Disaster Recovery*, all published by Course Technology.

Herbert Mattord, MBA, Ph.D. (ABD), CISM, CISSP completed 24 years of IT industry experience as an application developer, database administrator, project manager, and information security practitioner before joining the faculty of Kennesaw State University in 2002. Dr. Mattord is an assistant professor of information security and assurance and the coordinator for the bachelor of business administration in Information Security and Assurance program. He is the operations manager of the KSU Center for Information Security Education and Awareness (*infosec.kennesaw.edu*) as well as the coordinator for the KSU certificate in Information Security and Assurance. During his career as an IT practitioner, he has been an adjunct professor at Kennesaw State University; Southern Polytechnic State University in Marietta, Georgia; Austin Community College in Austin, Texas; and Texas State University: San Marcos. He currently teaches undergraduate courses in information security, data communications, local area networks, database technology, project management, systems analysis and design, and information resources management and policy. He was formerly the manager of corporate information technology security at Georgia-Pacific Corporation, where much of the practical knowledge found in this textbook was acquired. Professor Mattord is also the coauthor of *Principles of Information Security*, 4th edition; *Management of Information Security*, 3nd edition; *Readings and Cases in the Management of Information Security*; *Readings and Cases in Information Security: Law and Ethics; The Hands-On Information Security Lab Manual*, 3rd edition; *Roadmap to the Management of Information Security for IT and Information Security Professionals*; *Guide to Firewalls and VPNs*, 3rd edition; *Guide to Firewalls and Network Security*, 2nd edition; and *Principles of Incident Response and Disaster Recovery*, all published by Course Technology.

David Mackey, CISSP, GCIH is the director of ArcSight's security operations consulting practice. David has over 12 years of information security experience, working in security policy development, IT auditing, threat intelligence collection and analysis, security operations, and incident response with IBM, IT-ISAC, HP, and ArcSight. Mr. Mackey is part of the adjunct faculty with the Interdisciplinary Telecommunications Program (ITP) at the University of Colorado at Boulder, where he teaches graduate courses in network security. He is the author of *Web Security for Network and System Administrators*, published by Course Technology. Prior to his IT career, Mr. Mackey served as an intelligence specialist in the U.S. Army.

Andrew Green, MSIS is a lecturer in information security and assurance in the Information Systems Department of Michael J. Coles College of Business at Kennesaw State University, Kennesaw,

Georgia. Mr. Green has over 10 years of experience in information security. Prior to entering academia full time, he worked as an information security consultant, focusing primarily on the needs of small and medium-sized businesses. Prior to that, he worked in the healthcare IT field, where he developed and supported transcription interfaces for medical facilities throughout the United States. Mr. Green is also a full-time PhD student at Nova Southeastern University, where he is studying Information Systems with a concentration in Information Security. He is the coauthor of *Guide to Firewalls and VPNs*, 3rd edition, published by Course Technology.

Structure

Guide to Network Security is a developmental extension of two previous texts: Whitman and Mattord's *Guide to Firewalls and Network Security: With Intrusion Detection and VPNs*, 2nd edition, and Mackey's *Web Security for Network and Systems Administrators*. This textbook is organized into 12 chapters:

Chapter 1: Introduction to Information Security This chapter provides a primer on information security and an understanding of the terminology used throughout the text and the discipline. This chapter also presents the threats and attacks a technology user can expect to encounter while dealing with network security and firewalls. The chapter concludes with an examination of the need for a policy-driven approach coupled with an understanding of modern security standards organizations like ISO, NIST, and the IETF.

Chapter 2: Introduction to Networking This chapter, on the foundations of data communications and network security, begins with an introduction to modern networking fundamentals and exposure to the security issues associated with modern data communications technologies. The chapter examines network architectures, media, and technologies. It also examines the standards and protocols associated with data communications and networking, focusing on the two most relevant structures: the OSI reference model and TCP/IP. Using a layer-by-layer approach, the chapter moves through the structure of the OSI reference model, examining the security components of each stage.

Chapter 3: Cryptography This chapter serves as a primer on encryption systems by looking at the history of encryption and the basic principles of cryptography. It surveys popular cryptographic tools and the major protocols used for security communications. Finally, various attacks on cryptosystems are explored.

Chapter 4: Firewall Technologies and Administration This chapter explains how firewalls work, outlines the categories of firewalls, and explains how firewalls are used in an organization. It also examines rule sets used to configure firewalls, with an expansion of the study of firewall configuration.

Chapter 5: Network Authentication and Remote Access Using VPN This chapter examines authentication, authorization, and auditing; modern access control approaches and methodologies; and security issues associated with administering access controls. Specifically, the chapter examines how VPNs support network access control and security issues in deploying VPNs.

Chapter 6: Network Monitoring and Intrusion Detection and Prevention Systems This chapter begins an overview of network traffic and explains the anatomy of a network packet. It then transitions from network monitoring to Intrusion Detection and Prevention Systems (IDPS), focusing on their classifications, use, and deployment. Specific issues associated with IDPS are addressed, including product selection, deployment, and response strategies.

Chapter 7: Wireless Network Security This chapter continues the coverage of encryption-based network security technologies by examining in detail the implementation, configuration, and use of wireless protection mechanisms. The chapter also examines methods to secure wireless technologies and contemporary security issues associated with those technologies.

Chapter 8: Security of Web Applications This chapter examines the broad topics associated with Internet and Web communication, including specific protocols, programming languages, and other technologies. Critical attacks associated with Web servers are presented, along with recommendations on how best to address security vulnerabilities in these systems.

Chapter 9: Network Vulnerability Assessment This chapter discusses the standards, methods, tools, and techniques employed by network security professionals to evaluate the security of network security equipment, data servers, and other modern information systems. The chapter also provides an overview of the common vulnerability assessment methods. An emphasis on their use in remediating problems completes the chapter.

Chapter 10: Auditing, Monitoring, and Logging This chapter discusses system auditing and how systems record activities within the system. Data analysis of logs is then examined in the context of Security Information and Event Management (SIEM) and its overall tie-in to monitoring security within IT environments. This chapter also examines formal audit programs and how they relate to network security.

Chapter 11: Contingency Planning and Network Incident Response This chapter begins by reviewing the need for business contingency plans and the steps involved in developing, implementing, and testing those plans. It then discusses the role and responsibilities of the network security professional in incident response, which include planning, reacting, responding, and recovery operations.

Chapter 12: Digital Forensics This chapter examines the functions, tasks, and responsibilities of conducting digital forensics. The impact of legal and regulatory requirements on the forensics process is also reviewed. How to conduct and administer a digital forensics process is discussed in the context of an organization's decision to remediate the event and/or pursue prosecution.

Instructor's Materials

A variety of teaching tools support this textbook and offer many options to enhance the classroom learning experience.

Instructor Resources CD—All the supplements available with this book are provided to the instructor on a single CD-ROM (ISBN: 978-0-8400-2423-7) and can be found online at the textbook's Web site. Please visit *login.cengage.com* and log in to access instructor-specific resources.

Electronic Instructor's Manual—The Instructor's Manual includes suggestions and strategies for using this text, such as suggestions for lecture topics. It also includes answers to the Review Questions and suggested solutions to the Real-World Exercises at the end of each chapter.

Figure Files—Figure Files allow instructors to create their own presentations using figures taken from the text.

PowerPoint Presentations—This book comes with Microsoft PowerPoint slides for each chapter. These are a teaching aid that can be used for classroom presentation, made available to students on the network for chapter review, or printed for classroom distribution. Instructors can add their own slides for additional topics they introduce to the class.

ExamView—ExamView® is a powerful objective-based test generator that enables instructors to create paper, LAN, or Web-based tests from testbanks designed specifically for their Course Technology text. Instructors can utilize the ultra-efficient QuickTest Wizard to create tests in less than five minutes by taking advantage of Course Technology's question banks, or they can customize their own exams from scratch.

To access the instructor resources and additional course materials, please visit *www.cengagebrain.com*. At the *cengagebrain.com* home page, search for the ISBN of your title (from the back cover of your book) using the search box at the top of the page. This will take you to the product page where these resources can be found.

Lab Manual
Course Technology has developed a lab manual to accompany this and other books: *The Hands-On Information Security Lab Manual, 3rd edition*. The lab manual provides hands-on security exercises on footprinting, enumeration, and firewall configuration as well as a number of detailed exercises and cases that supplement the book as a laboratory component or as in-class projects.

Lab Manual: 978-1-4354-4156-9

Information Security Community Site
Stay secure with the Information Security Community Site! Connect with students, professors, and professionals from around the world, and stay on top of this ever-changing field.

Visit *www.cengage.com/community/infosec*

- Download resources such as instructional videos and labs.
- Ask authors, professors, and students the questions that are on your mind in our discussion forums.
- See up-to-date news, videos, and articles.
- Read author blogs.
- Listen to podcasts on the latest information security topics.

Coping with Change on the Web
Sooner or later, all the specific Web-based resources mentioned throughout the rest of this book will go stale or be replaced by newer information. In some cases, the URLs you find here may lead you to their replacements; in other cases, the URLs will lead nowhere, leaving you with the dreaded 404 error message: "File not found."

When that happens, please don't give up! There's always a way to find what you want on the Web, if you're willing to invest some time and energy. To begin with, most large or complex Web sites offer a search engine. As long as you can get to the site itself, you can use this tool to help you find what you need.

Don't be afraid to use general search tools like *www.google.com*, *www.bing.com*, or some other search engine to find related information. Although certain standards bodies may offer the most precise and specific information about their standards online, there are plenty of third-party sources of information, training, and assistance in this area as well. The bottom line is: If you can't find something where the book says it lives, start looking around. It's got to be around there somewhere!

Visit our World Wide Web Site Additional materials designed especially for you might be available for your course on the World Wide Web. Go to *www.course.com* and search for this book title periodically for more details.

Acknowledgments

The authors would like to thank their families for their support and understanding for the many hours dedicated to this project, hours taken away, in many cases, from family activities. Special thanks to Carola Mattord, Ph.D., professor of English at Kennesaw State University. Her reviews of early drafts and suggestions for keeping the writing focused on the students resulted in a more readable manuscript.

Contributors

Many people and organizations have contributed materials that were used in the preparation of this textbook, and we have acknowledged those contributions in each instance. We would like to especially thank the National Institute of Standards and Technology as the source of many references, tables, figures, and other content used throughout the textbook.

Reviewers

We are indebted to the following individuals for their contributions of perceptive feedback on the initial proposal, the project outline, and the chapter-by-chapter reviews of the text:

- Scott Domowicz, Erie Institute of Technology, Erie, Pennsylvania
- Rick Blazek, Robert Morris University, Springfield, Illinois
- Angela Herring, Wilson Community College, Wilson, North Carolina
- Guy Garrett, Gulf Coast Community College, Panama City, Florida

Special Thanks

The authors wish to thank the editorial and production teams at Course Technology. Their diligent and professional efforts greatly enhanced the final product:

- Michelle Ruelos Cannistraci, Senior Product Manager
- Kent Williams, Development Editor
- Steve Helba, Executive Editor
- Brooke Baker, Content Project Manager

In addition, several professional and commercial organizations and individuals have aided the development of the textbook by providing information and inspiration, and the authors wish to acknowledge their contribution:

- Tenable Network Security, Inc.
- Our colleagues in the Department of Information Systems, Kennesaw State University
- Professor Amy Woszczynski, interim chair of the Department of Information Systems, Kennesaw State University
- Dr. Kathy Schwaig, dean of the Michael J. Coles College of Business, Kennesaw State University

Our Commitment

The authors are committed to serving the needs of the adopters and readers of this book. We would be pleased and honored to receive feedback on the textbook and its supporting materials. You can contact us through "Ask the Author" on the Information Security Community Site. You can reach that interactive Web portal by going to *www.cengage.com/community/infosec* and, under the Community tab, selecting "Ask the Author."

chapter 1

Introduction to Information Security

The user's going to pick dancing pigs over security every time. — Bruce Schneier

Upon completion of this material, you should be able to:

- Explain the relationships among the component parts of information security, especially network security
- Define the key terms and critical concepts of information and network security
- Explain the business need for information and network security
- Identify the threats posed to information and network security, as well as the common attacks associated with those threats
- Distinguish between *threats* to information from within systems and *attacks* against information from within systems
- Describe the organizational roles of information and network security professionals
- Define management's role in the development, maintenance, and enforcement of information security policy, standards, practices, procedures, and guidelines
- Discuss how an organization institutionalizes policies, standards, and practices using education, training, and awareness programs

Learning to Crawl

Noah Atwater and Paige Davis have been working in the IT field for almost five years. They are members of the information technology (IT) staff at Elway Business Services, Inc.—a company that provides accounting and financial services to small businesses—and are responsible for the company's modest IT environment. Noah is responsible for the Windows servers, and Paige takes care of the Linux servers and network devices. Both are talented administrators and motivated workers.

In recent years, EBS has been moving more and more of its management and accounting services to the Web in order to attract more small businesses. A key aspect of this strategy has been enabling credit card transactions via the EBS Web site, which allows the company to provide quick service to its customers. However, the credit card companies, through the Payment Card Industry (PCI) Security Standards Council, require EBS and its card processing company to adhere to guidelines outlined in the council's Data Security Standard (PCI-DSS).

Noah and Paige have just met with EBS's chief information officer, Jeff Mobley. In order to meet the PCI-DSS requirements, Jeff is hiring a chief information security officer (CISO) to build the overall security program. Additionally, Jeff has asked that Noah and Paige immediately start designing the various network security program components necessary to meet PCI-DSS requirements. There's no time to wait for the new CISO.

When Noah and Paige left the meeting, they exchanged worried glances. Although they are EBS's most senior IT staff members, they have not spent much time worrying about an overall security program. With the constant technological demands of EBS's customers and staff, the IT department has barely kept the company's desktops, servers, networks, and applications running smoothly. The IT staff has had no governing program for building and reviewing security policies, identifying vulnerabilities, implementing controls, monitoring the day-to-day security, and responding to any suspicious activities. Noah and Paige have their work cut out for them.

Introduction

Network security is a critical component in the day-to-day IT operations of nearly every organization in business today. Before learning how to plan, design, and implement network security, it is important to understand the larger topic of information security and how the components of network security fit into this topic. Additionally, the field of information security has matured in the last 20 years and become so large that those who don't understand these concepts risk being unable to make the best business decisions regarding network security. This chapter offers an overview of the entire field of information security and its effects on network security.

What Is Information Security?

Information security (InfoSec) is the protection of information and its critical elements, including the systems and hardware that use, store, and transmit that information. Information security includes the broad areas of information security management, computer and data security, and network security (the primary topic of this book). To protect information and its related systems, organizations must integrate the following security layers:

- **Network security**—The protection of networking components, connections, and contents, which is the primary focus of this textbook

- **Physical security**—The protection of the physical items or areas of an organization from unauthorized access and misuse

- **Personal security**—The protection of the people who are authorized to access the organization and its operations

- **Operations security**—The protection of the details of a particular operation or series of activities

- **Communications security**—The protection of an organization's communications media, technology, and content

Information Security Terminology

This book uses a number of terms and concepts that are essential to any discussion of information security. Several of these terms are illustrated in Figure 1-1.

- **Access**—A subject or object's ability to use, manipulate, modify, or affect another subject or object. Authorized users have legal access to a system. Access controls regulate this access.

- **Asset**—The organizational resource that is being protected. An asset can be "logical," such as a Web site, information, or data, or it can be "physical," such as a person, computer system, or other tangible object. Assets, and particularly information assets, are the focus of security efforts; they are what those efforts are attempting to protect.

- **Attack**—An intentional or unintentional act that can cause damage to or otherwise compromise the information and/or the systems that support it. Attacks can be active or passive, intentional or unintentional, and direct or indirect. Someone casually reading sensitive information not intended for his or her use is a passive attack. A hacker attempting to break into an information system is an intentional attack. A lightning strike that causes a fire in a building is an unintentional attack. A direct attack is a hacker using a personal computer to break into a system. An indirect attack is a hacker compromising a system and using it to attack other systems—for example, as part of a botnet (slang for robot network). This group of compromised computers, running software of the attacker's choosing, can operate autonomously or under the attacker's direct control to attack systems and steal user information or

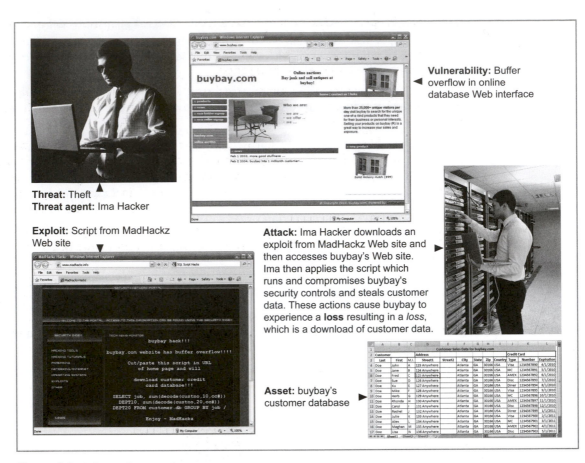

Figure 1-1 Information security terms
© Cengage Learning 2013 (Photo in the top left and right are © iStockphoto)

to conduct distributed denial-of-service attacks. Direct attacks originate from the threat itself. Indirect attacks originate from a compromised system or resource that is malfunctioning or working under the control of a threat.

- **Control, safeguard,** or **countermeasure**—Security mechanisms, policies, or procedures that can successfully counterattack, reduce risk, resolve vulnerabilities, and otherwise improve the security within an organization. The various levels and types of controls are discussed more fully in the following chapters.

- **Exploit**—A technique used to compromise a system. This term can be a verb or a noun. Threat agents may attempt to exploit a system or other information asset by using it illegally for their personal gain. Alternatively, an exploit can be a documented process used to take advantage of a vulnerability or exposure, usually in software, that is either inherent in the software or created by the attacker. Exploits make use of existing software tools or custom-made software components.

- **Exposure**—A condition or state of being exposed. In information security, exposure exists when a vulnerability known to an attacker is present.

- **Intellectual Property**—Often referred to as IP, intellectual property is defined as works of the mind, such as inventions, literature, art, logos, names, symbols, and other creative works. IP is protected by law, and any use, whether or not it requires payments or permission, should be properly credited.

- **Loss**—A single instance of an information asset suffering damage, unintended or unauthorized modification, or disclosure. When an organization's information is stolen, it has suffered a loss.

- **Protection profile** or **security posture**—The entire set of controls and safeguards (including policy, education, training and awareness, and technology) that the organization implements (or fails to implement) to protect the asset. The term "security program" also gets used for this, but it often includes managerial aspects of security, including planning, personnel, and subordinate programs.

- **Risk**—The probability that something unwanted will happen. Organizations must minimize risk to match their **risk appetite**—the quantity and nature of risk the organization is willing to accept.

- **Subjects** and **objects**—A computer can be either the **subject** of an attack—an agent entity used to conduct the attack—or the **object** of an attack—the target entity, as shown in Figure 1-2. A computer can be both the subject and object of an attack when, for example, it is compromised by an attack (object) and is then used to attack other systems (subject).

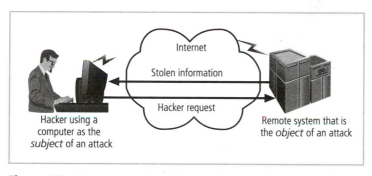

Figure 1-2   Computer as the subject and object of an attack
© Cengage Learning 2013

- **Threat**—A category of objects, persons, or other entities that presents a danger to an asset. Threats are always present and can be purposeful or undirected. For example, hackers purposefully threaten unprotected information systems, whereas severe storms incidentally threaten buildings and their contents.

- **Threat agent**—The specific instance of a threat or a particular component of a threat. For example, all hackers in the world present a collective threat, and Kevin Mitnick, who was convicted for hacking into phone systems, is a specific threat agent. Likewise, a lightning strike, hailstorm, or tornado is a threat agent that is part of the threat of severe storms.

- **Vulnerability**—Weaknesses or faults in a system or protection mechanism that open it to the possibility of attack or damage. Examples of vulnerabilities include a flaw in a software package, an unprotected system port, and an unlocked door. **Well-known vulnerabilities** are those that have been examined, documented, and published; others remain latent (or undiscovered).

Critical Characteristics of Information

The value of information comes from the characteristics it possesses. When a characteristic of information changes, the value of that information either increases or, more commonly, decreases. Although information security professionals and end users share an understanding of the characteristics of information, tensions can arise when the need to secure information from threats conflicts with the end users' need for unhindered access to the information. The following are important terms describing the characteristics of information:

- **Availability** enables authorized users—persons or computer systems—to access information without interference or obstruction, and to receive it in the required format.

- **Accuracy** means that information is free from mistakes or errors and has the value that the end user expects it to have.

- **Authenticity** is the quality or state of being genuine or original rather than a reproduction or fabrication. Information is authentic when it is the information that was originally created, placed, stored, or transferred.

- **Confidentiality** is the protection of information from disclosure or exposure to unauthorized individuals or systems. This means that *only* those with the rights and privileges to access information are able to do so. To protect any breach in the confidentiality of information, a number of measures can be used:

  - Information classification
  - Secure document storage
  - Application of general security policies
  - Education of information custodians and end users

- **Data owners** are those responsible for the security and use of a particular set of information. They are usually members of senior management and could be CIOs. The data owners usually determine the level of data classification associated with the data. The data owners work with subordinate managers to oversee the day-to-day administration of the data.

- **Data custodians** work directly with data owners and are responsible for the storage, maintenance, and protection of the information. Depending on the size of the organization, the custodian may be a dedicated position, such as the CISO, or it may be an additional responsibility of a systems administrator or other technology manager. The duties of a data custodian often include overseeing data storage and backups, implementing the specific procedures and policies laid out in the security policies and plans, and reporting to the data owner.

- **Data users** are end users who work with the information to perform their daily jobs supporting the mission of the organization, and who therefore share the responsibility for data security.

- **Integrity** means that information remains whole, complete, and uncorrupted. The integrity of information is threatened when the information is exposed to corruption, damage, destruction, or other disruption of its authentic state.

- **Utility** is the quality or state of having value for some purpose or end. To have utility, information must be in a format meaningful to the end user. For example, U.S. Census data can be overwhelming and difficult to understand; however, the data, when properly interpreted, reveals information about the voters in a district; which political parties they belong to; their race, gender, and age; and so on.

- **Possession** is the ownership or control of some object or item. Information is said to be in one's possession if one obtains it, independent of format or other characteristics.

- **Privacy** means that information is used in accordance with the legal requirements mandated for employees, partners, and customers. In the rush to protect data from theft or mischief, organizations often trample the rights of individuals. For example, customers may not want a company to use their names and personal information for marketing purposes. A comprehensive security strategy should take into account these privacy concerns.

Security Models

An information security model allows professionals to map abstract security goals to concrete ideas and blueprints for how to implement proper security controls. Current information security models evolved from a concept known as the C.I.A. triad, which was developed by the computer security industry. It is typically displayed as a triangle, as shown in Figure 1-3. The **C.I.A. triad** has been the industry standard for computer security since the development of the mainframe. It is based on three characteristics of information that form the foundation for many security programs: confidentiality, integrity, and availability.

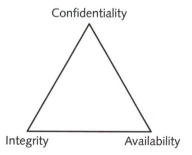

Figure 1-3   C.I.A. triad
© Cengage Learning 2013

These three characteristics are still important today, but the C.I.A. triad no longer adequately represents all the key security concepts that are used to address the constantly changing environment of the computer industry. Today's evolving threats—accidental or intentional damage or destruction, theft, unintended or unauthorized modification, and other misapplication—have prompted the development of a more robust security model that addresses the complexities of the current information security environment.

The definition of information security presented earlier in this chapter is based in part on a document called the U.S. National Training Standard for Information Security Professionals NSTISSI No. 4011, which was published by the U.S. Committee on National Security Systems (CNSS).[1] This document presents a comprehensive model for information security, known as the McCumber Cube, which is becoming a standard for the discussion of security of information systems.

Created by John McCumber in 1991, the **McCumber Cube** provides a graphical description of the architectural approach widely used in computer and information security.[2] As shown in Figure 1-4, it is a representation of a 3 x 3 x 3 cube, with the 27 cells representing areas that must be addressed to secure today's information systems. For example, the intersection between the technology, integrity, and storage areas requires a control or safeguard that addresses the need to use *technology* to protect the *integrity* of information while it is in *storage*. One such control is a system for detecting host intrusion, which protects the integrity of information by alerting the security administrators to the potential modification of a critical file.

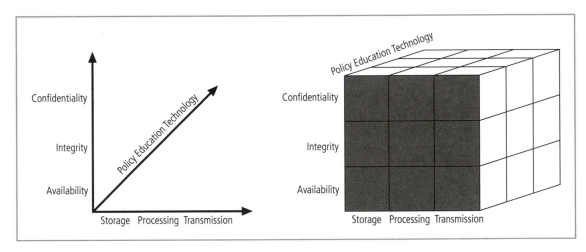

Figure 1-4 McCumber Cube
© Cengage Learning 2013

Balancing Information Security and Access

Information security must effectively balance protection and availability. Even with the best planning and implementation, it is impossible to obtain perfect information security; information security is a process, not a goal. A completely secure information system—if one existed— would not allow anyone access, ever, resulting in a complete lack of availability. On the other hand, it is possible to permit unrestricted access to a system, so that it is available to anyone, anywhere, anytime, through any means. However, this poses a danger to the confidentiality and integrity of the information.

To achieve balance—that is, to operate an information system to the satisfaction of the user and the security professional—the level of security must allow reasonable access, yet protect against threats. An imbalance between access and security can occur when the needs of the end user are undermined by too heavy a focus on protecting and administering the information systems. Both information security technologists and end users must exercise patience and cooperation when interacting with one another, as both groups share the same overall goals of the organization: to ensure that the data is available when, where, and how it is needed, with minimal delays or obstacles. In an ideal world, this level of availability is met even after concerns about loss, damage, interception, or destruction have been addressed.

Business Needs First

An information security program performs four important organizational functions:

- Protects the organization's ability to function
- Enables the safe operation of applications implemented on the organization's IT systems
- Protects the data the organization collects and uses
- Safeguards the technology assets in use at the organization

Protecting the Functionality of an Organization
Both general management and IT management are responsible for implementing information security that protects the organization's ability to function. Although many business and government managers shy away from addressing information security because they perceive it to be a technically complex task, implementing information security actually has more to do with management than with technology. Just as managing payroll has more to do with management than with mathematical wage computations, managing information security to protect an organization's ability to function has more to do with policy and enforcement than with the technology of its implementation.

Enabling the Safe Operation of Applications
Because the majority of a business's critical data resides in complex IT applications, today's organizations are under immense pressure to acquire and operate integrated, efficient, and capable applications. Securing the storage of business-critical data, ensuring the integrity of key business transactions, and making communication constantly available require protecting these applications, particularly those that are important elements of the organization's infrastructure—operating system platforms, electronic mail (e-mail), and instant messaging (IM) applications.

Protecting Data that Organizations Collect and Use
Any business, educational institution, or government agency that functions within the modern context of connected and responsive services relies on information systems to support its transactions. Even if the transaction is not online, information systems and the data they process enable the creation and movement of goods and services. Therefore, protecting *data in motion* and *data at rest* are both critical aspects of information security. The value of data motivates attackers to steal, sabotage, or corrupt it. An effective information security program

directed by management is essential to the protection of the integrity and value of the organization's data.

Safeguarding Technology Assets in Organizations To perform effectively, organizations must add secure infrastructure services matching the size and scope of the enterprise assets. In general, as the organization's network grows to accommodate changing needs, it may need more robust technology solutions. An example of a robust solution is a firewall, a device that keeps certain kinds of network traffic out of the internal network. Another example is caching network appliances, which are devices that store local copies of Internet content, such as Web pages that are frequently referred to by employees. In order to ensure effective business operations, these key technology assets must also be protected.

Threats to Information Security

Around 500 BC, the Chinese general Sun Tzu wrote a treatise on warfare called the *Art of War*. It contains military strategies that are still studied by military leaders and students. In one of his most famous passages, Sun Wu writes, "If you know the enemy and know yourself, you need not fear the result of a hundred battles. If you know yourself but not the enemy, for every victory gained you will also suffer a defeat. If you know neither the enemy nor yourself, you will succumb in every battle."[3] In the battle to protect information, you must know yourself—that is, be familiar with the information that needs protecting and the systems that store, transport, and process it. You must also know the enemy—that is, be informed about the various threats facing the organization, its people, applications, data, and information systems.

To understand the wide range of threats that pervade the interconnected world, researchers have interviewed practicing information security personnel and examined the information security literature on threats. Although the categorizations may vary, threats are relatively well researched and, consequently, fairly well understood.

The Computer Security Institute (CSI) Computer Crime and Security Survey is a representative study. The study found that approximately 50 percent of the organizations responding (skewed to primarily larger organizations) had experienced at least one security incident, with 45.6 percent of those respondents reporting that they had been the subject of a targeted attack.[4]

Table 1-1 presents 12 categories that are a clear and present danger to an organization's people, information, and systems, listed in order from most severe to least severe, as determined by the study's participants. Each organization must prioritize the dangers it faces, based on the particular security situation in which it operates, its organizational strategy regarding risk, and the exposure levels in which its assets operate. You'll notice that many of the threat examples could be listed in more than one category. For example, an act of theft performed by a hacker falls into the theft category, but such acts are often accompanied by defacement actions to delay discovery, thus they may also be placed within the sabotage-or-vandalism category.

Category	Examples
1. Human error or failure	Accidents, employee mistakes, or failure to follow established policies or procedures
2. Compromises to intellectual property	Theft or unauthorized use of written documents, trade secrets, copyrights, trademarks, and patents, including software piracy
3. Espionage or trespass	Unauthorized access and/or data collection, hacking
4. Information extortion	Blackmail or information disclosure
5. Sabotage or vandalism	Destruction of systems or information
6. Theft	Illegal confiscation of equipment or information
7. Software attacks	Malicious code or malware attacks, including viruses, worms, macros, denial-of-service, Trojan horses
8. Forces of nature	Fire, flood, earthquake, lightning, and electrostatic discharge
9. Deviations in quality of service	ISP, power, or WAN service issues from service providers
10. Hardware failures or errors	Equipment failure
11. Software failures or errors	Bugs, code problems, unknown loopholes
12. Obsolescence	Antiquated or outdated technologies

Table 1-1 Threats to Information Security[5]
© Cengage Learning 2013

Common Threats

- **Cracker**—An individual who "cracks" or removes software protection that is designed to prevent unauthorized duplication or use
- **Cyberterrorist**—An individual or group that hacks systems to conduct terrorist activities through a network or Internet pathway
- **Hackers**—Individuals who gain access to information or systems without explicit authorization, often illegally
- **Hacktivist or cyberactivist**—Individuals who interfere with or disrupt systems to protest the operations, policies, or actions of an organization or government agency
- **Malicious code (malcode) or malicious software (malware)**—Software components or programs designed to damage, destroy, or deny service to the target systems. Includes viruses, worms, Trojan horses, and an expanding taxonomy of other malicious software, such as:
  - **Computer viruses**—Segments of code that perform malicious actions, including the following:
    - **Macro virus**—One that is embedded in the automatically executing macro code common in word processors, spread sheets, and database applications
    - **Boot virus**—One that infects the key operating system files located in a computer's boot sector

- **Worms**—Malicious programs that replicate themselves constantly without requiring another program to provide a safe environment for replication (named for the tapeworms in John Brunner's novel *The Shockwave Rider*)
- **Trojan horses**—Software programs that reveal their designed behavior only when activated, often appearing benign until that time
- **Backdoor, trap door,** or **maintenance hook**—A component in a system that allows the attacker to access the system at will, bypassing standard login controls
- **Rootkit**—Malicious software designed to operate with administrative access while hiding itself from the operating system and monitoring tools

- **Packet monkeys**—Script kiddies who use automated tools to inundate a Web site with a barrage of network traffic, usually resulting in a denial of service
- **Phreaker**—An individual who hacks the public telephone network to make free calls or disrupt services
- **Script kiddies**—Hackers of limited skill who use expertly written software to attack a system
- **Shoulder surfing**—Observing others' passwords by watching system login activities
- **Software piracy**—The most common IP breach, the unlawful use or duplication of software-based intellectual property

Attacks on Information Security

An attack is an action that takes advantage of a vulnerability to compromise a controlled system. As described earlier, a threat is accomplished by a threat agent that damages or steals an organization's information or physical asset. Unlike threats, which are always present, attacks occur through specific actions that may cause a business loss. For example, the threat of damage from a thunderstorm is present during most of the summer in many places, but a thunderstorm attack and its associated risk of loss only exist for the duration of the actual thunderstorm. The following sections discuss each of the major types of attack used against controlled systems.

Malicious Code

Malicious code attacks, mentioned earlier, include the execution of viruses, worms, Trojan horses, and active Web scripts with the intent of destroying or stealing information. The state-of-the-art malicious code attack is the polymorphic, or multivector, worm. These attack programs use several known attack vectors to exploit a variety of vulnerabilities in commonly used software. Table 1-2 outlines the six categories of known attack vectors.

Vector	Description
IP scan and attack	The infected system scans a random or local range of IP addresses and targets any of several vulnerabilities known to hackers or left over from previous exploits.
Web browsing	If the infected system has write access to any Web pages, it makes all Web content files (.html, .asp, .cgi, and others) infectious, so that users who browse to those pages become infected.
Virus	Each infected machine infects certain common executable or script files on all computers to which it can write with virus code that can cause infection.
Unprotected shares	Using vulnerabilities in file systems and the way many organizations configure them, the infected machine copies the viral component to all locations it can reach.
Mass mail	By sending e-mail infections to recipients in the address book, the infected machine infects many users, whose mail-reading programs also automatically run the program and infect other systems.
Simple Network Management Protocol (SNMP)	By using the common passwords that were employed in early versions of this protocol, widely used for remote management of network and computer devices, the attacker program can gain control of a device.

Table 1-2 **Attack Replication Vectors**
© Cengage Learning 2013

Password Attacks

A number of attacks attempt to bypass access controls by guessing passwords; this is sometimes called **password cracking**. Such attacks range from making educated guesses based on the individual's background to guessing every possible combination of letters, numbers, and special characters. The most common password attacks are examined here:

Rainbow Tables   One popular password attack, variously called a **rainbow attack**, a precomputed hash attack, or a time-memory tradeoff attack, uses a database of precomputed hashes (or **rainbow tables**) derived from sequentially calculated passwords to look up the hashed password and read out the text version. A rainbow attack is used when a copy of the hash of the user's password has been obtained. When a match is found, the password has been cracked.

Brute Force Attacks   Using computing and network resources to try every possible combination of available characters, numbers, and symbols for a password is called a **brute force attack**. Because this often involves repeatedly guessing the passwords to commonly used accounts, it is sometimes called a **guessing attack**. If attackers can narrow the field of target accounts, they can devote more time and resources to attacking fewer accounts. That is one reason to change the names of common accounts from the manufacturer's default names.

Although often effective against low-security systems, brute force attacks are often not useful against systems that have adopted the usual security practices recommended by manufacturers. Controls that limit the number of attempts allowed per unit of elapsed time are very effective at combating these attacks. Defenses against brute force attacks are usually adopted early on in any security effort and are thoroughly covered in the SANS/FBI list of the Top 20 Most Critical Internet Security Vulnerabilities.[6]

Dictionary A variation on the brute force attack, the **dictionary attack** narrows the field by selecting specific target accounts and using a list of commonly used passwords (the dictionary) instead of random combinations. Organizations can use similar dictionaries to disallow passwords during the reset process and, thus, guard against easy-to-guess passwords. In addition, rules requiring additional numbers and/or special characters make the dictionary attack less effective.

Denial-of-Service (DoS) and Distributed Denial-of-Service (DDoS) Attacks

In a **denial-of-service** (DoS) attack, the attacker sends a large number of connection or information requests to a target (see Figure 1-5). So many requests are made that the target system cannot handle them along with other, legitimate requests for service. The system may crash, or it may simply be unable to perform ordinary functions. A **distributed denial-of-service** (DDoS) launches a coordinated stream of requests against a target from many locations at the same time. Most DDoS attacks are preceded by a preparation phase in which many systems, perhaps thousands, are compromised. The compromised machines are turned into **zombies** (or **bots**), machines that are directed remotely (usually via transmitted command) by the attacker to participate in the attack. DDoS attacks are the most difficult to defend against. There are, however, some cooperative efforts to enable DDoS defenses among groups of service providers; among them is the Consensus Roadmap for Defeating Distributed Denial of Service Attacks.[7] To use a popular metaphor, DDoS is considered a weapon of mass destruction on the Internet.[8]

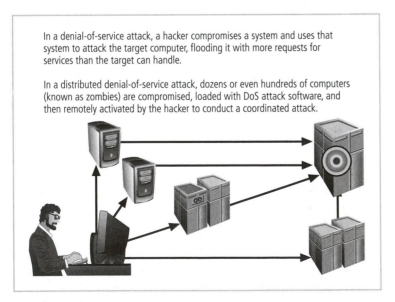

Figure 1-5 Denial-of-service attacks

Any system connected to the Internet that provides TCP-based network services (such as a Web server, FTP server, or mail server) is a potential target for denial-of-service attacks. Note that in addition to attacks launched at specific hosts, these attacks can be launched against routers or other network server systems if these hosts enable (or turn on) other TCP services (e.g., echo). Even though such attacks make use of a fundamental element of the TCP protocol used by all systems, the consequences of the attacks may vary, depending on the system.[9]

Spoofing

Spoofing is a technique used to gain unauthorized access to computers, wherein the intruder sends messages whose IP addresses indicate to the recipient that the messages are coming from a trusted host. To engage in IP spoofing, a hacker must first use a variety of techniques to find an IP address of a trusted host and then modify the packet headers (see Figure 1-6) so that it appears that the packets are coming from that host.[10] Newer routers and firewall arrangements can offer protection against IP spoofing.

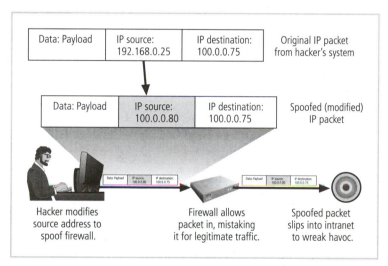

Figure 1-6 IP spoofing
© Cengage Learning 2013

Man-in-the-Middle Attacks

In the well-known **man-in-the-middle** attack, an attacker monitors (or sniffs) packets from the network, modifies them using IP spoofing techniques, and inserts them back into the network, allowing the attacker to eavesdrop as well as to change, delete, reroute, add, forge, or divert data.[11] In a variant attack, the spoofing involves the interception of an encryption key exchange, which enables the hacker to act as an invisible man-in-the-middle—that is, eavesdropper—in encrypted exchanges. Figure 1-7 illustrates these attacks by showing how a hacker uses public and private encryption keys to intercept messages.

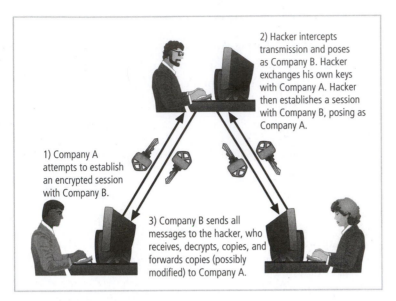

2) Hacker intercepts transmission and poses as Company B. Hacker exchanges his own keys with Company A. Hacker then establishes a session with Company B, posing as Company A.

1) Company A attempts to establish an encrypted session with Company B.

3) Company B sends all messages to the hacker, who receives, decrypts, copies, and forwards copies (possibly modified) to Company A.

Figure 1-7   Man-in-the-middle attack
© Cengage Learning 2013

E-Mail Attacks

A number of attacks focus on the use of e-mail to deny service to the user (a form of DoS), exploit the inexperience or vulnerability of the user, or trick the user into installing back-doors or viruses. In general, e-mail is more the vehicle for the attack than the attack itself. However, there are also specific e-mail attacks, including spam and mail bombing.

Spam **Spam,** or unsolicited commercial e-mail, has been used as a means of making mali-cious code attacks more effective. In some cases, malicious code is embedded in files that are included as attachments to spam.[12] The most significant impact of spam, however, is the waste of both computer and human resources. Many organizations attempt to cope with the flood of spam by using filtering technologies to stem the flow. Other organiza-tions simply tell users of the mail system to delete unwanted messages.

Mail Bomb Another form of e-mail attack is a **mail bomb,** in which an attacker routes large quantities of e-mail to the target system. This can be accomplished through social engineering (to be discussed shortly) or by exploiting various technical flaws in the Simple Mail Transport Protocol (SMTP). The target of the attack receives unmanageably large volumes of unsolicited e-mail. By sending large e-mails with forged header information, attackers can take advantage of poorly configured e-mail systems and trick them into sending many e-mails to an address chosen by the attacker. If many such systems are tricked into participating in the event, the target e-mail address is buried under thousands or even mil-lions of unwanted e-mails.

Sniffers

A **sniffer** is a program or device that monitors data traveling over a network. Sniffers can be used both for legitimate network management functions and for stealing information from a network. Unauthorized sniffers can be extremely dangerous to a network's security because they are virtually impossible to detect and can be inserted almost anywhere. This makes them a favorite weapon in the hacker's arsenal. Sniffers often work on TCP/IP networks, where they are sometimes referred to as **packet sniffers**.[13] Sniffers add risk to the network because many systems and users send information on local networks in clear text. A sniffer program shows all the data going by, including passwords, the data inside files (such as word-processing documents), and screens full of sensitive data.

Social Engineering

Within the context of information security, **social engineering** is the process of using social skills to convince people to reveal access credentials or other valuable information to the attacker. This can be done in several ways, and usually involves the perpetrator posing as a person higher in the organizational hierarchy than the victim. To prepare for this false representation, the perpetrator may have used social engineering against others in the organization to collect seemingly unrelated information that, when used together, makes the false representation more credible. For instance, anyone can call the main switchboard of a company and get the name of the CIO, but an attacker may find it just as easy to get even more information by calling others in the company and asserting (false) authority by mentioning the CIO's name. Social engineering attacks may involve individuals posing as new employees or as current employees who pathetically need assistance to avoid getting fired. Sometimes, attackers threaten, cajole, or beg to sway the target.

The Advance Fee Fraud (AFF), internationally known as the "419" fraud, is an example of a social engineering attack. Named after a section of the Nigerian penal code, these schemes often involve fictitious companies, such as the Nigerian National Petroleum Company, but the perpetrators may invent other entities as well—a bank, a government agency, or a nongovernmental organization, such as a lottery corporation. Funds are stolen from individuals who think they're participating in money-making ventures; first, they're asked to send money up front, then they're charged an endless series of fees. Some 4-1-9 schemes are suspected of involving kidnapping, extortion, and murder, and they have, according to the Secret Service, bilked over $100 million from unsuspecting Americans lured into disclosing personal banking information.

The infamous hacker Kevin Mitnick had this to say about attacks: "People are the weakest link. You can have the best technology, firewalls, intrusion-detection systems, biometric devices, [then] somebody calls an unsuspecting employee. That's all she wrote, baby. They got everything."[14]

Buffer Overflow

A **buffer overflow** is an application error that occurs when more data is sent to a buffer than it can handle. During a buffer overflow, the attacker can make the target system execute instructions, or the attacker can take advantage of some other unintended consequence of the failure. Sometimes, this is limited to a denial-of-service attack, when the attacked system crashes and is (until it is restarted) rendered unavailable to users. In either case, data on the attacked system loses integrity.[15] In 1998, Microsoft revealed that Internet Explorer it had been vulnerable to a buffer overflow problem, as described here:

> *Microsoft acknowledged that if you type a res:// URL (a Microsoft-devised type of URL) which is longer than 256 characters in Internet Explorer 4.0, the browser will crash. No big deal, except that anything after the 256th character can be executed on the computer. This maneuver, known as a buffer overrun, is just about the oldest hacker trick in the book. Tack some malicious code (say, an executable version of the Pentium-crashing FooF code) onto the end of the URL, and you have the makings of a disaster.*[16]

Timing Attacks

The **timing attack** works by measuring the time required to access a Web page and deducing that the user has visited the site before by the presence of the page in the browser's cache. Another attack by the same name is a side channel attack on cryptographic algorithms using measurements of the time required to perform cryptographic functions.[17]

Security Professionals and the Organization

It takes a wide range of professionals to support a diverse information security program. Senior management is the key component, but administrative support is also needed to develop and execute specific security policies and procedures, and technical expertise is needed to implement the details of the information security program. What follows are descriptions of the various positions that information security professionals hold in a typical organization.

Executive Management

The **chief information officer (CIO)** is often the senior technology officer. Titles such as vice president (VP) of information, VP of information technology, and VP of systems may also be used. The CIO is primarily responsible for advising the chief executive officer, president, or company owner on the strategic planning that affects the management of information in the organization.

The **chief information security officer (CISO)** is the individual primarily responsible for the assessment, management, and implementation of information security in the organization. The CISO may also be referred to as the manager for IT security, the security administrator, or a similar title. The CISO usually reports directly to the CIO, although in larger organizations it is common for one or more layers of management to exist between the two.

Information Security Project Team

The information security project team consists of a number of individuals who are experienced in one or more facets of the vast array of required technical and nontechnical areas. Many of the same skills needed to manage and implement security are needed to design the security system. Members of the security project team fill the following roles:

- *Champion*—A senior executive who promotes the project and ensures that it is supported, both financially and administratively, at the highest levels of the organization

- *Team leader*—A project manager (it may be a departmental line manager or staff unit manager) who understands project management, personnel management, and information security technical requirements

- *Security policy developers*—Individuals who understand the organizational culture, existing policies, and requirements for developing and implementing successful policies

- *Risk assessment specialists*—Individuals who understand financial risk assessment techniques, the value of organizational assets, and the security methods to be used

- *Security professionals*—Dedicated, trained, and well-educated specialists in all aspects of information security, both technical and nontechnical

- *Systems, network, and storage administrators*—Individuals with the primary responsibility for administering the systems, data storage, and networks that house and provide access to the organization's information

- *End users*—Those who will be most directly affected by new implementations and changes to existing systems. Ideally, a selection of users from various departments, levels, and degrees of technical knowledge assist the team in focusing on the application of realistic controls applied in ways that do not disrupt the essential business activities they seek to safeguard.

Information Security Policy, Standards, and Practices

A **policy** is guidance or instructions that an organization's senior management implements to regulate the activities of the organization members who make decisions, take actions, and perform other duties. Policies are like laws in that they dictate acceptable and unacceptable behavior within the organization. Like laws, policies define what is right and what is wrong, what the penalties are for violating policies, and what the appeal process is. **Standards**, although they have the same compliance requirement as policies, are more detailed descriptions of what must be done to comply with policy. The standards may be informal or part of an organizational culture; these are referred to as **de facto standards**. Alternatively, standards may be published, scrutinized, and ratified by a group; these are referred to as **de jure standards**. Practices, procedures, and guidelines effectively explain how to comply with policy. Figure 1-8 shows policies as the force that drives standards, which in turn drive practices, procedures, and guidelines.

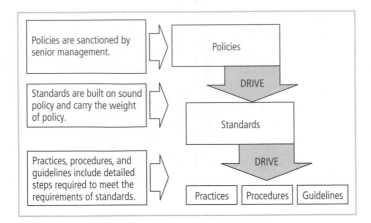

Figure 1-8   Policies, standards, and practices
© Cengage Learning 2013

Management must make policies the basis for all information security planning, design, and deployment. Policies direct how issues are addressed and how technologies are used. Policies do not specify the proper operation of equipment or software—this information should be placed in the standards, procedures, and practices of users' manuals and systems documentation. In addition, policy should never contradict governmental laws; this can create a significant liability for the organization.

Because information security is primarily a management problem, not a technical one, high-quality security programs begin and end with policy.[18] Policy obliges personnel to function in a manner that adds to the security of information assets rather than threatens them. Security policies are the least expensive control to design and disseminate—they require only the time and effort of the management team—but they are the most difficult to implement properly. Even if the management team hires an outside consultant to assist in the development of policy, the costs are minimal compared to those of technical controls.

For a policy to be effective and legally enforceable, it must meet the following criteria:

- *Dissemination (distribution)*—The organization must be able to demonstrate that the relevant policy has been made readily available for review by the employee. Common dissemination techniques include hard-copy and electronic distribution.

- *Review (reading)*—The organization must be able to demonstrate that it disseminated the document in an intelligible form, including versions for illiterate, non-English-reading, and reading-impaired employees. Often, organizations record versions of the policy in English and alternate languages.

- *Comprehension (understanding)*—The organization must be able to demonstrate that employees understood the requirements and content of the policy. Techniques include quizzes and other assessments.

- *Compliance (agreement)*—The organization must be able to demonstrate that employees have agreed to comply with the policy, either through act or affirmation. Techniques include log-on banners that require a specific action (mouse click or keystroke) to acknowledge agreement or documents that employees sign to indicate that they have read, understood, and agreed to comply with the policy.

- *Uniformity (equality of application)*—The organization must be able to demonstrate that the policy has been uniformly enforced throughout the organization.

Policies are put in place to support the organization's mission, vision, and strategic planning. The **mission** is a written statement of the organization's purpose. The **vision** is a written statement of the organization's long-term goals. (Where will it be in five years? Ten?) **Strategic planning** is the process of moving the organization towards its vision.

What the term *security policy* means depends on the context in which it is used. Governmental agencies discuss security policy in terms of national security and national policies to deal with foreign states. A security policy can also be a credit card agency's method of processing credit card numbers. In general, a **security policy** is a set of rules that protect an organization's assets. An **information security policy** provides rules for the protection of the information assets of the organization.

Management must define three types of security policies:

- Enterprise information security policies
- Issue-specific security policies
- Systems-specific security policies[19]

Each of these types of management policy is examined in greater detail in the sections that follow.

Enterprise Information Security Policy (EISP)

An **enterprise information security policy** (EISP) is also known as a **general security policy, IT security policy,** or **information security policy.** It is based on and directly supports the mission, vision, and direction of the organization and sets the strategic direction, scope, and tone for all security efforts. The EISP is an executive-level document, usually drafted by, or in cooperation with, the chief information officer of the organization. It is usually two to ten pages long and shapes the philosophy of security in the IT environment. The EISP usually needs to be modified only when there is a change in the strategic direction of the organization.

The EISP guides the development, implementation, and management of the security program. It specifies the requirements to be met by the information security blueprint or framework. It defines the purpose, scope, constraints, and applicability of the security program in the organization. It also assigns responsibilities for the various areas of security, including systems administration, maintenance of the information security policies, and the practices and responsibilities of the users. Finally, it addresses legal compliance in two areas:

- General compliance to ensure meeting the requirements to establish a program and the responsibilities assigned therein to various organizational components
- The use of specified penalties and disciplinary action[20]

When the EISP has been developed, the CISO begins forming the security team and initiating the necessary changes to the information security program.

EISP Components Although the specifics of EISPs vary from organization to organization, most EISP documents include the components shown in Table 1-3.[21]

Component	Description
Statement of Purpose	Answers the question "What is this policy for?" Provides a framework that helps the reader understand the document's intention. For example: "This document will:
	• Identify the elements of a good security policy
	• Explain the need for information security
	• Specify the various categories of information security
	• Identify the information security responsibilities and roles
	• Identify appropriate levels of security through standards and guidelines
	This document establishes an overarching security policy and direction for our company. Individual departments are expected to establish standards, guidelines, and operating procedures that adhere to and reference this policy while addressing their specific and individual needs."[22]
Information Technology Security Elements	Defines information security. For example: "Protecting the confidentiality, integrity, and availability of information while performing processing, transmission, and storage, through the use of policy, education and training, and technology."
	This section can also lay out security definitions or philosophies to clarify the policy.
Need for Information Technology Security	Provides information on the importance of information security in the organization and the obligation (legal and ethical) to protect critical information about customers, employees, and markets.
Information Technology Security Responsibilities and Roles	Defines the organizational structure designed to support information security. Identifies categories of individuals with responsibility for information security (IT department, management, users) and their information security responsibilities, including maintenance of this document.
Reference to Other Information Technology Standards and Guidelines	Lists other standards that influence and are influenced by this policy document, perhaps including relevant laws (federal and state) and other policies.

Table 1-3 Components of the EISP
© Cengage Learning 2013

Issue-Specific Security Policy (ISSP)

As an organization executes various technologies and processes to support routine operations, it must instruct employees on the proper use of those technologies and processes. The **issue-specific security policy** (ISSP), which requires frequent updates, addresses specific areas of technology, stating the organization's position on each issue.[23] Here are some of the issues it may cover:

- Use of company-owned networks and the Internet
- Use of telecommunications technologies (fax and phone)
- Use of e-mail
- Specific minimum configurations of computers to defend against worms and viruses
- Prohibitions against hacking or testing organization security controls

- Home use of company-owned computer equipment
- Use of personal equipment on company networks
- Use of photocopy equipment

Table 1-4 shows an outline of a sample ISSP, which can be used as a model. An organization should add to this structure any security procedures not covered by these general guidelines.

Component	Description

1. Statement of policy
   a. Scope and applicability
   b. Definition of technology addressed
   c. Responsibilities
	The policy should begin with a clear statement of purpose.

2. Authorized access and usage
   a. User access
   b. Fair and responsible use
   c. Protection of privacy
	Who can use the technology governed by the policy, and what can it be used for? An organization's information systems are the exclusive property of the organization, and users have no general rights of use. Each technology and process is provided for business operations. Use for any other purpose constitutes misuse.

3. Prohibited usage
   a. Disruptive use or misuse
   b. Criminal use
   c. Offensive or harassing materials
   d. Copyrighted, licensed, or other intellectual property
   e. Other restrictions
	Unless a particular use is clearly prohibited, the organization cannot penalize its employees for using it in that fashion.

4. Systems management
   a. Management of stored materials
   b. Employer monitoring
   c. Virus protection
   d. Physical security
   e. Encryption
	All systems-management responsibilities should be designated to the systems administrators or to the users; otherwise, each may infer that the responsibility belongs to the other.

5. Violations of policy
   a. Procedures for reporting violations
   b. Penalties for violations
	Users need to be instructed how to report suspected violations of policy. Allowing anonymous submissions may be the only way to convince them to report the unauthorized activities of other, more influential employees.

6. Policy review and modification a. Scheduled review of policy and procedures for modification	Each policy should contain procedures and a timetable for periodic reviews so that users do not begin circumventing policy as it grows obsolete.
7. Limitations of liability a. Statements of liability or disclaimers	The policy should state that the organization will not protect employees who violate a company policy or any law using company technologies, and that the company is not liable for such actions.

Table 1-4 Components of the ISSP
© Cengage Learning 2013

Systems-Specific Policy (SysSP)

Whereas issue-specific policies are written documents readily identifiable as policy, system-specific security policies (SysSPs) sometimes have a different look. They can be separated into two general areas, **managerial guidance** and **technical specifications**, or they can be combined into a single policy document.

Managerial Guidance SysSPs A managerial guidance SysSP document is created by management to guide the implementation and configuration of technology, as well as to regulate the behavior of people in the organization. For example, although the method for implementing a firewall belongs in the technical specifications SysSP, the firewall's configuration must follow guidelines established by management. An organization might not want its employees to have access to the Internet via the organization's network, for instance; in that case, the firewall would have to be implemented accordingly.

Technical Specifications SysSPs Whereas a manager can work with a systems administrator to create managerial policy, the system administrator may in turn need to create a policy to implement the managerial policy. Each type of equipment requires its own set of policies to translate the managerial intent into an enforceable technical approach. For example, an ISSP may require that user passwords be changed quarterly; a systems administrator can implement a technical control within a specific application to enforce this policy. There are two general methods for implementing such technical controls: access control lists and configuration rules.

Access control lists (ACLs) consist of the user access lists, matrices, and capability tables that govern the rights and privileges of users. ACLs can control access to file storage systems, software components, or network communications devices. A **capability table** specifies which subjects and objects users or groups can access; in some systems, capability tables are called user profiles or user policies. These specifications frequently take the form of complex matrices rather than simple lists or tables. The **access control matrix** includes a combination of tables and lists; organizational assets are listed along the column headers, and users are listed along the row headers. The resulting matrix contains ACLs in columns for a particular device or asset, and a row contains the capability table for a particular user.

Configuration rule policies are the specific instructions entered into a security system to regulate how it reacts to the data it receives. Rule-based policies are more specific to the operation of a system than ACLs are, and they may or may not deal with users directly. Many security systems—for example, firewalls, intrusion detection systems (IDSs), and proxy servers—use specific configuration rules to determine how the system handles each data element they process.

Frameworks and Industry Standards in Information Security

After the information security team has inventoried the organization's information assets and assessed and prioritized the threats to those assets, it must conduct a series of risk assessments using quantitative or qualitative analyses, as well as feasibility studies and cost-benefit analyses. These assessments, which include determining each asset's current protection level, are used to decide whether or not to proceed with any given control. Armed with a general idea of the vulnerabilities in the information technology systems, the security team develops a design blueprint for security, which is used to implement the security program.

This **security blueprint** is the basis for the design, selection, and implementation of all security program elements, including policy implementation, ongoing policy management, risk management programs, education and training programs, technological controls, and maintenance of the security program. The security blueprint, built on top of the organization's information security policies, is a scalable, upgradable, comprehensive plan to meet the organization's current and future information security needs. It is a detailed version of the **security framework,** which is an outline of the overall information security strategy and a roadmap for planned changes to the organization's information security environment. The blueprint specifies the tasks in the order in which they are to be accomplished.

To select a methodology by which to develop an information security blueprint, you can adapt or adopt a published information security model or framework. This framework can be an outline of steps to take to design and implement information security in the organization. There are a number of published information security frameworks, including ones from government sources, which are presented later in this chapter. Because each information security environment is unique, the security team may need to modify or adapt pieces from several frameworks; what works well for one organization may not precisely fit another.

The ISO 27000 Series

One of the most widely referenced security models is *Information Technology – Code of Practice for Information Security Management*, which was originally published as British Standard 7799. In 2000, this code of practice was adopted as an international standard framework for information security by the International Organization for Standardization (ISO) and the International Electrotechnical Commission (IEC) as ISO/IEC 17799 (or more commonly just ISO 17799). It was revised in 2005 (becoming ISO 17799:2005) and renumbered ISO 27002 in 2007 in order to align it with the document ISO 27001, which is discussed later in this chapter. Although the details of ISO 27002 are available to those who purchase the standard, its structure and general organization are well known. For a summary description, see Table 1-5.

1. Risk Assessment and Treatment
2. Security Policy
3. Organization of Information Security
4. Asset Management
5. Human Resource Security
6. Physical and Environmental Security
7. Communications and Operations
8. Access Control
9. Information Systems Acquisition, Development, and Maintenance
10. Information Security Incident Management
11. Business Continuity Management
12. Compliance

Table 1-5 Sections of the ISO/IEC 27002[24]

The stated purpose of ISO 27002 is to "give recommendations for information security management for use by those who are responsible for initiating, implementing, or maintaining security in their organization. It is intended to provide a common basis for developing organizational security standards and effective security management practice and to provide confidence in interorganizational dealings."[25] Whereas ISO/IEC 27002 offers a broad overview of the various areas of security, providing information on 127 controls over 12 broad areas, ISO/IEC 27001 provides information on how to implement ISO/IEC 27002 and how to set up an information security management system (ISMS). The overall methodology for this process and its major steps are presented in Figure 1-9.

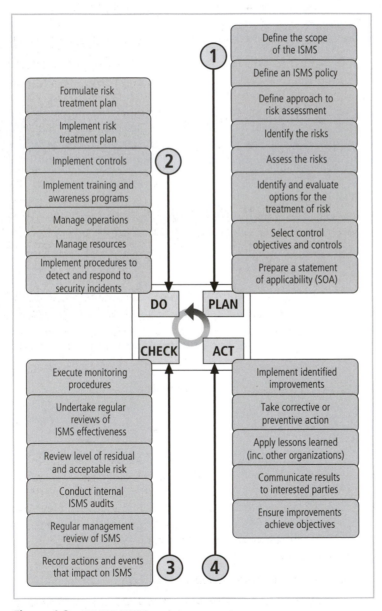

Figure 1-9   ISO/IEC 27002 major process steps
© Cengage Learning 2013

In 2007, ISO announced plans for the issuance of forthcoming standards related to information security issues and topics (see Table 1-6).

Standard	Status	Title or Topic	Comment
27000	Published 2009	Series Overview and Vocabulary	Typically, when ISO releases a series of standards, the first defines series terminology and vocabulary
27001	Published 2005	Information Security Management System Specification	Drawn from BS 7799:2
27002	Published 2010	Code of Practice for Information Security Management	Was renamed from ISO/IEC 17799, drawn from BS 7799:1
27003	Published 2010	Information Security Management Systems Implementation Guidelines	To provide guidance and assistance in implementing an ISMS
27004	Published 2009	Information Security Measurements and Metrics	To assist organizations in collecting, evaluating, and reporting metrics and performance measures
27005	Published 2008	ISMS Risk Management	Guidelines for InfoSec Risk Management—supporting requirement of ISO 27001
27006	Published 2007	Requirements for Bodies Providing Audit and Certification of an ISMS	Largely intended to support the accreditation of certification bodies providing ISMS certification
27007	Planned	InfoSec Management Systems Auditing	In preparation
27008	Planned	InfoSec Management Auditing – Security Controls	In preparation
27011	Published 2008	IT: InfoSec Management Guidelines for Telecomm	ISMS assistance for the implementation of InfoSec management in Telecom organizations

Table 1-6 ISO 27000 Series Current and Planned Standards (*www.27000.org/*)
© Cengage Learning 2013

NIST Security Models

Another approach to security standards is described in documents available from the Computer Security Resource Center of the National Institute for Standards and Technology (*csrc.nist.gov*). Because the NIST documents are publicly available, free, and have been available for some time, they have been broadly reviewed by government and industry professionals and were among the references cited by the federal government when it decided not to select the ISO 17799 standards. The following NIST documents can assist in the design of a security framework:

- SP 800-12: *An Introduction to Computer Security: The NIST Handbook*
- SP 800-14: *Generally Accepted Security Principles and Practices for Securing Information Technology Systems*

- SP 800-18 Rev. 1: *Guide for Developing Security Plans for Federal Information Systems*
- SP 800-30: *Risk Management Guide for Information Technology Systems*
- SP 800-53 Rev. 3: *Recommended Security Controls for Federal Information Systems and Organizations*

Although these are the more widely used documents, they are but a few of the documents available from *csrc.nist.gov/publications/PubsSPs.html*.

IETF Security Architecture

The Security Area Working Group acts as an advisory board for the protocols and areas developed and promoted by the Internet Society and the Internet Engineering Task Force (IETF), and although the group endorses no specific information security architecture, one of its requests for comment, RFC 2196: *Site Security Handbook*, offers a good discussion of important security issues. The handbook covers five basic areas of security, with detailed discussions on development and implementation. There are also chapters on such important topics as security policies, security technical architecture, security services, and security incident handling.

Benchmarking and Best Business Practices

Benchmarking and best practices are methods used by some organizations to assess security practices. They don't provide a complete methodology for the design and implementation of all the practices needed by an organization; however, it is possible to formulate the desired outcome of the security process and work backwards toward an effective design. The Federal Agency Security Practices (FASP) Web site (*fasp.nist.gov*) is a popular place to look up best practices. FASP provides best practices for public agencies, but these practices can be adapted easily to private institutions. The documents found at this site include specific examples of key policies and planning documents, implementation strategies for key technologies, and position descriptions for key security personnel.

A number of other public and private institutions provide information on best practices. One such group is the SANS Institute (*http://www.sans.org*), which is a cooperative information security research and education organization. The organization provides recommendations for security implementations and policies. Other widely referenced sources include the Computer Emergency Response Team Coordination Center (CERT/CC) at Carnegie Mellon University (*www.cert.org*) and the United States Computer Emergency Readiness Team (US-CERT, *http://www.us-cert.gov*). These organizations provide detailed and specific assistance on how to implement sound security methodologies.

Spheres of Security   The spheres of security, shown in Figure 1-10, are the foundation of the security framework. Generally speaking, they illustrate that information is under attack from a variety of sources. The sphere of use, on the left side of Figure 1-10, illustrates the ways in which people access information; for example, people read hard copies of documents but can also access information through systems. Information, as the most important asset in this model, is at the center of the sphere. Information is always at risk from the people and computer systems that have access to it. Networks and the Internet represent indirect threats, because a person attempting to access information from the

Internet must first go through the local networks and then access systems that contain the information. The sphere of protection, on the right side of Figure 1-10, illustrates that between each layer of the sphere of use there must exist a layer of protection to prevent access to the inner layer from the outer layer. Each shaded band is a layer of protection and control. For example, the items labeled "Policy & law" and "Education & training" are located between people and the information. Controls are also implemented between systems and the information, between networks and the computer systems, and between the Internet and internal networks. This reinforces the concept of defense in depth. As illustrated in the sphere of protection, a variety of controls can be used to protect the information. The items of control shown in the figure are not intended to be comprehensive, but they illustrate individual safeguards that can protect the various systems that are located closer to the center of the sphere. However, because people can directly access each ring, as well as the information at the core of the model, the side of the sphere of protection that attempts to control access by relying on people requires a different approach to security than the side that uses technology. The members of the organization must become a safeguard that is effectively implemented and maintained or else they too represent a threat to the information.

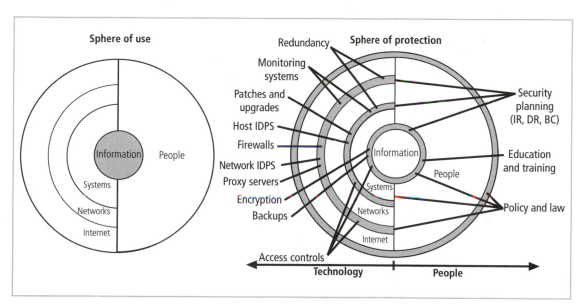

Figure 1-10 Spheres of security
© Cengage Learning 2013

Information security is designed and implemented in three layers: policies, people, and technology. Although the design and implementation of the people layer and the technology layer overlap, both must follow the sound management policies discussed earlier in this chapter. Each of the layers contains controls and safeguards that protect the valuable information and information system assets. Before any technical controls or other safeguards are put into place, however, the policies defining the management philosophies that guide the security process must already be in place.

Defense in Depth   One of the basic tenets of security architectures is the layered implementation of security. This layered approach is called **defense in depth**. To achieve defense in depth, an organization must establish multiple layers of security controls and safeguards, which can be organized into policy, training and education, and technology per the NSTISSC model. Although policy itself may not prevent attacks, it certainly prepares the organization to handle them, and coupled with other layers, it can deter attacks. This is true of training and education, which can also provide some defense against attacks stemming from employee ignorance and social engineering. Technology is also implemented in layers, with detection equipment working in tandem with reaction technology, all operating behind access control mechanisms. Implementing multiple types of technology and thereby preventing the failure of one system from compromising the security of information is referred to as **redundancy**. Redundancy can be implemented at a number of points throughout the security architecture—for example, firewalls, proxy servers, and access controls. Figure 1-11 illustrates the concept of building controls in multiple, sometimes redundant, layers. The figure shows the use of firewalls and intrusion detection systems (IDS) that use both packet-level rules (shown as the header in the diagram) and data content analysis (shown as 0100101011 in the diagram).

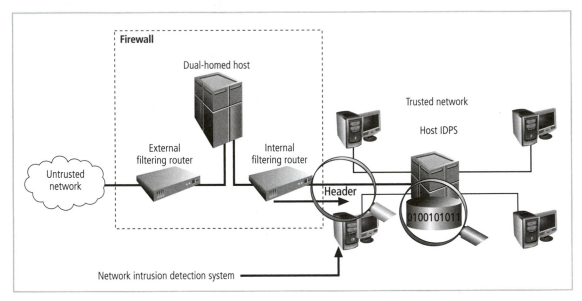

Figure 1-11   Defense in depth
© Cengage Learning 2013

Security Perimeter   A **security perimeter** defines the boundary between the outer limit of an organization's security and the beginning of the outside world. A security perimeter protects all internal systems from outside threats, as shown in Figure 1-12. There can be both an electronic security perimeter, usually at the organization's exterior network or Internet connection, and a physical security perimeter, usually at the gate to the organization's offices. Both require perimeter security. Security perimeters can be implemented as multiple technologies that segregate the protected information from potential attackers. Within security perimeters, the organization can establish **security domains**—areas of trust within which users can freely communicate. The assumption is that if individuals have access to one system within a security domain, they have authorized access to all systems within that particular domain. The security perimeter is an essential element of the overall security framework, and its implementation details are the core of the completed security blueprint. The key components used for planning the perimeter include firewalls, DMZs, proxy servers, and intrusion detection systems.

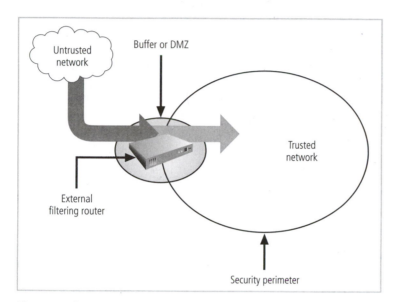

Figure 1-12   Security perimeters
© Cengage Learning 2013

It should be noted that the traditional boundaries of the perimeter are fading. The proliferation of endpoints, such as mobile devices, is destroying the traditional definition of an organization's perimeter.[26] Enterprises must carefully consider how these new technologies can redefine where the perimeter actually falls, or if a perimeter exists at all. Additionally, organizations are becoming more concerned with internal attacks from employee threats or on-site physical threats. These two major concerns violate the assumption that all systems within the security perimeter should be trusted.

Chapter Summary

- Before learning how to plan, design, and implement network security, it is important to understand the larger issue of information security. Learning about the overall picture of information security helps you become aware of these areas that affect firewalls and network security.

- Information security is the protection of information and its critical elements, including the systems and hardware that use, store, and transmit that information. The C.I.A. triad is based on the confidentiality, integrity, and availability of information and the systems that process it.

- The value of information comes from the characteristics it possesses. When a characteristic of information changes, the value of that information either increases or, more commonly, decreases.

- The CNSS Security model is known as the McCumber Cube and was created by John McCumber in 1991. It provides a graphical description of the architectural approach widely used in computer and information security.

- Information security cannot be an absolute; it is a process, not a goal. Information security should balance protection and availability. To achieve balance—that is, to operate an information system to the satisfaction of the user and the security professional—the level of security must allow reasonable access yet protect against threats.

- Information security performs four important organizational functions: protects the organization's ability to function, enables the safe operation of applications implemented on the organization's IT systems, protects the data the organization collects and uses, and safeguards the technology assets in use at the organization.

- A threat is an object, person, or other entity that represents a constant danger to an asset. Twelve categories have been developed to represent the dangers posed to an organization's people, information, and systems. They are: (1) human error or failure, (2) compromises to intellectual property, (3) espionage or trespass, (4) information extortion, (5) sabotage or vandalism, (6) theft, (7) software attacks, (8) forces of nature, (9) deviations in quality of service, (10) hardware failures or errors, (11) software failures or errors, and (12) obsolescence.

- An attack is an action that takes advantage of a vulnerability to compromise a controlled system. A vulnerability is an identified weakness in a controlled system. An attack is a specific action that may cause a potential loss. Types of attack include: malicious code, backdoors, password cracking, denial-of-service (DoS) and distributed denial-of-service (DDoS), spoofing, man-in-the-middle, spam, mail bombs, sniffers, social engineering, buffer overflow, and timing attacks.

- It takes a wide range of professionals and skills to support the information security program, from senior management and administrative support to technical expertise. The following job positions are involved with information security: chief information officer (CIO), chief information security officer (CISO), members of the information security project team (including team leader, security policy developers, risk assessment specialists, security professionals, systems, network and storage administrators, and end users. In order to most effectively secure its networks, an organization must establish a functional and well-designed information security program in the context of a well-planned and fully defined information policy and planning environment. The creation of an information security program requires information security policies, standards, and practices, an information security architecture, and a detailed information security blueprint.

- Management must make policy the basis for all information security planning, design, and deployment in order to direct how issues are addressed and how technologies are used. Policy must never conflict with laws, must stand up in court, if challenged, and must be properly administered through dissemination and documented acceptance. For a policy to be considered effective and legally enforceable, it must be disseminated, reviewed, understood, complied with, and uniformly enforced. Policy is implemented with an overall enterprise information security policy and as many issues-specific and system-specific policies as are required to meet the management team's policy needs.

Review Questions

1. What is information security? How does it differ from network security?

2. What are the three components of the C.I.A. triad?

3. How does a threat to information security differ from an attack?

4. List the vectors that malicious code uses to infect or compromise other systems.

5. What are the various types of malware? How do worms differ from viruses? Do Trojan horses carry viruses or worms?

6. What are some examples of violation of intellectual property?

7. What is the difference between an exploit and vulnerability?

8. What are the types of password attacks?

9. What is the difference between a denial-of-service attack and a distributed denial-of-service attack? Which is potentially more dangerous and devastating? Why?

10. For a sniffer attack to succeed, what must the attacker do? How can an attacker gain access to a network to use the sniffer system?

11. What is management's role with regard to information security policies and practices?

12. What are the differences between a policy, a standard, and a practice?

13. For a policy to be considered effective and legally enforceable, what criteria must be met?

14. What are the components of an effective EISP? How does the EISP differ from the ISSP?

15. What is the difference between a security framework and a security blueprint?

16. What is the ISO 27000 series of standards?

17. What documents are available from the NIST Computer Resource Center, and how can they support the development of a security framework?

18. Briefly describe the Spheres of Security. Who could benefit from understanding this approach to security?

19. What is a security perimeter, and what are the different types of perimeters organizations should look to implement?

20. What are the key components used for planning the security perimeter?

Real-World Exercises

Exercise 1-1

Using an existing security policy, build an effective security education presentation. The presentation should be geared to the computer layman, should highlight the important portions of the security policy, and should point end users to both the security policy and additional help. Additionally, list five different ways that you could deliver effective education to the necessary audience.

Exercise 1-2

Applying software patches to fix security vulnerabilities is one of the most effective security measures you can use to protect your environment. Find a reputable Internet source from which to receive security advisories. Now that the advisory information is flowing to you, develop a process to receive, assess, and distribute the advisories. In addition, the process should address how you identify all the systems to which the advisory applies and track the progress of testing and installing the proper patches.

Hands-On Projects

Project 1-1

The Annualized Loss Expectancy (ALE) is a risk assessment formula that calculates the potential financial loss from perceived threats. Based on the ALE calculation, one can determine which assets hold the greatest value, prioritize the protection of those assets, and determine which security measures will best benefit the business. The formula is as follows: ALE = SLE * ARO, where SLE refers to Single Loss Expectancy and ARO refers to Annualized Rate of Occurrence. SLE is determined by multiplying an asset's value by the Exposure Factor (EF). The first component of SLE, the asset value, is the total monetary amount determined from the cost of the hardware, software, training, support, and other costs of maintaining the system—otherwise known as total cost of ownership (TCO.) The asset value should also include the value to the organization of the applications and data on the system. The second component, Exposure Factor (EF), is the percentage of asset loss that is expected from a particular threat. In this project, you use the ALE formula to compute possible financial loss from computer attacks. To complete this project, you need a pencil and paper.

1. For this project, assume that an organization has five servers. Server 1 has a TCO of $25,000, Servers 2 and 3 have a TCO of $37,000 each, and the remaining two servers—Servers 4 and 5—have a TCO of $42,000 each. The servers are not used by internal employees but are used by Web visitors. The total income that all five servers brings in is $5 million a year (equally provided by all five servers). Compute the total asset value for each of the five servers.

2. In order to recover from an attack on any one server, it would take an estimated 14 hours to rebuild Servers 1, 2, 3, and 4 and 37 hours to rebuild Server 5. If each server is required to be online 8,760 hours a year, compute the EF for each server.

3. Since the security for the five Web servers is moderate, a Web attack is estimated to occur once per year. Compute the ARO for a Web attack.

4. What is the ALE for a Web attack for each of the five servers?

5. What is the total ALE for the entire organization for a Web attack that damages all five servers at the same time?

6. Based on the calculated ALE for an attack that damages all five servers, how much should the organization spend on security controls to prevent Web attacks on the five servers?

Endnotes

1. National Security Telecommunications and Information Systems Security, *National Training Standard for Information Systems Security (Infosec) Professionals*, 20 June 1994, File 4011. Accessed February 8, 2004 from *www.nstissc.gov/Assets/pdf/4011.pdf*.

2. McCumber, John. "Information Systems Security: A Comprehensive Model." *Proceedings 14th National Computer Security Conference. National Institute of Standards and Technology.* Baltimore, MD (October 1991).

3. Sun Tzu. *The Art of War* Chapter Three: "Planning Attacks." Accessed February 16, 2004 from *www.sonshi.com/sun3.html*.

4. Computer Security Institute, "2010/2011 CSI Computer Crime and Security Survey." Accessed November 4, 2011 from *http://gocsi.com/survey*.

5. Michael Whitman, "Enemy at the Gates: Threats to Information Security," *Communications of the ACM*, 46(8) August 2003, pp. 91–96.

6. SANS Institute, "The Twenty Most Critical Internet Security Vulnerabilities (Updated): The Experts' Consensus," *SANS Institute Online* (May 2, 2002). Accessed February 15, 2004 from *www.sans.org/top20.html*.

7. SANS Institute, "Consensus Roadmap for Defeating Distributed Denial of Service Attacks: A Project of the Partnership for Critical Infrastructure Security," *SANS Institute Online*, (February 23, 2000). Accessed February 15, 2004 from *www.sans.org/dosstep/roadmap.php*.

8. Paul Brooke, "DDoS: Internet Weapons of Mass Destruction," *Network Computing* 12, no. 1 (January 2001): 67.

9. CERT® Advisory CA-1996-21 TCP SYN Flooding and IP Spoofing Attacks, CERT, "TCP SYN Flooding and IP Spoofing Attacks," Advisory CA-1996-21.

10. Webopedia, "IP spoofing," *Webopedia Online* (4 June 2002). Accessed February 15, 2004 from *www.webopedia.com/TERM/I/IP_spoofing.html*.

11. Bhavin Bharat Bhansali, "Man-In-The-Middle Attack: A Brief." *SANS Institute Online* (February 16, 2001). Accessed 15 February 2004 from *www.giac.org/practical/gsec/Bhavin_Bhansali_GSEC.pdf*.

12. James Pearce, "Security Expert Warns of MP3 Danger," *ZDNet News Online* (March 18, 2002). Accessed February 15, 2004 from *zdnet.com.com/2100-1105-861995.html*.

13. Webopedia, "sniffer," *Webopedia Online* (February 5, 2002). Accessed February 15, 2004 from *www.webopedia.com/TERM/s/sniffer.html*.

14. Elinor Abreu, "Kevin Mitnick Bares All," *NetworkWorldFusion News Online* (28 September 2000). Accessed 15 February 2004 from *www.nwfusion.com/news/2000/0928mitnick.html*.

15. Webopedia, "buffer overflow," *Webopedia Online* (29 July 2003). Accessed 15 February 2004 from *www.webopedia.com/TERM/b/buffer_overflow.html*.

16. Scott Spanbauer, "Pentium Bug, Meet the IE 4.0 Flaw," *PC World* 16, no. 2 (February 1998): 55.

17. Gaël Hachez, François Koeune, and Jean-Jacques Quisquater, "Timing attack: what can be achieved by a powerful adversary?" *Proceedings of the 20th symposium on Information Theory in the Benelux* (May 1999), 63–70.

18. Charles Cresson Wood. "Integrated Approach Includes Information Security." *Security* 37, no. 2 (February 2000): 43–44.

19. National Institute of Standards and Technology. *An Introduction to Computer Security: The NIST Handbook*, SP 800-14, Accessed December 23, 2010 from *csrc.nist.gov/publications/nistpubs/800-14/800-14.pdf*.

20. National Institute of Standards and Technology. *An Introduction to Computer Security: The NIST Handbook*, SP 800-12.

21. Derived from a number of sources, the most notable of which is *www.wustl.edu/policies/infosecurity.html*.

22. Aalberts, R., Townsend, A. & Whitman, M. (1999). "Considerations for an Effective Telecommunications Use Policy." *Communications of the ACM* 42, no. 6, (101–109).

23. National Institute of Standards and Technology. *An Introduction to Computer Security: The NIST Handbook*, SP 800-12.

24. National Institute of Standards and Technology (2001). *Code of Practice for Information Security Management* (ISO/IEC 17799).

25. National Institute of Standards and Technology (2001). *Code of Practice for Information Security Management* (ISO/IEC 17799).

26. Kadrich, M. (2007) *Endpoint Security*. Boston: Addison-Wesley.

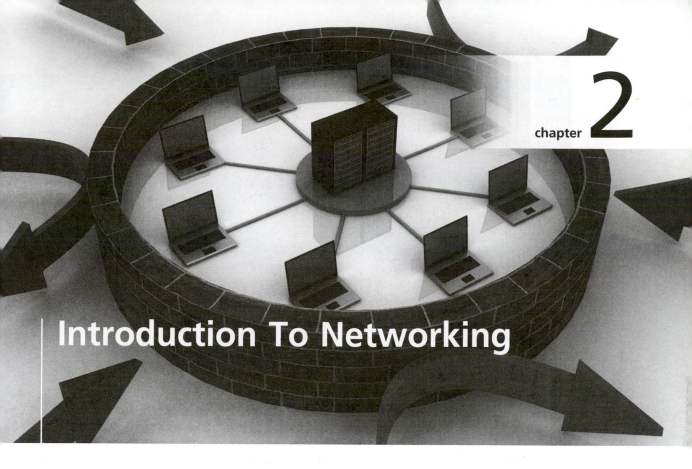

chapter 2

Introduction To Networking

There are three kinds of death in this world. There's heart death, there's brain death, and there's being off the network. – Guy Almes

Upon completion of this material, you should be able to:

- Describe the basic elements of computer-based data communication
- Discuss the key entities and organizations behind current networking standards, as well as the purpose of and intent behind the more widely used standards
- Explain the nature and intent of the OSI reference model as well as list and describe each of the model's seven layers
- Describe the nature of the Internet and the relationship between the TCP/IP protocol and the Internet

Running Case: Chatting with Partners

It has been several years since EBS established a connection in order to share real-time information with its suppliers. In order to efficiently replace office supplies, EBS's order management had given its business partner, Davis Office Megaplex, access to the EBS inventory management system. Enabled with this type of real-time access, Davis Office Megaplex periodically checks inventory levels and restocks office supplies when levels drop below certain thresholds. The order management project called for a new type of network connection: an extranet.

Until establishing that type of connection, EBS used an internal network, a small, protected network for Web servers called a demilitarized zone (or DMZ), and outbound access to the Internet. The extranet connection and partner relationship streamlined EBS's ordering process and allowed the OM department to reduce its staff. In addition, the other departments at EBS benefited by avoiding the problems caused by running out of office supplies at crucial times.

Now, the key for EBS in general, and its IT department in particular, is to make sure this critical network connection has the necessary security controls so that data is protected in transit and no unauthorized users can use the connection. Luckily, Paige Davis, the network administrator, is well versed in EBS's network architecture. However, it has been some time since she looked into the network technologies and devices involved with the extranet connection. To ensure security controls are properly in place for the upcoming audit, it is time to get back to basics and relearn the various network technologies involved.

Introduction

To computer users, the network is a transparent entity. A user logs on to his or her workstation and uses a variety of tools to communicate with other users and other computer systems. He or she expects e-mail, instant messaging, and Web browsing to work. After all, if the data is there in a timely fashion, who cares how it got there?

Network administrators care. Networks provide the blood flow for the computing environment and must be managed efficiently around the clock. Networks are typically composed of hundreds or even thousands of miles of data arteries and veins. Each network component is designed to ensure that information continues to flow efficiently to all consumers. The burden of maintaining this vital IT resource is left to the network administrators.

Hackers also care—those miscreants who seek to use computers and networks for unintended, unauthorized, and often illegal purposes. By design, the increasing complexity of network communication speeds up and increases the amount of data users can share. However, by mastering the complexity of network protocols, attackers can also subvert network devices and communications for malicious purposes. Security professionals must recognize this fact and help network administrators keep this vital arterial system protected. This chapter outlines many of the technologies that network administrators—and security professionals—must support and protect. It serves as a survey of the essentials of computer networking.

Networking Fundamentals

In a fundamental exchange of information between two parties, one party—the sender—communicates a message to a second party—the receiver—over some medium, as illustrated in Figure 2-1.

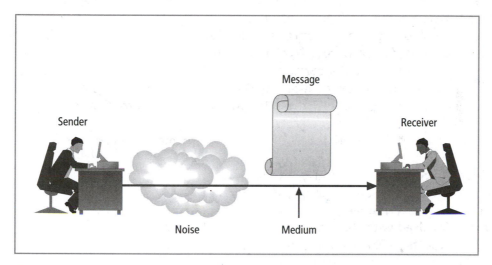

Figure 2-1 Basic communications model
© Cengage Learning 2013

Communication can only occur when the recipient is able to receive, process, and comprehend the message. This one-way flow of information from sender to receiver is referred to as a **channel**. When the recipient also becomes a sender—for example, by responding to the original sender's message—this two-way flow of information is called a **circuit**.

Reasons to Network

Data communications and networking go hand in hand. **Data communications** is the exchange of computer-based or other digital messages across a medium. **Networking** is the interconnection of groups or systems with the purpose of exchanging information. There are a number of reasons to build a network:

- Exchanging information—First and foremost, we create networks to exchange information among entities, both human and electronic. This information could be stored in databases, created in processing, or obtained from external inputs. The modern extensions of information exchange include e-mail, instant messaging, video conferencing, and online seminar broadcasting.

- Sharing scarce or expensive resources—A typical organization may not be able to afford expensive equipment for every member. For example, a standard laser printer may cost between $300 and $500. For an organization with 1,000 members, the costs to provide one to each member would be $300,000–$500,000. Instead, workgroups could share equipment that's more expensive, more reliable, and more full featured, thereby saving the organization money.

- Allowing distributed organizations to act as if centrally located—With the almost instant communications capabilities of today's Internet, interaction among members of an organization can be even faster and more productive than face-to-face meetings. Instead of the travel and scheduling complications of face-to-face meetings for dispersed groups, video conferencing can provide instant exchange of ideas. Communications has evolved to the point where an individual really does not need to care about where his or her peers are, only if they are able to respond in a timely manner.

Getting the Message Across

Communication requires the sender to get the message to the receiver successfully via a medium. The process of placing a message on a medium usually requires some modification or manipulation of the medium so that it can carry the message. This modification is referred to as **modulation**. The sender modulates the medium—the signal—to carry the message.

The method used to embed the message on the signal depends on the type of message and type of signal. As shown in Figure 2-2, there are two types of message (or information). Analog information, such as voice communications, is carried on a medium that is constantly changing, whereas digital information, such as computer communications, is discrete, alternating between a few values—in this case, 1s and 0s. Analog signals, such as those carried on the public phone network (the human voice and music, most commonly), use continuously varying waveforms, whereas discrete signals, such as those carried on computer networks, use discrete values in defined voltage levels. The grid shown in Figure 2-2 indicates that modulation may take one of four forms: analog to analog, analog to digital, digital to analog, or digital to digital.

Analog Information on an Analog Medium The public telephone network and commercial radio stations have been embedding information on an analog medium for over 90 years. The embedding or modulation of an analog data source onto an analog signal involves manipulating one or more of the three characteristics of a signal. As shown in Figure 2-3, the analog signal has height (**amplitude**), length (**frequency**), and a reference to an original wave starting point (**phase**). Frequency is measured in hertz—named after the scientist Heinrich Rudolf Hertz, who pioneered radio wave production and detection. One wave iteration or *cycle* per second is one **hertz (Hz)**, one thousand cycles per second is one kilohertz (KHz), and one million cycles per second is one megahertz (MHz), and so forth. By altering a wave's amplitude, frequency, and phase, analog information can be stored and transmitted. In modern communications, more than one characteristic may be modified at the same time.

Most common voice networks use a functional bandwidth of 4,000 hertz (4 KHz). Some of this bandwidth is used to provide a buffer between adjacent bandwidths, such as between the 0 and 4,000 Hz bandwidth and the 4,000 and 8,000 Hz bandwidth. These buffers typically result in a loss of 300 Hz on the lower end of the spectrum and 700 Hz on the upper end,

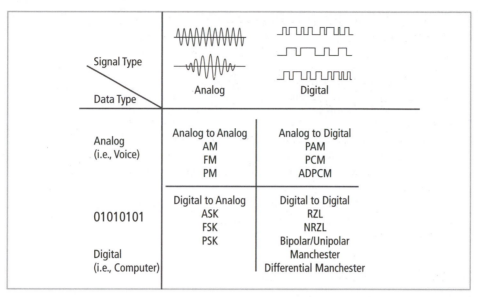

Figure 2-2 Data-to-signal modulation
© Cengage Learning 2013

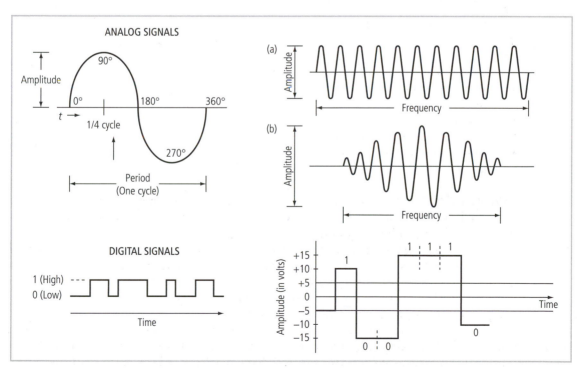

Figure 2-3 Analog and digital signals
© Cengage Learning 2013

resulting in a typical usable bandwidth of approximately 3 KHz. Because most of the audible component of human speech falls in this 300–3,300 Hz range, it has been commonplace for several decades, becoming a de facto standard.

Analog Information on a Digital Medium With the explosion in popularity of digital entertainment via CDs and DVDs, and with the rise of digital communications technologies like wireless telephony, digitizing analog data has become more commonplace. In fact, the same technologies noted earlier are required in order to digitize analog information found in older media formats so that they can be efficiently transmitted over a digital network. The technologies involved are based on **pulse amplitude modulation (PAM)**, which uses analog frequencies to encode one or more bits, by measuring the height of the signal. The height measurements correspond to a digital value: "0," "1," or some multi-bit combination. PAM incorporates the **Shannon-Nyquist theorem**, which states that if a signal is sampled at a rate at least twice the highest frequency and at regular intervals, the sample will contain all the relevant information of the original signal. The most common version of PAM, **pulse code modulation (PCM)**, uses an 8-bit sample size. If we were to use PCM on a standard voice channel of 4,000 Hz, then sampling at twice the highest frequency would provide 8,000 samples of 8 bits each, for an equivalent digital signal of 64,000 bits per second (bps). If we sample at greater rates (known as oversampling), the resulting signal will have even more data embedded but will require greater bandwidth. Figure 2-4 provides an illustration of PCM used in voice digitization.

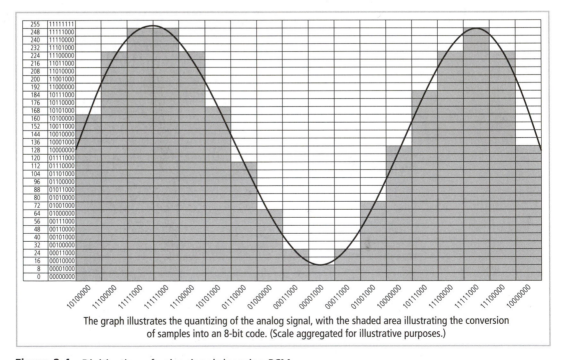

The graph illustrates the quantizing of the analog signal, with the shaded area illustrating the conversion of samples into an 8-bit code. (Scale aggregated for illustrative purposes.)

Figure 2-4   Digitization of voice signals by using PCM

© Cengage Learning 2013

An improvement on PCM—Adaptive Differential PCM (ADPCM)—requires only a 4-bit code, given that it measures only the difference between sequential waves, thus requires a low data rate to transmit. This technique is used in some voice over IP (VoIP) communications.

Digital to Analog In the early days of home Internet access, most people used a modem. This modulator-demodulator converted the native digital data into an analog form capable of traveling over the public phone networks. Modems embed digital data much the same way that radios embed voices over the airwaves: by manipulating the basic characteristics of the signal. As shown in Figure 2-5, the three techniques used to embed digital information onto an analog signal are **amplitude shift keying (ASK)**, **frequency shift keying (FSK)**, and **phase shift keying (PSK)**. Actually, a combination of these techniques is used to improve data throughput. In the early days of modems, the term **baud rate** was used to represent the speed of communications—that is, the number of signals transmitted per second. Now, with the ability to embed multiple bits of information in each signal, the term has fallen out of use in favor of **bits per second (bps)**. (This is not to be confused with bytes per second (Bps), used in describing the uploading and downloading of data files.)

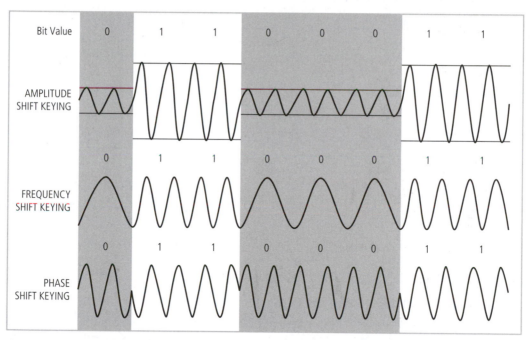

Figure 2-5 Shift keying
© Cengage Learning 2013

Digital to Digital Embedding digital information onto a digital signal is performed by computer hardware known as a transceiver (transmitter/receiver) or a network interface card (NIC), which connects a computer to its network. The NIC modulates the current carried over the network into a series of discrete voltage levels encoding the binary data. The more common versions are described as "unipolar" or "bipolar," which refers to whether the signal uses one pole or two. They are also described as "return to zero" or "non-return to zero" level, which refers to whether or not the signal drops to zero voltage, either between values or as a value (see Figure 2-6). By using multiple voltage levels, multiple bits can be transmitted at the same voltage level; for example, 4 volts could be 00, 3 volts could be 01, 2 volts could be 10, and 1 volt could be 11.

One of the challenges in digital communications is the transmission of a long string of values, given that this requires careful synchronization between systems to keep the bit count on long strings. The alternative is to embed a synchronization point in the bit stream—sort of like using a metronome for a music performance. Ethernet LANs use Manchester encoding, which provides a synchronization point in mid-bit, encodes a 1 bit as a transition between a low and high value and a 0 bit as a shift between a high and low value. Most modern Ethernet implementations use a voltage level of approximately +/- 1 volt, depending on the technology deployed.

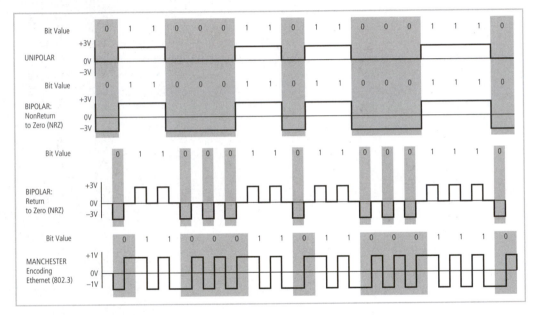

Figure 2-6   Digital communications
© Cengage Learning 2013

Combining Multiple Signals

Because the transmission of a single signal over long distances is inefficient, techniques have been developed to carry additional data over the same media. The first is multi-bit encoding, in which the signal levels described earlier are coded to allow the representation of more than one bit per signal level. The second is the combination of several inputs onto a high-bandwidth stream to carry multiple signals long distances. This method of combining signals is known as **multiplexing**. The three dominant multiplexing methods in use today are frequency division multiplexing, time division multiplexing, and wave division multiplexing.

Frequency Division Multiplexing   Frequency division multiplexing (FDM) is used primarily in analog communications to combine voice channels. The standard voice channel for analog communication on the telephone network is 0–4,000 Hz, with a built-in buffer to prevent the channels from interfering with one another. FDM works by temporarily shifting channels to higher frequencies, then moving them back on the far end of the high-capacity connection. This technique is illustrated in Figure 2-7.

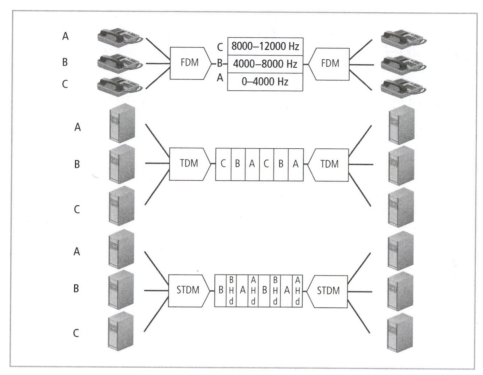

Figure 2-7   Multiplexing
© Cengage Learning 2013

Time Division Multiplexing   Time division multiplexing (TDM), used predominantly in digital communications, assigns a time block to each client, then polls each client in succession to transmit a set of information (predefined byte or block). Each station sends its information, which is recompiled into a cohesive data stream on the far end of the communication channel. If a station has no data to send, that time slot goes empty. Because this was viewed as inefficient, though, a variant on TDM—**statistical time division multiplexing (STDM)**, also known as statistical multiplexing —has eliminated the dedicated time slots by adding header information to each packet, allowing any station with traffic to transmit on an as-needed basis. These techniques are also illustrated in Figure 2-7.

Wave Division Multiplexing   Wave Division Multiplexing (WDM), found exclusively in fiber-optic communications, uses different colors of light to allow multiple light-based signals to travel on the same fiber-optic channel. This is a derivative of FDM, but only applies to fiber-optic channels.

Impedance to Communications

Any communications medium may be subject to various types of interference, which are collectively referred to as **noise**. Noise occurs in a variety of forms:[1]

- **Attenuation**—The loss of signal strength as the signal moves across media. Both wired and wireless communications suffer from attenuation. The higher quality the media, the less the degree of attenuation. Counteracting attenuation involves repeating or amplifying the signal or using a higher grade or type of media—for example, fiber-optic rather than copper cable.

- **Crosstalk**—The effect of one communications channel upon another. Crosstalk occurs when one transmission "bleeds" over to another (e.g., from one channel to another). Cable shielding can help minimize the possibility of crosstalk, as can changing from electrical or electromagnetic communications to photonic (fiber optic).

- **Distortion**—The unintentional variation of the communication over the media. Many items can affect the electrical or electromagnetic signal, including solar flares, magnetic interference from florescent lighting, and even electrical cables. The same techniques that mitigate crosstalk will counter the effects of distortion.

- **Echo**—The reflection of a signal because of equipment malfunction or poor design. The failure to properly terminate the physical medium (e.g., by failing to place a cap on the end of early coaxial cable-based networks) leads to signal reflection: the echoing of signals as they bounce back from the ends of the network. If you've ever heard your own voice on a telephone conversation, you've experienced echo. Repairing or replacing poorly designed or malfunctioning equipment usually resolves echo.

- **Impulse noise**—A sudden, short-lived increase in signal frequency or amplitude, also known as a spike. Like distortion, impulse noise causes a temporary loss in signal clarity. Some of the sources of distortion also cause impulse noise—solar flares, an overloaded electrical circuit, or a short in a data communications channel. Because these problems cannot be predicted or easily diagnosed, countering their effects is usually difficult.

- **Jitter**—Signal modification caused by malfunctioning equipment, such as a faulty network interface card or hub. Jitter usually involves extra signal components in (or unwanted modification of) the amplitude, frequency, or phase of the signal. If you've listened to a CD skipping or playing at the wrong speed with click sounds, you've heard jitter. Providing anti-jitter circuits (AJC) or buffers to provide some measure of delay helps to counter jitter occurrence.

- **White noise**—Unwanted noise from a signal coming across the media at multiple frequencies, also referred to as static noise. It can be the result of the heat of the electrons moving across electrical communications or poor-quality communication circuits. The background hiss heard in telephone communications is white noise. Moving from electrical to photonic communications can resolve this issue.

Types of Networks

Networks can be categorized by components, size, layout or topology, or media. These categories ensure that practitioners can speak a common language when referring to networks.

Networks Categorized by Components

Networks categorized by their components include peer-to-peer (or P2P) networks, server-based networks, and distributed multi-server networks. In peer-to-peer networks, the individual users or clients directly interact with one another, sharing resources without the benefit of a central repository or server. This level of connection is common in small office or home networks, where users may share hard drives, directories, or printers. An extension of the P2P network is the Servant model, where a client shares part of its resources, thereby serving as a pseudo-server—a device that provides services to others. The Servant model became very popular in the late-1990s, when music-sharing services like Napster were quickly adopted by end users. Even after legal issues associated with the unauthorized reproduction and distribution of copyrighted music caused Napster to be shut down and dramatically redesigned, other variants like Kazaa, LimeWire, iMesh, Morpheus, and BearShare adopted the model.

Server-based networks use a dedicated system to provide specific services to their clients. These services may be hosted on a single general service system, or individual services may be provided by multiple servers. These types of networks are discussed in the upcoming sections on local and wide area networks. Distributed multi-server networks add distance and additional services to this model by separating the services outside the organization from other organizations with other systems and servers.

Networks Categorized by Size

One of the most common methods of categorizing networks is by size. Originally, network sizes were described as either local area or wide area. The Institute of Electrical and Electronics Engineers (IEEE) first defined a **local area network (LAN)** as a network with less than 3 miles of total cabling. The current definition is of a network containing a dedicated server that provides services connecting systems within or between a few buildings, over a small geographic space. LANs are typically owned by a single organization and used to support its internal communications.

The next largest size is a **metropolitan area network (MAN)**, which typically covers a region the size of a municipality, county, or district. The informal definition of a MAN is that it is larger than a LAN but smaller than a wide area network (WAN).

A **wide area network (WAN)** is a very large network that covers a vast geographic region like a state, a country, or even the planet. There are two dominant WANs: the public telephone network and the Internet. (Note that *the* Internet begins with an uppercase I, whereas *an* internet—an internetwork or network of networks—begins with a lowercase i.) There are a host of other WANs, usually associated with one of the dominant communications infrastructure providers. A WAN can comprise a collection of LANs and MANs.

Since these definitions were developed, a host of variations has arisen, including: personal area networks, which typically connect a few devices owned by the same individual; file area networks, which connect a number of data storage technologies; campus area networks, which are large LANs or small MANs that connect two or more LANs, typically within adjacent buildings; and body area networks, which are personal devices carried on one's person that communicate with each other.

Networks Categorized by Topology

A **topology** is the pattern of associations among network components. The topology can be physical or logical. Physical topologies indicate how networks are cabled, whereas logical topologies indicate how they function. The most common physical topologies are ring, bus, star, hierarchy, mesh, and hybrid (see Figure 2-8), whereas the most common logical topologies are bus and star. A bus is a linear communication channel and its associated nodes, the messages being transmitted one at a time from one station or node to another, with each node taking turns. The messages can travel in either direction (in the case of a physical bus) or in just one direction (in the case of a physical ring). In a star logical topology, there is a central node to which each station or node transmits, after which the message is retransmitted to all the attached nodes.

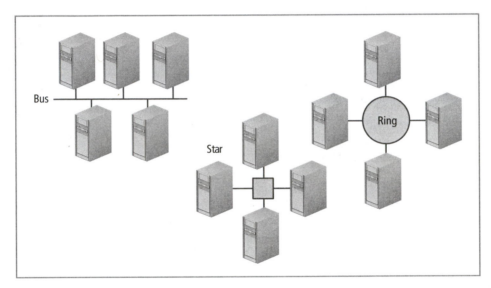

Figure 2-8   Physical network topologies
© Cengage Learning 2013

Networks Categorized by Media

There are two categories for network media: guided and unguided, also known as wired and wireless. Wired networks typically use electricity or light waves over cables to transmit messages, whereas wireless media networks use radio or infrared electromagnetic energy. Network media are discussed in the section on the TCP/IP Physical layer.

Standards Organizations

A number of organizations promote the standardization of data communication components. Some seek to standardize the use of data communications, whereas others work on standardizing the design of data communications technologies and **protocols**—that is, the rules for communications. Protocols that are widely accepted become standards. Some standards are formal, or **de jure**; these have been reviewed by a group of experts and endorsed by a standards body. Other standards are informal, or **de facto**; they have been widely adopted without having been formally reviewed. The Internet standards, such as TCP/IP, are de facto standards, whereas Ethernet standards (IEEE 802.3) are de jure standards.

Among the agencies that work on data communications standards are the Internet Society (ISOC), the Internet Assigned Numbers Authority (IANA), the American National Standards Institute (ANSI), the International Telecommunications Union (ITU), the Institute of Electrical and Electronics Engineers (IEEE), the Telecommunications Industry Association (TIA), and the International Organization for Standardization (ISO).

The Internet Society (ISOC)

ISOC seeks to formalize standards to facilitate the development of compatible technologies. It was formed in 1992 with a mission "to assure the open development, evolution, and use of the Internet for the benefit of all people throughout the world."[2] ISOC is an organizational umbrella under which a number of other organizations operate:

- Internet Engineering Task Force (IETF)
- Internet Research Task Force (IRTF)
- Internet Engineering Steering Group (IESG)
- Internet Architecture Board (IAB)

Internet Assigned Numbers Authority (IANA)

Originally part of the ISOC, IANA is responsible for the coordination of domain names, IP addresses and protocols, and port assignments. In recent years, IANA was transferred to the Internet Corporation for Assigned Names and Numbers (ICANN), an international non-profit organization set up by the ISOC. It is closely monitored by the U.S. government and ICANN to ensure that no inappropriate activities occur.

American National Standards Institute (ANSI)

The American National Standards Institute (ANSI) seeks to reinforce the position of U.S. government and industry while helping ensure the health and safety of consumers and protecting the environment. ANSI supervises the creation and use of thousands of standards and directives that directly affect companies and government agencies in almost every sector of the economy. It is also actively committed to accrediting programs that evaluate conformity to those standards.[3]

International Telecommunications Union (ITU)

ITU is the United Nations' principal agency for communication and information technologies. Acting as a focus for government interests and the private sector, ITU serves to help the world communicate in three critical sectors: radio communication, calibration, and development. It is based in Geneva, Switzerland, and its membership includes 191 member states and more than 700 member organizations and associations.[4]

Institute of Electrical and Electronics Engineers (IEEE)

A nonprofit organization, IEEE is the world's principal trade association for the advancement of technology. It is active in many industrial sectors, including computers and telecommunications, electric power, and electronics. Its members count on IEEE as an impartial source of information, resources, and engineering for both organizations and individual professionals. To stimulate an interest in the technology profession, IEEE is also active among university students around the world.

IEEE has:

- More than 400,000 total members (including more than 100,000 student members)
- 333 sections divided into 10 geographical areas
- 2,081 chapters that link the local members who have similar technical interests
- Over 1,855 student organizations at universities in 80 countries
- 533 student branch chapters of IEEE technical societies[5]

Telecommunications Industry Association (TIA)

TIA is a partnership among information, communications, and entertainment companies. It is active in the development of standards and has a role in the development of both domestic and international policy.[6] Standards for data communications are commonly published as dual standards with the Electronics Industry Association (EIA)—for example, the standards for wiring specifications (such as EIA/TIA T568A and T568B) in communications jacks (e.g., RJ-11s for telephones and RJ-45s for data cables).

International Organization for Standardization (ISO)

ISO is the global leader in developing and publishing international standards. The organization's initials are derived from its French title. It is a network of national standards bodies from 157 countries, with one member body per country. ISO is organized around a Central Secretariat based in Geneva, Switzerland, which coordinates activities across the system. It is a nongovernmental organization that bridges the gap between the public and private sectors. Many of its member institutes are governmental structures in their own countries, whereas others have their roots in the private economy. Therefore, ISO often represents a consensus for solutions that meet the requirements of business and the broader needs of society.[7]

OSI Reference Model

In 1978, ISO developed a layered model of networking that became known as the Open Systems Interconnection (OSI) Reference Model. This model rapidly became the dominant method for illustrating the functions of a network protocol in academic and industry environments. Developed jointly with the International Telecommunications Standardization Sector of the International Telecommunications Union (ITU-T), the project was to develop a vendor-neutral, nonproprietary set of network standards in an effort to establish a method of creating components for networking that would facilitate communications through common protocols, but it was quickly eclipsed by the rising popularity of the TCP/IP protocol stack of the Internet's predecessors, like the MILNET and BITNET.

The OSI Reference Model broke down the complex process of communications into seven distinct layers, each with specific functions and protocols. Whereas the protocols themselves became obsolete, the reference model layers are widely accepted as a common methodology for communications instruction. Figure 2-9 provides an overview of the OSI Reference Model layers and functions. Each layer is discussed in additional detail in the following sections.

OSI Model			
	Data Unit	**Layer**	**Function**
Host layers	Data	7. Application	Network process to application
		6. Presentation	Data representation and encryption
		5. Session	Interhost communication
	Segments	4. Transport	End-to-end connections and reliability (TCP)
Media layers	Packets	3. Network	Path determination and logical addressing (IP)
	Frames	2. Data Link	Physical addressing (MAC & LLC)
	Bits	1. Physical	Media, signal, and binary transmission

Figure 2-9 ISO OSI Reference Model
© Cengage Learning 2013

As shown in Figure 2-10, the premise of the OSI Reference Model is that information created by the user or client is translated and encoded through the various layers, from the top level at the Application layer to the bottom level at the Physical layer, where it is transmitted across a network, to a receiver, where it is broken down by the receiver's protocol stack in reverse order. Each layer provides a header with specific information on the function of that layer, then passes the data and header to the next-lower level, where it becomes the data payload for that layer.

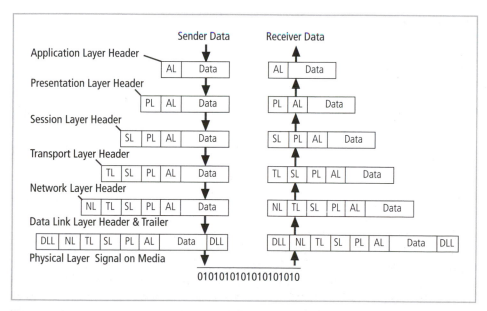

Figure 2-10 OSI Reference Model in action
© Cengage Learning 2013

Physical Layer

At the **Physical layer**, the primary function is to place the transmission signal carrying the message onto the communications media—in other words, put "bits on a wire." The following sections describe the primary functions and services.

Establishing and Terminating the Physical and Logical Connection to the Media
The physical standards and specifications are too various to discuss in this chapter. However, there are several common to networking, including cabling and connector standards. As mentioned earlier, media can be divided into two categories: guided media (including wire and cables) and unguided media (including wireless and microwave radio and infrared). The dominant media types and standards will be examined here.

Twisted Pair Wire Twisted pair wire consists of a number of colored wires twisted together to minimize the effect of external noise on the carried signal. There used to be two types of twisted pair wire in use: shielded twisted pair wire (STP) and unshielded twisted pair wire (UTP). STP was used primarily for token ring networks (discussed in the Data Link layer section) and is seldom seen in modern implementations. UTP cable is now the most common alternative, given that it is inexpensive, easy to work with, and physically small compared to other options. With no shielding, the twisting would only provide minimal protection, so the cable has a maximum effective limit of approximately 100 yards. (Note that this distance is between end nodes—i.e., a computer and the switch, not the length of cable between the computer and the wall outlet.)

As shown in Figure 2-11, the color coding follows a standard—**TIA 568 A/B**—issued by the Telecommunications Industry Association (an offshoot of the Electronics Industry Association) and is used to ensure that both ends of the cable are connected correctly between the endpoints. (The B standard, published in 2001, renders the A standard obsolete.) The jacks and ports used for these cables are part of a standard known as Radio Jack (RJ) 45 series.

The type of UTP cable used is rated by category. The categories currently listed include:

- Cat 1—Not a formal standard recognized by TIA/EIA; previously used for POTS telephone communications, ISDN, and doorbell wiring
- Cat 2—Not a formal standard recognized by TIA/EIA; previously was frequently used on 4-Mbps token ring networks
- Cat 3—Currently defined in TIA/EIA-568-B; used for data networks using frequencies up to 16 MHz; traditionally popular for 10-Mbps Ethernet networks
- Cat 4—Currently unrecognized by TIA/EIA; provided performance of up to 20 MHz and was frequently used on 16-Mbps token ring networks
- Cat 5—Currently unrecognized by TIA/EIA; provided performance of up to 100 MHz and was frequently used on 100-Mbps Ethernet networks; may be unsuitable for 1000BASE-T Gigabit Ethernet networks
- Cat 5e—Currently defined in TIA/EIA-568-B; provides performance of up to 100 MHz and is frequently used for both 100-Mbps and Gigabit Ethernet networks
- Cat 6—Currently defined in TIA/EIA-568-B; provides performance of up to 250 MHz,

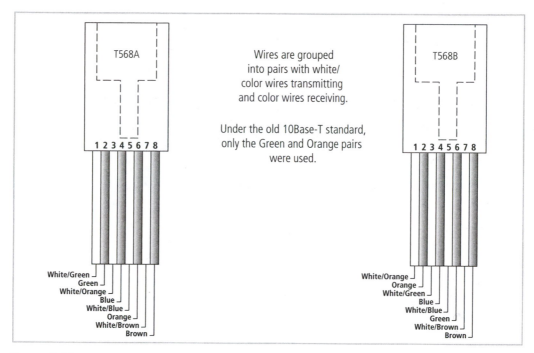

Figure 2-11   TIA 568A/B standard wiring specifications
© Cengage Learning 2013

- Cat 6a—Future specification for 10-Gbps applications
- Cat 7—An informal name applied to ISO/IEC 11801 Class F cabling; specifies four individually-shielded pairs (STP) inside an overall shield; designed for transmission at frequencies up to 600 MHz

Coaxial Cable   Coaxial cable consists of a solid core of copper surrounded by an insulating material surrounded by a mesh of conducting copper fibers, all of which is embedded in another insulating material like foil. Finally, the entire cable has a protective cover around it. Coaxial cable was one of the first local area networking cable types.

As shown in Figure 2-12, the primary purpose of the outer conductor is to absorb external noise that could interfere with the signal carried on the copper core. Coaxial cable, like fiber-optic cable, is a channel media, which means that it can only carry one message in one direction. A second cable is needed to return a message and complete the circuit. Some short-distance communications have been performed using the outer conductor in implementations like high-speed Internet over cable television installations from the home to the street connection point.

At the height of coaxial-based networks, there were two primary types of cable used: "thicknet" (RG-8) and "thinnet" (RG-58). Thicknet used a large auxiliary unit interface (AUI) cable connected to a "vampire tap" that connected to the large diameter cable to establish the connection. Thinnet ran station to station, connecting directly to the network interface card through a BNC connector. Today, coaxial cable is all but obsolete in data communications. The exception is its use in the cable television infrastructure to support cable modem-based high-speed Internet access for residences.

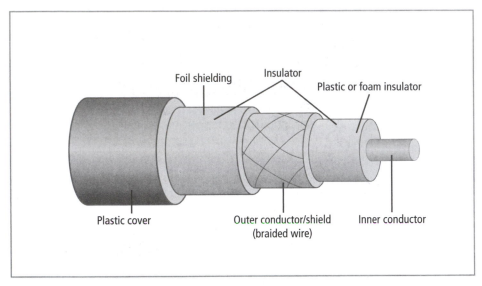

Figure 2-12   Coaxial cable structure
© Cengage Learning 2013

Fiber-Optic Cable   Fiber-optic cable is a tube of glass with an ultra-pure glass core that carries light waves through the length of the cable. As shown in Figure 2-13, there are a number of variants of fiber-optic cable. The simplest is single mode, in which a single beam of light is transmitted down the length of the cable. This provides data rates of approximately 10 Gbps over distances of up to approximately 35 miles.

If a sender desires to send more than one signal at the same time, a multi-mode variant can be used, such as graded-index or step-index. Typical transmission speeds for these variants are up to 100 Mbps for up to two miles, up to 1 Gbps for approximately 500 yards, and up to 10 Gbps for up to approximately 1/5 mile (300 yards). The two variants differ in the method they use to "bounce" the light down the path, with step-index using changes in the angle of transmission and graded-index modifying the wavelengths of light. Fiber-optic cable typically uses an "ST" or "SC" type connector.

Wireless LAN   When installing networks in buildings under construction, it is most beneficial to use physical cable like UTP. UTP is easy to work with, reliable, not subject to interception or eavesdropping, and relatively inexpensive. However, when installing networks in existing buildings, it becomes difficult and expensive to attempt to retrofit the facility with physical cable. The most commonly accepted alternative is to use a wireless local area network. Wireless LANS (also known as WLANs or by the brand name Wi-Fi, which stands for "wireless fidelity") are thought by many in the IT industry to be inherently insecure. The communication channel between the wireless network interface of any computing device and the access point that provides its services uses radio transmissions. Without some form of protection, these signals can be intercepted by anyone with a wireless packet sniffer. In order to prevent interception of these communications, these networks must use some form of cryptographic security control.

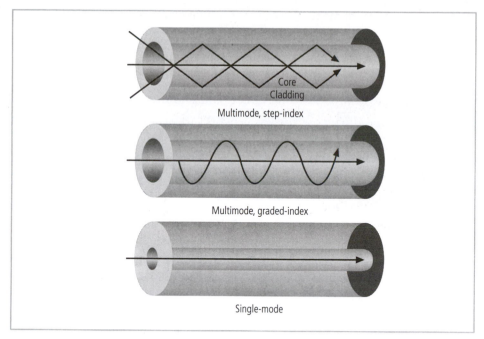

Figure 2-13   Fiber-optic cable modes
© Cengage Learning 2013

The advantages of WLANs include:

- Convenience—The wireless nature of such networks allows users to access network resources from nearly any convenient location within their primary networking environment (home or office).

- Mobility—With the emergence of public wireless networks, users can access the Internet even outside their normal work environment.

- Productivity—Users connected to a wireless network can maintain a nearly constant affiliation with their desired network as they move from place to place.

- Deployment—Initial setup of an infrastructure-based wireless network requires little more than a single access point.

- Expandability—Wireless networks can serve a suddenly increased number of clients with the existing equipment.

- Cost—Wireless networking hardware is at worst a modest increase from wired counterparts.

The disadvantages of WLANs include:

- Security—Wireless LAN transceivers are designed to serve computers throughout a structure with uninterrupted service using radio frequencies. Not only can the wireless packets be intercepted by a nearby adversary's computer, but more importantly, a user willing to spend a small amount of money on a good-quality antenna can pick up packets at a remarkable distance. In fact, there are even computer users, known as wardrivers, who are dedicated to locating and sometimes cracking into wireless networks.

- Range—The typical range of a common wireless network with standard equipment is on the order of tens of meters. Though sufficient for a typical home, it will be insufficient in a larger structure.

- Reliability—Like any radio frequency transmission, wireless networking signals are subject to a wide variety of interference as well as complex propagation effects that are beyond the control of the network administrator.

- Speed—The speed on most wireless networks (typically, 1 to 108 Mbps) is reasonably slow compared to the slowest common wired networks (100 Mbps up to several Gbps).

Wireless networks use wireless network interface cards to connect to an access control point (or AP). The AP provides the connection between the wireless network and the physical network. WLANs are organized into one of three architectures: peer to peer (P2P), basic service set (BSS), or extended service set (ESS). As shown in Figure 2-14, a P2P WLAN works much like its wired counterpart, with one client serving as the coordinating point for wireless access. All other clients connect by communicating with this coordinating client. A BSS works much like a true LAN, with a central AP serving as the hub or switch and with all the clients connecting through it. An extended service set is a collection of connected APs that allows the client to roam between BSSs much as a cellular phone customer can roam throughout a geographic region without being disconnected.

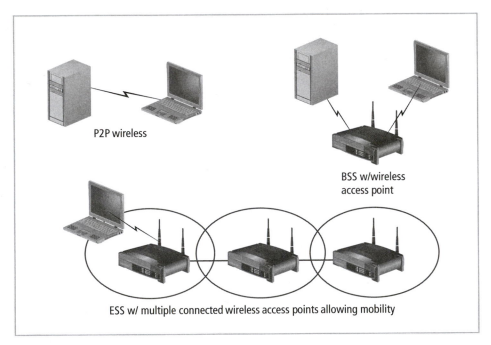

Figure 2-14 WLAN architectures
© Cengage Learning 2013

Bluetooth Bluetooth is now the de facto industry standard for short range wireless communications between devices. It is used to establish communications links between wireless telephones and headsets, between PDAs and desktop computers, and between laptops. It was established by scientists from the telecommunications company Ericsson, and soon they invited Intel, Nokia, IBM, and Toshiba to participate. Microsoft, Lucent Technologies, and 3Com joined the Bluetooth Special Interest Group shortly after its inception in order to support the new standard and technology.

The Bluetooth wireless communications link can be exploited by anyone within an approximately 30-foot range unless suitable security controls have been implemented. It has been estimated that there will be almost a billion Bluetooth-enabled devices by the end of the decade. In discoverable mode, devices can easily be discovered and accessed, much as a shared folder can on a networked computer. Even in nondiscoverable mode, the device is susceptible to access by other devices that have connected with it in the past.[8]

Infrared   Yet another variant is infrared wireless networks, which are currently not as popular as 802.11 or Bluetooth-based networks. At one time, there was a movement toward the use of Infrared Data connections between personal devices such as personal digital assistants (PDAs) and laptops. The Infrared Data Association (IrDA) defined several standards for use in short-range (typically less than 1 meter) infrared connections. This worked well for synchronizing personal computing equipment but was considered ineffective for networking because of its data rate (2.4 Kbps to 16 Mbps) and its line-of-sight requirement. Older infrared (IR) LANs mounted central APs in the ceiling as a networking option, but these were quickly replaced with 802.11 alternatives.

Physical Layer Networking Devices   At the Physical layer, a **hub** is a device that provides a physical connection between a system and a network. Although advances in networking technology have blurred the lines between hubs, switches, and even routers, the simplest connection is that of the hub. It works by accepting a transmission on the outbound wire or sets of wires connecting the computer to the network, then retransmitting it on all inbound connections (from the hub to other clients or network connections). Hubs were initially called concentrators because they concentrated the network connections for each network segment.

Hubs do little in the way of treating transmissions other than rebroadcasting them. Analog hubs (known as amplifiers) simply take incoming analog signals and retransmit them. Signals suffering from attenuation (drop in signal strength) are increased in amplitude (made louder or stronger) and rebroadcast. Unfortunately, weak signals with weak noise become strong signals with strong noise when amplified. Digital hubs (repeaters) recreate the digital bit stream from the incoming connection and thus virtually eliminate noise. However, in many cases, even hubs can only retransmit a few times before issues arise. In the early days of 10-Mbps Ethernet (described in the Data Link Section), networks were subject to the 3-4-5 rule: no more than three populated segments, connected by four repeater hops, with five total segments. This rule proved to be invalid with the advent of Fast Ethernet (100 Mbps).

Physical Layer Security   The primary focus of security at the Physical layer is the protection of the medium against unauthorized interception. Eavesdropping typically occurs through unauthorized access to connection devices like hubs, in which the attacker uses special software, called a packet sniffer, to capture and view the packets transmitted across the device. The problem is worst with wireless communications because of the pervasive nature of the transmissions. Fiber-optic cable is naturally resistant to eavesdropping given that it is less susceptible to physical interception. Although an attacker could tap into a wire connection such as UTP or Coax, the glass fibers that form the cable resist a physical interception.

However, the connection points are just as susceptible to interception and capture or rebroadcasting to unauthorized stations.

Data Link Layer

The **Data Link layer** (DLL) is the primary layer for networking support. It is referred to as the first "subnet" layer given that it provides the addressing, packetizing, media access control, error control, and some flow control for networks. In LANs, it is the primary level responsible for client-to-client and client-to-server communications. The DLL is further divided into two sublayers: the Logical Link Control (LLC) sublayer and the Media Access Control (MAC) sublayer. The LLC sublayer is primarily designed to support the multiplexing and demultiplexing protocols transmitted over the MAC sublayer. It also provides flow control and error detection and retransmission. The MAC sublayer is designed to manage access to the communications media—in other words, regulates which clients are allowed to transmit and when. The MAC sublayer and other functions of the DLL are further discussed in later sections.

DLL Protocols There are a number of protocols available for DLL support; however, the dominant protocols for local area networking are Ethernet (for wired networks) and Wireless Ethernet or Wi-Fi (for wireless networks). Other DLL LAN protocols include token ring, FDDI, PPP, PPTP, and L2TP. For WANs, Asynchronous Transfer Mode and Frame Relay are the dominant protocols.

Ethernet Standardized as IEEE Standard 802.3, Ethernet was originally developed by Xerox PARC in the mid-1970s. However, the developers failed to gain support for the protocol at Xerox. Eventually, Robert Metcalfe left Xerox and formed 3Com. He convinced Digital Equipment Corporation (DEC), Intel, and Xerox to work collaboratively to further develop the protocol, resulting in the original DIX Ethernet standard. In 1983, Ethernet was modified and adopted as IEEE 802.3. Original versions of 802.3 Ethernet worked at 10 Mbps over coaxial cable and UTP. In fact, the descriptors for Ethernet included information on its DLL protocol as well as physical media, as shown in Table 2-1. Most UTP installations have limits of 100 meters for the cables from the client to a powered repeater or switch.

For its MAC sublayer, Ethernet uses Carrier Sense Multiple Access with Collision Detection (CSMA/CD) for its wired protocols and Carrier Sense Multiple Access with Collision Avoidance (CSMA/CA) for its wireless protocols. These are described in a later section.

Wireless Ethernet The standard for wireless networks falls under IEEE 802.11 – Wireless Local Area Networks (WLAN). Currently, there are four standards (and a host of legacy systems) operating: 802.11a, 802.11b, 802.11g, and 802.11n. Although 802.11a was the first formal standard, it was hampered in development by regulation; as a result, 802.11b became the first widely accepted standard. Most modern equipment is downwardly compatible, meaning a device designed to work in the 802.11g range will work on a lower-level network. Table 2-2 provides an overview of available and planned WLAN standards.

Token Ring Ratified as IEEE Standard 802.5, IBM's Token Passing ring network used a logical ring topology and required stations to possess a token—essentially a data frame with no data—prior to being allowed to transmit data. In the logical ring, which could be implemented in a physical star with a standard hub (referred to as a multistation access unit, or MAU) connected to clients with UTP, the token travels to and from each workstation in turn. Because of the relatively cheap cost of Ethernet (originally referred to informally as cheapnet), token ring lost the market battle in spite of IBM's best marketing efforts.

Ethernet Variant	Description
10Base2	10 Mbps baseband (not multiplex) Ethernet over thin coaxial cable (RG-58 or similar)
10Base5	10 Mbps Ethernet over thick coaxial cable (RG-8 or similar)
10BaseT	10 Mbps Ethernet over unshielded twisted pair (Cat5 or similar)
10BaseF	10 Mbps Ethernet over fiber-optic cable
100BaseTX	100 Mbps Ethernet over UTP (a.k.a. Fast Ethernet)
100BaseFX	100 Mbps Ethernet over fiber-optic cable
100BaseT4	100 Mbps Ethernet over low-grade UTP
1000BaseX	Generic Term for 1000 Mbps Ethernet (a.k.a. Gigabit Ethernet)
1000BaseSX	1000 Mbps Ethernet over multimode fiber-optic cable
1000BaseLX	1000 Mbps Ethernet over single-mode fiber-optic cable
1000BaseCX	1000 Mbps Ethernet over balanced copper cable (obsolete)
1000BaseT	1000 Mbps Ethernet over UTP

Table 2-1 Ethernet Variants
© Cengage Learning 2013

Protocol	Release Date	Operational Frequency	Throughput (Type)	Data Rate (Max)	Indoor Range (Depends on Number and Types of Walls)	Outdoor Range (Includes One Wall)
Legacy	1997	2.4 GHz	0.9 Mbit/s	2 Mbit/s	~20 Meters	~100 Meters
802.11a	1999	5 GHz	23 Mbit/s	54 Mbit/s	~35 Meters	~120 Meters
802.11b	1999	2.4 GHz	4.3 Mbit/s	11 Mbit/s	~38 Meters	~140 Meters
802.11g	2003	2.4 GHz	19 Mbit/s	54 Mbit/s	~38 Meters	~140 Meters
802.11n	Sept. 2008	2.4 GHz5 GHz	74 Mbit/s	248 Mbit/s	~70 Meters	~250 Meters
802.11y	March 2008	3.7 GHz	23 Mbit/s	54 Mbit/s	~50 Meters	~5000 Meters

Table 2-2 WLAN Overview
© Cengage Learning 2013

Fiber Distributed Data Interface Fiber Distributed Data Interface (FDDI) was a standard similar to token ring that used two counterdirectional fiber-optic loops to provide network connections over large areas—up to about 120 miles. Similar to token ring, the MAC used by FDDI was based on a token and was referred to as token bus (from the IEEE 802.4 token bus protocol). This protocol allowed multiple stations to transmit by adding their packets onto the token, whether it already contained data or not. FDDI's advantage lay in its resiliency; even if the loop was severed, stations could still transmit using one loop to transmit to stations in one direction and the other for the opposite direction. Stations were natively attached to one or both loops, depending on their priority, and were thus known as single attached stations (SAS) or dual attached stations (DAS). The development of Fast Ethernet and Gigabit Ethernet and their relatively inexpensive implementations has made FDDI virtually obsolete.

Asynchronous Transfer Mode Asynchornous Transfer Mode (ATM) is a WAN packet-switching DLL protocol that uses fixed cell (frame) sizes of 53 bytes (48 bytes of data and 5 bytes of header information). Also known as Cell Relay, ATM is different from other protocols in that it is a connection-oriented DLL protocol rather than connectionless, like Ethernet. ATM provides support for virtual channels and virtual paths to expedite packet transmission. A virtual channel indicates that each cell has a similar identifier (VCI) guiding the cell through the network. The virtual channels may also share a common identifier, indicating a virtual path (VPI). A virtual path is a grouping of virtual channels with common endpoints. A virtual path may be established between two locations, with the channels representing communications between systems at those locations.

ATM can even be implemented in a LAN through a process of LAN emulation (LANE). There are still many ATM implementations in operation, given that its original 155 Mbps data rate has been upgraded to multi-gigabit speed. However, the current development of multi-gigabit Ethernet and the low costs associated with Ethernet networks threaten ATM's future.

Frame Relay Frame relay is another WAN protocol used to encapsulate voice and data transmitted between LANs. Unlike ATM, frame relay uses flexible-length frames and leaves error checking to the endpoints. Like ATM, frame relay uses virtual circuits for long distance point-to-point data delivery. Similar to ATM, developments in Gigabit Ethernet also threaten the future of frame relay.

PPP, PPTP, and L2TP This final set of DLL protocols is used most commonly for computer communications over dial-up telephone networks. Prior to the development of high-speed Internet access through cable modems, residential and most commercial connections to the Internet were made through modems. Protocols like the Point-to-Point Protocol (PPP) are used to make the connection from the client's system through a modem. DSL still uses PPP in its communication process, multiplexing the data signal with the home voice channel. PPP has replaced older protocols like the Serial Line Internet Protocol (SLIP), which had poor error-handling procedures. PPP over Ethernet is the most common implementation today, although PPP over ATM is also used.

Point-to-Point Tunneling Protocol (PPTP) and Layer 2 Tunneling Protocol (L2TP) are other protocols used for remote access and tunneling PPP packets over an IP network. Instead of communicating over modems for dial-up networking, the PPP packets are encapsulated using PPTP or L2TP and sent over an IP network. In order to secure communications over PPTP or L2TP, other encryption protocols, such as IPSec or EAP-TLS, must be used.

Packet Framing The first responsibility of the DLL is to convert the network layer packet into a DLL frame. Unlike higher levels, the DLL adds not only a header component but also a trailer. When necessary, the packet is fragmented into one or more frames, with corresponding information embedded into the frame header. As shown in Figure 2-15, the Ethernet II frame includes a preamble. The preamble is a series of bits (010101010) used to indicate the start of a frame, an SFD, the destination MAC address, the source MAC address, a specification of the type of Ethernet being used, the data payload, and the frame check sequence, which is a 32-bit cyclic redundancy check used in detecting errors in the frame.

Preamble	SFD	DestinationMACAddress	SourceMACAddress	Ethernet Type	Payload	FCS

Figure 2-15 Ethernet II frame
© Cengage Learning 2013

Addressing Networking addressing at the DLL is accomplished by a number embedded in the network interface card (NIC) by the manufacturer. This number, known as the MAC address, Ethernet Hardware Address, or simply hardware address, uniquely identifies the client system and, through the address resolution protocol, allows packets to be delivered to an endpoint. This 48-bit number is commonly denoted in hexadecimal format (e.g., 00-00-A3-6A-B2-1A). The first three octets (or hex sets) are assigned by IEEE as part of their organizationally unique identifier, or Company_id. The database of these addresses can be viewed at *http://standards.ieee.org/develop/regauth/oui/public.html*. Recent updates in MAC addresses allow the last octets to be assigned by the organization, overriding the burned-in addresses.

Media Access Control One of the primary functions of the DLL is the control of traffic flow—which station is allowed to transmit when. There are two general approaches to this task: deterministic (or control) and contention (or stochastic). Contention approaches such as CSMA/CA and CSMA/CD work on a first-come, first-served basis, whereas control approaches regulate flow, specifying requirements the client must follow before transmitting, as in the case of a token or central station permission.

Deterministic Approach With the **deterministic approach**, a "predetermined" or "controlled" method of allowing clients to transmit data is used. There are a number of ways this can be implemented. The first is a controlled network, in which the client must request permission to transmit. In **roll-call polling**, the central control unit, usually a server, polls each client to determine if it has traffic to transmit. If it does, it is allowed to send that data. If not, the next client on the list is contacted. In **go-ahead polling**, the first client on the list transmits data if it needs to; if it doesn't, it notifies the next client that it may transmit data if needed. Token passing rings and busses work on this principle, using the token as the control mechanism. Control approaches are superior in that they maintain a well-regulated network, in which traffic is transmitted in an orderly fashion, with an optimal data rate. They also facilitate a priority system, in that priority clients or servers can be polled more frequently than others. Token-based systems can also incorporate a priority set of bits that allows assignment of different classes, to facilitate the transmission of important and time-sensitive data, such as video.

Contention Approach The other dominant media access control method allows a first-come, first-served approach. With the **contention** approach, whenever a station needs to transmit data, it simply listens to determine if the network is currently being used, as when another client is transmitting data. If the channel is free, the station transmits. The downside to this approach is that more than one station may attempt to transmit at the same time. Thus, the contention approach must have mechanisms to deal with this event, which is referred to as a **collision**.

Carrier Sense Multiple Access (CSMA) is the dominant contention mechanism. Based on the Aloha Protocols, a set of communications protocols used in a radio-based data network in Hawaii, CSMA means that each station listens to the media (Carrier Sense) and all stations have equal access (Multiple Access). Two variants of CSMA are CSMA/CD and CSMA/CA. With CSMA, systems are set up so that if a collision is detected, both stations immediately emit a jamming signal to warn all other clients that a collision has occurred and must be resolved. How do clients know a collision has occurred? A client transmitting a specific voltage level on a wire will receive a voltage spike when more voltage is detected than is being transmitted. When these stations recognize a collision, they begin the Binary Exponential Backoff Algorithm. Beginning with 1 bit that has two values (0 or 1), each client randomly selects a value and waits that amount of time in milliseconds, then attempts to retransmit. If the two clients choose the same value, another collision is detected and the two stations move to 2 bits (four values) and try again. The clients continue until they are able to transmit or they reach 16 bits, at which time they give up and send an error message to their systems.

Collision avoidance differs from collision detection in that, before a client transmits, it sends a short "intent to transmit" message warning other clients not to transmit. The client then waits a short time to ensure that the channel is clear, then transmits its message, and waits for acknowledgement of receipt.

Networking Devices at the Data Link Layer

To connect networks at the DDL, specific technologies are employed. Although the hub connects networks at the Physical layer, that results in one large network. However, connecting networks with a Layer 2 switch maintains separate collision domains, given that this device is capable of bridging. **Bridging** is the process of connecting networks with the same DLL protocols (e.g., Ethernet) while maintaining the integrity of each network and only passing messages that need to be transmitted between the two. Bridges, which are no longer used, were specialized network equipment that connected multiple networks. They were capable of router-type operations in building bridging tables, tracking which clients were on which network. When moving frames between networks (referred to as filtering or forwarding), the bridge would hear a message transmitted for a specific destination client; if that client didn't respond, the bridge would forward the retransmitted message to its other network(s) to determine where that client resided. If a response was detected, the response was forwarded back to the original sender, and the bridge would update its table. That's why these devices became known as learning bridges. Bridges were replaced with Layer 2 switches, which perform the same tasks but can connect more than two networks.

From a security standpoint, switches increased the relative protection of networking communications. By creating a point-to-point connection between two stations, the switch prevents other nodes from eavesdropping on the digital conversation. This prevents the average user from running a packet sniffer program and listening in on a coworker's data communications. From a network administration standpoint, where using a packet sniffer is not only legal but advisable (to detect anomalous network performance), most switches have a monitoring port, which operates in "promiscuous mode" and allows the administrator to review all networking traffic.

Network Layer

The Network layer is the primary layer for communications between networks. This layer has three key functions: packetizing, addressing, and routing.

Packetizing The Network layer takes the segments handed down from the Transport layer and organizes them into one or more packets for transmission across a network. Each packet (also called a **datagram**) consists of two parts: the header and the data. The header contains information that is normally only read by computers, such as where the packet is coming from and its destination. The data is the part that end users actually see—for example, the body of an e-mail message or a Web page.

Understanding exactly what goes in a packet header is important because it can help you configure packet filters against possible attacks. Some firewall programs can give you a glimpse of the contents of a packet. To find out more about headers and their contents, go to the original Internet Protocol specification at *www.ietf.org*, click RFC Pages, and search for RFC 791.

An IP packet header is commonly illustrated according to the layers of information within it, as shown in Figure 2-16, which contains the following packet elements:

- Version—Identifies the version of IP that was used to generate the packet. As of early 2008, TCP/IP version 4 is still in common use. However, some larger organizations and ISPs have begun to deploy IPv6 on their internal networks.

- Internet header length—Describes the length of the header in 32-bit words and is a 4-bit value. The default value is 20.

- Type of service—Indicates which of four service options is used to transmit the packet: minimize delay, maximize throughput, maximize reliability, and minimize cost. However, this field is of limited value because most IP network setups don't enable an application to set this value.

- Total length—This 16-bit field gives the total length of the packet, to a maximum of 165,535 bytes.

- Identification—This 16-bit value aids in the division of the data stream into packets of information. The receiving computer (possibly a firewall) uses each packet's identification number to reassemble, in the correct order, the packets that make up the data stream.

- Flags—This 3-bit value tells whether this packet is a fragment of a whole packet and, more specifically, whether it's the last fragment or more fragments are to follow.

- Fragment offset—If the data received is a fragment, this value indicates where the fragment belongs in the sequence of fragments so that a packet can be reassembled.

- Time to live (TTL)—This 8-bit value identifies the maximum time the packet can remain in the system before it is dropped. Each router or device through which the packet passes reduces the TTL by a value of one. Having a TTL prevents a packet from getting caught in loops because it is undeliverable. When the value reaches zero, the packet is destroyed and an ICMP message is transmitted to the sender.

- Protocol—Identifies the IP protocol that was used in the data portion of the packet and should receive the data at its destination (e.g., TCP, UDP, or ICMP).

- Header checksum—A summing up of all the 16-bit values in the packet header in a single value.

- Source address—The address of the computer or device that sent the packet.

- Destination address—The address of the computer or device that is to receive the packet.

- Options—This element can contain a Security field, which enables the sender to assign a classification level to the packet (such as Secret, Top Secret, and so on), as well as several source routing fields by which the sender can supply routing information that gateways can use to send the packet to its destination.

- Data—The part that the end user actually sees, such as the body of an e-mail message.

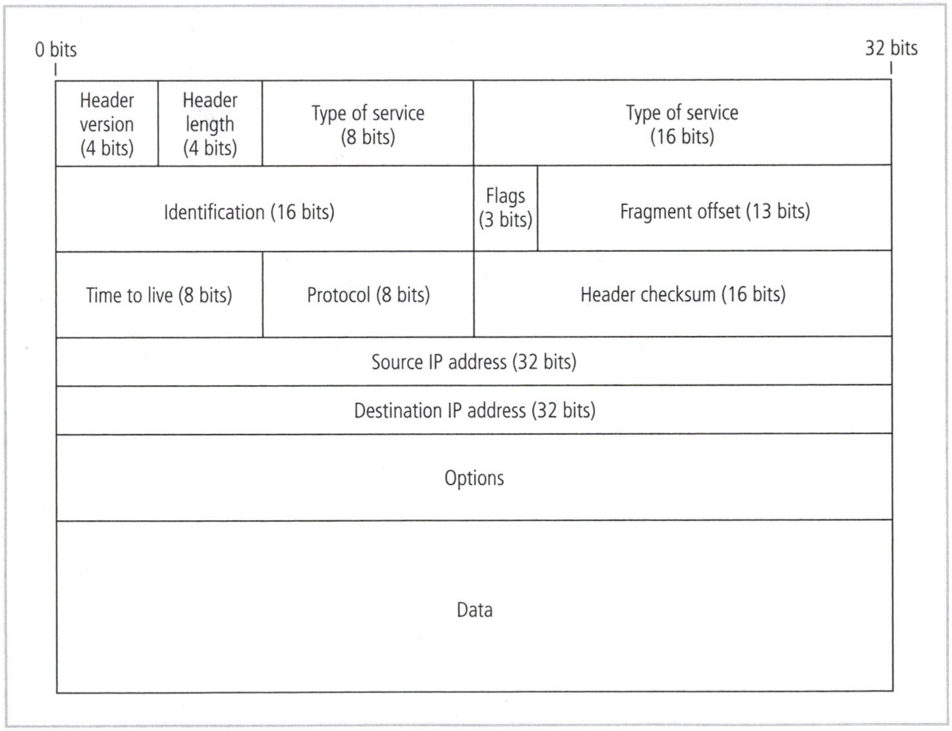

Figure 2-16 IP packet
© Cengage Learning 2013

Addressing The Network layer also assigns a Network layer address to uniquely identify a destination across multiple networks. A typical address consists of two components: the network identification, or netid, component and the host identification, or hostid, component, as shown in Figure 2-17. Note that the **dotted decimal notation** most commonly used (e.g., 192.168.2.118) is translated into binary for network use. In TCP/IP, the IP address is the Network layer address.

As shown in Figure 2-17, the IP address contains a source and destination IP address along with additional information on the packet.

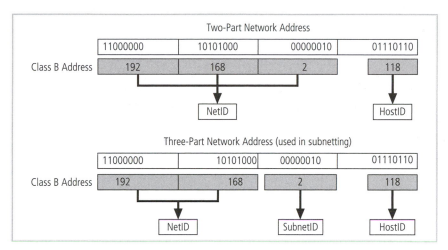

Figure 2-17 IP addresses
© Cengage Learning 2013

Addresses are maintained by the Internet Assigned Names Authority (IANA) and issued on an as-needed basis (see Table 2-3). In the early years of the Internet, these addresses were handed out in blocks or classes, as follows:

- Class A—A Class A address consists of a primary octet providing the netid and then three octets providing the hostid. This allows an organization to configure up to 16,777,214 hosts on its network. In practice, the final octet of an address cannot be 0 or 255. The eight binary 0s are used to represent the network address, and eight binary 1s are used to represent a broadcast address.

- Class B—A Class B address consists of two octets providing the netid and two octets providing 65534 hostids.

- Class C—A Class C address consists of three octets providing the netid and one octet providing 254 hostids.

- Class D and Class E addresses are reserved.

Unfortunately, this assignment has proven very inefficient. For example, a university might be issued a Class B address but have, at its peak, only 4,000–5,000 devices that need a network address. This means that 61,000 or more addresses are not used.

In 1993, a stop-gap measure was implemented by the IANA to slow the adoption of class-based addresses. Known as Classless Inter-Domain Routing (CIDR), this measure replaced the

Class	Address Range	Supports
Class A	1.0.0.1 to 126.255.255.254	Approximately 16 million hosts on each of 127 networks
Class B	128.1.0.1 to 191.255.255.254	Approximately 65,000 hosts on each of 16,000 networks
Class C	192.0.1.1 to 223.255.254.254	254 hosts on each of 2 million networks
Class D	224.0.0.0 to 239.255.255.255	Reserved for multicast groups
Class E	240.0.0.0 to 254.255.255.254	Reserved

Table 2-3   IP Address Classes
© Cengage Learning 2013

traditional class-based assignment system with a method that assigns only the addresses that an organization actually needs. Instead of defaulting to octet-based assignment, as was the case with the class-based system, CIDR issues addresses to organizations based on a binary method. Thus, an organization could be issued just the number of addresses it needs rather than the usual grouping size of addresses used in the class-based address scheme. CIDR notation designates this assignment as 192.168.2.0/30, where the /30 indicates the number of digits that are assigned as network address (versus host address) and the remaining digits indicate the number of host addresses available to the organization. With 30 of 32 bits dedicated to the network ID, only two bits remain for the host ID, resulting in four available host addresses: 00, 01, 10, and 11. A /24 is essentially a Class C address; however, organizations are no longer under constraints to be issued addresses in the class system.

The dwindling pool of addresses is one of the reasons the Internet is moving to IPv6, a new version of IP, which uses a 128-bit address instead of a 32-bit address. This substantially increases the number of available addresses (2^{128}). Because of the length of the IPv6 addresses, they are commonly expressed in hexadecimal format (e.g., 12a4:011c:0003:ba37:0000:0000:0000:1922) rather than dotted decimal notation. Two rules guide the notation of IPv6:

1. Leading zeros can be skipped within each octet (thus, the address above can be shortened to 12a4:11c:3:ba37:0:0:0:1922).

2. Consecutive zeros can be replaced with double colons (thus, the address above can be further shortened to 12a4:11c:3:ba37::1922).

IPv6 uses CIDR assignment rather than a new version of class-based assignment. Even though IPv6 has been around since 1981, it is deployed on only an estimated one percent of world networks.

Dynamic Addressing   Until IPv6 adoption is complete, many organizations are using other methods to manage their limited addresses—for example, dynamic addressing. **Dynamic addressing** assigns a pool of addresses to an address assignment server, using a protocol like Dynamic Host Configuration Protocol (DHCP). When a computer system starts up or "boots," it requests and receives an address and critical network configuration information, including the gateway address and the address of Domain Name Service servers. The advantage of this method is that a large group of systems may require only a smaller number of addresses. When a system shuts down, it returns the address to the pool, where it can be used by another system.

Network Address Translation In addition to CIDR, another mechanism supported at the Network layer that assists in the management of addresses is **Network Address Translation (NAT)**. NAT uses a device like a router to segregate the external Internet from an internal intranet or network. The device is provided with the addresses assigned to the organization. It maps these addresses to different addresses inside the intranet. This provides security but can also maximize network address assignment when combined with Port Address Translation, as described in the Transport layer section. The internal addresses could be any address; however, there are IP addresses reserved for private (nonroutable) networking. These include:

- 10.0.0.0—For those needing a Class A range
- 172.16.0.0–172.31.0.0—For those needing multiple Class B ranges
- 192.168.0.0—For those needing a single Class B range (the most commonly implemented range)

Subnetting Organizations are commonly assigned wider address pools than they need. Or, to keep things simple, they may want to divide their assigned addresses into logical network groups, such as LANs located in different buildings or on different floors of a building. In these cases, an organization may wish to subnet its addresses. **Subnetting** is the process of internally dividing a block of addresses into smaller logical groups for ease of organization. When configuring a system to be on a network, the administrator will specify a **subnet mask,** which is a notation that tells the network what parts of the address are subnet and what parts are host. Subnet masks are commonly presented in dotted decimal notation but are also commonly presented in CIDR notation—for example, 255.255.255.0/24, in which the 255 block indicates a network address, regardless of the size of the network address block assigned to the organization. By manipulating the subnet component (see Figure 2-16), the organization can increase or decrease the number of subnets or hosts per subnet that it manages.

Routing Routing is the process of moving a Network layer packet across multiple networks. The devices that connect multiple networks are called routers. Routers work at the Network layer to receive packets and direct them toward their ultimate destinations. The transmission links between routers work at the Data Link layer. In other words, the router has one or more types of Data Link layer protocols represented by an interface or network card. A router could have different types of data link protocols, as it receives the frame carrying the Network layer packet, and creates a new frame once it determines the outbound interface that represents the direction the packet needs to go. Routers accomplish this through the use of router tables. A router table is a text entry that contains information on destination addresses, outbound interfaces toward those addresses, and additional information on the status of the host or network.

There are a number of routing protocol categories. Static routing requires an administrator to manually enter the routing table information, whereas dynamic routing is done by the router itself. Routers do this by transmitting their router tables to their neighbors and updating their own tables with the information they received.

Internal Routing Protocols Internal routing protocols are used inside an **autonomous system (AS)**. An AS is a system owned or managed by a single entity and generally consisting of analogous technologies. The two dominant internal routing protocol methods are distance-vector routing protocols and link-state routing protocols. Distance-vector protocols base their routing decisions on a simple determination of the number of hops between the router and the destination. A hop is one connection from router to router. The two dominant distance-vector protocols are the **Routing Information Protocol (RIP)** and the **Interior Gateway Routing Protocol (IGRP)**. RIP is more widely used, although implementations are rapidly being replaced by link-state protocols. RIP routers originally transmitted their entire router tables every 30 seconds, resulting in a significant amount of network traffic. In order to manage the table sizes, RIP tables have a maximum hop count of 15. RIP has evolved through versions 1, 2, and next generation (ng).

Link-state protocols contain information about not only the distance to the destination but the states of the links, including traffic, throughput, and other components. The dominant link-state routing protocols are **Open Shortest Path First (OSPF)** and **Intermediate System to Intermediate System (IS-IS)**. OSPF is superior to RIP in that the entire router table is not transmitted, only information on the immediate neighbor routers. OSPF can also track and store information on the time to transmit and receive an update. Each neighbor router receives this information and then updates its table with that information, providing information on network traffic delays as calculating hop counts. OSPF also doesn't broadcast routing information on a regular basis; instead, it sends routing updates to select devices.

External Gateway Routing Protocols   External routing protocols are used to communicate between autonomous systems (AS). These provide translation between the possibly different internal routing protocols. The dominant external routing protocols are the **Exterior Gateway Protocol (EGP)** and the **Border Gateway Protocol (BGP)**. EGP is the older, now obsolescent Internet routing protocol developed in 1982. The replacement, BGP, is now the dominant protocol for the Internet; it is now in version 4. When used as an Internal Gateway Protocol, it is referred to as IBGP; when used externally, it is referred to as EBGP.

Network Layer Security

Network Layer Security   The security issues associated with the Network layer focus on the addresses and routing of these addresses. Many of the attacks discussed in Chapter 1, such as man-in-the-middle attacks and address spoofing, are targeted at the Internet Protocol, which is the dominant Network layer protocol. Other risks include packet storms (a form of denial-of-service attack), address conflicts, address redirects (in which packets aimed at one destination are redirected to a different location), and replay attacks (in which legitimate traffic is duplicated or delayed, possibly as part of one of the other attacks mentioned here).

Other security issues address other protocols used at this level, such as the Internet Control Message Protocol (ICMP), a simple tool for relaying messages between systems. Ping sweeps and port scanners, among other attacks, use ICMP to carry their queries to determine if systems are operational and, if so, what services are available. This information can facilitate a more directed attack. By disabling or limiting the use of this protocol, an administrator can greatly reduce the protocol implementation's susceptibility to attack.

Transport Layer

The primary function of the Transport layer is to provide reliable end-to-end transfer of data between user applications. Although the lower layers focus on networking and connectivity, the upper layers, beginning with the Transport layer, focus on application-specific services. The Transport layer can also provide support for a **virtual circuit,** a technique that allows for higher-level communications to occur without the overhead of packet reassembly. This type of communication is an example of a connection-oriented model. In a **connection-oriented model**, a connection is established between two points, and all communications occur over that dedicated end-to-end connection. Using a virtual circuit, each segment of the route has a path as well as a destination embedded into the packet, ensuring that the traffic will follow the predesigned path, without the overhead of establishing an actual connection. In a **connectionless protocol**, individual packets are transmitted separately, without prior negotiation, each with its own addressing information. These individual packets may take different paths, but they all end up at the same destination, where they are reassembled into the correct order. The Transport layer is also responsible for end-to-end error and flow control.

Error Control Error control is the process of handling problems with the transfer process, which result in modified or corrupted segments. Error control is broken into two components: error detection and error correction. Errors typically take one of two formats. A single-bit error only affects a single bit—typically, a 1 changing to a 0 or vice versa. Single-bit errors are easily detected. Multiple-bit errors are more complex in that they affect more than 1 bit, even bits in more than one location in the segment. Bit errors are most likely the result of noise interference and are detected through one of the following schemes:

- Repetition schemes—Repeating blocks of data a predetermined number of times. If an error doesn't affect each block, it may be detected. This overly simplistic method is inefficient, however, and only catches basic errors.

- Parity schemes—Including additional bits at the end of each byte of data. These additional "check bits" provide a measure of error detection. With odd parity, the sum of the values is expected to be odd. If it is odd, a 0 is added to the block; if not, a 1 is added, making the block sum odd. Similarly, with even parity, the check bits are added to make the sum even.

- Redundancy schemes—Calculating parities for blocks of data rather than for an individual byte. Longitudinal redundancy checking (LRC) examines a long row of blocks, then adds a byte of parity for the row. It is often used with vertical redundancy checking (VCR), which does the same task for a column of data. By placing the data into blocks and incorporating both LRC and VRC data, it becomes possible to detect even multi-bit errors easily. Cyclic redundancy checking uses a long-division computation, where the remainder becomes a block of data included with the segment. CRCs are often 16, 32, or 64 bits long. The receiver performs the same computation at its end, and if the remainder is different, there is a problem with the segment, and a retransmission is requested.

- Message authentication codes—Hash values of the entire message appended onto the message, also known as a message authentication code. This is used for advanced determination of errors, especially at the message level. These message hashes can be encrypted with a sender's private key (in public key encryption) to provide nonrepudiation as well as message-integrity checking.

Error Correction Errors are most commonly corrected through retransmission of the damaged segment. To manage the process of correcting errors, protocols are used to manage the flow of retransmission. The dominant error correction techniques are automatic repeat requests (or ARQs). The three most common ones are Stop-And-Wait ARQ, Go-Back-N ARQ, and

Selective Repeat ARQ. Stop-And-Wait ARQ works on a 1-datagram (or packet) premise. Each segment transmitted must be acknowledged (ACK) by the receiver before another segment is transmitted. This one-to-one operation is very slow and intensive. However, it is very reliable, in that if an error is detected the bad segment is requested for retransmission—most commonly by reacknowledging the last good segment received. Figure 2-18 illustrates the Stop-And-Wait ARQ.

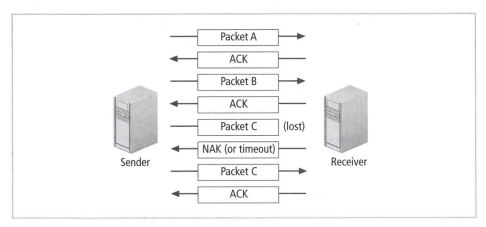

Figure 2-18   Stop-And-Wait ARQ
© Cengage Learning 2013

With the Go-Back-N ARQ, a number of packets can be transmitted before an acknowledgement must be received. The exact number is negotiated between the two stations, as part of the Sliding Window Protocol described in the following section on flow control. The WIN value (window size) determines how many segments can be transmitted. Once an acknowledgement is received, additional segments are transmitted. If an error is detected, the last good segment received before the error is acknowledged and all segments since that point are retransmitted. Although this is somewhat wasteful, given that all the segments received since the bad segment are discarded, it is much more efficient than Stop-And-Wait ARQ. Figure 2-19 illustrates the Go-Back-N ARQ

With Selective Repeat ARQ, only those segments that are determined to be bad are requested for retransmission. Thus, when a bad segment is received but followed by several good segments, the good segments are accepted and only the bad segment is re-requested. Figure 2-20 illustrates the Selective Repeat ARQ.

Flow Control Along with the error correction schemes, the Transport layer provides for flow control for end-to-end transfers. The purpose of flow control is to prevent a receiver from being overwhelmed with segments, which might prevent effective processing of each received segment. Some error correction techniques, like Stop-And-Wait ARQ, provide built-in flow control. In other techniques, some mechanism is needed to regulate the traffic. The dominant technique for flow control is a sliding window protocol, which provides a mechanism by which a receiver can specify the number of segments (or number of bytes) it can receive before the sender must wait. In TCP, this is implemented as a WIN value. A typical WIN value would be 4096 (or 4K).

2

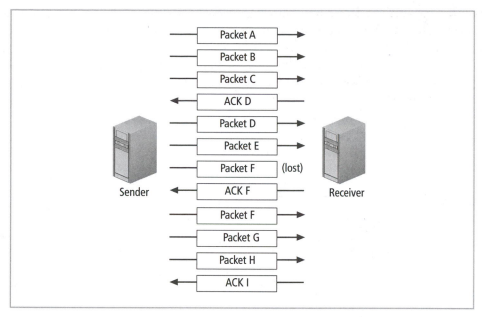

Figure 2-19 Go-Back-N ARQ
© Cengage Learning 2013

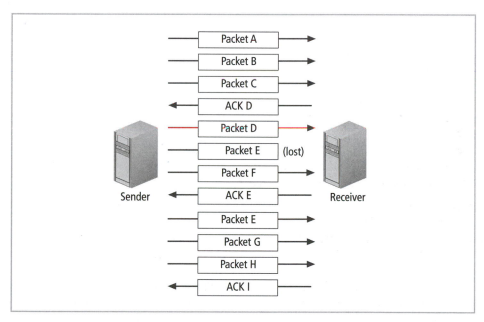

Figure 2-20 Selective Repeat ARQ
© Cengage Learning 2013

If the sender and receiver are using a maximum segment size of 1K, the sender can send four segments before it needs to wait for an acknowledgement of permission to continue transmitting. The implementation of a WIN value shows an overlap between flow control and error control because the wait for acknowledgement allows the receiver to determine if there are any problems with the received datagrams/segments. A window size is also flexible. As a receiver gains efficiency—possibly through the reduction in the number of concurrent sessions—it can widen a window. As the receiver gets overwhelmed with additional connection requests, it can reduce a window's size, slowing down each connection. Figure 2-21 illustrates a sliding window protocol process.

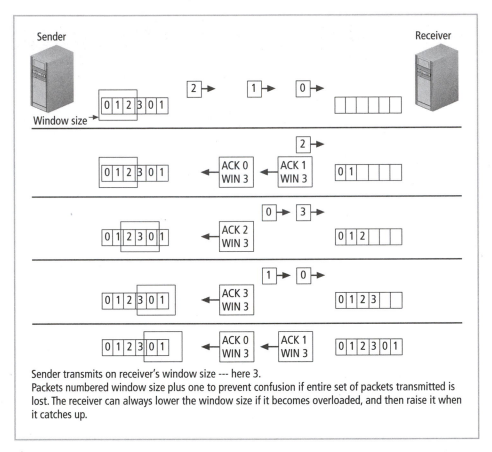

Figure 2-21   Sliding window protocol
© Cengage Learning 2013

Other Functions   The Transport layer is also responsible for assigning ports—uniquely identifying the service requested by the user. The combination of Network layer address and port is referred to as a **socket**. Table 2-4 provides a list of well-known port addresses. When users wish to establish a connection with a particular service, such as HTTP, they send a request to the well-known port address 80 as part of their socket. This tells the receiving server, which may have more than one type of service to provide, what specific Application layer service is requested. The sender's client system assigns a random port number outside the well-known port range (i.e., above 1023) as part of its socket, so that upon return the response can find its way to the corresponding application. This socket combination allows users to have multiple iterations of an application (e.g., multiple Web browsers) open while each maintains its own integrity. Similarly, it allows a home Internet user to have multiple systems working off a single dynamic IP address. The home router performs Port Address Translation and assigns a unique socket to each client request, along with an internal IP address, as described in the Network layer under Network Address Translation. Thus, multiple users with multiple applications all requesting external services through a common source address are able to accurately receive responses.

Port Number	Protocol
7	Echo
20	File Transfer [Default Data] (FTP)
21	File Transfer [Control] (FTP)
23	Telnet
25	Simple Mail Transfer Protocol (SMTP)
53	Domain Name Services (DNS)
80	Hypertext Transfer Protocol (HTTP)
110	Post Office Protocol version 3 (POP3)
161	Simple Network Management Protocol (SNMP)

Table 2-4 **Well-Known Port Numbers**
© Cengage Learning 2013

Tunneling protocols also work at the Transport layer. These work with Data Link layer protocols to provide secure connections. Additional information on tunneling is provided in the discussions of VPNs in later chapters.

Transport Layer Security Within the Transport layer, there are two great risks. The first is handling sequence numbers. TCP segments are assigned sequential numbers to track their sequences. By guessing these sequence numbers, attackers can hijack TCP communications and attack either endpoint. The other great risk is the port assignments given the various services provided at higher layers. The combined Network layer address and Transport layer port socket provides insight into the function and operation of network-available services. Knowing the ports available allows attackers to infer the listening services or applications and thus provide the necessary intelligence to use to stage an attack. Port scanners are commonly used to identify this information, as systems are commonly configured to respond to requests about available services as part of normal network operations.

Session Layer

The Session layer is responsible for establishing, maintaining, and terminating communications sessions between two systems. It also regulates whether communications are preformed in a simplex (one way only), half-duplex (one way at a time), or full-duplex (bidirectional) mode. In other words, when one station wishes to request services from a server, it requests a session, much as a person dials a telephone. The dialing, ringing, and opening conversation ("Hello, may I speak with Mr. Smith?") are part of the establishment of a communications session. Then, as data is transferred, the Session layer keeps the communications connected. Finally, once both parties have completed their transfers of information, the session is closed. In TCP/IP, this is referred to as a half-close, because even though the client may have completed its data transfer and is finished, the server may still have data to transmit and, therefore, maintains the connection until it has completed.

Session Layer Security Because the most common protocol, TCP/IP, does not have an explicit Session layer, Session layer protocols are not as common, and thus there are fewer attacks and risks associated with it. The two most common issues at the Session layer involve the Domain Name Service (DNS) and some implementations of Kerberos, an architecture used to provide session authentication to minimize the number of logins a user must provide to use recourses on a network. Kerberos is discussed in more detail in later chapters.

DNS, on the other hand, is a significant system with inherent weaknesses. It is part of the Application layer of the TCP/IP protocol stack but operates much the same as the Session layer. Most Web addresses involve a Uniform Resource Locator (URL), also known as a domain name or simply Web address (e.g., *www.course.com*). In TCP/IP, this is also referred to as an Application layer address. However, in order to route traffic to this location, the network needs a Network layer address, not an Application layer address. The DNS is a centralized database with information on the local database of addresses associated with a particular domain (e.g., course.com). It is a hierarchical structure organized by top-level domain (.com, .org, .net, .edu, etc.) and primary domain level (e.g., course.com). The database also contains information on the primary and secondary name servers responsible for all addresses within these primary domains. Basically, looking up a domain name in DNS is a lot like dialing 411 and asking for a phone number for a university switchboard. The 411 service converts the domain name (e.g., Kennesaw State University) to a switchboard phone number, then finds the specific address/number the requestor seeks from that switchboard. This system, given that it is inherently insecure, is very susceptible to interception, which is known as DNS hijacking, DNS redirection, or session hijacking. If you have ever typed in a Web address but ended up at a different site, you've been the victim of this type of attack.

Presentation Layer

The Presentation layer is responsible for data translation and encryption functions. For example, if one system is using the standard ASCII (American Standard Code for Information Interchange) and another system is using EBCDIC (Extended Binary Coded Decimal Interchange Code), the Presentation layer performs this translation. The Presentation layer also encapsulates the Application layer message prior to passing it down to the Transport layer.

Presentation Layer Security Like the Session layer, the Presentation layer has no direct counterpart in the TCP/IP protocol stack and thus harbors few risks. However, some technologies, like virtual private networks (VPNs), are encryption based and work at this layer. Thus, most encryption-oriented attacks and risks impact the Presentation layer. The protection of the encryption keys and endpoints becomes the primary concern at this layer.

Application Layer

At the Application layer, users are provided with a number of services they can use to exchange information. Although the term *application* is used for this layer of the OSF model, we are not necessarily dealing with communication among or between applications. Instead, we generally refer to discrete application *protocols* that support those applications. In the TCP/IP protocol suite, applications include e-mail (SMTP and POP), the World Wide Web, (HTTP and HTTPS), and file transfer (FTP and SFTP). However, users will still need a computer program (a generalized browser in some cases or a specific application program in other cases) to access the features of these protocols. Table 2-5 provides a more comprehensive list of Application layer protocols and their uses.

Protocols	Use
Bootstrap Protocol (BOOTP)	Assists a client in obtaining a network address on startup; replaced by DHCP.
Domain Name System (DNS) Protocol	Provides a translation between Application layer addresses or host names (i.e., HTTP Uniform Resource Locators (URLS)) and IP addresses; serves as a look-up resource for the Internet; also associated with the assignment of domain names and the Internet Domain Registry.
Dynamic Host Configuration Protocol (DHCP)	Used to assist a client in obtaining a network address from a central pool of available addresses. DHCP can also provide a number of other items, such as the subnet mask, the addresses of its gateway, and DNS servers.
File Transfer Protocol (FTP)	Used to transfer files from a server to a client and vice versa over the Internet; allows the user to manipulate (move, modify, and delete) these files.
HyperText Transfer Protocol (HTTP) & Secure HTTP (HTTPS)	Used for the retrieval and display of hypertext documents over the Internet; provides the foundation for the World Wide Web (frequently used for internal networks as well).
Internet Message Access Protocol (IMAP)	Allows clients to access their e-mail on a server; virtually all e-mail clients support both IMAP and POP.
Internet Relay Chat (IRC) Protocol	Used for near-real time chat support; allows one-to-one communications between users.
Lightweight Directory Access Protocol (LDAP)	Used for modifying and querying directory services; these directory structures are "trees" of entries, each with attributes that can be queried.
Multipurpose Internet Mail Extensions (MIME) & Secure MIME (S-MIME)	Used for extending e-mail formats beyond basic text; allows non-text attachments, non-ASCII character sets, and additional extensions to standard e-mail formats.
Post Office Protocol (POP)	Like IMAP, supports the retrieval of e-mail from an e-mail server. IMAP and POP are used by users' client e-mail programs to view, modify and send e-mail.
Remote Login (rlogin)	Used to remotely log onto a UNIX System.
Server Message Block (SMB)	Designed to support the sharing of files and peripherals (printers, drives, directories, etc.) between clients on a network; most commonly associated with Microsoft Windows systems under the name Microsoft Windows Network.

Table 2-5 Common Application Layer Protocols (*continues*)

Protocols	Use
Simple Mail Transfer Protocol (SMTP) & Extended SMTP (ESMTP)	De facto standard that supports e-mail transfer across the Internet. Extended SMTP improves upon the base SMTP protocol to support the use of service extensions.
Simple Network Management Protocol (SNMP)	Specifies a dictionary of predefined service queries for network systems; used to determine network management issues. The SNMP standard includes: • Management Information Base (MIB)—The database of queries • Agents—Remote utilities to collect information for the MIB • Network Management Station—Or a client system that serves to collect and present the information collected from the network systems.
Remote Desktop Protocol (RDP)	Allows user to operate a system by transmitting keyboard, video, and mouse commands from a remote location. Users are able to see and control the remote system as if they were sitting in front of it.
Secure Shell (SSH)	Establishes a secure channel between two systems; used heavily in electronic commerce. SSH uses public key encryption to support the establishment of this session.
Telnet	Older protocol used to allow connection to and control of dissimilar systems—for example, a PC user running Windows who is accessing an IBM mainframe running UNIX.
Trivial File Transfer Protocol (TFTP)	Very simple protocol for FTP-like services that takes little memory and is, therefore, useful for networking devices like switches and routers.
Whois	Used to determine the registrant (or owner) of an IP address or domain name.

Table 2-5 Common Application Layer Protocols (*continued*)
© Cengage Learning 2013

HTTP Many protocols, like HTTP, use a two-part transfer. The first part is a request from the client to the server that could be a request for information; this is known as a GET statement, a request to upload information, a PUT statement, or other file-modification statement (POST, DELETE, HEAD, etc.). The second part of the transfer is the response from the server—that is, the delivery of the requested material. This is known as a REPLY statement or some other service response.

The HTTP GET request message contains:

- A request line—that is, GET
- Header information—For example, specifying the language (EN) and HTTP version
- A message body, which is optional

Here is a sample HTTP GET request, to which the server would respond with the corresponding HTML files:

GET /index.html HTTP/1.1

Host: *www.course.com*

HTTP works with Hypertext Markup Language (HTML), which embeds multiple links inside one or more master documents. These documents do not actually have colors or graphics embedded in them; instead, they contain links that reference the needed fonts, graphics, and supplemental documents. Figure 2-22 shows some sample HTML code.

```
<html>
<head>
<title>KSU's Center for Information Security Education and Awareness</title>
</head>
<body bgcolor="#000000" text="#000000" link="#0000FF" vlink="#FF0033" leftmargin="0"
topmargin="0" bottommargin="0" rightmargin="0" marginwidth="0" marginheight="0" alink="#663399">
<table width="640" border="0" cellspacing="0" cellpadding="0" align="left" bgcolor="#FFFFFF">
  <tr>
        <font size="2" face="Arial, Helvetica, sans-serif"><a href="CAEIAE.html">
        <strong>&lt;&lt;Click here for more information&gt;&gt;</strong></a></font></p>
     <p align="left"><font face="Arial, Helvetica, sans-serif">
        Welcome to KSU's Center for Information Security Education. The primary purpose of the
Center is to provide information on information security educational opportunities and
initiatives in the KSU community. The Center also  serves to increase the level of information
security awareness in the KSU community. </font></p>
     <td width="26%"><div align="right"><img src="nsaseal.gif" width="112" height="106"><br>
        <img src="IMAGES/DHS.jpg" width="113" height="110"></div></td>
     <td width="67%">
       <p><font face="Arial, Helvetica, sans-serif">
        If you have any questions about  the Center, its charter, activities or  the content of
this Web site, please contact the Center Director: <br> Dr. Michael Whitman, CISM, CISSP, at
<a href="mailto:infosec@kennesaw.edu"> infosec@kennesaw.edu</a>.</font></p>
        <p><strong>KSU is a National Center for Academic Excellence <br> in Information Assurance
Education </strong></p>
  </tr>
</table>
<p> </p>
</body>
</html>
```

Figure 2-22 Sample HTML code
© Cengage Learning 2013

IMAP, POP, and SMTP There are two dominant protocols used to support retrieval of e-mail messages from an e-mail server by client applications: IMAP and POP. POP, the Post Office Protocol, is currently in version 3 (POP3), whereas IMAP, the Internet Message Access Protocol, is currently in version 4 (IMAP4). Most e-mail clients allow users to select whether or not messages are left with the server or deleted from the server as they are retrieved. However, POP3 clients download messages to the client system and then delete them from the server. IMAP client connections allow both online and offline (or discon-nected) operation. Many IMAP clients will default to leave messages on the server, and users must explicitly delete them. POP3 clients tend to operate like a mail drop; the mes-sages exist on the server only until retrieved. When considering POP3 messages, the copy located at the client will be considered authoritative. On the other hand, IMAP messages are considered authoritative at the server. Client e-mail protocols are designed to pull e-mail from a server to a client.

On the server site, SMTP (Simple Mail Transfer Protocol) is the de facto standard for transfer-ring e-mail between post office servers across the Internet. SMTP is a text-based transfer pro-tocol. SMTP is designed to transmit e-mail from one server to another.

FTP FTP, the File Transfer Protocol, is designed to support the transfer of files between two computers—typically, a client and a server. According to RFC 959, the objectives of FTP are:

- To promote sharing of files (computer programs and/or data)
- To encourage indirect or implicit (via programs) use of remote computers
- To shield a user from variations in file storage systems among hosts
- To transfer data reliably and efficiently[9]

FTP establishes an FTP session and transfers data between a protocol interpreter (PI) and a data transfer process (DTP). It operates in one of three modes once a session is requested: active, passive, and extended passive. In active mode, the client actively seeks an FTP session from a server listening on TCP port 21. Once the session is established, the server will send data from TCP port 20. In passive mode, the server transmits its FTP information, which the client picks up. Extended passive is similar to passive, but less server information is transmitted—in fact, only the port number.

RPC The Application layer also involves the use of RPC, or remote procedure calls, which allows a computer program to call for information from another program or service without the user specifically requesting it. This "unsupervised" computer-to-computer communications can have severe security implications.

Application Layer Security Most of the applications and programs that give the network and the Internet value reside at the Application layer. Therefore, this is where the largest number of risks and attacks are. Each protocol has its inherent weaknesses and must be examined, evaluated, and then implemented only if truly needed by the organization. In many cases, there is a secure alternative to the protocols presented here. For example, instead of using FTP, secure FTP (SFTP) could be deployed, with increased security measures and fewer vulnerabilities. The same can be said for SHTTP and other protocols. The remainder of this book is devoted to a number of these security issues and ways to mitigate those risks.

The Internet, WWW, and TCP/IP

The Internet is simply a network of networks; in fact, the word *Internet* is an abbreviation for *internetwork*. The Internet today incorporates the networks of millions of small, independent networked systems, connected by major common carriers such as AT&T, Verizon, Global Crossing, and Sprint. Most of the services we associate with the Internet are e-mail, the Web, FTP, and instant messaging (IM). Given that the Internet and the World Wide Web are such vast topics, this section provides only a cursory overview of the primary protocols, TCP and IP.

By March 2011, almost 2.095 billion people were using the Internet, according to Internet World Stats, as shown in Figure 2-23. Writing in the Harvard International Review, philosopher N. J. Slabbert, a writer on policy issues for the Washington, DC–based Urban Land Institute, has asserted that the Internet is fast becoming a basic feature of global civilization, so that what has traditionally been called "civil society" is now becoming identical with information technology society as defined by Internet use.[10]

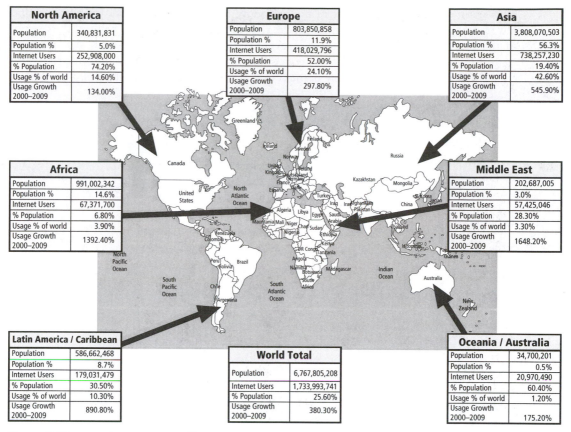

Figure 2-23 World Internet usage[11]
© Cengage Learning 2013

The World Wide Web

It is important to distinguish the Internet from the World Wide Web (WWW). The Internet is a physical set of networks, whereas the WWW is a set of applications that runs on top of the Internet. Most notably, the WWW is based on a series of hyperlinked documents that allow the creation and retrieval of information at a number of locations using uniform resource locators or URLs. Working at CERN in Geneva, Switzerland, Sir Tim Berners-Lee created the WWW in 1989. Since then, he has helped guide the development of many WWW standards, including markup language like HTML and XML.

The WWW works through Web browsers (like Mozilla, Firefox or Internet Explorer)—applications that take the requested information from the user or WWW resource and present it by integrating text, video, graphics, and sound through hyperlinks. Figure 2-24 illustrates how DNS is used to access a WWW document. In this illustration, a user, through a browser, seeks to find a specific Web page. As described earlier, DNS plays a key role in finding this information. First, the root-level WWW servers provide information on the primary name server responsible for containing the information about the specific host containing the requested resource, including its IP address. Next, the primary name server points the browser to the IP address of the host, where the browser goes for the actual resource. By separating the resolution of the primary domain from that of the secondary (and tertiary) domain, there are significantly fewer changes that need to be made to the root servers. Any changes beyond the assignment of the primary domain name are the responsibility of the primary (and secondary) name server. ISPs frequently provide this service for small networks. Many organizations provide their own primary and secondary name services. Once a browser has visited a specific site, it can cache this information to facilitate subsequent visits.

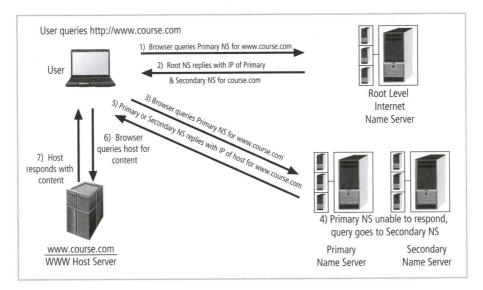

Figure 2-24   How DNS works
© Cengage Learning 2013

TCP/IP

TCP/IP is a suite of protocols used by the Internet to facilitate communications. Developed before the OSI Reference Model, it is similar in concept but differs in various details, as shown in Figure 2-25.

The TCP/IP network model is less formal that the OSI Reference Model discussed earlier. In fact, the TCP/IP protocol stack is a compilation of many discrete elements that work more or less in concert to provide network services. It is sometimes useful to view these many parts and pieces as working within a set of layers. Each layer, like those in the OSI Reference Model, attempts to solve a group of networking problems that are involved in delivering certain aspects of necessary network services. Also like the OSI Reference Model, each layer provides well-defined services to the layer above it and also expects services to be provided to it from the layer below. Higher level layers are logically closer to the user and are more abstract, whereas lower level layers are closer to the connection where signaling occurs and are in forms that can physically transmitted over various media channels.

Each of the four layers of the TCP/IP model is described in the following sections.

Application Layer   As defined earlier, the Application layer consists of the utility protocols designed to provide value to the end user. Data from the end user's utilities (the message) is passed down to the Transport layer for processing, as shown in Figure 2-26.

	OSI Layers	Included Protocols		TCP/IP Layers
7	Application	SNMP	FTP	
6	Presentation	TFTP NFS	Telnet Finger	Application
5	Session	DNS BOOTP	SMTP POP	
4	Transport	UDP	TCP	Host-to-Host Transport
3	Network	IP		Internet
2	Data Link	Network Interface Cards		Subnet
1	Physical	Transmission Media		

Figure 2-25 TCP/IP layers compared to OSI layers
© Cengage Learning 2013

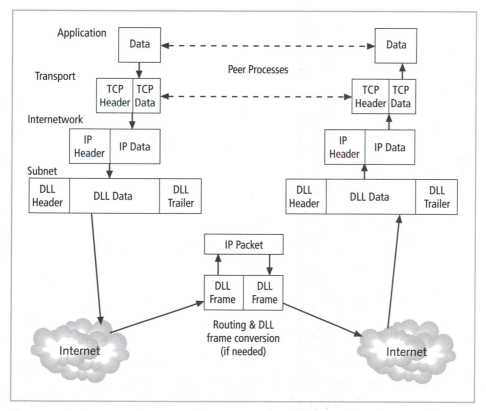

Figure 2-26 Application layer interconnection
© Cengage Learning 2013

There is a wide variety of Application layer protocols available to support use of the Internet, including SMTP and POP for e-mail, FTP for data transfer, and HTTP for the transfer of WWW content, all of which have been discussed earlier.

Transport or Host-to-Host Layer The Transport layer's responsibilities include end-to-end message transfer capabilities independent of the underlying network along with error control, fragmentation, and flow control. End-to-end-message transmissions and the connection of applications at the Transport layer can be categorized as either connection-oriented (e.g., TCP) or connectionless (e.g., UDP).

The Transport layer is literally a transport mechanism—that is, a vehicle that is responsible for making sure its contents (passengers/goods) reach their destination safely and soundly (unless a higher or lower layer is responsible for safe delivery). The Transport layer connects applications through the use of ports. Because IP provides only a best-effort delivery, the Transport layer is the first layer of the TCP/IP stack to offer reliability. Note that IP can run over a reliable data link protocol such as the High-Level Data Link Control (HDLC). Protocols above Transport, such as RPC, can also provide reliability. For example, TCP is a connection-oriented protocol that addresses the following reliability issues to provide a reliable byte stream:

- Data arrives in the right order.
- Data has minimal errors (i.e., has correctness).
- Duplicate data is discarded.
- Lost/discarded packets are re-sent.
- Congestion in traffic is reduced.

A newer element of the Transport layer is Stream Control Transmissions Protocol (SCTP). This was created to provide efficiencies for telephony but is also useful for situations that call for connection-oriented services that are reliable. It is a stream-oriented protocol (unlike the byte-stream-oriented nature of TCP) and multiplexes multiple streams with a single connection. It also offers redundant addressing in which an endpoint can be denoted as multiple IP addresses, thus providing failover support without interruption.

UDP is a connectionless datagram protocol. Like IP, it is a best-effort or "unreliable" protocol. Reliability is addressed through error detection using a weak checksum algorithm. UDP is typically used for applications such as streaming media (audio, video, Voice over IP, etc.), where on-time arrival is more important than reliability, or for simple query/response applications like DNS lookups, where the overhead of setting up a reliable connection is disproportionately large.

Both TCP and UDP are used to implement many applications or services. The applications at any given network address are distinguished by their TCP or UDP port. By convention, certain well-known ports are associated with specific applications.

Internetwork or Internet Layer The Internet layer serves to move packets across one or more networks, relying on the Link layer to get the messages up from the host systems and on the Transport layer to make sure that the traffic is correct and gets delivered properly. For the most part, this layer is concerned with two key functions: (1) host addressing and identification and (2) routing the packets across the Internet, getting data packets from source to destination. One example of this is the X.25 protocol.

Link or Network Interface Layer The subnet layers for TCP/IP include the Data Link layer and the Physical layer. TCP/IP relies on whatever native Network subnet layers are present. If the user's network is Ethernet, then the IP packets are encapsulated into Ethernet frames. As such, TCP/IP provides no specification for the Data Link layer or Physical layer.

2

Chapter Summary

- Communication can only occur when the recipient is able to receive, process, and comprehend the message. This one-way flow of information is referred to as a channel. Any communications medium may be subject to various types of interference, which is commonly called noise.

- Data communications and networking go hand in hand. Data communications is the exchange of messages across a medium, and networking is the interconnection of groups or systems with the purpose of exchanging information. Networks come in a variety of types and can be categorized by size (LAN, MAN, WAN), topology (bus, ring, star), or other criteria.

- A number of organizations promote standardized components of data communications. Some standards are formal, or de jure; these standards have been reviewed by a group of experts and endorsed by a standards body. Other standards are informal, or de facto; these have been widely adopted without having been formally reviewed.

- Among the agencies that work on data communications standards are the Internet Society (ISOC), the American National Standards Institute (ANSI), the International Telecommunications Union (ITU), the Institute of Electrical and Electronics Engineers (IEEE), the Telecommunications Industry Association (TIA), and the International Organization for Standardization (ISO).

Review Questions

1. What are the two parties to any communication channel called?

2. What is interference in communications channels called?

3. List and describe the various types of noise.

4. What are the reasons to create a computer network?

5. How is analog (voice) information placed onto an analog signal?

6. How is analog (voice) information placed onto a digital signal?

7. How is digital (computer) information placed onto an analog signal?

8. How is digital (computer) information placed onto a digital signal?

9. What are the various ways in which networks can be categorized?

10. List and describe the various sizes of networks.

11. List and describe network logical topologies.

12. List the advantages and disadvantages of WLANs.

13. List the various networking standards-setting organizations.

14. List and describe the various forms of multiplexing.

15. Describe the difference between the Internet and the World Wide Web (WWW).

16. List and describe the dominant error correction techniques.

17. Describe the difference between Source Address and Destination Address in an IP packet.

18. List each layer of the OSI Reference Model and its primary function.

19. List and describe the two parts contained within an IP packet.

20. What are the objectives of FTP?

Real-World Exercises

Exercise 2-1

Using an Internet search engine, look up "world internet usage." What is the most recent estimate of worldwide Internet usage, and when was it assessed? What percentage of the world's population is using the Internet?

Exercise 2-2

Using an Internet search engine, look up "Ethernet Standards." Read the content from at least two of the resulting links, then answer these questions:

a. Who invented Ethernet and when?

b. What is the IEEE standard number for all Ethernet standards?

c. What is the highest-rated speed for Ethernet?

Exercise 2-3

Using an Internet search engine, look up "Overview of the IETF." Read the page '"IETF Overview" and answer these questions:

a. Where can you find the IETF mission statement? What is the mission of the IETF, and how does it relate to the Internet?

b. What is an IETF working group area? What working group areas are currently defined?

Exercise 2-4

Using a Web browser, go to **www.protocols.com/protocols.htm**, then answer these questions:

   a. What is your estimate of how many protocols are shown on this page?

   b. How many families of protocols are listed on the right side of the page?

   c. Select one of the protocol families that interests you. Now, select one of the protocols on that page. Identify the protocol you have chosen and then describe the section headings for that protocol.

Exercise 2-5

Using an Internet search engine, look up "PPP." After reading at least two pages about the Point-to-Point Protocol, define it in your own words.

Exercise 2-6

Using an Internet search engine, look up "Network Access Control." After reading at least two pages about Network Access Control, define it in your own words.

Hands-On Projects

Project 2-1

Imagine that your department or lab has decided to upgrade from IP version 4 (IPv4) to IP version 6 (IPv6).

1. Inventory the current devices on the network. Gather rough counts, manufacturers, and models of the NICs, switches, routers, and other network devices that participate on the network.

2. Research the various network devices and determine if they are already IPv6 compatible.

3. For those devices that only support IPv4, determine how much it would cost to replace the device with one that provides the same functionality but supports IPv6.

4. Total the costs and organize your findings into an executive-level presentation to convince management of the need (or lack thereof) to upgrade. Base your recommendation on whether the benefits of IPv6 outweigh the costs.

Endnotes

1. Forouzan, B. Business Data Communications. McGraw-Hill Professional, 2002.

2. Internet Society. "About The Internet Society." Accessed 18 November 2011 from *www.isoc.org/isoc/*.

3. American National Standards Institute, "About ANSI." Accessed 18 November 2011 from *www.ansi.org/about_ansi/overview/overview.aspx?menuid=1*.

4. International Telecommunications Union, "About ITU." Accessed 18 November 2011 from *www.itu.int/en/about/Pages/default.aspx*.

5. IEEE, "IEEE At a Glance." Accessed November 18, 2011 from *www.ieee.org/about/today/at_a_glance.html*.

6. Telecommunications Industry Association, "About TIA." Accessed November 18, 2011 from *www.tiaonline.org/business/about/*.

7. International Organization for Standardization, "About ISO." Accessed November 18, 2011 from *www.iso.org/iso/about.htm*.

8. Bialoglowy, M. "Bluetooth Security Review, Part I: Introduction to Bluetooth." Accessed April 15, 2007 from *www.securityfocus.com/infocus/1830*.

9. Postel, J. & Reynolds, J., "Request for Comments: 959." Accessed November 18, 2011 from *tools.ietf.org/html/rfc959*.

10. EdChange, "Multicultural Education and Equity Awareness Quiz." Accessed November 18, 2011 from *www.edchange.org/multicultural/quiz/quiz_key.pdf*.

11. Internet World Stats. "Internet Usage Statistics: The Internet Big Picture, World Internet Users and Population Stats." Accessed February 24, 2010 from *www.internetworldstats.com/stats.htm*.

chapter 3

Cryptography

There are no secrets better kept than the secrets that everybody guesses. — George Bernard Shaw

Upon completion of this material, you should be able to:
- Chronicle the most significant events and discoveries in the history of cryptology
- Explain the basic principles of cryptography
- Describe the operating principles of the most popular cryptographic tools
- List and explain the major protocols used for secure communications
- Discuss the nature and execution of attacks used against cryptosystems

Talking in Code

The EBS IT team was still preparing for the PCI audit. Things were going well, and the necessary tasks were being documented. One of the key areas of concern involved PCI Data Security Standard's (DSS) Requirement 4, which governs the transmission of cardholder data across public networks. Specifically, Requirement 4.1 calls for an organization to "use strong cryptography and security protocols (SSL/TLS, IPSec, SSH, etc.) to safeguard sensitive cardholder data during transmission over open, public networks."[1]

At the time, EBS's extranet with Davis Office Megaplex wasn't being used to transmit credit card data; however, during recent planning sessions at EBS, the Davis group had outlined a solution that would allow EBS to resell office supplies to EBS customers. This would allow EBS to provide business services to customers and also sell office supplies to those same customers. However, this type of service would require the transmission of customer credit card data across the extranet. To do so, the IT staff would have to make sure the proper encryption was in place at all communications levels to ensure that the credit card data was transmitted safely.

Paige Davis knew that there were encryption products out there that would resolve the company's extranet issue as well as other security problems. However, she needed to do some research. Which encryption products would best fit EBS's business needs? Which products would provide the most security for the lowest cost? What encryption algorithms would be used for the selected product to provide the most security with the greatest performance while still meeting the PCI DSS requirements? Paige dived in to learning more about encryption.

Introduction

The science of cryptography is not as enigmatic as you might think. Various cryptographic techniques are used in everyday life. For example, open your newspaper to the entertainment section and you may find the Daily Cryptogram, which is a word puzzle that involves unscrambling letters to find a hidden message. Also, although it is a dying art, many court reporters still use stenography—an abbreviated, symbolic writing method—to take rapid dictation during legal proceedings. A form of cryptography is even used in knitting patterns, where directions are written in coded form—for example, K1P1 (knit 1, purl 1), which only an initiate can understand. These examples illustrate one common application of cryptography: the efficient and rapid transmission of information.

In this textbook, we focus on the other critical aspects of cryptography: protecting and verifying information transmitted via information systems. **Cryptography**, which comes from the Greek words *kryptos*, meaning "hidden," and *graphein*, meaning "to write," is the process of making and using codes to secure the transmission of information. The science of encryption, known as **cryptology**, encompasses both cryptography and cryptanalysis. **Cryptanalysis** is the process of obtaining the original message (called the **plaintext**) from an encrypted message (called the **ciphertext**) without knowing the keys used to perform the encryption. (Note: the algorithms used in most current encryption are freely available and published to allow academic and professional review.) **Encryption** is the process of converting an original message into a form that is unreadable to unauthorized individuals—that is, to anyone without the tools to convert the encrypted message back to its original format. **Decryption** is the process of converting the ciphertext message back into plaintext so that it can be readily understood. These are key terms that will be used throughout the book.

The field of cryptology is so complex it can fill volumes; this textbook seeks to provide only a general overview of cryptology and some specific information about cryptographic tools. The early sections of this chapter provide background on cryptology and general definitions of key concepts in cryptography. In later sections, you will learn about common cryptographic protocols and some of the attack methods used against cryptosystems.

Terminology

To help you understand the fundamentals of cryptography, here are a number of additional definitions:

- **Algorithm**—The programmatic steps used to convert an unencrypted message into an encrypted sequence of bits that represents the message; sometimes refers to the programs that enable the cryptographic processes

- **Cipher** or **cryptosystem**—An encryption method or process encompassing the algorithm, key(s) and/or cryptovariable(s), and procedures used to perform encryption and decryption

- **Ciphertext** or **cryptogram**—The encoded message resulting from an encryption

- **Code**—The process of converting components (words or phrases) of an unencrypted message into encrypted components

- **Decipher**—To decrypt, decode, or convert ciphertext into the equivalent plaintext

- **Encipher**—To encrypt, encode, or convert plaintext into the equivalent ciphertext

- **Key** or **cryptovariable**—The information used in conjunction with an algorithm to create the ciphertext from the plaintext or derive the plaintext from the ciphertext; it can be a series of bits used by a computer program, or it can be a passphrase used by humans that is then converted into a series of bits used by a computer program

- **Keyspace**—The entire range of values that can be used to construct an individual key

- **Link encryption**—A series of encryptions and decryptions among a number of systems, wherein each system in a network decrypts the message sent to it and then re-encrypts it using different keys and sends it to the next neighbor, with this process continuing until the message reaches the final destination

- **Nonrepudiation**—Verification that a message was sent by a particular sender and cannot be refuted

- **Plaintext** or **cleartext**—The original unencrypted message, or a message that has been successfully decrypted

- **Steganography**—The hiding of messages in such a way that no one but the sender and intended recipient of the message even knows a message exists—for example, within the digital encoding of a picture or graphic

- **Substitution**—The process of replacing plaintext values with other values to form ciphertext

- **Transposition:** The process of rearranging plaintext values to form ciphertext

- **Work factor**—The amount of effort (usually in hours) required to decode an encrypted message when the key and/or algorithm is unknown

History of Cryptology

Cryptology has a long history among the cultures of the world. Table 3-1 provides an overview.

1900 BC	Egyptian scribes used nonstandard hieroglyphs while inscribing clay tablets; this is the first documented use of written cryptography.
1500 BC	Mesopotamian cryptography surpassed that of the Egyptians. This is demonstrated in a tablet that was discovered to contain an encrypted formula for pottery glazes; the tablet used special symbols that appear to have different meanings from the usual symbols used elsewhere.
500 BC	Hebrew scribes writing the book of Jeremiah used a reversed alphabet substitution cipher known as the Atbash.
487 BC	The Spartans of Greece developed the scytale, a system consisting of a strip of papyrus wrapped around a wooden staff. Messages were written down the length of the staff, and the papyrus was unwrapped. The decryption process involved wrapping the papyrus around a shaft of similar diameter.
50 BC	Julius Caesar used a simple substitution cipher to secure military and government communications. To form an encrypted text, Caesar shifted the letter of the alphabet three places. In addition to this monoalphabetic substitution cipher, Caesar strengthened his encryption by substituting Greek letters for Latin letters.
Fourth and fifth centuries AD	The Kama Sutra of Vatsayana listed cryptography as the 44th and 45th of the 64 arts (yogas) that men and women should practice: "44) The art of understanding writing in cipher, and the writing of words in a peculiar way"; "45) The art of speaking by changing the forms of the word."
725	Abu 'Abd al-Rahman al-Khalil ibn Ahman ibn 'Amr ibn Tammam al Farahidi al-Zadi al Yahmadi wrote a book (now lost) on cryptography; he also solved a Greek cryptogram by guessing the plaintext introduction.
855	Abu Wahshiyyaan-Nabati, a scholar, published several cipher alphabets that were used to encrypt magic formulas.
1250	Roger Bacon, an English monk, wrote *Epistle of Roger Bacon on the Secret Works of Art and of Nature and Also on the Nullity of Magic*, in which he described several simple ciphers.
1392	*The Equatorie of the Planetis*, an early text possibly written by Geoffrey Chaucer, contained a passage in a simple substitution cipher.

Table 3-1 **History of Cryptology**

1412	*Subhalasha*, a 14-volume Arabic encyclopedia, contained a section on cryptography, including both substitution and transposition ciphers, and ciphers with multiple substitutions, a technique that had never been used before.
1466	Leon Battista Alberti, the "father of Western cryptography," worked with polyalphabetic substitution and also designed a cipher disk.
1518	Johannes Trithemius wrote the first printed book on cryptography and invented a steganographic cipher in which each letter was represented as a word taken from a succession of columns. He also described a polyalphabetic encryption method using a rectangular substitution format that is now commonly used. He is credited with introducing the method of changing substitution alphabets with each letter as it is deciphered.
1553	Giovan Batista Belaso introduced the idea of the passphrase (password) as a key for encryption; this polyalphabetic encryption method is misnamed for another person who later used the technique, today called the *Vigenère cipher*.
1563	Giovanni Battista Porta wrote a classification text on encryption methods, categorizing them as transposition, substitution, and symbol substitution.
1623	Sir Francis Bacon described an encryption method employing one of the first uses of steganography; he encrypted his messages by slightly changing the typeface of a random text so that each letter of the cipher was hidden within the text.
1790s	Thomas Jefferson created a 26-letter wheel cipher, which he used for official communications while ambassador to France; the concept of the wheel cipher would be reinvented in 1854 by Charles Babbage, and again in 1913.
1861–1865	During the U.S. Civil War, Union forces used a substitution encryption method based on specific words, and the Confederacy used a polyalphabetic cipher whose solution had been published before the start of the Civil War.
1914–1917	During World War I, the Germans, British, and French used a series of transposition and substitution ciphers in radio communications. All sides expended considerable effort toward intercepting and decoding communications, and they thereby created the science of cryptanalysis. British cryptographers broke the Zimmerman Telegram, in which the Germans offered Mexico U.S. territory in return for Mexico's support. This decryption helped to bring the United States into the war.
1917	William Frederick Friedman, the father of U.S. cryptanalysis, and his wife, Elizabeth, were employed as civilian cryptanalysts by the U.S. government. Friedman later founded a school for cryptanalysis in Riverbank, Illinois.
1917	Gilbert S. Vernam, an AT&T employee, invented a polyalphabetic cipher machine that used a nonrepeating random key.
1919	Hugo Alexander Koch filed a patent in the Netherlands for a rotor-based cipher machine; in 1927, Koch assigned the patent rights to Arthur Scherbius, the inventor of the Enigma machine, which was a mechanical substitution cipher.
1927–33	During Prohibition, criminals in the United States began using cryptography to protect the privacy of messages used in criminal activities.
1937	The Japanese developed the Purple machine, which was based on principles similar to those of Enigma and used mechanical relays from telephone systems to encrypt diplomatic messages. By late 1940, a team headed by William Friedman had broken the code generated by this machine and constructed a machine that could quickly decode Purple's ciphers.

Table 3-1 History of Cryptology (*continues*)

1939–1942	The Allies secretly broke the Enigma cipher, undoubtedly shortening World War II.
1942	Navajo code talkers entered World War II; in addition to speaking a language that was unknown outside a relatively small group within the United States, the Navajos developed code words for subjects and ideas that did not exist in their native tongue.
1948	Claude Shannon suggested using frequency and statistical analysis in the solution of substitution ciphers.
1970	Dr. Horst Feistel led an IBM research team in the development of the Lucifer cipher.
1976	A design based upon Lucifer was chosen by the U.S. National Security Agency as the Data Encryption Standard (DES) and found worldwide acceptance.
1976	Whitefield Diffie and Martin Hellman introduced the idea of public-key cryptography with the Diffie-Hellman key exchange.
1977	Ronald Rivest, Adi Shamir, and Leonard Adleman developed a practical public-key cipher for both confidentiality and digital signatures; the RSA family of computer encryption algorithms was born.
1978	The initial RSA algorithm was published in the Communication of ACM.
1991	Phil Zimmermann released the first version of PGP (Pretty Good Privacy); PGP was originally released as freeware and became the worldwide standard for public cryptosystems.
2000	The Rijndael cipher, developed by Joan Daemen and Vincent Rijmen, was selected as the Advanced Encryption Standard (AES).

Table 3-1 History of Cryptology (*continued*)
© Cengage Learning 2013

Cipher Methods

There are two contemporary methods for encrypting plaintext: the bit stream method and the block cipher method. In the bit stream method, each bit in the plaintext is transformed into a cipher bit, 1 bit at a time. In the block cipher method, the message is divided into blocks—for example, sets of 8-, 16-, 32-, or 64-bit blocks—and then each block of plaintext bits is transformed into an encrypted block of cipher bits using an algorithm and a key. Bit stream methods commonly use algorithm functions like the exclusive OR operation (XOR), whereas block methods can use substitution, transposition, XOR, or some combination of these operations. Note that most computer-based encryption methods operate on data at the level of its binary digits (bits), but some operate at the byte or character level.

Substitution Cipher

With a **substitution cipher**, you substitute one value for another. For example, you can replace a letter in the alphabet with the letter three values to the right. Alternatively, you can replace one bit with a bit that is four places to its left. A three-character substitution to the right results in the following transformation of the standard English alphabet:

Initial alphabet   ABCDEFGHIJKLMNOPQRSTUVWXYZ

Encryption alphabet DEFGHIJKLMNOPQRSTUVWXYZABC

Within this substitution scheme, the plaintext MOM would be encrypted into the ciphertext PRP.

This is a simple enough method by itself but very powerful if combined with other operations. This type of substitution is based on a **monoalphabetic substitution** because it only uses one alphabet. More advanced substitution ciphers use two or more alphabets and are referred to as **polyalphabetic substitutions**.

To extend the previous example, consider the following block of text:

Plaintext	ABCDEFGHIJKLMNOPQRSTUVWXYZ
Substitution cipher 1	DEFGHIJKLMNOPQRSTUVWXYZABC
Substitution cipher 2	GHIJKLMNOPQRSTUVWXYZABCDEF
Substitution cipher 3	JKLMNOPQRSTUVWXYZABCDEFGHI
Substitution cipher 4	MNOPQRSTUVWXYZABCDEFGHIJKL

The first row is the plaintext, and the next four rows are four sets of substitution ciphers, which when taken together constitute a single **polyalphabetic** substitution cipher. To encode the word TEXT with this cipher, you substitute a letter from the second row for the first letter in TEXT, a letter from the third row for the second letter, and so on—a process that yields the ciphertext WKGF. Note how the plaintext letter T is transformed into a W or an F, depending on its order of appearance in the plaintext. Complexities like these make this type of encryption substantially more difficult to decipher when one doesn't have the algorithm (in this case, the rows of ciphers) and the key, which is the method used (in this case, the use of the second row for first letter, third row for second, and so on). A logical extension of this process is to randomize the cipher rows completely in order to create a more complex operation.

One example of a substitution cipher is the cryptogram in the daily newspaper (see Figure 3-1); another is the once-famous "Radio Orphan Annie" decoder pin, which consisted of two alphabetic rings that could be rotated to a predetermined pairing to form a simple substitution cipher. The device was made to be worn as a pin so one could always be at the ready. As mentioned in Table 3-1, Julius Caesar reportedly used a three-position shift to the right to encrypt his messages (so A became D, B became E, and so on), thus was this particular substitution cipher given its name—the *Caesar Cipher*.

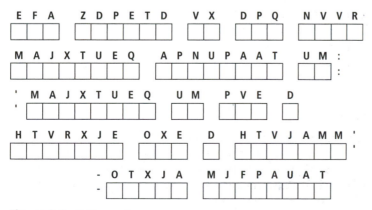

Figure 3-1 Daily cryptogram
© Cengage Learning 2013

An advanced type of substitution cipher that uses a simple polyalphabetic code is the **Vigenère cipher**. It is implemented using the Vigenère Square (or table), which is made up of 26 distinct cipher alphabets. Figure 3-2 illustrates the setup of the Vigenère Square. In the header row, the alphabet is written in its normal order. In each subsequent row, the alphabet is shifted one letter to the right until a 26 x 26 block of letters is formed. There are a number of ways to use the Vigenère Square. You could perform an encryption by simply starting in the first row and finding a substitute for the first letter of plaintext, and then moving down the rows for each subsequent letter of plaintext. With this method, the word SECURITY in plaintext would become TGFYWOAG in ciphertext.

```
    A B C D E F G H I J K L M N O P Q R S T U V W X Y Z
A   A B C D E F G H I J K L M N O P Q R S T U V W X Y Z
B   B C D E F G H I J K L M N O P Q R S T U V W X Y Z A
C   C D E F G H I J K L M N O P Q R S T U V W X Y Z A B
D   D E F G H I J K L M N O P Q R S T U V W X Y Z A B C
E   E F G H I J K L M N O P Q R S T U V W X Y Z A B C D
F   F G H I J K L M N O P Q R S T U V W X Y Z A B C D E
G   G H I J K L M N O P Q R S T U V W X Y Z A B C D E F
H   H I J K L M N O P Q R S T U V W X Y Z A B C D E F G
I   I J K L M N O P Q R S T U V W X Y Z A B C D E F G H
J   J K L M N O P Q R S T U V W X Y Z A B C D E F G H I
K   K L M N O P Q R S T U V W X Y Z A B C D E F G H I J
L   L M N O P Q R S T U V W X Y Z A B C D E F G H I J K
M   M N O P Q R S T U V W X Y Z A B C D E F G H I J K L
N   N O P Q R S T U V W X Y Z A B C D E F G H I J K L M
O   O P Q R S T U V W X Y Z A B C D E F G H I J K L M N
P   P Q R S T U V W X Y Z A B C D E F G H I J K L M N O
Q   Q R S T U V W X Y Z A B C D E F G H I J K L M N O P
R   R S T U V W X Y Z A B C D E F G H I J K L M N O P Q
S   S T U V W X Y Z A B C D E F G H I J K L M N O P Q R
T   T U V W X Y Z A B C D E F G H I J K L M N O P Q R S
U   U V W X Y Z A B C D E F G H I J K L M N O P Q R S T
V   V W X Y Z A B C D E F G H I J K L M N O P Q R S T U
W   W X Y Z A B C D E F G H I J K L M N O P Q R S T U V
X   X Y Z A B C D E F G H I J K L M N O P Q R S T U V W
Y   Y Z A B C D E F G H I J K L M N O P Q R S T U V W X
Z   Z A B C D E F G H I J K L M N O P Q R S T U V W X Y
```

Figure 3-2 Vigenère Square
© Cengage Learning 2013

A much more sophisticated way to use the Vigenère Square would be to use a keyword to represent the shift. To accomplish this, you begin by writing a keyword above the plaintext message. For example, suppose the plaintext message was "SACK GAUL SPARE NO ONE" and the keyword was "ITALY." We, thus, end up with the following:

ITALYITALYITALYITA

SACKGAULSPARENOONE

Now, you use the keyword letter and the message (plaintext) letter below it in combination. Returning to the Vigenère Square, notice how the first column of text, like the first row, forms the normal alphabet. To perform the substitution, start with the first combination of keyword and message letters, IS. Use the keyword letter to locate the column, and the message letter to find the row, and then look for the letter at their intersection. Thus, for column "I" and row "S," you will find the ciphertext letter "A." After you follow this procedure for each of the letters in the message, you will produce the encrypted ciphertext ATCVEINLDNIKEYMWGE.

3

One weakness of this method is that any keyword-message letter combination containing an "A" row or column reproduces the plaintext message letter. For example, the third letter in the plaintext message, the C (of SACK), has a combination of AC and thus is unchanged in the ciphertext. To minimize the effects of this weakness, you should avoid choosing a keyword that contains the letter "A."

Transposition Cipher

Like the substitution operation, the transposition cipher is simple to understand, but it can, if properly used, produce ciphertext that is difficult to decipher. In contrast to the substitution cipher, however, the **transposition cipher** (or **permutation cipher**) simply rearranges the values within a block to create the ciphertext. This can be done at the bit level or at the byte (character) level. For example, consider this transposition key pattern:

Key pattern: 1→4, 2→8, 3→1, 4→5, 5→7, 6→2, 7→6, 8→3

In this transposition key, the bit or byte (character) in position 1 (with position 1 being at the far left as if transmitted from right to left) moves to position 4, and the bit or byte in position 2 moves to position 8, and so on. This is similar to another newspaper puzzle favorite: the Word Jumble, as shown in Figure 3-3.

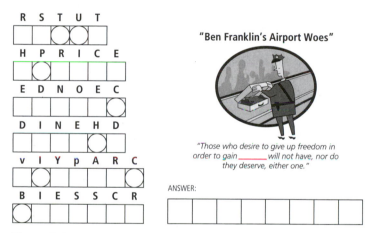

Figure 3-3 Word Jumble
© Cengage Learning 2013

Using that same transposition key, consider this plaintext message, sent from left to right starting with the 0 bit: 001001010110101110010101. What follows are the bit locations, the plaintext, and the ciphertext that are produced when the key pattern is applied to the plaintext, all three broken into 8-bit blocks for ease of discussion:

```
Bit Locations:  1 2 3 4 5 6 7 8 | 1 2 3 4 5 6 7 8 | 1 2 3 4 5 6 7 8
Plaintext:      0 0 1 0 0 1 0 1 | 0 1 1 0 1 0 1 1 | 1 0 0 1 0 1 0 1
Ciphertext:     1 1 1 0 0 0 0 0 | 1 0 1 0 0 1 1 1 | 0 1 1 1 1 0 0 0

Bit locator:    1 2 3 4 5 6 7 8 | 1 2 3 4 5 6 7 8 | 1 2 3 4 5 6 7 8
```

Reading from left to right, the first bit of plaintext (position 1 of the first byte) becomes the fourth bit (in position 4) of the first byte of the ciphertext. Similarly, the second bit of the plaintext (position 2) becomes the eighth bit (position 8) of the ciphertext, and so on. To further examine how this transposition key works, let's see its effects on a plaintext message composed of letters instead of bits. Using the same transposition cipher, here's what we get when we replace the 8-bit block of plaintext with the plaintext message "SACK GAUL SPARE NO ONE":

```
Letter Locations:   1 2 3 4 5 6 7 8 | 1 2 3 4 5 6 7 8 | 1 2 3 4 5 6 7 8
Plaintext:          S A C K _ G A U | L _ S P A R E _ | N O _ O N E _ _
Ciphertext:         C G U S K _ A A | S R _ L P E A _ | _ E _ N O _ N O
```

Remember the transposition pattern is: 1→4, 2→8, 3→1, 4→5, 5→7, 6→2, 7→6, 8→3. So, in this example, reading from left to right, the letter in block 1, position 1 of the first block of the plaintext (this is the letter "S") moves to the position in block 1, character 4 in the ciphertext. Then, still in block 1, we move the character found in position 2 (it is an "A") to the 8th position. Continuing, we move the third character (a letter "C") to the first position. This continues for all characters in block 1 and then repeats for subsequent blocks. So, the "P" that is the fourth letter of the plaintext in block 2 is the same "P" found as the fifth letter of the ciphertext in block 2. Note that the spaces in the original text are transposed as well.

In addition to being credited with inventing a substitution cipher, Julius Caesar was associated with an early version of the transposition cipher. In the Caesar block cipher, the recipient of the coded message fits the text to a prime number square (a square of text consisting of a prime number of rows and columns). In practice, this means that if there are fewer than 25 characters, the recipient uses a 5 x 5 square. For example, if you were the recipient of the Caesar ciphertext shown below, you would make a square of 5 columns and 5 rows, then write the letters of the message into the square, filling the slots from left to right, top to bottom. You would then read the message from the opposite direction—that is, from top to bottom, left to right.

```
Ciphertext:      S G S _ N A A P N E C U A O _ K L R _ _ _ _ E O _
5 X 5 Square:
```

```
            S G S _ N
            A A P N E
            C U A O _
            K L R _ _
            _ _ E O _
```

Reading from top to bottom, left to right reveals the plaintext "SACK GAUL SPARE NO ONE."

When mechanical and electronic cryptosystems became more widely used, transposition ciphers and substitution ciphers were combined to produce highly secure encryption processes. To make the encryption even stronger (more difficult to cryptanalyze), the keys and block sizes can be made much larger (up to 128 bits), which produces substantially more complex substitutions or transpositions.

Exclusive OR Operation

The **exclusive OR operation (XOR)** is a function of a binary operation in which two bits are compared and (1) if the two bits are identical, the result is a binary 0, and (2) if the two bits are not the same, the result is a binary 1. XOR encryption is a very simple symmetric cipher that is used in many applications where security is not a defined requirement. Table 3-2 shows an XOR truth table with the results of all the possible combinations of two bits.

First Bit	Second Bit	Result
0	0	0
0	1	1
1	0	1
1	1	0

Table 3-2 XOR Truth Table
© Cengage Learning 2013

To see how XOR works, consider the plaintext "CAT." The binary representation of the plaintext is "01110000 01100101 1000000." In order to encrypt the plaintext, a secret key value needs to be selected for the encryption operation. In this case, the bit pattern for the letter "V" (10000101) is used, and it is repeated for each character to be encrypted, left to right. Performing the XOR operation on the two bit streams (the plaintext and the key) produces the result shown in Table 3-3.

Text Value	Binary Value
CAT as bits	01110000 01100101 10000000
Key (in this case, V three times)	10000101 10000101 10000101
Cipher	11110101 11100000 00000101

Table 3-3 Example of XOR Encryption (Spaces Added for Easy Viewing)
© Cengage Learning 2013

The row of Table 3-3 labeled "Cipher" contains the bit stream that will be transmitted; when this cipher is received, it can be decrypted using the key value of "V." Note that the XOR encryption method is very simple to implement and equally simple to break, *if* you have the key. The XOR encryption method should not be used by itself when an organization is transmitting or storing sensitive data. Actual encryption algorithms used to protect data typically use the XOR operator as part of a more complex encryption process.

You can combine the XOR operation with a block cipher operation to produce a simple but powerful operation. In the example that follows, the first row shows the character message that requires encryption: "5E5+•". The second row shows this message in binary notation. In order to apply an 8-bit block cipher method, the binary message is broken into 8-bit blocks in the row labeled "Message Blocks." The fourth row shows the 8-bit key (01010101) chosen for the encryption. To encrypt the message, you must perform the XOR operation on each 8-bit block by using the XOR function on the message bit and the key bit to determine the bits of the ciphertext until the entire message is enciphered. The result is shown in the row labeled "Ciphertext." This ciphertext can now be sent to a receiver, who will be able to decipher the message by simply knowing the algorithm (XOR) and the key (01010101).

Message (text):	"5E5+•"
Message (binary):	0011010101000101001101010010101110010101
Message blocks:	00110101 01000101 00110101 00101011 10010101
Key:	01010101 01010101 01010101 01010101 01010101
Ciphertext:	01100000 00010000 01100000 01111110 11000000

If the receiver cannot apply the key to the ciphertext and derive the original message, either the cipher was applied with an incorrect key or the cryptosystem was not used correctly.

Vernam Cipher

Also known as the one-time pad, the **Vernam cipher**, which was developed at AT&T, uses a set of characters only one time for each encryption process (hence, the name *one-time pad*). The pad in the name comes from the days of manual encryption and decryption, when the key values for each ciphering session were prepared by hand and bound into an easy-to-use form—that is, a pad of paper. To perform the Vernam cipher encryption operation, the pad values are added to numeric values that represent the plaintext that needs to be encrypted. Each character of the plaintext is turned into a number, and a pad value for that position is added to it. The resulting sum for that character is then converted back to a ciphertext character for transmission. If the sum of the two values exceeds 26, then 26 is subtracted from the total. (Note that the process of keeping a computed number within a specific range is a key concept in modular arithmetic. Requiring that all numbers be in the range 1–26 is referred to as *modulo 26*. In modulo 26, if a number is larger than 26, then 26 is sequentially subtracted from it until the number is in the proper range.)

To examine the Vernam cipher and its use of modular arithmetic, consider the following example, which uses "SACK GAUL SPARE NO ONE" as plaintext. In the first step of this encryption process, the letter "S" is converted into the number 19 (because it is the 19th letter of the alphabet), and the same conversion is applied to the rest of the letters of the plaintext message, as shown below. Rows 3 and 4 show, respectively, the one-time pad text and the corresponding value that was chosen for this encryption.

Plaintext:	S	A	C	K	_	G	A	U	L	_	S	P	A	R	E	_	N	O	_	O	N	E
Plaintext value:	19	01	03	11	_	07	01	21	12	_	19	16	01	18	05	_	14	15	_	15	14	05
One-time pad text:	F	P	Q	R	_	N	S	B	I	_	E	H	T	Z	L	_	A	C	_	D	G	J
One-time pad value:	06	16	17	18	_	14	19	02	09	_	05	08	20	26	12	_	01	03	_	04	07	10
Sum of plaintext and pad:	25	17	20	29	_	21	20	23	21	_	24	24	21	44	17	_	15	18	_	19	21	15
After modulo subtraction:	25	17	20	03	_	21	20	23	21	_	24	24	21	18	17	_	15	18	_	19	21	15
Ciphertext:	Y	Q	T	C	_	U	T	W	U	_	X	X	U	R	Q	_	O	R	_	S	U	O

As you can see, the pad value, like the plaintext value, is derived from the position of each pad text letter in the alphabet; thus, the pad text letter "F" is assigned the value of 06. This conversion process is repeated for the entire one-time pad text. Next, the plaintext value and the one-time pad value are added together; the first such sum is 25. Because 25 is in the range of 1 to 26, no modulo 26 subtraction is required. The sum remains 25, and yields the ciphertext "Y." Skipping ahead to the fourth character of the plaintext, "K," the plaintext value for it is 11. The pad text is "R," and the one-time pad value is 18. The sum of 11 and 18 is 29. Because 29 is larger than 26, 26 is subtracted from it, which yields the value 03. The ciphertext for this plaintext character is then the third letter of the alphabet, "C."

Decryption of any ciphertext generated from a one-time pad requires either knowledge of the pad values or the use of elaborate and (the encrypting party hopes) very difficult cryptanalysis. Using the pad values and the ciphertext, the decryption process works as follows: "Y" becomes the number 25, from which we subtract the pad value for the first letter of the message, 06. This yields a value of 19, or the letter "S." This pattern continues until the fourth letter of the ciphertext, where the ciphertext letter is "C" and the pad value is 18. Subtracting 18 from 3 yields negative 15. Because modulo 26 is employed, which requires that all numbers be in the range of 1–26, you must add (not subtract) 26 to negative 15. This gives a sum of 11, which means that the fourth letter of the message is "K."

Book or Running Key Cipher

One encryption method made popular by spy movies involves using the text in a book as the key to decrypt a message. The ciphertext consists of a list of codes representing the page number, line number, and word number of the plaintext word. The algorithm is the mechanical process of looking up the references from the ciphertext and converting each reference to a word by using the ciphertext's value and the key (the book). For example, from a copy of a particular popular novel, one may send the message 259, 19, 8; 22, 3, 8; 375, 7, 4; 394, 17, 2. Although almost any book can be used, dictionaries and thesauruses are typically the most popular sources, as they are likely to contain almost any word that might be needed. The recipient of a running key cipher must first know which book is used—in this case, let's say the science fiction novel *A Fire Upon the Deep* (1992 TOR edition). To decrypt the ciphertext, the receiver acquires the book and turns to page 259, finds line 19, and selects the eighth word in that line (which is "SACK"). The receiver then turns to page 22, line 3, and selects the eighth word again, and so forth. In this example, the resulting message is "SACK ISLAND SHARP PATH." If dictionaries are used, the message could consist of only the page number and the number of the word on the page. An even more sophisticated version might use multiple books, perhaps even in a particular sequence for each word or phrase.

Another variation of the book cipher is the **grille cipher**, which uses a stencil or template with holes cut out. When the template is applied to a particular message, book, or other document, the message is revealed in the holes (apertures). This also represents a form of steganography. Not only must the template be possessed, the reader must know the sequence of revealed letters or words in order to understand the message.

Hash Functions

In addition to ciphers, an important encryption technique that is often incorporated into cryptosystems is the hash function. **Hash functions** are mathematical algorithms that generate a message summary or digest (sometimes called a fingerprint) that can be used to confirm the identity of a specific message and/or confirm that there have not been any changes to the content. Although they do not create a ciphertext, hash functions confirm message identity and integrity, both of which are critical functions in e-commerce.

Hash algorithms are mathematical functions that create a hash value, also known as a message digest, by converting variable-length messages into a single fixed-length value. The **message digest** is a "fingerprint" of the author's message, which is compared with the recipient's locally calculated hash of the same message. If the two hashes are identical after transmission, the message has arrived without modification. Hash functions are considered one-way operations in that the same message always provides the same hash value, but the hash value itself cannot be used to determine the contents of the message.

Hashing functions do not require the use of keys, but it is possible to attach a **message authentication code (MAC)**—a key-dependent, one-way hash function that allows only specific recipients (symmetric key holders) to access the message digest. Because hash functions are one-way, they are used in password verification systems to confirm the identity of the user. In such systems, the hash value, or message digest, is calculated based upon the originally issued password, and this message digest is stored for later comparison. When the user logs on for the next session, the system calculates a hash value based on the user's password input, and this value is compared against the stored value to confirm identity.

The **Secure Hash Standard (SHS)** is a standard issued by the National Institute of Standards and Technology (NIST). The Federal Information Processing Standard (FIPS) 180-2 specifies the Secure Hash Algorithm 1 (SHA-1) as a secure algorithm for computing a condensed representation of a message or data file. SHA-1 produces a 160-bit message digest, which can be used as an input to a digital signature algorithm. SHA-1 is based on principles modeled after MD4 (which is part of the MDx family of hash algorithms created by Ronald Rivest). Other hash algorithms (SHA-224, SHA-256, SHA-384, and SHA-512) have also been specified in FIPS 180-2 as standards, with digests of 224, 256, 384, and 512 bits, respectively. The number of bits used in the hash algorithm is a measurement of the strength of the algorithm against collision attacks. SHA-256 is essentially a 256-bit block cipher algorithm that creates a key by encrypting the intermediate hash value with the message block functioning as the key. The compression function operates on each 512-bit message block and a 256-bit intermediate message digest.[2] As shown in Figure 3-4, there are free tools that can calculate hash values by using a number of popular algorithms.

In general, if attackers gain access to a list of hashed passwords, they can use a combination of brute force and dictionary attacks to reveal user passwords. Passwords that are dictionary words or poorly constructed can be easily cracked. However, an attack method called **rainbow cracking** has generated significant concern about the strength of the processes used for password hashing—even for well-constructed passwords. Using a **rainbow table**—a database of precomputed hashes from sequentially calculated passwords—the rainbow cracker simply looks up the hashed password in the massive list and reads out the text version, with no brute force required. This type of attack is more properly classified as a **time-memory trade-off attack**.

To defend against this type of attack, you must first protect the file of hashed passwords and implement strict limits to the number of attempts allowed per login session. You can also use an approach called password hash salting. **Salting** is the process of providing a nonsecret,

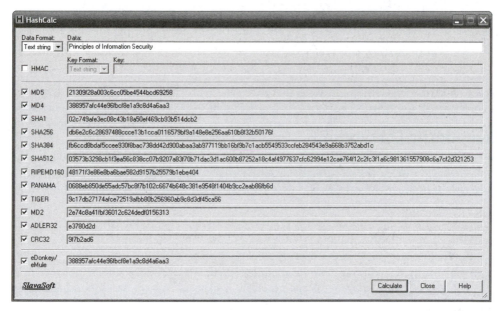

Figure 3-4   HashCalc hash calculation tool

Source: HashCalc

random piece of data to the hashing function when the hash is first calculated. The salt value is not kept a secret; it is stored along with the account identifier so that the hash value can be recreated during authentication.[3] The use of a salt value creates a different hash, and when a large set of salt values is used, rainbow cracking fails because it makes the reverse calculation of the time-memory tradeoff attack of no value to the attacker.

Cryptographic Algorithms

Cryptographic algorithms are often grouped into two broad categories—symmetric and asymmetric—but today's most popular cryptosystems use a combination of symmetric and asymmetric algorithms. These are distinguished by the types of keys they use for encryption and decryption operations, and how those keys are distributed. This section begins with an examination of the notation methods used to describe how these algorithms function.

Cryptographic Notation

The notation used to describe an encryption process varies, depending on the source describing the encryption. The notation used in this textbook uses the letter "M" to represent the original message, "C" to represent the resulting ciphertext, and "E" to represent the encryption process—thus, the formula, $E(M) = C$.[4] This formula represents the application of encryption (E) to a message (M) to create ciphertext (C). Also in this notation scheme, the letter "D" represents the decryption or deciphering process—thus, the formula $D[E(M)] = M$, which states that if you decipher (D) an enciphered message (E(M)), you get the original message (M). This can also be stated as $D[C]=M$, or the deciphering of the ciphertext (remember that C=E(M)) results in the original message M. Finally, the letter "K" is used to represent the key; therefore, E(M,K) = C states that encrypting (E) the message (M) with the key (K) results in the ciphertext (C). Similarly, D(C,K) = D[E(M,K),K] = M, which states that deciphering the ciphertext with key K results in the original plaintext message. Or, to translate this formula even more precisely: deciphering with key K the message encrypted with key K results in the original message.

Symmetric Encryption

Encryption methodologies that require the same **secret key** to encipher and decipher the message are using **private key encryption** or **symmetric encryption.** Symmetric encryption methods use mathematical operations that can be programmed into extremely fast computing algorithms so that the encryption and decryption processes are executed quickly by even small computers. As you can see in Figure 3-5, one of the challenges is that both the sender and the recipient must have the secret key. Also, if either copy of the key falls into the wrong hands, messages can be decrypted by others and the sender and intended receiver may not know the message has been intercepted. The primary challenge of symmetric key encryption is getting the key to the receiver, a process that must be conducted out-of-band (i.e., through a channel or band other than the one carrying the ciphertext) to avoid interception.

Data Encryption Standard (DES) There are a number of popular symmetric encryption cryptosystems. One of the most widely known is **Data Encryption Standard (DES)**, which was developed by IBM and is based on the company's Lucifer algorithm, which uses a key length of 128 bits. Using a 64-bit block size and a 56-bit key, DES

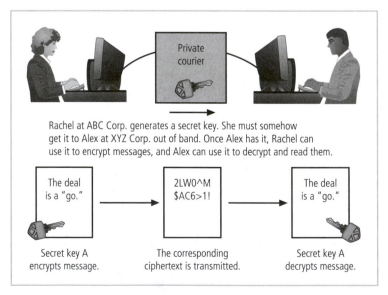

Figure 3-5 Example of symmetric encryption
© Cengage Learning 2013

was adopted by NIST in 1976 as a federal standard for encryption of nonclassified information, after which it became widely employed in commercial applications. It enjoyed increasing popularity for almost 20 years, until 1997, when users realized that a 56-bit key size did not provide an acceptable level of security. In 1998, a group called the Electronic Frontier Foundation (*www.eff.org*), using a specially designed computer, broke a DES key in just over 56 hours. Since then, it has been theorized that a dedicated attack supported by the proper hardware (not necessarily a specialized computer) can break a DES key in less than four hours.

Triple DES (3DES) Triple DES (3DES) was created to provide a level of security far beyond that of DES. Triple DES encryption is the same as that of standard DES, except it is repeated three times. 3DES was an advanced application of DES, and although it did deliver on its promise of encryption strength beyond DES, it too soon proved too weak to survive indefinitely—especially as computing power continued to double every 18 months (known as Moore's law).

3DES takes three 64-bit keys for an overall key length of 192 bits. It can be employed using two or three keys and a combination of encryption or decryption, for additional security. The most common implementations involve encrypting and/or decrypting with two or three different keys, a process that is described next. 3DES employs 48 rounds in its encryption computation, generating ciphers that are approximately 256 (72 quadrillion) times stronger than standard DES ciphers but require only three times longer to process. Three types of 3DES encryption operations are illustrated here:

1. In the first option, 3DES encrypts the message with Key 1, then decrypts it with Key 2, then encrypts it again with Key 1. In cryptographic notation, this is [E{D[E(M,K1)],K2}, K1]. Decrypting with a different key is essentially another encryption, but it reverses the application of the traditional encryption operations.

2. In the second option, 3DES encrypts the message with Key 1, then encrypts it again with Key 2, then encrypts it a third time with Key 1 again—that is, [E{E[E(M,K1)], K2},K1].

3. In the third option, 3DES encrypts the message three times with three different keys—that is, [E{E[E(M,K1)],K2},K3]. Of the three options, this is the most secure encryption operation possible with 3DES.

The Advanced Encryption Standard (AES) The successor to 3DES is **Advanced Encryption Standard (AES)**. AES is a Federal Information Processing Standard (FIPS) that specifies a cryptographic algorithm used within the U.S. government to protect information in federal agencies that are not a part of the national defense infrastructure. (Agencies that are considered a part of national defense use other, more secure methods of encryption, which are provided by the National Security Agency.)

AES was developed to replace both DES and 3DES. Although 3DES remains an approved algorithm for some uses, its expected useful life is limited. Historically, cryptographic standards approved by FIPS have been adopted on a voluntary basis by organizations outside government. The AES selection process involved cooperation between the U.S. government, private companies, and universities around the world.

Of the many ciphers that were submitted from around the world for consideration in the AES selection process, five finalists were chosen: MARS, RC6, Rijndael, Serpent, and Twofish. On October 2, 2000, NIST announced the selection of Rijndael as the cipher to be used as the basis for the AES, and this block cipher was approved by the secretary of commerce as the official federal governmental standard as of May 26, 2002.

AES implements a block cipher called the Rijndael Block Cipher, with a variable block length and a key length of 128, 192, or 256 bits. Experts estimate that the special computer used by the Electronic Frontier Foundation to crack DES within a couple of days would require approximately 4.7×10^{24} (or 4,698,864 quintillion years) to crack AES.

AES can use a multiple-round-based system. Depending on the key size, the number of rounds varies between 9 and 13. For a 128-bit key, 9 rounds plus one end round are used; for a 192-bit key, 11 rounds plus one end round are used; and for a 256-bit key, 13 rounds plus one end round are used. Once Rijndael was adopted as the AES, the ability to use variably sized blocks was standardized to a single 128-bit block, for simplicity.

Asymmetric Encryption

Whereas symmetric encryption uses a single key to both encrypt and decrypt a message, **asymmetric encryption** uses two different but related keys, and either key can be used to encrypt or decrypt the message. If, however, Key A is used to encrypt the message, only Key B can decrypt it, and if Key B is used to encrypt a message, only Key A can decrypt it. Asymmetric encryption can be used to provide elegant solutions to problems of secrecy and verification. This technique has its highest value when one key is used as a private key, which means that it is kept secret (much like the key of symmetric encryption), known only to the owner of the key pair, and the other key serves as a public key, which means that it is stored in a public location where anyone can use it. This is why the more common name for asymmetric encryption is **public-key encryption**.

Consider the following example, illustrated in Figure 3-6. Alex at XYZ Corporation wants to send an encrypted message to Rachel at ABC Corporation. Alex goes to a public-key registry and obtains Rachel's public key. Remember that the foundation of asymmetric encryption is that the same key cannot be used to both encrypt and decrypt the same message. So when Rachel's public key is used to encrypt the message, only Rachel's private key can be used to decrypt the message, and that private key is held by Rachel alone. Similarly, if Rachel wants to respond to Alex's message, she goes to the registry where Alex's public key is held and uses it to encrypt her message, which can only be read by Alex's private key. This approach, which keeps private keys secret and encourages the sharing of public keys in reliable directories, is an elegant solution to the key management problems of symmetric key applications.

Asymmetric algorithms are one-way functions. A one-way function is simple to compute in one direction but complex to compute in the opposite direction. This is the foundation of public-key encryption. Public-key encryption is based on a hash value, which, as you learned earlier in this chapter, is calculated from an input number using a hashing algorithm. This hash value is essentially a summary of the original input values. It is virtually impossible to

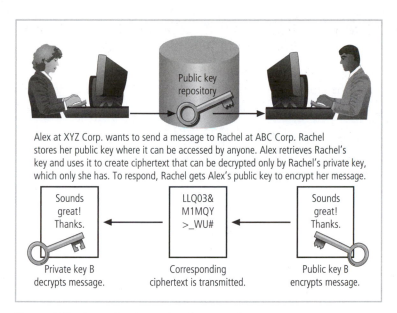

Figure 3-6 Example of asymmetric encryption
© Cengage Learning 2013

derive the original values without knowing how those values were used to create the hash value. For example, if you multiply 45 by 235, you get 10,575. But if you are simply given the number 10,575, can you determine which two numbers were multiplied to arrive at this number? Now, let's assume that each multiplier is 200 digits long and a prime number. The multiplicative product would be up to 400 digits long. Imagine the time you'd need to factor that out.

Note that there is a shortcut, however. In mathematics, it is known as a trapdoor (which is different from a software trapdoor). A mathematical **trapdoor** is a "secret mechanism that enables you to easily accomplish the reverse function in a one-way function."[5] With a trapdoor, you can use a key to encrypt or decrypt the ciphertext, but not both, thus it requires two keys. The public key becomes the true key, and the private key is derived from the public key using the trapdoor.

RSA Algorithm Function One of the most popular asymmetric key cryptosystems is RSA, the name of which is derived from Rivest-Shamir-Adleman, the algorithm's developers. The **RSA algorithm** was the first asymmetric, or public-key, encryption algorithm developed (in 1977) and published for commercial use. It is very popular and has been embedded in most Web browsers to enable them to provide security for e-commerce applications. The patented RSA algorithm has in fact become the de facto standard for public use encryption applications.

If you understand modular arithmetic, you can appreciate the complexities of the RSA algorithm. It is based on the large amount of computational work required in factoring large composite numbers and computing the so-called e^{th} roots modulo, a composite number for a specified odd integer (e). Encryption in RSA is accomplished by raising the message M to a nonnegative integer power e. The product is then divided by the nonnegative modulus n

(which should have a bit length of at least 1024), and the remainder is the ciphertext C. This process results in one-way operation (shown below) when n is a very large number.

$$C = Me \; / \; \text{mod} \; n$$

In the decryption process, the ciphertext C is raised to the power d, a nonnegative integer, as follows:

$$d = e\text{-1} \; \text{mod} \; ((p\text{-1})(q\text{-1}))$$

C is then reduced by modulo n. In order for the recipient to calculate the decryption key, the p and q factors must be known. The modulus n, which is a composite number, is determined by multiplying two large nonnegative prime numbers, p and q (in these discussions, * is used as the symbol for multiplication):

$$n = p \; {}^* \; q$$

In RSA's asymmetric algorithm, which is the basis of most modern Public Key Infrastructure (PKI) systems (a topic covered later in this chapter), the public and private keys are generated using the following procedure, created by the RSA Corporation:

- Choose two large prime numbers, p and q, of equal length, and compute $p \; {}^* \; q = n$, which is the public modulus.
- Choose a random public key, e, so that e and $(p\text{-1})(q\text{-1})$ are relatively prime.
- Compute $e \; {}^* \; d = 1 \; \text{mod} \; (p - 1)(q - 1)$, where d is the private key.
- Thus, $d = e^{-1} \text{mod}[(p - 1)(q - 1)]$ where (d, n) is the private key; (e, n) is the public key. Plaintext P is encrypted to generate ciphertext C as C = Pe mod n, and is decrypted to recover the plaintext P as P = Cd mod n.

The RSA algorithm has three major operations:

1. Key generation—Prime factors p and q are selected by a statistical technique known as probabilistic primality testing and then multiplied together to form n. The encryption exponent e is selected, and the decryption exponent d is calculated.

2. Encryption—M is raised to the power of e, reduced by modulo n, and remainder C is the ciphertext.

3. Decryption—C is raised to the power of d and reduced by modulo n.

The sender publishes the public key, which consists of modulus n and exponent e. The remaining variables—d, p, and q—are kept secret. If p and q are not big enough for the cipher to be secure, they must be made bigger. The strength of this encryption algorithm relies on how difficult it is to factor p and q from n if n is known. If n is not known, the algorithm is even harder to break, of course.

A message can then:

- Be encrypted by: $C = M^e$(recipient) mod n(recipient)
- Be digitally signed by: $C' = M'^d$(sender) mod n(sender)
- Be verified by: $M' = C'^e$(sender) mod n(sender)
- Be decrypted by: $M = C^d$(recipient) mod n(recipient)

Hybrid Cryptography Systems

The problem with asymmetric encryption, as was shown in Figure 3-6 is that holding a single conversation between two parties requires four keys. Moreover, if four organizations want to exchange communications, each party must manage its own private key and four public keys. In such scenarios, determining which public key is needed to encrypt a particular message can become a rather confusing problem, and with more organizations in the loop, the problem expands. This is why asymmetric encryption is sometimes regarded by experts as inefficient in terms of CPU computations. Consequently, hybrid systems are more commonly used.

The most common hybrid system is based on the **Diffie-Hellman key exchange**, which is a method for exchanging private keys using public-key encryption. Figure 3-7 shows a simplified example of how the key exchange works.

Mathematically the two users share a prime number and a base (p & g). They each think up a secret number and use the two values to create a product (g^a mod p = A, for example). The other person creates his or her version (g^b mod p = B), and the two values are exchanged. They can then both calculate a shared secret value (B^a mod p = s = A^b mod p) and use that secret key for future data exchanges.

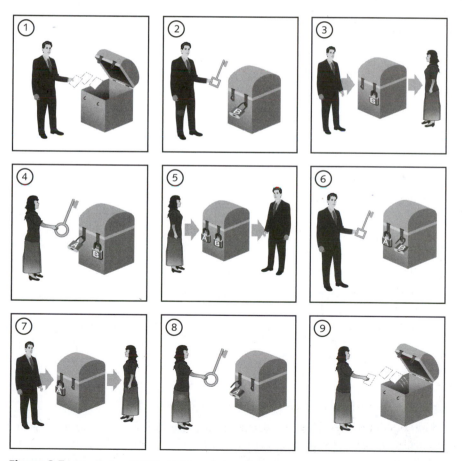

Figure 3-7   Example of Diffie-Hellman key exchange

Created in 1976 by Whitfield Diffie and Martin Hellman, the Diffie-Hellman key exchange uses asymmetric encryption to exchange **session keys.** These are limited-use symmetric keys for temporary communications; they allow two organizations to conduct quick, efficient, secure communications based on symmetric encryption. Diffie-Hellman provides the foundation for subsequent developments in public key-encryption. Because symmetric encryption is more efficient than asymmetric for sending messages, and because asymmetric encryption doesn't require out-of-band key exchange, asymmetric encryption can be used to transmit symmetric keys in a hybrid approach. Diffie-Hellman protects data from exposure to third parties, which is sometimes a problem when keys are exchanged out-of-band.

A hybrid encryption approach is illustrated in Figure 3-8. Here, Alex at XYZ Corp. wants to communicate with Rachel at ABC Corp., so Alex first creates a session key. He encrypts a message with this session key, then gets Rachel's public key. Alex uses Rachel's public key to encrypt both the session key and the message, which is already encrypted. He then transmits the entire package to Rachel, who uses her private key to decrypt the package containing the session key and the encrypted message, then uses the session key to decrypt the message. Rachel can continue to use only this session key for electronic communications until the session key expires. The asymmetric session key is used in the much more efficient asymmetric encryption and decryption processes. After the session key expires (usually in a few minutes), a new session key is chosen and shared using the same process.

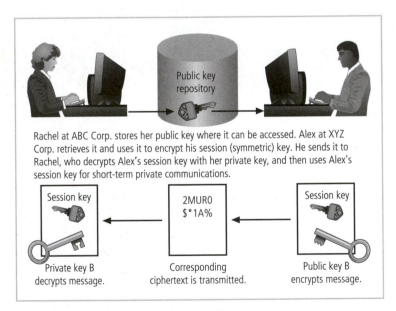

Figure 3-8 Example of hybrid encryption

Encryption Key Size

When deploying ciphers, users have to decide on the size of the cryptovariable or key. This is very important, because the strength of many encryption applications and cryptosystems is measured by key size. How exactly does key size affect the strength of an algorithm? Typically, the length of the key increases the number of random guesses that have to be made in order to break the code. Creating a larger number of possibilities increases the time required to make guesses, and thus a longer key directly influences the strength of the encryption.

It may surprise you to learn that when it comes to cryptosystems, the security of encrypted data is not dependent on keeping the encrypting algorithm secret; in fact, algorithms should be (and often are) published, so that research to uncover their weaknesses can be done. The security of any cryptosystem depends on keeping some or all of the elements of the crypto-variable(s) or key(s) secret, and effective security is maintained by manipulating the size (bit length) of the keys and by following proper procedures and policies for key management.

For a simple example of how key size is related to encryption strength, suppose you have an algorithm that uses a three-bit key. You may recall from earlier in the chapter that keyspace is the entire range of characters from which the key can be drawn. Also, you may recall that in binary notation, 3 bits can be used to represent values from 000 to 111, which correspond to the numbers 0 to 7 in decimal notation and, thus, a keyspace of eight keys. This means that an algorithm that uses a 3-bit key has eight possible keys (the numbers 0 to 7 in binary are 000, 001, 010, 011, 100, 101, 110, 111). If you know how many keys you have to choose from, you can program a computer to try all the keys to attempt to crack the encrypted message.

The preceding paragraph presumes a few things: (1) you know the algorithm, (2) you have the encrypted message, and (3) you have time on your hands. It is easy to satisfy the first criterion. The encryption tools that use DES can be purchased over the counter. Many of these tools are based on encryption algorithms that are standards, as is DES itself; therefore, it is relatively easy to get a cryptosystem based on DES that would enable you to decrypt an encrypted message if you possess the key. The second criterion requires the interception of an encrypted message, which is illegal but not impossible. As for the third criterion, the task required is a brute force attack, in which a computer randomly (or sequentially) selects possible keys of the known size and applies them to the encrypted text or a piece of the encrypted text. If the result is plaintext, bingo! But as indicated earlier in this chapter, it can take quite a long time to exert brute force on the more advanced cryptosystems. In fact, the strength of an algorithm is determined by how long it takes to guess the key.

When it comes to keys, however, how big is enough? As you learned earlier in this section, a 3-bit system has eight possible keys. Furthermore, an 8-bit system has 256 possible keys. Note, however, that a 32-bit system, puny by modern standards, has almost 16.8 million possible keys. Even so, an average PC, such as the one described in Table 3-4, could discover this key in mere seconds. However, as Table 3-4 shows, the amount of time needed to crack a cipher by guessing its key grows very quickly—that is, exponentially with each additional bit.

Although the estimated time to crack an encryption key grows rapidly with respect to the number of bits in the encryption key, it is not impossible to crack the key. Table 3-4 doesn't account for the fact that computing power has increased (and continues to increase). Therefore, these days even the once-standard 56-bit encryption can't stand up to brute force attacks by personal computers, especially if multiple computers are used to crack these keys. Each additional computer reduces the amount of time needed. Two computers can divide the possibilities and crack the key in approximately half the time, and so on. Thus, 285 computers can crack a 56-bit key in one year; ten times as many would do it in a little over a month.

Key Length (bits)	Maximum Number of Operations (Guesses)	Maximum Time to Crack	Estimated Average Time to Crack
8	256	0.0000000085 seconds	0.0000000043 seconds
16	65,636	0.0000022 seconds	0.00000109 seconds
24	16,777,216	0.00056 seconds	0.00028 seconds
32	4,294,967,296	0.143 seconds	0.072 seconds
56	72,057,594,037,927,900	27.800 days	13.9 days
64	1.844674E+19	19.498 years	9.7 years
128	3.40282E+38	3.596761E+20 years	1.798381E+20 years
256	1.15792E+77	1.2E+59 years	6.1E+103 years
512	1.3408E+154	1.4E+136 years	7.1E+135 years

Table 3-4 Encryption Key Power

Note: In most cases, it takes one operation to calculate a password and then at least one operation to test the password; however, this example assumes that each guess only requires one operation. Doubled, tripled, or even quadrupled, the relative values of the times don't vary much: 56-bit or less is insufficient for sensitive data, 64-bit is marginal, and 128-bit and larger is more than sufficient. The modern standards are 128- and 256-bit (AES), with 512- and 1024-bit encryption available.

© Cengage Learning 2013

Multiple Encryption Methods

Why do encryption systems such as DES incorporate multiple elements or operations? Consider this: if you use the same operation (XOR, substitution, or transposition) multiple times, you gain no additional benefit. For example, if, using a substitution cipher, you substitute B for A, then R for B, then Q for R, it has the same effect as if you had substituted Q for A. Similarly, if you transpose a character in position 1 to position 4, then to position 3, you could more easily transpose the character from position 1 to position 3. There is no net advantage for sequential operations unless each subsequent operation is different. Therefore, if you substitute, then transpose, then XOR, then substitute again, you will have dramatically scrambled, substituted, and recoded the original plaintext with ciphertext that is untraceable without the key.

Encrypted Communications

Much of the software programs currently used to protect the confidentiality of information are not true cryptosystems. Instead, they are applications to which cryptographic protocols have been added. This is perhaps particularly true of Internet protocols; some experts claim that the Internet and its corresponding protocols were designed without any consideration for security, which was added as an afterthought. Whether or not this is true, the lack of threats in the environment in which it was launched allowed the Internet to grow rapidly. As the number of threats grew, however, so did the need for additional security measures.

3

Securing Network Communications with IPSec and SSH

Internet Protocol Security (IPSec) and Secure Shell (SSH) are widely used to enable secure network communications across LANs, WANs, and the Internet. IPSec is most often used to create a secure virtual private network (VPN) over an insecure medium like the Internet, and SSH is used to secure remote logins. Both use encryption to ensure that the confidentiality and integrity of transmitted data is protected.

IPSec Internet Protocol Security (IPSec) is an open-source protocol framework for security development within the TCP/IP family of protocol standards. It is used to secure communications across IP-based networks such as LANs, WANs, and the Internet by protecting data integrity, user confidentiality, and authenticity at the IP packet level. IPSec is the cryptographic authentication and encryption product of the IETF's IP Protocol Security Working Group. It is often described as the security system from IP version 6 (the future version of the TCP/IP protocol), retrofitted for use with IP version 4 (the current version). IPSec is defined in Request for Comments (RFC) 1825, 1826, and 1827 and is widely used to create VPNs.

IPSec includes the IP Security protocol itself, which specifies the information to be added to an IP packet as well as how to encrypt packet data, and the Internet Key Exchange (IKE), which uses an asymmetric-based key exchange and negotiates the security associations. IPSec operates in two modes: transport and tunnel. In transport mode, only the IP data are encrypted, not the IP headers. This allows intermediate nodes to read the source and destination addresses. In tunnel mode, the entire IP packet is encrypted and then placed into the content portion of another IP packet. This requires other systems at the beginning and end of the tunnel to act as proxies and to send and receive the encrypted packets. These systems then transmit the decrypted packets to their true destinations.

IPSec uses several different cryptosystems:

- Diffie-Hellman key exchange for deriving key material between peers on a public network
- Public-key cryptography for signing the Diffie-Hellman exchanges to guarantee the identity of the two parties
- Bulk encryption algorithms, such as DES, for encrypting the data
- Digital certificates signed by a certificate authority to act as digital ID cards[6]

Within IPSec, IP layer security is achieved by means of an authentication header protocol or an encapsulating security payload protocol. The authentication header (AH) protocol provides system-to-system authentication and data integrity verification but does not provide secrecy for the content of a network communication. The encapsulating security payload (ESP) protocol provides secrecy for the contents of network communications, as well as system-to-system authentication and data integrity verification. When two networked systems form an association that uses encryption and authentication keys, algorithms, and key lifetimes, they can implement either the AH or the ESP protocol, but not both. If the security functions of both the AH and ESP are required, multiple security associations must be bundled to provide the correct sequence through which the IP traffic must be processed to deliver the desired security features.

The AH protocol is designed to provide data integrity and IP packet authentication. Although AH does not provide confidentiality protection, IP packets are protected from replay attacks and address spoofing as well as other types of cyberattacks against open networks. Figure 3-9 shows the packet format of the IPSec AH protocol. As shown in this diagram, the security parameter index (SPI) references the session key and algorithm used to protect the data being transported. Sequence numbers allow packets to arrive out of sequence for reassembly. The integrity check value (ICV) of the authentication data serves as a checksum to verify that the packet itself is unaltered. Whether used in IPv4 or IPv6, authentication secures the entire packet, excluding mutable fields in the new IP header. In tunnel mode, however, the entire inner IP packet is secured by the authentication header protocol. The ESP protocol provides confidentiality services for IP packets across insecure networks. ESP can also provide the authentication services of AH.

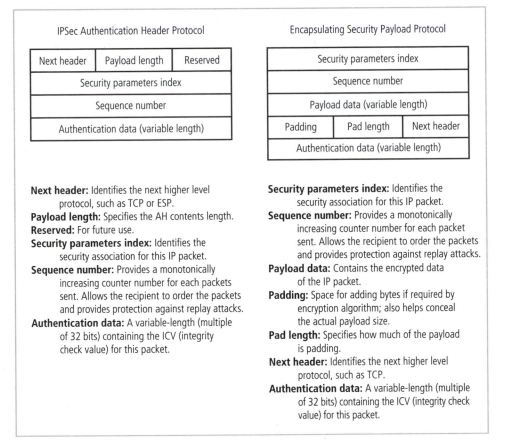

Figure 3-9 IPSec headers

© Cengage Learning 2013

Figure 3-9 also shows information on the ESP packet header. ESP in tunnel mode can be used to establish a VPN, assuring encryption and authentication between networks communicating via the Internet. In tunnel mode, the entire IP packet is encrypted with the attached ESP header. A new IP header is attached to the encrypted payload, providing the required routing information.

An ESP header is inserted into the IP packet prior to the TCP header, and an ESP trailer is placed after the IPv4 packet. If authentication is desired, an ESP authentication data field is appended after the ESP trailer. The complete transport segment is encrypted, in addition to the ESP trailer. In an IPv6 transmission, the ESP header is placed after the hop-by-hop and routing headers. Encryption under IPv6 covers the transport segment and the ESP trailer. Authentication in both IPv4 and IPv6 covers the ciphertext data plus the ESP header. IPSec ESP-compliant systems must support the implementation of the DES algorithm utilizing the CBC (cipher block chaining) mode, which incorporates the following encryption algorithms: Triple DES, IDEA, RC5, CAST, and Blowfish.

SSH The Secure Shell (SSH) protocol was developed in order to provide a secure method for accessing systems over an insecure medium. The latest version of the protocol, SSH-2, offers a number of improved security features over its predecessor, SSH-1. SSH is most commonly used to access UNIX and Linux system shells as a replacement for the less secure remote login protocols, like Telnet. SSH also supports a number of encryption technologies in order to provide a secure communications channel between client and server.

Securing Web Communications with SSL and S-HTTP

Secure Sockets Layer (SSL) and Secure Hypertext Transfer Protocol (S-HTTP) are designed to enable secure Web communications for e-commerce, banking, and a number of other sensitive uses. By adding encryption to standard HTTP and TCP communication, SSL and S-HTTP ensure TCP/IP security via different mechanisms and can be used independently or together.

SSL The Secure Sockets Layer (SSL) protocol is used for public-key encryption to secure a channel over the Internet. Most popular browsers, including Internet Explorer, Firefox, Safari, and Chrome, use SSL and can thank the group that created the original Netscape browser for creating SSL. In addition to providing data encryption, integrity, and server authentication, SSL can, when properly configured, provide client authentication.

SSL uses a number of algorithms but mainly relies on RSA for key transfer and on IDEA, DES, or 3DES for encrypted symmetric-key-based data transfer. Figure 3-10 illustrates the kind of certificate and SSL information that is displayed when you are checking out of an e-commerce site. If your Web connection does not automatically display such certificates, you can right-click in your browser's window and select Properties to view the connection encryption and certificate properties.

The SSL protocol works as follows. During a normal client/server HTTP session, when the client requests access to a portion of the Web site that requires secure communication, the server sends a message to the client indicating that a secure connection must be established. The client sends its public key and security parameters. This handshaking phase is complete when the server finds a public-key match and sends a digital certificate to the client in order to authenticate itself. Once the client verifies that the certificate is valid and trustworthy, the SSL session is established. Until the client or the server terminates the session, any amount of data can be transmitted securely via the SSL session.

SSL provides two protocol layers within the TCP framework: SSL Record Protocol and Standard HTTP. The SSL Record Protocol provides basic security and communications services

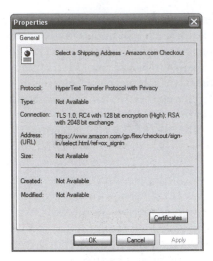

Figure 3-10 Digital certificate

Source: Internet Explorer

to the top levels of the SSL protocol stack and is responsible for the fragmentation, compression, encryption, and attachment of an SSL header to the plaintext prior to transmission. Received encrypted messages are decrypted and reassembled for presentation to the higher levels of the protocol. Standard HTTP provides the Internet communications services between client and host without considering encryption of the data that is transmitted between client and server.

S-HTTP Secure HTTP (S-HTTP) is an extended version of HTTP that provides for the encryption of individual messages transmitted via the Internet between a client and server. S-HTTP allows the encryption of all information passing between two computers through a protected and secure virtual connection. Unlike SSL, in which a secure channel is established for the duration of a session, S-HTTP is designed for sending individual messages over the Internet; therefore, a session for each individual exchange of data must be established. To establish a session, the client and server must have compatible cryptosystems and agree on the configuration. The S-HTTP client and the server then agree on a session key, computed by the server. The session key from the server is then encrypted with the client's public key and returned to the client. The client decrypts the key using its private key, and the client and server now possess identical session keys, which they can use to encrypt the messages sent between them. S-HTTP can provide confidentiality, authentication, and data integrity through a variety of trust models and cryptographic algorithms. In addition, this protocol is designed for easy integration with existing HTTP applications and for implementation in conjunction with HTTP.

Securing E-mail with S/MIME and PGP

A number of cryptosystems have been adapted to work with the dominant e-mail protocols in an attempt to incorporate some degree of security into this notoriously insecure communications medium. Some of the more popular adaptations are Secure Multipurpose Internet Mail Extensions (S/MIME) and Pretty Good Privacy (PGP).

S/MIME The first commonly used Internet e-mail standard was SMTP/RFC 822, also called SMTP, but it has had problems and limitations, such as an inability to transmit executable files and binary objects or to handle character sets other than 7-bit ASCII. These limitations make SMTP unwieldy for organizations that need greater security and support for international character sets. MIME (Multipurpose Internet Mail Extension) extends SMTP to overcome these limitations. In Table 3-5, you can see that MIME's message header fields are designed to identify and describe the e-mail message and to handle a variety of e-mail content. In addition to the message header fields, the MIME specification includes predefined content types and conversion transfer encodings, such as 7-bit, 8-bit, binary, and radix-64, which it uses to deliver e-mail messages reliably across a wide range of systems.

Header Field	Function
MIME-version	States conformity to RFCs 2045 and 2046
Content-ID	Identifies MIME entities
Content-type	Describes data in body of message
Content-description	Describes body object
Content-transfer-encoding	Identifies type of conversion used in message body

Table 3-5 MIME Message Header Fields
© Cengage Learning 2013

Secure Multipurpose Internet Mail Extensions (S/MIME) builds on the encoding format of the MIME protocol and uses digital signatures based on public-key cryptosystems to secure e-mail; it is the second generation of enhancements to the SMTP standard. MIME and S/MIME have the same message header fields, except for those added to support new functionality. Like MIME, S/MIME uses a canonical form format, which allows it to standardize message content type among systems, but it has the additional ability to sign, encrypt, and decrypt messages. Table 3-6 summarizes the functions and algorithms used by S/MIME. It should be mentioned that PGP is functionally similar to S/MIME, incorporates some of the same algorithms, and can, to some degree, interoperate with S/MIME.

Function	Algorithm
Hash code for digital signatures	Secure Hash Algorithm 1(SHA-1)
Digital signatures	DSS
Encryption session keys	ElGamal (variant of Diffie-Hellman)
Digital signatures and session keys	RSA
Message encryption	3DES, RC2

Table 3-6 S/MIME Functions and Algorithms
© Cengage Learning 2013

PGP Pretty Good Privacy (PGP) was developed by Phil Zimmermann and is a hybrid cryptosystem that combines some of the best available cryptographic algorithms and has become the open-source de facto standard for encryption and authentication of e-mail and file storage applications. Both commercial and desktop versions of PGP are available for a wide variety of platforms. Table 3-7 lists a number of PGP functions.

Function	Algorithm	Application
Public-key encryption	RSA/SHA-1 or DSSISHA-1	Digital signatures
Conventional encryption	3DES, RSA, IDEA or CAST	Message encryption
File management	ZIP	Compression

Table 3-7 PGP Functions[7]
© Cengage Learning 2013

PGP provides six services: authentication by digital signatures, message encryption, compression, e-mail compatibility, segmentation, and key management. As shown in Table 3-7, one of the algorithms used in the PGP public-key encryption is Secure Hash Algorithm 1 (SHA-1), which is used to compute hash values for calculating a 160-bit hash code based on the plaintext message. The hash code is then encrypted with DSS or RSA and appended to the original message. The recipient uses the sender's public key to decrypt and recover the hash code. Using the same encryption algorithm, the recipient then generates a new hash code from the same message. If the two hash codes are identical, the message and the sender are authentic.

A sender may also want the entire contents of the message protected from unauthorized viewing; 3DES, IDEA, or CAST, which are all standard algorithms, may be used to encrypt the message contents with a unique, randomly generated 128-bit session key. The session key is encrypted by RSA, using the recipient's public key, then appended to the message. The recipient uses his private key with RSA to decrypt and recover the session key. The recovered session key is used to decrypt the message. Authentication and message encryption can be used together by first digitally signing the message with a private key, encrypting the message with a unique session key, then encrypting the session key with the intended recipient's public key.

In order to save space, PGP also uses the ZIP algorithm to compress the message after it has been digitally signed but before it is encrypted. This generates a more secure encrypted document because a smaller file offers an attacker fewer chances to look for patterns in the data and fewer characters with which to perform frequency analysis. PGP also uses a process known as Radix-64, which encodes nontextual data and ensures that encrypted data can be transferred using e-mail systems by maintaining the required 8-bit blocks of ASCII text. The format maps three octets of binary data into four ASCII characters and appends a cyclic redundancy check (CRC) to detect transmission errors.

Because many Internet facilities impose restrictions on message size, PGP can automatically subdivide messages into a manageable stream size. This segmentation is performed after all other encryption and conversion functions have been processed. At the recipient end, PGP reassembles the segment's message blocks prior to decompression and decryption. PGP does not impose a rigid structure for public-key management, but it can assign a level of trust within the confines of PGP, although it does not specify the actual degree of trust the user should place in any specific key. Trust can be addressed and assured by using the public-key ring structure. In a public-key ring structure, each specific set of public-key credentials is associated with a key legitimacy field, a signature trust field, and an owner trust field. These fields contain a trust-flag byte that identifies whether the credential is trusted in each of these three fields. In the event that the trust of a given credential has been broken, as occurs when a key is compromised, the owner can issue a digitally signed key revocation certificate that updates the credential trust bytes when the credential is next verified.

Securing Wireless Networks with WEP and WPA

Wireless LANs (also known by the brand name Wi-Fi, or wireless fidelity networks) are thought by many in the IT industry to be inherently insecure. The communications channel between the wireless network interface of any computing device and the access point that provides its services uses radio transmissions. Without some form of protection, these signals can be intercepted by anyone with a wireless packet sniffer. In order to prevent interception of these communications, these networks must use some form of cryptographic security control. Two sets of protocols are currently widely used to help secure wireless transmissions: Wired Equivalent Privacy (WEP) and Wi-Fi Protected Access (WPA). Both are designed for use with the IEEE 802.11 wireless networks.

Wired Equivalent Privacy (WEP) WEP was an early attempt to provide security with the 802.11 network protocol. It is now considered too cryptographically weak to provide any meaningful protection from eavesdropping, but for a time it did provide some measure of security for low-sensitivity networks. WEP uses the RC4 cipher stream to encrypt each packet using a 64-bit key. This key is created using a 24-bit initialization vector and a 40-bit key value. The packets are formed using an XOR function to use the RC4 key value stream to encrypt the data packet. A 4-byte integrity check value (ICV) is calculated for each packet and then appended.[8] According to many experts, WEP is too weak for use in most network settings for the following reasons: [9]

- Key management is not effective because most networks use a single shared secret key value for each node. Synchronizing key changes is a tedious process, and no key management is defined in the protocol, so keys are seldom changed.

- The initialization vector (IV) is too small, resulting in the recycling of IVs. An attacker can reverse-engineer the RC4 cipher stream and decrypt subsequent packets, or can forge future packets. In 2007, this was accomplished in less than one minute.[10]

In summary, an intruder who collects enough data can threaten a WEP network in just a few minutes by decrypting or altering the data being transmitted, or by forging the WEP key to gain unauthorized access to the network. WEP also lacks a means of validating user credentials to ensure that only those who should be on the network are allowed to access it.[11]

Wi-Fi Protected Access (WPA and WPA2) WPA was created to resolve the issues with WEP. WPA has a key size of 128 bits, and instead of static, seldom-changed keys it uses dynamic keys created and shared by an authentication server. WPA accomplishes this through the use of the Temporal Key Integrity Protocol (TKIP), which is a suite of algorithms that attempts to deliver the best security that can be obtained given the constraints of the wireless network environment. The algorithms are designed to work with legacy networking devices. TKIP adds four new algorithms to those that were used in WEP:

- A cryptographic message integrity code, or MIC, called Michael, to defeat forgeries
- A new IV sequencing discipline, to remove replay attacks from the attacker's arsenal
- A per-packet key mixing function, to de-correlate the public IVs from weak keys
- A rekeying mechanism, to provide fresh encryption and integrity keys, undoing the threat of attacks stemming from key reuse[12]

Although it offered dramatically improved security over WEP, WPA was not the most secure wireless protocol design. Some compromises were made in the security design to allow compatibility with existing wireless network components. Protocols to replace TKIP are currently under development. Table 3-8 provides a summary of the differences between WEP and WPA. In 2004, WPA2 was made available as a replacement for WPA. WPA2 provided many of the elements missing from WPA, most notably AES-based encryption. Beginning in 2006, WPA2 became mandatory for all new Wi-Fi devices. WPA2 is backwardly compatible with WPA, although some older network cards have difficulty using it.

	WEP	WPA
Encryption	Broken by scientists and hackers	Overcomes all WEP shortcomings
	40-bit key	128-bit key
	Static key—The same value is used by everyone on the network.	Dynamic keys—Each user is assigned a key per session with additional keys calculated for each packet.
	Manual key distribution—Each key is typed by hand into each device.	Automatic key distribution
Authentication	Broken; used WEP key itself for authentication	Improved user authentication, utilizing stronger 802.1X and EAP

Table 3-8 Comparison of WEP and WPA

Source: Wi-Fi Alliance[13]

© Cengage Learning 2013

Next-Generation Wireless Protocols

Robust Secure Networks (RSN), a protocol planned as a replacement for TKIP in WPA, uses AES along with 802.1x and EAP. It extends AES with the Counter Mode CBC MAC Protocol (CCMP). AES supports key lengths up to 256 bits but is not compatible with older hardware. However, a specification called Transitional Security Network (TSN) allows RSN and WEP to coexist on the same wireless local area network (WLAN). Note, however, that a WLAN on which devices are still using WEP is not optimally secured.

The RSN protocol functions as follows:

1. The wireless NIC sends a probe request.
2. The wireless access point sends a probe response with an RSN Information Exchange (IE) frame.
3. The wireless NIC requests authentication via one of the approved methods.

4. The wireless access point provides authentication for the wireless NIC.

5. The wireless NIC sends an association request with an RSN IE frame.

6. The wireless access point sends an association response.[14]

Cryptographic Tools

The ability to conceal the contents of sensitive messages and to verify the contents of messages and the identities of their senders can be useful in all areas of business. However, to be practical to organizations, these cryptographic capabilities must be embodied in tools that allow IT and information security practitioners to apply the elements of cryptography in the everyday world of computing. This section discusses a number of the more widely used tools that bring the functions of cryptography to the world of information systems.

Public Key Infrastructure (PKI)

Public Key Infrastructure (PKI) is an integrated system of software, encryption methodologies, protocols, legal agreements, and third-party services that enables users to communicate securely. PKI systems are based on public-key cryptosystems and include digital certificates and certificate authorities (CAs).

Digital certificates are public-key container files that allow computer programs to validate the key and identify to whom it belongs. (More information about digital certificates appears in later sections of this chapter.) PKI and the digital certificate registries they contain enable the protection of information assets by making verifiable digital certificates readily available to business applications. This, in turn, allows the applications to implement several of the key characteristics of information security and to integrate these characteristics into business processes across an organization. These processes include the following:

- *Authentication*—Individuals, organizations, and Web servers can validate the identity of each of the parties in an Internet transaction.

- *Integrity*—Content signed by the certificate is known to be unaltered while being moved from host to host or server to client.

- *Privacy*—Information is protected from being intercepted during transmission.

- *Authorization*—The validated identity of users and programs can enable authorization rules that remain in place for the duration of a transaction. This reduces some of the overhead and allows for more control of access privileges for specific transactions.

- *Nonrepudiation*—Customers or partners can be held accountable for transactions, such as online purchases, which they cannot later dispute.

A typical PKI solution protects the transmission and reception of secure information by integrating the following components:

- A **certificate authority (CA)**, which issues, manages, authenticates, signs, and revokes users' digital certificates, which typically contain the user name, public key, and other identifying information.

- A **registration authority (RA)**, which operates under the trusted collaboration of the certificate authority and can handle day-to-day certification functions, such as verifying registration information, generating end-user keys, revoking certificates, and validating user certificates.

- Certificate directories, which are central locations for certificate storage that provide a single access point for administration and distribution.

- Management protocols, which organize and manage the communications between CAs, RAs, and end users. This includes the functions and procedures for setting up new users, issuing keys, recovering keys, updating keys, revoking keys, and enabling the transfer of certificates and status information among the parties involved in the PKI's area of authority.

- Policies and procedures, which assist an organization in the application and management of certificates, the formalization of legal liabilities and limitations, and actual business use.

Common implementations of PKI include: systems to issue digital certificates to users and servers, directory enrollment, key-issuing systems, tools for managing the key issuance, and verification and return of certificates. These systems enable organizations to apply an enterprise-wide solution that provides users within the PKIs area of authority the means to engage in authenticated and secure communications and transactions.

The CA performs many housekeeping activities regarding the use of keys and certificates that are issued and used in the zone of authority for which it is established. Each user authenticates him or herself with the CA, and the CA can issue new or replacement keys, track issued keys, provide a directory of public-key values for all known users, and perform other management activities. When a private key is compromised or when the user loses the privilege of using keys in the area of authority, the CA can revoke the user's keys. The CA periodically distributes a **certificate revocation list (CRL)** to all users. When important events occur, specific applications can make a real-time request to the CA to verify any user against the current CRL.

The issuance of certificates (and the keys inside of them) by the CA enables secure, encrypted, nonrepudiable e-business transactions. Some applications allow users to generate their own certificates (and the keys inside them), but a key pair generated by the end user can only provide nonrepudiation, not reliable encryption. A central system operated by a CA or RA can generate cryptographically strong keys that are considered by all users to be independently trustworthy and can provide services for users such as private key backup, key recovery, and key revocation.

The strength of a cryptosystem relies on both the raw strength of its key (secrecy and length) and the overall quality of its key management security processes. PKI solutions can provide several mechanisms for limiting access and possible exposure of the private keys. These mechanisms include password protection, smart cards, hardware tokens, and other hardware-based key storage devices that are memory-capable (like flash memory or PC memory cards). PKI users should select the key security mechanisms that provide a level of key protection appropriate to their needs. Managing the security and integrity of the private keys used for nonrepudiation or the encryption of data files is a critical activity for all the users of encryption and nonrepudiation services within the PKI's area of trust.[15]

Digital Signatures

Digital signatures were created in response to the rising need to verify information transferred using electronic systems. Currently, asymmetric encryption processes are used to create digital signatures. When an asymmetric cryptographic process uses the sender's private key to encrypt a message, the sender's public key must be used to decrypt the message. When the decryption happens successfully, it provides nonrepudiation, which is the principle of cryptography that underpins the authentication mechanism collectively known as a digital signature. **Digital signatures** are, therefore, encrypted messages that can be mathematically proven authentic.

The management of digital signatures has been built into most Web browsers. The Internet Explorer digital signature management screen is shown in Figure 3-11. In general, digital signatures should be created using processes and products that are based on the Digital Signature Standard (DSS). When processes and products are certified as DSS compliant, it means they have been endorsed by U.S. federal and state governments (as well as many foreign governments) as a means of authenticating the author of an electronic document. NIST has approved a number of algorithms that can be used to generate and verify digital signatures. These algorithms can be used in conjunction with the sender's public and private keys, the receiver's public key, and the Secure Hash Standard (described later in this chapter) to quickly create messages that are both encrypted and nonrepudiable. This process first creates a message digest using the hash algorithm, which is then inputted into the digital signature algorithm along with a random number that is used to generate the digital signature. The digital signature function also depends on the sender's private key and other information provided by the CA. The resulting encrypted message contains the digital signature, which can be verified by the receiver using the sender's public key.

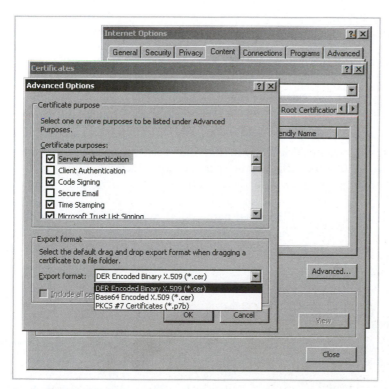

Figure 3-11 Managing digital signatures

Source: Internet Explorer

Digital Certificates

As you learned earlier in this chapter, a digital certificate is an electronic document or container file that holds a key value and identifying information about the entity that controls the key. The certificate is often issued and certified by a third party, usually a certificate authority. A digital signature attached to the certificate's container file certifies the file's origin and integrity. This verification process often occurs when you download or update software via the Internet. The pop-up window back in Figure 3-10 shows, for example, that the downloaded files do, in fact, come from the purported originating agency, Amazon.com, and thus can be trusted.

Unlike digital signatures, which help authenticate the origin of a message, digital certificates authenticate the cryptographic key that is embedded in the certificate. When used properly, these certificates enable diligent users to verify the authenticity of an organization's certificates. This is much like what happens when the Federal Deposit Insurance Corporation issues its FDIC logo to banks to assure customers that their banks are authentic. Different client/server applications use different types of digital certificates to accomplish their assigned functions:

- The CA application suite issues and uses certificates (keys) that identify and establish a trust relationship with a CA to determine what additional certificates (keys) can be authenticated.

- Mail applications use S/MIME certificates for signing and encrypting e-mail as well as for signing forms.

- Development applications use object-signing certificates to identify signers of object-oriented code and scripts.

- Web servers and Web application servers use SSL certificates to authenticate servers via the SSL protocol in order to establish an encrypted SSL session.

- Web clients use client SSL certificates to authenticate users, sign forms, and participate in single sign-on solutions via SSL.

Two popular certificate types are those created using Pretty Good Privacy (PGP) and those created using applications that conform to International Telecommunication Union's (ITU-T) X.509 version 3. The X.509 v3 certificate, the structure for which is outlined in Table 3-9, is an ITU-T recommendation for defining a directory service that maintains a database (also known as a repository) of information about a group of users holding X.509 v3 certificates. An X.509 v3 certificate binds a **distinguished name** (DN), which uniquely identifies a certificate entity, to a user's public key. The certificate is signed and placed in the directory by the CA for retrieval and verification by the user's associated public key. The X.509 v3 standard's recommendation does not specify an encryption algorithm, although RSA, with its hashed digital signature, is typically used.

Steganography

The word *steganography*—the art of secret writing—is derived from the Greek words *steganos*, meaning "covered," and *graphein*, meaning "to write." The Greek historian Herodotus described one of the first steganographers, a fellow Greek who sent a message to warn of an imminent invasion by writing it on the wood beneath a wax writing tablet.[16] Although steganography is technically not a form of cryptography, it is another way of protecting the

Version
Certificate serial number
Algorithm ID •   Algorithm ID •   Parameters
Issuer name
Validity •   Not before •   Not after
Subject name
Subject public key info •   Public-key algorithm •   Parameters Subject public key
Issuer unique identifier (optional)
Subject unique identifier (optional)
Extensions (optional) •   Type •   Criticality Value
Certificate signature algorithm
Certificate signature

Table 3-9 X.509 v3 Certificate Structure[17]
© Cengage Learning 2013

confidentiality of information in transit. The most popular modern version of steganography involves hiding information within files that contain digital pictures or other images.

To understand how this form of steganography works, you must first know a little about how images are stored. Most computer graphics standards use a combination of three color values—red, blue, and green (RGB)—to represent a picture element, or pixel. Each of the three color values requires an 8-bit code for that color's intensity (e.g., 00000000 for no red and 11111111 for maximum red). Each color image pixel therefore requires 24 bits to represent the color mix and intensity. (Actually, some image encoding standards use more or fewer bits per pixel.) When a picture is created (by a digital camera or a computer program), the number of horizontal and vertical pixels captured and recorded is known as the image's resolution. For example, if 1,024 horizontal pixels and 768 vertical pixels are captured and recorded, the image has a 1024 x 768 resolution and is said to have 786,432 pixels, which is over three-fourths of a megapixel (MP). In other words, it contains 786,432 groups of 24 bits each to represent the red, green, and blue data. The raw image size can be calculated as 1024 x 768 x 24, or approximately 1.9 megabytes (MB). There are plenty of bits in this picture data file in which to hide a secret message.

To the naked eye, there is no discernible difference between a pixel with a red intensity of 00101001 and another slightly different pixel with a red intensity level of 00101000. This provides the steganographer with one bit per color (or three bits per pixel) to use for encoding data into an image file. If a steganographic process uses three bits per pixel for all 786,432 pixels, it will be able to store 236 kilobytes (KB) of hidden data within the uncompressed image.

Some steganographic tools can calculate the maximum size image that can be stored before being detectable. Messages can also be hidden in nonimage computer files that do not utilize all their available bits by placing the data in places where software ignores it and humans almost never look. Some applications can hide messages in .bmp, .wav, .mp3, and .au files, as well as in otherwise unused storage space on CDs and DVDs. One program can take a text or document file and hide a message in the unused whitespace.

Even before the attacks of September 11, 2001, U.S. federal agencies believed that terrorist organizations were "hiding maps and photographs of terrorist targets and posting instructions for terrorist activities on sports chat rooms, pornographic bulletin boards, and other Web sites" by means of steganographic methods. No documented proof of this activity has been made public.[18]

Attacks on Cryptosystems

Historically, attempts to gain unauthorized access to secure communications have used brute force attacks in which the ciphertext is repeatedly searched for clues that can lead to the algorithm's structure. These ciphertext attacks involve a hacker searching for a common text structure, wording, or syntax in the encrypted message that can enable him or her to calculate the number of each type of letter used in the message. This process, known as frequency analysis, is used along with published frequency of occurrence patterns of various languages and can allow an experienced attacker to crack almost any code quickly with a large enough sample of the encoded text. To protect against this, modern algorithms attempt to remove the repetitive and predictable sequences of characters from the ciphertext.

Occasionally, an attacker may obtain duplicate texts, one in ciphertext and one in plaintext, and thus reverse-engineer the encryption algorithm in a **known-plaintext attack** scheme. Alternatively, attackers may conduct a **selected-plaintext attack** by sending potential victims a specific text that they are sure the victims will forward to others. When the victim does encrypt and forward the message, it can be used in the attack if the attacker can acquire the outgoing encrypted version. At the very least, reverse-engineering can usually lead the attacker to discover which cryptosystem is being employed.

Most publicly available encryption methods are released to the information and computer security communities to test the encryption algorithm's resistance to cracking. In addition, attackers are kept informed of which methods of attack have failed. Although the purpose of sharing this information is to develop a more secure algorithm, it does prevent attackers from wasting their time, freeing them up to find new weaknesses in the cryptosystem or new, more challenging means of obtaining encryption keys.

In general, attacks on cryptosystems fall into four general categories: man-in-the-middle, correlation, dictionary, and timing. Although several of these attacks were discussed in Chapter 2, they are discussed here to evaluate their impact on cryptosystems.

3

Man-in-the-Middle Attack

A **man-in-the-middle attack**, as you learned in Chapter 1, attempts to intercept a public key or even to insert a known key structure in place of the requested public key. Thus, attackers attempt to place themselves between the sender and receiver, and once they've intercepted the request for key exchanges, they send each participant a valid public key, which is known only to them. To the victims of such attacks, encrypted communications appears to be occurring normally, but in fact the attacker is receiving each encrypted message and decoding it (with the key given to the sending party), then encrypting and sending it to the intended recipient. Establishing public keys with digital signatures can prevent the traditional man-in-the-middle attack, as the attacker cannot duplicate the signatures.

Correlation Attacks

As the complexity of encryption methods has increased, so too have the tools and methods of cryptanalysts. **Correlation attacks** are a collection of brute force methods that attempt to deduce statistical relationships between the structure of the unknown key and the cipher-text generated by the cryptosystem. Differential and linear cryptanalysis, advanced methods of code breaking beyond the scope of this text, have been used to mount successful attacks on block cipher encryptions such as DES. If these advanced approaches can calculate the value of the public key, and if this can be achieved in a reasonable time, all messages written with that key can be decrypted. The only defense against this attack is the selection of strong cryptosystems that have stood the test of time, thorough key management, and strict adherence to the best practices of cryptography in the frequency of key changes.

Dictionary Attacks

In a **dictionary attack**, the attacker encrypts every word in a dictionary by applying the same cryptosystem as used by the target in an attempt to locate a match between the target ciphertext and the list of encrypted words. Dictionary attacks can be successful when the ciphertext consists of relatively few characters—for example, files that contain encrypted usernames and passwords. An attacker who acquires a system password file can run hundreds of thousands of potential passwords from the dictionary he or she has prepared against the stolen list. Most computer systems use a well-known one-way hash function to store passwords in such files, but an attacker can almost always find at least a few matches in any stolen password file. After a match is found, the attacker has essentially identified a potential valid password for the system.

Timing Attacks

In a **timing attack**, the attacker eavesdrops on the victim's session and uses statistical analysis of patterns and inter-keystroke timings to discern sensitive session information. Although timing analysis may not directly result in the decryption of sensitive data, it can be used to gain information about the encryption key and perhaps the cryptosystem. It may also eliminate some algorithms, thus narrowing the attacker's search and increasing the odds of eventual success. Having broken an encryption, the attacker may launch a **replay attack**, which is an attempt to resubmit a recording of the deciphered authentication to gain entry into a secure source.

Defending Against Attacks

Encryption is a very useful tool in protecting the confidentiality of information that is in storage and/or transmission. However, it is just that—another weapon in the information security administrator's arsenal. Frequently, uninformed IT personnel describe information security exclusively in terms of encryption (and possibly firewalls and antivirus software), but encryption is simply the process of hiding the true meaning of information. Over millennia, mankind has developed dramatically more sophisticated means of hiding information from those who should not see it, but no matter how sophisticated encryption and cryptosystems have become, they retain the flaw that was present in the very first such system: If you discover the key (i.e., the method used to perform the encryption), you can read the message. Thus, key management is less the management of technology than the management of people.

Encryption can, however, protect information when it is most vulnerable—that is, when it is outside the organization's systems. Information in transit through public or leased networks is outside the organization's control, and with loss of control can come loss of security. Encryption helps organizations secure information that must travel through public and leased networks by guarding the information against the efforts of those who sniff, spoof, and otherwise skulk around. As such, encryption is a vital piece of the security puzzle.

Chapter Summary

- Encryption is the process of converting a message into a form that is unreadable to unauthorized individuals.

- The science of encryption, known as cryptology, encompasses cryptography (making and using encryption codes) and cryptanalysis (breaking encryption codes).

- Cryptology has a long history and continues to change and improve.

- Two basic processing methods are used to convert plaintext data into encrypted data: bit stream and block ciphering. The other major methods used for scrambling data include substitution ciphers, transposition ciphers, XOR function, the Vigenère cipher, and the Vernam cipher.

- The strength of many encryption applications and cryptosystems is determined by key size. All other things being equal, the longer the size of the key, the greater the strength of the encryption.

- Hash functions are mathematical algorithms that generate a message summary or digest that can be used to confirm the identity of a specific message and to confirm that the message has not been altered.

- Most cryptographic algorithms can be grouped into two broad categories: symmetric and asymmetric. In practice, most popular cryptosystems combine symmetric and asymmetric algorithms.

- IPSec and SSH provide encrypted communications for various types of networks. SSL and S-HTTP provide encrypted communications, typically for Web sessions. And S/MIME and PGP offer encryption for enhanced e-mail and file security.

- Public Key Infrastructure (PKI) is an integrated system of software, encryption methodologies, protocols, legal agreements, and third-party services that enables users to communicate securely. PKI includes digital certificates and certificate authorities.

- Digital signatures are encrypted messages that are independently verified by a central facility and which provide nonrepudiation. A digital certificate is an electronic document, similar to a digital signature, that is attached to a file to certify that the file is from the organization it claims to be from and has not been modified from its original format.

- Steganography is the hiding of information, and although it is not properly a form of cryptography, it is used to protect confidential information while in transit, as cryptography is.

- Unauthorized attempts to access communications often use brute force or ciphertext attacks that perform frequency analysis on the encoded text. Therefore, modern algorithms attempt to remove the repetitive and predictable statistical bias from the ciphertext. If attackers obtain duplicate texts, one in ciphertext and one in plaintext, they can reverse-engineer the encryption algorithm. This is referred to as a known-plaintext attack or a selected-plaintext attack. Attacks against cryptosystems include the man-in-the-middle attack, correlation attacks, dictionary attacks, and timing attacks.

- Most well-known encryption methods are released to the information and computer security communities for testing, which leads to the development of more secure algorithms.

Review Questions

1. What are cryptography and cryptoanalysis?

2. What were some of the first uses of cryptography?

3. What is a key, and what is it used for?

4. List and describe the two contemporary methods of encrypting plaintext.

5. What is a hash function, and what can it be used for?

6. Why is it important to exchange keys "out of band" in symmetric encryption?

7. What is the fundamental difference between symmetric and asymmetric encryption?

8. How does the Public Key Infrastructure (PKI) protect information?

9. List the four general categories that attacks on cryptosystems fall into.

10. List and describe the encryption method made popular by spy movies.

11. What is the difference between digital signatures and digital certificates?

12. List and discuss the different cryptosystems used by IPSec.

13. What is steganography, and what can it be used for?

14. What is PGP?

15. List the six services provided by the PGP security solution.

16. Using a modern personal computer, how long would it take to crack a cryptosystem that is based on a 32-bit key? 56-bit key? 64-bit key?

17. What is the average key size of a "strong encryption" system in use today?

18. What is the standard for encryption currently recommended by NIST?

19. What are the two sets of protocols currently used to help secure wireless transmissions?

20. Why is the size of a key important?

Real World Exercises

Exercise 3-1

Make a list of five symmetric encryption algorithms other than those mentioned in this chapter. Include the key length, number of rounds, and block sizes (if a block cipher is used). Also, list one application that uses the algorithm.

Exercise 3-2

Research two other asymmetric encryption algorithms not listed in this chapter. For each algorithm, list the key lengths used, outline the encryption process, and name at least one application that uses the algorithm.

Exercise 3-3

Research the hash algorithm used to store Windows NT 4.0 user passwords. Why are these passwords easier to break than those used in other operating systems?

Exercise 3-4

Make a list of 10 software applications or hardware devices that use RSA asymmetric encryption. What is the key length used in each product?

Exercise 3-5

Make a list of 10 software applications or hardware devices that continue to use DES symmetric encryption. Why do these products continue to use DES instead of 3DES or AES?

Hands-On Projects

Project 1-1

In these exercises, you will use TrueCrypt to create and manage secure, encrypted file storage containers. This lab uses TrueCrypt version 7.0a. The TrueCrypt installer can be found at *www.truecrypt.org/downloads*. Installation and setup is outside the scope of this exercise.

First, we will create a TrueCrypt container to store sensitive data in.

1. Click **Start, All Programs, TrueCrypt,** and then click **TrueCrypt** again. You should see the main TrueCrypt window, as shown in Figure 3-12.

Figure 3-12   TrueCrypt
Source: TrueCrypt

2. Click **Create Volume,** which will start the Creation Wizard, as shown in Figure 3-13.

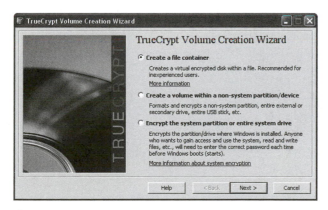

Figure 3-13   TrueCrypt Volume Creation Wizard
Source: TrueCrypt

3. Ensure the **Create a file container** option is selected, and then click **Next.** TrueCrypt volumes can be stored in separate files or can occupy an entire drive or partition. In the next window, select **Standard TrueCrypt volume** and click **Next.** You should see the Volume Location window, as shown in Figure 3-14.

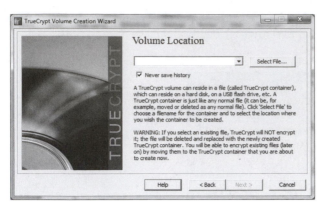

Figure 3-14 TrueCrypt select volume type
Source: TrueCrypt

4. Now, we specify where the volume will be located. Click **Select File**, browse to Desktop, type <*yourname*-truecrypt> in the File name text box (where you substitute your first initial and last name for *yourlastname*, as in agreen), then click **Save**. Once you are returned to the previous window, click **Next**.

5. In the Encryption Options window, as shown in Figure 3-15, leave AES as the Encryption Algorithm and RIPEMD-160 as the Hash Algorithm, and then click **Next**.

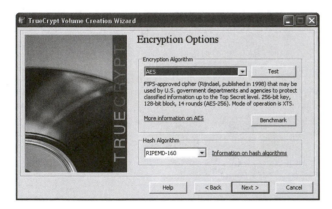

Figure 3-15 TrueCrypt Encryption Options
Source: TrueCrypt

6. In the Volume Size window, specify the size of the TrueCrypt volume. The larger the size, the longer it will take to generate the volume. Type **2** in the text box, and then click **Next**.

7. In the Volume Password window, as shown in Figure 3-16, specify your password to access the file.

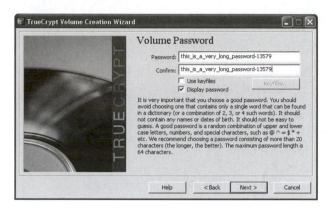

Figure 3-16 TrueCrypt Volume Password generation
Source: TrueCrypt

8. The longer your password, the more secure the container is. Type your password again in the Confirm text box, making sure to type the same password in both text boxes. Note: if you forget your password, the data stored in the encrypted container will not be accessible.

9. Once you have entered your passwords in both fields, click **Next**. If you have chosen a weak password, TrueCrypt will warn you in a pop-up message. If this happens, click **Yes** to close the pop-up window.

10. Now, TrueCrypt will generate a random pool of values from which to draw your encryption key. Move your mouse in quick, random motions for at least 30 seconds to generate a sufficiently large key pool, and then click **Format**.

11. Because we built a small volume, TrueCrypt should finish creating values within a few seconds. Click **OK** in the pop-up-windows indicating the volume has been successfully created, and then click **Exit**.

   Now that we have created an encrypted volume, we can use TrueCrypt to mount the volume as a logical drive and interact with it as you would any other drive.

Endnotes

1. PCI Security Standards Council (2010). *Navigating PCI DSS: Understanding the Intent of the Requirements, Version 2.0.* Accessed October 2010 from *fttps://www.pcisecurity standards.org.*

2. Anderson, T. (1999). Polyalphabetic Substitution. Accessed June 21, 2007 from *cvni.net/radio/nsnl/nsnl010/nsnl10poly.html.*

3. Varughese, S. (2006). Rainbow Cracking and Password Security. Accessed June 21, 2007 from *palisade.plynt.com/issues/2006Feb/rainbow-tables/.*

4. Krutz, R. and Vines, R.D. (2001) *The CISSP Prep Guide: Mastering the Ten Domains of Computer Security* (p. 131). Hoboken, NJ: John Wiley and Sons.

5. National Institute of Standards and Technology (1999). *Data Encryption Standards (DES)* (pp. 46–3).

6. Cisco Systems, Inc. (2000) White Paper: IPSec. Accessed July 1, 2002 from *www.cisco.com/warp/public/cc/so/neso/sqso/eqso/ipsec_wp.htm.*

7. The International PGP Home Page. PGPI Online. Accessed 21 June 21, 2007 from *www.pgpi.org/.*

8. NetworkWorld (2007) WEP (Wired Equivalent Privacy). Accessed April 10, 2007 from *www.networkworld.com/details/715.html.*

9. iLabs Wireless Security Team (2002). What's Wrong with WEP? Accessed April 9, 2007 from *www.networkworld.com/research/2002/0909wepprimer.html.*

10. Leyden, J. (2007). WEP Key Wireless Cracking Made Easy. Accessed June 30, 2007 from *www.theregister.co.uk/2007/04/04/wireless_code_cracking.*

11. Wi-Fi Alliance (2003). Wi-Fi Protected Access: Strong, standards-based, interoperable security for today's Wi-Fi Networks. Accessed 9 April 2007 from *www.wi-fi.org/files/wp_8_WPA%20Security_4-29-03.pdf.*

12. Walker, J. "802.11 Security Series Part II: The Temporal Key Integrity Protocol (TKIP)." Accessed April 10, 2007 from *http://cache-www.intel.com/cd/00/00/01/77/17769_80211_part2.pdf.*

13. Wi-Fi Alliance (2003). Wi-Fi Protected Access: Strong, standards-based, interoperable security for today's Wi-Fi networks. Accessed April 9, 2007 from *www.wi-fi.org/files/wp_8_WPA%20Security_4-29-03.pdf.*

14. Tech-FAQ. RSN (Robust Secure Network) Accessed 21 June 2007 from *www.tech-faq.com/rsn-robust-secure-network.html.*

15. Kelm, S. (2007). The PKI Page. Accessed June 21, 2007 from *www.pki-page.info/roo/.*

16. Conway, M. Code Wars: Steganography, Signals Intelligence, and Terrorism. Accessed June 21, 2007 from *transactionpub.metapress.com/app/home/contribution.asp?referrer=parent&backto=issue,6,9;journal,14,30;linkingpublicationresults,1:105285,1.*

17. Internet X.509 Public Key Infrastructure Certificate and CRL Profile. Accessed November 28, 2011 from *www.ietf.org/rfc/rfc2459.txt.*

18. McCullagh, D. Bin Laden: Steganography Master? Accessed June 21, 2007 from *www.wired.com/news/politics/0,1283,41658,00.html.*

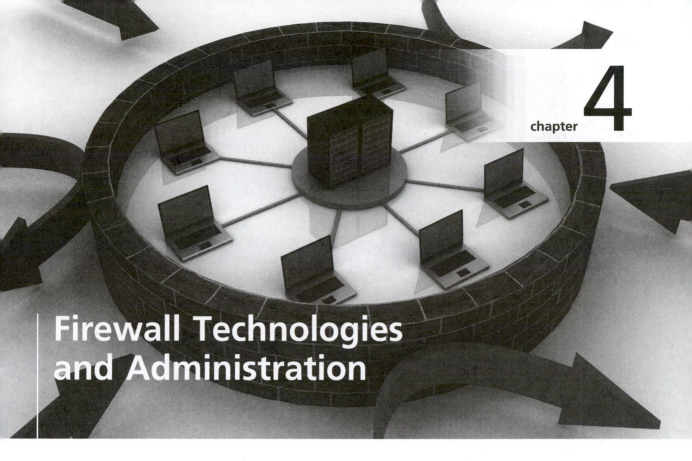

chapter 4

Firewall Technologies and Administration

As security or firewall administrators, we've got basically the same concerns [as plumbers]: the size of the pipe, the contents of the pipe, making sure the correct traffic is in the correct pipes, and keeping the pipes from splitting and leaking all over the place. Of course, like plumbers, when the pipes do leak, we're the ones responsible for cleaning up the mess, and we're the ones who come up smelling awful. — Marcus J. Ranum

Upon completion of this material, you should be able to:

- Describe what a firewall does
- Explain how a firewall restricts access to a network
- List the types of firewall protection as well as the types of firewall implementations and the ways they are used
- Describe how firewall rules are created and how they are used to control the behavior of the firewall
- Explain how instruction detection and prevention systems are related and how they may be made to interact with one another

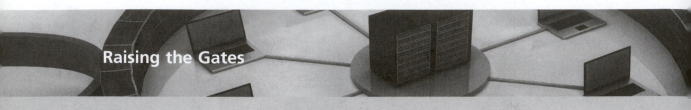

Raising the Gates

Cryptography had helped the EBS IT team solve a critical challenge by providing a means to secure communication with one of EBS's suppliers, Davis Office Megaplex. Now, it was time for the team to focus on a fundamental security control that had been in place for years: firewalls. The IT team had heard the latest security news: cyberthreats were more likely to come from company insiders, the mobile phone had erased the perimeter, and "click-and-own" threats were making botnets of company computers. However, firewalls still represented a fundamental way of protecting the company's network traffic and were, therefore, indispensable. Like locking the doors to the company building, there will always be a need to deter threats, and although a firewall—like a locked door—won't stop all attacks, it still provides a minimum baseline for protecting the IT environment.

The EBS IT team went to work auditing the current firewall rules and reviewing the overall firewall architecture. The team even mapped out some time to determine whether the current technology met its goals in protecting against outside threats as well as threats from partners like Davis Office Megaplex.

Introduction

No security system can provide absolute certainty that it will protect all of an organization's information all the time. However, firewalls—used in conjunction with other technical controls, deployed according to the requirements of security policies and programs, and maintained and upgraded on a regular basis—are one of the most effective security tools a network administrator has. Just as security policy lays the foundation for a corporate security program, firewalls lay the foundation for network security. A firewall can effectively enforce general security guidelines, such as disallowing audio streaming, controlling Internet access, and providing a virtual blockade from unknown network traffic.

A firewall is not necessarily a single router, computer, VPN gateway, or software program. Any firewall is a combination of multiple software and hardware components and is designed for a number of crucial security tasks, such as the following:

- Firewalls restrict traffic between networks. Whether the traffic flow originates on the Internet and is destined for a private corporate network or the traffic flow is between two important networks within the same company, the firewall provides a critical blockade. Using an access control list, packet inspection, or other techniques, a firewall ensures that only legitimate, authorized traffic can travel into or out of a network.

- Firewalls provide a checkpoint—that is, a single point of entry or exit. As in military planning, a checkpoint is an effective defense because all activities can be directed to it. These activities can include monitoring network traffic for attacks or unauthorized traffic, pursuing network security policies using one central control mechanism, or blocking any of a number of network protocols.

- Firewalls record network activity. In cases of abuse or intrusion, they can reveal the who, when, and how of network traffic.

This chapter provides an overview of the issues involved in planning and designing firewalls. First, you learn what a firewall is *not* so that you can begin to understand what it actually is, then you learn about security policies and the rules and procedures that govern how a firewall works. Next, you learn about the types of firewall protection, the limitations of firewalls, and hardware firewall implementations. The chapter concludes with evaluations of firewall software packages.

Firewall Overview

Most people have heard of the term "firewall," but not in connection with computer networks. They may know about the fireproof barrier between the engine of a car and its interior or may have heard the term used to describe a brick wall or other fireproof barrier. Such firewalls are intended to slow or even completely prevent the movement of a dangerous element—specifically, fire—from passing from one side to the other.

Comparisons with physical firewalls have led to the false notion that a computer firewall is designed to prevent all attackers, viruses, and would-be intruders from entering a computer or computer network. Instead, firewalls are designed to simply enable authorized traffic to pass through and block unauthorized traffic. In general, a **firewall** is anything, whether hardware or software (or a combination of hardware and software), that can filter the transmission of packets of digital information as they attempt to pass through a boundary of a network. Figure 4-1 shows a general architecture using firewalls to help establish network boundaries.

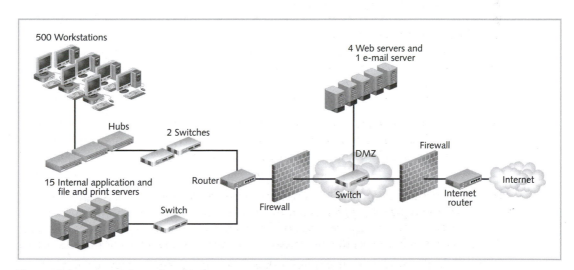

Figure 4-1 General firewall architecture

Network firewalls bear many resemblances to real-life security checkpoints, like those you encounter in an airport:

- Entry and exit points (called ports) are specified for different types of passengers—in our case, network traffic. (For example, Web page content typically travels through TCP port 80.)

- Information that meets specified security criteria (such as an approved IP address) is allowed to pass, whereas other data is filtered—that is, it can't pass through freely.

- Logging of unauthorized (as well as authorized) accesses both into and out of a network.

In addition to these fundamental functions of a firewall, manufacturers have added a slew of features that blur the lines between firewalls and other security devices (such as intrusion prevention systems, or IPS). These advanced features include the following:

- Functioning as a sort of electronic metal detector, scanning for viruses and repairing infected files before they invade the network

- Sending out alert messages if viruses are detected and to notify staff of break-ins

- Providing a virtual private network (VPN) link to another network

- Authenticating users who provide usernames and passwords so that they can be identified and given access to the services they need

- Shielding hosts inside the network so that attackers cannot identify them and use them as staging areas for sustained attacks

- Caching data so that files that are repeatedly requested can be called from the cache to reduce the server load and improve Web site performance

- Filtering content that is considered inappropriate (such as video streams) or dangerous (such as mail attachments)

- Offering all-in-one feature sets that include antivirus scanning, network intrusion prevention, firewall technology, and other security features. This type of technology is referred to as Unified Threat Management, or UTM.

Firewall Uses

Before you can understand how a firewall works, it is helpful to understand how firewalls are used and applied in various situations and organizations. The following sections outline some of the major firewall applications.

Protecting a System

For a single home user who regularly surfs the Web, exchanges e-mail, and uses instant messaging, a firewall's primary job is to keep viruses from infecting files and prevent Trojan horses from entering the system through hidden openings called **back doors**. Most commercial home "firewall" software—for example, Norton Internet Security, McAfee Personal Firewall Plus, and CA Internet Security Suite—have antivirus programs that alert users when an e-mail attachment or file containing a known virus is found.

Restricting Access to the Network

The most obvious goal of a firewall is to regulate which packets of information can enter the network. To do so, the firewall examines each packet to determine whether it meets the necessary "authorized" criteria. The criteria might be protocols or IP addresses on an "approved" list. Anything not on the list is excluded. Such packet filtering is discussed in more detail later in this chapter.

As a professional network administrator or security expert, you need to become familiar with firewalls that function as checkpoints, protecting large companies or other organizations from outside attackers and thieves. The firewall is positioned at the border of the network (zone of trust), providing security for all the computers within it, so that each individual server user or workstation does not have to provide its own security. This checkpoint establishes a network perimeter.

A **perimeter** is a boundary between two zones of trust. For example, an organization's internal network is more trusted than the Internet, and it is common to install a firewall at this boundary to inspect and control the traffic that flows across it, as shown in Figure 4-2. There are additional zones of trust within the organization's network, such as among the Web, application, and database tiers of a three-tiered application.

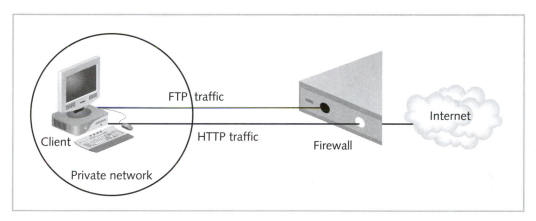

Figure 4-2   Firewall at the perimeter
© Cengage Learning 2013

Placing the firewall at the perimeter has one obvious benefit: it enables you to set up a checkpoint where you can block attacks and malware before they pass the perimeter. However, it has less obvious benefits, too. A perimeter firewall enables you to log passing traffic, protecting the whole network at one time. If an attack does occur, having defined network boundaries—especially those that include firewalls—can minimize the damage.

A perimeter firewall also centralizes security for the organization it protects. It simplifies the security-related activities of the network administrator, who typically has many other responsibilities. Having a firewall on the perimeter gives the network administrator a single location from which to configure security policies and monitor arriving and departing traffic.

Extending the Network

If you have an **extranet**—an extended network that shares part of an organization's network with a third party (e.g., a business partner)—the location of the "perimeter" becomes a bit murky. A firewall is an ideal endpoint for VPN, which connects two companies' networks over the Internet. A VPN is one of the safest ways to exchange information online. You find out more about VPNs later in this chapter.

If the extranet operates over a VPN, the VPN should have its own perimeter firewall because your network boundary technically extends to the end of the VPN. To be really secure, you should install a firewall on the partner's VPN host, as shown in Figure 4-3.

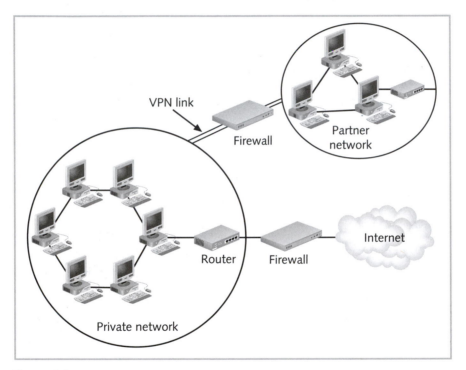

Figure 4-3 VPN perimeters
© Cengage Learning 2013

Mobile devices such as laptops, PDAs, and smartphones blur the perimeter boundary even more because they may extend an organization's network into Internet cafes, coffee shops, and so forth. This, however, does not remove the need for a firewall. Firewalls become more needed in order to extend the network but still provide necessary layers of protection for the internal network.

Preventing Malicious Traffic from Leaving the Network

It is sometimes easier to protect a network from the Internet than from an inside attack. Whether they are disgruntled or just ignorant of the proper security procedures, employees can be a major source of trouble. Users inside your network could exploit security tools to conduct attacks against other organizations or networks, or users may be duped by a spam message to visit a malicious Web site and install malware. This malware, in turn, can conduct attacks against other organizations from your network.

Firewalls can be configured to recognize these types of malicious attacks and prevent this type of traffic from leaving your network. It won't reduce the threat to your own networks, but it will prevent the use of your systems as platforms for external attacks. A firewall can also be configured to recognize packets or to prevent access to protected files from internal as well as external hosts. Note, however, that remote access and social-engineering attacks will still require that the organization make use of training and raise awareness about security procedures.

Along with preventing traffic from leaving the network, firewalls can selectively permit traffic to go from inside the network to the Internet or other networks to provide more precise control of how employees inside the network use external resources. In other words, the firewall can act as a **proxy server** that makes high-level application connections on behalf of internal hosts and other systems. Application proxies can restrict internal users who want to gain unrestricted access to the Internet. A single firewall product can provide both outbound packet filtering (shown in Figure 4-4) and outbound proxy services.

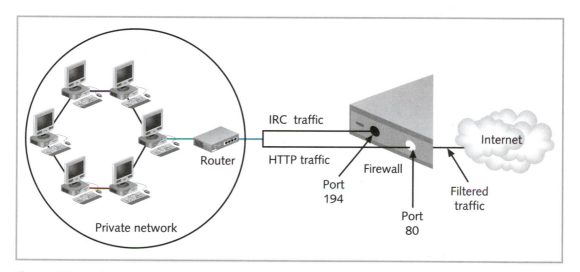

Figure 4-4 Outbound packet-filtering
© Cengage Learning 2013

Application proxies are control devices that can restrict internal users from unlimited access to the Internet. Keep in mind, though, that some technically sophisticated users might be able to circumvent the security measures you set up. They might, for instance, dial into the office using remote access, thus opening a potential security hole. They might use a remote access program like gotomypc.com, which provides client software that they install on both their home and work computers. The software is configured so that every 15 or 20 seconds the work computer sends out the query "Does anyone want to connect to me?" (The target port is TCP port 80, the commonly used HTTP port.) Such traffic may well go through the firewall unchecked, and it presents an obvious security risk because home networks are seldom as well defended as corporate networks are, and attackers may be able to first attack a user's home network and, thus, gain access to the more valuable corporate network. Note that some sophisticated users may use anonymizing sites that appear to be innocuous Web servers but can allow unfettered access to anywhere else on the Internet.

Protecting Critical Resources

In order to provide true defense in depth, organizations deploy firewalls to segment networks within an organization. This can be done to provide a tiered architecture in which Web servers are separated by a firewall from their supporting application servers. The application servers, in turn, are sequestered by the firewall from their supporting database servers. This tiered architecture allows administrators to position firewalls to provide several layers of protection for the organization's most critical systems and resources.

Enabling an Audit Trail

Every firewall should be configured to provide information to the network administrator in the form of log files. These log files record attempted intrusions and other suspicious activity as well as mundane events such as legitimate file accesses, unsuccessful connection attempts, and the like. Looking through log files is tedious, but they can help a network administrator identify weak points in the security system so that they can be strengthened.

Log files can also identify intruders so that they can be apprehended in case theft or damage occurs. Regular review and analysis of the log file data is what makes firewalls effective because methods of attack change all the time. The firewall rules must be evaluated and adjusted to account for the many new and emerging threats.

Providing for Authentication

You are probably familiar with authentication—the process of logging in to a server with credentials before being allowed access to protected information. Only users who have registered credentials are recognized by the server and allowed to enter. The authentication process can also be performed at the firewall and make use of encryption to protect credentials transmitted from client to server (or client to firewall).

How Do Firewalls Work?

In this section, we discuss the various features of firewalls and the ways they work. Firewalls perform two basic security functions:

- Packet filter—First and foremost, a firewall must be able to determine whether to allow or deny the passage of packets of digital information, based on established security policy rules.
- Application proxy—In some cases, a firewall may provide network services to users while shielding individual host computers. This is done by breaking the IP flow (i.e., the traffic into and out of the network) between the network being protected and the network outside.

Firewalls can be complex, but if you thoroughly understand only these two functions, you'll make a lot of progress toward being able to choose the right firewall and configure it to protect a computer or network.

Firewalls work at many levels of the seven-layer OSI networking model, which is one reason they're so effective. Table 4-1 provides examples of firewall functions and the corresponding layers at which they operate.

Layer Number	OSI Reference Model Layer	Firewall Functions
7	Application	Application-level gateway
6	Presentation	Encryption
5	Session	SOCKS proxy server
4	Transport	Packet filtering (based on port)
3	Network	NAT and packet filtering (based on address alone)
2	Data Link	MAC address-filtering
1	Physical	N/A

Table 4-1 **Network Layers and Firewalls**
© Cengage Learning 2013

Protocols

Firewalls affect the transmission of packets based on the protocols used. You, therefore, need to understand how the various Internet protocols function. Here are brief descriptions:

- Internet Protocol (IP)—The rules used for all parts of the IP protocol control the overall flow of IP traffic through your network. If you have identified a computer or network that you want to block from your company's network, you would specify Source IP or Destination IP rule criteria. These rules will affect the entire TCP/IP suite of protocols (ICMP, UDP, or TCP).

- Internet Control Message Protocol (ICMP)—IP, by itself, has no way of letting the host that originated a request know whether a packet was received at its destination in its entirety. It can, however, use ICMP to report any errors that occurred in the transmission. Utilities such as Ping and Traceroute use ICMP. The danger is that ICMP packets can be filled with false information that can trick your hosts into redirecting or stopping communications.

- User Datagram Protocol (UDP)—This protocol further handles the addressing of a message. UDP breaks a message into numbered segments so that it can be transmitted. UDP then reassembles the message when it reaches the destination computer. UDP is connectionless; it simply sends segments of messages without performing error-checking or waiting for an acknowledgment that the message has been received. Such a protocol is useful for video and audio broadcasts on the Internet. TCP and UDP are often mentioned together in discussions of firewalls because both transmit data through ports and thus open up vulnerabilities. It's useful to set up rules to block UDP traffic on ports 21 and below and to block traffic on ports that control hardware such as keyboards, hubs, and routers; see Chapter 2 for more information.

- Transmission Control Protocol (TCP)—The rules used to control filtering of TCP packets are similar to those used for UDP packets. For example, you should block packets that use ports below 20, and you can block specific protocols—for example, Telnet connections on port 23. Unlike UDP, however, TCP provides connections for error checking and for ensuring that transmissions have been sent and received successfully.

Ports

UDP and TCP ports work like apartment numbers in that they allow many network services to share a network address. Tenants in an apartment building have their own apartment numbers but share a street address; likewise, network services have their own port numbers but share a network address. To send a specific letter to a specific tenant, a sender would address the envelope with the street and the apartment number. The sender then adds her own address to the envelope, including the apartment number at her own building. This combination of a sender's full address (network address plus port) and receiver's address (network address plus port) makes up what is called a **socket.** To initiate a connection to a network service, the sender specifies both his IP address and port number and the recipient's IP address and port number.

A port is a network subaddress (assigned a number between 0 and 65,535) through which a particular type of data is allowed to pass. There are two types of ports: **well-known ports** (those numbered at 1023 and below) and **ephemeral ports** (those numbered from 1024 through 65535). Well-known ports are defined for most common services—the Web (port 80), SSH (port 22), Simple Mail Transport Protocol (port 25), POP Mail (port 110), and many others. Ephemeral port numbers are dynamically assigned as needed and have no special meaning outside the connection using them.

So, for example, when a user requests a connection to a Web server running at address 192.168.5.203, the Web browser would know to attempt the connection at port 80. Exposed network services—such as an unplanned mail server running on a corporate Web server—are one of the biggest vulnerabilities that firewalls can protect against. A firewall can block external access to such unplanned services so that, for example, mail server connection requests are always routed to the actual mail server and not to any other system that may have inadvertently set up a mail server.

Packet filtering, which virtually all firewalls do, protects networks from port scanning and other types of attacks. In a port scanning attack, special software scans a series of network addresses, attempting to connect to each one. If a connection is made, it gives the attacker a target. A properly configured firewall only allows authorized connection attempts to the ports on the network it protects.

Packet-Filtering Firewalls

Packet filtering is a key function of any firewall. In fact, packet filters were one of the first types of firewalls. Packet filters are an effective element in any perimeter security setup.

As you learned in Chapter 2, at the Physical layer, data is referred to as a bit stream. At the Data Link layer, the bit stream is encapsulated in a frame. At the Network layer, frames are used to encapsulate packets (or datagrams). Both the frame and the packet contain two types of information:

- The **header,** which consists of general information about the size of the packet, the protocol that was used to send it, and the IP addresses of the source computer and the destination.

- The data, which is the information you view and use—for example, the text of an e-mail message, the contents of a Web page, a piece of a file being transferred, or the bits of a digital photograph. The data of a packet also includes the Data Link layer frame in its entirety.

- A frame also includes a **trailer** (or **footer**) at its end, after the data field. The trailer can contain error-checking data.

A packet-filtering firewall installed on a TCP/IP-based network typically functions at the IP level and determines whether to alert the sender that a packet will not be delivered (reject), ignore a packet (drop), or forward it to the next network connection (allow) based on the rules programmed into the firewall. Packet-filtering firewalls examine every incoming packet header and can selectively filter packets based on header information such as destination address, source address, packet type, and other key information. Figure 4-5 shows the general structure of an IPv4 packet.

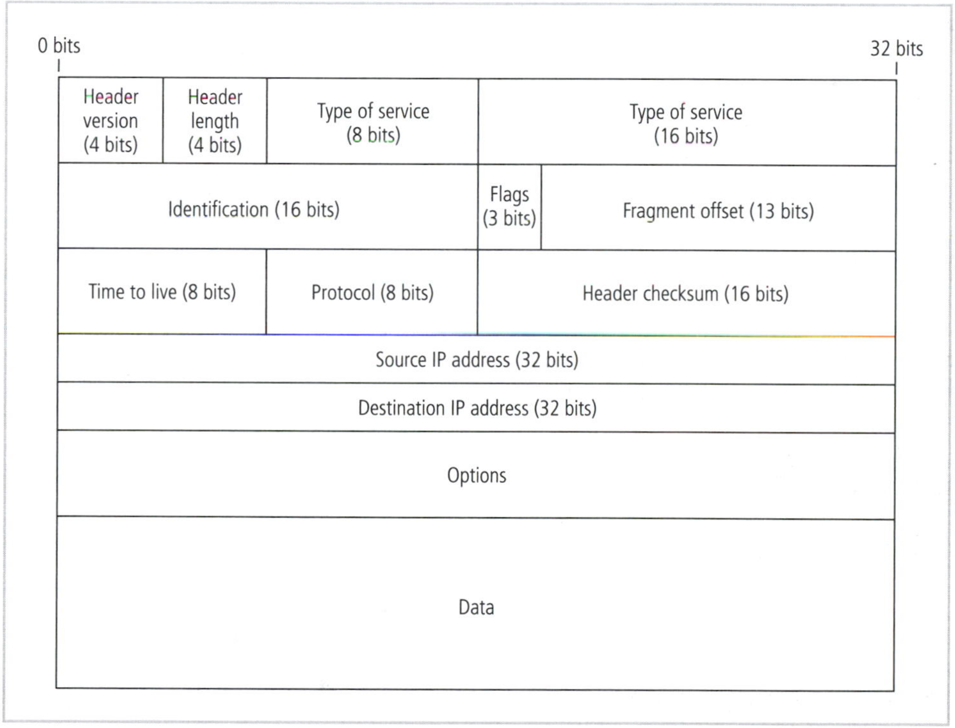

Figure 4-5 IPv4 packet structure
© Cengage Learning 2013

Packet-Filtering Rules Simple firewall models examine two components of the packet header: the destination address and the source address. They enforce address restrictions rules and prohibit packets with specific addresses or incomplete addresses from passing through the device. These restrictions are defined in **access control lists (ACLs)**, or **firewall rules,** which are created and modified by the firewall administrators. Typically, a rule specifies a protocol (such as ICMP, UDP, or HTTP), the IP address or address range, the TCP or UDP ports, and the desired firewall action.

To better understand firewall rules, consider Table 4-2. If an administrator were to configure three firewall rules based on the content of Table 4-2, any connection from an external computer or network device would be denied access to systems in the 10.10.x.x address range (10.10.0.0–10.10.255.255) unless they were communicating over HTTP to 10.10.10.25 or over FTP to 10.10.10.10.

Source Address	Destination Address	Service (HTTP, SMTP, FTP, Telnet, etc.)	Action (Allow or Deny)
Any	10.10.x.x	Any	Deny
192.168.x.x	10.10.10.25	HTTP	Allow
192.168.x.x	10.10.10.10	FTP	Allow

Table 4-2 Sample Firewall Rule and Format
© Cengage Learning 2013

Note that the order of the rules is very important. Rules are executed in order, and later rules can override a previous rule. Therefore, a best practice is to start with the rule to drop all incoming traffic; this blocks all traffic and then adds back specific ports or programs to achieve the functionality that is needed. The subsequent rules identify the specific types of communication you want to permit. The allowances may be based on a specific program being executed, a precise time of day, a specific port, a known IP address, or other specific criteria.

Packet-Filtering Best Practices The following list outlines some best practices in setting up the packet-filtering rules:

- Any outbound packet must have a source address that is in your internal network.
- Any outbound packet must not have a destination address that is in your internal network.
- Any inbound packet must not have a source address that is in your internal network.
- Any inbound packet must have a destination address that is in your internal network.
- Any packet that enters or leaves your network must have a source or destination address that falls within the range of addresses in your network. Your network may use (but does not have to use) private addresses or addresses listed in RFC1918. These include 10.x.x.x/8, 172.16.x.x/12, or 192.168.x.x/16 as well as the loopback network 127.0.0.0/8.
- All traffic from the trusted network is filtered. This allows members of the organization to access the services they need but prevents botnet behaviors or other internal threats from affecting other Internet denizens. Filtering and logging outbound traffic is possible when indicated by specific organizational policy goals. However, when the organization

4

wants to control outbound traffic, a separate firewall is used to minimize the load on the inbound firewall.

- The firewall device should never be managed or configured directly from the public network. Almost all management access to the firewall device is denied to internal users as well. Only authorized firewall administrators access the device via secure authentication mechanisms, with preference for a method based on cryptographically strong authentication using two-factor access control techniques.

- All inbound traffic that is not a response to an outbound request is routed to the appropriate, well-configured server or it is dropped. For example, Simple Mail Transport Protocol (SMTP) data is allowed to pass through the firewall, but all of it is routed to a well-configured SMTP gateway to filter and route messaging traffic securely. Web services are only allowed to go to either the Web or e-commerce servers or (as described in the next guideline) to a proxy server.

- When Web services are offered outside the firewall, HTTP traffic is prevented from reaching your internal networks via the implementation of some form of proxy access or DMZ architecture. That way, if any employees are running Web servers for internal use on their desktops, the services will be invisible to the outside Internet.

- If your Web server is located behind the firewall, you need to allow HTTP or HTTPS (S-HTTP) data through for the Internet at large to view it. The best solution is to place the Web servers containing critical data inside the network and to use proxy services from a DMZ (screened network segment).

- It is also advisable to restrict incoming HTTP traffic to internal network addresses so that the traffic must be responding to requests originating at internal addresses. This restriction can be accomplished through NAT or firewalls that support stateful inspection or are directed at the proxy server itself. All other incoming HTTP traffic should be blocked. If the Web servers contain only advertising (static Web pages), they should be placed in the DMZ and rebuilt if and when they are compromised.

- All ICMP data is denied. Known as the ping service, use of ICMP traffic is a common method for hacker reconnaissance and should be turned off to prevent snooping.

- Access to all network communication services that are not explicitly required is blocked. If internal users need to reach an organization's network that is outside the firewall, use a virtual private network (VPN) client or other secure authentication system to allow this kind of access.

- Eliminate packets bound for all ports that should not be available to the Internet, such as NetBIOS, but allow Internet-related traffic, such as SMTP, to pass.

- Drop all packets that use the IP header source routing feature. In IP source routing, the originator of a packet can attempt to partially or completely control the path through the network to the destination. Source routing is widely considered a suspect activity from a security standpoint because this is a favorite technique of network attackers; few legitimate uses exist for this kind of route control.

- Drop all other inbound connections; allow only outbound connections on port 80 (HTTP), port 443 (HTTPS), and port 25 (SMTP) unless users can demonstrate a business need to access other protocols.

Stateless Packet-Filtering Firewalls Stateless inspection, also called stateless packet filtering, is firewall packet inspection that ignores the state of the connection between the internal computer and the external computer. A firewall that conducts stateless packet-filtering blocks or allows a packet based on the information in the header.

Static packet-filtering firewalls scan network data packets looking for compliance with, or violation of, the rules of the firewall's database. Filtering firewalls inspect packets at the Network layer (Layer 3) of the OSI model. If the device finds a packet that violates a rule, it stops the packet from traveling from one network to another. The restriction criteria most commonly implemented in packet-filtering firewalls are based on a combination of the following:

- IP source and destination address
- Direction (inbound or outbound)
- TCP or UDP source and destination port
- ICMP message types and codes

Packet structure varies, depending on the nature of the packet. The server that receives the packet makes use of the details of its packet structure when it processes the packet. The two primary service types are TCP and UDP. Figures 4-6 and 4-7 show the structures of these two major elements of the combined protocol known as TCP/IP.

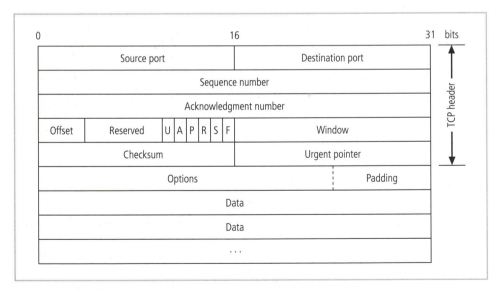

Figure 4-6 TCP packet structure
© Cengage Learning 2013

Packet-Filtering Router The ability to restrict a specific service is now standard in most routers and is invisible to the user. Unfortunately, such routers are unable to detect whether packet headers have been modified, which occurs in some advanced attack methods, including IP spoofing attacks. **IP spoofing** is the falsification of the source IP address in a packet's header so that it appears to have come from a trusted or legitimate sender. In some cases, attackers spoof using a source IP address that belongs to the target in order to make it look as though the packet is coming from a computer within the organization.

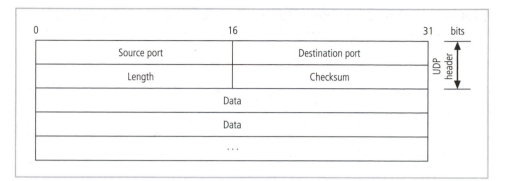

Figure 4-7   UDP packet structure
© Cengage Learning 2013

Figure 4-8 shows how a packet-filtering router can be used as a simple firewall to filter data packets from inbound connections and allow outbound connections unrestricted access to the public network.

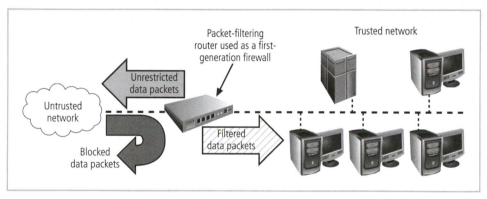

Figure 4-8   Packet-filtering router
© Cengage Learning 2013

Stateful Packet-Filtering Firewalls

Stateful inspection, also called **stateful packet filtering**, is an examination of the data contained in a packet as well as the state of the connection between internal and external computers. This information, known as the state table, is kept in a memory location called the cache. Stateful inspection is superior to stateless inspection because it uses the connection state to make decisions on whether to allow the traffic. A **state table** tracks the state and context of each packet in the conversation by recording which station sent what packet and when. Whereas simple packet-filtering firewalls allow or deny certain packets based only on their addresses, stateful packet filtering can allow incoming packets that have been sent in response to internal requests. If the stateful firewall receives an incoming packet that it cannot match in its state table, it defaults to its ACL to determine whether to allow the packet to pass.

The primary disadvantage of this type of firewall is the additional processing required to manage packets and verify them against the state table, which can leave the system vulnerable to a DoS or DDoS attack. In such an attack, the system receives a large number of external packets, which slows down the firewall because it attempts to compare all the incoming packets first to the state table and then to the ACL.

On the positive side, these firewalls can track connectionless packet traffic, such as UDP and remote procedure calls (RPCs) traffic. Dynamic stateful-filtering firewalls maintain a dynamic state table, making changes (within predefined limits) to the filtering rules based on events as they happen.

A sample state table is shown in Table 4-3. The state table contains the source IP and port, the destination IP and port, information on the protocol used (i.e., UDP or TCP), the total time (in seconds), and the time remaining (in seconds). Many state table implementations allow a connection to remain in place for up to 60 minutes without any activity before the state entry is deleted. The state table shown in Table 4-3 shows this in the column labeled "Total Time." The Time Remaining column shows a countdown of the time that is left until the entry is deleted.

Source Address	Source Port	Destination Address	Destination Port	Time Remaining (in Seconds)	Total Time (in Seconds)	Protocol
192.168.2.5	1028	10.10.10.7	80	2725	3600	TCP

Table 4-3 State Table Entries
© Cengage Learning 2013

Stateful inspection also blocks packets that are sent from an external computer that does not have a currently active connection to an internal computer.

Application-Level Gateways

Another type of firewall protection is the application-level gateway, also known as a proxy server. An **application-level gateway** works at the Application layer, the top layer of the OSI model of network communications, as described in Chapter 2. This level of functionality allows the firewall to act as a intermediary between two systems that wish to communicate.[1]

The application-level gateway runs special software that enables it to act as a proxy for a specific service request. For example, an organization that runs a Web server can avoid exposing the server to direct user traffic by installing such a **proxy server**, configured with the registered domain's URL. This proxy server receives requests for Web pages, accesses the Web server on behalf of the external client, and returns the requested pages to the users. These servers can store the most recently accessed pages in their internal cache, which is why they are also called "cache servers."

By setting up a proxy service, an application-level gateway can control the way applications inside the network access external networks. The proxy service acts as a substitute for the client, making requests for Web pages or sending and receiving e-mail on behalf of individual users who are thus shielded from directly connecting with the Internet. This shielding minimizes the effect of viruses, worms, Trojan horses, and other malware.

The benefits of using an application-level gateway are significant. For one, the gateway is placed in an unsecured area of the network or in the demilitarized zone (DMZ)—an intermediate area between a trusted network and an untrusted network—so that it, rather than the Web server, is exposed to the higher levels of risk from the less-trusted networks. Additional filtering routers can be implemented behind the gateway, limiting access to the more secure internal system and thereby further protecting internal systems.

One common example of an application-level gateway implementation is a firewall that blocks all requests for and responses to requests for Web pages and services from the organization's internal computers and instead makes all such requests and responses go to intermediate computers (or proxies) in the less-protected areas of the organization's network. This technique is still widely used to implement e-commerce functions, although most users of this technology have upgraded to take advantage of the DMZ approach.

4

The primary disadvantage of application-level gateways is that they are designed for a specific protocol and cannot easily be reconfigured to protect against attacks on other protocols. Because application-level gateways work at the Application layer (hence the name), they are typically restricted to a single application (e.g., FTP, Telnet, HTTP, SMTP, or SNMP). The processing time and resources necessary to read each packet down to the Application layer diminish the ability of these firewalls to handle multiple types of applications.

An application-level gateway provides you with one especially valuable security benefit. Unlike a packet filter, which decides whether to allow or deny a request based on the information contained in the packet header, the gateway understands the contents of the requested data. It can be configured to allow or deny (both of which actions can be taken as a result of filtering) specific content, such as viruses and executables.

Content filtering is only one of the tasks that application-level gateways perform that give them the edge over merely blocking specified IP addresses. Among the other tasks are:

- Load balancing—If an airport security checkpoint has not one but two secure entrances, the number of people passing through each can be reduced substantially. In the same way, large organizations commonly install more than one firewall and divide the traffic load between them.

- IP address mapping—This is a type of NAT in which a static IP address assigned by an ISP is mapped to the private IP address of a computer on the local network; it is sometimes called "address vectoring" or "static IP mapping." The benefit to an internal network is that it shields actual internal IP addresses from the prying eyes of unauthorized external clients.

- Filtering specific content—An application proxy server can be set up to filter on specific criteria. You can block files that have a certain filename or part of a filename, a keyword, an e-mail attachment, or a content type.

- URL filtering—This can be used to block a site's Domain Name System (DNS) name, such as *www.criminalactivity.com*.

- Fragmentation attack prevention—A natural feature of IP communication allows packets to be split (i.e., fragmented) prior to sending to allow for the transmission of large packets of data. The recipient then uses the information to reassemble the packets upon receipt. Attacks like Tiny Fragment and Overlapping Fragment[2] abuse this IP routing feature to carry out actions. An application-level gateway can prevent these attacks because it reassembles packets, discards those that are malformed, and sends only valid packets to the client.

Multi-Layer Filtering

Larger organizations use multiple firewall technologies in a DMZ perimeter security setup. They might use a router that functions as a static packet filter, a stateful packet filter that has been set up in a bastion host, and firewall software, as shown in Figure 4-9.

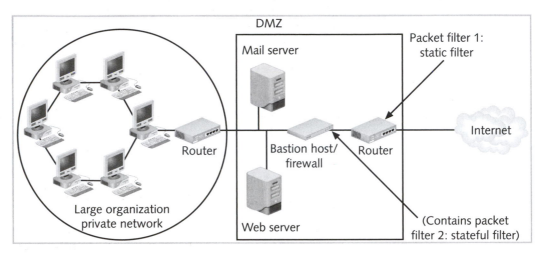

Figure 4-9   Multiple packet filters
© Cengage Learning 2013

Additionally, firewalls were dedicated to one specific type of technology, with each appliance serving as either a packet-filtering firewall, stateful packet-filtering firewall, or an application-level gateway. Modern advances in firewall technologies now allow a firewall to serve as a true hybrid device, performing stateful packet inspection with the option of conducting more detailed analysis down into the Application layer on demand.

This detailed analysis is referred to as **deep packet inspection**. Deep packet inspection combines stateful packet filtering with the ability to analyze Application-layer protocols used in communication and determine if there are any inconsistencies, deviations, or malformed packets. Firewalls with this ability are called application firewalls.[3]

Deep packet inspection is implemented through the use of **jump rules**. Jump rules enable the firewall (when certain conditions are met) to execute a separate set of rules that examines the packet in question in much greater detail. Jump rules work the same way as nested programming code, in which the program flows until a specified condition is met. Once that condition is met, the device pulls up a separate, referenced set of code and follows its instructions.

A simple example is provided by modern Web pages using HTML. When you read a Web page, you find links to other pages. These links bring up additional content referred to in the master page. This linking allows each section of code—or, in the case of firewalls, each rule set—to be managed independently, keeping the master set of rules much neater and better organized. The administrator can also assign responsibility for maintenance of the subsets to different individuals or departments, increasing the efficiency of firewall management.

Multi-layer filtering does have its disadvantages. Every time the jump rule is triggered, it slows down the processing of that packet. However, with the advances in modern computing technology, this is no longer dramatic enough to overcome the advantages of being able to determine if a particular packet carries a substantial threat. Before multi-layer filtering was available, two or more different devices were required to perform this function: a core packet-filtering (or stateful packet-filtering) firewall to perform base analysis and a separate application-level gateway to handle the examination of each higher-level protocol. Now, one firewall device can do the work of many.

Circuit-Level Gateways

Another approach, the circuit-level gateway, operates at the Transport layer and is different from both packet-filtering firewalls and application-level gateways. Connections are authorized based on addresses. Like filtering firewalls, circuit gateway firewalls do not usually examine traffic flowing between one network and another, but they do prevent direct connections between one network and another. They accomplish this by creating tunnels connecting specific processes or systems on each side of the firewall and then allowing only authorized traffic, such as a specific type of TCP connection for authorized users, in these tunnels. A circuit gateway is a firewall component often included in the category of application gateway, but it is in fact a separate type of firewall. Writing for NIST in SP 800-10, John Wack describes the operation of a circuit gateway as follows:

> A circuit-level gateway relays TCP connections but does no extra processing or filtering of the protocol. For example, the TELNET application gateway example provided here would be an example of a circuit-level gateway, since once the connection between the source and destination is established, the firewall simply passes bytes between the systems. Another example of a circuit-level gateway would be for NNTP, in which the NNTP server would connect to the firewall, and then internal systems' NNTP clients would connect to the firewall. The firewall would, again, simply pass bytes.[4]

Although not as well known or widely referenced as the firewall approaches discussed previously, MAC layer firewalls are designed to operate at the media access control sub-layer of the Data Link layer (Layer 2) of the OSI network model. This enables these firewalls to consider the specific host computer's identity, as represented by its MAC or network interface card (NIC) address, in its filtering decisions. Using this approach, the MAC addresses of specific host computers are linked to ACL entries that identify the specific types of packets that can be sent to each host, and all other traffic is blocked.

Figure 4-10 shows where in the OSI model each of the firewall processing modes inspects data.

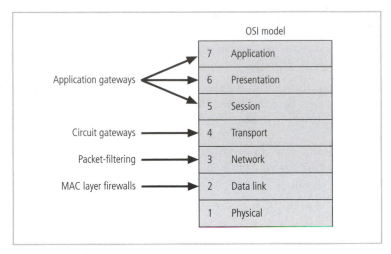

Figure 4-10 Firewalls in the OSI Model
© Cengage Learning 2013

Firewall Form Factors

Firewalls can be categorized by generations or by form factor. Technologically, firewalls are categorized into generations, the later generations being more recently developed and more complex. However, there is no standard definition of which generation refers to which type of firewall. Additionally, the advanced features of modern firewalls cause "blurring" of which firewalls fit into which generation.

Instead, in this text, we will categorize firewalls by form factor. This type of categorization refers to whether a firewall is a residential-grade or commercial-grade, hardware-based or software-based, or appliance-based device.

Most commercial-grade firewalls are dedicated appliances—stand-alone units running on fully customized computing platforms that provide both the physical network connection and firmware programming necessary to perform their functions. Some use highly customized, sometimes proprietary hardware systems that are developed exclusively as firewall devices. Others are off-the-shelf, general-purpose computer systems that use custom application software running on either standard operating systems like Windows or Linux/UNIX or on specialized variants of these operating systems. Most small-office or residential-grade firewalls are either simplified dedicated appliances running on computing devices or application software installed directly on the user's computer.

Firewall Appliances

Firewall appliances are stand-alone, self-contained combinations of computing hardware and software. These devices frequently have many of the features of a general-purpose computer with the addition of firmware-based instructions that increase their reliability and performance and minimize the likelihood of their being compromised. The customized software operating system that drives the device can be periodically upgraded but can only be modified by using a direct physical connection or by using extensive authentication and authorization protocols. The firewall rule sets are stored in non-volatile memory, and thus they can be changed by technical staff when necessary but are available each time the device is restarted.

These appliances may be manufactured from stripped-down, general-purpose computer systems, and/or they can be designed to run a customized version of a general-purpose operating system. These variant operating systems are tuned to meet the type of firewall activity built into the application software that provides the firewall functionality. Examples of the current firewall appliances include:[5]

- Cisco Systems Adaptive Security Appliance (ASA)
- Fortinet Fortigate
- McAfee Firewall Enterprise
- Palo Alto Networks PA-4000 Series
- SonicWALL E-Class Network Security Appliance (NSA)

Firewall Systems A commercial-grade firewall system consists of application software that is configured for the firewall application and runs on a general-purpose computer. Organizations can install firewall software on an existing general-purpose computer system, or they can purchase hardware that has been configured to specifications that yield optimum firewall performance. These systems exploit the fact that firewalls are essentially application software packages that use common general-purpose network connections to move data from one network to another. Full-featured, commercial-grade firewall packages include:

- Check Point Software Technologies Firewall Software Blade
- Barracuda Networks NG Firewall
- Microsoft Forefront Threat Management Gateway 2010

Virtual Firewalls With the widespread adoption of virtualized server environments or cloud-based infrastructures, more and more enterprise systems exist as virtual systems. To protect these virtual systems, a variety of virtualized firewalls have been introduced. A virtual firewall has the same features and functions of its physical brethren but is built on a virtual server or is implemented as a virtual security appliance. The virtual security appliance is similar to the firewall appliance in that the firewall is bundled with a hardened operating system and virtualized hardware.[6] As its name implies, the virtual server option is similar to a firewall system, but the firewall software is installed on a virtual server. Examples of virtual firewalls include:[7]

- Juniper Networks vGW Series
- Altor v4.0
- McAfee Firewall Enterprise, Virtual Appliance

Small Office/Home Office (SOHO) Firewall Appliances Most small businesses and residences have fast Internet connections. Therefore, they are more vulnerable to attacks. What many small-business and work-from-home users don't realize is that these high-speed services are always on; thus, the computers connected to them are more visible to the scans performed by attackers. Coupled with the typically lax security configured by users on systems running modern home computing operating systems, these systems are vulnerable to outside intrusion.

Newer operating systems such as Windows 7 and Mac OS X have improved security "out of the box," but users can still benefit from having solid SOHO networking security in place. Just as organizations must protect their information, residential users must implement some form of firewall to prevent loss, damage, or disclosure of personal information.

One of the most effective methods for improving computing security in the SOHO setting is using a SOHO or residential-grade firewall. These devices, also known as broadband gateways or DSL/cable modem routers, connect the user's local area network (LAN) or a specific computer system to the Internet working device—in this case, the cable modem or DSL router provided by the Internet service provider (ISP). The SOHO firewall serves first as a stateful firewall to enable inside-to-outside access and can be configured to allow limited TCP/IP port forwarding and/or screened subnet capabilities (see the later sections of this chapter for definitions of these terms).

In recent years, the broadband router devices that can function as packet-filtering firewalls have been enhanced to combine the features of wireless access points (WAPs) and small stackable LAN switches in a single device. These convenient combination devices give the residential/SOHO user the strong protection that comes from the use of NAT services. NAT assigns nonrouting local addresses to the computer systems in the LAN and uses the single ISP-assigned address to communicate with the Internet. Because the internal computers are not visible to the public network, they are much less likely to be scanned or compromised. Many users implement these devices primarily to allow multiple internal users to share a single external Internet connection. Figure 4-11 shows a few examples of the SOHO firewall devices currently available on the market.

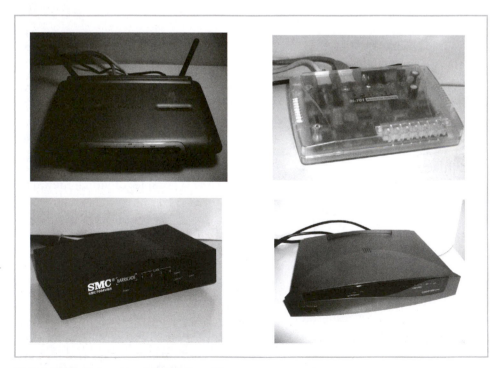

Figure 4-11   Examples of SOHO firewalls

Many of these firewalls provide more than simple NAT services. As illustrated by the screenshots in Figures 4-12 through 4-16, some SOHO/residential firewalls include packet-filtering, port-filtering, and simple intrusion detection systems, and some can even restrict access to specific MAC addresses. Users may be able to configure port forwarding and enable outside users to access specific TCP or UDP ports on specific computers on the protected network.

Figure 4-12 shows the MAC Address filter setup screen from the SMC Barricade residential broadband router, which can be used to identify the computers inside a trusted network that may access the Internet.

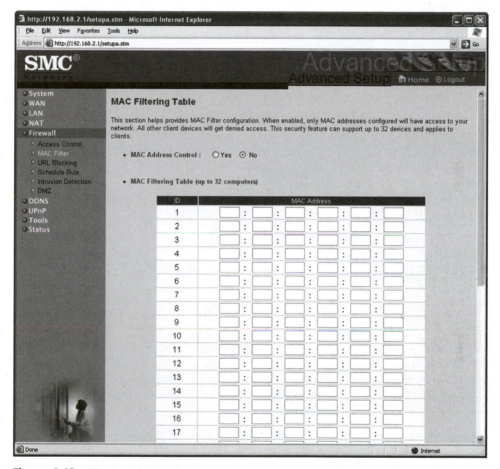

Figure 4-12   Filtering MAC addresses
Source: SMC Barricade

Some firewall devices provide a limited intrusion detection capability. Figure 4-13 shows the configuration screen from the SMC Barricade residential broadband router that enables the intrusion detection feature. When enabled, this feature detects specific intrusion attempts that are defined in the currently installed detection library—that is, attempts to compromise the protected network that are known to the device manufacturer and are detectable based on the nature of the attack. In addition to recording intrusion attempts, the router can be configured to use the contact information to notify the firewall administrator when an intrusion attempt occurs.

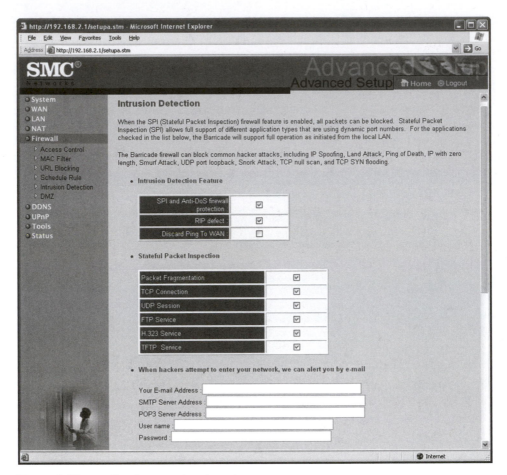

Figure 4-13 Configuring Intrusion detection

Source: SMC Barricade

Figure 4-14 shows a continuation of the configuration screen for the intrusion detection feature. Note that the intrusion criteria are limited in number but that the actual threshold levels of the various activities detected can be customized by the administrator.

Figure 4-15 illustrates that even simple residential firewalls can be used to create a logical screened subnetwork (often called a DMZ) that can provide Web services. This screen shows how the Barricade can be configured to allow port forwarding to be established so that Internet users can be allowed access to servers inside the trusted network for services at specific port numbers. The network administrator is expected to ensure that the exposed servers are sufficiently secured for this type of exposure.

Firewall Software Many people have installed software firewalls on the systems they use. Firewall software looks at network communication to and from the system on which it's installed. This specific focus on a single system gives the system operator a greater degree of granularity in specifying what applications are allowed to communicate as well as determining which users can interact with the system. Additionally, these firewalls are more

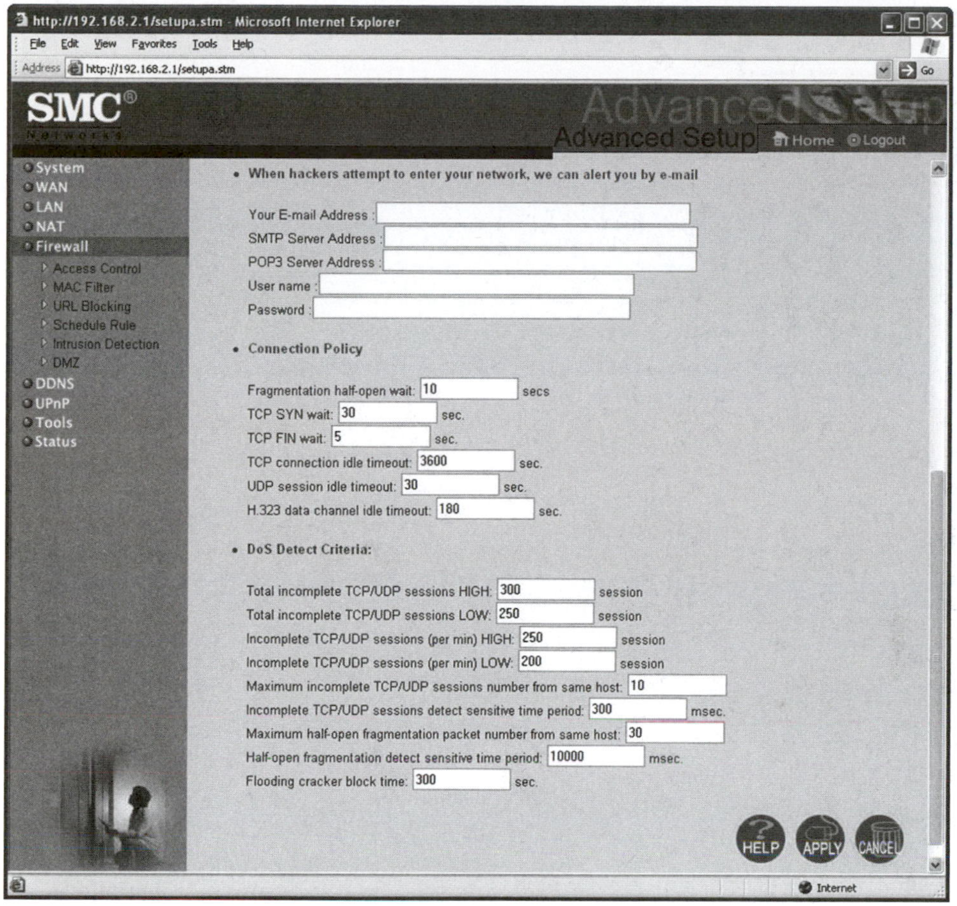

Figure 4-14 Configuring intrusion detection
Source: SMC Barricade

commonly bundled into overall security suites that offer intrusion prevention, antivirus, and other security features. Examples of the security suites include:[8]

- Bitdefender Total Security 2012
- Norton Internet Security 2012
- Webroot SecureAnywhere Complete
- ZoneAlarm Extreme Security 2012

Software vs. Hardware: The SOHO Firewall Debate Should a residential user implement a software-based firewall or a hardware-based firewall? Look at it this way: When would you rather defend against an attacker? If you use a software-based firewall, the attacker is inside your computer, battling a piece of software (free software, in some cases) that may not have been correctly installed, configured, patched, upgraded, or designed. If the software happens to have a known vulnerability, the attacker can bypass the software and gain unrestricted access to your system.

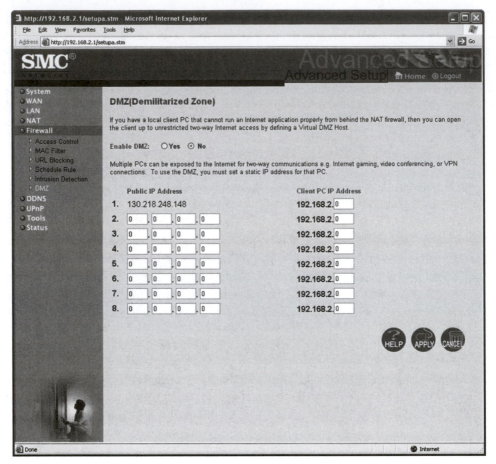

Figure 4-15   Configuring port forwarding
Source: SMC Barricade

If you use a hardware-based firewall, even if the attacker manages to crash the firewall system, your computer and information are still safely behind the now-disabled connection, which is assigned a nonroutable IP address, making it virtually impossible to reach from the outside. A former student of one of the authors responded to this debate by installing a hardware firewall, then visiting an attacker chat room. He challenged the group to penetrate his system. A few days later, he received an e-mail from an attacker claiming to have accessed his system. The attacker included a graphic of a screen showing a C:\ prompt, which he claimed was from the student's system. After doing a bit of research, the student found out that the firewall had an image stored in firmware that was designed to distract attackers. It was an image of a command window with a DOS prompt. The hardware (NAT) solution had withstood the challenge.

There are, however, a number of recent attacks taking place against home routers and firewalls in which the administrator password is compromised or software vulnerability is exploited.[9] Whether a hardware-based firewall or a software-based firewall is used, you must choose difficult admin passwords, harden the systems, and continue to update software as new vulnerabilities are discovered.

Free Firewall Tools on the Internet Most of the free firewall software available on the Internet (including the packet-filter ipchains, iptables, and TIS Firewall Toolkit) also run on a free operating system (such as Linux, the Berkeley Software Design variety of UNIX (BSD), or DOS).

Free firewall programs aren't perfect. Their logging capabilities aren't as robust as some commercial products, they can be difficult to configure, and they usually don't include a way to monitor the firewall in real time. Nonetheless, they have a place in networking because of their convenience, simplicity, and unbeatable price.

Examples of free firewall products include:

- Windows Firewall—Starting with Windows XP SP2, the current versions of Microsoft Windows operating systems include the Windows Firewall. Early versions only allowed for blocking incoming traffic, but since Windows Vista, outgoing traffic is also filtered.[10]

- Application Firewall—Apple Mac OS X 10.5 and later includes the Application Firewall that allows users to filter traffic on a per-application basis.[11]

- Netfilter and iptables—Netfilter and iptables comes with the Linux 2.4 and 2.6 kernels and is a powerful solution for stateless and stateful packet filtering, NAT, and packet processing.[12] Netfilter doesn't have all the features of commercial programs such as VPN, but it does one thing very well: logging. Netfilter records copious information about the traffic that passes through it, but that information is well organized and easy to review.

- ZoneAlarm Free Firewall—ZoneAlarm offers a free firewall that provides basic ingress and egress filtering. ZoneAlarm provides a full security suite via the for-sale version.

Firewall Architectures

Each of the firewall devices described earlier can be configured in a number of network connection architectures. These approaches are sometimes mutually exclusive and sometimes can be combined.

The configuration that works best for a particular organization depends on three factors: the objectives of the network, the organization's ability to develop and implement the architectures, and the budget available for the function. Although hundreds of variations exist, there are four common architectural implementations of firewalls. These implementations are packet-filtering routers, screened host firewalls, dual-homed firewalls, and screened subnet firewalls. Each of these is examined in more detail in the following sections.

Packet-Filtering Routers

Most organizations with an Internet connection have some form of router at the perimeter, between the organization's internal networks and the external service provider. Many of these routers can be configured to reject packets that the organization does not allow into the network. This is a simple but effective way to lower the organization's risk from external attack. The drawbacks to this type of system include a lack of auditing and a lack of strong authentication. Also, the complexity of the ACLs used to filter the packets can degrade network performance.

Screened Host Firewalls

Screened host firewalls combine the packet-filtering router with a separate, dedicated firewall, such as an application proxy server. This approach allows the router to prescreen packets to minimize the network traffic and load on the internal proxy. The application proxy examines an Application layer protocol, such as HTTP, and performs the proxy services. This separate host is often referred to as a bastion host; it can be a rich target for external attacks and should be very thoroughly secured.

Even though the bastion host/application proxy actually contains only cached copies of the internal Web documents, it can still present a promising target, because compromise of the bastion host can disclose the configuration of internal networks and possibly provide external sources with internal information. Because the bastion host stands as a sole defender on the network perimeter, it is also commonly referred to as the sacrificial host. To its advantage, this configuration requires the external attack to compromise two separate systems before the attack can access internal data. In this way, the bastion host protects the data more fully than the router alone. Figure 4-16 shows a typical configuration of a screened host architecture.

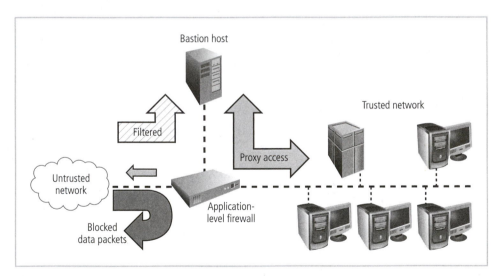

Figure 4-16   Screened host architecture
© Cengage Learning 2013

Dual-Homed Host Firewalls

The next step up in firewall architectural complexity is the dual-homed host. When this architectural approach is used, the bastion host contains two NICs rather than one, as in the bastion host configuration. One NIC is connected to the external network, and one is connected to the internal network, providing an additional layer of protection. With two NICs, all traffic must physically go through the firewall to move between the internal and external networks. This architecture often makes use of NAT—mapping real, valid, external IP addresses to special ranges of nonroutable internal IP addresses—thereby creating yet another barrier to intrusion from external attackers. If the NAT server is a multi-homed bastion host, it translates between the true, external IP addresses assigned to the organization by public network naming authorities and the internally assigned, nonroutable IP addresses. NAT translates by dynamically assigning addresses to internal communications and tracking the conversations with sessions to determine which incoming message is a response to which outgoing traffic. Figure 4-17 shows a typical configuration of a dual-homed host firewall that uses NAT and proxy access to protect the internal network.

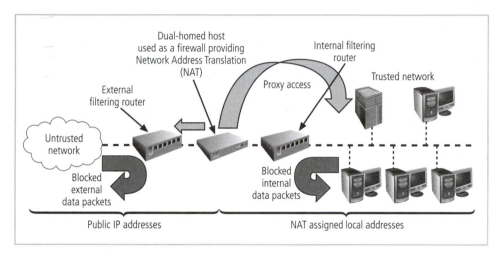

Figure 4-17   Dual-homed host
© Cengage Learning 2013

Another benefit of a dual-homed host is its ability to translate many different protocols at their respective Data Link layers, including Ethernet, Token Ring, Fiber Distributed Data Interface (FDDI), and Asynchronous Transfer Method (ATM). On the downside, if this dual-homed host is compromised, it can disable the connection to the external network, and as traffic volume increases, it can become overloaded. Compared to more complex solutions, however, this architecture provides strong overall protection with minimal expense.

Screened Subnet Firewalls (with DMZ)

The dominant architecture used today is the screened subnet firewall. The architecture of a screened subnet firewall provides a DMZ. The DMZ can be a dedicated port on the firewall device linking a single bastion host, or it can be connected to a screened subnet, as shown in Figure 4-18. Until recently, servers providing services through an untrusted network were commonly placed in the DMZ. Examples of these include Web servers, File Transfer Protocol (FTP) servers, and certain database servers. More recent strategies using proxy servers have provided much more secure solutions.

A common arrangement is a subnet firewall consisting of two or more internal bastion hosts behind a packet-filtering router, with each host protecting the trusted network. There are many variants of the screened subnet architecture. The first general model consists of two filtering routers, with one or more dual-homed bastion hosts between them. In the second general model, the connections are routed as follows:

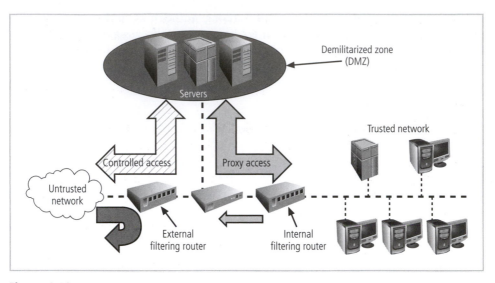

Figure 4-18 Screened subnet
© Cengage Learning 2013

- Connections from the outside or untrusted network are routed through an external filtering router.

- Connections from the outside or untrusted network are routed into—and then out of—a routing firewall to the separate network segment known as the DMZ.

- Connections into the trusted internal network are allowed only from the DMZ bastion host servers.

The screened subnet is an entire network segment that performs two functions: it protects the DMZ systems and information from outside threats by providing a network of intermediate security (more secure than the general public networks but less secure than the internal network), and it protects the internal networks by limiting how external connections can gain access to them. Though extremely secure, the screened subnet can be expensive to implement and complex to configure and manage. The value of the information it protects must justify the cost.

Another facet of the DMZ is the creation of an area known as an extranet. An extranet is a segment of the DMZ where additional authentication and authorization controls are put in place to provide services that are not available to the general public. An example is an online retailer that allows anyone to browse the product catalog and place items into a shopping cart but requires extra authentication and authorization when the customer is ready to check out and place an order.

Limitations of Firewalls

Firewalls can do a lot, but they can't be expected to do it all. Firewalls should not be the only form of protection for a network. They should be part of an overall security plan and should be used in conjunction with other forms of protection, including intrusion prevention, antivirus, and encrypted communication. Even the most elaborate firewall can't protect against an employee who brings a USB flash drive to work containing files that have been infected with a virus, or employees who use a host inside the firewall to gain unauthorized access to sensitive information.

There are a number of things that must be considered when deploying and maintaining a firewall infrastructure:

- Packet filtering has limitations—Filtering does not hide the IP addresses of the hosts that are on the network inside the filter. The IP addresses are contained in the outbound traffic, which makes it easy for attackers to target individual hosts behind the filter to attack them. Filters also don't check to make sure the protocols inside packets are legitimate. Packet filtering can limit addresses based only on the source IP address listed in the packet's header, and thus it does not protect against IP spoofing. For these reasons, firewalls that perform only packet filtering do not provide adequate network protection.

- Firewalls can be circumvented—Technically sophisticated attackers or technologies can circumvent the firewall security measures you've set up. Here's how that might happen:

  - An attacker might use a remote access service provider like GoToMyPC (gotomypc.com). The service provider will have the user install an application program, typically on both their home and work computers. Once the application is installed, the service provider can allow the user to move network traffic between the two endpoints. The traffic that the user is transferring may well go through the firewall unchecked, and it presents an obvious security risk because home networks are seldom as well defended as corporate networks.

  - An employee might bring to the office portable media (memory sticks, CD/DVDs, etc.) that contain malware.

  - An attacker might obtain confidential information by contacting employees and deceiving them into giving up passwords, IP addresses, server names, and so on (i.e., **social engineering**).

  - An employee might open an e-mail attachment that launches a program capable of spreading to other computers using the recipient's e-mail address book. The program might then damage files on the host machine or undertake any number of harmful activities.

- Firewalls are not fortresses—There are two key concepts to firewall deployment: defense in depth and the principle of least privilege. In connection to firewalls, the defense-in-depth concept mandates that a single firewall should not be your only defense. Deploy a sound network firewall architecture, deploy host-based firewalls, and use IPS and other security technologies to ensure that if a firewall is breached, the attacker is stopped elsewhere. The principle of least privilege mandates that users be given the minimum amount of privilege to do their jobs. With firewalls, this principle translates into starting with default firewall rules that deny all traffic and then gradually allowing more traffic as the business needs dictate.

- Firewalls are not impenetrable—Like any IT hardware or software, firewalls must be updated with the latest patches and fixes to keep up with the latest security threats. Firewalls must also be supported by trained and experienced firewall administrators.

- Firewall rules are not always simple—Firewall rules can become quite complex. They should be audited and updated regularly to ensure that they don't conflict and aren't not unnecessarily permissive.

- Firewalls can't protect network segments they're not attached to—The placement of firewalls in the overall IT environment is crucial. To ensure the level of protection you want, know your network topology and ensure that the firewall is connected to the intended networks.

- Firewalls cannot create your security policy—The organization must develop a solid security policy. Although there are a number of best practices in deploying firewalls, there are business-specific needs that should be mandated in a security policy, then translated into firewall rules.

- Firewalls cannot read your security policy—In order to properly maintain a firewall infrastructure, you must have trained administrators who understand network protocols and the organization's security policy. If the security policy states that the IT environment must not allow FTP from outside the organization, a trained network administrator would know to translate that requirement into blocking not only the control session on port 21 but the FTP's data session that occurs on port 20.

- Firewalls cannot speed up network traffic—A firewall will always introduce latency to network traffic based on its need to examine packets before forwarding them to the intended recipient. Make sure you properly scope the firewall equipment to minimize the overall latency to the network and/or IT systems.

Chapter Summary

- A firewall is hardware or software (or a combination of hardware and software) that filters the transmission of packets of digital information as they attempt to pass through a boundary of a network. Firewalls perform two basic security functions: packet filtering and implementing proxy access for specific services.

- A firewall can contain many components, including a packet filter, a proxy server, an authentication system, and software that can perform port forwarding. Some firewalls can encrypt traffic, and some help establish VPNs.

- Packet filtering is a key function of any firewall. In fact, packet filters were one of the first types of firewalls. Packet filters are an effective element in any perimeter security setup. A packet-filtering firewall may be stateless or stateful. Stateless packet filtering ignores the state of the connection between the internal computer and the external computer. Stateful packet filtering is an examination of the data contained in a packet, with a memory of the state of the connection between client and internal and external computers.

- Application-level gateways, also known as proxy servers, control the way applications inside the network access external networks by setting up proxy services. This service acts as a substitute (i.e., proxy) for the client, making requests for Web pages or sending and receiving e-mail on behalf of individual users, who are thus shielded from directly connecting with the Internet.

■ Firewalls can be categorized by generation or form factor. Technologically, firewalls are categorized into generations, the later generations being more recently developed and more complex. Categorizing firewalls by form factor refers to whether they are residential-grade or commercial-grade, hardware-based or software-based, or appliance-based devices.

■ Each of the firewall devices described in this chapter can be configured in a number of network connection architectures. The configuration that works best for a particular organization depends on three factors: the objectives of the network, the organization's ability to develop and implement the architectures, and the budget available for the function. There are four common architectural implementations of firewalls: packet-filtering routers, screened host firewalls, dual-homed firewalls, and screened subnet firewalls.

Review Questions

1. Why is it important that a firewall provide a centralized security checkpoint for a network?

2. What are the two basic functions of a firewall?

3. What advanced security features can be incorporated into a firewall?

4. What technology was used in the earliest firewalls?

5. What components are found in many firewalls?

6. Why is packet filtering alone inadequate for security purposes?

7. When does packet filtering offer an advantage over other security methods, such as proxy services?

8. What is load balancing?

9. Web site requests are routed to which TCP port by default?

10. What can TCP do that UDP cannot do?

11. How is a firewall configured to allow Web access to a Web server?

12. At how many ports can a computer offer services?

13. What is a stateless firewall?

14. What is a stateful firewall?

15. List the benefits of locating your firewall on the perimeter of a network.

16. What network information do attackers initially try to find?

17. List two reasons why a hardware firewall solution is a good choice compared with software-only solutions.

18. Which protocol is connectionless?

19. For what kinds of communication is a connectionless protocol useful?

20. What is a proxy server and what can it do?

Real World Exercises

Exercise 4-1

You are assigned by upper management to purchase a firewall and hardware, but first you have to prepare a report that (1) describes your organization's network, (2) lists three primary goals of a firewall, and (3) compares two different firewall packages that seem to be good options. Prepare the report based on your classroom's network.

Exercise 4-2

Create a diagram of your classroom's network. Be sure to determine where the network connects with the larger network—your school's network or the Internet. Indicate on the diagram where a firewall would go by drawing a miniature brick wall.

Hands-On Projects

Project 4-1

To get an idea of how vulnerable your computer is to attackers, go to one of the Web sites that run security tests on machines. If your lab computer is already equipped with a firewall, so much the better. Even if it is not equipped, you can get an idea of the kinds of sensitive information you need to protect. Follow these steps:

1. If your computer is not powered up, power it up now.

2. When the Log on to Windows dialog box appears, in the User Name text box, type **administrator.**

3. In the Password text box, type **password.** (If this does not work, ask your instructor for the password.)

4. Double-click the **Internet Explorer** icon on the desktop to start your browser.

5. In the Address box, type **www.securityspace.com/smysecure/index.html.**

6. Press **Enter.** The Security Space Security Audits page will appear in the browser window.

7. In order to run a free security scan on your workstation, you need to register with the site's owner, Security Space. Registration is free. Scroll down the page to the How to Order/Run Audit section. Under New User, enter your e-mail address, and then enter a username and password of your choosing. Deselect the two check boxes asking if you want to receive e-mail notifications from this site, and then click **Register.** A Member Services page appears, telling you your registration has been accepted and directing you to check your e-mail.

8. Open the program you usually use to receive e-mail. Retrieve the e-mail message with the subject line Member Services Registration Request, and click the link included in the e-mail message. A Member Services Web page appears stating that your registration has been confirmed.

9. In the Registered User section of the same Member Services page, enter the UserID and password you just created, and then click **Login.**

10. The Security Space Member Services page appears. Click the link **Security Audits**.

11. Scroll down the page and click **No Risk Audit**. Click the **Run Audit** button. In the Web page that appears, choose **No Risk Audit** from the Audit Type drop-down list.

12. Click **Begin Audit**. A Web page appears stating either that the test is being run or is in a queue behind other tests. Check your e-mail periodically for a message entitled Security Audit Alert. Open the message and click the link supplied in the body of the message. A Web page appears with a detailed report about any vulnerabilities found on your system.

Project 4-2

In this project, you install iptables for Red Hat Linux.

1. Log in to the Linux console using your normal user account.

2. At the command line, type **su –**. This command allows you to switch the user to the root account. You will be prompted to enter the root account's password.

3. During the typical installation of Red Hat Linux, iptables is installed by default. However, to check whether iptables is installed, run the following command from the command line: **rpm -q iptables**. If RPM Package Manager (RPM) returns a version number, then iptables is installed and you can skip the following step, because this project is complete.

4. If RPM returns the message indicating that the package named iptables is not installed, you must install iptables manually. For that, you will have to install the package. To do so, insert the Red Hat Linux installation CD (you may have to insert several of the installation CDs to complete the setup process) and enter the following commands at the command line:

```
mount -t iso9660 /dev/cdrom /mnt/cdrom
cd /mnt/cdrom
rpm -ivh iptables-1.2.5-3.i386.rpm
```

(Note: the file name might be different based on the version number included with your version of Red Hat Linux)

5. Again check whether iptables is installed by running the following command from the command line: **rpm -q iptables**. If RPM returns a version number, then iptables was installed successfully.

Project 4-3

In this project, you configure iptables to deny all incoming traffic but allow all outgoing traffic.

1. After installing iptables, log in to Linux console using your normal user account.

2. At the command line, type **su –** . This command allows you to switch the user to the root account. You will be prompted to enter the root account's password.

3. Type **iptables --flush**. What does this command do? Why is it important to run this command?

4. Next, set up the policy governing the incoming network traffic by typing **iptables -P INPUT DROP**.

5. Set up the policy governing the network traffic leaving your system by typing **iptables -P OUTPUT ACCEPT**. What is the difference between the ACCEPT and DROP options? Are there other options to use?

6. Type **iptables -P FORWARD DROP**. What network routing behavior does the FORWARD policy control?

7. After you have made the configuration changes, run the command **ping google.com** (or use another remote host or IP address) from your Linux workstation. Do you receive a response? Why or why not?

8. Try pinging the network address of your Linux workstation from another system. Do you receive a response? Why or why not? (Note: to list the IP address of your Linux workstation, type **ifconfig**.)

 When running iptables, you may encounter an error similar to the following: "/lib/modules/2.4.17-0.1/kernel/net/ipv4/netfilter/ip_tables.o: init_module: Device or resource busy." This may occur if both firewall packages, the ipchains and the iptables, are started at the same time. To fix the problem, run the following command: **chkconfig—del ipchains**. Then, reboot your Linux workstation.

Project 4-4

In this hands-on project, you configure iptables to simulate a firewall that only allows incoming network traffic to the organization's Web servers.

1. After installing iptables, log in to the Linux console using your normal user account.

2. At the command line, type **su - **. This command allows you to switch user to the root account. You will be prompted to enter the root account's password.

3. Type **iptables -A INPUT -p tcp --destination-port 80 -j ACCEPT**. What does the –j command line option do?

4. Type **iptables -A INPUT -p tcp --destination-port 443 -j ACCEPT**. Why is it necessary to allow traffic over both ports 80 and 443? What option would you use to open UDP ports 80 and 443?

5. To view the rules in effect for iptables, type **iptables --list or iptables -L**. What is the current output?

Project 4-5

In this project, you configure iptables to block a certain IP address. This exercise demonstrates a situation in which a visitor is abusing his or her access to your Web site. In order to prevent access, the abuser's IP address is blocked at the iptables firewall.

1. After installing iptables, log in to the Linux console using your normal user account.

2. At the command line, type **su - **. This command allows you to switch the user to the root account. You will be prompted to enter the root account's password.

3. Type **iptables –A INPUT –s 192.168.100.50 tcp --destination-port 80 –j DROP**. What does the –s command line option do? How would you block a range of IP addresses? In what situations would this command be useful?

4. How would you block network traffic *destined* for a specific IP address?

Project 4-6

In this project, you review your network configuration.

1. Log in to the Linux console using your normal user account.

2. At the command line, type **su –** . This command allows you to switch the user to the root account. You will be prompted to enter the root account's password.

3. Type **ifconfig**. Write down the following information:

   • Your network card's MAC address

   • Your workstation's IP address

   • Your workstation's default network mask

Based on this information, on what class of IP network does your workstation participate (e.g., Class C)? How many other systems can participate on the same network?

Endnotes

1. National Institute of Standards and Technology, "Guidelines on Firewalls and Firewall Policy." September 2009. Accessed November 27, 2011 from *csrc.nist.gov/publications/nistpubs/800-41-Rev1/sp800-41-rev1.pdf*.

2. Cisco Systems, Inc. "Access Control Lists and IP Fragments." August 10, 2005. Accessed November 27, 2011 from *www.cisco.com/en/US/tech/tk827/tk369/technologies_white_paper09186a00800949b8.shtml*.

3. National Institute of Standards and Technology, "Guidelines on Firewalls and Firewall Policy." September 2009. Accessed November 28, 2011 from *csrc.nist.gov/publications/nistpubs/800-41-Rev1/sp800-41-rev1.pdf*.

4. Wack, John. "Keeping Your Site Comfortably Secure: An Introduction to Internet Firewalls." 16 Oct 2002. Accessed 7 March 2007 from *www.windowsecurity.com/whitepaper/Keeping_Your_Site_Comfortably_Secure__Introduction_to_Firewalls.html*.

5. SC Magazine. "2011 SC Awards U.S. Finalists." Accessed November 27, 2011 from *www.scmagazineus.com/2011-sc-awards-us-finalists/section/1908/*.

6. Wikipedia. "Virtual Server Appliance." Accessed November 27, 2011 from *en.wikipedia.org/wiki/Virtual_security_appliance*.

7. VMWare. "Virtual Appliances: Virtual Firewall." Accessed November 27, 2011 from *www.vmware.com/appliances/directory/cat/5863*.

8. *PC Magazine*. "The Best 2012 Security Suites." Accessed November 27, 2011 from *www.pcmag.com/article2/0,2817,2369749,00.asp*.

9. Greenberg, Andy. "'Millions' of Home Routers Vulnerable to Web Hack." Forbes.com. July 13, 2010. Accessed November 27, 2011 from *www.forbes.com/sites/firewall/2010/07/13/millions-of-home-routers-vulnerable-to-web-hack/*.

10. Microsoft Corporation. "Windows Firewall." Accessed November 27, 2011 from *technet.microsoft.com/en-us/network/bb545423*.

11. Apple Inc. "Mac OS X v10.5, 10.6: About the Application Firewall." Accessed November 27, 2011 from *support.apple.com/kb/ht1810*.

12. Netfilter.org. "What can I do with netfilter/iptables?" Accessed November 27, 2011 from *www.netfilter.org*.

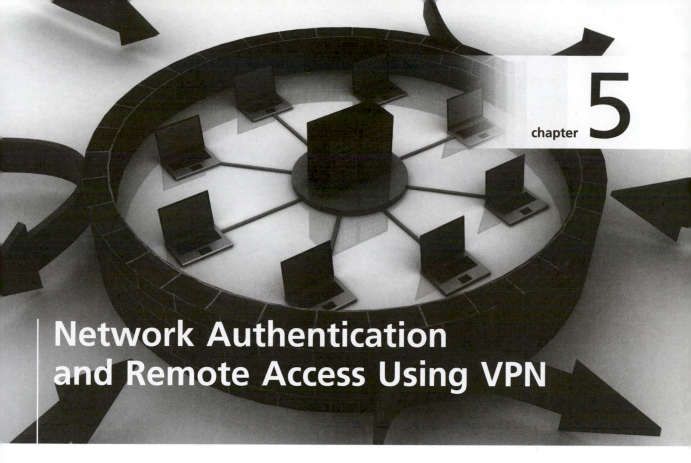

chapter 5

Network Authentication and Remote Access Using VPN

The whole notion of passwords is based on an oxymoron. The idea is to have a random string that is easy to remember. Unfortunately, if it's easy to remember, it's something nonrandom like "Susan." And if it's random, like "r7U2*Qnp," then it's not easy to remember. — Bruce Schneier

Upon completion of this material, you should be able to:

- Define access control and identify the various ways it can be implemented
- Explain why authentication is a critical aspect of network access control
- Identify the component parts of virtual private networks (VPNs)
- List and define the essential activities that an VPN must be able to perform
- Explain the various VPN architectures in common use

Strong Authentication; Weak Business Case

The PCI audit preparation was continuing at EBS. As part of the PCI prep, Paige Davis worried about usernames and passwords. A large number of the Sales staff and other traveling workers needed to access EBS remotely via the company's virtual private network (VPN). Strictly enforced password policies for accessing the network remotely had resulted in users writing down their passwords on sticky notes that they attached to their computer monitors or on pieces of paper they tacked to the bulletin board. On the other hand, lax password policies would give abusers an open door to the company's user accounts. It seemed there was no easy answer... until Paige discovered two-factor authentication.

With two-factor authentication, employees could authenticate themselves to EBS's VPN using a password and a code displayed randomly by a key token. Employees would still have user IDs; however, they would also need (1) something they knew (i.e., their passwords) and (2) something they had (i.e., the key tokens)—the two factors. Given that it would cost around $25 per workstation, the plan seemed reasonable.

It was reasonable to Paige, anyway. To authenticate the 500 users at EBS using key tokens, the cost would be a mere $12,500. When Paige eagerly presented the plan to the EBS CIO for approval, however, the CIO just as eagerly denied the request and declared that usernames and passwords were sufficient security controls. "Why do business concerns always win?" Paige asked herself, glumly. The battle for secure authentication remained to be won.

Introduction

Unlike some strategies used to secure information systems, network security strategies authenticate machines rather than individuals. For example, a firewall filters traffic based on a machine's IP address, not on the end user sending or receiving that traffic. Some network security devices—for example, Network Access Control (NAC) and virtual private network (VPN) access controllers—can perform a stronger level of authentication. That is, they typically deploy stronger authentication mechanisms to determine whether persons or entities are who they claim to be. This level of authentication is important because if an unauthorized user gains access to protected resources, the whole purpose of the firewall has been defeated. For this reason, many network devices implement user authentication schemes to support their other security approaches.

In this chapter, you will learn what authentication is and why it is important to network security in general. Because passwords are a critical part of all the aforementioned authentication schemes, you'll explore password security issues and learn about special password security tools, including one-time passwords. Then you'll learn how and why network security devices perform authentication services. This chapter also introduces the main types of authentication performed by network security devices—client, user, and session authentication—as well as the different types of centralized authentication methods that network security devices can use, including Kerberos, TACACS+, and RADIUS.

VPNs function like private leased lines: They encapsulate and encrypt the data being transmitted, and they use authentication to ensure that only approved users can access the VPN. However, rather than using an expensive leased line, VPNs provide a means of secure point-to-point communications over the public Internet. In this chapter, you will also learn the role VPNs play in providing remote access to end users.

5

Access Control

Access control enables organizations to restrict access to information, information assets, and other tangible assets to those who have a bona fide business need. Access controls regulate the admission of users into trusted areas of the organization—both logical access to the information systems and physical access to the organization's facilities. Access control is maintained by means of a collection of policies, programs to carry out those policies, and technologies that enforce those policies. Access control comprises four processes: obtaining the identity of the entity that requests access to a logical or physical area (**identification**), confirming the identity of the entity that seeks access to a logical or physical area (**authentication**), determining which actions an authenticated entity can perform in that physical or logical area (**authorization**), and documenting the activities of the authenticated individual and systems (**accountability**).

We will cover accountability in more detail in Chapter 10, "Auditing and Logging."

Access control is built on several key principles, including:

- **Least privilege**—This is the principle by which members of the organization are allowed to access the minimal amount of information for the minimal amount of time necessary to perform their required duties. Under this principle, users are given access appropriate to the level required for their assigned duties. For example, if a task requires only the reading of data, the user is given read-only access, which does not allow the creation, updating, or deletion of data.

- **Need to know**—This principle limits a user's access to the specific information required to perform the currently assigned task, not some category of data required for a general work function. For example, a manager who needs to change a specific employee's pay rate is granted access to read and update that data but is restricted from accessing pay data for other employees. This principle is most frequently associated with data classification.

- **Separation of duties**—This principle requires that tasks be split up in such a way that more than one individual is responsible for their completion. For example, in accounts payable situations, one person may set up a vendor, another may request payments for the vendor, and a third may authorize the payments. Separation of duties reduces the chance of an individual violating information security policy and breaching the confidentiality, integrity, and availability of the information.

Categories of Access Control

There are a number of ways to categorize access controls. One way is by their functional characteristics, each control falling into one of the following categories:

- Deterrent—Discourages or deters an incipient incident
- Preventative—Helps an organization avoid an incident
- Detective—Detects or identifies an incident or threat when it occurs
- Corrective—Remedies a circumstance or mitigates the damage done during an incident
- Recovery—Restores operating conditions to normal
- Compensating—Resolves shortcomings[1]

A second approach, described in the NIST Special Publication SP800-12 (*http://csrc.nist.gov/publications/PubsSPs.html*), categorizes security controls into three general classes:

- Management—"Techniques and concerns that are normally addressed by management in the organization's computer security program. In general, they focus on the management of the computer security program and the management of risk within the organization."

- Operational (or administrative)—"Controls that are … implemented and executed by people (as opposed to systems). These controls are put in place to improve the security of a particular system (or group of systems). They often require technical or specialized expertise and often rely upon management activities as well as technical controls."

- Technical—"Controls that the computer system executes. These controls are dependent upon the proper functioning of the system for their effectiveness. The implementation of technical controls, however, always requires significant operational considerations and should be consistent with the management of security within the organization."[2]

Table 5-1 shows examples of controls categorized by both the approaches just described.

A third approach categorizes controls by the degree of flexibility under which they are applied. Controls can be mandatory, discretionary, or nondiscretionary; each category regulates access to a particular type or collection of information.

Mandatory Access Controls A **mandatory access control (MAC)** is one in which the computer system enforces the controls without the input or intervention of the system or data owner. In order to implement MAC, a strict user and data classification scheme is required. For example, if data is classified as "Super Sensitive," then the user must also have been through the proper administrative procedures to be allowed access to data

	Deterrent	Preventative	Detective	Corrective	Recovery	Compensating
Management	Policies	Registration procedures	Periodic violation report reviews	Employee or account termination	Disaster recovery plan	Separation of duties, job rotation
Operational	Warning signs	Gates, fences, and guards	Sentries, CCTVs	Fire suppression systems	Disaster recovery procedures	Defense in depth
Technical	Warning banners	Login systems, Kerberos	Log monitors and IDPSs	Forensics procedures	Data backups	Key logging and keystroke monitoring

Table 5-1 **Examples of Controls Categorized by Operational Level and Functional Characteristics**
Source: Official (ISC)2 Guide to the CISSP CBK
© Cengage Learning 2013

rated as "Super Sensitive." These ratings are often referred to as sensitivity levels. When MACs are implemented, users and data owners have little to no control over setting access to information resources.

U.S. Military Classification Scheme The U.S. Department of Defense (DoD) is perhaps the best-known user of data classification schemes that assign MAC sensitivity levels. In fact, many developments in data communications and information security are the result of military-sponsored research and development. As you might expect, military classification schemes rely on a more complex set of sensitivity levels than those at most corporations. For most of its information, the military uses a five-level classification scheme that is defined in Executive Order 12958:

- *Unclassified data—Generally free for distribution to the public; poses no threat to U.S. national interests.*

- *Sensitive but unclassified (SBU) data—Any information of which the loss, misuse, or unauthorized access to, or modification of, might adversely affect U.S. national interests, the conduct of Department of Defense (DoD) programs, or the privacy of DoD personnel. Common designations include For Official Use Only, Not for Public Release, or For Internal Use Only.*

- *Confidential data—Any information or material the unauthorized disclosure of which reasonably could be expected to cause damage to the national security. Examples of damage include the compromise of information that indicates strength of ground, air, and naval forces in the United States and overseas areas; disclosure of technical information used for training, maintenance, and inspection of classified munitions of war; and revelation of performance characteristics, test data, design, and production data on munitions of war.*

- *Secret data—Any information or material the unauthorized disclosure of which reasonably could be expected to cause serious damage to the national security. Examples of serious damage include disruption of foreign relations significantly affecting the national security; significant impairment of a program or policy directly related to the national security; revelation of significant military plans or intelligence operations; compromise of significant military plans or intelligence operations; and compromise of significant scientific or technological developments relating to national security.*

- *Top secret data—Any information or material the unauthorized disclosure of which reasonably could be expected to cause exceptionally grave damage to the national security. Examples of exceptionally grave damage include armed hostilities against the United States or its allies; disruption of foreign relations vitally affecting the national security; the compromise of vital national defense plans or complex cryptologic and communications intelligence systems; the revelation of sensitive intelligence operations; and the disclosure of scientific or technological developments vital to national security. This classification comes with the general expectation of "cradle to grave" protection, meaning that individuals entrusted with top secret information are expected to honor the classification of the information for life, even after they are no longer employed in the role that originally allowed them to access the information.[3]*

These data classifications are then applied to data to ensure the optimal level of protection. In concert, the personnel security clearance structure ensures that each user of an information asset is assigned an authorization level that identifies the level of information classification he or she can access. Individuals who then need to access the data must also hold the same security clearance level to access the data. For example, an employee must hold a personal security clearance level of Top Secret in order to access Top Secret information. Thus, the scheme enforces a MAC model that does not allow flexibility of data access based on individuals or data.

The military further divides information into compartments to ensure that only individuals with the "Need to Know" can access information, regardless of the information's data classification level. There are also specialty classification ratings, such as Personnel Information and Evaluation Reports, to protect related areas of information. Federal agencies such as the FBI and CIA also use specialty classification schemes, such as Need-to-Know and Named Projects. Obviously, Need-to-Know authorization allows access to information by individuals who need the information to perform their work. Named Projects are clearance levels based on a scheme similar to Need-to-Know. When an operation, project, or set of classified data is created, the project is assigned a code name. Next, a list of authorized individuals is created and assigned to either the Need-to-Know or the Named Projects category.

Discretionary Access Controls Discretionary access controls (DACs) are implemented at the discretion of the data owner. Sharing resources in a peer-to-peer configuration allows users to control access to information or resources at their disposal. This can mean allowing general, unrestricted access, or it can mean allowing specific individuals or sets of individuals to access these resources. For example, suppose that a user has a hard drive containing information to be shared with office coworkers. This user can allow specific individuals to access this drive by listing their names in the share control function. Most personal computer operating systems use the DAC model.

An example of a DAC model is an access control matrix, which arranges users in rows and objects in columns. At the intersections of each row and column, an individual user's rights are specified. As shown in Figure 5-1, each business unit's shared file directory is a column (these are called objects) and the users are listed as rows (these are called subjects). The intersection of each row and column identifies the access rights for that subject for that object. This type of table can be easily checked to determine which user has access to which object.

	Finance Shared Files	HR Shared Files	IT Shared Files	Legal Shared Files	Manufacturing Shared Files
John	r	rwx		r	
Stephanie			rwx		r
Steve					rwx
Jennifer	r	r		rwx	
Todd	rwx	r			

Access Legend:
r = Read
w = Write
x = Execute

Figure 5-1 Sample access control matrix
© Cengage Learning 2013

Another example of a DAC model is rule-based access controls, in which access to information is granted based on a set of rules specified by a central authority. This is a DAC model because the individual user is the one who decides which rules apply. Role-based models, described in the following section, can also be implemented under DAC if an individual system owner wants to create the rules for other users of that system or its data.

Nondiscretionary Controls Nondiscretionary controls are determined by a central authority and can be either role-based access controls (RBAC) or task-based controls. Task-based controls can, in turn, be based on lists maintained on either subjects or objects. Role-based controls are tied to the role that a particular user performs in an organization, whereas task-based controls are tied to a particular assignment or responsibility.

Using role- and task-based controls makes it easier to maintain access permissions and restrictions, especially if the person performing the role or task changes often. Instead of constantly assigning and revoking the privileges of people who come and go, the administrator simply assigns the associated access rights to the role or task. The person assigned to that role or task automatically receives the corresponding access. The administrator can easily remove people's associations with roles and tasks, thereby revoking their access.

Other Forms of Access Control Access control is developing rapidly, both in the principles it's based on and the technology that is used. Other forms of access control include:

- Content-dependent—Making access to specific information dependent on its content. For example, the marketing department might be given access to marketing data, the accounting department is given access to accounting data, and so forth.

- Constrained user interfaces—Restricting what information an individual user can access. The most common example is a bank's automated teller machine (ATM), which restricts authorized users to simple account queries, transfers, deposits, and withdrawals.

- Temporal (time-based) isolation—Putting a time-of-day constraint on information access. An example is a time-release safe, found in most convenience and fast-food establishments. The safe can only be opened during a specific time frame, even if by an authorized user (e.g., the store manager).

 Should access controls be centralized or decentralized? A collection of users who have access to the same data typically has a centralized access control authority, even under a discretionary access control model. The level of centralization varies by organization and by the type of information being protected. The less critical the protected information, the more decentralized the controls tend to be. When critical information assets are being protected, the use of a highly centralized access control toolset is indicated.

Identification

Identification is the process by which a computer system recognizes a user's identity.[4] Most often, identification is performed by means of a user account. In network security, accounts are stored in one of two places:

- Local accounts—A server maintains a local file of usernames and passwords to which it refers for matching the username-password pair being supplied by a client. This is the most common form of authentication, the weakness of which is that passwords can be forgotten, stolen, or accidentally revealed, thus compromising the user's account.

- Centralized accounts—A centralized server handles user accounts for a number of different systems on the network. For example, Microsoft's Active Directory (AD) provides a centralized mechanism whereby users can authenticate themselves once to their user account but gain access to multiple network and server resources.

Default Accounts All operating systems come with a preinstalled user account (or accounts). This account—for example, "root" in the UNIX operating system or "administrator" in Windows operating systems—generally has administrative access to the system and is used to create additional accounts. Attackers know which default accounts are included with an operating system, so these accounts need to be renamed. By doing so, you force attackers to spend more time discerning or guessing a username.

In addition, a large number of applications use a default user account when the application needs to log into the operating system. Default application usernames can also be determined quite easily from the manufacturer's documentation. Like default operating system accounts, application user accounts should be renamed to make intrusion more difficult for abusers.

Because of the high level of access and control that these accounts have over the operating system, system administrators should take every precaution to protect these accounts, including the use of strong passwords, as discussed later in this chapter.

Periodic Reviews Network administrators should periodically review user accounts. There are two types of checks. One check determines if the employee still works at the company. (If the employee is not found in the company's human resources system, the account can be removed or disabled for a period of time and later removed.) The other check determines if the employee still requires an account on a particular system or application. This requires more user intervention because the owning user or manager must validate that the business need still exists.

Authentication

Authentication is the act of confirming the identity or user account. Once the identity is confirmed as authentic, that user is authorized to perform specific actions on the system or network. Potential users (sometimes called supplicants) first propose an identity (a process known as **identification**) and then verify (or authenticate) that identity by providing some combination of the following:

- Something you know—A piece of information known to the supplicant, such as a password or passphrase
- Something you have—Proof of physical possession of something, such as a **smart card** (a plastic card with an embedded microchip that can store data about the owner) or a metal key
- Something you are—A piece of information that indicates something about the supplicant's physical nature. This piece of information can refer to a physical attribute (a fingerprint or an iris scan) or it can rely on pattern recognition (a voiceprint or a keyboard typing pattern).

Most commonly, authentication is completed by requiring a user to enter a password at some point, which, if that is all that is required, is an example of **single-factor authentication**. The user needs to know only one item (the password) to initiate the authentication process.

Physical objects such as smart cards or other kinds of physical **tokens** offer the more stringent level of two-factor authentication in which users need to have something (the token) and know something (the PIN or password) to gain access. For example, you withdraw cash from a debit account with a bank card. Along with the card (something you have), you also need to enter a PIN (something you know) to authenticate yourself to the bank's network. After you are authenticated, the ATM gives you access to your account. An authentication system that, like the bank ATM example, uses two different forms of confirmation for the proposed identity is known as **strong authentication** or **two-factor authentication**.

Biometrics (retinal scans, fingerprints, and the like) are mainly used for authentication by large security-minded entities such as banking institutions and credit card centers for regulating access to sensitive information, but biometrics are also gaining ground in the general corporate world.

Password Security Issues

Many authentication systems depend in part or entirely on passwords. In fact, the simplest forms of authentication require typing a username and a reusable password. The following sections discuss password security issues that you need to be aware of to prevent your network from being accessed by unauthorized users.

Cracking The traditional access control mechanism consists of both a username and a password. However, because system administrators tend to follow some sort of standard convention (e.g., first initial and last name—jdoe), usernames are usually easy to guess. Defending access control, therefore, rests with protecting the password.

The generally accepted definition of **cracking** refers to guessing, breaking, and/or stealing passwords to gain access to a system or application. Usually, once a password is obtained, the attacker logs in by impersonating an authorized user. Most operating systems and applications use a password scheme that takes a user account's password, passes it through a hash algorithm, and stores it somewhere on the system. The purpose of the hash is to transform the password into an unreadable format that makes it impossible to reverse the transformation back into the original password text.

To obtain passwords, crackers try dictionary and brute force attacks. A **dictionary attack** throws every known word (sometimes in many languages) into the authentication system until something matches what's stored on the system. For example, using "fox" as a password presents a problem because it is only three characters long and is a common animal name. A dictionary attack against this password would succeed in a very short time.

A **brute-force attack** tries every possible character, number, and symbol combination to guess the password. These processes are time-intensive, so they are rarely aimed at the target system in general. Instead, crackers steal the password files from the target systems, crack the passwords on their local systems, and then use the stolen passwords to log into the target system.

Crackers can also use published **rainbow tables** to help with password lookups. Rainbow tables contain hash outputs for a myriad of different password combinations using different hash algorithms. These tables can save time because the cracker can look up a suspected password, get the hash output from the rainbow table, and then see if that hash output occurs within the password file.

Security professionals who lecture on the need for password complexity are trying to prevent cracking attacks. The more characters and combinations of letters, numbers, and symbols that a password contains, the more difficult it is to carry out a cracking attack. Password complexity should be required by a company's security policy and included within the password policies of computer and network systems.

Password Policies To protect against cracking, each password must be hard to guess, must be changed often, and must be used by only one person. Luckily, most network devices and systems accommodate policies that restrict the configuration of passwords by creating a

password policy. The following password policy guidelines help enforce password confidentiality by making attacks too time-consuming to attempt. Passwords should:

- Be at least eight characters long
- Contain at least one uppercase character
- Contain at least one lowercase character
- Contain at least one number
- Contain at least one symbol (#,$, %, ^, &, etc.)
- Contain no part of the user's name
- Contain no words commonly found in a dictionary
- Contain no repeating characters
- Be combined with a **salt** when calculating hashes. A salt is a secret value that is combined with the plaintext password to create the final stored password hash. That way, even if the password file is stolen, rainbow tables can't be used to reverse-engineer the value.

A password policy should also have a number of restrictions. The login policy should require that the password system do the following:

- Force users to change passwords at a minimum of every 90 days.
- Remember, at minimum, 10 previous passwords used on that system so that the user cannot reuse old passwords when it's time to change them.
- Lock accounts after, say, three to five invalid login attempts.
- Disable accounts when the lockout threshold has been met, after which users must be required to contact a help desk or administrator to reset the account.

Lax Security   Lax security practices can also contribute to compromised passwords. Things to avoid include:

- Using simple passwords or words that are easy to remember
- Storing passwords on pieces of paper displayed in readily visible areas
- Using the same password to access different systems
- Sharing passwords with others

The chance that passwords will be guessed can be reduced by telling users to choose passwords that are not words contained in the dictionary (e.g., "purple"), simple keyboard tricks (e.g., "qwerty"), or memorable dates (e.g., your birthday.) A simple trick is to use a combination of words and a number that's complicated enough not to be guessed easily (e.g., "purple1qwerty").

Another option is to have users use passphrases, which are similar to passwords but longer. Like passwords, passphrases should not simply consist of a combination of dictionary words, and they should contain uppercase and lowercase characters, numeric values, and special characters. For example, you could make the basis of your passphrase "Go Bama, Roll Tide!" but remove the spaces and replace some of the characters with numeric values and special characters, leaving you with the passphrase "G0Bama,R0ll+1d3!"

Users should also be told to memorize the passwords rather than write them down and to never reveal their passwords to anyone, even though recent developments in PDA and smartphone applications allow users to securely store system information in an encrypted format without additional concern for disclosure.

One-Time Password Software The risks introduced by poor password management can be offset by passwords that are generated for one-time use during a single session and then discarded. Three types are available:

- Challenge-response passwords—Each time the user logs in, the authenticating computer or firewall generates a new random number (the challenge) and sends it to the user, who enters a secret PIN or password (the response). If the challenge and PIN or password match the information stored on the authenticating server, the user gains access.

- Password list passwords—The user enters a seed phrase, and the password system generates a list of passwords the user can use. The user picks one from the list and submits it along with the seed phrase to gain access.

- Token generators—An even higher level of security is realized by firewalls that work with hardware devices called token generators, which automatically generate and display the next password the user types.

Implementing Authentication

Most operating systems are equipped with authentication schemes. Web servers can be configured to authenticate clients who want to access certain protected content. Firewalls and VPN access controllers can also perform **user authentication**. In fact, many organizations depend on these devices to provide more secure authentication than conventional systems. Authentication is a key function because firewalls exist to give external users (such as mobile users and telecommuters) access to protected resources.

Authentication comes into play when a network security device such as a firewall is called upon to apply its set of rules to specific individuals or groups of users. For instance, the IT staff may need remote access to all the computers in the organization; thus, a higher level of security is needed to ensure that only the proper individuals are granted such a level of access. On the other hand, the head of a company's accounting department may need remote access to the company once a quarter or once a year—not frequently enough to warrant the establishment of a dedicated network connection.

A firewall uses authentication to identify individuals so that it can apply rules that have been associated with those individuals. Some firewalls use authentication to give employees access to common resources, such as the Web or file transfer protocol (FTP). Some identify the user associated with a particular IP address; after the user is authorized, the IP address can then be used to send and receive information between hosts on the internal network.

The exact steps that firewalls follow to authenticate users may vary, but the general process is as follows:

1. The client makes a request to access a resource.
2. The firewall intercepts the request and prompts the user for name and password.

3. The user submits the requested information to the firewall.

4. The user is authenticated.

5. The request is checked against the firewall's rule base.

6. If the request matches an existing allow rule, the user is granted access.

7. The user accesses the desired resources.

The "plain English" version of the exchange between external client and authenticating firewall is illustrated in Figure 5-2.

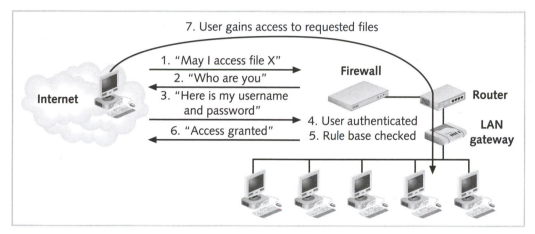

Figure 5-2 Basic user authentication
© Cengage Learning 2013

User Authentication Some firewalls provide for a variety of authentication methods. User authentication is the simplest type and the one with which you are most likely to be familiar. Upon receiving a request, a program prompts the user for a username and password. When the information is submitted, the software checks the information against a list of user-names and passwords in its database. If a match is made, the user is authenticated.

User authentication can enable the following users to access your internal servers:

- Remote or work-at-home employees
- Traveling employees
- Contractors
- Guests or visitors with a genuine "need to know"
- Special employees: interns, temporary, or conditional employees
- Employees of partner companies
- Members of the public who need to get into your internal network to make purchases, change contact information, or review account information

Authorized users should be added to your **access control lists (ACLs)**. An ACL is a list of authorization rights attached to an object—in other words, who can access that device or application and what can they do with it. These can be organized by directory or even by individual files, but most often they are organized by groups of users because this simplifies administration. How you organize the ACL depends on how many users you have, how many resources you need to protect, and how much time you have to administer the ACL.

Client Authentication   Of course, not every outside user should gain access to everything on the network. Client authentication can help you establish limits to user access. **Client authentication** is similar to user authentication but with the addition of usage limits. The firewall enables the authenticated user to access the desired resources for a specific period of time (e.g., one hour) or for a specific number of times.

To configure client authentication, the administrator needs to set up one of two types of authentication systems:

- **Standard sign-on**—The client, after being authenticated, is allowed to access whatever resources the user needs to perform any desired functions, such as transferring files or viewing Web pages.

- **Specific sign-on**—The client must authenticate each time it accesses a server or uses a service on the protected network.

Network Access Control (NAC)   As the threats posed by internal users on local networks grow, IT organizations have turned to **Network Access Control** (**NAC**) technologies to help solve the problem of verifying the security of various endpoints that connect to the local network. This client authentication technology intercepts attempts to access the network and scans the system to determine the security of the system. If the system meets the internal security policy, the system is then allowed to connect to the network.

Although there are a number of different NAC technologies on the market, the basic idea behind NAC is that before a device is allowed to communicate on a network, it must first prove that it:

- Has authorized user credentials needed to access the network
- Has the appropriate security tools installed
- Has the appropriate system configuration
- Has OS patches installed and software versions that are up to date
- Complies with established security standards (e.g., no P2P software installed)

Once the endpoint is verified as meeting the NAC thresholds, the system can communicate on the wireless or local network with the typical network access. If, however, the endpoint does not pass these initial tests, the system is denied access or quarantined on a special subnet, where it can access the appropriate security remediation software and instructions.

Session Authentication   **Session authentication** requires authentication whenever a client system attempts to connect to a network resource and establish a session (a period when communications are exchanged). Session authentication can be used with any service. The client system wishing to be authenticated is usually equipped with a software agent that enables the authentication process; the server or firewall detects the agent when the connection request is made. When necessary, the firewall intercepts the connection request and contacts the agent. The agent performs the authentication, and the firewall allows the connection to the required resource.

Some advanced firewalls offer multiple authentication methods. Which one should you choose? It depends on the client operating system and the applications you need to authenticate. Choose user authentication if the protocols that you want authorized users to use include FTP, HTTP, HTTPS, rlogin, or Telnet. Choose client authentication or session authentication when only a single user will be coming from a single IP address. Table 5-2 gives the reasons for using each authentication method.

Method	Use When...
User Authentication	• You want to scan the content of IP packets. • The protocol in use is HTTP, HTTPS, FTP rlogin, or Telnet. • You need to authenticate for each session separately.
Client Authentication	• The user to be authenticated will use a specific IP address. • The protocol in use is not HTTP, HTTPS, FTP, rlogin, or Telnet. • You want a user to be authenticated for a specific length of time.
Session Authentication	• The individual user to be authenticated will come from a specific IP address. • The protocol in use is not HTTP, HTTPS, FTP, rlogin or Telnet. • You want a client to be authenticated for each session.

Table 5-2 Authentication Methods
© Cengage Learning 2013

Centralized Authentication

Large corporations often develop complex sets of security requirements that are difficult to maintain and require different types of authentication control for different purposes. Fortunately, deploying a centralized authentication server can greatly simplify such enterprise-wide authentication. This centralized server maintains all the authorizations for users regardless of where a user is located and how the user connects to the network.

In a centralized authentication setup, a server—sometimes referred to as an **authentication, authorization, and auditing (or accountability) (AAA) server**—alleviates the need to provide each server on the network with a separate database of usernames and passwords, each of which has to be updated every time a password changes or a user is added. The process of centralized authentication is illustrated in Figure 5-3. It begins with a client on a local network requesting access to a program held on an application server. First, though, the client must be authenticated using the authentication server. Two levels of trust are involved: The client trusts that the authentication server holds the correct information, and the application server trusts that the authentication server can correctly identify and authorize the client. The scenario illustrated in Figure 5-3 has a substantial downside: The authentication server becomes a single point of failure. Organizations that use this method should have contingency plans for getting the server back online or should have alternative servers to limit downtime.

Centralized authentication can use a number of different authentication methods. The following sections examine some of the most common ones, including Kerberos, TACACS+, and RADIUS.

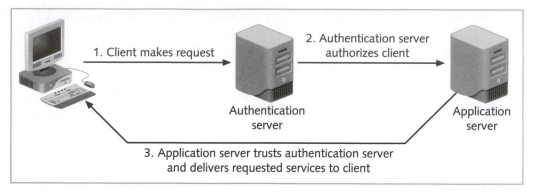

Figure 5-3 Centralized authentication
© Cengage Learning 2013

Kerberos Developed at MIT, **Kerberos** is designed to provide authentication and encryption on standard clients and servers. Instead of a server having to trust a client over an untrusted network, both client and server place their trust in the Kerberos server. Kerberos provides an effective network authentication system that is used internally on Windows 7 and Windows XP systems. It also has backward compatibility with Microsoft's NTLM protocol, which is used in Windows NT 4.0 and earlier. Although Kerberos is useful for authentication to a local system, care must be taken when authenticating via a Kerberos system on the network. As in all situations regarding the passing of credentials on the network, proper steps must be taken to ensure they are not passed in plaintext. Remote users should make use of encrypted transmissions or one-time passwords, which are discussed later in this chapter.

The Kerberos system of granting access to a client that requests a service is quite involved (and thus quite secure). The steps are as follows:

1. The client requests a file or other service.

2. The client is prompted for a username and password.

3. The client submits a username and password. The request goes to a Kerberos Authentication Server (AS) that is part of the Kerberos system. The AS creates an encrypted code called a **session key** that is based on the client's password plus a random number associated with the service being requested. The session key functions as a ticket-granting ticket (TGT).

4. AS grants the TGT.

5. The client presents the TGT to a ticket-granting server (TGS), which is also part of the Kerberos system and that may or may not be the same server as the AS.

6. The TGS grants a session ticket. The TGS forwards the session ticket to the server holding the requested file or service.

7. The client gains access.

The Kerberos authentication server is also known as a key distribution center (KDC). In Windows networks, a domain controller also functions as an authentication server. The Kerberos server must be highly secured because of the strong level of trust placed in it.

One great advantage of using the Kerberos ticket system is that passwords are not stored on the system and, thus, cannot be intercepted by hackers. The tickets issued are specific to the individual user who made the request and to the services the user is attempting to access. Tickets have a time limit (typically, eight hours, although this can be configured by the security administrator). Before a ticket expires, the client may make additional requests using the same ticket without reauthenticating itself. Another advantage is that Kerberos is widely used in the UNIX environment, which enables authentication to take place across operating systems—for example, a Windows client can be authenticated by a UNIX server, or vice versa. The authentication process is illustrated in Figure 5-4. You can download trial versions of both the Kerberos client and server from the MIT Kerberos Distribution page at *http://web.mit.edu/Kerberos/dist/index.html*.

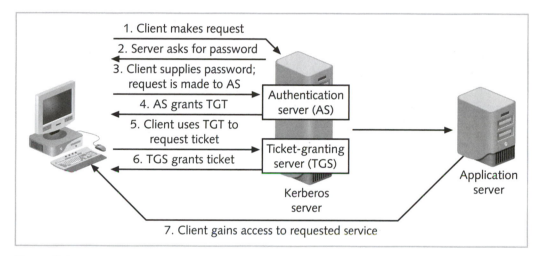

Figure 5-4 Kerberos authentication
© Cengage Learning 2013

TACACS+ **Terminal Access Controller Access Control System Plus (TACACS+)**—commonly called "tac-plus"—is the latest and strongest version of a set of authentication protocols developed by Cisco Systems. TACACS+ replaces its less secure predecessor protocols, TACACS and XTACACS. TACACS+ and its predecessor protocols all provide authentication for dial-in users and are used primarily on UNIX-based networks. TACACS+ uses the **MD5 algorithm** (a hash algorithm developed in 1991 by Ron Rivest of RSA that produces a 128-bit code called a message digest) to encrypt data.

It provides centralized authentication services so that a network access server such as a router or firewall doesn't have to handle dial-in user authentication. An organization might have to use TACACS+ or RADIUS (described in the following section) if its firewall doesn't support authentication or if its authentication needs are so extensive that they might slow down other tasks the firewall is called on to perform. For more information about the MD5 algorithm and other security tools, visit the Internet RFC repository site at *http://www.ietf.org/rfc/rfc1321.txt*.

Remote Authentication Dial-In User Service (RADIUS) **Remote Authentication Dial-In User Service (RADIUS)** is the other common protocol used to provide dial-in authentication. Note that RADIUS still transmits unencrypted authentication packets across the network, which means they are vulnerable to attacks from packet sniffers. RADIUS is generally considered to provide a lower level of security than TACACS+, even though it's more widely supported.

TACACS+ and RADIUS Compared If you authenticate users who connect to your network from remote locations, chances are you'll use either TACACS+ or RADIUS. Table 5-3 compares the two protocols.

TACACS+	RADIUS
Uses TCP	Uses UDP
Full packet encryption between client and server	Encrypts only passwords—other information is unencrypted
Independent authentication, authorization, and auditing	Combines authentication and authorization
Passwords in the database may be encrypted	Passwords in the database are in cleartext

Table 5-3 **Characteristics of TACACS+ and RADIUS**
© Cengage Learning 2013

As you can tell from Table 5-3, TACACS+ provides stronger security than RADIUS. TCP, which TACACS+ uses, is considered more secure than UDP, an alternative network communications protocol, because when a host sends a TCP packet, it expects a packet to be sent in response, with the ACK bit to show that a connection has been established. ACK (for acknowledgement), which is one of the flags in the TCP header part of a packet, indicates that the destination computer has received the packets that were previously sent. UDP, in contrast, is considered "connectionless." If a UDP packet is sent, an acknowledgement packet is not sent. If the destination host doesn't receive the packet, it simply asks for the packet to be re-sent.

TCP traffic can be filtered by firewalls based on the presence of the ACK bit. TACACS+ also does full-packet encryption, and it handles accounting (i.e., auditing or logging) as well as authentication and authorization; RADIUS stores passwords in cleartext. Note, however, that if you use both a firewall and an authentication server, the encryption benefits of TACACS+ aren't as dramatic because the firewall receives communications directly from the Internet, and because the firewall and authentication server communicate with one another over a trusted network. RADIUS can be a viable solution in this type of network configuration.

Filtering Characteristics TACACS+ uses TCP Port 49, so in order to use it you need to set up rules that enable clients to exchange authorization packets with the TACACS+ or RADIUS server. RADIUS uses UDP Port 1812 for authentication and UDP Port 1813 for accounting. Table 5-4 shows a set of packet-filtering rules that enables users on an internal network protected by a firewall to be authenticated by a TACACS+ or RADIUS server.

Direction	Protocol	Source Port	Destination Port	Remarks
Inbound	TCP	All ports > 1023	49	Enables external client to connect to internal TACACS+ server
Outbound	TCP	49	All ports > 1023	Allows internal TACACS+ server to respond to external client
Inbound	UDP	All ports > 1023	1812	Allows external client to connect to internal RAIDIUS server
Outbound	UDP	1812	All ports > 1023	Allows internal RAIDIUS server to respond to external client
Inbound	UDP	All ports > 1023	1813	Enables auditing when external client connects to RADIUS server
Outbound	UDP	1813	All ports > 1023	Enables auditing when internal RADIUS server responds to a client

Table 5-4 **Filtering Rules for TACACS+ and RADIUS**
© Cengage Learning 2013

Proxy Characteristics Note that RADIUS doesn't work with generic proxy systems. However, a RADIUS server can function as a proxy server, speaking to other RADIUS servers or other services that do authorization, such as Windows domain authentication.

TACACS+ does work with generic proxy systems. Because some TACACS+ systems use the same IP address to generate the key, you may need a dedicated proxy that has its own encryption key.

NAT Characteristics RADIUS doesn't work with NAT. As mentioned in Chapter 2, NAT translates public IP addresses to private IP addresses. Addresses that are intended to go through NAT need to be static, not dynamic. TACACS+ should work with NAT systems, but because TACACS+ supports encryption using a secret key shared between server and client, there is no way for the server to know which key to use if different clients make use of different keys. Static IP address mappings work best because some TACACS+ systems use the source IP address to create the encryption key.

Virtual Private Networks

The networks that organizations create are seldom used only by people at that location. When connections are made between one network and another, the connections are arranged and managed carefully. Installing such network connections requires using leased lines or other data channels provided by common carriers, and therefore these connections are usually permanent and secured under the requirements of a formal service agreement. However, when individuals—whether employees working from home, employees who are traveling, or contract workers hired for specific assignments—seek to connect to an organization's network(s), a more flexible option must be provided.

In the past, organizations provided these remote connections exclusively through dial-up services like Remote Authentication Service (RAS). Although connections via dial-up and leased lines are becoming less popular, they are still quite common. It is widely believed, however, that these unsecured, dial-up connection points represent a substantial exposure to attack. An attacker who suspects that an organization has dial-up lines can use a device called a **war dialer** to locate the connection points. A war dialer is an automatic phone-dialing program that dials every phone number in a configured range (e.g., from 555–1000 to 555–2000) and checks to see if a person, answering machine, or modem answers. If a modem answers, the war dialer program makes a note of the number and then moves to the next target number. The attacker then attempts to hack into the network via the identified modem connection using a variety of techniques. Dial-up network connectivity is usually less sophisticated than that deployed with Internet connections. For the most part, simple username and password schemes are the only means of authentication. However, some technologies, such as RADIUS and TACACS+ password systems (discussed earlier in this chapter), have improved the authentication process, and there are even systems now that use strong encryption.

Because the Internet continues to permeate the developed world, other options such as virtual private networks (VPNs) have become more popular than dial-up and other dedicated remote connection technologies. Organizations rely on firewalls to protect networked information assets, and they have come to rely on VPN technologies to enable users to make secure connections, using the public Internet, between where they are working and the company networks they depend on for communication and access to critical information.

Organizations routinely join two or more LANs to facilitate point-to-point communications over a secure line. Private **leased lines** are often used to connect remote users or branch offices to a central administrative site. However, private leased lines, such as the **frame relay** high-speed network connections mentioned in Chapter 2, don't scale well; the cost of leased lines and the complexity of the technology used to support them often make this an expensive, if more reliable, option than using the public Internet infrastructure. The growth and widespread use of the Internet has been coupled with the use of encryption technology to produce a solution for specific types of private communication channels: **virtual private networks** (**VPNs**). VPNs function like private leased lines; they encapsulate and encrypt the data being transmitted, and they use authentication to ensure that only approved users can access the VPN. However, unlike a leased line, VPNs provide a means of secure point-to-point communications over the public Internet.

Extranets and Intranets

Whether you use the hub-and-spoke, mesh, or hybrid network topologies (discussed in Chapter 2), creating VPNs that connect business partners and other branches of your own organization raises a number of questions and considerations.

Each end of the VPN represents an extension of your corporate network to a new location; you are, in effect, creating an **extranet**. An extranet is really an extension of your organization's network using the Internet. The same security measures you take to protect your own network should be applied to the endpoints of the VPN. Each remote user or business partner should have firewalls and antivirus software enabled, for instance.

An **intranet** is basically an internal network restricted to employees within the organization, also using Internet technologies. VPNs can also be used to restrict access to other areas of the intranet. For example, a large corporation that has facilities spread across several locations can use a VPN to allow the IT staff in one location to monitor servers in the other location, or accounting staff to adjust the financial records or job records in a server located in another building. However, leaving the VPN connection "always on" can enable unscrupulous staff members to gain access to corporate resources they are not allowed to use. Therefore, VPN users inside your organization should have usage limits and antivirus and firewall protection, just as outside users should, as shown in Figure 5-5.

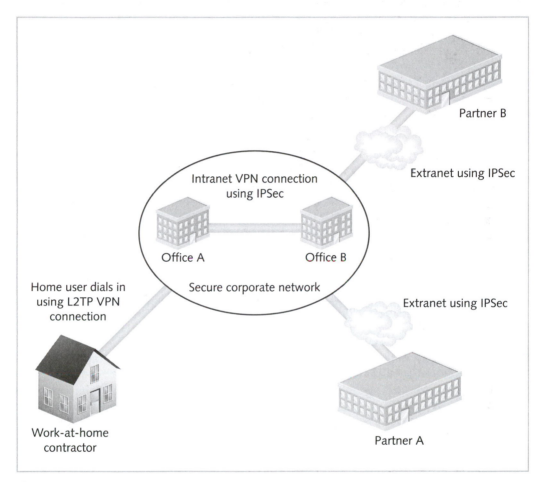

Figure 5-5 VPN for intranets and extranets
© Cengage Learning 2013

VPN Components and Operations

Many telecommunications companies provide VPN services. VPNs can be set up with special hardware or with firewall software that includes VPN functionality. Many firewalls have VPN systems built into them, because the rules that apply to the VPN are part of the firewall's existing security policy. When set up correctly, a VPN can become a critical component in an organization's perimeter security configuration.

The goal of VPNs is to provide a cost-effective and secure way to connect business locations to one another and connect remote workers to office networks. When each remote branch office has a secure connection to the central office using a VPN, all branches can communicate via a higher-level Application-layer protocol that cannot normally be routed over the Internet, like Windows' use of NetBIOS or Mac OS X's use of AppleTalk for resource sharing.

VPN Components VPNs consist of two different types of components: hardware devices and the software that performs security-related activities. This section briefly discusses the components of a VPN.

Each VPN tunnel has two **endpoints** or **terminators**. Endpoints are hardware devices or software modules that perform encryption to secure data, perform authentication to make sure the host requesting the data is an approved user of the VPN, and perform encapsulation to protect the integrity of the information being sent.

A VPN connection occurs within the context of a TCP/IP **tunnel**. A tunnel is a channel or pathway over a packet network used by the VPN; it runs through the Internet from one endpoint to another. The term "tunnel" can be misleading, because it implies that there is a single cable joining one endpoint to another and that no one but approved users can send or receive data using that cable. In reality, a VPN uses a virtual tunnel between two endpoints; this virtual tunnel makes use of Internet-based hosts and servers to conduct data from one network station to another, just as with any other TCP/IP data transmission. Although using the Internet's system of networks, subnetworks, and servers makes it relatively easy to set up a VPN, it also adds a level of uncertainty to VPN communications because so many systems are involved.

In drawings of networks that employ VPNs, you'll often see a single line used to join the two endpoints, as shown in Figure 5-6. This very simplified picture illustrates that a VPN is essentially a communications path through the Internet that provides a heightened degree of security for two participants.

Figure 5-7, on the other hand, illustrates that VPNs in fact traverse the public Internet and must therefore handle the Internet's protocols and procedures. The figure shows one set of endpoints for a VPN: routers that support Internet Security Protocol (IPSec). Each LAN's communications first go to its ISP's server, then to a **network access point** (a point that is on a high-speed part of the Internet called the backbone) and several intermediate servers.

Figure 5-8 shows a typical configuration used for VPN services. You may notice that it is more complicated because the ISPs involved may or may not be connected to the Internet backbone, and there are probably more than three servers lying between one LAN and the other. Not only that, more than one VPN may be involved when different offices that are part of the same corporate network attempt to share information. Figure 5-8 illustrates the complexity of the Internet environment in which VPNs are deployed.

The devices that form the endpoints of the VPN (they are often said to "terminate" the VPN) can be one of the following:

- A server running a tunneling protocol
- A VPN appliance, which is a special hardware device devoted to setting up VPN communications
- A firewall/VPN combination. Many high-end firewall programs support VPN setups as part of their built-in features.

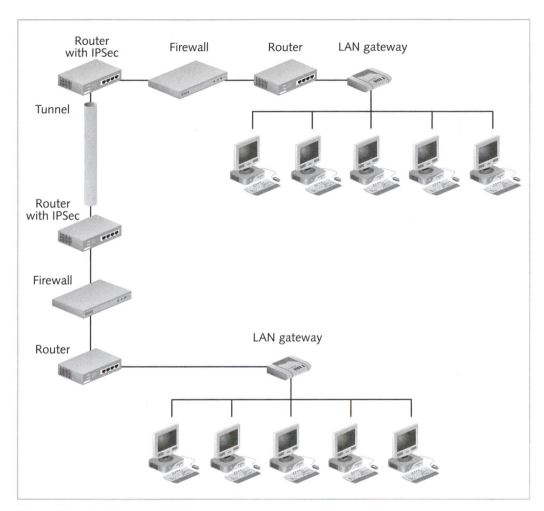

Figure 5-6 Simplified model VPN
© Cengage Learning 2013

- A router-based VPN. Routers that support IPSec can be set up at the perimeter of the LANs to be connected. These are sometimes called **IPSec concentrators,** and they use a complex set of security protocols to protect information, including Internet Key Exchange (IKE), which provides for the exchange of security keys between the machines in the VPN.

The final component in a VPN scenario is a certificate server, which manages certificates, if they are required, and manages client computers that run VPN client software; this lets remote users connect to the LAN over the VPN.

Essential Activities of VPNs

Because the VPN uses the Internet to transfer information from one computer or LAN to another, the data needs to be well protected. The essential activities that protect data transmitted over a VPN are IP encapsulation, data payload encryption, and encrypted authentication.

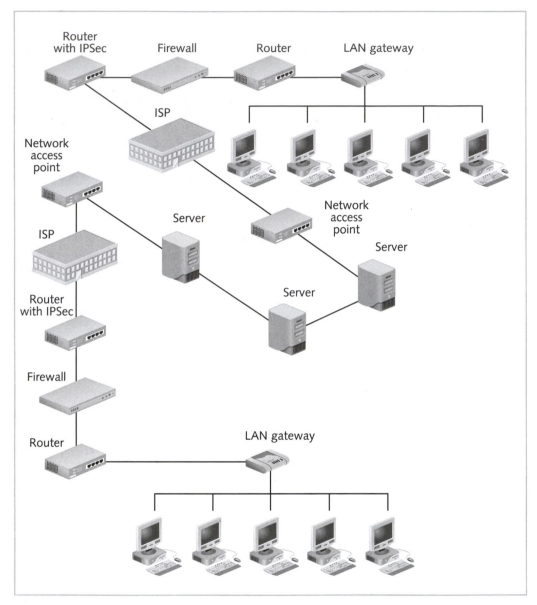

Figure 5-7 Model VPN
© Cengage Learning 2013

IP Encapsulation You already know from Chapter 2 that information passing to and from TCP/IP-based networks travels in manageable chunks called packets. VPNs protect packets by performing IP encapsulation, the process of enclosing a packet within another one that has different IP source and destination information.

Encapsulating IP packets within other packets hides the source and destination information of the encapsulated packets; the encapsulating packet uses the source and destination addresses

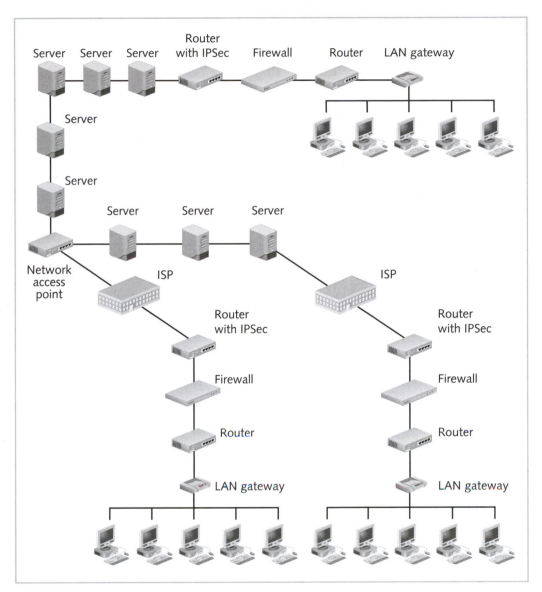

Figure 5-8   Common VPN
© Cengage Learning 2013

of the VPN gateway. In the cases where a VPN tunnel is being used, the source and destination IP addresses of the encapsulated packets can be in the private reserved blocks that are not usually routable over the Internet, such as the 10.0.0.0/8 addresses or the 192.168.0.0/16 reserved network blocks.

Data Payload Encryption   One of the big benefits of using VPNs is that they can be implemented to fully or partially encrypt the data portion of the packets that are passing through them. The encryption can be accomplished in one of two ways:

- Transport method—The host encrypts traffic when it is generated; the data parts of packets are encrypted, but not the headers.

- Tunnel method—The traffic is encrypted and decrypted in transit, somewhere between the source computer that generated it and its destination. In addition, both the header and the data portions of packets are encrypted.

Figure 5-9 illustrates a simple view of IP encapsulation using both the transport and tunneling methods discussed in the next section.

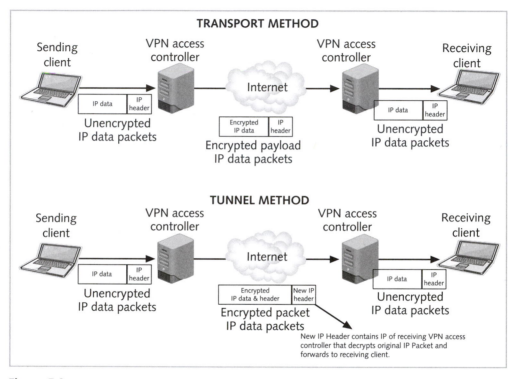

Figure 5-9   VPN IP encapsulation with transport encryption and tunnel encryption methods
© Cengage Learning 2013

These techniques were illustrated in Figure 5-7. The level of encryption applied by the firewall or VPN hardware device varies: The higher the number of data bits used to generate keys, the stronger the encryption. As you'll recall from Chapter 3, a key is the value used by the cryptographic formula or algorithm to either produce or decrypt ciphertext. The length of a key affects the strength of the encryption.

Encrypted Authentication   Some VPNs use the term **encryption domain** to describe everything in the protected network behind the gateway. The same cryptographic system that protects the information within packets can be used to authenticate computers that use the VPN. Authentication is essential because hosts in the network that receive VPN communications need to know that the host originating the communications is an approved user of the VPN.

Types of VPNs

There are two types of VPN setups. The first type links two or more networks and is called a **site-to-site VPN**. The second type makes a network accessible to remote users who need dial-in access; it is called a **client-to-site VPN**. The two types of VPNs are not mutually exclusive; many large corporations link the central office to one or more branch locations using site-to-site VPNs while providing dial-in access to the central office by means of a client-to-site VPN.

Because of their cost-effectiveness, VPNs are growing steadily in popularity. Accordingly, you can choose among a number of options for configuring VPNs—various hardware systems and software systems as well as hybrids that combine hardware and software. When choosing a system, keep in mind that any type of VPN, whether it consists of hardware or software or both, needs to be able to work with any number of different operating systems or types of computers.

VPN Appliances

One way to set up a VPN is to use a hardware device, such as a router that has been configured to use IPSec or another VPN protocol. Another option is to obtain a **VPN appliance**, a hardware device specially designed to terminate VPNs and join multiple LANs. VPN appliances can permit connections among large numbers of users or multiple networks, but they don't provide other services, such as file sharing and printing.

Commercial VPN hardware devices (like those provided by Cisco, Checkpoint, and Sonic-WALL) have a large number of VPN appliance options. At one end of the product spectrum is a product designed for a small business or a branch office. It can support multiple (commonly 10, 25, or 50) simultaneous VPN connections along with stateful packet filtering, NAT, and even antivirus protection. A Web-based interface and wizard installations make these products good for basic VPN support and a minimal amount of management.

At the other end of the product spectrum are products that can support up to 500 concurrent VPN connections at speeds greater than 1.5 Gbps. Designed to deliver a high-performance VPN solution, these VPN products come with redundant power supplies that can be replaced without turning the unit off. It provides mission-critical safety for large organizations that need the highest level of security. Some of these products also feature an automatic backup that enables dial-up connections using an external modem in the event of a service disruption to ensure continuous connectivity.

The advantage of using a hardware VPN appliance (see Figure 5-10) is that it enables you to connect more tunnels and users than software systems do. If the server goes offline or crashes for some reason (as shown in the left half of the figure), the hardware VPN appliance doesn't go offline (as shown in the right half of the figure).

Software VPNs Software VPNs are generally less expensive than hardware systems, and they tend to scale better on fast-growing networks. These products support: traveling employees who need private access to a corporate LAN or intranet from any dial-up location, IT staff who need to secure internal networks and partition parts of the network, and corporate partners who require secure connections to a company's data network for business collaboration. Most of these software-based applications support Windows, Linux, and Solaris SPARC clients and servers as well as gateways.

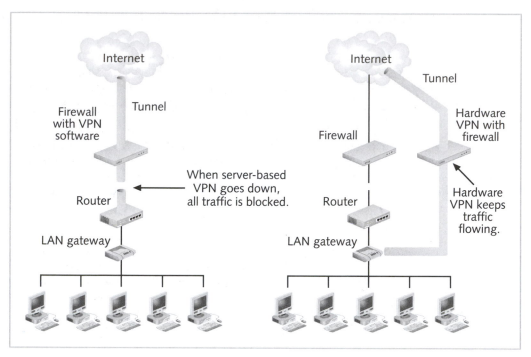

Figure 5-10   Hardware VPN
© Cengage Learning 2013

Some software VPNs use policy manager systems for enterprise-wide software distribution, policy creation, and management. Security settings for the entire corporate network using VPN can be made from the administrator's computer. Settings can be based on "role-based policies." This allows the creation of multiple configuration profiles for end users—for example, "out-of-office," "at-home," or "in-office." In addition, all installations and maintenance can usually be performed from a single central location.

Many software-based VPN applications are designed to integrate into existing directory services such as Novell and Microsoft in order to simplify VPN management and administration. These applications authenticate users through the directory service to ensure that only authorized users are permitted to access the VPN. Administrators can control access through the same interface used to manage other network users, as it is not necessary to maintain a separate directory of information for VPN users.

An increasingly popular alternative for remote access to Web-enabled applications is SSL-based VPNs. These VPNs make use of the SSL protocol (instead of IPSec) but only allow access to Web-enabled applications.

VPN Combinations of Hardware and Software   You may also use VPN systems that implement a VPN appliance at the central network and use client software at the remote end of each VPN connection. Several vendors (Cisco, for example) offer VPN concentrators that come with a variety of features and capabilities. These VPN concentrators provide solutions for the smallest office or branch location all the way up to the largest enterprise. Access levels can be set either by individual user or by groups, which allows for easy configuration and maintenance of company security policies.

Most VPN concentrator appliances give users the choice of operating in one of two modes: client mode or network extension mode. In client mode, the concentrator acts as a software client, enabling users to connect to another remote network via a VPN. In network extension mode, the concentrator acts as a hardware device, enabling a secure site-to-site VPN connection.

You may have to operate a VPN system that is "mixed"—that is, one that uses hardware and software from different vendors. You might have one company that issues certificates, another that handles the client software, another that handles the VPN termination, and so on. The challenge is to get all these pieces to communicate with one another successfully. To do this, pick a standard security protocol that is widely used and supported by all the devices, such as IPSec.

5

VPN Architectures

If there are only two participants in a VPN, the configuration is relatively straightforward in terms of expense, technical difficulty, and time. When three or more networks or individuals need to be connected, there are several options: a mesh, hub-and-spoke, or hybrid configuration.

Mesh Configuration In a **mesh configuration**, each participant (i.e., each network, router, or computer) in the VPN has an approved relationship, called a **security association** (**SA**), with every other participant. In configuring the VPN, you need to specifically identify each of these participants to every other participant that uses the VPN. Before initiating a connection, each VPN hardware or software terminator checks its routing table or **SA table** to see if the other participant has an SA with it.

In Figure 5-11, four LANs are joined in a mesh VPN. Each LAN has the ability to establish VPN communications with all the other participants in the LAN. If a new LAN is added to the VPN, all other VPN devices must be updated to include information about the new users in the LAN. Thus, each host can be added to the state table. In addition, every host that needs to use the VPN in each of the LANs must be equipped with sufficient memory to operate the VPN client software and to communicate with all other hosts in the VPN. The problem with VPNs is the difficulty associated with expanding the network and updating every VPN device whenever a host is added. That's why, for fast-growing networks, a hub-and-spoke configuration is preferable.

Hub-and-Spoke Configuration In a **hub-and-spoke configuration**, a single VPN router contains records of all SAs in the VPN. Any LANs or computers that want to participate in the VPN need only connect to the central server, not to any other machines in the VPN. This setup makes it easy to increase the size of the VPN as more branch offices or computers are added. Figure 5-12 illustrates a hub-and-spoke configuration. Here, the central VPN router resides at the organization's central office because that is where the main IT staff resides; this is the most common arrangement. A hub-and-spoke VPN is ideally suited for communications within an organization that has a central main office and a number of branch offices.

The problem with hub-and-spoke VPNs is that this requirement that all communications flow into and out of the central router slows down communications, especially if branch offices are located on different continents around the world. In addition, the central router must have

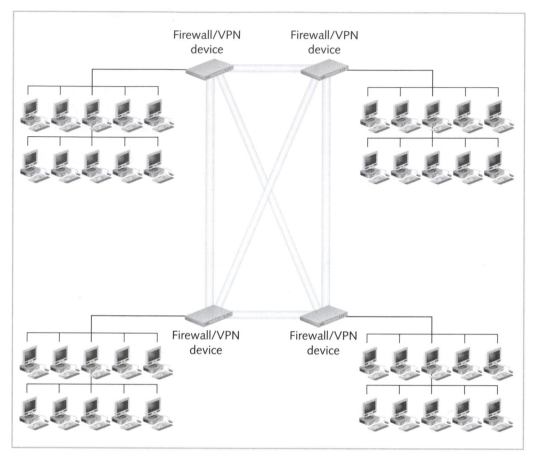

Figure 5-11   Mesh VPN
© Cengage Learning 2013

double the bandwidth of other connections in the VPN because it must handle inbound and outbound traffic at the same time. The high-bandwidth charge for such a router can easily amount to several thousand dollars per month. However, in a situation where all communications need to go through the central office, a hub-and-spoke configuration makes sense because of the heightened security it gives to all participants.

Hybrid Configuration As organizations grow, a VPN that starts out as a mesh configuration or a hub-and-spoke configuration often evolves into a mixture of the two. Mesh configurations tend to operate more efficiently; therefore, the central core linking the most important branches of the network should probably be a mesh configuration. However, as branch offices are added, they can be added as spokes that connect to a central VPN router at the central office.

Any time-critical communications with branch offices should be part of the mesh configuration. However, far-flung offices, such as overseas branches, can be part of a hub-and-spoke configuration. A hybrid setup that combines the two configurations benefits from the strengths of each one—the scalability of the hub-and-spoke configuration and the speed of the mesh

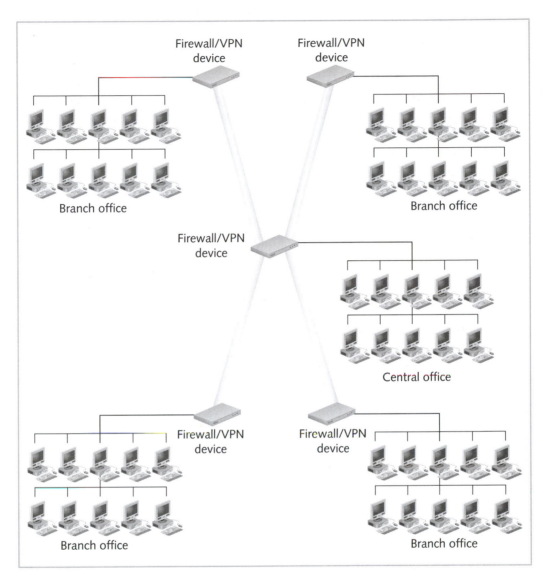

Figure 5-12 Hub-and-spoke VPN
© Cengage Learning 2013

configuration. If at all possible, try to have the branch offices that participate in the VPN use the same ISP. That will minimize the number of "hops" between networks.

Tunneling Protocols Used with VPNs

In the past, firewalls that provided for the establishment of VPNs used proprietary protocols—that is, protocols established by a single vendor and only implemented in that vendor's products. Such firewalls would only be able to establish connections with remote LANs that used the same brand of firewall. Today, the widespread acceptance of IPSec with the IKE system means that proprietary protocols are used far less often.

IPSec/IKE Developed by the Internet Engineering Task Force (IETF), IPSec is a standard for secure encrypted communications. It provides for (1) encryption of the data part of packets, (2) authentication to guarantee that packets come from valid sources, and (3) encapsulation between two VPN hosts.

IPSec utilizes two security methods: Authenticated Headers (AH) and Encapsulating Security Payload (ESP). AH is used to authenticate packets, whereas ESP encrypts the data portion of packets. The two methods can be combined.

IPSec works in two different modes: transport mode and tunnel mode. Transport mode is used to provide secure communications between hosts over any range of IP addresses. Tunnel mode is used to create secure links between two private networks. Tunnel mode is the obvious choice for VPNs; however, there are some concerns about using tunnel mode in a client-to-site VPN because IPSec by itself does not provide for user authentication. However, when combined with an authentication system like Kerberos, IPSec can authenticate users.

IPSec is commonly combined with IKE as a means of using public-key cryptography to encrypt data between LANs or between a client and a LAN. IKE provides for the exchange of public and private keys. The key exchange is used to tell the hosts wishing to initiate a VPN connection that each is a valid user of the system. IKE can also determine which encryption protocols should be used to encrypt data that flows through the VPN tunnel. The process of establishing an IPSec/IKE VPN connection works as follows:

1. The host or gateway at one end of the VPN sends a request to a host or gateway at the other end asking to establish a connection. (Both hosts have obtained the same key, called a **preshared key**, from the same trusted authority.)

2. The remote host or gateway generates a random number and sends a copy of the number back to the machine that made the original request.

3. The original machine encrypts its preshared key using the random number and sends the preshared key to the remote host or gateway.

4. The remote host decrypts the preshared key and compares it to its own preshared key or, if it has multiple keys, to a set of keys called a keyring. If the preshared key matches one of its own keys, the remote host encrypts a public key using the preshared key and sends it back to the machine that made the original request.

5. The original machine uses the public key to establish a security association (SA) between the two machines, which establishes the VPN connection.

Even though many firewalls support IPSec and IKE, they sometimes use different versions of these protocols. If your VPN uses more than one kind of firewall and you plan to implement an IPSec/IKE VPN, check with the manufacturers of those firewalls to see if their products will work with the other firewalls you have, and ask about any special configuration you have to perform.

PPTP **Point-to-Point Tunneling Protocol** (PPTP) is commonly used by remote users who need to connect to a network using a dial-in modem connection. PPTP uses Microsoft Point-to-Point Encryption (MPPE) to encrypt data that passes between the remote computer and the remote access server. It's an older technology than the other dial-in tunneling protocol, L2TP, but it is useful if support for older clients is needed. It's also useful because packets sent using

PPTP can pass through firewalls that perform NAT. This is in contrast to L2TP, which is incompatible with NAT but provides a higher level of encryption and authentication.

L2TP Layer 2 Tunneling Protocol (L2TP) is an extension of PPP. It uses IPSec rather than MPPE to encrypt data sent over PPP. It provides secure authenticated remote access by separating the process of initiating a connection from the process of forwarding the data encapsulated in PPP communications. Using L2TP, a host machine can make a connection to a modem and then have its PPP data packets forwarded to another, separate remote access server. When the data reaches the remote access server, its payload is unpacked and forwarded to the destination host on the internal network.

PPP over SSL/PPP over SSH Point-to-Point Protocol (PPP) over Secure Sockets Layer (SSL) and **Point-to-Point Protocol (PPP) over Secure Shell (SSH)** are two UNIX-based methods for creating VPNs. Both combine an existing tunnel system (PPP) with a way of encrypting data in transport (SSL or SSH). As you probably know already, PPP can be used to establish a connection between two hosts over an IP system.

SSL is a public-key encryption system used to provide secure communications over the World Wide Web. (See Chapter 7 for more on SSL). SSH is the UNIX secure shell, which was developed when serious security flaws were identified in Telnet. SSH enables users to perform secure authenticated logons and encrypted communications between a client and host. SSH can be configured so that it requires that both client and host have a secret key in advance—a preshared key—in order to establish a connection.

Which protocol should you use in a VPN you establish, and why? Table 5-5 lists the protocols mentioned in this section along with situations in which they might be used.

Protocol	Recommended Usage
IPSec/IKE	Rapidly becoming the protocol of choice for VPN connections of all sorts and should be used when the other protocols are not acceptable
PPTP	When a dial-up user has an old system that doesn't support L2TP and needs to use PPP to establish a VPN connection to your network
L2TP	When a dial-up user needs to establish a VPN connection with your network (L2TP provides stronger protection than PPTP)
PPP Over SSL	When a UNIX user needs to create a VPN connection "on the fly" by connecting to the SSL port on a server
PPP Over SSH	When a UNIX user needs to create a VPN connection "on the fly" over the UNIX secure shell (SSH) and both parties know the secret key in advance

Table 5-5 VPN Protocols and Their Uses
© Cengage Learning 2013

VPN Best Practices

The successful operation of a VPN depends not only on its hardware and software components and overall configuration but also on a number of best practices. These include security policy rules that specifically apply to the VPN, the integration of firewall packet filtering with VPN traffic, and auditing the VPN to make sure it is performing acceptably.

Need for a VPN Policy In a corporate setting, the VPN is likely to be used by many different workers in many different locations. A VPN policy is essential for identifying who can use the VPN and for ensuring that all users know what constitutes proper use of the VPN. This can be a separate stand-alone policy, or it can be a clause within a larger security policy.

The VPN policy should spell out who is permitted to have VPN access to your corporate network. For example, vendors might be granted access to the network through a VPN connection, but they may only be allowed to access information pertaining to their own company's accounts. The vendor VPN solution should have controls that allow the administrator to restrict where vendors can go on the corporate network. On the other hand, managers and full-time employees who access the network through a VPN while traveling should be granted more comprehensive access to network resources.

The VPN policy should also state whether authentication is to be used and how it is to be used, whether **split tunneling** (two connections over a VPN line) is permitted, how long users can be connected using the VPN at any one session, whether virus protection is included, and so on. The SANS Institute is an information security research and education organization; it provides a sample VPN policy at *http://www.sans.org/security-resources/policies/Virtual_Private_Network.pdf*.

Packet Filtering and VPNs When configuring a VPN, you must decide early on where data encryption and decryption will be performed in relation to packet filtering. You can decide to do encryption and decryption either outside the packet-filtering perimeter or inside it. Figure 5-13 shows encryption and decryption outside the packet-filtering perimeter.

In the scenario shown in Figure 5-13, the firewall/VPN combination is configured to perform transport encryption. Packets are encrypted at the host as soon as they are generated. Packets that are already encrypted pass through the packet filters at the perimeter of either LAN and are not filtered. In this scenario, if the LAN that generates the communications has been infected by a virus or is compromised in some way, the packets that pass through the packet filters could be infected and could then infect the destination LAN.

Figure 5-14 illustrates the alternative: encryption and decryption performed inside the packet-filtering perimeter using the tunnel method. Keep in mind that the network configurations illustrated in this figure and in Figure 5-13 depict a packet filter that is separate from the firewall; this is done for clarity of explanation. In fact, packet filtering might be done by the firewall itself; the same firewall may provide VPN services, or a separate VPN appliance may be used instead of a firewall-based VPN.

In Figure 5-14, packet filtering is performed before the data reaches the VPN. Mangled packets can be dropped before they reach the firewall/VPN, thus providing additional protection for the destination LAN.

Benefits and Drawbacks of VPNs

One of the benefits of VPNs is secure networking without the expense of establishing and maintaining leased lines. VPNs also allow the packet encryption/translation overhead to be handled on dedicated systems, decreasing the load placed on production machines. They also allow you to control the physical setup and, therefore, decide on data encryption levels as well as decide whether to encrypt data at the physical level or at the application level.

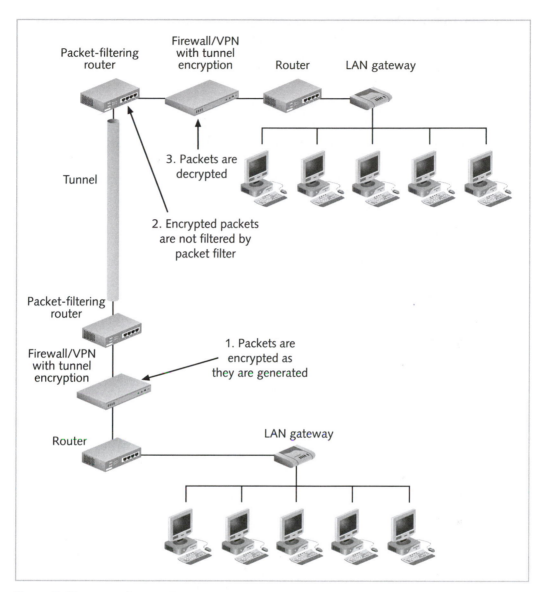

Figure 5-13 External encryption
© Cengage Learning 2013

VPNs do have some significant drawbacks. They are complex and, if configured improperly, can create significant network vulnerabilities. Leased lines may be more expensive, but the chance of introducing vulnerabilities is not as great because they create point-to-point connections. VPNs also make use of the unpredictable and often unreliable Internet. Multinational VPNs, in particular, can experience problems because packets being routed through various hubs can encounter slowdowns or blockages that you can neither predict nor resolve. You then have to explain to administration that the problem is occurring thousands of miles away and they'll just have to wait until it is fixed there.

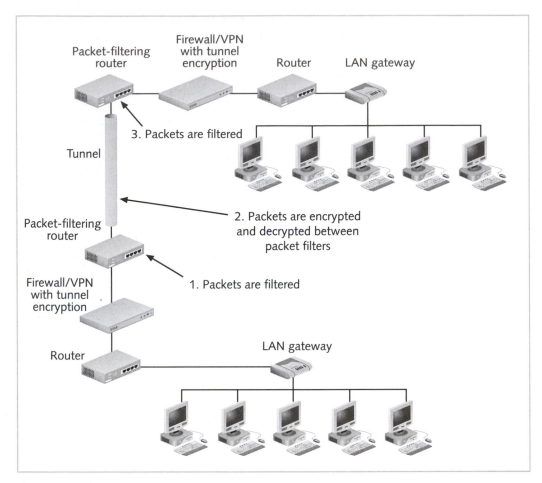

Figure 5-14   Internal encryption
© Cengage Learning 2013

Another problem involves authorization: If your VPN's authorization is not configured properly, you can easily expose your corporate network. In addition, some vendor solutions have more documented security issues than others.

VPNs Extend Network Boundaries

High-speed Internet connections such as cable modem and DSL lines are changing the role of VPNs in the corporate setting. Only a few years ago, when high-speed connections were expensive and relatively hard to come by, remote users primarily used VPNs to dial into a network using modems. They were connected to the corporate network through the VPN only for the length of the dial-up connection. Because many ISPs charged by the minute or placed restrictions on the number of hours a customer could be connected each month, the remote user was likely to hang up as soon as business was completed.

Now, it's increasingly likely that the contractors, vendors, and telecommuters who connect to an organization's internal network through a VPN will have a high-speed connection that is "always on." Unless you specifically place limits on how long such employees can use the

VPN, they can be connected to your network around the clock. Thus, each VPN connection extends your network to a location that is out of your control, and each such connection can open up your network to intrusions, viruses, or other problems. You need to take extra care with users who connect to the VPN through always-on connections. Here are some suggestions for how to deal with the increased risk:

- **Multifactor authentication**—As described earlier, this uses two or more authentication factors to authenticate remote users. This means combining something the user possesses, such as a token or smart card, with something physically associated with the user, such as fingerprints or retinal scans. For such a system to work, each remote user needs to have a smart card reader, a fingerprint reader, a retinal scanner, or some other (potentially expensive) device along with a computer.

- Integrated virus protection—Make sure each user's computer is equipped with up-to-date antivirus software that scans the computer continually, screening out any viruses as soon as they enter the system. After files are encapsulated, encrypted, and sent through the VPN tunnel, any viruses in those files will make it through the firewall into the corporate network. Virus-scanning software needs to be present on the network to catch any viruses, of course; however, requiring vendors, partners, or contractors to use their own antivirus software will reduce the chance of viruses entering the system in the first place.

- NAC—NAC solutions vary in complexity; some check for installed antivirus software, current antivirus updates, and relevant security patches. More sophisticated solutions can remediate identified defects by installing the appropriate items.[5]

- Usage limits—VPNs should be configured to inform all VPN participants that they need to terminate VPN sessions as soon as they are done with them. Configuration of the VPN software can enforce the policy limits.

Such countermeasures should be supported by the organization's security policies, and requirements for their enforcement should be written into any agreements with business partners or contractors. As with all security policies, they should be explained to employees and business partners during orientation and security awareness sessions.

Chapter Summary

- Network security devices such as firewalls require authentication when they need to assign different levels of authorization to different users and groups. By determining that users or computers are really who or what they claim to be, the firewall can then grant access to the needed network resources.

- Network security devices can make use of many types of authentication schemes, including user, client, and session authentication. In general, these schemes require users to supply either something they have (such as a smart card) or something they know (such as a password), or both. The most recent authentication systems measure or evaluate a physical attribute, such as a fingerprint or voiceprint.

- In a centralized authentication system, the firewall works in tandem with an authentication server. The authentication server handles the maintenance (or generation) of usernames and passwords as well as login requests and auditing, which is the process of recording who is and who is not authenticated and what level of access is granted. Kerberos is a centralized authentication system used for LAN authentication, whereas TACACS+ and RADIUS are systems used to authenticate remote users who remotely connect to the network.

- Password management is an important part of virtually every authentication system. It takes one of two forms:
  - Single-word, static passwords
  - One-time passwords generated dynamically each time the user attempts to log on

- The growth and widespread use of the Internet has coupled with the use of encryption technology to produce a solution for specific types of private communication channels: virtual private networks (VPNs). VPNs provide a means of secure point-to-point communications over the public Internet.

- VPNs are used for e-commerce and telecommuting and are becoming widespread. They can be set up with special hardware or with firewall software that includes VPN functionality. Many firewalls have VPN systems built into them, and VPN is a critical component in an organization's perimeter security configuration.

- Because the VPN uses the Internet to transfer information from one computer or LAN to another, the data needs to be well protected. The essential activities that protect data transmitted over a VPN are: IP encapsulation, data payload encryption, and encrypted authentication.

- There are two types of VPN: site-to-site and client-to-site. One way to set up a VPN is to use a hardware device, such as a router that has been configured to provide a VPN protocol, use a VPN appliance, or run VPN software on a general-purpose server.

- VPN configuration for three or more networks or individuals results in combinations of mesh, a hub-and-spoke arrangement, or a hybrid setup. In a mesh configuration, each participant in the VPN has an approved relationship with every other participant. In a hub-and-spoke configuration, a single, central VPN router contains records of all associations in the VPN, and any other participants need only connect to the central server, not to any other machines in the VPN. As organizations grow, a VPN that starts out as a mesh design or hub-and-spoke design often evolves into a mixture of the two.

- Firewalls that use proprietary protocols can only establish connections with remote LANs that use the same brand of firewall. Today, the widespread use of the IPSec protocol with the Internet Key Exchange (IKE) system means that proprietary protocols are used far less often. IPSec provides two security methods: Authenticated Headers (AH) and Encapsulating Security Payload (ESP). AH is used to authenticate packets, whereas ESP encrypts the data portion of packets. You can use the methods together.

- Point-to-Point Tunneling Protocol (PPTP) is commonly used by remote users who need to connect to a network using a dial-in modem connection. Layer 2 Tunneling Protocol (L2TP) is an extension of the protocol long used to establish dial-up connections on the Internet, Point-to-Point Protocol (PPP).

- Point-to-Point Protocol (PPP) over Secure Sockets Layer (SSL) and Point-to-Point Protocol (PPP) over Secure Shell (SSH) are two UNIX-based methods for creating VPNs. Both of them combine an existing tunnel system (PPP) with a way of encrypting data in transport (SSL or SSH).

- A VPN is a good way to secure communications with users who need to connect remotely by dialing into their ISP, or who use their cable or DSL Internet connections to initiate the VPN connection. To enable a remote user to connect to a VPN, you need to issue VPN client software to that user. You should make sure the user's computer is equipped with antivirus software and a firewall. You may need to obtain a key for the remote user if you plan to use IPSec to make the VPN connection.

- The successful operation of a VPN depends not only on its hardware and software components and overall configuration but also on a number of best practices. These include security policy rules that specifically apply to the VPN, the integration of firewall packet filtering with VPN traffic, and auditing the VPN to make sure it is performing acceptably.

5

Review Questions

1. What is authentication? What is a supplicant?

2. What are the factors on which authentication may be based?

3. Which authentication factors are being used by an authenticating server that responds to a login request by generating a random number or code and expects to receive that code plus a secret password in return?

4. How is local authentication different from centralized authentication? How is it the same?

5. Identify and define the three elements associated with AAA services.

6. Which type of network environment is not suitable for Kerberos authentication services?

7. In addition to a password, which is "something you know," what might be the second factor in a two-factor authentication system?

8. What is a token? How is a token different from a biometric measurement? How is it the same?

9. When should a firewall require authentication?

10. How are client and session authentication the same? How are they different?

11. What is the advantage of TACACS+ over RADIUS?

12. What do VPNs do that firewalls cannot do?

13. What are the disadvantages of using leased lines to set up a private network?

14. In the context of VPNs, how can the term "tunnel" be misleading?

15. What is the downside of using a proprietary VPN protocol?

16. Why is authentication an essential part of a VPN?

17. When is a hub-and-spoke VPN configuration most useful?

18. Which VPN protocol is most widely used today?

19. What is one potential drawback to using IPSec in tunnel mode?

20. PPTP is an older VPN protocol that is mainly used with older client computers, but it has one advantage over the more recent L2TP. What is it?

Real World Exercises

Exercise 5-1

You need to restrict your company's rank-and-file employees to using the Internet only during regular working hours (9 am to 5 pm, five days a week). However, as network administrator, you want to be able to access the network at any time of the day or night, seven days a week. How can you meet the needs of the employees and yourself?

Exercise 5-2

A group of freelance designers who work at home using DSL or cable modem connections needs to gain access to a set of your company publication files to redesign them. How can you enable this?

Exercise 5-3

Your network uses basic authentication that centers on usernames and passwords. However, you have two ongoing problems: Usernames and passwords are frequently lost by negligent users, and hackers have, on occasion, fooled employees into giving up their authentication information. Identify two things you can do to strengthen the use of basic username and password authentication.

Exercise 5-4

You have configured your firewall to authenticate a group of 100 users within your company. You set up the user database with the firewall's own user management software. As your network grows and security items are added, other network components need to access the same database of users. What strategies can you employ to provide the other network components with access to the user database?

Exercise 5-5

Using an Internet search engine, look up "one-time password." Access several Web sites that define the term. After reading at least two definitions, write your own definition of the term.

Exercise 5-6

Using an Internet search engine, look up "biometric user authentication." Access several Web sites that define the term. Write a paragraph expressing your opinion on whether and when this will be the dominant way that users authenticate when using home computers.

Hands-On Projects

Project 5-1

In this project, we examine how users and groups are managed in Open-SUSE. Managing users and groups is a common activity for security professionals and administrators alike. User management will provide the basis for access control and rights management. First, we will use the YaST GUI utility provided by OpenSUSE, and then we will use command line applications.

To complete this project, you will need to have an installation of OpenSUSE available for use. This can be achieved either by installing OpenSUSE on an available computer or by building a virtual instance using virtualization software, such as Oracle's VirtualBox or VMware's Player.

The instructions in this lab were verified on OpenSUSE 11.4. If you use another operating system or version, your results may vary.

1. Open the YaST utility. Click the **OpenSUSE** icon in the lower-left corner of the desktop, then click **Computer**, and then click **YaST**. When prompted, enter the administrator password.

2. Click **Security and Users**, and then click **Users and Group Management**.

3. Click **Add**. A new local user window should appear that looks like what is shown in Figure 5-15.

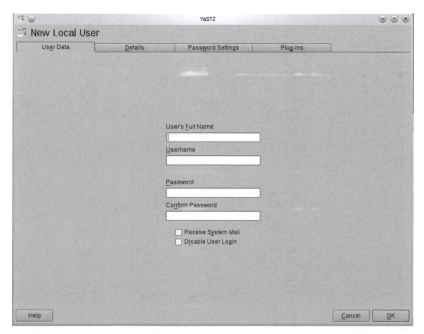

Figure 5-15   User management console

Source: OpenSuse

4. Make up a name and username for the new user we will be adding to our system. Give the new user a password. Click **OK**.

5. Click **Groups** and then click **Add**. A new local group window should appear.

6. Enter a name for a new group. Leave the password blank. Check the box next to your username and the new username you just made. Click **OK**.

7. Click **Users**. Make sure the new user is selected. Click **Delete**. Click **Yes**, confirming the choice.

8. Click **Groups**. Click the group you made and click **Edit**. Remove yourself from the group by unchecking the box next to your username. A group must be empty in order to remove it. Click **OK**.

9. Click the group you made and then click **Delete**. Click **Yes** to confirm your choice. Click **OK** to close the User and Group Administration window.

Endnotes

1. Tiller, J. S. "Access Control," in *Official (ISC)2 Guide to the CISSP CBK*. Tipton, H. & Henry, K. (eds), Boca Raton, FL: Auerbach Publishers, 2007.

2. National Institute of Standards and Technology (NIST). "An Introduction to Computer Security: The NIST Handbook." SP800-12. Accessed 1 December 2011 from *http://csrc. nist.gov/publications/nistpubs/800-12/handbook.pdf*.

3. Exec. Order No. 12958. Accessed December 4, 2011 from *www.dtic.mil/dtic/pdf/ customer/STINFOdata/EO_12958.pdf*.

4. National Institute of Standards and Technology (NIST). "The Impact of the FCC's Open Network Architecture on NS/NP Telecommunications Security." SP800-11. Access December 2011 from *csrc.nist.gov/publications/nistpubs/800-11/node26.html*.

5. For more information, see Mark Kadrich, *Endpoint Security*, Boston, MA: Addison-Wesley, 2007.

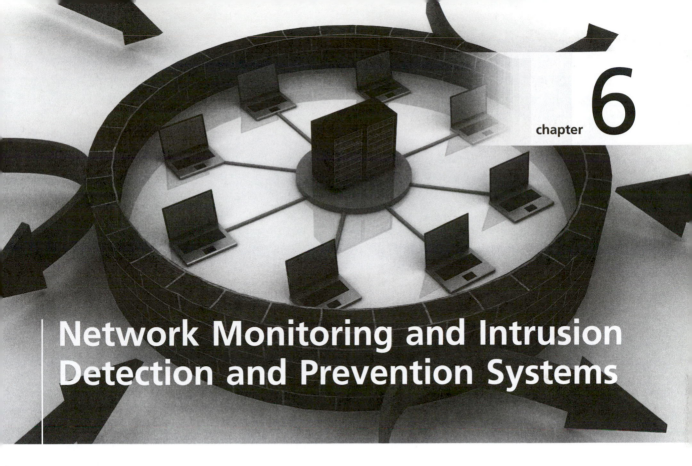

chapter 6

Network Monitoring and Intrusion Detection and Prevention Systems

You can't hold firewalls and intrusion detection systems accountable. You can only hold people accountable. — Daryl White, U.S. Department of the Interior CIO

Upon completion of this material, you should be able to:

- Define the basic concepts of network packet analysis
- Explain the various network packet formats and standards
- Describe how packet analysis forms the basis of network intrusion detection
- Discuss the various types of intrusion detection and prevention
- Explain intrusion detection and prevention deployments and response strategies
- Describe various honeypot technologies

Getting Visibility

Paige Davis had been given a mission from on high regarding the PCI audit. She was to deploy an IDS solution that would monitor activities within the EBS IT infrastructure and provide the IT department with a better understanding of activity taking place on the network. Paige's first act was to deploy a network IDS that would monitor the critical attack avenue from the Internet.

In teaming up with Noah Atwater, Paige was able to sketch out a rough plan. Because management, out of fear, had authorized a "blank check" to purchase network IDS equipment, Paige chose to use a commercial product from IBM, called Proventia Network Intrusion Prevention System. She laid the foundation of the infrastructure by deploying an appliance located on the main DMZ network segment. The appliance would collect data from the network intrusion prevention system (NIPS) sensors, correlate the data, and issue alerts on high-severity suspicious activity.

Paige then deployed a NIPS appliance at each of the critical network junctures with the user network and servers. She also instituted authentication mechanisms so that the sensors could prove their identity to the central collection point—Proventia Management SiteProtector—and she instituted encryption so that the sensors could pass back data without the fear of eavesdropping. This would be crucial because Paige would have to allow communication through the internal firewall. Authentication and encryption would mitigate the overall risk of opening a door to the internal network.

The final architecture gave Paige two important tools. First, any critical alerts could be sent via pager to the IT team for an immediate response. Second, all data would be archived, which would allow Paige to run reports presenting a view of the malicious activity taking place on the network.

Introduction

As part of a prudent approach to keeping an eye on their networks, organizations should consider continuous monitoring programs that involve two key components: network-monitoring software, such as packet sniffers, and Intrusion Detection and Prevention Systems (IDPSs).[1] Network-monitoring software is the organization's data collection utility, whereas IDPSs provide the analysis component to detect any abnormal activity or suspicious traffic.

Network-Monitoring Software: Packet Sniffers

As you learned in Chapter 1, a packet sniffer (also known as a network sniffer) is a program or device that can view data traversing a network. Sniffers can be used maliciously to intercept usernames, passwords, and other sensitive transmitted information. However, sniffers have long been used to help network administrators troubleshoot a variety of problems with network communications. Also, sniffers have helped security administrators by monitoring attacks on the network and helping prevent or remediate damage.

Capturing Network Traffic

Capturing network traffic is fairly easy. The simple concept is that enabling a network adapter to communicate in promiscuous mode allows the adapter to then see all traffic, whether it is destined to the host or not. Usually, network cards (also known as network interface cards or NICs) operate in a mode in which they only receive and pass on traffic addressed to their system. However, with appropriate privileges, a NIC can be reconfigured to pass on all received traffic to allow the interception and viewing of that traffic. This is known as **promiscuous mode**. (Enabling promiscuous mode differs by operating system and network device. Refer to information provided by the vendor for more details on enabling promiscuous mode.) There are, however, a number of considerations for capturing network traffic:

- Capturing network traffic could be deemed illegal unless you are authorized by the network owner to use a sniffer. Obtain permission first!

- The computer must be placed on the proper network segment on which you want to capture traffic. It does no good to place a sniffer on an Internet segment if your true goal is to capture network traffic behind the border firewall.

- In addition to knowing the network segment, you must do your homework on how your sniffer is connected to the network. For example, if you are using a laptop to capture network traffic, you cannot just connect it to a switch and expect to see all traffic on the network segment, as a switch is smart enough to route traffic to the specific MAC address destinations. More sophisticated switches have a spanning port or the ability to enable switch port mirroring, which allows the administrator to connect one device to a designated port to view all traffic that flows through the switch. Alternatively, you can install a hub, which typically does not apply the advanced switching techniques that prohibit one station from viewing all traffic that passes through the device.

- A sniffer cannot decipher encrypted traffic.

Packet Analysis

In order to use a sniffer effectively, the operator must understand the fundamental structure of network packets. With this understanding, a security professional can make sense of what type of traffic is being transmitted, who is sending, who is receiving, when the information is being sent, and even what applications may be involved. This type of analysis is called packet analysis, and it requires training on normal network packets, the RFC specifications, and then training on spotting suspicious packets.

The first step in understanding how packet sniffers work is to understand normal TCP/IP communications. As a quick review, Figure 6-1 displays the IP packet first shown in Figure 2-16 in Chapter 2. This figure shows the various fields necessary in the IPv4 header and where the transmitted data is stored. However, in this rendering, the packet has been broken down by bit. This type of understanding is necessary when viewing network packets in hexadecimal (hex) or other renderings that sniffers may provide. Additionally, Figure 6-2 shows the IP packet structure for IPv6.

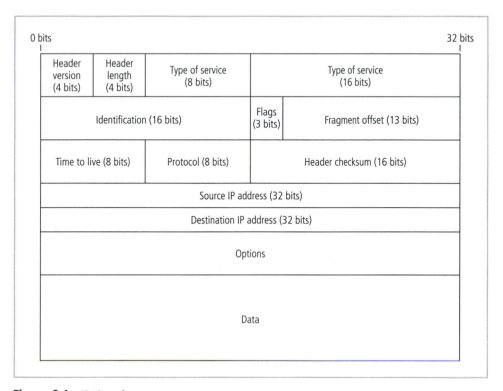

Figure 6-1 IPv4 packet structure
© Cengage Learning 2013

Figure 6-2 IPv6 packet structure
© Cengage Learning 2013

IP headers are important, but it is also important to understand the structures for TCP and UDP, which are encapsulated in IP packets. These headers transmit additional information that is important for understanding more details about the nature of the data traffic. Figures 6-3 and 6-4 detail these packet structures.

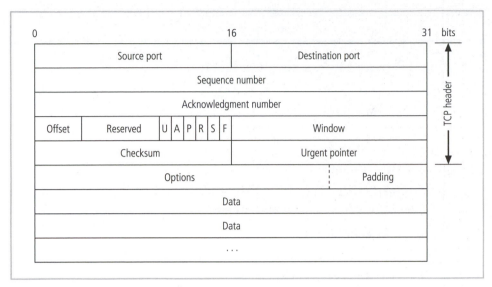

Figure 6-3   TCP packet structure
© Cengage Learning 2013

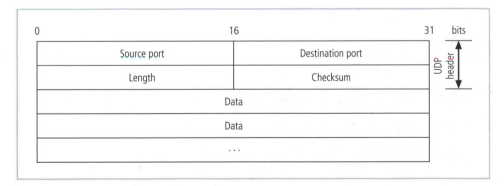

Figure 6-4   UDP packet structure
© Cengage Learning 2013

ICMP packets are another common traffic packet. Their structure is shown in Figure 6-5.

Tcpdump

Once you understand the structure of network packets and what you would expect to see in normal TCP/IP communications, it is time to invest in learning a tool and its output format to perform packet analysis. Because of its ubiquity in UNIX/Linux systems, tcpdump has become the *de facto* standard in network sniffing. It was originally written by Van Jacobson,

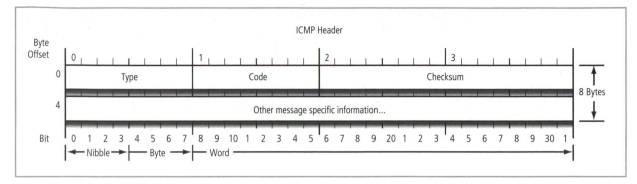

Figure 6-5 ICMP packet structure
© Cengage Learning 2013

Craig Leres, and Steven McCanne, who worked for Lawrence Berkeley National Laboratory at the University of California, Berkeley.[2]

Tcpdump—like many UNIX/Linux-based utilities—has a number of case-sensitive command line options. Here are some useful options to get you started:

- -i—Define network interface to use.
- -r—Read network capture data from file.
- -w—Write network capture data to file.
- -n—Don't convert addresses to names.
- -c—Specify the number of packets to capture.
- -A—Print data (without the link-level header) in ASCII.
- -X—Print data (without the link-level header) in hex and ASCII.
- -xx—Print data (with the link-level header) in hex.

The real power of tcpdump, however, comes in its ability to select which network packets to capture. Tcpdump uses expressions to allow the operator to narrow down traffic. If no expressions are used, then all network traffic is dumped. Here are a number of simple but useful expressions:

- `tcpdump host 192.168.1.100`—Only captures traffic originating from and destined to 192.168.1.100
- `tcpdump src 192.168.1.100`—Only captures traffic originating from 192.168.1.100
- `tcpdump dst 192.168.1.100`—Only captures traffic destined to 192.168.1.100
- `tcpdump net 192.168.1.0/24`—Only captures traffic destined to or originating from the 192.168.1.0 network
- `tcpdump tcp`—Only captures TCP traffic
- `tcpdump tcp and dst port 1025`—Only captures TCP traffic destined to TCP port 1025
- `tcpdump portrange 21-23`—Only captures traffic destined to or originating from ports 21, 22, or 23

Tcpdump Examples It is important to see examples in order to better understand tcpdump output. By default, tcpdump will just print packet header information, as shown in Figure 6-6.

```
14:40:09.801833 IP 192.168.1.124 >
192.168.1.2: ICMP echo request, id
20385, seq 0, length 8

14:40:09.804572 IP 192.168.1.2 >
192.168.1.124: ICMP echo reply, id
20385, seq 0, length 8
```

Figure 6-6   Tcpdump example #1
Source: Linux

In Figure 6-6, two network packets are represented. The first shows the host 192.168.1.124 sending host 192.168.1.2 an ICMP echo request. Host 192.168.1.2 replies shortly thereafter with an ICMP echo reply. The first field lists a timestamp. The second field indicates that the packet is IP. The third field shows the source IP address. The fourth field shows the destination IP address. Following those standard fields in the tcpdump output, there is additional information to indicate that ICMP is used and what message format is used.

```
09:48:59.548280 IP 192.168.253.128.49244
> 192.168.1.13.ftp: S
3455425427:3455425427(0) win 5840 <mss
1460,sackOK,timestamp 5170829
0,nop,wscale 2>

09:48:59.566468 IP 192.168.1.13.ftp >
192.168.253.128.49244: S
90249632:90249632(0) ack 3455425428 win
64240 <mss 1460>

09:48:59.566541 IP 192.168.253.128.49244
> 192.168.1.13.ftp: . ack 1 win 5840
```

Figure 6-7   Tcpdump example #2
Source: Linux

In Figure 6-7, we see an FTP session initiation in which 192.168.253.128 sets up a session with the FTP server at 192.168.1.13. In these series of packets—because we have communications over TCP—we also have TCP port information along with TCP flag information. In the first packet, for example, we see the S indicator, which indicates the SYN flag being set in the header of the packet. The second packet shows the S as well as the ack indicator. This shows the second step in the three-way handshake for SYN/ACK. Finally, the third packet shows ack to indicate the final step in session initiation. In addition, tcpdump shows the TCP session ID numbers to help the operator line up packets to the individual TCP session communications.

Figure 6-8 shows off tcpdump's ability to include not only the packet header information but the packet contents. The tcpdump tool will output both the header and packet contents into hex format. If we felt so inclined, we could decipher the hex content directly into packet header information by referring to the RFC specifications for the various protocols. Although the protocol diagrams seem overwhelming, using these blueprints helps to decipher the information from a network sniffer. For example, the first hex 4 in Figure 6-8's output indicates that we are viewing IPv4. The 06 at position 19 and 20 indicates that TCP is encapsulated in the IP packet. This type of information is deduced by mapping the packet positions to the hex output.

```
17:36:09.758756 IP 192.168.253.1.1094 > 192.168.253.129.80: . 1:1461
(1460) ack 1 win 65535
0x0000:  4500 05dc 62e8 4000 8006 165f c0a8 fd01  E...b.@...._....
0x0010:  c0a8 fd81 0446 0050 56a6 4cf8 d5c0 0b31  .....F.PV.L....1
0x0020:  5010 ffff 90f9 0000 5345 4152 4348 202f  P.......SEARCH./
0x0030:  4141 4141 4141 4141 4141 4141 4141 4141  AAAAAAAAAAAAAAAA
0x0040:  4141 4141 4141 4141 4141 4141 4141 4141  AAAAAAAAAAAAAAAA
0x0050:  4141 4141 4141 4141 4141 4141 4141 4141  AAAAAAAAAAAAAAAA
0x0060:  4141 4141 4141 4141 4141 4141 4141 4141  AAAAAAAAAAAAAAAA
0x0070:  4141 4141 4141 4141 4141 4141 4141 4141  AAAAAAAAAAAAAAAA
0x0080:  4141 4141 4141 4141 4141 4141 4141 4141  AAAAAAAAAAAAAAAA
0x0090:  4141 4141 4141 4141 4141 4141 4141 4141  AAAAAAAAAAAAAAAA
0x00a0:  4141 4141 4141 4141 4141 4141 4141 4141  AAAAAAAAAAAAAAAA
0x00b0:  4141 4141 4141 4141 4141 4141 4141 4141  AAAAAAAAAAAAAAAA
0x00c0:  4141 4141 4141 4141 4141 4141 4141 4141  AAAAAAAAAAAAAAAA
0x00d0:  4141 4141 4141 4141 4141 4141 4141 4141  AAAAAAAAAAAAAAAA
0x00e0:  4141 4141 4141 4141 4141 4141 4141 4141  AAAAAAAAAAAAAAAA
0x00f0:  4141 4141 4141 4141 4141 4141 4141 4141  AAAAAAAAAAAAAAAA
0x0100:  4141 4141 4141 4141 4141 4141 4141 4141  AAAAAAAAAAAAAAAA
0x0110:  4141 4141 4141 4141 4141 4141 4141 4141  AAAAAAAAAAAAAAAA
0x0120:  4141 4141 4141 4141 4141 4141 4141 4141  AAAAAAAAAAAAAAAA
```

Figure 6-8 Tcpdump example #3
Source: Linux

Additionally, we have the raw packet content. In this case, we have a large number of As being sent to a Web server, which we deduce by the destination port of 80. This attack tries to exploit a Microsoft Windows vulnerability in the ntdll.dll library, where the attack vector is WebDAV using IIS.[3] By using the hex output, we are able to understand that this packet is part of an attack (or security test) on the network. This fundamental ability to decipher headers and peek into packet contents forms the basis for modern network intrusion detection and prevention systems.

Intrusion Detection and Prevention Systems

An **intrusion** occurs when an attacker attempts to gain entry or disrupt the normal operations of an information system, almost always with the intent to do harm. Even when such attacks are self-propagating, as in the case of viruses and distributed denial-of-service attacks, they are almost always instigated by an individual whose purpose is to harm an organization. Often, the differences among intrusion types lies with the attacker. Some intruders don't care which organizations they harm and prefer to remain anonymous, whereas others crave notoriety.

Intrusion detection consists of procedures and systems that identify system intrusions. **Intrusion prevention** consists of activities that deter an intrusion. Some important intrusion prevention activities are writing and implementing good enterprise information security policy, planning and performing effective information security programs, installing and testing technology-based information security countermeasures (such as firewalls and intrusion detection systems), and conducting and measuring the effectiveness of employee training and awareness activities. **Incident response** (covered in more depth in Chapter 11) encompasses the actions an organization takes when an intrusion is detected. These actions seek to limit the loss from an intrusion and return operations to a normal state as rapidly as possible. Incident management activities also finalize the restoration of operations to a normal state and seek to identify the source and method of the intrusion in order to ensure that the same type of attack cannot occur again—thus, reinitiating intrusion prevention.

Information security **intrusion detection systems (IDSs)** became commercially available in the late-1990s. An IDS works like a burglar alarm in that it detects a violation (some system activity analogous to an opened or broken window) and activates an alarm. This alarm can be audible and/or visual (producing noise and lights, respectively), or it can be silent (an e-mail message or pager alert). With almost all IDSs, system administrators can choose the configuration of the various alerts and the alarm levels associated with each type of alert. Many IDSs enable administrators to configure the systems to notify them directly of trouble via e-mail or pagers. The systems can also be configured—again, like a burglar alarm—to notify an external security service organization of a "break-in." The configurations that enable IDSs to provide customized levels of detection and response are quite complex. An extension of IDS technology is the **intrusion prevention system (IPS)**, which can detect an intrusion and also prevent that intrusion from successfully attacking the organization by means of an active response. Because the two systems often coexist, the combined term **intrusion detection/ prevention system (IDPS)** can be used to describe current anti-intrusion technologies.

IDPS Terminology

In order to understand IDPS operational behavior, you must first become familiar with some IDPS terminology. The following is a list of common IDPS terms and definitions:

- **Alert** or **alarm**—An indication that a system has detected a possible attack. IDPS alerts and alarms take the form of audible signals, e-mail messages, pager notifications, or pop-up windows.

- **Confidence**—A value placed on an IDPS event's ability to correctly detect and identify certain types of attacks. The confidence value an organization places on the IDPS, IDPS signatures, or specific events is based on experience and past performance measurements.

- **Evasion**—The process by which an attacker changes the format of the network packets and/or timing of their activities to avoid being detected by the IDPS.

- **Events**—IDPS events that are accurate and noteworthy but do not pose a significant threat to information security. Inappropriate system use, policy violations, and events triggered by scanning and enumeration tools fall into this category.

- **False negative**—The failure of an IDPS to react to an actual attack event. This is the most grievous failure because the purpose of an IDPS is to detect and respond to attacks.

- **False positive**—An alert or alarm that occurs in the absence of an actual attack. A false positive can sometimes be produced when an IDPS mistakes normal system activity for an attack. False positives tend to make users insensitive to alarms and, thus, reduce their reactivity to actual intrusion events. Also referred to as *noise*.

- **Filtering**—The process of reducing IDPS events in order to receive a better confidence in the alerts received. For example, the administrator may set the IDPS to discard alarms produced by false positives or normal network operations. Event filters are similar to packet filters in that they can filter items by their source or destination IP addresses, but they can also filter by operating systems, confidence values, alarm type, or alarm severity.

- **Tuning**—The process of adjusting an IDPS to maximize its efficiency in detecting true positives while minimizing both false positives and false negatives. This process may also include grouping almost identical alarms that happen at close to the same time into a single higher-level alarm. This consolidation reduces the number of alarms generated, thereby reducing administrative overhead, and also identifies a relationship among multiple alarms. This type of clustering may be based on combinations of frequency, similarity in attack signature, similarity in attack target, or other criteria that are defined by the system administrators.

Why Use an IDPS?

According to the NIST's documentation on industry best practices, there are several compelling reasons to acquire and use an IDPS:

- To reduce the likelihood of bad behavior by making users and maybe even intruders think they would be at a higher risk of discovery and punishment if they attacked or otherwise abused the system

- To detect attacks and other security violations that may not be prevented by other security measures

- To detect and react to common preambles of attacks (commonly experienced as network probes and other "doorknob rattling" activities)

- To document existing threats that may exist in an organization

- To act as a quality control measure for the security design and ongoing operation of security measures, especially for large and complex enterprises

- To provide useful information about intrusions that do take place, allowing improved diagnosis, recovery, and correction of causative factors[4]

One of the best reasons to install an IDPS is to provide an organization with overall situational awareness—or a better overall understanding—of the activities that take place on the network. Without this type of technology, most IT and network administrators would not have the detailed, real-time understanding of what attacks may be occurring at a given time.

Another reason to install an IDPS is to cover the organization when its network cannot protect itself against known vulnerabilities or is unable to respond to a rapidly changing threat environment. There are many factors that can delay or undermine an organization's ability to make its systems safe from attack and subsequent loss:

- Even though popular information security technologies such as scanning tools allow security administrators to evaluate the readiness of their systems, they may still fail to detect or correct a known deficiency, or they may perform the vulnerability detection process too infrequently.

- When a vulnerability is detected in a timely manner, it cannot always be corrected quickly. Because corrective measures usually require that the administrator install patches and upgrades, addressing the vulnerabilities is subject to fluctuations in the administrator's workload.

- To further complicate the matter, sometimes services known to be vulnerable cannot be disabled or otherwise protected because they are essential to ongoing operations.

At such times—that is, when there is a known vulnerability or deficiency in the system—an IDPS can be set up to detect attacks or attempts to exploit existing weaknesses, thus becoming an important part of the strategy of defense in depth to mitigate the overall risk to the business.

IDPSs can also help administrators detect the preambles to attacks. Most attacks begin with an organized and thorough probing of the organization's network environment and its defenses. This initial estimation of the defensive state of an organization's networks and systems is called *doorknob rattling* and is conducted first through activities collectively known as *footprinting* (which involves gathering information about the organization and its network activities and assets), and then through another set of activities collectively known as *fingerprinting* (in which network locales are scanned for active systems, and then the network services offered by the host systems on that network are identified). A system capable of detecting the early warning signs of footprinting and fingerprinting functions like a neighborhood watch that spots potential burglars testing doors and windows; this enables administrators to prepare for a potential attack or to take actions to minimize potential losses from an attack.

Another reason for acquiring an IDPS is threat documentation. The implementation of security technology usually requires that project proponents document the threat from which the organization must be protected. IDPSs are one means of collecting such data. (To collect statistics measuring the types of attack information you could expect in support of an IDPS implementation, you can begin with a freeware IDPS tool such as Snort.)

Data collected by an IDPS can also help management with quality assurance and continuous improvement; they consistently pick up information about attacks that have successfully compromised the outer layers of the network security architecture, such as a firewall or another control. This information can be used to identify and repair emergent or residual flaws in the security and network architectures and, thus, help the organization expedite its incident response process and make other continuous improvements.

Finally, even if an IDPS fails to prevent an intrusion, it can still assist in the after-attack review by providing information on how the attack occurred, what the intruder accomplished, and which methods the attacker employed. This information can be used to remedy deficiencies and to prepare the organization's network environment for future attacks. The IDPS may also provide forensic information that may be useful should the attacker be caught and prosecuted or sued.[5]

NIST SP 800-94 distinguishes between IPS and IDS as follows:

> *IPS technologies are differentiated from IDS technologies by one characteristic: IPS technologies can respond to a detected threat by attempting to prevent it from succeeding. They use several response techniques, which can be divided into the following groups:*
>
> - *The IPS stops the attack itself. Examples of how this could be done are as follows:*
>   - *Terminate the network connection or user session that is being used for the attack*
>   - *Block access to the target (or possibly other likely targets) from the offending user account, IP address, or other attacker attribute*
>   - *Block all access to the targeted host, service, application, or other resource*

- *The IPS changes the security environment. The IPS could change the configuration of other security controls to disrupt an attack. Common examples are reconfiguring a network device (e.g., firewall, router, switch) to block access from the attacker or to the target, and altering a host-based firewall on a target to block incoming attacks. Some IPSs can even cause patches to be applied to a host if the IPS detects that the host has vulnerabilities.*

- *The IPS changes the attack's content. Some IPS technologies can remove or replace malicious portions of an attack to make it benign. A simple example is an IPS removing an infected file attachment from an e-mail and then permitting the cleaned email to reach its recipient. A more complex example is an IPS that acts as a proxy and normalizes incoming requests, which means that the proxy repackages the payloads of the requests, discarding header information. This might cause certain attacks to be discarded as part of the normalization process.*[6]

Types of IDPSs

IDPSs operate as network- or host-based systems and work together to protect the network, as shown in Figure 6-9. A network-based IDPS is focused on protecting network information assets. Two specialized subtypes of network-based IDPS are the wireless IDPS and the network behavior analysis (NBA) IDPS. The wireless IDPS focuses on wireless networks, as the name indicates, whereas the NBA IDPS examines traffic flow on a network in an attempt to recognize abnormal patterns like DDoS, malware, and policy violations.

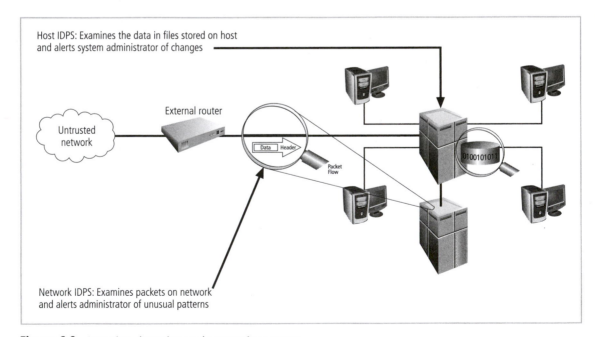

Host IDPS: Examines the data in files stored on host and alerts system administrator of changes

External router

Untrusted network

Data | Header

Packet Flow

0100010101

Network IDPS: Examines packets on network and alerts administrator of unusual patterns

Figure 6-9 Intrusion detection and prevention system
© Cengage Learning 2013

A host-based IDPS protects the server or host's information assets by monitoring both network connection activity and current information states on host servers. The application-based model works on one or more host systems that support a single application and defends that specific application from special forms of attack.

Network-Based IDPS A **network-based IDPS** (NIDPS) resides on a computer or appliance connected to a segment of an organization's network and monitors network traffic on that network segment—much like tcpdump—looking for indications of ongoing or successful attacks. When the NIDPS identifies activity that it is programmed to recognize as an attack, it responds by sending notifications to administrators. When examining incoming packets, an NIDPS looks for patterns within network traffic, such as large collections of related items of a certain type, which could indicate that a denial-of-service attack is underway, or the exchange of a series of related packets in a certain pattern, which could indicate that a port scan is in progress. An NIDPS can detect many more types of attacks than a host-based IDPS, but it requires a much more complex configuration and maintenance program.

As shown in Figure 6-10, an NIDPS is installed at a specific place in the network (such as on the inside of an edge router) from where it is possible to monitor the traffic going into and out of a particular network segment. The NIDPS can be deployed to monitor a specific grouping of host computers on a specific network segment, or it may be installed to monitor all traffic between the systems that make up an entire network.

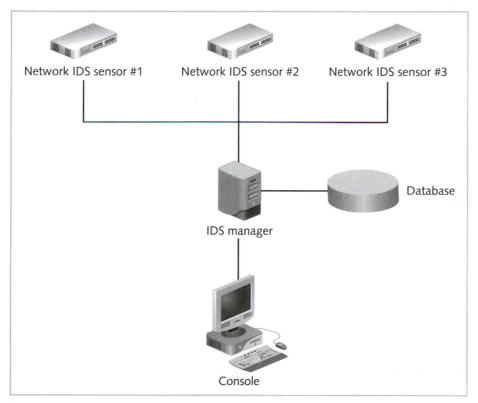

Figure 6-10 Simple network IDPS model
© Cengage Learning 2013

When placed next to a hub, switch, or other key networking device, the NIDPS may use that device's monitoring port. The **monitoring port,** also known as a switched port analysis (SPAN) port or mirror port, is a specially configured connection on a network device that is capable of viewing all the traffic that moves through the entire device. In the early 1990s, before switches became standard for connecting networks in a shared-collision domain, hubs were used. Hubs receive traffic from one node and retransmit it to all other nodes. This configuration allows any device connected to the hub to monitor all traffic passing through the hub. Unfortunately, it also represents a security risk because anyone connected to the hub can monitor all the traffic that moved through that network segment. Switches, on the other hand, create dedicated point-to-point links between their ports. These links create a higher level of transmission security and privacy, and they effectively prevent anyone from capturing, and thus eavesdropping on, the traffic passing through the switch. Unfortunately, the ability to capture the traffic is necessary for the use of an IDPS. Thus, monitoring ports are required. These connections enable network administrators to collect traffic from across the network for analysis by the IDPS as well as for occasional use in diagnosing network faults and measuring network performance.

Figure 6-11 shows a sample screen from SQueRT, a Web application used to query and view event data generated by IDPS applications like the Snort Network IDPS Engine (see *www.snort.org*) and OSSEC.

To determine whether an attack has occurred or is underway, NIDPSs compare measured activity to known signatures in their knowledge base. This is accomplished by means of a special implementation of the TCP/IP stack that reassembles the packets and applies protocol stack verification, application protocol verification, or other verification and comparison techniques.

In the process of **protocol stack verification**, the NIDPSs look for invalid data packets—that is, packets that are malformed under the rules of the TCP/IP protocol. A data packet is verified when its configuration matches that defined by the various Internet protocols. The elements of these protocols (IP, TCP, UDP, and application layers such as HTTP) are combined in a complete set called the *protocol stack* when the software is implemented in an operating system or application. Many types of intrusions, especially DoS and DDoS attacks, rely on the creation of improperly formed packets to take advantage of weaknesses in the protocol stack in certain operating systems or applications.

In **application protocol verification**, the higher-order protocols (HTTP, FTP, Telnet) are examined for unexpected packet behavior or improper use. Sometimes, an attack uses valid protocol packets, but in excessive quantities (in the case of the Tiny Fragment Packet attack, the packets are also excessively fragmented). Although the protocol stack verification looks for violations in the protocol packet structure, the application protocol verification looks for violations in the protocol packet use. One example of this kind of attack is DNS cache poisoning, in which valid packets exploit poorly configured DNS servers to inject false information to corrupt the servers' answers to routine DNS queries from other systems on the network. Unfortunately, this higher-order examination of traffic can have the same effect on an IDPS as it can on a firewall—that is, it slows the throughput of the system. It may be necessary to have more than one NIDPS installed, with one of them performing protocol stack verification and one performing application protocol verification.

Advantages of operational NIDPSs include:

- A smaller investment in NIDPS can often provide more coverage than the same investment in HIDPS because good network design and placement of NIDPS devices can enable an organization to use a few devices to monitor a large network.

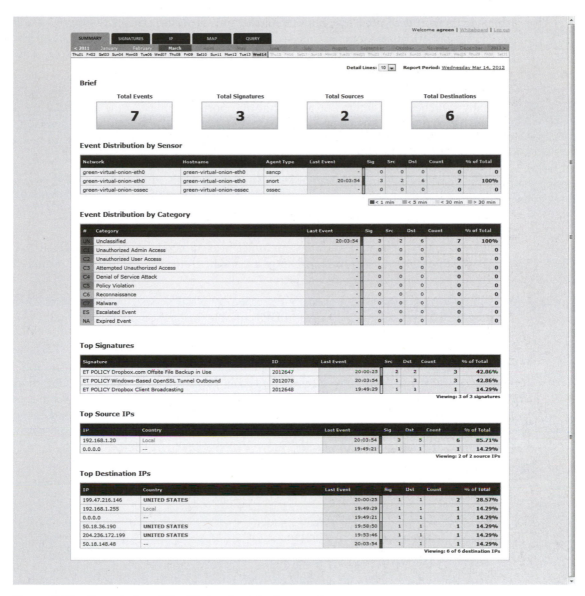

Figure 6-11 Example from SQueRT showing intrusion events
Source: SQueRT

- NIDPSs operating in a detection-only mode can be deployed in existing networks with little or no disruption to normal network operations.

- NIDPSs are not usually susceptible to direct attack and, in fact, may not be detectable by attackers.[7]

Disadvantages of operational NIDPSs include:

- NIDPSs can become overwhelmed by network volume and fail to recognize attacks they might otherwise have detected. Some IDPS vendors are accommodating the need for ever-faster network performance by improving the processing of detection algorithms in dedicated hardware circuits to gain a performance advantage. Additional efforts to optimize rule set processing may also reduce NIDPSs' overall effectiveness in detecting attacks.

- NIDPSs require access to all traffic that's to be monitored. The broad use of switched Ethernet networks has replaced the ubiquity of shared collision domain hubs. Since many switches have limited or no monitoring port capability, some networks are not capable of providing aggregate data for analysis by a NIDPS. Even when switches do provide monitoring ports, they may not be able to mirror all activity with a consistent and reliable time sequence.

- NIDPSs cannot analyze encrypted packets, making some of the network traffic invisible to the process. The increasing use of encryption that hides the contents of some or all of the packet by some network services (such as SSL, SSH, and VPN) limits the effectiveness of NIDPSs.

- NIDPSs cannot reliably ascertain if an attack was successful or not. This requires the network administrator to be engaged in an ongoing effort to evaluate the results of the logs of suspicious network activity.

- Some forms of attack are not easily discerned by NIDPSs, specifically those involving fragmented packets. In fact, some NIDPSs are particularly susceptible to malformed packets and may become unstable and stop functioning.[8]

Wireless IDPS   A wireless IDPS monitors and analyzes wireless network traffic looking for potential problems with the wireless protocols (layers 2 and 3 of the OSI model). Products like Motorola's AirDefense, Fluke's AirMagnet, and the open-source Kismet have to be deployed physically around the protected site in order to monitor the broad range of wireless signals able to reach the facility. In many cases, this type of functionality can be built into the wireless access point itself.

Wireless IDPS can help detect:

- Unauthorized WLANs and WLAN devices
- Poorly secured WLAN devices
- Unusual usage patterns
- Use of wireless network scanners
- Denial-of-service (DoS) attacks and conditions
- Impersonation and man-in-the-middle attacks[9]

Sensors for wireless networks can be located at the access points, installed on specialized sensor components, or incorporated into selected mobile stations. Centralized management stations collect information from these sensors, much the same way that other network-based IDPSs do, and aggregate the information into a comprehensive assessment of wireless network intrusions. Issues associated with the implementation of wireless IDPSs include:

- Higher protocol monitoring—Wireless IDPSs cannot evaluate and diagnose issues with higher-layer protocols like TCP and UDP. As such, Wireless IDPSs are unable to detect certain passive wireless protocol attacks in which the attacker monitors network traffic without active scanning and probing.

- Physical security—Unlike wired network sensors, which can be physically secured, many wireless sensors are located in public areas such as conference rooms, assembly areas, and hallways in order to attain the widest possible network range. Some of these locations may even be outdoors, as more and more organizations are deploying networks in external locations. Thus, the physical security of these devices is an issue and is likely to require additional security configuration and monitoring. The best configured IDPS in the world cannot withstand an attack from a well-placed brick.[10]

- Sensor range—A wireless device's range can be affected by atmospheric conditions, building construction, and the quality of both the wireless network card and access point. Some IDPS tools allow an organization to identify the optimal location for sensors by modeling the wireless footprint based on signal strength. Sensors are most effective when their footprints overlap.

- Access point and wireless switch locations—Wireless components with bundled IDPS capabilities must be carefully deployed to optimize the IDPS sensor detection grid. The minimum range is just that; you must guard against the possibility of an attacker connecting to a wireless access point from a range far beyond the minimum.

- Wired network connections—Wireless network components work independently of the wired network when sending and receiving between stations and access points. However, a network connection eventually integrates wireless traffic with the organization's wired network. Where there is no available wired network connection, it may be impossible to deploy a sensor.

- Cost—The more sensors deployed, the more expensive the configuration. Wireless components typically cost more than wired counterparts; thus, the total cost of both wired and wireless varieties should be carefully considered.[11]

Network Behavior Analysis System Network behavior analysis (NBA) systems examine network traffic in order to identify problems related to the flow of traffic. They use a version of the anomaly detection method described later in this section to identify excessive packet flows such as might occur in the case of equipment malfunction, denial-of-service attacks, virus and worm attacks, and some forms of network policy violations. NBA IDPSs typically monitor internal networks but occasionally monitor connections between internal and external networks. Typical flow data particularly relevant to intrusion detection and prevention includes the following:

- Source and destination IP addresses
- Source and destination TCP or UDP ports or ICMP types and codes
- Number of packets and bytes transmitted in the session
- Starting and ending timestamps for the session[12]

Most NBA sensors can be deployed in **passive mode** only, using the same connection methods (e.g., network tap, switch spanning port) as network-based IDPSs. Passive sensors that are performing direct network monitoring should be placed so that they can monitor key network locations, such as the divisions between networks, and key network segments, such as demilitarized zone (DMZ) subnets. **Inline sensors** are typically intended for network perimeter use, so they would be deployed in close proximity to the perimeter firewalls, often between the firewall and the Internet border router to limit incoming attacks that could overwhelm the the firewall.

The types of events most commonly detected by NBA sensors include the following:

- Denial-of-service (DoS) attacks (including distributed denial-of-service [DDoS] attacks)
- Scanning
- Worms
- Unexpected application services (e.g., tunneled protocols, backdoors, use of forbidden application protocols)
- Policy violations

NBA sensors offer various intrusion prevention capabilities, including the following (grouped by sensor type):

- Passive only, ending the current TCP session—A passive NBA sensor can attempt to end an existing TCP session by sending TCP reset packets to both endpoints.

  - Inline only, performing inline firewalling—Most inline NBA sensors offer firewall capabilities that can be used to drop or reject suspicious network activity.

- Both passive and inline, reconfiguring other network security devices—Many NBA sensors can instruct network security devices, such as firewalls and routers, to reconfigure themselves to block certain types of activity or route it elsewhere, such as to a quarantine virtual local area network (VLAN).

- Running a third-party program or script—Some NBA sensors can run an administrator-specified script or program when certain malicious activity is detected.[13]

Host-Based IDPS Whereas a network-based IDPS resides on a network segment and monitors activities across that segment, a **host-based IDPS** resides on a particular computer or server, known as the host, and monitors activity only on that system. HIDPSs are also known as **system integrity verifiers** because they benchmark and monitor the status of key system files and detect when an intruder creates, modifies, or deletes monitored files.[14] An HIDPS has an advantage over NIDPS in that it can be enabled to access encrypted information that is decrypted at the system level and use it to make decisions about potential or actual attacks. Also, because the HIDPS works on only one computer system, all the traffic it needs to make decisions comes to the system on which the HIDPS is running. The nature of the network packet delivery, whether switched or in a shared-collision domain, is not a factor.

A HIDPS is also capable of monitoring system configuration databases, such as Windows registries or stored configuration files like .ini, .cfg, and .dat files. Most HIDPSs work on the principle of configuration or change management, which means that they record the sizes, locations, and other attributes of system files. The HIDPS triggers an alert when one of the following occurs: file attributes change, new files are created, or existing files are deleted. A HIDPS can also monitor systems logs for predefined events. The HIDPS examines these files and logs to determine if an attack is underway or has occurred, and if the attack is succeeding or was successful. The HIDPS maintains its own log file so that an audit trail is available even when hackers modify files on the target system to cover their tracks.

Once properly configured, a HIDPS is very reliable. The only time it produces a false positive alert is when an authorized change occurs for a monitored file. This action can be quickly reviewed by an administrator, who may choose to disregard subsequent changes to the same set of files. If properly configured, a HIDPS can also detect when users attempt to modify or exceed their access authorization level.

A HIDPS classifies files into various categories and then sends notifications when changes occur. Most HIDPSs provide only a few general levels of alert notification. For example, an administrator can configure a HIDPS to report changes in a system folder (e.g., in C:\Windows or C:\WINNT) and changes to a security-related application (such as C:\TripWire). The configuration rules may classify changes to a specific application folder (e.g., C:\Program Files\Office) as normal, and hence unreportable. Administrators can configure the system to log all activity but to page them or e-mail them only if a reportable security event occurs. Because internal application files (such as dictionaries and configuration files) and data files are frequently modified, a poorly configured HIDPS can generate a large volume of false alarms.

As shown in Figure 6-12, a managed HIDPS service can monitor multiple computers simultaneously by creating a configuration file on each monitored host and by making each HIDPS report back to a master console system, which is usually located on the system administrator's computer. This master console monitors the information provided by the managed hosts and notifies the administrator when it senses recognizable attack conditions.

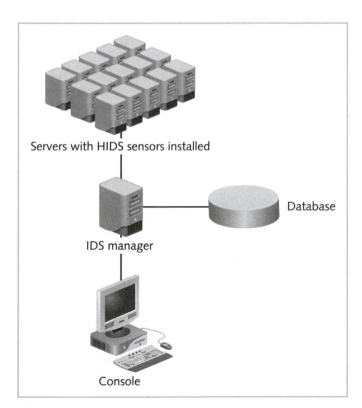

Figure 6-12 Simple HIDPS monitoring model
© Cengage Learning 2013

Advantages of HIDPSs include:

- A HIDPS can detect local events on host systems and also detect attacks that may elude a network-based IDPS.

- A HIDPS functions on the host system, where encrypted traffic will have been decrypted and is available for processing.

- The use of switched network protocols does not affect a HIDPS.

- A HIDPS can detect inconsistencies in how applications and systems programs were used by examining the records stored in audit logs. This can enable it to detect some types of attacks, including Trojan horse programs.[15]

Disadvantages of HIDPSs include:

- HIDPSs pose more management issues because they are configured and managed on each monitored host. This means that it requires more management effort to install, configure, and operate a HIDPS than a comparably sized NIDPS solution.

- A HIDPS is vulnerable both to direct attacks and to attacks against the host operating system. Either circumstance can result in the compromising and/or loss of HIDPS functionality.

- A HIDPS is not optimized to detect multi-host scanning, nor is it able to detect the scanning of non-host network devices, such as routers or switches. Unless complex correlation analysis is provided, the HIDPS will not be aware of attacks that span multiple devices in the network.

- A HIDPS is susceptible to some denial-of-service attacks.

- A HIDPS can use large amounts of disk space to retain the host OS audit logs; to function properly, it may require that disk capacity be added to the system.

- A HIDPS can inflict a performance overhead on its host systems and, in some cases, may reduce system performance below acceptable levels.[16]

IDPS Detection Methods

IDPSs use a variety of detection methods to monitor and evaluate network traffic. Three methods dominate: the signature-based approach, the statistical-anomaly approach, and the stateful packet inspection approach.

Signature-Based IDPS

A **signature-based IDPS** examines network traffic in search of patterns that match known **signatures**—that is, preconfigured, predetermined attack patterns. Signature-based IDPS technology is widely used because many attacks have clear and distinct signatures. Examples include:

- Footprinting and fingerprinting activities—Described in detail earlier in this chapter, these have an attack pattern that includes the use of ICMP, DNS querying, and e-mail routing analysis.

- Exploits—These involve a specific attack sequence designed to take advantage of a vulnerability to gain access to a system.

- Denial-of-service (DoS) and distributed denial-of-service (DDoS) attacks—During these, the attacker tries to prevent the normal usage of a system, which entails overloading the system with requests so that the system's ability to process them efficiently is compromised/disrupted and it begins denying services to authorized users.[17]

The problem with the signature-based approach is that as new attack strategies are identified, the IDPS's database of signatures must be continually updated; otherwise, attacks that use new strategies will not be recognized and might succeed. Another weakness of the signature-based method is that a slow, methodical attack might escape detection if the relevant IDPS attack signature has a shorter time frame. The only way for a signature-based IDPS to resolve this vulnerability is for it to collect and analyze data over longer periods of time, a process that requires substantially larger data storage capability and additional processing capacity.

Statistical Anomaly–Based IDPS

The **statistical anomaly–based IDPS (stat IDPS)**, or **behavior-based IDPS,** collects statistical summaries by observing traffic that is known to be normal. This normal period of evaluation establishes a performance baseline. Once the baseline is established, the stat IDPS periodically samples network activity and, using statistical methods, compares the sampled network activity to this baseline. When the measured activity is outside the baseline parameters—exceeding what is called the **clipping level**—the IDPS sends an alert to the administrator. The baseline data can include variables such as host memory or CPU usage, network packet types, and packet quantities.

The advantage of the statistical anomaly-based approach is that the IDPS can detect new types of attacks because it looks for abnormal activity of any type. Unfortunately, these systems require much more overhead and processing capacity than signature-based IDPSs because they must constantly compare patterns of activity against the baseline. Another drawback is that these systems may not detect minor changes to system variables and may generate many false positives. If the actions of the users or systems on a network vary widely, with periods of low activity interspersed with periods of heavy packet traffic, this type of IDPS may not be suitable because the dramatic swings from one level to another will almost certainly generate false alarms. Because of its complexity and impact on the overhead computing load of the host computer, as well as the number of false positives it can generate, this type of IDPS is less commonly used than the signature-based type.

Stateful Protocol Analysis IDPS

As you learned in Chapter 4, stateful inspection firewalls track each network connection between internal and external systems using a state table to record which station sent which packet and when, essentially pairing communicating parties. An IDPS extension of this concept is stateful protocol analysis. According to SP 800-94, "**Stateful protocol analysis (SPA)** is a process of comparing predetermined profiles of generally accepted definitions of benign activity for each protocol state against observed events to identify deviations. Stateful protocol analysis relies on vendor-developed universal profiles that specify how particular protocols should and should not be used."[18] Essentially, the IDPS knows how a protocol, such as FTP, is supposed to work and, therefore, can detect anomalous behavior. By storing relevant data detected in a session and then using that data to identify intrusions that involve multiple requests and responses, the IDPS can better detect specialized, multi-session attacks. This process is sometimes called *deep packet inspection* because SPA closely examines packets at the Application layer for information that indicates a possible intrusion.

SPA can also examine authentication sessions for suspicious activity, as well as for attacks that incorporate "unexpected sequences of commands, such as issuing the same command repeatedly or issuing a command without first issuing a command upon which it is dependent, as well as 'reasonableness' for commands such as minimum and maximum lengths for arguments."[19]

The models used for SPA are similar to signatures in that they are provided by vendors. These models are based on industry protocol standards established by such entities as the Internet Engineering Task Force, but they vary along with the protocol implementations in such documents. Also, proprietary protocols are not published in sufficient detail to enable the IDPS to provide accurate and comprehensive assessments.

Unfortunately, this type of IDPS method has a drawback: the analytical complexity of session-based assessments, which is further complicated by the amount of processing overhead in tracking multiple, simultaneous connections. Additionally, unless the protocol violates its fundamental behavior, this type of IDPS method may completely fail to detect the intrusion. One final issue is the possibility that the IDPS may in fact cause problems with the protocol it's examining, especially with client- and server-differentiated operations.[20]

Log File Monitors A **log file monitor** (LFM) IDPS is similar to an NIDPS. Using LFM, the system reviews the log files generated by servers, network devices, and even other IDPSs, looking for patterns and signatures that may indicate that an attack or intrusion is in process or has already occurred. Although an individual host IDPS is only able to examine the activity in one system, the LFM is able to look at multiple log files from a number of different systems. The patterns that signify an attack can be subtle and hard to distinguish when one system is examined in isolation, but they may be much easier to identify when the entire network and its systems are viewed. Of course, this holistic approach requires the allocation of considerable resources because it involves the collection, movement, storage, and analysis of very large quantities of log data.

IDPS Response Behavior

IDPSs responds to external stimulation in different ways, depending on their configurations and functions. Some respond in active ways, collecting additional information about the intrusion, modifying the network environment, or even taking action against the intrusion. Others respond in passive ways—for example, by setting off alarms or notifications or by collecting passive data through SNMP traps.

IDPS Response Options When an IDPS detects possible intrusion, it has a number of response options, depending on the implementing organization's policy, objectives, and system capabilities. When configuring an IDPS's responses, the system administrator must exercise care to ensure that a response to an attack (or potential attack) does not inadvertently exacerbate the situation. For example, if an NIDPS reacts to suspected DoS attacks by severing the network connection, the attack is a success, and such attacks repeated at intervals will thoroughly disrupt an organization's business operations.

An analogy to this approach would be the case of a potential car thief who walks up to a desirable target in the early hours of the morning, strikes the car's bumper with a rolled-up newspaper, and then ducks into the bushes. When the car alarm is triggered, the car owner wakes up, checks the car, determines there is no danger, resets the alarm, and goes back to bed. The thief repeats the triggering actions every half hour or so until the owner disables the alarm. The thief is now free to steal the car without worrying about triggering the alarm.

IDPS responses can be classified as active or passive. An active response is a definitive action automatically initiated when certain types of alerts are triggered; this can include collecting additional information, changing or modifying the environment, or taking action against the intruders. Passive response IDPSs simply report the information they have collected and wait for the administrator to act. Generally, the administrator chooses a course of action after analyzing the collected data. The passive IDPS is the most common implementation, although most systems allow some active options that are disabled by default.

The following list illustrates some of the responses an IDPS can be configured to produce. Note that some of these apply only to a network-based or a host-based IDPS, whereas others are applicable to both.[21]

- Audible/visual alarm—The IDPS can trigger a .wav file, beep, whistle, siren, or other audible or visual notification to alert the administrator of an attack. The most common type of such notifications is the computer pop-up window. This display can be configured with color indicators and specific messages, and it can also contain specifics about the suspected attack, the tools used in the attack, the level of confidence the system has in its own determination, and the addresses and/or locations of the systems involved.

- SNMP traps and plug-ins—The Simple Network Management Protocol contains trap functions, which allow a device to send a message to the SNMP management console indicating that a certain threshold has been crossed, either positively or negatively. The IDPS can execute this trap, telling the SNMP console an event has occurred. Some of the advantages of this operation include the relatively standard implementation of SNMP in networking devices, the ability to configure the network system to use SNMP traps in this manner, the ability to use systems specifically to handle SNMP traffic, including IDPS traps, and the ability to use standard communications networks.

- E-mail message—The IDPS can e-mail an individual to notify him or her of an event. Many administrators use personal digital assistants (PDAs) to check their e-mail frequently. Organizations should use caution in relying on e-mail systems as the primary means of communication between the IDPS and security personnel; e-mail is inherently unreliable, and an attacker could compromise the e-mail system and block such messages.

- Text or phone message—The IDPS can be configured to dial a phone number and produce an alphanumeric text or leave a message.

- Log entry—The IDPS can enter information about the event (addresses, time, systems involved, protocol information, etc.) into an IDPS system log file or operating system log file. These files can be stored on separate servers to prevent skilled attackers from deleting entries about their intrusions.

- Evidentiary packet dump—Organizations that require an audit trail of the IDPS data may choose to record all log data in a special way. This method allows the organization to perform further analysis on the data and also to submit the data as evidence in a civil or criminal case. Once the data has been written using a cryptographic hashing algorithm (discussed in detail in Chapter 3), it becomes evidentiary documentation—that is, suitable for criminal or civil court use. This packet logging can, however, be resource-intensive, especially in denial-of-service attacks.

- Take action against the intruder—It has become possible, though not advisable, to take action against an intruder. Known as trap and trace, back-hacking, or traceback, this response option involves configuring intrusion detection systems to trace the data

6

from the target system to the attacking system in order to initiate a counterattack. Although this may sound tempting, it is ill-advised and may not be legal. An organization only owns a network to its perimeter, and conducting traces or back-hacking to systems outside that perimeter may make the organization just as criminally liable as the individual(s) who began the attack. Also, in some cases the "attacking system" is in fact a compromised intermediary system, and in other cases attackers use address spoofing; either way, any counterattack would actually only harm an innocent third party. Any organization planning to configure any sort of retaliation effort into an automated intrusion detection system is strongly encouraged to seek legal counsel.

- Launch program—An IDPS can be configured to execute a specific program when it detects specific types of attacks. A number of vendors have specialized in tracking, tracing, and response software that could be part of an organization's intrusion response strategy.

- Reconfigure firewall—An IDPS could send a command to the firewall to filter out suspected packets by IP address, port, or protocol using one of the following methods:

  - Establishing a block for all traffic from the suspected attacker's IP address, or even from the entire source network from which the attacker appears to be operating. This blocking might be set for a specific period of time and be reset to normal rules after that period has expired.

  - Establishing a block for specific TCP or UDP port traffic from the suspected attacker's address or source network, blocking only the services that seem to be under attack.

  - Blocking all traffic to or from a network interface (such as the organization's Internet connection) if the severity of the suspected attack warrants that level of response.[22]

  - Terminating the session by using the TCP/IP protocol specified as packet *TCP close*. This is a simple process, and some attacks would be deterred or blocked by session termination, but others would simply continue when the attacker issues a new session request.

  - Terminating the organization's internal or external connections should be the last resort for an IDPS under attack, given that terminating network connections may be exactly what the attacker wants. Smart switches can cut traffic to/from a specific port, should that connection be linked to a system that is malfunctioning or otherwise interfering with efficient network operations.

It is, unfortunately, still possible for a skilled attacker to break in by simply spoofing a different address, shifting to a different port, or changing the protocols used in the attack.

Reporting and Archiving Capabilities Many, if not all, commercial IDPSs provide capabilities to generate routine reports and other detailed information documents. Some of these can output reports of system events and intrusions detected over a particular reporting period (e.g., a week or a month). Some provide statistics or logs generated by the IDPSs in formats suitable for inclusion in database systems or for use in report generating packages.[23]

Fail-Safe Considerations for IDPS Responses When choosing an IDPS product, you must consider the fail-safe features of the IDPS design or product. Fail-safe features protect the IDPSs from being circumvented or defeated by an attacker. There are several areas that require fail-safe measures. For instance, IDPSs need to provide silent, reliable monitoring of attackers. Should the response function of an IDPS break this silence by broadcasting alarms and alerts in plaintext over the monitored network, attackers can detect the presence of the IDPS and might then directly target the IDPS as part of the attack. Encrypted tunnels or other cryptographic measures that hide and authenticate IDPS communications are excellent ways to secure and ensure the reliability of the IDPS.[24]

Selecting IDPS Approaches and Products

The wide array of intrusion detection products available today addresses a broad range of organizational security goals and considerations; the process of selecting products that represent the best fit for any particular organization is challenging. The following considerations and questions may help you prepare a specification for acquiring and deploying an intrusion detection product.[25]

Technical and Policy Considerations

In order to determine which IDPS best meets an organization's needs, first consider the organizational environment in technical, physical, and political terms.

What Is Your System's Environment? The first hurdle a potential IDPS must clear is functioning in your systems environment. This is important; if an IDPS is not designed to accommodate the information sources that are available on your systems, it will not be able to see anything that goes on—neither normal activity nor an attack—in your systems. When considering an IDPS product, you must ask yourself the following questions:

- *What are the technical specifications of your systems environment?*—First, specify the technical attributes of your systems environment. These include: the number and locations of hosts, as specified by network diagrams and maps; operating systems for each host; the number and types of network devices, such as routers, bridges, and switches; the number and types of terminal servers and dial-up connections; and descriptors of any network servers, including types, configurations, and application software and versions running on each. If you run an enterprise network management system, specify it here.

- *What are the technical specifications of your current security protections?*—Describe the security protections you already have in place. Specify numbers, types, and locations of network firewalls, identification and authentication servers, data and link encryptors, antivirus packages, access control products, specialized security hardware (such as crypto accelerator hardware for Web servers), virtual private networks, and any other security mechanisms on your systems.

- *What are the goals of your enterprise?*—Some IDPSs have been developed to accommodate the special needs of certain industries or market niches such as electronic commerce, health care, or financial services. Define the functional goals of your enterprise (there can be several goals associated with a single organization) that are supported by your systems.

- *How formal is the system environment and management culture in your organization?*—Organizational styles vary, depending on the function of the organization and its traditional culture. For instance, the military and other organizations that deal with national security issues tend to operate with a high degree of formality, especially when contrasted with university or other academic environments. Some IDPSs support enforcement of formal use policies, with configuration options built into them by the manufacturer that can handle the particulars from commonly used

6

issue-specific security policies or system-specific security policies, as well as provide a library of reports for commonly encountered policy violations, along with other reporting capabilities.[26]

What Are Your Security Goals and Objectives? Once you've specified the technical landscape of your organization's systems as well as its existing security mechanisms, it's time to articulate the goals and objectives you wish to attain by using an IDPS. Ask yourself the following:

- *Is the organization's primary goal protecting itself from threats originating outside the organization?*—Perhaps the easiest way to identify security goals is by categorizing your organization's threat concerns. Identify the various concerns your organization has regarding external threats.

- *Is your organization more concerned about an insider attack—that is, threats originating within the organization?*—This can encompass not only a user who attacks the system from within (such as a shipping clerk who attempts to access and alter the payroll system) but also the authorized external user who exceeds his privileges, thereby violating organizational security policy or laws (such as a customer service agent who, driven by curiosity, accesses earnings and payroll records for public figures).

- *Does your organization want to use the output of your IDPS to determine new needs?*—System usage monitoring is sometimes provided as a generic system management tool to determine when system assets require upgrading or replacement. When such monitoring is performed by an IDPS, the needs for upgrade can show up as anomalous levels of user activity.

- *Does your organization want to use an IDPS to maintain managerial control (non-security-related) over network usage?*—In some organizations, there are system use policies that may be classified as personnel management rather than system security issues. These might include accessing questionable Web sites (such as ones containing pornography) or using organizational systems to send e-mail or other messages for the purpose of harassing individuals. Some IDPSs provide features that detect such violations of management controls.[27]

What Is Your Existing Security Policy? At this time, you should review your existing organization security policy. This will serve as the template against which the features of your IDPS will be configured. During your review, look for the following items (or augment the policy if these items do not exist):

- *How is it structured?*—It is helpful to articulate the goals outlined in the security policy in terms of the standard security goals (integrity, confidentiality, and availability) as well as in terms of more generic management goals (privacy, protection from liability, manageability).

- *What are the general job descriptions of your system users?*—List the general job functions of system users (there are commonly several functions assigned to a single user), as well as the data and network accesses that each function requires.

- *Does the policy include reasonable use policies or other management provisions?*—As mentioned earlier, many organizations have system use policies included as part of security policies.

- *Has your organization defined processes for dealing with specific policy violations?*—It is helpful to have a clear idea of what the organization wishes to do when the IDPS detects that a policy has been violated. If the organization doesn't intend to react to such violations, it may not make sense to configure the IDPS to detect them. If, on the other hand, the organization wishes to actively respond to such violations, the IDPS's operational staff should be informed of the response policy so that they can deal with alarms in an appropriate manner.[28]

Organizational Requirements and Constraints Your organization's operational goals, constraints, and culture will affect the selection of the IDPS and other security tools and technologies to protect your systems. Here are some questions to ask:[29]

What Requirements Are Levied from Outside the Organization?

- Is your organization subject to oversight or review by another organization? If so, does that oversight authority require IDPSs or other specific system security resources?

- Are there requirements for public access to information on your organization's systems? Do regulations or statutes require that information on your system be accessible by the public during certain hours of the day or during certain date or time intervals?

- Are there other security-specific requirements levied by law? Are there legal requirements for protection of personal information (such as earnings information or medical records) stored on your systems? Are there legal requirements for investigation of security violations that divulge or endanger that information?

- Are there internal audit requirements for security best practices or due diligence? Do any of these audit requirements specify functions that the IDPSs must provide or support?

- Is the system subject to accreditation? If so, what is the accreditation authority's requirement for IDPSs or other security protection?

- Are there requirements for law enforcement investigation and resolution of security incidents? Do these specify any IDPS functions, especially those having to do with collection and protection of IDPS logs as evidence?[30]

What Are Your Organization's Resource Constraints? IDPSs can protect the systems of an organization, but at a price. It makes little sense to incur additional expense for IDPS features if your organization does not have sufficient systems or personnel to handle the alerts generated by the system. Here are some of the questions an organization must ask:

- *What is the budget for acquisition and life-cycle support of intrusion detection hardware, software, and infrastructure?*—Remember that the acquisition of IDPS software is not the only element that counts toward the total cost of ownership; you may also have to acquire a system on which to run the software, obtain specialized assistance to install and configure the system, and train your personnel. Ongoing operations may also require additional staff or outside contractors.

- *Is there sufficient existing staff to monitor an intrusion detection system full time?*— Some IDPSs require that systems personnel attend them around the clock. If you do not anticipate having such personnel available, you may wish to explore those systems that accommodate less than full-time attendance.

- *Does your organization have authority to instigate changes based on the findings of an intrusion detection system?*—It is critical that you and your organization be clear

6

about what you plan to do about the problems uncovered by an IDPS. If you are not empowered to handle the incidents that arise as a result of the monitoring, you should consider coordinating your selection and configuration of the IDPS with the party who is empowered.[31]

IDPS Product Features and Quality

The IDPSs on the market provide a bewildering array of capabilities and features that may or may not be relevant to the needs of a particular organization. In selecting a specific product or a set of product features, you should consider the questions discussed in the following sections.[32]

Is the Product Sufficiently Scalable for Your Environment? Many IDPSs struggle to function within large or widely distributed enterprise network environments. Most of this is because of the product's inability to handle the high volume of network traffic. The demands of a large environment can take several different forms:

- The product cannot support the network throughput required to inspect packets and pass benign packets on to their destinations. This causes latency to overall network communications.

- Because of the large number of sensors that large enterprises must deploy to cover the various logical networks, management of the sensors can be unwieldy. Products without centralized management and monitoring of the sensors will quickly overwhelm the IDPS support staff.

- Large enterprises typically have many offices or many logical networks. Without proper placement of IDPS sensors, the organization may have a false sense of security, believing they are seeing all traffic in cases where entire network segments may not be monitored.[33]

How Has the Product Been Tested? Simply asserting that an IDPS has certain capabilities is not sufficient to demonstrate that those capabilities are real. You should request demonstrations of how suitable a particular IDPS is to your environment and goals. You should also get answers to these questions:

- *Has the product been tested against functional requirements?*—What assumptions has the vendor made regarding the goals and constraints of customer environments?

- *Has the product been tested against attack?*—Ask vendors for details of the security testing that its products have been subjected to. If the product includes network-based vulnerability assessment features, ask whether test routines that produce system crashes or other denials of service have been identified and flagged in system documentation and interfaces.[34]

What Is the User Level of Expertise Targeted by the Product? Different IDPS vendors target users with different levels of technical and security expertise. Ask vendors what their assumptions are regarding the users of their products. Any organization planning on deploying IDPS should budget knowledgeable, trained support staff who can maintain the infrastructure and ensure that the IDPS operates according to plan.[35]

Is the Product Designed to Evolve as the Organization Grows? The product you choose should be able to adapt to your needs over time. To ensure that happens, you should ask vendors the following questions:

- *Can the product adapt to growth in user expertise?*—Can the IDPS's interface be configured (with shortcut keys, customizable alarm features, and custom signatures) on the fly? Are these features documented and supported?

- *Can the product adapt to growth and change of the organization's systems infrastructure?*—This question has to do with the ability of the IDPS to scale to an expanding and increasingly diverse network. Most vendors have experience in adapting their products as target networks grow. Ask about commitments to support new protocol standards and platform types.

- *Can the product adapt to growth and change of the security threat environment?*— This is especially critical given the current Internet threat environment, in which 30 to 40 new attacks are published to the Web every month.[36]

What Are the Support Provisions for the Product? Like other systems, IDPSs require maintenance and support over time. These needs should be identified and prepared in a written report. Questions to ask include:

- *What are the commitments for product installation and configuration support?*— Many vendors provide expert assistance to customers in installing and configuring IDPSs; others expect that your own staff will handle these functions and, therefore, provide only telephone or e-mail help-desk functions.

- *What are the commitments for ongoing product support?*—In this area, ask about the vendor's commitment to supporting your use of its IDPS product.

- *Are subscriptions to signature updates included?*—Most IDPSs are signature based, so the value of the product is only as good as the signature database against which events are analyzed. Most vendors provide subscriptions to signature updates for some period of time (a year is typical).

- *How often are subscriptions updated?*—In today's threat environment, this is a critical question.

- *How quickly after a new attack is made public will the vendor ship a new signature?*— If you are using IDPSs to protect highly visible or heavily traveled Internet sites, it is especially critical that you receive the signatures for new attacks as soon as possible.

- *Are software updates included?*—Most IDPSs are software products and, therefore, subject to bugs and revisions. Ask the vendor about support for software updates and bug patches and determine to what extent they are included in the product you purchase.

- *How quickly will software updates and patches be issued after a problem is reported to the vendor?*—Because software bugs can allow attackers to nullify an IDPS's protective effect, it is extremely important that problems be fixed reliably and quickly.

- *Are technical support services included? What is the cost?*—Technical support services means vendor assistance in tuning or adapting your IDPS to accommodate special needs, whether that's monitoring a custom or legacy system within your enterprise or reporting IDPS results in a custom protocol or format.

- *What are the provisions for contacting technical support (e-mail, telephone, online chat, Web-based reporting)?*—The contact provisions will likely tell you whether these technical support services are accessible enough to support incident handling or other time-sensitive needs.

- *Are there any guarantees associated with the IDPS?*—As with other software products, IDPSs traditionally have few guarantees associated with them; however, in an attempt to gain market share, some vendors are initiating guarantee programs.

- *What training resources does the vendor provide?*—Once an IDPS is selected, installed, and configured, it must still be operated by your personnel. In order for these people to make optimal use of the IDPS, they should be trained in its use. Some vendors provide this training as part of the product package.

- *What additional training resources are available from the vendor and at what cost?*— If the IDPS vendor does not provide training as part of its IDPS package, you should budget appropriately to train your operational personnel.[37]

Strengths and Limitations of IDPSs

Although IDPSs are a valuable addition to an organization's security infrastructure, there are things they do well and things they do not do well. As you plan the security strategy for your organization's systems, it is important to understand what IDPSs should be trusted to do and what goals might be better served by other types of security mechanisms.

Strengths of IDPSs IDPSs perform the following functions well:

- Monitoring and analysis of system events and user behaviors
- Testing the security states of system configurations
- Baselining the security state of a system, then tracking any changes to that baseline
- Recognizing patterns of system events that correspond to known attacks
- Recognizing patterns of activity that statistically vary from normal activity
- Managing operating system audit and logging mechanisms and the data they generate
- Alerting appropriate staff by appropriate means when attacks are detected
- Measuring enforcement of security policies encoded in the analysis engine
- Providing default information security policies
- Allowing non-security experts to perform important security monitoring functions[38]

Limitations of IDPSs IDPSs cannot perform the following functions:

- Compensating for weak or missing security mechanisms in the protection infrastructure, such as firewalls, identification and authentication systems, link encryption systems, access control mechanisms, and virus detection and eradication software
- Instantaneously detecting, reporting, and responding to an attack when there is a heavy network or processing load
- Detecting newly published attacks or variants of existing attacks
- Effectively responding to attacks launched by sophisticated attackers
- Automatically investigating attacks without human intervention
- Resisting all attacks that are intended to defeat or circumvent them
- Compensating for problems with the fidelity of information sources
- Dealing effectively with switched networks

There is also the considerable challenge of configuring an IDPS to respond accurately to a perceived threat. Once a device is empowered to react to an intrusion by filtering or even severing a communication session, or by severing a communication circuit, the impact from a false positive becomes increasingly significant. It's one thing to fill an administrator's e-mail box or compile a large log file with suspected attacks; it's quite another to shut down critical communications. Some forms of attacks are designed to trip the organization's IDPS, essentially causing the organization to conduct its own DoS attack by overreacting to an actual, but insignificant, attack.[39]

Deployment and Implementation of an IDPS

Deploying and implementing an IDPS is not always a straightforward task. The strategy should consider a number of factors, the foremost being how the IDPS will be managed and where it will be placed. These factors determine the number of administrators needed to install, configure, and monitor the IDPS, as well as the number of management workstations, the size of the storage needed for retention of the data generated by the systems, and the ability of the organization to detect and respond to remote threats.

IDPS Control Strategies
An IDPS can be implemented via one of three basic control strategies. A control strategy determines how an organization exerts influence and maintains the configuration of an IDPS. It also determines how the input and output of the IDPS is to be managed. The three commonly utilized control strategies are centralized, partially distributed, and fully distributed. The IT industry has been exploring technologies and practices to enable the distribution of computer processing cycles and data storage for many years. These explorations have long considered the advantages and disadvantages of the centralized strategy versus strategies with varying degrees of distribution. In the early days of computing, all systems were fully centralized, resulting in a control strategy that provided high levels of security and control as well as efficiencies in resource allocation and management. During the 1980s and 1990s, with the rapid growth in networking and computing capabilities, the trend was to implement a fully distributed strategy. In the mid-1990s, however, the high costs of a fully distributed architecture became apparent, and the IT industry shifted toward a mixed strategy of partially distributed control. A strategy of partial distribution, in which some features and components are distributed and others are centrally controlled, is now recognized as the recommended practice for IT systems in general and for IDPS control systems in particular.

Centralized Control Strategy
In a **centralized IDPS control strategy**, all IDPS control functions are implemented and managed in a central location, which is depicted by the large square symbol labeled "IDPS Console" in Figure 6-13. The IDPS console includes the management software, which collects information from the remote sensors (depicted in the figure by triangular symbols), analyzes the systems or networks monitored, and determines whether the current situation has deviated from the preconfigured baseline. All reporting features are also implemented and managed from this central location. The primary advantages of this strategy are related to cost and control. With one central implementation, there is one management system, one place to go to monitor the status of the systems or networks, one location for reports, and one set of administrative management. This centralization of IDPS management supports task specialization because all managers are either located near the IDPS management

console or can acquire an authenticated remote connection to it, and technicians are located near the remote sensors. This means that each person can focus specifically on the assigned task. In addition, the central control group can evaluate the systems and networks as a whole, and because it can compare pieces of information from all sensors, the group is better positioned to recognize a large-scale attack.

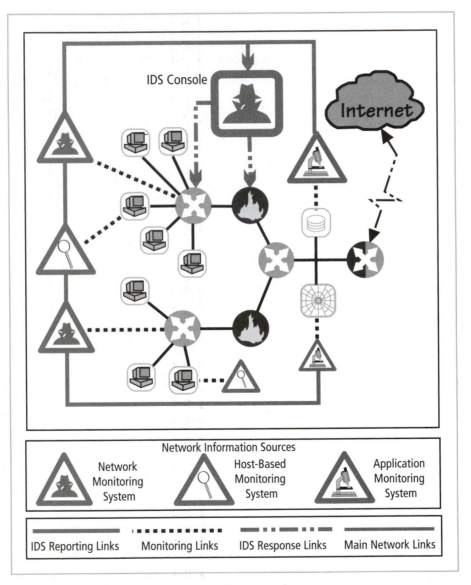

Figure 6-13   Centralized intrusion detection approach
© Cengage Learning 2013

Fully Distributed Control Strategy   As shown in Figure 6-14, a **fully distributed IDPS control strategy** is the opposite of the centralized strategy. Note in the figure that all control functions (which appear as small square symbols enclosing a computer icon) are applied at the physical location of each IDPS component. Each monitoring site uses its own paired sensors to perform its own control functions to achieve the necessary detection, reaction, and response functions. Thus, each sensor/agent is best configured to deal with its own environment. Because the IDPSs do not have to wait for a response from a centralized control facility, their reaction time to individual attacks is greatly increased.

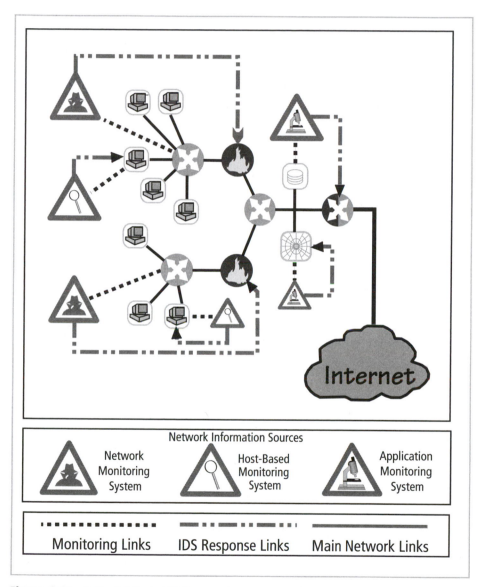

Figure 6-14   Fully distributed IDPS control

© Cengage Learning 2013

Partially Distributed Control Strategy

A **partially distributed IDPS control strategy**, shown in Figure 6-15, combines the best of the other two strategies. Although the individual agents can still analyze and respond to local threats, they report to a hierarchical central facility, which enables the organization to detect widespread attacks. This blended approach to reporting is one of the more effective methods of detecting intelligent attackers, especially those who probe an organization through multiple points of entry, trying to scope out the systems' configurations and weaknesses, before they launch a concerted attack. The partially distributed control strategy also allows the organization to optimize for economy of scale in the implementation of key management software and personnel, especially in the reporting areas. When the organization can create a pool of security managers to evaluate reports from multiple distributed IDPS systems, it becomes better able to detect these distributed attacks before they become unmanageable.

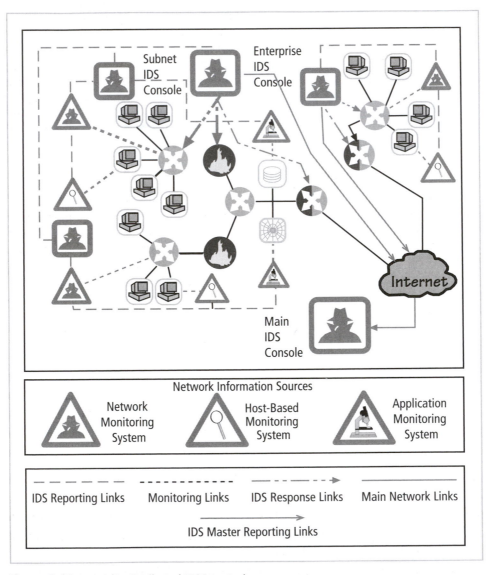

Figure 6-15 Partially distributed IDPS control

IDPS Deployment Given the highly technical skills required to implement and configure IDPSs and the imperfection of the technology, great care must be made in the decisions about where to locate the components, both in their physical connection to the network and host devices and in how they are logically connected to each other and the IDPS administration team. Because IDPSs are designed to detect, report, and even react to anomalous stimuli, placing IDPSs in an area where such traffic is common can result in excessive reporting. Moreover, the administrators monitoring systems located in such areas can become desensitized to the information flow and may fail to detect actual attacks in progress.

As an organization selects an IDPS and prepares for implementation, planners must select a deployment strategy that is based on a careful analysis of the organization's information security requirements and that integrates with the organization's existing IT infrastructure but, at the same time, causes minimal impact. After all, the purpose of the IDPS is to detect anomalous situations, not create them. One consideration is the skill level of the personnel required to install, configure, and maintain the systems. An IDPS is a complex system in that it involves numerous remote monitoring agents (on both individual systems and networks) that require proper configuration to gain the proper authentication and authorization. As the IDPS is deployed, each component should be installed, configured, fine-tuned, tested, and monitored. A mistake in any step of the deployment process may produce a range of problems, from a minor inconvenience to a network-wide disaster. Thus, both the individuals installing the IDPS and the individuals using and managing the system require proper training.

NIDPS and HIDPS can be used in tandem to cover both the individual systems that connect to an organization's networks and the networks themselves. To do this, it is important for an organization to use a phased implementation strategy so as not to affect the entire organization all at once. A phased implementation strategy also allows security technicians to resolve the problems that do arise without compromising the very information security the IDPS is installed to protect. In terms of sequencing the implementation, first the organization should implement the network-based IDPS, as this type of IDPS is less problematic and easier to configure than their host-based counterparts. After the NIDPSs are configured and running without issue, the HIDPSs can be installed to protect the critical systems on the host server. Next, after both are considered operational, it would be advantageous to scan the network with a vulnerability scanner such as Nmap or Nessus to determine if (1) the scanners pick up anything new or unusual and (2) the IDPS can detect the scans.

Deploying Network-Based IDPSs As discussed earlier, the placement of the sensor agents is critical to the operation of all IDPSs, but this is especially critical in the case of NIDPSs. As shown in Figure 6-16, NIST recommends four locations for NIDPS sensors:

Location 1: Behind each external firewall, in the network DMZ

Advantages:

- The IDPS sees attacks that originate on the Internet and may penetrate the network's perimeter defenses.

- The IDPS can identify problems with the network firewall policy or performance.

- The IDPS sees attacks that might target the Web server or ftp server, both of which commonly reside in this DMZ.

- Even if the incoming attack is not detected, the IDPS can sometimes recognize, in the outgoing traffic, patterns that suggest that the server has been compromised.

Location 2: Outside an external firewall

Advantages:

- The IDPS documents the number of attacks originating on the Internet that target the network.
- The IDPS documents the types of attacks originating on the Internet that target the network.

Location 3: On major network backbones

Advantages:

- The IDPS monitors a large amount of a network's traffic, thus increasing its chances of spotting attacks.
- The IDPS detects unauthorized activity by authorized users within the organization's security perimeter.

Location 4: On critical subnets

Advantages:

- The IDPS detects attacks targeting critical systems and resources.
- The location allows organizations with limited resources to focus these resources on the network assets considered of greatest value.[40]

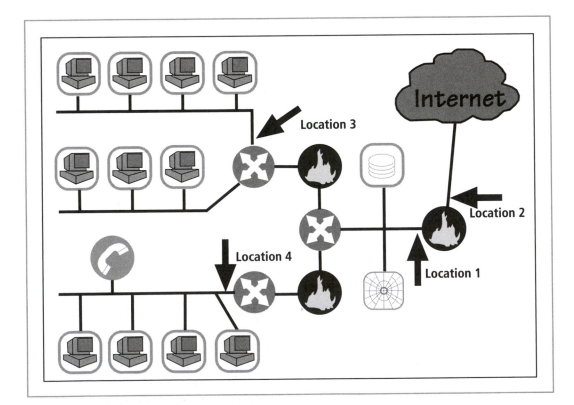

Figure 6-16 Network IDPS sensor locations
© Cengage Learning 2013

Deploying Host-Based IDPSs Implementing HIDPSs can be a painstaking and time-consuming task, as each HIDPS must be custom configured to its host systems. Deployment begins with implementing the most critical systems first. This poses a dilemma for the deployment team because the first systems to be implemented are mission critical, and any problems in the installation could be catastrophic to the organization. Therefore, it may be beneficial to practice an implementation on one or more test servers configured on a network segment that resembles the mission-critical systems. Practicing will help the installation team gain experience and also help determine if the installation might trigger any unusual events. Gaining an edge on the learning curve by training on nonproduction systems will benefit the overall deployment process by reducing the risk of unforeseen complications.

Installation continues until either all systems are installed or the organization reaches the planned degree of coverage it is willing to live with in regard to the number of systems or percentage of network traffic. To provide ease of management, control, and reporting, each HIDPS should, as discussed earlier, be configured to interact with a central management console.

Just as technicians can install the HIDPS in offline systems to develop expertise and identify potential problems, users and managers can gain expertise and understanding of the operation of the HIDPS by using a test facility. This test facility could use the offline systems configured by the technicians, but it could also be connected to the organization's backbone to allow the HIDPS to process actual network traffic. This setup also enables technicians to create a baseline of normal traffic for the organization. During the system testing process, training scenarios can be developed that enable users to recognize and respond to common attack situations. To ensure effective and efficient operation, the management team can establish policy for the operation and monitoring of the HIDPS.

Measuring the Effectiveness of IDPSs
When selecting an IDPS, one typically looks at four measures of comparative effectiveness:

- Thresholds—A threshold is a value that sets the limit between normal and abnormal behavior. Thresholds usually specify a maximum acceptable level, such as x failed connection attempts in 60 seconds or x characters for a filename length. Thresholds are most often used for anomaly-based detection and stateful protocol analysis.

- Blacklists and whitelists—A blacklist is a list of discrete entities, such as hosts, TCP or UDP port numbers, ICMP types and codes, applications, usernames, URLs, filenames, or file extensions, that have been previously determined to be associated with malicious activity. Also known as hot lists, blacklists are typically used to allow IDPSs to recognize and block activity that is highly likely to be malicious; they may also be used to assign a higher priority to alerts that match entries on the blacklists. Some IDPSs generate dynamic blacklists that are used to temporarily block recently detected threats (e.g., activity from an attacker's IP address). A whitelist is a list of discrete entities that are known to be benign. Whitelists are typically used on a granular basis, such as protocol by protocol, to reduce or ignore false positives involving known benign activity from trusted hosts. Blacklists and whitelists are most commonly used in signature-based detection and stateful protocol analysis.

- Alert settings—Most IDPS technologies allow administrators to customize each alert type. Examples of actions that can be performed on an alert type include (1) toggling it on or off, (2) setting a default priority or severity level, (3) specifying what information should be recorded and what notification methods (e.g., e-mail, pager) should be used, and (4) specifying which prevention capabilities should be used. Some products also suppress alerts if an attacker generates many alerts in a short period of time; they may also temporarily ignore all future traffic from the attacker. This is to prevent the IDPS from being overwhelmed by alerts.

- Code viewing and editing—Some IDPS technologies permit administrators to see some or all of the detection-related code. This is usually limited to signatures, but some technologies allow administrators to see additional code, such as programs used to perform stateful protocol analysis.[41]

Once implemented, IDPSs are evaluated using two sets of measurements. First, administrators evaluate the number of attacks detected in a known collection of probes. Second, they examine the level of use (commonly measured in megabits per second of network traffic) at which the IDPSs fail. An IDPS evaluation might read something like this: "At 100 Mbps, the IDPS was able to detect 97 percent of directed attacks." This is a dramatic change from the previous method used for assessing IDPS effectiveness, which was based on the total number of signatures the system was currently running—a sort of "more is better" approach. This evaluation method of assessment was flawed for several reasons. Not all IDPSs use simple signature-based detection. Some systems, as discussed earlier, can use the almost infinite combination of network performance characteristics of statistical-anomaly-based detection to detect a potential attack. Also, some more sophisticated signature-based systems actually use *fewer* signatures/rules than older, simpler versions, which, in direct contrast to the signature-based assessment method, suggests that less may actually be more.

The recognition that the size of the signature base is an insufficient measure of an IDPS's effectiveness led to the development of stress test measurements for evaluating IDPS performance. These only work, however, if the administrator has a collection of known negative and positive actions that can be proven to elicit a desired response. Because developing this collection can be tedious, most IDPS vendors provide testing mechanisms for verifying that their systems are performing as expected. These testing processes enable the administrator to:

- Record and retransmit packets from a real virus or worm scan
- Record and retransmit packets from a real virus or worm scan with incomplete TCP/IP session connections (missing SYN packets)
- Conduct a real virus or worm scan against an invulnerable system

This last measure is important because future IDPSs will probably include much more detailed information about the overall site configuration. With the rapid growth in technology, each new generation of IDPSs will require new testing methodologies. However, the measured values that will continue to be of interest to IDPS administrators and managers will, most certainly, include some assessment of how much traffic the IDPS can handle, the numbers of false positives and false negatives it generates, and the IDPS's ability to detect actual attacks. Vendors of IDPS systems could also include a report of the alarms sent and the relative accuracy of the system in correctly matching the alarm level to the true seriousness of the threat. Some planned metrics for IDPSs may include the flexibility of signatures and detection policy customization.

IDPS administrators may soon be able to purchase tools that test IDPS effectiveness. Until these tools are available from a neutral third party, the diagnostics from the IDPS vendors will always be suspect. No vendor, no matter how reliable, would provide a test that their system would fail.

One note of caution: There may be a strong tendency among IDPS administrators to use common vulnerability assessment tools, like Nmap or Nessus, to evaluate the capabilities of an IDPS. Although this may seem like a good idea, it will not work as expected, because most IDPS systems are equipped to recognize the differences between a locally implemented vulnerability assessment tool and a true attack.

In order to perform a true assessment of the effectiveness of IDPS systems, the test process should be as realistic as possible in its simulation of an actual event. This means coupling realistic traffic loads with realistic levels of attacks. You cannot expect an IDPS to respond to a few packet probes as if they represent a denial-of-service attack. In one reported example, a program was used to create a synthetic load of network traffic made up of many TCP sessions, with each session consisting of a SYN (or synchronization) packet, a data exchange, and ACK (or acknowledgement) packets, but no FIN or connection termination packets. Of the several IDPS systems tested, one of them crashed because of lack of resources while it waited for the sessions to be closed. Another IDPS passed the test with flying colors because it did not perform state tracking on the connections. Neither of the tested IDPS systems worked as expected, but the one that didn't perform state tracking was able to stay operational and was, therefore, given a better score on the test.[42]

Honeypots and Honeynets

A class of powerful security tools that go beyond routine intrusion detection is known variously as honeypots, honeynets, or padded cell systems. To understand the value, you must first understand how they differ from a traditional IDPS. **Honeypots** are decoy systems designed to lure potential attackers away from critical systems. In the industry, they are also known as decoys, lures, and fly-traps. When a collection of honeypots connects several honeypot systems on a subnet, it may be called a **honeynet**. A honeypot system (or in the case of a honeynet, an entire subnetwork) contains pseudo-services that emulate well-known services but are configured in ways that make them look vulnerable to attacks. This combination is meant to lure potential attackers into committing an attack, thereby revealing themselves—the idea being that once organizations have detected these attackers, they can better defend their networks against future attacks against real assets. In sum, honeypots are designed to:

- Divert an attacker from critical systems
- Collect information about the attacker's activity
- Encourage the attacker to stay on the system long enough for administrators to document the event and perhaps respond

Because the information in a honeypot appears to be valuable, any unauthorized access to it constitutes suspicious activity. Honeypots are equipped with sensitive monitors and event loggers that detect attempts to access the system and collect information about the potential attacker's activities.

IDPS researchers have used honeypot systems since the late-1980s, but until recently no commercial versions of these products were available. It is important to seek guidance from legal counsel before deciding to use either of these systems in your operational environment, because using an attractant and then launching a back hack or counterstrike might be illegal and make the organization subject to a lawsuit or a criminal complaint.

The advantages of using the honeypot approach are:

- Attackers can be diverted to targets that they cannot damage.

- Administrators have time to decide how to respond to an attacker.

- Attackers' actions can be easily and more extensively monitored, and the records can be used to refine threat models and improve system protections.

- Honeypots may be effective at catching insiders who are snooping around a network.

The disadvantages of using a honeypot approach are:

- The legal implications of using such devices are not well defined.

- An expert attacker, once diverted into a decoy system, may become angry and launch a more hostile attack against an organization's systems.

- Administrators and security managers need a high level of expertise to use these systems.

- Administrators should also be wary of the wasp trap syndrome. In this syndrome, a concerned homeowner installs a wasp trap in his backyard to trap the few insects he sees flying about. Because these traps use scented bait, however, they wind up attracting far more wasps than were originally present. Security administrators should keep the wasp trap syndrome in mind before implementing honeypots.

- Special care must be taken in order to ensure that a honeypot cannot be compromised in a way that could lead to further attacks on your networks or systems.[43]

Trap-and-Trace Systems

Trap-and-trace applications, which are an extension of the attractant technologies discussed in the previous section, are growing in popularity. These systems use a combination of techniques to detect an intrusion and trace it back to its source. The trap usually consists of a honeypot and an alarm. While the intruders are distracted, or trapped, by what they perceive to be successful intrusions, the system notifies the administrator of their presence. The trace feature is an extension to the honeypot. The trace—similar to caller ID—is a process by which the organization attempts to determine the identity of someone discovered in unauthorized areas of the network or systems. If the intruder is someone inside the organization, the administrators are completely within their power to track the individual and turn him or her over to internal or external authorities. If the intruder is outside the security perimeter of the organization, then numerous legal issues arise.

On the surface, trap-and-trace systems seem like an ideal solution. Security is no longer limited to defense. Now, the security administrators can go on the offense. They can track down the perpetrators and turn them over to the appropriate authorities. Under the guise of justice, some less scrupulous administrators may even be tempted to **back hack**, or hack into a hacker's system to find out as much as possible about the hacker. Vigilante justice would be a more appropriate term for these activities, which are in fact deemed unethical by most codes of professional conduct. In tracking the hacker, administrators may end up wandering through other organizations' systems, especially when the wily hacker has used IP spoofing, compromised systems, or a myriad of other techniques to throw trackers off the trail. The back-hacking administrator becomes the hacker.

There are more legal drawbacks to trap and trace. The trap portion frequently involves the use of honeypots or honeynets. When using honeypots and honeynets, administrators should be careful not to cross the line between enticement and entrapment. **Enticement** is the process of attracting attention to a system by placing tantalizing information in key locations. **Entrapment** is the act of luring an individual into committing a crime to get a conviction. Enticement is legal and ethical, whereas entrapment is not. It is difficult to gauge the effect such a system can have on the average user, especially if the individual has been nudged into looking at the information.

Active Intrusion Prevention

6

Some organizations would like to do more than simply wait for the next attack; they want to implement active countermeasures to stop attacks. One tool that provides active intrusion prevention is known as LaBrea (*http://labrea.sourceforge.net/labrea-info.html*). LaBrea works by taking up the unused IP address space within a network. When LaBrea notes an ARP request, it checks to see if the IP address requested is actually valid on the network. If the address is not currently being used by a real computer or network device, LaBrea pretends to be a computer at that IP address and allows the attacker to complete the TCP/IP connection request, known as the three-way handshake. Once the handshake is complete, LaBrea changes the TCP sliding window size to a low number to hold open the TCP connection from the attacker for many hours, days, or even months. Holding the connection open but inactive greatly slows down network-based worms and other attacks. It allows the LaBrea system time to notify the system and network administrators about the anomalous behavior on the network.

Chapter Summary

- An intrusion detection and prevention system (IDPS) works like a burglar alarm by detecting network traffic that is a violation of the rules with which it is configured and activating an alarm. Intrusion detection systems (IDSs) are designed to detect possible intrusion activity and sound an alarm. Intrusion prevention systems (IPSs) work like IDSs but also take action to defend the network they are designed to protect.

- A network-based IDPS (NIDPS) monitors network traffic and, when a predefined event occurs, responds and notifies the appropriate administrator. A host-based IDPS (HIDPS) is a system that resides on a particular computer or server and monitors the system's activity.

- Signature-based IDPSs, also known as knowledge-based IDPSs, examine data traffic for patterns that match signatures, which are preconfigured, predetermined attack patterns. Statistical anomaly-based IDPSs, also known as behavior-based IDPSs, collect data from normal traffic and establish a baseline. When an activity is found to be outside the baseline parameters (or clipping level), these IDPSs activate an alarm to notify the administrator.

■ Selecting IDPS products that best fit an organization's specific needs is a challenging and complex process because there is a wide array of products and vendors available, each with its own approach and capabilities.

■ Deploying and implementing IDPS technology is a complex undertaking that will require the sponsoring organization to have some experience with the technology or else hire the necessary expertise to complete the process successfully. After such a deployment, each organization should measure the effectiveness of its IDPS and then continue to periodically assess its effectiveness after the initial deployment.

■ Honeypots are decoy systems, which means they are designed to lure potential attackers away from critical systems. In the security industry, these systems are also known as decoys, lures, or fly-traps.

■ Trap-and-trace applications are designed to react to intrusion events by tracing them back to their sources. This process is fraught with professional and ethical issues in that some observers may perceive the back hack in the trace process as being as inappropriate as the initial attack.

Review Questions

1. What are some of the considerations to be taken into account when capturing network traffic?

2. Define packet analysis.

3. What is the general structure of the IP packet?

4. What is tcpdump?

5. What is an intrusion, as the term is used in this chapter?

6. Define *intrusion detection*, *intrusion prevention*, and *incident response*.

7. What common security system often found in the home or business is an IDPS most like?

8. What is a false positive alarm?

9. What is a false negative alarm?

10. From a security perspective, which is least desirable, a false positive or a false negative alarm?

11. What is filtering, as applied to IDPS technology?

12. What is tuning, as applied to IDPS technology?

13. What is the best single reason to use IDPS technology?

14. How does a network-based IDPS differ from a host-based IDPS?

15. How does a signature-based IDPS differ from a behavior-based IDPS?

16. What is the optimal location for a network-based IDPS? Host-based IDPS?

17. What is a monitoring (or SPAN) port? What is it used for?

18. What is a honeypot? How is it different from a honeynet?

19. What is a trap-and-trace system? Why might we not choose to use one?

20. What is active intrusion prevention?

Real World Exercises

Exercise 6-1

A key feature of hybrid IDPS systems is event correlation. After researching event correlation online, define the following terms as they are used in this process: *compression, suppression,* and *generalization.*

6

Exercise 6-2

ZoneAlarm is a PC-based firewall and IDPS tool. Visit the product manufacturer at *www. zonelabs.com* and find the product specification for the IDPS features of ZoneAlarm. Which of the ZoneAlarm products offer these features?

Exercise 6-3

Using the Internet, search for commercial IDPS systems. What classification systems and descriptions are used, and how can these be used to compare the features and components of each IDPS? Create a comparison spreadsheet identifying the classification systems you find.

Hands-On Projects

Project 6-1

In this project, you will set up and configure Valhala, a Windows-based honeypot. Then, you will examine how network scanning applications like Nmap detect and report services enabled in Valhala using different types of scanning options.

To complete this exercise, you need to have an installation of Windows 7 Professional available for use. This can either be achieved by installing Windows 7 Professional on an available computer or by building a virtual instance using virtualization software such as Oracle's VirtualBox or VMWare's VMware player. Additionally, you will need the Nmap application available for use on a separate system, which we will use to "attack" the honeypot system.

1. Using a Web browser on the Windows 7 system, visit *http://sourceforge.net/projects/ valhalahoneypot* and click the green **Download** button to begin downloading Valhala. When prompted, save the ZIP file to your desktop.

2. Once the download process is complete, close the browser window, then open the ZIP file by double-clicking the icon on your desktop.

3. Drag the honeypot application from the ZIP folder to copy it onto the desktop, then close the ZIP file window. Now, you will disable the Windows Firewall for demonstration purposes. Click the **Network** icon in the system tray and select **Open Network and Sharing Center**.

4. Select *Windows Firewall*.

5. Select **Turn Windows Firewall on or off**.

6. Select **Turn off Windows Firewall (not recommended)** for both the Private and Public network settings, then click **OK**.

7. Close the Control Panel.

8. Now, we will run a quick Nmap scan to verify which services are available on the Windows 7 system before we configure and start the honeypot. On the system with Nmap installed, type this Nmap command: **Nmap -sS <IP address of Windows 7 system>**, then press **Enter**.

9. There should be few, if any, services available. Make a note of the services available for comparison later on.

10. Start Valhala by double-clicking the **honeypot** icon on the desktop. If prompted, uncheck the **Always ask before opening this file** option, then click **Run** to allow the software to run. You should now see the Valhala main menu, as displayed in Figure 6-17. Now, we will enable a telnet honeypot server, which will provide a fake server for attackers to access.

Figure 6-17 Valhala honeypot menu
Source: Valhala

11. Click **Server Config**, then click **Options** under TELNET Server.

12. Click the white box to the left of **Enable Telnet Service** to enable the service; the box should turn blue.

13. Click the white box to the left of **No login required** to allow anonymous logins; the box should turn blue. When done, your screen should look like what is shown in Figure 6-18.

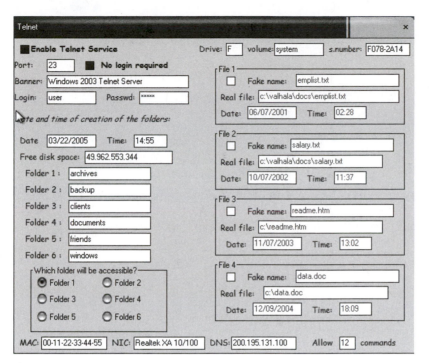

Figure 6-18 Telnet Server menu
Source: Valhala

14. Close the setup screen by clicking the **X** in the upper-right corner of the window, which will return you to the Server Config menu. Now, you will enable the FTP honeypot server, which will provide another fake server for attackers to access.

15. Click **Options** under FTP Server.

16. Click the white box to the left of **Enable FTP Service** to enable the service; the box should turn blue.

17. Close the setup screen by clicking the **X** in the upper-right corner of the window, which will return you to the Server Config menu. Note that both TELNET Server and FTP Server have changed from red to green, as shown in Figure 6-19.

18. Close the Server Config menu by clicking the **X** in the upper-right corner of the window, which will return you to the Main menu.

19. To enable the honeypot, click **Monitoring** in the vertical menu. The application will minimize to the system tray.

20. Execute the Nmap command listed in Step 9 again. This time, you will see a new Telnet service available on port 23 as well as an FTP service available on port 21, as shown in Figure 6-20.

This type of scan may be enough to fool most attackers into believing a telnet or FTP server is available. However, attackers may run a more in-depth Nmap scan and collect more data about the target. In cases like this, a honeypot may return data that indicates a service is not

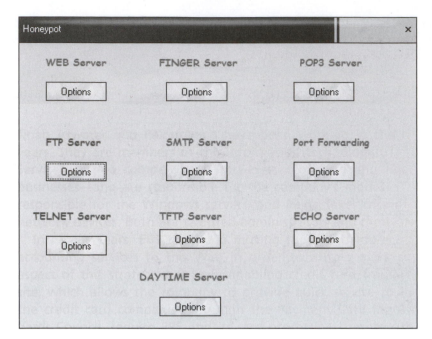

Figure 6-19   Server configuration menu
Source: Valhala

```
root@bt:~# nmap -sS 192.168.1.118

Starting Nmap 5.61TEST2 ( http://nmap.org ) at 2011-12-23 01:34 EST
Nmap scan report for win7-pro-virtua (192.168.1.118)
Host is up (0.00041s latency).
Not shown: 987 closed ports
PORT      STATE SERVICE
21/tcp    open  ftp
23/tcp    open  telnet
135/tcp   open  msrpc
139/tcp   open  netbios-ssn
445/tcp   open  microsoft-ds
5357/tcp  open  wsdapi
12345/tcp open  netbus
49152/tcp open  unknown
49153/tcp open  unknown
49154/tcp open  unknown
49155/tcp open  unknown
49156/tcp open  unknown
49157/tcp open  unknown
MAC Address: 00:0C:29:B1:C5:95 (VMware)

Nmap done: 1 IP address (1 host up) scanned in 2.21 seconds
root@bt:~# █
```

Figure 6-20   Nmap scan results
Source: Linux

actually what is being advertised. To see what additional data can be returned, run a different Nmap scan by typing the following command: **nmap -sV <IP address of Windows 7 system>**, then press **Enter**.

Your results should look similar to what is shown in Figure 6-21. Note that the results returned now include a "VERSION" column, which returns suspicious data for the Telnet server. Instead of returning an expected telnet service banner, Nmap displays suspicious version details that may indicate a Telnet server isn't actually running on that port, and the "SERVICE" column now displays "backdoor" instead of "telnet." Results like this could possibly alert an attacker to the possibility that this is a honeypot, thus minimizing its effectiveness as a decoy.

```
root@bt:~# nmap -sV 192.168.1.118

Starting Nmap 5.51 ( http://nmap.org ) at 2011-07-19 23:19 EDT
Nmap scan report for win7-pro-virtua (192.168.1.118)
Host is up (0.00059s latency).
Not shown: 988 closed ports
PORT      STATE SERVICE      VERSION
21/tcp    open  ftp
23/tcp    open  backdoor     OptixPro backdoor (**BACKDOOR**)
135/tcp   open  msrpc        Microsoft Windows RPC
139/tcp   open  netbios-ssn
445/tcp   open  netbios-ssn
5357/tcp  open  http         Microsoft HTTPAPI httpd 2.0 (SSDP/UPnP)
12345/tcp open  tcpwrapped
49152/tcp open  msrpc        Microsoft Windows RPC
49153/tcp open  msrpc        Microsoft Windows RPC
49154/tcp open  msrpc        Microsoft Windows RPC
49155/tcp open  msrpc        Microsoft Windows RPC
49156/tcp open  msrpc        Microsoft Windows RPC
1 service unrecognized despite returning data. If you know the service/version, please submit the following fingerprint at http:
//www.insecure.org/cgi-bin/servicefp-submit.cgi :
SF-Port21-TCP:V=5.51%I=7%D=7/19%Time=4E26492C%P=i686-pc-linux-gnu%r(NULL,1
SF:3,"220\x20Wu-ftpd\x201\.7\.0\r\n")%r(GenericLines,57,"220\x20Wu-ftpd\x2
SF:01\.7\.0\r\n500\x20'\r':\x20command\x20not\x20understood\.\r\n500\x20'\
SF:r':\x20command\x20not\x20understood\.\r\n")%r(Help,38,"220\x20Wu-ftpd\x
SF:201\.7\.0\r\n500\x20'HELP':\x20command\x20not\x20understood\.\r\n")%r(S
SF:MBProgNeg,13,"220\x20Wu-ftpd\x201\.7\.0\r\n");
MAC Address: 00:0C:29:B1:C5:95 (VMware)
Service Info: OS: Windows

Service detection performed. Please report any incorrect results at http://nmap.org/submit/ .
Nmap done: 1 IP address (1 host up) scanned in 50.62 seconds
root@bt:~#
```

Figure 6-21 Nmap scan results – version details

Source: Linux

Valhala also displays alerts as a result of intrusive scans like the ones we just ran. These alerts are also saved in text files in the location we specified earlier in this exercise. The visual alert is displayed in Figure 6-22.

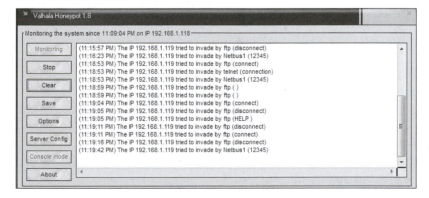

Figure 6-22 Valhala alert screen

Source: Valhala

Endnotes

1. Dempsey, K., Chawla, N. Johnson, A., Johnson, R. Jones, A. Orebaugh, A. Scholl, M, and Stine, K. (2011) *Information Security Continuous Monitoring (ISCM) for Federal Information Systems and Organizations.* NIST Special Publication 800-137, Sep. 2011. WWW Document viewed 12/26/2011 from *http://csrc.nist.gov/publications/nistpubs/800-137/SP800-137-Final.pdf.*

2. TCPDUMP main page. Accessed June 15, 2011 from *www.tcpdump.org/tcpdump_man.html.*

3. Microsoft Security Bulletin MS03-007: "Unchecked Buffer in Windows Component Could Cause Server Compromise (815021)." Accessed June 17, 2011 from *www.microsoft.com/technet/security/bulletin/MS03-007.mspx.*

4. Scarfone, K. & Mell, P. (2007) "Guide to Intrusion Detection and Prevention Systems (IDPS)" NIST Special Publication 800-94. Accessed June 21, 2007 from *csrc.nist.gov/publications/nistpubs/800-94/SP800-94.pdf.*

5. Scarfone, K. & Mell, P. (2007) "Guide to Intrusion Detection and Prevention Systems (IDPS)" NIST Special Publication 800-94. Accessed June 21, 2007 from *csrc.nist.gov/publications/nistpubs/800-94/SP800-94.pdf.*

6. Scarfone, K. & Mell, P. (2007) "Guide to Intrusion Detection and Prevention Systems (IDPS)" NIST Special Publication 800-94. Accessed June 21, 2007 from *csrc.nist.gov/publications/nistpubs/800-94/SP800-94.pdf.*

7. Scarfone, K. & Mell, P. (2007) "Guide to Intrusion Detection and Prevention Systems (IDPS)" NIST Special Publication 800-94. Accessed June 21, 2007 from *csrc.nist.gov/publications/nistpubs/800-94/SP800-94.pdf.*

8. Scarfone, K. & Mell, P. (2007) "Guide to Intrusion Detection and Prevention Systems (IDPS)" NIST Special Publication 800-94. Accessed June 21, 2007 from *csrc.nist.gov/publications/nistpubs/800-94/SP800-94.pdf.*

9. Scarfone, K. & Mell, P. (2007) "Guide to Intrusion Detection and Prevention Systems (IDPS)" NIST Special Publication 800-94 Accessed June 21, 2007 from *csrc.nist.gov/publications/nistpubs/800-94/SP800-94.pdf.*

10. Scarfone, K. & Mell, P. (2007) "Guide to Intrusion Detection and Prevention Systems (IDPS)" NIST Special Publication 800-94 Accessed June 21, 2007 from *csrc.nist.gov/publications/nistpubs/800-94/SP800-94.pdf.*

11. Scarfone, K. & Mell, P. (2007) "Guide to Intrusion Detection and Prevention Systems (IDPS)" NIST Special Publication 800-94 Accessed June 21, 2007 from *csrc.nist.gov/publications/nistpubs/800-94/SP800-94.pdf.*

12. Scarfone, K. & Mell, P. (2007) "Guide to Intrusion Detection and Prevention Systems (IDPS)" NIST Special Publication 800-94 Accessed June 21, 2007 from *csrc.nist.gov/publications/nistpubs/800-94/SP800-94.pdf.*

13. Scarfone, K. & Mell, P. (2007) "Guide to Intrusion Detection and Prevention Systems (IDPS)" NIST Special Publication 800-94 Accessed June 21, 2007 from *csrc.nist.gov/publications/nistpubs/800-94/SP800-94.pdf.*

14. Graham, R. (2000) "FAQ: Intrusion Detection Systems." March 2000. Viewed online on 4/9/07. Accessed June 21, 2007 from *linuxsecurity.com/resource_files/intrusion_detection/network-intrusion-detection.html*.

15. Scarfone, K. & Mell, P. (2007) "Guide to Intrusion Detection and Prevention Systems (IDPS)" NIST Special Publication 800-94 Accessed June 21, 2007 from *csrc.nist.gov/ publications/nistpubs/800-94/SP800-94.pdf*.

16. Scarfone, K. & Mell, P. (2007) "Guide to Intrusion Detection and Prevention Systems (IDPS)" NIST Special Publication 800-94 Accessed June21, 2007 from *csrc.nist.gov/ publications/nistpubs/800-94/SP800-94.pdf*.

17. Graham, R. (2000) "FAQ: Intrusion Detection Systems." March 2000. Viewed online on 4/9/07. Accessed June 21, 2007 from *linuxsecurity.com/resource_files/intrusion_detection/network-intrusion-detection.html*.

18. Scarfone, K. & Mell, P. (2007) "Guide to Intrusion Detection and Prevention Systems (IDPS)" NIST Special Publication 800-94 Accessed June 21, 2007 from *csrc.nist.gov/ publications/nistpubs/800-94/SP800-94.pdf*.

19. Scarfone, K. & Mell, P. (2007) "Guide to Intrusion Detection and Prevention Systems (IDPS)" NIST Special Publication 800-94 Accessed June 21, 2007 from *csrc.nist.gov/ publications/nistpubs/800-94/SP800-94.pdf*.

20. Scarfone, K. & Mell, P. (2007) "Guide to Intrusion Detection and Prevention Systems (IDPS)" NIST Special Publication 800-94 Accessed June 21, 2007 from *csrc.nist.gov/ publications/nistpubs/800-94/SP800-94.pdf*.

21. Graham, R. (2000) "FAQ: Intrusion Detection Systems." March 2000. Viewed online on 4/9/07. Accessed June 21, 2007 from *linuxsecurity.com/resource_files/intrusion_detection/network-intrusion-detection.html*.

22. Scarfone, K. & Mell, P. (2007) "Guide to Intrusion Detection and Prevention Systems (IDPS)" NIST Special Publication 800-94. Accessed June 21, 2007 from *csrc.nist.gov/ publications/nistpubs/800-94/SP800-94.pdf*.

23. Scarfone, K. & Mell, P. (2007) "Guide to Intrusion Detection and Prevention Systems (IDPS)" NIST Special Publication 800-94. Accessed June 21, 2007 from *csrc.nist.gov/ publications/nistpubs/800-94/SP800-94.pdf*.

24. Scarfone, K. & Mell, P. (2007) "Guide to Intrusion Detection and Prevention Systems (IDPS)" NIST Special Publication 800-94. Accessed June 21, 2007 from *csrc.nist.gov/ publications/nistpubs/800-94/SP800-94.pdf*.

25. Scarfone, K. & Mell, P. (2007) "Guide to Intrusion Detection and Prevention Systems (IDPS)" NIST Special Publication 800-94. Accessed June 21, 2007 from *csrc.nist.gov/ publications/nistpubs/800-94/SP800-94.pdf*.

26. Scarfone, K. & Mell, P. (2007) "Guide to Intrusion Detection and Prevention Systems (IDPS)" NIST Special Publication 800-94. Accessed June 21, 2007 from *csrc.nist.gov/ publications/nistpubs/800-94/SP800-94.pdf*.

27. Scarfone, K. & Mell, P. (2007) "Guide to Intrusion Detection and Prevention Systems (IDPS)" NIST Special Publication 800-94. Accessed June 21, 2007 from *csrc.nist.gov/ publications/nistpubs/800-94/SP800-94.pdf*.

6

28. Scarfone, K. & Mell, P. (2007) "Guide to Intrusion Detection and Prevention Systems (IDPS)" NIST Special Publication 800-94. Accessed June 21, 2007 from *csrc.nist.gov/publications/nistpubs/800-94/SP800-94.pdf*.

29. Scarfone, K. & Mell, P. (2007) "Guide to Intrusion Detection and Prevention Systems (IDPS)" NIST Special Publication 800-94. Accessed June 21, 2007 from *csrc.nist.gov/publications/nistpubs/800-94/SP800-94.pdf*.

30. Scarfone, K. & Mell, P. (2007) "Guide to Intrusion Detection and Prevention Systems (IDPS)" NIST Special Publication 800-94. Accessed June 21, 2007 from *csrc.nist.gov/publications/nistpubs/800-94/SP800-94.pdf*.

31. Scarfone, K. & Mell, P. (2007) "Guide to Intrusion Detection and Prevention Systems (IDPS)" NIST Special Publication 800-94. Accessed June 21, 2007 from *csrc.nist.gov/publications/nistpubs/800-94/SP800-94.pdf*.

32. Scarfone, K. & Mell, P. (2007) "Guide to Intrusion Detection and Prevention Systems (IDPS)" NIST Special Publication 800-94. Accessed June 21, 2007 from *csrc.nist.gov/publications/nistpubs/800-94/SP800-94.pdf*.

33. Scarfone, K. & Mell, P. (2007) "Guide to Intrusion Detection and Prevention Systems (IDPS)" NIST Special Publication 800-94. Accessed June 21, 2007 from *csrc.nist.gov/publications/nistpubs/800-94/SP800-94.pdf*.

34. Scarfone, K. & Mell, P. (2007) "Guide to Intrusion Detection and Prevention Systems (IDPS)" NIST Special Publication 800-94. Accessed June 21, 2007 from *csrc.nist.gov/publications/nistpubs/800-94/SP800-94.pdf*.

35. Scarfone, K. & Mell, P. (2007) "Guide to Intrusion Detection and Prevention Systems (IDPS)" NIST Special Publication 800-94. Accessed June 21, 2007 from *csrc.nist.gov/publications/nistpubs/800-94/SP800-94.pdf*.

36. Scarfone, K. & Mell, P. (2007) "Guide to Intrusion Detection and Prevention Systems (IDPS)" NIST Special Publication 800-94. Accessed June 21, 2007 from *csrc.nist.gov/publications/nistpubs/800-94/SP800-94.pdf*.

37. Scarfone, K. & Mell, P. (2007) "Guide to Intrusion Detection and Prevention Systems (IDPS)" NIST Special Publication 800-94. Accessed June 21, 2007 from *csrc.nist.gov/publications/nistpubs/800-94/SP800-94.pdf*.

38. Scarfone, K. & Mell, P. (2007) "Guide to Intrusion Detection and Prevention Systems (IDPS)" NIST Special Publication 800-94. Accessed June 21, 2007 from *csrc.nist.gov/publications/nistpubs/800-94/SP800-94.pdf*.

39. Scarfone, K. & Mell, P. (2007) "Guide to Intrusion Detection and Prevention Systems (IDPS)" NIST Special Publication 800-94. Accessed June 21, 2007 from *csrc.nist.gov/publications/nistpubs/800-94/SP800-94.pdf*.

40. Scarfone, K. & Mell, P. (2007) "Guide to Intrusion Detection and Prevention Systems (IDPS)" NIST Special Publication 800-94. Accessed June 21, 2007 from *csrc.nist.gov/publications/nistpubs/800-94/SP800-94.pdf*.

41. Scarfone, K. & Mell, P. (2007) "Guide to Intrusion Detection and Prevention Systems (IDPS)" NIST Special Publication 800-94. Accessed June 21, 2007 from *csrc.nist.gov/publications/nistpubs/800-94/SP800-94.pdf*.

42. Scarfone, K. & Mell, P. (2007) "Guide to Intrusion Detection and Prevention Systems (IDPS)" NIST Special Publication 800-94. Accessed June 21, 2007 from *csrc.nist.gov/publications/nistpubs/800-94/SP800-94.pdf*.

43. Scarfone, K. & Mell, P. (2007) "Guide to Intrusion Detection and Prevention Systems (IDPS)" NIST Special Publication 800-94. Accessed June 21, 2007 from *csrc.nist.gov/publications/nistpubs/800-94/SP800-94.pdf*.

6

chapter 7

Wireless Network Security

I do not think that the wireless waves I have discovered will have any practical application. — Heinrich Rudolf Hertz, 19th century

Upon completion of this material, you should be able to:

- Identify various wireless technologies and standards
- Recognize the topology and architecture of wireless networks
- Define popular wireless security protocols
- Describe various WLAN security concerns
- Discuss the security issues regarding Bluetooth technology

Meeting the Standard

The EBS folks were hitting their stride with all the PCI remediation activities. They had defined the Cardholder Data Environment (CDE), so they knew all the networks and systems where credit card information was transferred, processed, or stored. They had also addressed a number of security concerns involving encryption on their extranet with Davis Office Megaplex, audited their firewall rules and architecture, and ensured that proper intrusion detection was implemented—or at least being planned—in the IT environment. They were feeling confident about meeting their deadlines ahead of schedule.

A prep team had come in to help conduct an informal audit of the PCI standards to identify any remaining gaps. Over the course of a week, the EBS IT team had worked with the audit prep team reviewing system configurations, walking through processes, and showing proof of their security efforts.

At the outbriefing, the prep team went through their findings. The biggest shock to EBS? Its CDE used a wireless connection that allowed financial analysts to connect to the cardholder systems to conduct business. The EBS IT staff had overlooked the fact that the network architecture allowed wireless access.

For EBS to pass the PCI audit, it would have to prove that it met the standards put forth in the PCI DSS Wireless Guideline. In other words, the EBS team had more work to do. According to the Wireless Guideline: "In the case where an organization has decided to deploy a WLAN [Wireless LAN] for any purpose whatsoever, and connect the WLAN to the CDE, then that WLAN is now a part of the CDE and is therefore in scope within the PCI DSS and within the scope of this document."[1] It would need to investigate the EBS wireless network and ensure that all of the PCI security measures EBS deployed for the LAN also covered the wireless network—or disallow the connection altogether. The end goal seemed further away.

Introduction

"Wireless," in its simplest form, means without wire (or cable). We usually construe this to mean that the signal is transmitted without physical media and is instead sent using some form of radiated signal—radio, light, or some other part of the electromagnetic spectrum. The application of this technology will be implemented differently, depending on whether you are working with wireless computer networks, wireless telephony, or one of a number of other wireless connectivity solutions. For the purposes of this chapter, we will be examining wireless computer networking and the security needs for this particular application of technology.

What makes wireless network security so difficult compared to wire-based networking? In wire-based networking, network administrators can control the infrastructure—the physical media (wires and cables) and the access points (hubs and switches). In wireless networking, once the radio signal leaves the access points (known as **wireless access points** or **WAPs**), an organization has little control over the signal. The WAP is the radio transmitter/receiver that takes the signal from the wired network and broadcasts it to wireless receivers, and vice versa. Although it is possible to restrict the footprint of the wireless network (the area the radio signal reaches) by controlling the strength of the broadcast signal, without the use of some very specialized technologies an organization can do little to guide or restrict the wireless signal itself. Instead, the organization must protect the data carried on the signal and the way the signal connects to other networks. The former is accomplished through encryption, which was covered in Chapter 3. The latter is accomplished through access controls, which were covered in Chapter 5. We will revisit each of these as we examine the form, function, and controls associated with wireless network security.

When installing networks in existing buildings, it may prove difficult and expensive to retrofit the facility with physical cable (as described in Chapter 2). A widely used alternative is a wireless LAN. A **wireless local area network**, also known as **WLAN** or by the branding label *Wi-Fi* (wireless fidelity), is a group of interconnected networking nodes operating within a limited geographic area that offers network access by the use of broadcast rather than physical media. Because the vast majority of WLANs use radio-based communications, that will be the focus of the discussion here. WLANs are thought by many in the IT industry to be inherently insecure. The communication channel between the wireless network interface of any computing device and the access point that provides its services uses radio transmissions, which are subject to accidental or purposeful interference or interception.

Wireless networks are inherently different from networks that use physical media like wires or cables. The IEEE has documented the differences, noting that wireless networks:

- Use a method of signaling that does not have readily observable boundaries, requiring special equipment to discern where the signal is present or where it is not

- Are susceptible to signals that come from other devices that are not part of the network as planned or built but that share the wireless medium being used

- Operate using a medium that is less reliable than a wired medium

- Often use dynamic topologies in which the number or even the nature of the devices being networked changes often and with little or no notice

- May lack full connectivity among nodes and invalidate the assumptions made about networking station visibility

- Operate in environments in which signal propagation is less certain and in which signal timing and symmetry may be unverifiable

- Are subject to interference from other networks when the signal area overlaps, even when the other networks are conforming to standards[2]

This chapter examines the differences between wireless networks and networks that use physical media, focusing on technologies and standards, topologies and architectures, and security mechanisms.

Wireless Technologies and Standards

WLANs became popular in the 1990s, with the emergence of commercial products that connected computers wirelessly using radio transmissions in the 900-megahertz band, which yielded data transmission rates of approximately 1 megabit per second (Mbps). Before that, radio-based teletypewriters and specialized communications terminals had been used by the military and news networks, but they were seldom used in corporate networks. Before long, though, data rates improved dramatically, and the bandwidths assigned to radio-based computer communications began to vary more widely—into the 2.4 gigahertz (GHz) range, yielding data rates of up to 54 Mbps.[3]

WLANs often combine a number of standards and technologies. The basic building blocks of the modern WLAN are wireless modulation technologies and IEEE Standard 802.11. We will cover these topics in the following sections.

Wireless Modulation Technologies

WLANs place the data onto the wireless radio signal using a host of modulation techniques. As described in Chapter 2, modulation is the method of manipulating the medium signal to carry the source data. Two sets of technology are involved in wireless communications modulation. The first set involves the placement of the data bits onto the electrical signal using Quadrature Amplitude Modulation (QAM) and/or Quadrature Phase Shift Keying (QPSK) as described here:

- QAM—This is a modulation technique that combines digital and analog signaling to encode data into radio signals. It functions by encoding two message channels at the same time. This is done by modulating (or changing) the amplitudes of two carrier waves, using the amplitude-shift keying (ASK) digital modulation scheme or the amplitude modulation (AM) analog modulation scheme. In the case of digital QAM, at least two phases and at least two amplitudes are used. A simple version of the modulation method, using four data values (4-QAM), is illustrated in Figure 7-1. In practice, the number of values encoded can reach 256 bits, transmitting an 8-bit code for each signal measurement.[4]

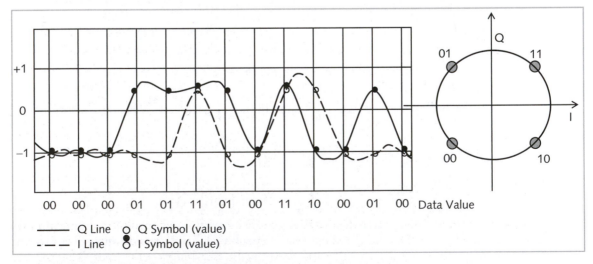

Figure 7-1   Quadrature Amplitude Modulation
© Cengage Learning 2013

- QPSK—This is a modulation technique that provides multi-bit carrying capability for the encoding of digital data on an analog signal. It is an enhancement of Binary Phase Shift Keying (BPSK), which uses two signal states that are 180 degrees out of phase to carry two signal values (0 and 1). QPSK uses four signal states that are 90 degrees out of phase to carry four signal values. PSK modulators (such as QPSK) are often implemented with QAM principles, but they are not considered QAM because the amplitude of the carrier is not modulated.[5]

The second set of technologies involved in wireless communications modulation, collectively known as spread-spectrum transmission, addresses the transmission of the data stream that has been properly encoded onto the radio signal. Spread-spectrum approaches have a number of advantages over the transmission of data using fixed frequencies:

- Narrowband interference is reduced by the use of spread-spectrum signals. The processes used to send and receive data literally spread out the signal across multiple frequencies and thus reduce the interference.

- Interceptions of signals are less likely. To a narrowband receiver, the spread-spectrum signals appear to be background noise. A potential eavesdropper is only able to intercept a transmission if the pseudorandom noise codes are known and the timing is synchronized with the sender.[6]

- Interference is minimized between spread-spectrum and narrowband transmissions because multiple devices can safely operate in one band of frequencies. The spread-spectrum signals add minimal noise to the narrow-frequency communications, and vice versa. As a result, bandwidth can be utilized more efficiently.[7]

Three technologies provide spread-spectrum security and transport features for the data stream:

- **Frequency Hopping Spread Spectrum (FHSS)**—This is a method of transmitting radio signals by jumping (hopping) rapidly among a number of predefined frequencies. This hopping follows a pattern known as a pseudorandom sequence, which must be programmed into the sending and receiving stations.

- **Direct-Sequence Spread Spectrum (DSSS)**—This works by taking the original data stream and breaking it up into small bits, then transmitting each of those on a different frequency channel simultaneously. It also combines the data signal with another data sequence, known as a *chipping code,* much like the XOR technique that was described in Chapter 5. The chipping code helps the signal resist interference and also enables the original data to be recovered if data bits are damaged during transmission.[8]

- **Orthogonal frequency-division multiplexing (OFDM)**—Frequency-division multiplexing (FDM) schemes were described in Chapter 2. This one is used to carry multiple digital signals. OFDM splits the data stream across several parallel channels. It may use QAM or QPSK to encode the data on each channel.[9]

IEEE 802.11 Standards

The IEEE ratified the 802.11 standard for WLANs in 1997. The original standard encompassed transmission of data using three defined methods, one of which was radio transmission in the 2.4 GHz band. In 1999, the standard was ratified with two amendments: 802.11a and 802.11b. These more clearly defined the use of radio transmission methods. The 802.11a standard operated in the 5 GHz range and offered speeds up to 54 Mbps. The 802.11b standard operated in the 2.4 GHz range and offered data rates up to 11 Mbps. Although the 802.11a standard offered greater speeds, it operated efficiently at shorter distances compared to 802.11b.[10] This factor helped to push 802.11b as the dominant standard in the marketplace. IEEE 802.11b was intended to provide performance, throughput, and security features comparable to wired LANs.

In 2003, the 802.11g amendment was released. It specified a radio transmission method that supported data rates of up to 54 Mbps. It is noteworthy that IEEE 802.11g-compliant products are backward compatible with IEEE 802.11b-compliant products.

In 2009, yet another amendment to the 802.11 standard was released. Known as 802.11n, the standard introduced: techniques for security improvements, multiple antennae to receive information simultaneously, the ability to operate in the 2.4 GHz and 5 GHz ranges, and the ability to transfer data at up to 600 Mbps.[11] Table 7-1 compares the basic characteristics of IEEE 802.11, 802.11a, 802.11b, and 802.11g. Wireless networking that follows 802.11 is also known as Wi-Fi.

The IEEE has defined standards for communications between most modern computer and electronic system operations in a document called *IEEE Standard for Information Technology – Telecommunications and Information Exchange Between Systems - Local and Metropolitan Area Networks - Specific Requirements - Part 11: Wireless LAN Medium Access Control (MAC) and Physical Layer (PHY) Specifications.*[12] The areas covered include:

- The basic functionality offered by 802.11-compliant devices operating in a peer-to-peer fashion or part of a wired network. As part of this functionality, the standard outlines the abstraction needed to ensure communications are seamless among the various wireless communication systems.
- Operations where an 802.11 device operates with multiple overlapping wireless LANs.
- The confidentiality of data transmitted over a WLAN, as well as mechanisms for 802.11 devices to authenticate themselves.
- Techniques that operate at the physical and data link layers to ensure efficient and reliable wireless data transfers.
- Mechanisms to "satisfy regulatory requirements for operation in the 5 GHz band."[13]

Standard	Data Rate	Technology	Band	Date Published	Notes
802.11	2 Mbps		2.4 GHz	1997	
802.11a	54 Mbps	OFDM	5 GHz	1999	Not compatible with 802.11b
802.11b	11 Mbps	DSSS	2.4 GHz	1999	
802.11g	54 Mbps	OFDM & DSSS	2.4 GHz	2003	Backwardly compatible with 802.11b
802.11n	600 Mbps	OFDM	2.4 GHz & 5 GHz	2009	Newest standard, still being deployed

Table 7-1 IEEE 802.11 WLAN Technologies

Source: NIST SP 800-97

In general, the estimated range of 802.11b and 802.11g networks is up to 150 feet indoors and up to 450 feet outdoors, with 802.11a having approximately one-third that range. Most specifications in the 802.11 range provide a bandwidth of 20-40 MHz. Under the 802.11y standard amendment, the FCC allows licensees to implement equipment with much higher power by using the standards in Table 7-1, increasing ranges up to 3 miles and operating in the 3650–3700 MHz band.

Wi-Fi Alliance Certifications

In 1999, as the 802.11 technology was coming to market, a group called the Wi-Fi Alliance was created to certify the interoperability of 802.11b products.[14] This group felt a need to reduce the ambiguity found in the marketplace when standards are emerging and manufacturers are creating products while trying to innovate and gain market share. Although they waited for 802.11 standards to mature, they wanted to assure consumers that some interoperability was available. In 2002, the Wi-Fi Alliance created the Wi-Fi Protected Access (WPA) security protocol, which implements a large portion of the 802.11i standard, which was then in the draft stage. Perhaps the largest difference between WPA and the 802.11i was that WPA called for supporting the Advanced Encryption Standard (AES), which would have required more computing power than many devices could muster at that time.[15] Later, with the ratification of the IEEE 802.11i amendment, the Wi-Fi Alliance introduced WPA2. This is a branding term for interoperable equipment that is capable of supporting IEEE 802.11i requirements. The Wi-Fi Alliance began testing IEEE 802.11i products for WPA2 certification shortly after the IEEE 802.11i amendment was finalized.[16]

Other Wireless Standards

Although 802.11 and Wi-Fi are the dominant wireless networking standards, there are others. Most prevalent among them are Bluetooth, WiMedia, ZigBee, and WiMax.

Bluetooth   Bluetooth is an open standard for short-range wireless communications between computers and small computing devices, including cell phones, earpieces, and computer accessories. It has been included in IEEE standard 802.15.1. It was established by scientists at the Swedish telecommunications company Ericsson and soon included Intel, Nokia, IBM, and Toshiba. Soon thereafter, Microsoft, Lucent Technologies (a 1996 AT&T spin-off that included Bell Labs), and 3Com joined the industry group. Bluetooth and its security concerns are covered in more detail later in this chapter.

WiMAX   WiMAX (Worldwide Interoperability for Microwave Access), IEEE 802.16e is a Wireless Metropolitan Area Network (WMAN) standard for devices in facilities that are geographically dispersed. WiMAX works in the 10–66 GHz transmission band, with a range of up to 30 miles, and provides a data rate of up to 75 Mbps.[17] A projected update to the standard, IEEE 802.16m (known as WiMAX 2), is expected to increase this data rate to approximately 1 Gbps. WiMAX adoption is promoted through the WiMAX forum (*www.wimaxforum.org*), which currently reports deployment of over 592 WiMAX networks in 149 countries.

WiMAX Security Concerns In SP800-127, NIST states:

> *WiMAX wireless interface threats focus on compromising the radio links between WiMAX nodes. These radio links support both line-of-sight (LOS) and non-line-of-sight (NLOS) signal propagation. Links from LOS WiMAX systems are generally harder to attack than those from NLOS systems because an adversary would have to physically locate equipment between the transmitting nodes to compromise the confidentiality or integrity of the wireless link. WiMAX NLOS systems provide wireless coverage over large geographic regions, which expands the potential staging areas for both clients and adversaries. Like other networking technologies, all WiMAX systems must address threats arising from denial of service attacks, eavesdropping, man-in-the-middle attacks, message modification, and resource misappropriation.*[18]

To help improve an organization's security posture relative to WiMAX, NIST recommends the following:

- Develop a robust WMAN security policy and enforce it.
- Assess WiMAX technical countermeasures before implementing a vendor's WiMAX technology.
- Require mutual authentication for WiMAX devices.
- Implement Federal Information Processing Standard (FIPS)-validated encryption algorithms employing FIPS-validated cryptographic modules to protect data communications.[19]

WiMedia WiMedia is outlined in the IEEE standard 802.15.3 and was the first standard for ultra-wideband radio technology. WiMedia provides a Wireless Personal Area Network (WPAN) standard for a low-cost, low-power-consumption network. One of the first practical applications of WiMedia was the use of Wireless USB (WUSB) to allow USB accessories to communicate remotely with their host system. WiMedia is assigned a wide range of frequencies in the GHz range in order to avoid interference with other wireless devices. Data rates of around 480 Mbps can be achieved over short distances.[20]

WiMedia Security Concerns Because of the novelty of this technology and its limited deployment so far, there are no published concerns about WiMedia. As with all new technologies, however, there is the inherent concern that issues and exploits will be discovered as it is deployed.

ZigBee ZigBee is outlined in the IEEE 802.15.4 standard for low-rate ultra-wideband wireless communications. ZigBee is another WPAN standard used for monitoring and control devices, such as building lighting and heating, ventilation, and air conditioning (HVAC) climate control systems, as well as short-range sensors like shipping container tracking devices.[21]

ZigBee Security Concerns The largest areas of concern with regard to security in ZigBee lie in accidental key reuse, which could lead to breaking of the encryption mechanism and loss of access control list data because of power loss. Because many of the ZigBee devices are expected to be battery powered, loss of power could potentially result in corrupted or lost ACL table data.[22]

Wireless Architectures and Topologies

Technology standards and hardware and software that follow them are not enough to create functional networks. One also needs to have clearly defined ways of assembling the pieces into functional networks that deliver business functionality. Wireless architectures define ways to use interoperating devices to create structured solutions without the need to prepare each deployment from scratch. This architecture can make the adoption of these technologies much more useful and cost-effective.

Wireless Architectures

The basic building block of the wireless network is a set of clients using wireless connectivity interfaces or wireless network interface cards (WNIC) to connect to a WAP. The WAP provides the connection between various wireless clients as well as between the clients and other networks. These other networks may be other wireless networks, but most commonly the WAP provides a connection to wired LANs and through those LANs to the Internet.

This basic model of wireless clients within a defined network area is referred to as the **basic service set (BSS)**. Individual **stations,** or **STAs** (IEEE terminology for a client with wireless connectivity capabilities), are authorized as members of a particular BSS. Once they leave the range of the BSS, as shown in Figure 7-2, they lose connectivity and can no longer function on the network. This BSS range is also known as a **basic service area (BSA)**.[23]

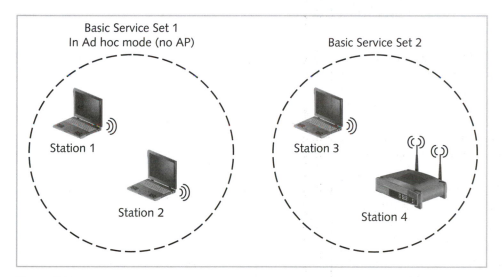

Figure 7-2 Basic service
© Cengage Learning 2013

The simplest form of BSS is an independent BSS (IBSS), which consists of a set of stations that are members of one BSA only. If a station moves within the range of a different BSA, it is unable to join without previous authorization. According to the 802.11 standard:

> *An STA's membership in a BSS is dynamic (STAs turn on, turn off, come within range, and go out of range). To become a member of a BSS, an STA joins the BSS using the synchronization procedure. To access all the services of an infrastructure*

> BSS, an STA shall become 'associated.' These associations are dynamic and involve the use of the distribution system service (DSS).[24]

Each BSS is uniquely identified with a BSSID. In the infrastructure BSS, the MAC address of the WAP is used. In an IBSS, the BSSID is a randomly generated 46-bit number. A BSSID of all 1s is used as a broadcast address for all nodes on the BSS.

To connect multiple BSSs, a **distributed system (DS)** may provide wireless internetworking connectivity. A DS works as a backbone network that WAPs use to connect other networks, but the DS contains no independent stations of its own, as shown in Figure 7-3. The DS provides a **distributed system service (DSS)** that enables the access points to provide cross domain (BSS) connectivity for clients. In order to accomplish this task, the WAP works as a switch or bridge to connect multiple networks—thus, it is multi-homed (contains more than one integral network interface card). Note that the DS backbone could be wireless or wired, as the environment mandates.

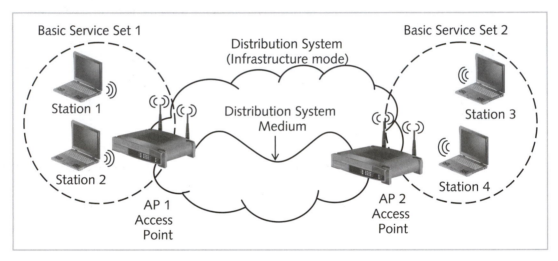

Figure 7-3   Distributed system
© Cengage Learning 2013

A collection of BSSs connected by one or more DSs is referred to as an extended service set (ESS), as illustrated in Figure 7-4. Essentially, an ESS creates a large "virtual" network consisting of all BSS logical segments connected by the various DSs. Clients don't realize the size or scope of the network, only that connectivity occurs. All data flows through the network from the client stations to the various access points, across one or more distributed system backbones, eventually arriving at the designated receiver station.

Wireless Topologies

Many of the physical and logical topologies discussed in Chapter 2 can be applied to wireless networks. If you remember, networks are configured—physically or logically—in one of these basic layouts:

- Star—A central node connected directly to all the other nodes
- Bus—A linear connection from node to node to node
- Ring—A circular bus in which the last station is connected to the first

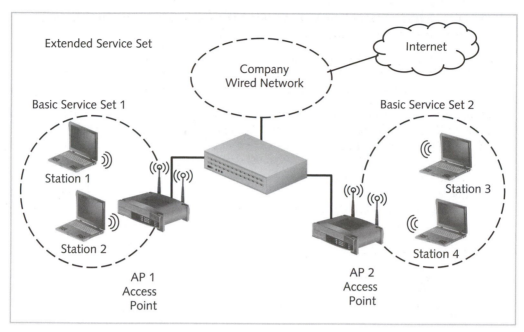

Figure 7-4 Extended service
© Cengage Learning 2013

- Hierarchical—A set of connected stars, with higher-level nodes connecting multiple stars by communicating directly with the central nodes

- Mesh—A multipoint-to-multipoint connection in which each node is connected to multiple other nodes

- Hybrid—Some combination of the above

Of these, only the star, mesh, hierarchical, and hybrid layouts are generally applied to wireless networks.

Star Wireless Topology Most BSS networks are configured as simple stars. In the "center" of the star topology, as shown in Figure 7-5, is the WAP, providing connectivity to the various stations directly. This topology is also known as a hub-and-spoke model, as it bears a resemblance to a wagon wheel. In this topology, the stations are unable to communicate directly to peers, instead having to route all traffic through the center WAP. This can become an issue if, for some reason, the client station is unable to communicate directly to the WAP and, thus, falls off the network.

Mesh Wireless Topology In the mesh wireless topology, there may be no dominant WAP. Instead, all stations on the network are equal peers and, thus, are capable of communicating through each other. As shown in Figure 7-6, mesh wireless topologies lack clearly defined boundaries. The lack of boundaries may result in challenges in which the network has difficulty determining which stations should relay a message from the sending station.

If multiple stations are able to communicate with a sending node, some mechanism (described later in this chapter) is needed to ensure that multiple copies of the same transmission are not routed through the network, creating additional problems. The primary advantage of this configuration is the flexibility of the network. If a station goes down, the rest of the network compensates for its loss. This model is also capable of "stringing out" over longer distances, as the station-to-station-to-station links become very linear—almost buslike—in their physical

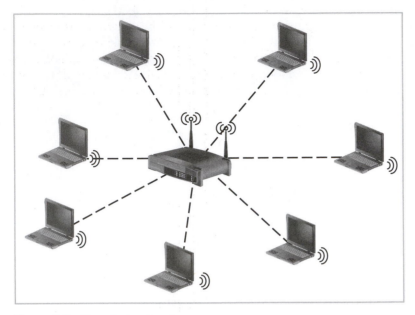

Figure 7-5 Star wireless topology
© Cengage Learning 2013

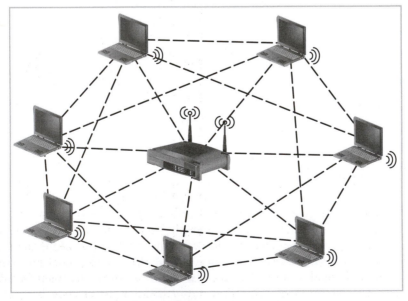

Figure 7-6 Mesh wireless topology
© Cengage Learning 2013

configuration. This allows the network to operate over larger areas than the centralized star counterpart.

Hierarchical Wireless Topologies One method of combining multiple star topologies is to create a hierarchy of stars in which individual stations connect to a WAP, which in turn connects to a higher-level WAP. These higher-level WAPs connect multiple WAPs and provide much larger geographic coverage. Unless the network provides centralized authentication, however, the individual stations are usually unable to move between lower-level WAPs (BSSs) and, thus, are constrained by the same geographic connectivity issues as the star topology. Figure 7-7 illustrates a simple hierarchical wireless topology. The primary advantage of this model is the increased number of connections among stations, which allows greater connectivity.

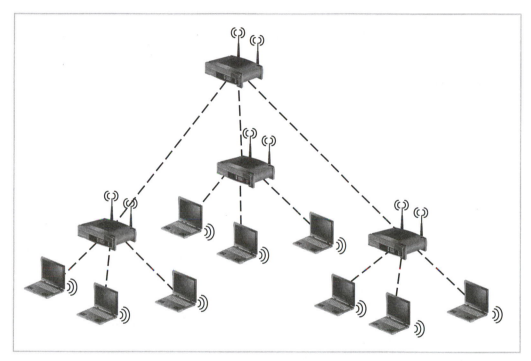

Figure 7-7 Hierarchical wireless topology
© Cengage Learning 2013

Hybrid Wireless Topologies As shown in Figure 7-8, the hybrid wireless topology combines the star and mesh topologies. Stations primarily communicate to WAPs, as in the star topology. However, if a station is unable to directly connect to a WAP but can communicate with another station, it creates a temporary mesh. The intermediate station serves as a secondary WAP, resulting in fault tolerance, like with the mesh topology. If the station is able to reconnect to its WAP, the mesh connection is discarded. This model provides much greater mobility for individual stations, as they are able to move between WAPs. This approach will require some form of centralized authentication to provide both the mesh and mobile star connectivity models.[25]

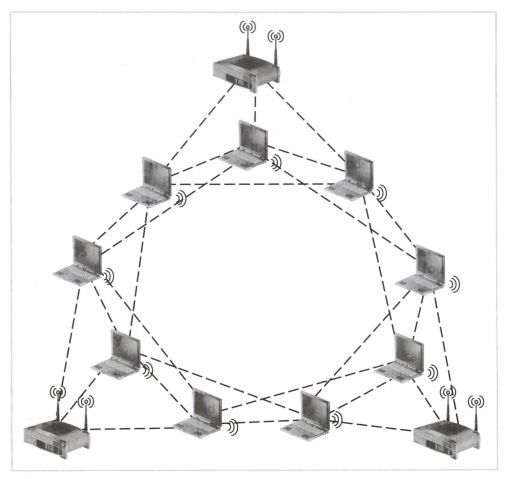

Figure 7-8   Hybrid wireless topology
© Cengage Learning 2013

Wireless Architectures

The implementation of these topologies brings up the basic wireless connection architectures that are incorporated into the topologies. In general, wireless networks can be categorized according to one of two descriptors:

- Implementation (ad hoc and infrastructure)
- Connectivity (point-to-point, point-to-multipoint, and multipoint)

Implementation Models Wireless networks can be implemented in one of two approaches, although hybrids of the two also exist. In the first approach, the ad hoc approach, networks are established as users on local stations need them. In the second approach, the organization establishes permanent, persistent connection points, typically providing centralized authentication to control access.

Ad Hoc Implementation Ad hoc wireless models rely on the existence of multiple stations to provide connectivity. In ad hoc mode, there are no formal access points, only peer stations. In order for higher-level connectivity to occur, however, at least one station has to have connectivity to an infrastructure WAP. This peer-to-peer (P2P) connection, in which the WLAN consists almost exclusively of wireless communications between multiple peer stations, creates a hybrid role for each station—part access point, part client. This ad hoc networking is convenient for connection between computers and peripherals, between multiple computers for file and resource sharing, and to create temporary networks for a particular purpose—like computer gaming.

The primary drawback associated with these networks is that they are inherently unreliable. If a single station is disconnected from the network, many individual stations may be without connectivity. Given that the ad hoc networks are typically not formally supported by an organization, they tend to be reliant on a diverse set of underlying computing technologies, which creates additional issues with security (discussed later in this chapter) and reliability. Figure 7-9 shows Windows 7 ad hoc network configuration screens. As a caution, Figure 7-9 shows an open access ad hoc network (no password). It is strongly recommended that wireless networks never be implemented without at least some level of access control protection.

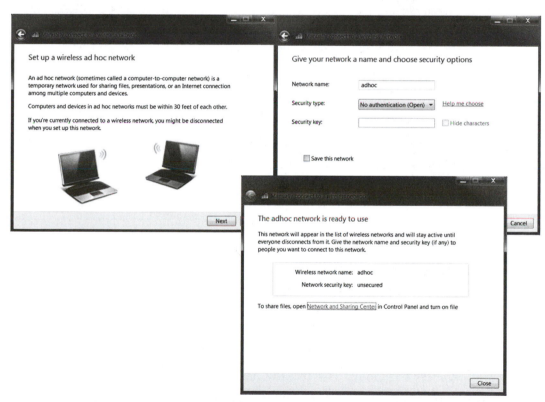

Figure 7-9 Wireless ad hoc network configuration screens
Source: Microsoft Windows 7

Infrastructure Model Most installed wireless networks use the infrastructure model, in which a WAP is installed and connected to wired networks to provide connectivity. This is usually done to create a wireless network footprint in a defined area for ongoing communications.

This model meets users' expectations for reliable connectivity for the stations connecting within the established perimeter of the WLAN. Infrastructure model-based networks tend to be much more scalable than ad hoc networks, and they are usually better organized, supported, and managed. In fact, for most Wi-Fi users, ad hoc networks are relegated to those who want to put up a temporary capability, often away from their central facility.

Connectivity Models Another component of the discussion around wireless networks is how they communicate. Closely related to the models discussed in the previous section, these architectures reflect whether the wireless communications channels are unicast (only sent to one station) or broadcast (sent to multiple stations simultaneously). Between unicast and broadcast is multicast, in which a message is sent to multiple recipients (but not all) in the same transmission. The most commonly defined approaches to these architectures are point-to-point, point-to-multipoint, and mesh (multipoint).

Point-to-Point As the name implies, a point-to-point wireless network is a direct link between two stations, implemented typically in the ad hoc manner. One station is configured to allow connection (reception), and another station initiates the connection. Point-to-point networks provide a dedicated circuit between the two stations and can offer higher data transfer rates than other shared options. Point-to-point networks can be extended to point-to-point-to-point networks, which allows longer-range communications. This is similar to a radio relay model used for long-distance communications, in which intermediate stations provide connectivity for very remote stations.

Point-to-Multipoint A point-to-multipoint wireless network is most commonly found in the star and hierarchical topologies discussed earlier. In this model, a single access point provides connectivity for a number of clients within a BSS. In telephony, the modern wireless phone (formerly cellular phone) network is a point-to-multipoint wireless network.

Mesh Multipoint The next iteration of point-to-multipoint communication is the mesh topology. This is when any station can directly send and receive data to and from any other station. Also known as a multipoint-to-multipoint network, the mesh multipoint network, including the hybrid network topology, is a more recent approach to networking, allowing end users to decide what wireless networks they need. Many new devices are capable of establishing this type of topology.

Roaming Though not a true connectivity model, the roaming model is the logical extension of the previously discussed models and implementations. It not only provides point-to-multipoint connectivity, but it allows the station to move between adjacent BSSs without losing connectivity. Although this technology was pioneered decades ago with wireless telephony, only recently has it been available to true wireless networking. Many organizations have been implementing roaming between multiple access points in relatively small LANs, but its availability for larger geographic areas is still being rolled out.

WiMAX, discussed earlier, is the latest roaming implementation for wide-scale wireless networking. Once end-users purchase WiMAX, they are able to move throughout the WMAN (within the WiMAX coverage area) while maintaining connectivity.

Mobile Hotspots and Wireless Networking Mobile hotspots and mobile device relays are an increasingly popular choice for users of personal digital assistants, smartphones, and other portable wireless devices. A **mobile hotspot** is a service usually provided by a wireless telephony service provider to allow users to connect their wireless devices to a specific commercial wireless service. It typically consists of a wireless network card or similar device that the customer can use to access wireless services over the provider's network.

Another innovation related to the mobile hotspot is the use of wireless devices to serve as a wireless network access point relay. Smartphones can serve as personal mobile hotspots to allow users to connect their laptops or tablet computers to a service provider's network by relaying the network traffic between the computer and the network. Though efficient and convenient for the user, unless proper access controls are implemented in the relay device, the technique can result in exploitation of the mobile device used for the relay and exploitation of all computers connected to the device.

Wireless Security Protocols

Without some form of protection, the radio transmission signals used in WLANs can be intercepted by anyone with a receiver and a wireless packet sniffer. In order to prevent interception of these communications, these networks must use some form of cryptographic security control. Two sets of protocols are currently widely used to help secure wireless transmissions: Wired Equivalent Privacy (WEP) and Wi-Fi Protected Access (WPA). Both are designed for use with the IEEE 802.11 wireless networks.

Wired Equivalent Privacy (WEP)

WEP was an early attempt to provide security with the 802.11 network protocol. It is now considered too weak cryptographically to provide any meaningful protection from eavesdropping, but for a time it did provide some measure of security for low-sensitivity networks. Using a 64-bit key, WEP uses the RC4 cipher stream to encrypt each packet. This key is created using a 24-bit initialization vector and a 40-bit key value. The packets are formed using an XOR function with the RC4 key value stream to encrypt the data packet. A 4-byte integrity check value (ICV) is calculated for each packet and then appended. Acording to many experts, WEP is too weak for use in most network settings for these reasons:

- Key management is not effective because most networks use a single shared secret key value for each node. Synchronizing key changes is a tedious process, and no key management is defined in the protocol, so keys are seldom changed.

- The initialization vector (IV) is too small, resulting in the recycling of IVs. An attacker can reverse-engineer the RC4 cipher stream and decrypt subsequent packets or forge future packets. In 2007, this was accomplished in less than one minute.

- There are a number of tools available that allow automatic cracking of the WEP key because of these WEP weaknesses—Aircrack-ng, WEPCrack, and Cafe Latte, to name a few. Most tools collect network packets broadcast over the air to nearby wireless networks (or wireless clients). In turn, the cracking tools sift through the captured packets to reverse-engineer the WEP key.

In summary, an intruder who collects enough data can threaten a WEP network in just a few minutes by decrypting or altering the data being transmitted, or by forging the WEP key to gain unauthorized access to the network. WEP also lacks a means of validating user credentials to ensure that only those who should be on the network are allowed to access it.[26]

Wi-Fi Protected Access (WPA and WPA2)

The Wi-Fi Alliance introduced WPA to resolve the issues with WEP. WPA has a key size of 128 bits, and instead of static, seldom-changed keys, it uses dynamic keys created and shared by an authentication server. WPA accomplishes this through the use of the Temporal Key Integrity Protocol (TKIP), a suite of algorithms that attempts to deliver the best security given the constraints of a wireless network environment. The algorithms are designed to work with legacy networking devices. TKIP adds four new algorithms to those that were used in WEP:

- A cryptographic message integrity code (MIC), called Michael, to defeat forgeries
- A new IV sequencing discipline to remove replay attacks from the attacker's arsenal
- A per-packet key-mixing function to de-correlate the public IVs from weak keys
- A rekeying mechanism to provide fresh encryption and integrity keys, thereby undoing the threat of attacks stemming from key reuse

Although it offered dramatically improved security over WEP, WPA was not the most secure wireless protocol design. Some compromises were made in the security design to allow compatibility with existing wireless network components. Protocols to replace TKIP are currently under development. Table 7-2 provides a summary of the differences between WEP and WPA.

	WEP	WPA
Encryption	Broken by scientists and hackers	Overcomes all WEP shortcomings
	40-bit key	128-bit key
	Static key—same value used by everyone on the network	Dynamic keys; each user assigned a key per session, with additional keys calculated for each packet
	Manual key distribution—each key typed by hand into each device	Automatic key distribution
Authentication	Broken, used WEP key itself for authentication	Improved user authentication, utilizing stronger 802.1X and EAP

Table 7-2 WEP versus WPA

Source: www.wi-fi.org/files/wp_8_WPA%20Security_4-29-03.pdf

© Cengage Learning 2013

TKIP TKIP is a "wrapper" used to enhance the WEP protocol. It was proposed as a way to implement improved security on slower platforms without performance degradation. The most fundamental improvement changes the key used in each packet by combining an encryption key, the MAC address of the transmitting station, and a serial number for the packet.[27]

TKIP offers these fundamental security features for IEEE 802.11 WLANs:

- Confidentiality with the RC4 algorithm
- Integrity using the Michael message digest algorithm (through generation of a MIC)
- Replay prevention through a frame sequencing technique
- Use of a new encryption key for each frame
- Implementation of countermeasures when encountering a frame with a MIC error, which is a strong indicator of an active attack

TKIP also provides encapsulation, which enhances the WEP encapsulation technique without requiring hardware changes. It uses three distinct keys: two integrity keys and an encryption key. Validation checks are performed on the frames as they are unencapsulated. For example, if a violation of proper frame sequencing is detected, the frame is discarded. Also, for each frame, the MIC is recomputed and compared with the MIC transmitted in the packet; if these do not match, the frame is discarded and TKIP countermeasures are invoked.[28]

WPA2

In 2004, WPA2 was made available as a replacement for WPA. Beginning in 2006, WPA2 became mandatory for all new Wi-Fi devices. WPA2 is backwardly compatible with WPA, although some older network cards have difficulty using it. Although WPA met a subset of requirements from the 802.11i standard, WPA2 was designed to meet all requirements. One of the important security concepts introduced with 802.11i was the idea of **Robust Security Networks (RSN)**. An RSN is a network that only allows connections that are **Robust Security Network Associations (RSNAs)**—in other words, wireless connections that provide encryption to protect against WLAN security threats.[29]

The most notable of the features added to WPA2 were AES-based encryption, CCMP encryption protocol, and EAP authentication protocol, which are described in the following sections.

The RSN protocol functions as follows:

1. The wireless NIC sends a probe request.
2. The WAP sends a probe response with an RSN Information Exchange (IE) frame.
3. The wireless NIC requests authentication via one of the approved methods.
4. The WAP provides authentication for the wireless NIC.
5. The wireless NIC sends an association request with an RSN Information Exchange (IE) frame.
6. The WAP sends an association response.[30]

CCMP Counter Mode with Cipher Block Chaining Message Authentication Code (CBC-MAC) Protocol (**CCMP**) is an encryption protocol that enhances the confidentiality and integrity of wireless LAN protocols implemented with the 802.11i amendment to the 802.11 standard. CCMP can be implemented as a negotiated cipher suite when creating a Robust Security Network Association (RSNA).

CCMP was created to meet the security requirements for secure wireless connections without the constraint of interoperation with legacy hardware, and it is considered the long-term solution to the confidentiality requirement in RSNs. The use of CCMP is required to achieve RSN compliance.

CCMP draws from the authenticated cipher mode of the AES standard: Counter Mode with CBC-MAC (CCM). CCM is a mode of operation defined for any block cipher with a 128-bit block size. CCMP protects the integrity of both the packet data and portions of the IEEE 802.11 header. CCM combines two well-known and proven cryptographic techniques to achieve robust security: CTR for confidentiality and Cipher Block Chaining MAC (CBC-MAC) for both authentication and integrity protection. For IEEE 802.11, CCM employs a single 128-bit session key (TK) to protect the duplex data channel. The CCMP key space has size 2^{128} and uses a 48-bit packet number (PN) to construct a nonce to prevent replay attacks. In cryptographic terms, a **nonce** is an arbitrary number used only once in communications. The construction of the nonce allows the key to be used for both integrity and confidentiality without compromising either.

CCM uses a new Temporal Key every session—with every new STA-AP association. Unlike TKIP, the use of AES at the core of CCM obviates the need to have per-packet keys. As a result, the two-phase key-mixing functions of TKIP encapsulation are not present in the CCMP encapsulation. Figure 7-10 depicts the CCMP encapsulation, illustrating the various functions and their sequence in the encapsulation process.[31]

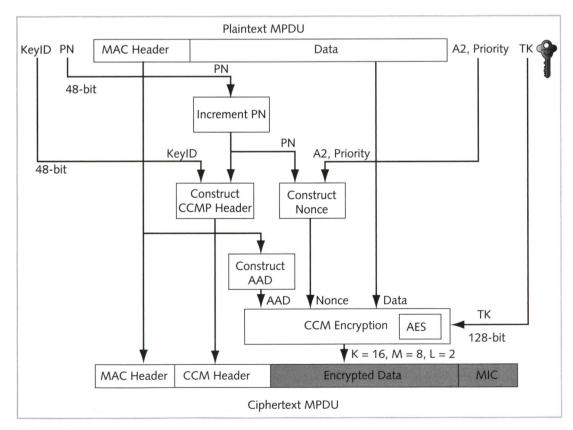

Figure 7-10 CCMP encapsulation diagram
© Cengage Learning 2013

Extensible Authentication Protocol (EAP) NIST Standard 800-97 provides the following overview of EAP:

> *IEEE 802.11 RSN uses the Extensible Authentication Protocol (EAP) for the authentication phase of establishing an RSNA. EAP supports a wide variety of authentication methods, also called EAP methods. They include authentication based on passwords, certificates, smart cards, and tokens. EAP methods also can include combinations of authentication techniques, such as a certificate followed by a password, or the option of using either a smart card or a token. This flexibility allows EAP to integrate with nearly any environment to which a WLAN might connect.*[32]

It is important to understand that EAP is a framework for device-to-device authentication but not an actual authentication mechanism. Do not confuse authentication between devices, which is used to ensure trust between network nodes, with the authentication required from users connecting to systems or networks. Originally, EAP was developed as a way to expand authentication mechanisms for Point-to-Point Protocol (PPP) dial-up communications beyond the standard Password Authentication Protocol (PAP) and Challenge-Handshake Authentication Protocol (CHAP). EAP's use, however, has expanded to other communications methods, such as WLANs. Because it's a framework, EAP supports many different authentication mechanisms, such as:

- Lightweight Extensible Authentication Protocol (LEAP)—A proprietary EAP authentication mechanism developed by Cisco
- EAP-TLS—Uses TLS protocol and an authentication server like RADIUS
- EAP-PSK—Uses a preshared key (PSK) to establish a mutual authentication method

Other authentication mechanisms are continually being added. It is important to understand the specific authentication mechanism and whether it employs strong cryptographic methods to provide strong authentication mechanisms.

Robust Security Network (RSN) In addition to the stations and access points discussed earlier in this chapter, the Robust Security Network (RSN) concept includes a new component: authentication servers (ASs). AS systems include RADIUS and KERBEROS servers, discussed in earlier chapters. By including an AS, a traditional WLAN can be upgraded to an RSN. NIST Special Publication 800-97, *Establishing Wireless Robust Security Networks: A Guide to IEEE 802.11i*, provides significant detail on this subject and thus has served as the foundation for much of the material in this chapter. The most common protocol used in support of an RSNA is EAP. The security of legacy 802.11 implementations is addressed in NIST SP 800-48.

RSN Operations According to NIST SP800-97, IEEE 802.11 RSN operation may be thought of as occurring in five distinct phases:

> 1. *RSN Operation Phase 1: Discovery. The STA identifies an AP for a WLAN with which it wishes to communicate. The STA locates an AP either by receiving one of the AP's periodic transmissions of Beacon frames, or by sending a Probe Request to solicit a Probe Response from an AP. After the STA has identified an AP, the STA and the AP exchange frames to negotiate various parameters for their communications. By the end of the phase, the STA and AP have agreed on an authentication method.*

2. *RSN Operation Phase 2: Authentication. During this phase, the STA and AS prove their identities to each other. The authentication frames pass through the AP, which also blocks non-authentication traffic from the STA using IEEE 802.1X port-based access control. The actual authentication mechanism is implemented by the STA and AS using EAP. EAP provides a framework that allows the use of multiple methods for achieving authentication, including static passwords, dynamic passwords, and public key cryptography certificates. After authentication has been completed, the AAA key is installed in the STA and AS. It serves as a root key to enable the generation of other keys used to secure communications between the STA and AP.*

3. *RSN Operation Phase 3: Key Generation and Distribution (KGD). During the KGD phase, the AP and the STA perform several operations that cause cryptographic keys to be generated and placed on the AP and the STA. The KGD phase employs two handshakes: a 4-Way Handshake and a Group Key Handshake. During the 4-Way Handshake, the STA and AP establish a security policy that specifies several key security capabilities, such as data confidentiality and integrity protocols for protecting data traffic, and a key distribution approach. Both handshakes employ message encryption and integrity checking, using one of two confidentiality and integrity algorithms. For both types of handshakes, NIST requires the use of AES Key Wrap with HMAC-SHA-1-128 instead of RC4 encryption with HMAC-MD5 because AES and SHA-1 are FIPS-approved algorithms, and RC4 and MD5 are not. Selecting CCMP as the cipher suite will ensure the use of the appropriate key wrap algorithms.*

4. *RSN Operation Phase 4: Protected Data Transfer. The STA and AP share data securely, using the security policy and cryptographic keys established during the first three phases. Because secure data transfer occurs between the STA and the AP only, organizations need to consider carefully the security of the data during the rest of its transit (e.g., on the DS).*

5. *RSN Operation Phase 5: Connection Termination. During this phase, the STA and AP tear down their secure connection and delete their association, thereby terminating their wireless connection.[33]*

WLAN Security Concerns

In deploying a wireless network, it's important to understand the various threats to the network in order to better defend against them. Here are some of the most notable threats to running a secure WLAN:

*   **Rogue APs**—There are two categories of threats that arise when an unauthorized access point is erected in a nearby physical location. The first is generally referred to as a rogue access point. This occurs when an employee sets up a WAP connected to the wired LAN. The problem is that the WAP is not tracked by the organization and may not be properly secured, resulting in a weak point on the network. The second threat category is generally referred to as an evil twin. This refers to the man-in-the-middle attack, in which an attacker sets up an access point to lure unsuspecting victims, who

think the WAP is part of the legitimate WLAN, into connecting. The attacker, using software like Airsnarf, tricks the users into providing legitimate user names and passwords or other information—an example of social engineering.

- **Key cracking**—There are a number of tools available—Aircrack, AirSnort, and WEPCrack, for example—that allow an attacker to sniff a large number of wireless network packets and then use the data to crack the encryption key. These types of attacks are fairly easy to pull off when wireless networks use WEP; they're even possible with WPA. Using strong passkeys and WPA2 are currently the best protection against these types of attacks.

- **Wardriving**—Because of the very nature of wireless communications, it is possible for an attacker to locate himself within the radio boundaries of the WLAN. By doing so, he can carry out key cracking on encrypted WLAN or just simply join unencrypted WLANs. The attacker can then roam the network like a trusted employee. There are also a number of antennae that can be used to increase how far away an attacker can be and still communicate with the WLAN. The term *wardriving* refers to the practice of driving around looking for and mapping insecure WLANs.

- **ARP poisoning**—As with the ARP poisoning attacks on wired networks, WLANs typically cannot verify that an ARP reply sent by a host on the wireless network was in response to a valid ARP request from another host. Because of this lack of verification, an attacker can send an ARP reply stating that its MAC address owns a particular IP address. If the attacker can poison the cache of two systems, mapping the IP address of System A on System B to the attacker system and mapping the IP address of System B on System A to the attacker system, the attacker can initiate a man-in-the-middle attack, effectively routing communication between the two hosts. Tools like Ettercap make ARP poisoning fairly easy to accomplish.

- **DoS attacks**—Like wired networks, WLANs are susceptible to DoS attacks that overwhelm the WAP with 802.1x handshake attempts, 802.1x authentication attempts, or even legitimate traffic. However, WAPs are also susceptible to radio jamming attacks, in which the attacker sends a more powerful signal to nearby clients and disallows radio communication with the legitimate WAP.

WLAN Security Solutions

WLAN technology has had a number of problems with protocols like WEP and WPA, which has creasted the perception that WLANs are inherently insecure. However, after a number of improvements, it is now possible to have sufficient security layers to protect wireless communication. Here are a number of recommendations to help secure your wireless network:

- Mandate the use of WPA2 and strong passkeys to encrypt wireless communications and to provide a basic layer of authentication.

- Employ wireless IDS to help spot rogue access points, evil twins, wardriving, and other probes of the network.

- Use mutual authentication methods—like EAP-TLS—in order to provide a level of trust by authenticating not only the client to server but also the server to the client.

- For an added security layer, ensure that wireless connections authenticate via a VPN prior to gaining access to the wired network resources.

WLAN Security Myths

There are a number of recommendations that have been passed from organization to organization with regards to securing wireless networks. Unfortunately, many of these recommendations don't provide an adequate level of security or are a waste of time.[34] Here are some of the most popular myths:

- **MAC filtering**—Most WAPs allow administrators to limit the connections to only listed MAC addresses. The idea is that only trusted computers can connect to the WAP, whereas untrusted (unlisted) MAC addresses cannot. The problem is that anyone sniffing wireless communications can intercept the MAC addresses of trusted systems. From there, the attacker only has to spoof the trusted MAC address to gain access to the network.

- **SSID hiding**—The usual advice is to have the administrator disable the WAP's SSID beaconing ability. The thinking is that, then, attackers are unable to discover the wireless network and, therefore, won't attack it. Unfortunately, tools like Kismet or NetStumbler make it incredibly easy to scan the local area in order to find wireless networks, regardless of whether or not they actively advertise their SSIDs via beaconing.

- **Disable DHCP**—Many organizations believe that by disabling DHCP for wireless network participants, they can prevent an attacker from obtaining a legitimate IP address and, therefore, prevent the attacker from participating on the network. Unfortunately, as just mentioned, wireless sniffing allows an attacker to easily determine what IP addresses are valid. From there, it's a simple matter to assign an IP address to participate.

- **LEAP authentication**—Cisco created the Lightweight Extensible Authentication Protocol (LEAP) for its wireless devices in order to provide an additional security layer to networks using WEP. Unfortunately, a researcher named Joshua Wright released a tool called Asleap, which is easily able to crack LEAP passwords. Since then, Cisco has released updates to LEAP, but there have also been a number of new tools able to attack LEAP. At this point, LEAP does not provide stronger security than WPA2 and is likely ineffective in providing a proper security layer.

- **Signal suppression**—Many organizations believe that by placing WAPs away from the physical boundaries of the building or campus or by reducing the signal strength, attackers will not be able to connect to the wireless network. Unfortunately, there are a number of antennae on the market that allow attackers to increase signal strength for both transmission and better reception. These antennae will quickly overcome most attempts to reposition WAPs or reduce signal strength.

Bluetooth

Like 802.11 standards, Bluetooth defines a wireless communication standard that allows mobile phones, computers, cars, and other industrial equipment to communicate with various accessories. Bluetooth has a physical limitation based on the type of radio used in the device. Class 3 radios provide a communication range of about 3 feet. Class 2 radios, found in most mobile devices, have a range of 33 feet. Finally, Class 1 radios, found in industrial applications, have a range of 300 feet. According to the Bluetooth Core Specification, Bluetooth operates in the industrial, scientific, and medical (ISM) radio frequency band of 2.4 GHz.[35] Originally, Bluetooth had a maximum data rate of around 720 Kbps. The improved Bluetooth 2.0 increased the data rate to around 3 Mbps.

Bluetooth networks are referred to as *piconets*. When multiple piconets are connected through common devices, the entire network structure is referred to as a *scatternet*. In discoverable mode—which allows other Bluetooth systems to detect and connect—devices can easily be accessed, much the way that a shared folder can be accessed on a networked computer. Even in nondiscoverable mode, the device is susceptible to access by other devices that have connected with it in the past. Here are some key benefits of Bluetooth technology:[36]

- Removes wired cables—To reduce clutter or some distance, a number of computer and phone peripherals have moved to remote Bluetooth connections.

- Share and synchronize data—Bluetooth-enabled devices can operate on piconets in order to transfer files from PC to PC, share data between connected phones, or synchronize phone books from PC to phone.

- Serve as an Internet hotspot—A Bluetooth-enabled device can be connected to the Internet and share that connectivity via Bluetooth to other Bluetooth-connected devices.

Bluetooth Security Concerns

Bluetooth has been consistently criticized as an insecure wireless communications standard, but it is still widely used for wireless telephony, mobile device accessories, and point-to-point data exchange. By default, Bluetooth does not authenticate connections; however, it does implement some degree of security when devices access certain services, such as dial-up accounts and local-area file transfers. Paired devices—usually a computer or phone and a peripheral that a user plans to connect to it—require that the same passkey be entered on both devices. This key is used to generate a session key, which is used for all future communications.

There are a number of attacks that exploit the simple security mechanisms implemented in Bluetooth devices. The Bluetooth attacks, however, must overcome the previously mentioned physical range in order to carry out attacks (although recent attacks have proved capable of using directional antennae to increase the range to over a mile).[37] Here are some of the most notable attacks:

- **Bluesnarf**—Bluetooth devices employ an object exchange (OBEX) profile that is intended to allow the easy transfer of business cards, contact information, and other items. A Bluesnarf attack is one in which the attacker exploits the OBEX connection to grab e-mail, text messages, contact information, pictures, or other information off the intended target. Most modern Bluetooth devices require that the two devices be paired in order for the attack to be successful. Bluesnarfer and Bloover are popular tools to carry out Bluesnarf attacks.

- **Bluejacking**—A Bluejack attack also exploits the OBEX connection, but instead of stealing data from the target device, the attacker sends a fake vCard for the target. Within the vCard, the attacker uses the name field to send a message to the unsuspecting victim. This type of attack has been used in guerilla marketing campaigns or just to see the reactions of nearby mobile users.

- **BlueBug**—The name BlueBug refers to a security vulnerability in Bluetooth-enabled mobile phones that allows a nearby attacker to issue commands to an unsuspecting target phone. If the exploit is successful, the attacker can initiate phone calls, read text messages, and read other information from the phone.[38]

- **Evil twin**—If an attacker uses a device to simulate a Bluetooth access point, he or she can trick the user into connecting his or her devices to the fake access point. The fake access point—or evil twin—can capture and store all communications, including the passkey submission. (This attack can also be classified as a man-in-the-middle attack and is a very serious concern for WLANs.)

Bluetooth Security Solutions

There are two general principles to keep in mind when securing Bluetooth-enabled devices: (1) Turn off Bluetooth when you do not intend to use it, and (2) do not accept an incoming communications pairing request unless you know who the requester is.

Although earlier versions of Bluetooth were inherently insecure, later versions, including Bluetooth 2.1 +Enhanced Data Rate, provide a new security mechanism called Secure Simple Pairing (SSP). NIST SP 800-121 describes the four security modes of Bluetooth:

Cumulatively, the various versions of Bluetooth specifications define four security modes. Each version of Bluetooth supports some, but not all, of the four modes. Each Bluetooth device must operate in one of the four modes, which are described below.

Security Mode 1 is non-secure. Security functionality (authentication and encryption) is bypassed, leaving the device and connections susceptible to attackers. In effect, Bluetooth devices in this mode are "promiscuous" and do not employ any mechanisms to prevent other Bluetooth-enabled devices from establishing connections. Security Mode 1 is only supported in v2.0 + EDR (and earlier) devices.

In Security Mode 2, a service level-enforced security mode, security procedures are initiated after LMP link establishment but before L2CAP channel establishment. L2CAP resides in the data link layer and provides connection-oriented and connectionless data services to upper layers. For this security mode, a security manager (as specified in the Bluetooth architecture) controls access to specific services and devices. The centralized security manager maintains policies for access control and interfaces with other protocols and device users. Varying security policies and trust levels to restrict access may be defined for applications with different security requirements operating in parallel. It is possible to grant access to some services without providing access to other services. In this mode, the notion of authorization—the process of deciding if a specific device is allowed to have access to a specific service—is introduced. It is important to note that the authentication and encryption mechanisms used for Security Mode 2 are implemented at the LMP layer (below L2CAP), just as with Security Mode 3. All Bluetooth devices can support Security Mode 2; however, v2.1 + EDR devices can only support it for backward compatibility with v2.0 + EDR (or earlier) devices.

In Security Mode 3, the link level-enforced security mode, a Bluetooth device initiates security procedures before the physical link is fully established. Bluetooth devices operating in Security Mode 3 mandates authentication and encryption for all connections to and from the device. This mode supports authentication (unidirectional or mutual) and encryption. The authentication and encryption features are based on a separate secret link key that is shared by paired devices, once the pairing has been established. Security Mode 3 is only supported in v2.0 + EDR (or earlier) devices.

Similar to Security Mode 2, Security Mode 4 (introduced in Bluetooth v2.1 + EDR) is a service level enforced security mode in which security procedures are initiated after link setup. Secure Simple Pairing uses Elliptic Curve Diffie Hellman (ECDH) techniques for key exchange and link key generation. Device authentication and encryption algorithms are identical to the algorithms in Bluetooth v2.0 + EDR and earlier versions. Security requirements for services protected by Security Mode 4 must be classified as one of the following: authenticated link key required, unauthenticated link key required, or no security required. Whether or not a link key is authenticated depends on the Secure Simple Pairing association model used. Security Mode 4 is mandatory for communication between v2.1 + EDR devices.

There are two methods in which link key generation is performed for Bluetooth. Security Modes 2 and 3 use one method, while Security Mode 4 uses another. For Bluetooth v2.0 + EDR (and earlier), operating in Security Mode 2 or 3, two associated devices simultaneously derive link keys during the initialization phase when users enter an identical PIN into one or both devices, depending on the configuration and device type. After initialization is complete, devices automatically and transparently authenticate and initiate the encryption procedure to secure the wireless link, if encryption is enabled. The PIN code used in Bluetooth devices can vary between one and 16 bytes. The typical four-digit PIN may be sufficient for low-risk situations; a longer PIN should be used for devices that require a higher level of security.

Secure Simple Pairing (SSP) was introduced in Bluetooth v2.1 + EDR for use with Security Mode 4. SSP simplifies the pairing process by providing a number of association models that are flexible in terms of device input capability. The four association models offered in SSP are as follows:

- Numeric Comparison was designed for the situation where both Bluetooth devices are capable of displaying a six-digit number and allowing a user to enter a "yes" or "no" response. During pairing, a user is shown a six-digit number on each display and provides a "yes" response on each device if the numbers match.

- Passkey Entry was designed for the situation where one Bluetooth device has input capability (e.g., Bluetooth-enabled keyboard), while the other device has a display but no input capability. In this model, the device with only a display shows a six-digit number that the user then enters on the device with input capability.

- Just Works was designed for the situation where one (or both) of the pairing devices has neither a display nor a keyboard for entering digits (e.g., Bluetooth-enabled headset). It performs Authentication Stage 1 in the same manner as the Numeric Comparison model, except that a display is not available.

The user is required to accept a connection without verifying the calculated value on both devices, so MITM protection is not provided.

- *Out of Band (OOB) was designed for devices that support a wireless technology other than Bluetooth for the purposes of device discovery and cryptographic value exchange. In the case of NFC, the OOB model allows devices to pair by simply "tapping" one device against the other, followed by the user accepting the pairing via a single button push.*

Security Mode 4 requires Bluetooth services to mandate an authenticated link key, an unauthenticated link key, or no security at all. Of the association models described above, all but the Just Works model provide authenticated link keys.[39]

Chapter Summary

- Wireless security is problematic. Unlike wire-based networking, which allows network administrators control over the physical media (wires and cables) and the access points (hubs and switches), wireless networking allows little control over the signal. An organization can restrict a wireless network's footprint, but it can do little to guide or restrict the wireless signal itself.

- A wireless local area network, also known as a WLAN or by the branding label Wi-Fi (wireless fidelity), is a group of interconnected networking nodes operating within a limited geographic area that offers network access by the use of radio waves.

- Wireless networks are inherently different from networks that use physical media like wires or cables.

- WLANs often combine a number of standards and technologies to provide communications. The basic building blocks of the modern WLAN are wireless modulation technologies and the IEEE Standard 802.11.

- WLANS place the data onto the wireless radio signal by using modulation techniques, such as Quadrature Amplitude Modulation (QAM) and Quadrature Phase Shift Keying (QPSK).

- Three technologies provide spread-spectrum security and transport features for the data stream: Frequency Hopping Spread Spectrum (FHSS), Direct-Sequence Spread Spectrum (DSSS), and Orthogonal frequency-division multiplexing (OFDM).

- In 1997, the IEEE ratified the 802.11 standard, which encompassed the transmission of data using three defined methods, one of which was radio transmission in the 2.4 GHz band. In 1999, the standard was ratified with two amendments: 802.11a and 802.11b.

- As the 802.11 technology was coming to market and the 802.11i amendment was being discussed, a group called the Wi-Fi Alliance proposed an interoperability agreement and a branding arrangement.

- Although 802.11 and Wi-Fi are the dominant wireless networking standards, there are others. Most prevalent among the non-802.11-style networking standards are Bluetooth, WiMedia, Zigbee, and WiMax.

- A wireless network consists of a set of clients using wireless network interface cards to connect to a WAP. The WAP provides the connection between various wireless clients as well as between the clients and other networks. This is considered a basic service set (BSS). Individual stations or STAs are authorized as members of a particular BSS. A BSS's range is known as a Basic Service Area (BSA).

- A collection of multiple BSSs is referred to as an extended service set (ESS), which creates a virtual network consisting of all BSS subnets.

- Wireless networks can be implemented in one of two approaches, although hybrids of the two certainly exist. In the ad hoc approach, networks are established as users on local stations need them, and connections are made between end points as needed. In another approach, the organization establishes permanent, persistent connection points, typically providing centralized authentication to control access.

- Another component of wireless networks is how they communicate. Point-to-point wireless is a direct link between two stations, typically implemented in the ad hoc manner. Point-to-multipoint wireless is most commonly found in the star and hierarchical topologies. A more complete instantiation of a multipoint network is the mesh topology, in which all stations can directly send to and receive from all other stations.

- WLANs are thought by many in the IT industry to be inherently insecure. Two sets of protocols are currently widely used to help secure wireless transmissions: Wired Equivalent Privacy (WEP) and Wi-Fi Protected Access (WPA).

- WEP was an early attempt to provide security with the 802.11 network protocol.

- WPA was introduced by the Wi-Fi Alliance to resolve the issues with WEP.

- Robust Secure Network (RSN) is a wireless security network that provides moderate to high levels of assurance against WLAN security threats through use of a variety of cryptographic techniques.

- The various threats to wireless security include Rogue Aps, Key cracking, ARP poisoning, and DoS attacks.

- Recommendations to help secure your wireless network include: mandating the use of WPA2 and strong passkeys to encrypt wireless communications and to provide a basic layer of authentication; employing wireless IDS to help spot rogue access points, evil twins, wardriving, and other probes of the network; and ensuring that wireless connections authenticate via a VPN prior to gaining access to the wired network's resources.

- Bluetooth is a wireless communication standard that allows mobile phones, computers, cars, and other industrial equipment to communicate with various accessories. Bluetooth networks are referred to as *piconets*. Bluetooth has been consistently criticized as an insecure wireless communications standard, but it is still widely used for wireless telephony, mobile device accessories, and point-to-point data exchange. There are two general principles for securing Bluetooth-enabled devices: (1) Turn off Bluetooth when you do not intend to use it, and (2) do not accept an incoming communications pairing request unless you know who the requester is.

Review Questions

1. What is wireless networking?

2. Why is wireless networking considered so difficult?

3. What is a WAP? What does it do?

4. According to the IEEE, what are the differences between wired and wireless networks?

5. What is the basic IEEE standard that defines WLAN technology?

6. What are the two technologies that are used to manipulate the radio medium to carry data?

7. What are three technologies that provide spread-spectrum security and transport features for the data stream?

8. What is the Wi-Fi Alliance?

9. What are some wireless standards in use other than 802.11?

10. What does "basic service set" mean in the context of Wi-Fi?

11. What is a star wireless topology?

12. What is a mesh wireless topology?

13. What are the two manners in which wireless networks are implemented?

14. What are the two widely used sets of IEEE wireless security protocols?

15. What is WEP, and why is it falling out of favor as a means of securing wireless networks?

16. What is Wi-Fi Protected Access (WPA) and WPA2?

17. What are the most notable threats to running a secure WLAN?

18. What are the recommended practices for running a secure WLAN?

19. What is Bluetooth networking?

20. What are the two general principles for securing BlueTooth-enabled devices?

Real World Exercises

Exercise 7-1

Use your preferred Web browser and search engine to shop for a WAP. What brand seems to have the most models under $50? What brand seems to be consistently the most expensive? Why do you think this is so?

Exercise 7-2

Use your preferred Web browser and search engine to investigate the technology known as *spread spectrum*. When was it invented? Can you find a relationship between a Hollywood starlet and this technology?

Exercise 7-3

Use your preferred Web browser and search engine to investigate the IEEE. When was it founded? What is its primary mission?

Exercise 7-4

Use your preferred Web browser and search engine to investigate the Wi-Fi Alliance. When was it founded? What is its primary mission?

Hands-On Projects

Project 7-1

This project examines the increased amount of protection provided to wireless network traffic when basic encryption is introduced. We will be using several tools in the "BackTrack" security distribution to capture and inspect wireless network traffic. This project assumes that you are authorized to work on a wireless network and can attach systems to the network as well as enable and disable encryption.

You will also need two systems and a wireless USB NIC to complete this exercise. One system will be used to run BackTrack 5, R1 in a virtual environment such as VMWare or VirtualBox. Setting up BackTrack in a virtual environment is outside the scope of this exercise, but there are numerous tutorials available on the Internet. (This system will need an open USB port for use.) The second system needs to be capable of attaching to the wireless network and doing simple Web browsing. Finally, you need an Atheros-based USB Wi-Fi card capable of passing the aireplay injection test. A list of such devices is available from the BackTrack Web site at *www.backtrack-linux.org/wiki/index.php/Wireless_Drivers*.

First, we will disable any encryption on the wireless network, so that all traffic is being sent cleartext. Next, we will configure BackTrack to capture that traffic. We will then use the second system to generate simple HTTP traffic to capture, and we will examine it. Then, we will enable network encryption and repeat these steps to examine our results with encrypted traffic.

1. Start the BackTrack virtual image and insert the USB Wi-Fi card into an open USB port. Configure the virtual environment to ensure that the USB Wi-Fi card is being passed through to the BackTrack environment. This configuration is outside the scope of this exercise, but numerous tutorials are available on the Internet to assist with this setup for both VMWare and VirtualBox.

2. Once BackTrack has started and you have logged in, start the GUI by typing **startx** and pressing **Enter,** then open a terminal by clicking the **Terminal** icon in the taskbar.

3. Type **iwconfig** and press **Return.** You should see output similar to that shown in Figure 7-11. Your wireless USB device should be named "wlan0" or something similar. If the wireless device does not appear, you must resolve this before moving forward with the exercise.

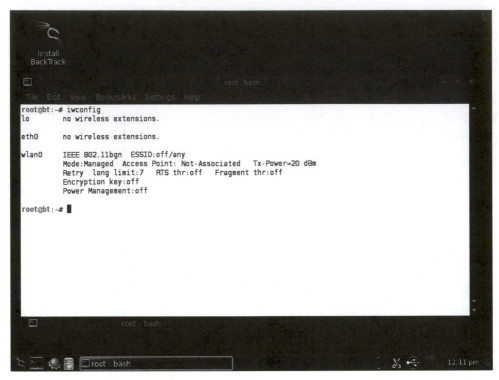

Figure 7-11   iwconfig output
Source: BackTrack

4. Note that the device details show it is in "managed" mode, which will not allow us to capture traffic. To put the device into "monitor" mode to allow traffic capture, we will use the airmon-ng utility. Type **airmon-ng** and press **Return**. This will show the interfaces that can be used to capture wireless traffic. Your wireless device should appear here, as shown in Figure 7-12. Make note of the interface name for later use.

5. Type **airmon-ng start <interface name>** and press **Return** to place the wireless device into monitor mode. After completion, airmon-ng will inform you the device was put into monitor mode on a newly created interface. Make note of the name for use going forward. As displayed in Figure 7-13, the interface name we will use is mon0.

6. At this point, you need to disable any encryption currently in place on your wireless test network. How to do this depends on your wireless network setup and is outside the scope of this exercise.

7. Type **wireshark** and press **Enter**. This will start the Wireshark application, and you should see the GUI. Take note that the mon0 interface is listed as available for use in Wireshark, as shown in Figure 7-14. Click on the mon0 interface to begin capturing wireless traffic.

8. Now, attach the second system to the unencrypted wireless network and open a Web browser. Visit the Web site located at *www.kennesaw.edu*

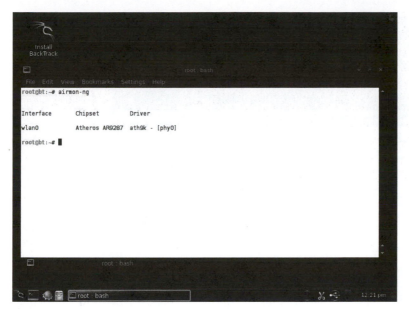

Figure 7-12   airmon-ng output
Source: BackTrack

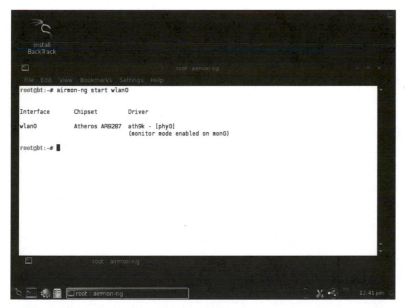

Figure 7-13   airmon-ng monitor output
Source: BackTrack

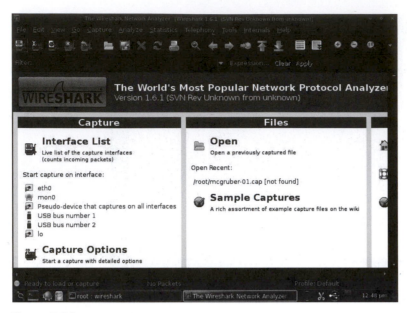

Figure 7-14   Wireshark main menu
Source: Wireshark

9. After the page loads on the second system, stop the Wireshark capture by clicking the icon with the network card and the red "x," as displayed in Figure 7-15. The icon has a green circle around it, for easier viewing in the figure.

10. In the Filter window, type `tcp.port eq 80` and click the **Apply** button. This will filter out unwanted traffic from the view.

11. Scroll down to locate the first packet that has "HTTP" as the protocol and "GET" in the Info column. Right-click on this packet and choose **Follow TCP Stream**, as displayed in Figure 7-16.

12. A new window will pop up, allowing you to read the entire contents of the HTTP request from the Kennesaw.edu Web site. Scroll down to view the content, noting that it is all in plaintext.

   Now, we will capture traffic from an encrypted wireless network and examine the differences between the two.

13. Enable encryption on your wireless test network. How to do this depends on your wireless network setup and is outside the scope of this exercise.

14. Type `wireshark` and press **Enter**.

15. Now, attach the second system to the encrypted wireless network and open a Web browser. Visit the Web site located at www.kennesaw.edu.

16. After the page loads on the second system, stop the Wireshark capture.

17. In the Filter window, type `tcp.port eq 80` and click the **Apply** button.

   As you will note, there are no packets displayed in the window at all. This is because traffic has been encrypted and is unable to be viewed without having the proper decryption keys.

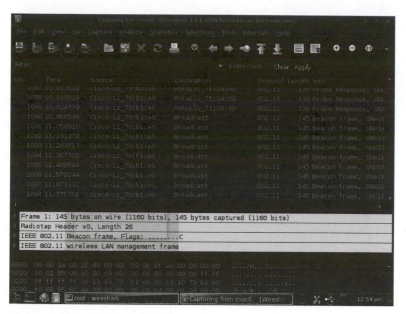

Figure 7-15   Stop Wireshark capture
Source: Wireshark

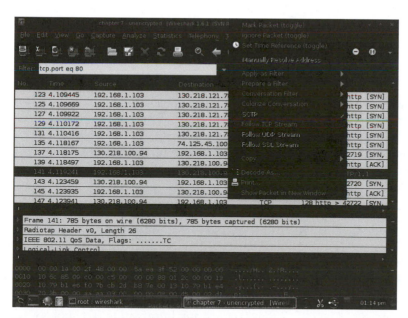

Figure 7-16   Wireshark packet analysis
Source: Wireshark

Endnotes

1. PCI Security Standards Council Wireless Special Interest Group (SIG) Implementation Team. "Information Supplement: PCI DSS Wireless Guideline." Accessed December 19, 2001 @ *https://www.pcisecuritystandards.org/pdfs/PCI_DSS_Wireless_Guidelines.pdf*.

2. IEEE. "IEEE Std 802.11-2007 IEEE Standard for Information Technology - Telecommunications and Information Exchange Between Systems - Local and Metropolitan Area Networks - Specific Requirements - Part 11: Wireless LAN Medium Access Control (MAC) and Physical Layer (PHY) Specifications." Accessed January 5, 2011 @ *http://standards.ieee.org/getieee802/download/802.11-2007.pdf*.

3. Frankel, S., Eydt, B., Owens, L., and Scarfone, K. *NIST Special Publication 800-97 - Establishing Wireless Robust Security Networks: A Guide to IEEE 802.11i*. Accessed January 5, 2011 @ *http://csrc.nist.gov/publications/nistpubs/800-97/SP800-97.pdf*.

4. National Instruments. "Quadrature Amplitued Modulation (QAM)." Accessed January 5, 2011 @ *http://zone.ni.com/devzone/cda/tut/p/id/3896*.

5. National Instruments. "Quadrature Amplitude Modulation (QAM)." Accessed January 5, 2011 @ *http://zone.ni.com/devzone/cda/tut/p/id/3896*.

6. Prabakaran, Prabakar. "Tutorial on Spread Spectrum Technology." *EE Times*. Accessed December 19, 2011 @ *http://www.eetimes.com/design/communications-design/4008962/Tutorial-on-Spread-Spectrum-Technology*.

7. "Frequency Hopping Spread Spectrum PHY of the 802.11 Wireless LAN Standard." Accessed January 5, 2011 @ *http://www.ieee802.org/11/Tutorial/FH.pdf*.

8. "direct sequence spread spectrum (DSSS) or direct sequence code division multiple access (DS-CDMA)." Accessed January 6, 2011 @ *http://searchnetworking.techtarget.com/definition/direct-sequence-spread-spectrum*.

9. Edfors, O., Sandell, M., van de Beek, J., Landstrom, D., and Sjoberg, F. "An introduction to orthogonal frequency-division multiplexing." Accessed January 5, 2011 @ *http://www.digitalsignallabs.com/esb96rc.pdf*.

10. Geier, J. "The BIG Question: 802.11a or 802.11b?" *Wi-Fi Planet*. Accessed January 25, 2012 @ *www.wi-fiplanet.com/columns/article.php/961181*.

11. Broadcom. "802.11n: Next-Generation Wireless LAN Technology." Accessed December 20, 2011 @ *http://www.broadcom.com/collateral/wp/802_11n-WP100-R.pdf*.

12. IEEE. "IEEE Std 802.11-2007 IEEE Standard for Information Technology - Telecommunications and Information Exchange Between Systems - Local and Metropolitan Area Networks - Specific Requirements - Part 11: Wireless LAN Medium Access Control (MAC) and Physical Layer (PHY) Specifications." Accessed January 5, 2011 @ *http://standards.ieee.org/getieee802/download/802.11-2007.pdf*.

13. IEEE. "IEEE Std 802.11-2007 IEEE Standard for Information Technology - Telecommunications and Information Exchange Between Systems - Local and Metropolitan Area Networks - Specific Requirements - Part 11: Wireless LAN Medium Access Control (MAC) and Physical Layer (PHY) Specifications." Accessed January 5, 2011 @ *http://standards.ieee.org/getieee802/download/802.11-2007.pdf*.

14. Wi-Fi Alliance. "Wi-Fi Celebrates Its Third Birthday." Accessed December 20, 2011 @ *http://www.wi-fi.org/news_articles.php?f=media_news&news_id=47.*

15. Frankel, S., Eydt, B., Owens, L., and Scarfone, K. *NIST Special Publication 800-97 Establishing Wireless Robust Security Networks: A Guide to IEEE 802.11i.* Accessed January 5, 2011 @ *http://csrc.nist.gov/publications/nistpubs/800-97/SP800-97.pdf.*

16. Frankel, S., Eydt, B., Owens, L., and Scarfone, K. *NIST Special Publication 800-97 Establishing Wireless Robust Security Networks: A Guide to IEEE 802.11i.* Accessed January 5, 2011 @ *http://csrc.nist.gov/publications/nistpubs/800-97/SP800-97.pdf.*

17. Frankel, S., Eydt, B., Owens, L., and Scarfone, K. *NIST Special Publication 800-97 Establishing Wireless Robust Security Networks: A Guide to IEEE 802.11i.* Accessed January 5, 2011 @ *http://csrc.nist.gov/publications/nistpubs/800-97/SP800-97.pdf.*

18. Scarfone, K., Tibbs, C., and Sexton, M. *NIST Special Publication 800-127 Guide to Securing WiMAX Wireless Communictions.* Accessed January 12, 2011 @ *http://csrc.nist.gov/publications/nistpubs/800-127/sp800-127.pdf.*

19. Scarfone, K., Tibbs, C., and Sexton, M. *NIST Special Publication 800-127 Guide to Securing WiMAX Wireless Communictions.* Accessed January 12, 2011 @ *http://csrc.nist.gov/publications/nistpubs/800-127/sp800-127.pdf.*

20. Frankel, S., Eydt, B., Owens, L., and Scarfone, K. *NIST Special Publication 800-97 Establishing Wireless Robust Security Networks: A Guide to IEEE 802.11i.* Accessed January 5, 2011 @ *http://csrc.nist.gov/publications/nistpubs/800-97/SP800-97.pdf.*

21. Frankel, S., Eydt, B., Owens, L., and Scarfone, K. *NIST Special Publication 800-97 Establishing Wireless Robust Security Networks: A Guide to IEEE 802.11i.* Accessed January 5, 2011 @ *http://csrc.nist.gov/publications/nistpubs/800-97/SP800-97.pdf.*

22. Sastry, N. and Wagner, D. "Security Concerns for IEEE 802.15.4 Networks" *WiSE'04,* October 1, 2004.

23. IEEE. "IEEE Std 802.11-2007 IEEE Standard for Information Technology - Telecommunications and Information Exchange Between Systems - Local and Metropolitan Area Networks - Specific Requirements - Part 11: Wireless LAN Medium Access Control (MAC) and Physical Layer (PHY) Specifications." Accessed January 5, 2011 @ *http://standards.ieee.org/getieee802/download/802.11-2007.pdf.*

24. IEEE. "IEEE Std 802.11-2007 IEEE Standard for Information Technology - Telecommunications and Information Exchange Between Systems - Local and Metropolitan Area Networks - Specific Requirements - Part 11: Wireless LAN Medium Access Control (MAC) and Physical Layer (PHY) Specifications." Accessed January 5, 2011 @ *http://standards.ieee.org/getieee802/download/802.11-2007.pdf.*

25. Pacelle, M. "Selecting the Right Wireless Mesh Topology" *EE Times.* Accessed January 4, 2011 @ *www.eetimes.com/design/industrial-control/4012553/Selecting-the-Right-Wireless-Mesh-Topology.*

26. Tews, E., and Beck, M. "Practical Attacks Againat WEP and WPA." WiSec '09 Proceedings of the Second ACM Conference on Wireless Network Security. 2009.

27. Snyder, J., Thayer, R. "Explaining TKIP." *Network World.* Accessed December 20, 2011 @ *http://www.networkworld.com/reviews/2004/1004wirelesstkip.html.*

7

28. Frankel, S., Eydt, B., Owens, L., and Scarfone, K. *NIST Special Publication 800-97 Establishing Wireless Robust Security Networks: A Guide to IEEE 802.11i.* Accessed January 5, 2011 @ *http://csrc.nist.gov/publications/nistpubs/800-97/SP800-97.pdf.*

29. Frankel, S., Eydt, B., Owens, L., and Scarfone, K. *NIST Special Publication 800-97 Establishing Wireless Robust Security Networks: A Guide to IEEE 802.11i.* Accessed December 20, 2011 @ *http://csrc.nist.gov/publications/nistpubs/800-97/SP800-97.pdf.*

30. Frankel, S., Eydt, B., Owens, L., and Scarfone, K. *NIST Special Publication 800-97 Establishing Wireless Robust Security Networks: A Guide to IEEE 802.11i.* Accessed January 5, 2011 @ *http://csrc.nist.gov/publications/nistpubs/800-97/SP800-97.pdf.*

31. Frankel, S., Eydt, B., Owens, L., and Scarfone, K. *NIST Special Publication 800-97 Establishing Wireless Robust Security Networks: A Guide to IEEE 802.11i.* Accessed January 5, 2011 @ *http://csrc.nist.gov/publications/nistpubs/800-97/SP800-97.pdf.*

32. Frankel, S., Eydt, B., Owens, L., and Scarfone, K. *NIST Special Publication 800-97 Establishing Wireless Robust Security Networks: A Guide to IEEE 802.11i.* Accessed January 5, 2011 @ *http://csrc.nist.gov/publications/nistpubs/800-97/SP800-97.pdf.*

33. Frankel, S., Eydt, B., Owens, L., and Scarfone, K. *NIST Special Publication 800-97 Establishing Wireless Robust Security Networks: A Guide to IEEE 802.11i.* Accessed January 5, 2011 @ *http://csrc.nist.gov/publications/nistpubs/800-97/SP800-97.pdf.*

34. Ou, George. "Wireless LAN security myths that won't die." Accessed June 26, 2011 @ *www.zdnet.com/blog/ou/wireless-lan-security-myths-that-wont-die/454.*

35. "A Look at the Basics of Bluetooth Wireless Technology." Accessed June 26, 2011 @ *www.bluetooth.com/Pages/Basics.aspx.*

36. Scarfone, K. and Padgette, J. *NIST SP 800-121 Guide to Bluetooth Security.* Accessed January 10, 2011 @ *http://csrc.nist.gov/publications/nistpubs/800-121/SP800-121.pdf.*

37. "Long Distance Snarf." Accessed June 26, 2011 @ *http://trifinite.org/trifinite_stuff_lds.html.*

38. "BlueBug." Accessed June 26, 2011 @ *http://trifinite.org/trifinite_stuff_bluebug.html.*

39. Scarfone, K. and Padgette, J. *NIST SP 800-121 Guide to Bluetooth Security.* Accessed January 10, 2011 @ *http://csrc.nist.gov/publications/nistpubs/800-121/SP800-121.pdf.*

chapter 8

Security of Web Applications

If you spend more on coffee than on Web application security, you will be hacked. What's more, you deserve to be hacked. — Richard Clarke, Former White House Cybersecurity Advisor

Upon completion of this material, you should be able to:

- List the various Internet services in use
- Identify threats to Internet services and basic countermeasures
- Describe the basics of Web client-server communication
- Identify the various Web languages and describe their uses
- Identify various Web threats and attacks
- Discuss the steps necessary to secure a Web server

Tangled Web

It was finally time. After all the effort analyzing network and system vulnerabilities, the EBS IT team had to turn its attention to the Web environment. Although Noah Atwater had spent many of his years at EBS maintaining the Web servers, he had little knowledge of the various applications running atop the infrastructure. There was a separate programmer responsible for maintaining the applications and creating the necessary content for EBS.

In order to properly address the security of the Web environment, Noah and Paige were going to have to address the security of the network architecture supporting the Web servers, analyze the security of the Web servers themselves, and then move up the stack to investigate the applications, protocols, and programming languages to discover what vulnerabilities existed. The complexity of the challenge intimidated the team, but it couldn't be avoided—they were going to become entangled in the Web.

Introduction

As mentioned in Chapter 2, it is important to delineate the Internet from the **World Wide Web (WWW)**. The **Internet** is a physical set of networks (the hardware, if you will), whereas the WWW is a set of applications (the software) that runs on top of the Internet. In fact, the Internet supports a host of services to help users access their information, entertainment, and communication needs. The laundry list of services available is beyond the scope of this book. Technically, the Web consists exclusively of documents linked via **Hypertext Transfer Protocol (HTTP)**. For our purposes, however, it will include many related applications that are generally described as "the Web"—applications like the File Transfer Protocol (FTP), the Simple Mail Transfer Protocol (SMTP), and the Post Office Protocol 3 (POP3).

This chapter focuses on the key Internet services in use, their vulnerabilities, the attacks upon them, and the various countermeasures, with the most attention paid to Web applications. This is simply because the majority of Internet attacks are still aimed at these applications.

Internet Services

It's a common misconception that the Web sites we use every day comprise the entirety of the Internet. In fact, a recent article in *Wired* magazine argued that the Web is dead, given that other services available on the Internet, such as video, e-mail, and peer-to-peer services, have surpassed the Web in popularity.[1] Figure 8-1 shows Cisco's analysis of the Cooperative Association for Internet Data Analysis (CAIDA) data, indicating the trends of various Internet communications. The point is that Internet security depends not only on securing Web sites (although we will focus mostly on that) but also on securing the various services that use the interconnected networks. This section briefly explains some of the more popular services, their vulnerabilities, and the security solutions that protect them. Some key information about the most common Internet services is provided in Table 8-1.

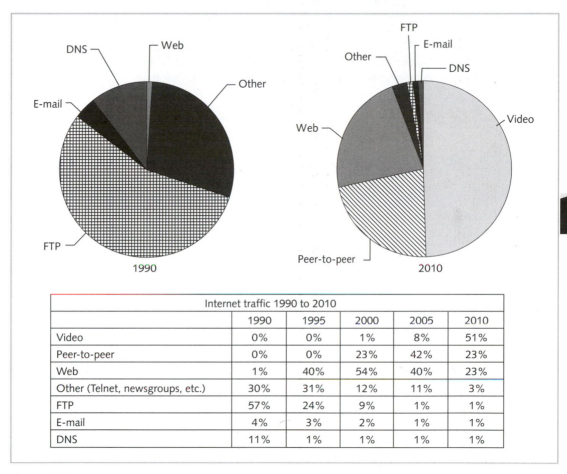

Internet traffic 1990 to 2010					
	1990	1995	2000	2005	2010
Video	0%	0%	1%	8%	51%
Peer-to-peer	0%	0%	23%	42%	23%
Web	1%	40%	54%	40%	23%
Other (Telnet, newsgroups, etc.)	30%	31%	12%	11%	3%
FTP	57%	24%	9%	1%	1%
E-mail	4%	3%	2%	1%	1%
DNS	11%	1%	1%	1%	1%

Figure 8-1 Overall Internet usage by service
© Cengage Learning 2013

SMTP, POP, and IMAP

The **Simple Mail Transfer Protocol (SMTP)** is used to send Internet mail, whereas the **Post Office Protocol 3 (POP3)** and the **Internet Message Access Protocol (IMAP)** are used to receive Internet mail. For example, if an organization installs an e-mail server like Microsoft Exchange to allow the company to share e-mail over the Internet, the e-mail server normally has SMTP and POP3 enabled to facilitate this communication. Both are higher-layer protocols that operate within the Application layer of the OSI reference model. For e-mail communication, SMTP uses TCP and UDP ports 25, POP3 uses TCP and UDP ports 110, and IMAP uses TCP and UDP ports 143.

Service	Function	TCP Port	UDP Port	RFC Number
SMTP	Sending Internet mail	25	25	RFC 2821
POP3	Receiving Internet mail	110	110	RFC 1939
IMAP	Receiving Internet mail	143	143	RFC 1203
FTP	Transferring files	21 – command 20 – data	NA	RFC 959
TFTP	Transferring files	NA	69	RFC 1350
Telnet	Remote system administration	23	NA	RFC 854
DNS	Translating domain names into IP addresses	53	53	RFC 1035
SNMP	Network monitoring	161, 162	161, 162	RFC 1157
LDAP	Directory services	389	389	RFC 2251
NNTP	Newsgroup information	119	NA	RFC 977

Table 8-1 Quick Reference Guide for Some of the Most Common Internet Services
© Cengage Learning 2013

For more information on SMTP, POP3, and IMAP, refer to RFCs 2821, 1939, and 1203, respectively, at *www.rfc-editor.org*.

Attacks on E-mail The bulk of e-mail attacks involve an attacker or malicious software that uses an e-mail server to send messages from the victim organization. In its early stages, SMTP had no way of authenticating users prior to e-mail being sent. Eventually, the Internet community realized that some form of user authentication was needed in order to minimize the amount of spam being generated on a daily basis. The SMTP-AUTH feature was included in the Extended SMTP (ESMTP) protocol to address this need. Unfortunately, attackers were soon able to use the SMTP-AUTH feature itself to attack SMTP servers or to send spam by compromising a legitimate user's account.

Another major attack involving an SMTP server occurs when an e-mail server administrator does not restrict who can use the SMTP server to send e-mail. This type of configuration is referred to as an **open relay**. Attackers will scan the Internet looking for open relays that they can use to send spam. This allows the attackers to use the e-mail system to send e-mail anonymously. In the case of worms, malicious software can also use the open relay to propagate itself across the Internet.

Mail bombing is another threat to e-mail servers. During this type of attack, a malicious user sends a flood of e-mail to the e-mail server—essentially, an e-mail-based denial of service (DoS) attack.

Security Solutions The most effective methods for preventing mail attacks are to apply security patches and restrict mail relayed on the e-mail server. Unfortunately, many e-mail server software packages either fully allow relaying or fully deny it. However, with the help of third-party software, organizations can maintain more precise control over the messages that come into and go out of the organization. In general, the following policies should be observed:

- A sender with a valid internal IP address should be allowed to send e-mail to internal e-mail addresses.

- A sender with a valid internal IP address should be allowed to send e-mail to external e-mail addresses.

- A recipient with a valid internal e-mail address should be allowed to receive e-mail from external e-mail addresses.

- A sender with an external e-mail address should be prohibited from sending e-mail to other external e-mail addresses.[2]

Server administrators should test their e-mail server configurations to be sure the server is not incorrectly set up as an open relay. Several publically accessible Web sites can be used to test a server configuration—for example, *www.spamhelp.org/shopenrelay* or *www.abuse.net/relay.html*.

Real-time blacklisting (RBL) lists are another way to defend against spam attacks. RBLs are collections of IP addresses of known spam sources on the Internet, and they can be easily integrated into most SMTP server configurations. When a connection request is received by the SMTP server, it checks the IP address of the requester against the RBL and denies the connection if the address is on the list.

The "POP before SMTP" authentication method is another way to defend against improper use of an SMTP server. With this method, a user must be authenticated against an associated POP server before being allowed to send mail through the SMTP server. Once authenticated, the SMTP server records the IP address of the sender and allows mail to be sent from there for a period of time. Care should be taken with how long that period lasts, though; an opening could be created from which attackers at that same IP address could later send e-mail.

FTP

Most users are familiar with the **File Transfer Protocol** (FTP), which is a simple method of transferring files between computer systems. An example of a popular freeware FTP client (CoreFTP Lite) is shown in Figure 8-2. FTP operates in the Application layer of the OSI reference model and only uses TCP for communication. It actually requires two TCP ports for communication: a command port and a data port. The command port communicates over TCP port 21, and the data port normally uses TCP port 20.

In active mode, the FTP client connects from a TCP source port greater than 1024 (N) to the FTP server's destination TCP port 21. The FTP client then starts listening on TCP port (N+1) and identifies for the FTP server the port to which it is listening. The server then connects to the destination port (N+1) on the client side and sends data from the server's TCP port 20. As shown in Figure 8-3, in active mode, the server must be able to establish a connection to the client for data transfer.

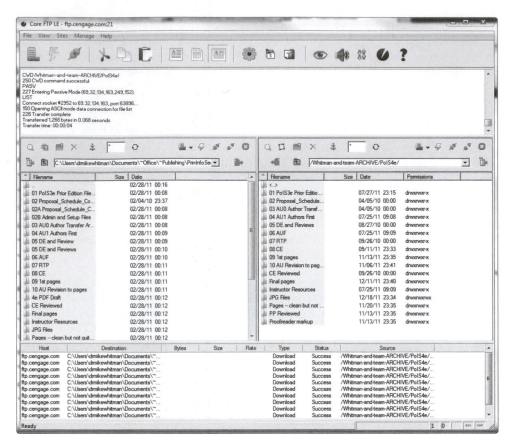

Figure 8-2 CoreFTP Lite
Source: CoreFTP Lite

In passive mode, the FTP client does not listen and wait for the server connection. Instead, it initiates a connection from a TCP source port greater than 1024 (N) to the FTP server port 21. The FTP client, as shown in Figure 8-4, makes another connection from TCP port N+1 to the FTP server's port 20 to transfer data.

With passive mode, a trusted internal FTP client makes an outgoing request to the FTP server. With active mode, the untrusted FTP server makes a connection to the listening client. Using the passive mode, an intervening firewall is more likely to allow FTP traffic because the trusted client is initiating the connection.

TFTP The **Trivial File Transfer Protocol** (TFTP) is very similar to FTP. TFTP is used to transfer data files as well, and it too operates within the Application layer of the OSI reference model. Most often, TFTP is used on network appliances to transfer configuration files, backups, and boot files. However, TFTP differs from FTP in the following ways:

- It is implemented over UDP instead of TCP, which allows for less overhead and more speed.
- It is a lightweight implementation of FTP that has far fewer features.
- It does not allow for authentication.
- It does not require two different communication links and only uses UDP port 69 for data transfers.

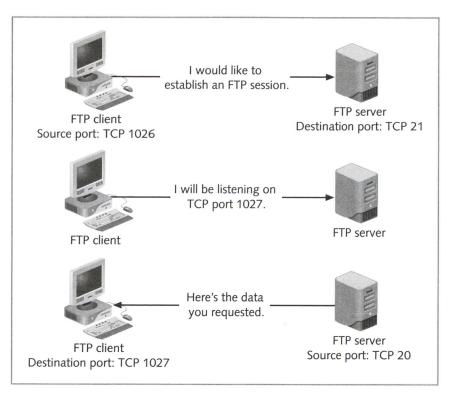

Figure 8-3 Example of FTP session established in active mode
© Cengage Learning 2013

For more information on FTP and TFTP, refer to RFC 959 and RFC 1350, respectively.

Attacks on FTP and TFTP When configuring an FTP server, administrators can set up anonymous FTP access. This can lead to a major problem with FTP in that it allows anyone with a network connection and an FTP client to access the FTP server and the files served. When properly configured to afford anonymous users only very limited access, the FTP server works well. However, in many cases, administrators mistakenly give an anonymous user too many rights to the server or do not restrict the areas in which a visitor can read files.

Another major problem with FTP is that data is transferred in plaintext. If an abuser is able to sniff the network traffic using a packet sniffer, he or she will be able to see usernames, passwords, and any other sensitive data.

In addition to the previous weaknesses, TFTP has an additional threat exposure in that it does not allow authentication. Because TFTP is typically shipped with a variety of systems and even network devices, an abuser can use TFTP to simply transfer sensitive data off the system. This poses a serious threat to both computer systems and network devices.

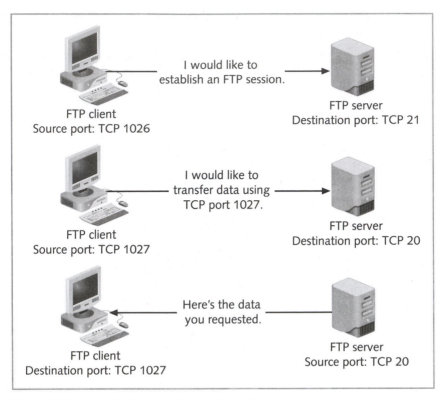

Figure 8-4   Example of FTP session established in passive mode
© Cengage Learning 2013

Security Solutions To reduce the overall risk, the best option is to not enable an FTP or TFTP server at all. Both actions pose serious threats because they have the potential of resulting in a server not requiring authentication, and because they send data in plaintext.

If FTP or TFTP must be used, then encryption and authentication should be employed. Both FTP implemented over SSL and Secure Copy (SCP) are secure substitute methods of transferring files. Each employs encryption techniques to hide data while in transit. Also, each enables only users with the proper credentials to gain access to the FTP server.

Anonymous FTP access should be avoided whenever possible. When it is not possible to avoid it, you should apply and maintain the latest patches for the operating system and FTP server software. Additionally, you should ensure that anonymous users have only limited access to files and directories. Remember, because the FTP connection is anonymous, everyone has access; worse, there's no record of who accessed your files.

Telnet

Like FTP, **Telnet** is an Application-layer protocol that allows users to connect to a remote computer. However, instead of transferring files, Telnet allows users to connect a remote shell to run programs, view files, and perform a variety of other operations as if they were using the system locally. For example, PuTTY, shown in Figure 8-5, is a free Telnet client that also supports Secure Shell (SSH).

There are still some servers that have Telnet enabled, which is good for functionality but bad for security. Therefore, a special effect must be made to close any unnecessary security holes. Telnet communicates over TCP port 23, whereas SSH communicates over TCP port 22.

```
192.168.1.194 - PuTTY
Welcome to Microsoft Telnet Service

login: demo
password:

*===============================================================
Microsoft Telnet Server.
*===============================================================
C:\Users\Demo>cd \tmp

C:\tmp>dir
 Volume in drive C has no label.
 Volume Serial Number is 88A9-03F9

 Directory of C:\tmp

12/26/2010  09:22 AM    <DIR>          .
12/26/2010  09:22 AM    <DIR>          ..
12/26/2010  09:20 AM         7,549,814 USB3_V2040_XpVistaWin7.zip
12/26/2010  09:22 AM        79,946,859 VIA_Audio_V6018700a_XpVistaWin7.zip
               2 File(s)     87,496,673 bytes
               2 Dir(s)   1,907,154,235,392 bytes free

C:\tmp>
```

Figure 8-5 Example of a PuTTY Telnet session to a Windows 7 System
Source: PuTTY

For more information on Telnet, refer to RFC 854. For more information on SSH, refer to RFC 4253.

NOTE

Attacks on Telnet Like FTP, Telnet is susceptible to misconfiguration and poor administration. The security of the Telnet server can be undermined by guest users with too many rights, users with no passwords, or a policy of requiring no passwords at all.

However, the biggest threat exposure is that the Telnet protocol sends traffic unencrypted over the network. This opens the door for sniffers to monitor Telnet sessions.

Security Solutions As with FTP, the best security practice is to not use Telnet at all. Use Secure Shell (SSH) or some other encrypted remote session tool instead. In addition, make sure that all users have the appropriate rights and strong passwords that change regularly.

If Telnet must be used, avoid having the server available to the Internet. Then, look to have external users attach to the internal network using a virtual private network (VPN). This is by no means a perfect solution, as the traffic from the VPN server to the Telnet server would still be in plaintext, but it does reduce the overall attack surface on the Telnet server.

SNMP

The **Simple Network Management Protocol (SNMP)**, as its name implies, is an Application-layer management protocol that is used to monitor the status and performance of network devices and systems. For example, the HP Network Management Center (used to be OpenView) product is able to monitor SNMP-enabled devices (and other network communications) to provide IT organizations with real-time information on the overall health of the environment, as shown in Figure 8-6.

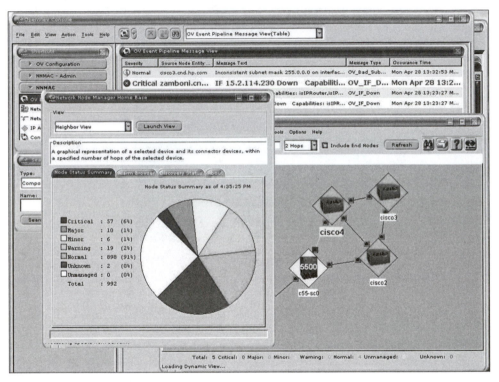

Figure 8-6 Example of HP Network Node Manager showing information provided by SNMP
Source: HP Network Node Manager

To provide monitoring, an SNMP agent must be installed on a desired host or network device. The SNMP agent then monitors and collects information according to the instructions and format of a particular **management information base (MIB)**. A MIB is designed to translate information sent from a particular agent or class of agents. This information can then be communicated to a central management system via SNMP traps. A **trap** is a simple message providing status information about the monitored device.

SNMP traffic occurs over TCP port 161 and UDP port 161. SNMP traps are sent back to the server over TCP port 162 and UDP port 162.

For more information on SNMP, refer to RFC 1157.

Attacks on SNMP SNMP provides information about the monitored system, such as IP address, operating system and version, host name, and a variety of other configuration options. Most of the weaknesses with SNMP occur with Version 1 of SNMP. SNMP v1 agents need a community string, which acts as a simple password, in order to allow read or write operations. In many cases, administrators do not change these strings from the default of "public." This allows an attacker to gain access to the SNMP agent to read information or use the `setRequest` command to perform actions on the target system. Because SNMP v1 uses only simple authentication and sends data over the network in plaintext, it is ripe for both break-in and eavesdropping.

Security Solutions Upgrading SNMP to a newer version (e.g., v3) affords network administrators encryption, stronger authentication, and other security tools to protect SNMP traffic. Additionally, for all SNMP agents, community strings must be changed to a value that is hard to guess. Another strong security measure is to ensure that SNMP-enabled systems are not connected to the Internet, thereby eliminating a public avenue of attack.

LDAP

The **Lightweight Directory Access Protocol (LDAP)** is another Application-layer protocol that rides on top of IP. Its purpose is to provide a communication framework with centralized directories that hold a variety of useful data. For example, manufacturers implement LDAP to communicate to a central database of users, user rights, and user properties that have access to particular systems or applications.

The LDAP protocol defines six standard operations that can be performed:

- Authenticating to the directory
- Searching the directory
- Reading attributes from the directory
- Adding entries to the directory
- Modifying entries in the directory
- Removing entries from the directory

LDAP communicates over TCP port 389 and UDP port 389.

For more information on LDAP, refer to RFC 4511.

Attacks on LDAP Like any sensitive data store, LDAP is a target because of the sensitive nature of the data it stores (e.g., user attributes). It's crucial that LDAP servers be hardened and patched regularly. The most common attacks on LDAP servers are very similar to SQL injection attacks (SQL injection attacks are covered in more detail later in this chapter) in that the attack manipulates the data sent from a Web page or Web application to the LDAP server.[3] These LDAP injection attacks seek to insert, modify, or delete data from the LDAP server without proper authentication.

8

Security Solutions Because LDAP servers and applications tend to send sensitive data, such as usernames and attributes, it is important to protect these servers with the typical security controls: physical security, user ID management, and rights management. Again, make sure these servers are patched regularly.

To thwart LDAP injection attacks, it is critical that any Web page or application gathering data from the user first scrub the data to only pass valid information back to the LDAP server. This countermeasure, called input validation, serves to prevent a variety of Web attacks.

NNTP

Many users like to communicate with other users in the forum-type environment of newsgroups. Designed to facilitate Usenet newsgroup communications, the **Network News Transfer Protocol (NNTP)** is similar to SMTP in architecture and function. NNTP runs over TCP port 119 and is another Application-layer protocol. Clients use a newsgroup client, like the one shown in Figure 8-7, to connect via NNTP to a central newsgroup server to download and post selective messages.

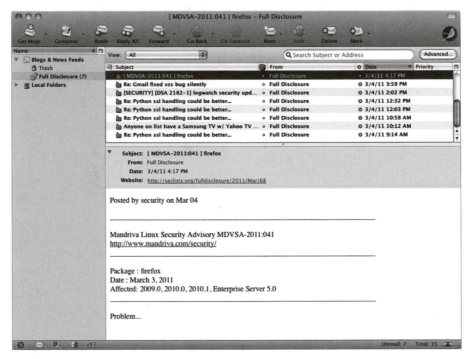

Figure 8-7   Example of newsgroup usage using SeaMonkey
Source: Sea Monkey

For more information on NNTP, refer to RFC 3977.

Attacks on NNTP News servers tend to reside in a DMZ and are accessible from the Internet, which places more risk on the server. Though not an attack on NNTP itself, Usenet groups and various sites carrying user forums tend to post links to malicious files or Web sites.

Security Solutions Many users will have access to the system, so make sure NNTP servers are patched regularly and the newsgroup content is continuously scanned for malware. If you happen to moderate a user forum, police the posts for malicious or inappropriate content. Additionally, you should implement user authentication, when possible.

DNS

For a domain name typed into a Web browser, there must be a helper service to translate that domain name into an IP address for proper routing. This is accomplished by **Domain Name System (DNS)** servers that are installed within organizations, at ISPs, and at key points within the Internet. DNS operates within the Application layer and allows clients to access these various DNS servers to perform the translation. The distributed nature of this information store allows users to type a domain name (e.g., facebook.com) into a Web browser and get the same response regardless of where the user is located.

DNS also helps Internet services other than the Web—for example, FTP and newsgroups—make the translation between domain names and IP addresses. The DNS software performs a query to the DNS server over UDP port 53. Using UDP makes the query quick and efficient.

DNS Overview DNS operations are split among three components: DNS servers, the DNS protocol, and DNS clients (otherwise known as resolvers). On the Internet, **BIND (Berkeley Internet Name Domain)** software is the most prevalently used software for DNS servers. Fortunately, almost all modern operating systems include a DNS client to make effective DNS queries. A typical DNS query exchange for a host that exists within the same organization is shown in Figure 8-8. A DNS typical query for an Internet system is shown in Figure 8-9.

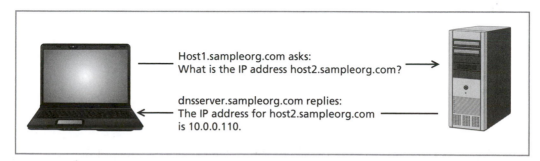

Figure 8-8 Typical DNS query confined to a local organization
© Cengage Learning 2013

DNS queries are initiated by clients to resolve a **fully qualified domain name (FQDN)** to its IP address. A FQDN uniquely identifies a host by representing the host name, subdomain, **second-level domain (SLD)**—or possibly a **country code second-level domain (ccSLD)**—and

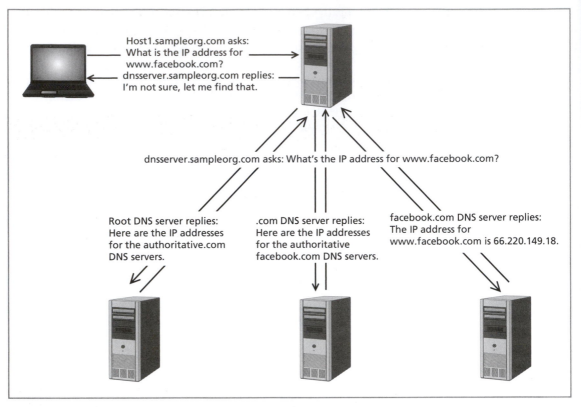

Figure 8-9 Typical DNS query for a public Internet system (iterative query)
© Cengage Learning 2013

top-level domain (TLD) separated by dots or periods. For example, the FQDN of mailserver1.mail.sampleorg.com can be broken down as follows:

- Host name or service: mailserver1
- Subdomain: mail
- SLD: sampleorg
- TLD: com

An international example is mailserver1.mail.sampleorg.co.uk, which can broken down as follows:

- Host name or service: mailserver1
- Subdomain: mail
- SLD: sampleorg
- ccSLD: co
- TLD: uk

The top-level domains are all managed by the Internet Assigned Numbers Authority (IANA) in the root zone. The root zone signifies the highest level of the domain hierarchy and ultimately is controlled by the **IANA Name Registration Authority**. Note that the complete listing of TLDs can be found on the IANA Web site at *www.iana.org/domains/root/db/*.

These FQDNs are stored in a resource record (RR) within the DNS database. The RR indicates key attributes that help to direct traffic within a specific domain. Table 8-2 lists some of the major types outlined in RFC 1035.

TYPE	Value
A	Host address
NS	Authoritative name server
CNAME	Canonical name for an alias
SOA	Marks the start of a zone of authority
MX	Mail exchange

Table 8-2 DNS Record Types
© Cengage Learning 2013

8

DNS Zones In addition, the Internet DNS infrastructure is divided into zones. Zones provide a mechanism to divide ownership responsibility among various DNS servers and the organizations they serve. For example, each zone contains all the hosts and subdomains that end with the zone's domain name. The DNS server considered authoritative—that is, holding the most accurate information for the zone—is identified by the first record in the zone, called the **Start of Authority** or **SOA** for the zone.[4]

A zone's NS server must get the latest DNS translation information from the organization's ISP. The ISP, in turn, must synchronize the data store with the TLD owner. These bulk transfers of data are called zone transfers. To allow the reliable exchange of this information, DNS switches to TCP for zone transfers on port 53.

For more information on DNS, refer to RFCs 1034 and 1035.

Attacks on DNS Attacks on DNS communication usually come in three varieties. The first type, the **DNS open resolver**, is similar to e-mail open relays in that the DNS server is open for anyone internal or external to the organization to query all the information from the DNS server to see the zone's complete list of hosts and their translations to IP addresses. An attacker can then use this information to footprint, or perform reconnaissance, on the target organization.

The second type of attack, called **DNS poisoning**, consists of inserting incorrect translation information within the DNS server (or within the communication between the resolver and server) in order to take a legitimate domain name and point the resolver to a malicious server, thereby secretly subverting the session. This can be accomplished by inserting malicious information into the **DNS cache** (used to speed up communication by allowing the DNS server to provide translation results without having to look up frequent queries), modifying the DNS records themselves, performing a man-in-the-middle attack on the DNS communication, or by tricking DNS servers into believing a malicious system is the authoritative name server, which is what infamously happened with the so-called Kaminsky bug.[5]

The third type of attack seeks to cause a DNS denial of service by asking the DNS server to perform a large number of recursive lookups or searches for domain information not located within its own zone, as shown in Figure 8-10. Most DNS servers have this recursive ability enabled by default so that the DNS server can perform an added service to its clients; however, the recursive queries can easily be manipulated.

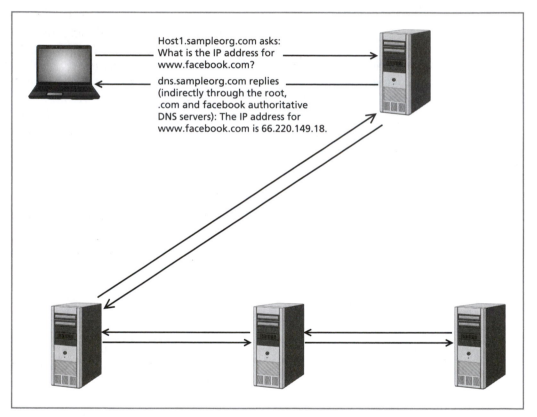

Host1.sampleorg.com asks: What is the IP address for www.facebook.com?

dns.sampleorg.com replies (indirectly through the root, .com and facebook authoritative DNS servers): The IP address for www.facebook.com is 66.220.149.18.

Figure 8-10   DNS query using recursive queries
© Cengage Learning 2013

Security Solutions There are a number of countermeasures to secure DNS communication:[6]

- Secure your DNS servers, and update the DNS software regularly.

- Block incoming DNS traffic. Outgoing DNS traffic should be allowed in order for clients or the internal DNS servers to communicate with DNS servers outside the organization; however, external users should not be able to query internal DNS servers.

- Limit zone transfers to trusted IP addresses. An attacker should not be able to trick a DNS server into performing a zone transfer with a malicious system.

- Employ DNSSEC (Domain Name System Security Extensions) to digitally sign information provided to the resolver. DNSSEC attempts to provide a level of authenticity to the DNS communication to avoid DNS poisoning attacks. DNSSEC is outlined in RFCs 4033, 4034, and 4035.

- Disable recursive query ability to avoid DoS attacks on the DNS server.

Web Overview

Despite arguments to the contrary, the Web continues to be actively used. In this textbook, we distinguish the Web from the Internet itself. The Internet is that worldwide network of interconnected data communication networks that interoperate using the IP protocol. The Web is the HTTP-driven content that is transmitted over the Internet. As security professionals, therefore, we must continue to protect our organizations from Web attacks that seek to subvert the information we publish to the Web and the services we offer to our customers over the Web. In order for you to be prepared to protect that content, we will begin with a discussion of the fundamentals of Web communication, how it makes use of servers, and how it delivers content and services to browser clients.

Web Client/Server Architecture

There are three fundamental aspects of Web communication: the server, the client, and the communication protocol. Although a particular Web server may also be a Web client (and vice versa), the key distinction is that a server hosts Web content and a client requests access to content. Throughout this section, these broad definitions will continue to apply.

Web Server There are some fundamental requirements that systems need to meet in order to serve as a Web server. The obvious one is that the system needs to be connected to the Internet (for a public Web server) or to an internal network (for an intranet Web server). The system must also have a Web server installed. Popular packages include: Apache HTTP Server, from the Apache Software Foundation; Internet Information Services (IIS), from Microsoft; and NGINX, from the NGINX open-source community.[7] To be a useful Web server, the system must also have content to share and allow incoming connections to access the content. For traditional HTTP traffic (more on that in a moment), incoming TCP/UDP ports 80 need to be open for incoming requests, and for encrypted HTTP traffic, TCP port 443 must allow incoming connections.

Web Client There are numerous ways that client systems can access Web servers, but the most common way is to use a Web browser like Mozilla's Firefox, Microsoft's Internet Explorer, Google's Chrome, or Apple's Safari. These applications hide much of the details of the HTTP communications from the user and translate the host of Web programming language automatically for content display. For those users who are too paranoid to allow the client to translate the numerous programming elements automatically, Linux and UNIX distributions allow command-line Web clients like Lynx or wget.

HTTP Communication Hypertext Transfer Protocol (HTTP) is the basis for Web communication. (The 1.1 version of HTTP is explained in RFC 2616.) It consists of requests and responses. These form the basis for the client requesting information from the Web server and the Web server sending information to the client. Table 8-3 outlines some common HTTP request methods. Table 8-4 lists some common response codes, and Figure 8-11 shows how a typical HTTP session is initiated.

Request Method	Use
OPTIONS	Allows a client to identify the various communication options available
GET	Retrieves information from the resource signified by the Uniform Resource Identifier (URI)
HEAD	Retrieves meta-information only from the resource signified in the URI
POST	Used to send information to the Web server; the actual action varies, depending on the server functions offered
PUT	A request to store information at the specified URI
DELETE	Removes the resource specified in the URI
TRACE	A troubleshooting request that tells the Web server to mirror the request for viewing

Table 8-3 Common HTTP Request Methods
© Cengage Learning 2013

Common Codes	Response Status Code Family	Description
100 Continue	100s: Informational	The server has sent a provisional response that consists of a status and optional headers.
200 OK	200s: Success	The server successfully processed the request.
300 Multiple Choices 301 Moved Permanently 302 Found 304 Not Modified	300s: Redirection	The client must take further action to fulfill the request.
400 Bad Request 401 Unauthorized 403 Forbidden 404 Not Found 410 Gone	400s: Client Error	An error has occurred on the client side.
500 Internal Server Error 501 Not Implemented 503 Service Unavailable 504 Gateway Timeout 505 HTTP Version Not Supported	500s: Server Error	An error has occurred on the server side.

Table 8-4 Common HTTP Response Codes[8]
© Cengage Learning 2013

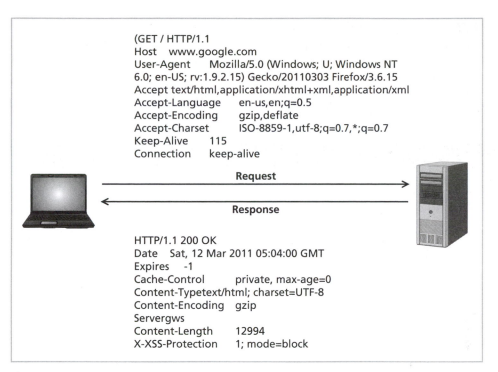

(GET / HTTP/1.1
Host   www.google.com
User-Agent   Mozilla/5.0 (Windows; U; Windows NT
6.0; en-US; rv:1.9.2.15) Gecko/20110303 Firefox/3.6.15
Accept text/html,application/xhtml+xml,application/xml
Accept-Language   en-us,en;q=0.5
Accept-Encoding   gzip,deflate
Accept-Charset   ISO-8859-1,utf-8;q=0.7,*;q=0.7
Keep-Alive   115
Connection   keep-alive

Request

Response

HTTP/1.1 200 OK
Date   Sat, 12 Mar 2011 05:04:00 GMT
Expires   -1
Cache-Control   private, max-age=0
Content-Typetext/html; charset=UTF-8
Content-Encoding   gzip
Servergws
Content-Length   12994
X-XSS-Protection   1; mode=block

Figure 8-11   Typical HTTP request and response exchange
© Cengage Learning 2013

HTTP communication and its encrypted counterpart, HTTPS, form the foundation for Web communication and for sessions between clients and servers. There are a number of tools for viewing these communications at the OSI Application layer. Traditional network sniffers, such as tcpdump or Wireshark, are always a good option. However, there are a number of HTTP-specific sniffers that can manipulate the HTTP commands being used—for example, HttpFox (shown in Figure 8-12) and HttpWatch.

Web Programming Languages

Although the Web was built on the basis of **Hypertext Markup Language** (HTML), the use of various programming languages has greatly expanded the content, use, and user experience of the Web. This section covers HTML and some of the more popular programming languages.

HTML HTML is a key component of the Web, working in conjunction with HTTP to move content from servers to clients. Similar to the formatting in a word-processing application, HTML, using tags, tells Web browsers how to format the content displayed to the user. Table 8-5 displays some of the common HTML tags.

HTML Versions Since its inception, HTML has gone through a number of changes. The list that follows documents the various major versions and the functionality introduced with each.

- HTML 1.0—A set of informal standards based on the **Standard Generalized Markup Language** (SGML), a system for "marking up" documents by "representing structural,

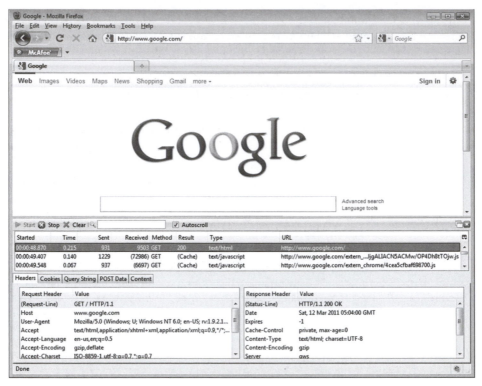

Figure 8-12 Screenshot from the HTTP sniffer HttpFox
Source: HttpFox

HTML Tag	Description
`<html> </hmtl>`	Signifies the start and end of an HTML document. To end formatting, start a tag with a backward slash (/).
`<head> </head>`	Specifies meta-information about the HTML document. This information is typically not displayed within the Web page.
`<body> </body>`	Starts and ends an HTML document's content.
`<h1> </h1>`	Provides formatting for headers.
`<p> </p>`	Starts and ends a paragraph of information.
`<b> </b>`	Bolds text.
`<i> </i>`	Italicizes text.
`<a href="http://www.domainname.tld/">Visit Our website</a>`	Links text to another Web site—also known as a hyperlink.

Table 8-5 Common HTML Tags and Their Uses
© Cengage Learning 2013

presentational, and semantic information alongside content."[9] HTML added the HREF tag invented by Tim Berners-Lee to link documents.[10]

- HTML 2.0—Formed first official HTML standard (RFC 1866). Codified many of the informal tags and HTML usage already in existence.[11]

- HTML 3.2—Provided support for style sheets, tables, footnotes, forms, and a host of additional features.[12]

- HTML 4.01—Provided improvements on features such as style sheets, tables, and forms and extended the feature set by adding mechanisms for scripting, frames, embedding objects, and mixed direction text.[13]

- HTML 5—This standard is still a work-in-progress but promises to provide a single language that can be written in HTML or XML syntax, improve interoperability among implementations, make improvements to the markup language, and provide support for emerging Web applications.[14]

CSS CSS (**Cascading Style Sheets**) standardizes the HTML formatting for an entire Web site by allowing developers to customize fonts, tables, and other page elements. For example, if changes need to be made to the font used on the Web site, the developer can change the font within the CSS, thereby updating all the uses of that font on the Web site, rather than have to manually put <font> tags on every single page.

CSS styles are typically saved within a .css file, and within a particular Web page, they are linked to using the following tag: <link rel="stylesheet" type="text/css" href="example.css" />. Figure 8-13 shows the interaction between the standard HTML tags, their customization using an external style sheet, and the modified display.

XML One of the limitations of HTML is that it was designed as a display language. You use it to format text and other elements so as to direct the client in how to view the data. However, if developers want to send or store data easily, they have to use the **Extensible Markup Language** (XML). XML is an extension to HTML that allows developers to define their own tags for structure. In other words, they can come up with their own dictionaries of tags—what each tag means and how the Web application or browser will handle the XML as it is passed to the client.

Here is a simple example of XML that defines a small retail catalog:

```
<retail_catalog>
    <clothing>
        <sku>3489222</sku>
        <description>Women's Cotton Blouse</description>
        <price>$34.95</price>
    </clothing>
    <jewelry>
        <sku>1299001</sku>
        <description>Women's Gold Watch</description>
        <price>$126.99</price>
    </jewelry>
</retail_catalog>
```

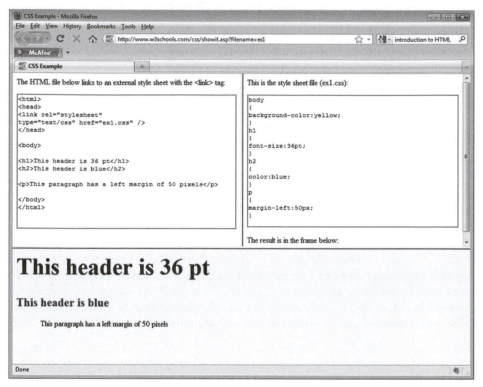

Figure 8-13 CSS example from w3schools.com

Source: w3school.com

CGI A common misconception is that the **Common Gateway Interface (CGI)** is a programming language in and of itself. Actually, CGI is an **API (application programming interface)** that allows external programs or scripts to interact with a Web server. As defined in RFC 3875, CGI provides a simple interface for running external programs or scripts on an HTTP server.[15]

Perl One of the first programming languages used for its CGI capability, **Perl** was developed in 1987 by Larry Wall as an interpreted language (based on C syntax) that helps provide a more robust scripting capability for UNIX. One of the biggest strengths of Perl is its text-manipulation abilities. Using regular expressions, Perl can easily parse text for a variety of purposes. Here is a sample Perl script used as a CGI program, in which the program queries various Web server variables and uses those for creating dynamic HTML output based on the user properties.

```
#!/usr/local/bin/perl

$remoteIp = $ENV{'REMOTE_ADDR'};
$remoteClient = $ENV{'HTTP_USER_AGENT'};

print "content-type: text/html \n\n";
print "<html> \n";
```

```
print "<h1>Welcome to my first CGI script!</h1> \n";
print "<p>You're visiting from the following IP address: ",
$remoteIp, "</p> \n";
print "<p>You're using the following Web browser: ",
$remoteClient, "</p> \n";
print "</html>";
exit (0);
```

This script creates the following HTML for display on the client side:

```
<html>
<h1>Welcome to my first CGI script!</h1>
<p>You're visiting from the following IP address: 10.1.23.129</p>
<p>You're using the following Web browser: Mozilla/5.0
(Macintosh; U; Intel Mac OS X 10.6; en-US; rv:1.9.2.15)
Gecko/20110303 Firefox/3.6.15</p>
</html>
```

PHP **PHP: Hypertext Preprocessor** (or simply PHP as a recursive abbreviation) was developed specifically to allow developers to create dynamically generated HTML content. PHP was originally developed by Rasmus Lerdorf in 1995 and named after his set of Perl scripts called Personal Home Page/Forms Interpreter. The modern versions of PHP are based on the wholesale rewrite to version 3.0 by Andi Gutmans and Zeev Suraski in 1997.[16]

Like most CGI scripts, PHP languages are interpreted on the server-side prior to content being delivered to the user. This allows the use of server variables, connections to databases, and a number of other features that create dynamic content. The following is a simple PHP script to determine whether the user agent reported by the Web server contains MSIE—thus, indicating the use of Internet Explorer.

```
<html>
<h1>Welcome to my first PHP script!</h1>
<p>Looking for Internet Explorer...</p>
<?php
if (strpos($_SERVER['HTTP_USER_AGENT'], 'MSIE') !== FALSE) {
  echo 'You are using Internet Explorer.<br />';
}
else {
echo 'You must be using a browser other than Internet Explorer.';
}
?>
</html>
```

This script then generates the following HTML to display to the client Web browser:

```
<html>
<h1>Welcome to my first PHP script!</h1>
<p>Looking for Internet Explorer...</p>
You must be using a browser other than Internet Explorer.
</html>
```

8

JavaScript In 1995, Netscape, to coincide with its release of Netscape Navigator 2.0, was looking to add support for Java applets. Brendan Eich was hired to lead the team that created this support via a scripting language called **JavaScript**. The syntax of the language is based on Java and has a fairly low "barrier to entry" compared with other scripting languages, such as Perl.[17]

JavaScript was originally developed as a client-side language, which means the code is interpreted on the client side instead of on the Web server. (Today, this has evolved so that various implementations of JavaScript can now be interpreted on the Web server side using customized Web applications.) The following HTML page with embedded JavaScript demonstrates a simple use of displaying text if scripting is enabled on the client side.

```
<html>
<h1>Welcome to my first JavaScript!</h1>

<script type="text/javascript">
 document.write('Hello World!');
</script>
<noscript>
<p>Your browser either does not support JavaScript, or you have JavaScript
turned off.</p>
</noscript>
</html>
```

Using a browser with scripting enabled, the following HTML is generated. You can see that the client gets all the content since no server-side interpretation is involved.

```
<html>
<h1>Welcome to my first JavaScript!</h1>
<script type="text/javascript">
 document.write('Hello World!');
</script>
<noscript>
<p>Your browser either does not support JavaScript, or you have JavaScript
turned off.</p>
</noscript>
</html>
```

AJAX The term "AJAX" was coined by Jesse James Garrett in an article published in 2005.[18] In the article, Garrett described a new approach to Web applications that allowed a more interactive user experience. "AJAX" stands for "**Asynchronous JavaScript and XML**" and does not refer to a new programming language but to a new use of existing technologies. The idea is to have a number of mini-requests from the client to the server to make the content seem dynamic. This illusion is achieved by implementing a program exchange like the one illustrated in Figure 8-14. The key aspect of this exchange is centered on the XMLHttpRequest function in JavaScript. This request will gather XML data from the server and load the response directly into a script.[19] This approach has revolutionized Web site interactions, as seen in examples like Google's implementation of the Google Talk instant messaging client within the Gmail Web site.

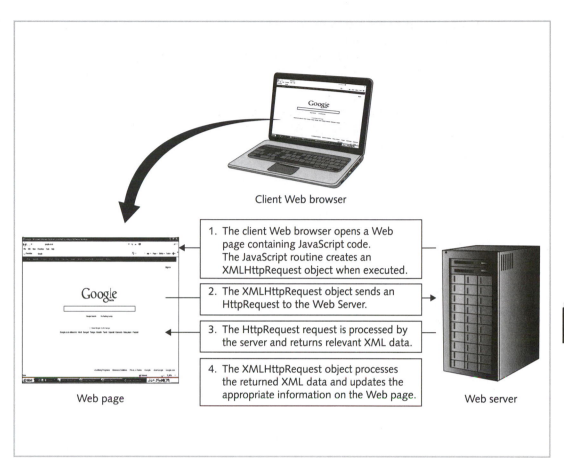

Figure 8-14   Client and server interaction using AJAX
© Cengage Learning 2013

Other Languages   There are a number of other programming languages in use around the Web. Most notably, Ruby and Python have made huge gains in Web programming mindshare in recent years. Microsoft has developed technologies specific for Windows that use Internet Explorer and Jscript or VBScript as programming languages of choice. We won't cover these languages in detail, given that most of them are similar to languages like Perl, PHP, and JavaScript and don't, on their own, add much to the security discussion about Web applications.

Threats and Vulnerabilities in Web Applications

The Open Web Application Security Project (OWASP) is an organization dedicated to collaboration, discussion, and education regarding the security of Web applications. OWASP is a nonprofit organization that releases all its materials under a free and open-source software license. This section will use OWASP's Top Ten Project (see *www.owasp.org/index.php/ Category:OWASP_Top_Ten_Project*) as the basis to discuss the top risks to Web applications.

Injection

In 2010, OWASP determined that injection attacks were the top risk to Web applications. Most notably, these attacks use a variety of techniques to inject data into a SQL command and thereby add, modify, or remove data from the back-end database communicating with the Web application. There are other injection attacks against LDAP, the underlying OS, or other components tied to the Web server using similar techniques.

The basic concept behind a **SQL injection** attack involves modifying the data sent via a URL or via an HTML form to the Web server. For example, a Web form might ask a user for a name in order to look up the person's e-mail address. That data is then passed to the database in the form of the following SQL statement:

```
SELECT email FROM users WHERE name = '<name field contents>';
```

The statement is asking the database to return the email field from the table users when the name field equals a particular value. Thus, if the Web visitor enters the name "David," the SQL passed is the following:

```
SELECT email FROM users WHERE name = 'David';
```

The result of the query would then be the e-mail address associated with David.

An attacker, however, can manipulate the data returned by simply modifying the data entered into the form field. For example, an attack can enter the following text:

```
' or 1=1;--
```

The data passed then creates the following SQL statement:

```
SELECT email FROM users WHERE name = '' or 1=1;--';
```

This statement translates to return the e-mail address for the user with the name field blank or in instances where 1=1. In SQL, the "--" denotes a comment, so the database will ignore the proceeding characters. The fact that 1 will always equal 1 makes the SQL statement always true and effectively turns the SQL statement into:

```
SELECT email FROM users;
```

That statement will return all e-mail addresses stored within the table named users. A more nefarious attack could perform a task more damaging by passing the following value:

```
'; drop table users;--
```

This value would then translate to the following SQL statement:

```
SELECT email FROM users WHERE name = ''; drop table users;--';
```

The statement would effectively destroy the table named users, assuming the attacker had the appropriate privileges to do so within the database.

Security Solutions Here are some preventative measures to ward off an SQL injection attack:[20]

- Make sure there is limited access to the Web application within the database, to prevent attacks that remove data.

- Use prebuilt statements that do not take user input. This creates more work for the developer, given that all possible SQL queries have to be predefined, but it also eliminates the direct translation of user input into a query that interacts with the database.

- Instead of sending SQL queries to the database, invoke stored procedures to take the appropriate actions on the database data. Stored procedures are saved within the database and do not allow user interaction. A key to using stored procedures is to make sure the Web application does not have too high a privilege to access administrative stored procedures.

- Scrub all user input to make sure no invalid characters are passed in the SQL statement. Although this approach is still prone to problems when the attacker obfuscates characters with ASCII codes, the idea is to remove quotes, parentheses, dashes, and other SQL characters that can affect the behavior of the SQL query.

- Alternatively, use a "white list" or simply indicate which type of data is acceptable and discard the rest. For example, instead of removing quotes from the user input, check to see if letters exist, then discard everything else.

Cross-Site Scripting (XSS)

Cross-site scripting (XSS) vulnerabilities may be the least understood in that the attack code is not sent from the client to the server, as with injection attacks. Instead, a server sends unverified data to the client, and the client, in turn, executes code that exploits the Web browser. This type of attack should be rare, in that the majority of Web sites are trusted and legitimate. However, the attack occurs because a legitimate Web site has a vulnerability that can be exploited by attackers who then cause the Web site to send malicious code to the client.

A simple approach to an XSS attack is to find Web sites that take user input and redisplay the results to the user, without scrubbing results. As an example, Acunetix hosts an HTML form at *http://testasp.vulnweb.com/search.asp* that is susceptible to an XSS attack. By entering the following HTML code as a search result, the form accidentally processes the script instead of looking for search terms:

```
<script>location.replace("http://www.yahoo.com");</script>
```

The result is that the user is redirected to yahoo.com without his knowledge. The key to this attack, then, is to find a way to pass that to a user. In this case, the trick is to entice a user into clicking the following link:

http://testasp.vulnweb.com/search.asp?tfSearch=<script>location.replace("http://www.yahoo.com")%3B<%2Fscript>

A user might only look to see that the URL points to a trusted Web site and ignore the odd script command contained within the URL. He then clicks the link expecting to be taken to a known Web site, only to be automatically redirected to a malicious site. Or better yet, we can transform the link so the user can't see the script contents by substituting hex codes for URL encoding, to form:

http://testasp.vulnweb.com/search.asp?tfSearch=%3C%73%63%72%69%70%74%3E%
6C%6F%63%61%74%69%6F%6E%2E%72%65%70%6C%61%63%65%28%27%
68%74%74%70%3A%2F%2F%77%77%77%2E%79%61%68%6F%6F%2E%63%
6F%6D%27%29%3B%3C%2F%73%63%72%69%70%74%3E

URL encoding allows the transmission of characters outside the standard ASCII character set by performing a simple ASCII code lookup, prefixing the hexadecimal value with a percentage sign.

Security Solutions Here are some preventative measures to ward off an XSS attack:[21]

- Make sure that untrusted data cannot be inserted into the HTML that is returned to a client or into URL parameters passed to the Web application. In particular, don't allow any JavaScript to be inserted that is automatically run on the client side.

- If untrusted data must be inserted into the returned HTML, all accepted input must be scrubbed prior to its return. This means removing special characters, script tags, and other characters that have special meaning to browsers, such as &, <, >, and ", or '.

- Again, if untrusted data must be used to form a URL parameter, scrub all characters to remove special URL characters.

Broken Authentication and Session Management

This is a broad category of vulnerabilities that occur when Web developers create applications with custom-made systems to authenticate users and manage the authentication during an active Web session. The most obvious example is when the Web application does not automatically end an authenticated session. For example, a user with a public kiosk computer can log in to her bank's Web site to check her account balances. She finishes, closes the Web browser (without logging off from the bank's Web site), and walks away. An attacker watches the exchange, visits the bank's Web site, and, with the user's credentials, is able to restart the same session. From there, the attacker has the same access as the user to the user's bank account information and transactions.

Security Solutions Here are some preventative measures to strengthen authentication or session vulnerabilities:[22]

- Require complex passwords for authentication. To avoid easy guessing, simple and short passwords should not be allowed. Even better, use two-factor authentication, such as tokens, to replace simple username and password combinations.

- Use encrypted communication to transmit password information. Use a VPN, Secure Socket Layer (SSL), or Transport Layer Security (TLS).

- Make sure all user sessions are disconnected after a certain amount of inactivity. For good measure, set an upper limit on a session, regardless of activity. Unfortunately, this will require a legitimate user to authenticate again, but it will also disconnect an attacker in the middle of a hijacked session.

- Do not give away too much information in an authentication error message. Make sure the error message lets a legitimate user know that the login attempt failed and he has to retry, but don't let an attacker know that, although the password is incorrect, the username is valid.

- Make sure an account is locked out after a certain number of invalid login attempts. This prevents brute force password attacks.

- Make sure session IDs are random and encrypted. This prevents attackers from guessing valid sessions and hijacking them.

Insecure Direct Object References

In many cases, an HTML form will restrict the choices a user has by way of a drop-down list, check box, or radio button, as shown in Figure 8-15. Most developers will then assume that the choices or data passed to the Web application will be limited by these forced choices. Unfortunately, that assumption is rarely valid.

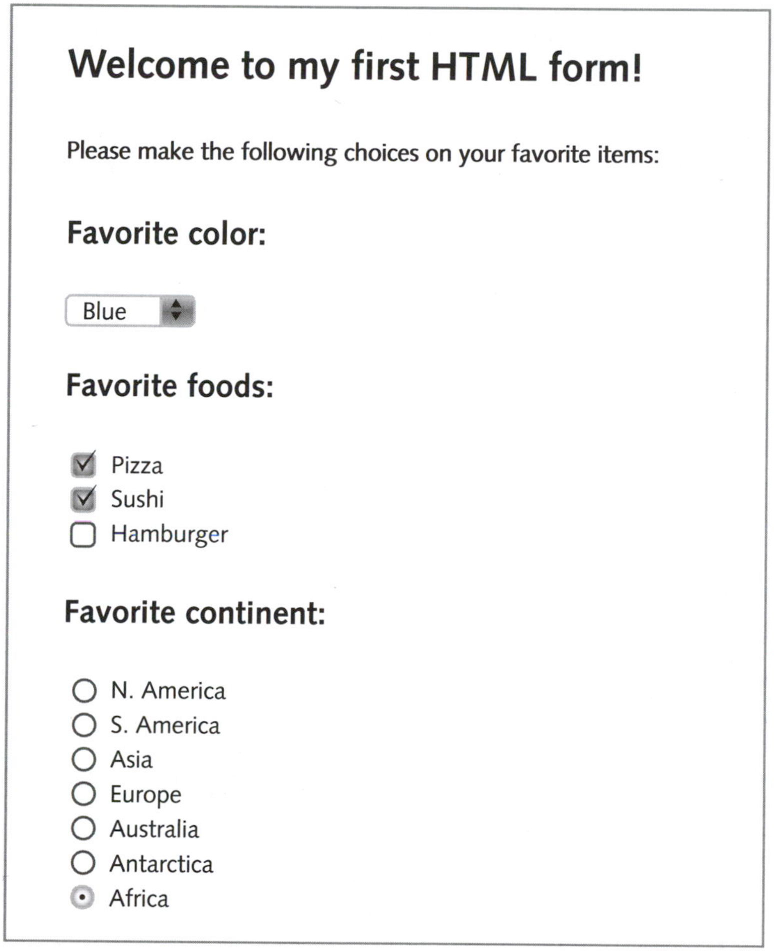

Welcome to my first HTML form!

Please make the following choices on your favorite items:

Favorite color:

Blue

Favorite foods:

☑ Pizza
☑ Sushi
☐ Hamburger

Favorite continent:

○ N. America
○ S. America
○ Asia
○ Europe
○ Australia
○ Antarctica
⊙ Africa

Figure 8-15   Sample HTML form
© Cengage Learning 2013

The trick is that the data from the form is passed in either the URL or via an HTML POST command. In both cases, an attacker can intercept the request, modify the choice, and try to gain access to an object or values to which she would not normally be given access. One example of this vulnerability is called directory traversal. A Web site's URL could be the following: *www.sampleorg.com/reference.php?view=article1.html.*

The intent is that the PHP script takes a variable called "view" that stores the page with the article information the user wants to view. However, an attacker, seeing the exposed variable, changes the URL to the following to expose a file unintended by the Web site developer or administrator:

www.sampleorg.com/reference.php?view=../../../../etc/passwd.

Security Solutions Here are some preventative measures to avoid improper access to files, database objects, or other data:[23]

- Analyze your Web server's settings to make sure the server prevents directory traversal and other forms of insecure object access. Upgrade or modify the configuration to ensure restrictions are added.

- Check the access of the user whenever he is accessing authorized (or unauthorized) objects. For example, within a database access request, make sure the user is authenticated and has authorization to the requested data. Do not assume that, because the data is coming from the Web server, that user's input has been verified by the Web application or Web server.

- Avoid exposing key names, variable types, or other attributes that help the attacker understand what has been passed. For example, map a list of file names to numbers so the attacker has no control over changing the mapped data.

Cross-Site Request Forgery (CSRF)

A **cross-site request forgery** (CSRF—pronounced "sea-surf") is an attack that exploits a Web site's trust or previous authentication of a user. Let's assume a food-delivery Web site allows you to order food online. You choose the food items and drinks, and pay via credit card. The food is delivered in due time. However, the Web site performs the ordering tasks using predictable variables and actions, as shown in the following URL:

www.favoritefoodexample.com/app/orderFood.asp?food=pizza&foodamt=2&drink=2ltrCola &drinkamt=2.

The URL passes parameters that define the type and amount of food ordered. The attacker, however, does not want to modify his own order. He wants you to modify yours—better yet, he wants you to enter an order when you did not intend to. To get you to do this, he might create an invisible image and trick you into visiting the image on a Web site, using the following HTML:

```
<img src =
"www.favoritefoodexample.com/app/orderFood.asp?food=pizza&foodam
t=2&drink=2ltrCola&drinkamt=2" width="0" height="0" />
```

The image is not visible to the user, but the user hopefully has session credentials or a valid cookie that automatically logs him into the food-delivery site, initiates the order, and results in the food being delivered. Now, imagine this same scenario, only with a banking application in which money is transferred. That could be much more costly than a couple of pizzas.

Security Solutions Here are some preventative measures to keep attackers from tricking users into inadvertently using CSRFs:[24]

- Generate random tokens with the various HTML forms used by a user. These tokens are then passed to the server for each of the sensitive Web application actions. In this way, random parameters cannot be passed via URL (or form) to initiate these actions. Make sure the secret token is sufficiently random to keep an attacker from guessing a token identifier.

- Use another challenge-response mechanism when the action is initiated. Mechanisms like **CAPTCHA (Completely Automated Public Turing Test to Tell Computers and Humans Apart)** allow a Web site to make sure that an automated script or system is NOT making the request. A Web site can also simply insist that a user reauthenticate himself for sensitive transactions.

- On the client side, make sure users log off of every session to prevent an automatic reinitiation of the same session.

Security Misconfiguration

Web servers are fairly complex to administer correctly. Like any system, there is always the concern of keeping the underlying hardware and operating system secure. However, there is the added concern of maintaining the Web server, any installed Web applications, and any developer framework necessary to run the applications. If administrators do not stay up on the latest patches, configuration changes, and versions, the Web server can be compromised.

Security Solutions There are a number of steps a system administrator can take to ensure the security of the Web server:[25]

- Stay informed of OS, Web server, and application updates as they are released from the vendor.

- Treat the Web server as a bastion host. Remove unnecessary applications, services, daemons, accounts, or other components.

- Secure application and development frameworks to make sure the applications do not open vulnerabilities to the system.

- Limit user accounts to those that are absolutely essential, and make sure that complex passwords are used for the remaining user accounts.

- Limit error messaging to Web visitors in order to limit the information an attacker can use to find vulnerabilities.

Insecure Cryptographic Storage

Given the threat of leaking sensitive personal information or personally identifiable information (PII), more and more organizations are turning to encryption to make sure the data is stored in a format that cannot be leaked if a system is compromised. Organizations must first determine what data they want to encrypt, then they must make sure they are properly encrypting the data in storage. In some cases, the data is encrypted while resting in a database but not when sent to backup, or the encryption key is included on the backup. In other cases, data is automatically decrypted when requested from a Web server, which could allow an attacker to gain access to the data through an injection attack.

Security Solutions Here are a number of ways to properly encrypt Web data at rest:[26]

- Use strong encryption algorithms, keys, and methods to encrypt sensitive information.
- Encrypt backups of the data, but manage keys separately.
- Verify that data can only be decrypted by authorized users or processes.

Failure to Restrict URL Access

URLs indicate the resources the client would like to request from a server. The following URL indicates the client would like access to the orderFood.asp script:

www.favoritefoodexample.com/app/orderFood.asp.

However, there is nothing stopping a user from manipulating the URL to access resources that are not normally accessible. For example, an attacker may venture a guess by trying the following URL:

www.favoritefoodexample.com/app/admin_orderFood.asp.

If the Web server does not check for authorization, the user may be able to access a script meant only for the administrator.

Security Solutions Here are some ways to restrict URL access:[27]

- Make sure sensitive pages require authentication.
- Check each user to make sure he or she has authorization to the specific page. Do not assume that if users are authenticated, they have access.

Insufficient Transport Layer Protection

A network sniffer is a tool that can capture traffic traversing a network with both the packet headers and the packet data. If the data is not encrypted, the sniffer can display the text included in the packet. Similar to the need to encrypt data in storage, it is important for sensitive information to be encrypted while in transit.

Security Solutions Here are some ways to make sure data is properly encrypted while in transit:[28]

- When sensitive information is transferred from the client to the server (and vice versa), make sure it is encrypted with SSL and TLS.
- Use the "secure" flag on all sensitive cookies.
- Make sure the SSL is valid and issued by a trusted Internet certificate authority.
- Make sure communications from the Web server to other back-end systems are encrypted.

Unvalidated Redirects and Forwards

There are a number of instances where a Web site might need to redirect visitors to another page. When pages are updated, edited, moved, or removed, a site administrator may want to direct visitors to the new location or page. For example, an administrator may want to redirect visitors from *www.sampleorg.com/old.html* to *www.sampleorg.com/new.html*. This can be done a number of ways, but one way is to create a .htaccess file with the following entry:

```
Redirect 301 /old/old.html /new/new.html
```

Security Solutions Here are some preventative measures to make sure redirects are not manipulated:[29]

- Do not use them at all.

- If they have to be used, make sure no parameters are fed to the redirects. An attacker should not be able to inject the ultimate target of the redirect.

- If you can, determine whether the parameters are valid and the user is authorized to create a redirect.

Securing a Web Server

Like any system, there are a number of best practices with regards to securing a Web server. NIST has published detailed guidelines for securing public Web servers in SP 800-44.[30] Web system administrators should use the following best practices:

- Upgrade and patch the underlying operating system and Web server software.

- Remove or disable unnecessary applications, services, and communications.

- Limit user accounts, enforce a strong password policy, and monitor user activity.

- Limit access to sensitive OS and Web resources.

- Configure various security settings within the Web server and make sure the application does not run with administrative privileges.

- Do not use links in the public Web content to point to other files or directories on the host or other network systems.

- Disallow search engine indexing on sensitive Web directories.

- Control access to specific pages and directories to ensure proper authorization.

Chapter Summary

- It is important to delineate the Internet from the World Wide Web (WWW). The Internet is a physical set of networks (the hardware, if you will), whereas the WWW is a set of applications (the software) that runs on top of the Internet. Internet security depends not only on securing Web sites but on securing the various services that use the interconnected networks.

- The Simple Mail Transfer Protocol (SMTP) is used to send Internet mail, whereas the Post Office Protocol 3 (POP3) and the Internet Message Access Protocol (IMAP) are used to receive Internet mail. The most effective methods for preventing mail attacks is to apply security patches and restrict mail relayed on the e-mail server.

- File Transfer Protocol (FTP) and Trivial File Transfer Protocol (TFTP) are simple methods of transferring files between computer system. They are often considered unsecurable unless used in conjunction with SSL or some other additional means of securing the communication channel they use.

- Telnet is an Application-layer protocol that allows users to connect to a remote computer, run programs, view files, and perform a variety of other operations as if they were using the system locally. Like FTP, it must be used over a secured network link in order to be used safely.

- The Simple Network Management Protocol (SNMP) is an Application-layer management protocol that is used to monitor the status and performance of network devices and systems.

- The Lightweight Directory Access Protocol (LDAP) is an Application-layer protocol that provides a communication framework with centralized directories that hold a variety of useful data.

- Network News Transfer Protocol (NNTP) is an Application-layer protocol that allows users to use a distributed protocol to download and post messages.

- The Domain Name System (DNS) operates within the Application layer and allows clients to perform the translation of domain names to network addresses. A related protocol, Domain Name System Security Extensions (DNSSEC), is employed to digitally sign information provided to the resolver and attempts to provide a level of authenticity to the DNS communication to avoid DNS poisoning attacks.

- There are three fundamental aspects of Web communication: the server, the client, and the communication protocol. A Web server shares content to incoming connections. The most commonly encountered Web client is a Web browser, which hides much of the details of HTTP communication and provides an easy-to-use interface for users. Hypertext Transfer Protocol (HTTP) is the basis for Web communication.

- The Web was built on the basis of Hypertext Markup Language (HTML), but the use of various programming languages has greatly expanded the content, use, and user experience of the Web:
  - Similar to the formatting in a word-processing application, HTML, using tags, tells Web browsers how to format the content displayed to the user.
  - CSS (Cascading Style Sheets) standardizes the HTML formatting for an entire Web site by allowing developers to customize fonts, tables, and other page elements.
  - XML is an extension to HTML that allows developers to define their own tags for structure.
  - CGI is an application programming interface (API) that allows external programs or scripts to interact with a Web server.
  - Perl is an interpreted language (based on C syntax) that helps provide a more robust scripting capability.
  - PHP: Hypertext Preprocessor was developed to allow developers to create dynamically generated HTML content.
  - JavaScript was developed as a client-side language, which means the code is interpreted on the client side instead of on the Web server. It has evolved to a hybrid model that runs on clients and servers.
  - "AJAX" stands for "Asynchronous JavaScript and XML"; it does not refer to a new programming language but to a new use of existing technologies. The idea is

to have a number of mini-requests from the client to the server to make the content seem dynamic.

- There are a number of other programming languages in use on the Web, such as Ruby, Python, and VBScript.

- Web Applications are subject to a variety of attacks, including:

  - Injection attacks, which use a variety of techniques to inject data into the communication channel from the client to the back-end server or database that is communicating with the Web application

  - Cross-site scripting (XSS), in which, instead of attack code being sent from the client to the server, a server sends unverified data to the client, and then the client executes code that exploits the Web browser

  - Broken authentication and session management, insecure direct object references, cross-site request forgery, general security misconfiguration, insecure cryptographic storage, failure to restrict URL access, insufficient transport layer protection, unvalidated redirects and forwards

Review Questions

1. What is SMTP used for? What are some common attacks against SMTP servers?

2. What are some ways to protect SMTP servers?

3. What is FTP used for?

4. What are some common attacks against FTP servers?

5. What is the difference between active and passive mode in FTP sessions?

6. Are you more likely to use active or passive mode FTP when located behind a firewall, and why?

7. What is Telnet used for?

8. What are some ways to protect Telnet servers?

9. Why is v3 of the SNMP protocol a step forward from previous versions?

10. What is LDAP used for?

11. What are the common attacks faced by LDAP servers?

12. What are some ways to protect LDAP servers from attacks?

13. What are the most common types of attacks against DNS servers?

14. What are some ways to harden DNS servers?

15. What are some recommended methods to combat SQL injection?

16. What is an XSS attack?

17. What are some ways to combat XSS attacks?

18. What are some ways to prevent authentication or session vulnerabilities?

19. What are some ways to properly encrypt data on a Web server?

20. What are some ways to harden a Web server?

Real-World Exercises

Exercise 8-1

Using your preferred Web browser on a system connected to the Internet, search for "OWASP." What is OWASP? Find the most current OWASP Top Ten Web-application security risks. What is Number One right now? How does the attack that exploits this risk work?

Exercise 8-2

You may have heard about the "client-server model" of computing, which is sometimes considered the same as n-tier computing. First, summarize in a sentence or two what the client-server model of computing is, after using a Web search tool and reading about that technology. Then, discuss at least two of the alternatives to this computing model.

Hands-On Projects

In this project, we will examine various methods that attackers use to exploit vulnerable Web-based applications. To complete this exercise, we will use Badstore, a deliberately insecure Web-based application designed for educational purposes. Badstore is available from the Badstore Web site at *www.badstore.net*.

To complete this exercise, you will need to download the Badstore ISO and set it up to run in a virtual environment. This setup is outside the scope of this exercise. Note that Badstore is a vulnerable application by design. It should only be set up to run in a test environment, not in a production environment on the Internet.

1. Start the Badstore virtual machine. After startup is complete, type **ifconfig** and press **Enter**. Take note of the IP address assigned to the interface, as you will need this going forward.

2. Open a Web browser and enter **http://<ip address>** in the address window. You should see the front page of the Web site, as shown in Figure 8-16. Note that the site greets you as {Unregistered User}.

One of the most basic methods of attack against Web sites involves the use of SQL injection. Attackers can leverage SQL injections to inflict damage, gain unauthorized access to an application, or create new users and subsequently grant those users (i.e., themselves) unauthorized privileges.

3. Click the **Login / Register** link in the site menu. In the "Login to Your Account" section, enter **' or 1=1 or '** in the Email Address field, as shown in Figure 8-17.

Figure 8-16   BadStore home page

Source: www.badstore.net

Figure 8-17   SQL injection attack

Source: www.badstore.net

4. Click **Login**. Note that the greeting has changed from "Unregistered User" to "Test User," indicating that the SQL injection was successful.

5. Frequently, attackers gain information about an application via error messages. Click the magnifying glass icon in the "Quick Item Search" area of the page, being careful to leave the search field blank. As displayed in Figure 8-18, the application returns an error message that provides valuable information about the structure of one of the tables being used in the database. Attackers can use this information to make informed guesses about the names and structures of the other tables used by the application.

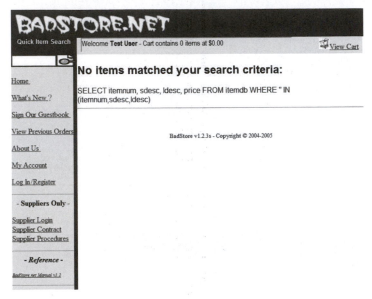

Figure 8-18 SQL error message

6. Attackers can also gain information about an application by viewing a Web page's source code. Click the **Login / Register** link in the site menu. After the page loads, right-click the page and choose the option to view the source code.

7. Copy the source code and paste it into a new document in a text editor.

8. Take a few minutes to examine the code. Toward the bottom of the code, you will see the section that allows users to register for a new account. Careful observation will show that the form has a hidden input value. The hidden value has the name "role" and a value of "U." Although you cannot be certain at this point, it seems reasonable to think that these attributes set the new user account with "user" access. It may be possible to escalate privileges to administrator by changing the value from "U" to "A." To test this theory, we will need to submit the form with this changed value. Most attackers will use some type of proxy application, such as Paros, to trap and change values like this in transit. However, for this exercise, we will make the changes manually to the source code, then load the modified source code in a browser and execute it.

9. In the text editor, change the value from "U" to "A," as shown in Figure 8-19.

```
<INPUT TYPE="hidden" NAME="role" VALUE="A">
```

Figure 8-19   Edited Hidden Value

Source: wwwbadstore.net

10. In order for this HTML to communicate with the server, it is necessary to change the ACTION value associated with the POST command for this form. Search the code until you find the text "Register for a New Account." Behind that text is the beginning of the FORM command that creates the new user account. Edit the ACTION value by adding **http://<IP address of Badstore>** in front of the "/cgi-bin/badstore.cgi?action= register" value already present. When done, your code should look like what is shown in Figure 8-20.

```
<FORM METHOD="POST" ACTION="http://192.168.1.138/cgi-bin/badstore.cgi?action=register"
```

Figure 8-20   Edited POST Value

Source: www.badstore.net

11. Save the HTML code as a file, using a .HTML extension.

12. Open the saved file in a Web browser. Enter **illegal admin** in the Full Name field, **crook@badstore.net** in the Email Address field, and **crook** in the Password field. See Figure 8-21 for details. Then, click **Register**.

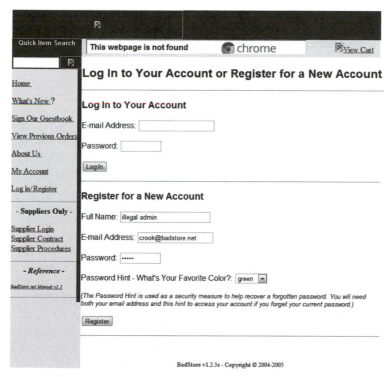

Figure 8-21   Creating admin user

Source: www.badstore.net

13. In the upper-left corner of the Web page, note that you are logged in as "illegal user."

14. Now, we will determine if this user has administrative privileges. To do this, we will engage in basic URL manipulation. URL manipulation is the act of changing values in a Web site's URL, submitting the changes to the Web server, and observing what happens. Currently, the URL is *http://<IP ADDRESS>/cgi-bin/badstore.cgi?action=register*. To manipulate this URL, replace "register" with "admin" and submit the page to the server. You are now taken to the secret administration menu, as shown in Figure 8-22. This figure also shows what the manipulated URL should look like.

Figure 8-22 Secret admin menu

Source: www.badstore.net

15. From here, we can effectively function as an application administrator, giving us access to all types of data and functionality. For example, we can now view credit card data by selecting **View Sales Reports** and clicking **Do It**. The report is shown in Figure 8-23.

Further examination of the available menu options shows that we can now reset user passwords, add and delete users, view user details, view technical details about the Web server, and create a database backup that we can view in a Web browser.

Figure 8-23 Sales report with CC data

Source: www.badstore.net

8

Endnotes

1. Anderson, C. and Wolff, M. (2010, August). "The Web Is Dead. Long Live the Internet." *Wired* magazine. Accessed March 5, 2011 @ *www.wired.com/magazine/2010/08/ff_webrip/all/1*.

2. JANET. "Repairing open mail relays." JANET. Accessed December 26, 2011 @ *www.ja.net/services/mail/janet-spam-relay-tester-and-notification-system/repairing-open-mail-relays.html*.

3. OWASP. "LDAP Injection — OWASP." *Owasp.org*. OWASP, April 7, 2009. Accessed March 11, 2011 @ *www.owasp.org/index.php/LDAP_injection*.

4. Microsoft. "DNS Architecture." *Microsoft TechNet: Resources for IT Professionals*. Microsoft. Accessed March 6, 2011 @ *http://technet.microsoft.com/en-us/library/dd197427(WS.10).aspx*.

5. Davis, Joshua. "Secret Geek A-Team Hacks Back, Defends Worldwide Web." *Wired.com. Wired* magazine, Nov. 24, 2008. Accessed March 6, 2011 @ *www.wired. com/techbiz/people/magazine/16-12/ff_kaminsky.*

6. USA. NIST. Computer Security Division. *Secure Domain Name System (DNS) Deployment Guide.* By Chandramouli, R. and Rose, S. Apr. 2010. Accessed March 6, 2011 @ *csrc.nist.gov/publications/nistpubs/800-81r1/sp-800-81r1.pdf.*

7. Netcraft. "March 2011 Web Server Survey." *Internet Research, Anti-Phishing and PCI Security Services | Netcraft.* Netcraft, Mar. 2011. Accessed March 7, 2011 @ *http:// news.netcraft.com/archives/2011/03/09/march-2011-web-server-survey.html.*

8. Web Hosting Help Guy. "HTTP Status Codes: A Guide To The Most Common Responses." *Web Hosting Help Guy by InMotion Hosting.* Accessed 9 March, 2011 @ *webhostinghelpguy.inmotionhosting.com/website-optimization/http-status-codes-a-guide-to-the-most-common-responses.*

9. W3C. "HTML 4.01 Specification." Accessed December 28, 2011 @ *www.w3.org/TR/ html4/intro/sgmltut.html.*

10. Raggett, D., Lam, J., Alexander, I., and Kmiec, M. "A history of HTML." Accessed December 27, 2011 @ *www.w3.org/People/Raggett/book4/ch02.html.*

11. Raggett, D., Lam, J., Alexander, I., and Kmiec, M. "A history of HTML." Accessed December 27, 2011 @ *www.w3.org/People/Raggett/book4/ch02.html.*

12. Raggett, D., Lam, J., Alexander, I., and Kmiec, M. "A history of HTML." Accessed December 27, 2011 @ *www.w3.org/People/Raggett/book4/ch02.html.*

13. W3C. "HTML 4.01 Specification." Accessed December 28, 2011 @ *www.w3.org/TR/ html401/intro/intro.html#h-2.2.1.*

14. W3C. "HTML5 Differences from HTML4." Accessed December 28, 2011 @ *www.w3. org/TR/html5-diff/.*

15. Robinson, D. and Coar, K. "RFC 3875: The Common Gateway Interface (CGI) Version 1.1." Accessed July 1, 2011 @ *www.rfc-editor.org/rfc/rfc3875.txt.*

16. The PHP Group. "PHP: History of PHP - Manual." *PHP: Hypertext Preprocessor.* Accessed 12 March, 2011 @ *www.php.net/manual/en/history.php.php.*

17. Flanagan, David. "JavaScript: How Did We Get Here? - O'Reilly Media." *O'Reilly Media - Technology Books, Tech Conferences, IT Courses, News.* 6 Apr. 2001. Accessed March 12, 2011 @ *http://oreilly.com/pub/a/javascript/2001/04/06/js_history. html.*

18. Garrett, Jesse James. "Ajax: A New Approach to Web Applications." *Adaptive Path » Product Experience Strategy and Design.* Adaptive Path, Feb. 18, 2005. Accessed March 12, 2011 @ *www.adaptivepath.com/ideas/essays/archives/000385.php.*

19. W3C. "XMLHttpRequest." *World Wide Web Consortium (W3C).* Aug. 3, 2010. Accessed March 12, 2011 @ *www.w3.org/TR/XMLHttpRequest.*

20. Wichers, Dave. "SQL Injection Prevention Cheat Sheet - OWASP." *Main Page - OWASP.* Accessed March 12, 2011 @ *www.owasp.org/index.php/SQL_Injection_ Prevention_Cheat_Sheet.*

21. Williams, J., and Manico, J. "XSS (Cross Site Scripting) Prevention Cheat Sheet - OWASP." *Main Page - OWASP*. Accessed March 12, 2011 @ *www.owasp.org/index. php/XSS_(Cross_Site_Scripting)_Prevention_Cheat_Sheet*.

22. Keary, Eoin. "Authentication Cheat Sheet - OWASP." *Main Page - OWASP*. Accessed March 12, 2011 @ *www.owasp.org/index.php/Authentication_Cheat_Sheet*.

23. OWASP Foundation. "Top 10 2010-A4-Insecure Direct Object References - OWASP." *Main Page - OWASP*. Accessed March 12, 2011 @ *www.owasp.org/index.php/Top_ 10_2010-A4*.

24. Petefish, P., Sheridan, E., and Wichers, D. "Cross-Site Request Forgery (CSRF) Prevention Cheat Sheet - OWASP." *Main Page - OWASP*. Accessed March 12, 2011 @ *www. owasp.org/index.php/Cross-Site_Request_Forgery_(CSRF)_Prevention_Cheat_Sheet*.

25. OWASP Foundation. "Top 10 2010-A6-Security Misconfiguration - OWASP." *Main Page - OWASP*. Accessed March 12, 2011 @ *www.owasp.org/index.php/Top_ 10_2010-A6*.

26. OWASP Foundation. "Top 10 2010-A7-Insecure Cryptographic Storage - OWASP." *Main Page - OWASP*. Accessed March 12, 2011 @ *www.owasp.org/index.php/ Top_10_2010-A7*.

27. OWASP Foundation. "Top 10 2010-A8-Failure to Restrict URL Access - OWASP." *Main Page - OWASP*. Accessed March 12, 2011 @ *www.owasp.org/index.php/ Top_10_2010-A8*.

28. Coates, M., Wichers, D., Boberski, M., and Reguly, T. "Transport Layer Protection Cheat Sheet - OWASP." *Main Page - OWASP*. Accessed March 12, 2011 @ *www. owasp.org/index.php/Transport_Layer_Protection_Cheat_Sheet*.

29. OWASP Foundation. "Top 10 2010-A10-Unvalidated Redirects and Forwards - OWASP." *Main Page - OWASP*. Accessed March 12, 2011 @ *www.owasp.org/index. php/Top_10_2010-A10*.

30. USA. NIST. Computer Security Division. *Guidelines on Security Public Web Servers*. By Tracy, M., Jansen, W., Scarfone, K., and Winograd, T. Sep. 2007. Accessed March 6, 2011 @ *src.nist.gov/publications/ nistpubs/800-44-ver2/SP800-44v2.pdf*.

8

chapter 9

Network Vulnerability Assessment

For years I've been saying security consists of protection, detection and response—and you need all three to have good security. Before you can do a good job with any of these, you have to assess your security. And done right, penetration testing is a key component of a security assessment. — Bruce Schneier, renowned security technologist and author, blog post from May 15, 2007

Upon completion of this material, you should be able to:
- Name the common categories of vulnerabilities
- Discuss common system and network vulnerabilities
- Find network vulnerabilities using scanning tools and in-depth penetration testing
- Access sources of information about vulnerabilities and determine how best to remediate those vulnerabilities

Knowing What We Don't Know

Paige Davis was thinking about several computer attacks that had recently been mentioned in the news. In one case, government, nonprofit, and commercial documents had been stolen and posted on the Web. In another, several high-profile commercial organizations had had malware lurking inside their networks for months. In yet another, Internet infrastructure servers had been subjected to DoS attacks. Without a doubt, some of these incidents resulted from the fact that the necessary security controls had not been implemented. That didn't explain all the attacks, however; even diligent security measures could not thwart dedicated, persistent attackers.

Even beyond prepping the PCI audit, EBS saw the value in conducting regular security testing. By constantly testing the network and system defenses, it found problems before abusers did. What Paige needed to do was determine whether the findings from these tests were being taken seriously and whether the vulnerabilities were being addressed. How easily were the company's networks being compromised?

Introduction

To maintain secure networks, information security professionals must be prepared to identify network vulnerabilities, whether by hiring vulnerability assessment experts or by conducting self-assessments using scanning and penetration tools. The term "vulnerability," like so many terms in information security, has a variety of meanings. To a systems developer, a vulnerability may be a poorly designed input buffer that is at risk of an overflow attack, or it may be a badly designed exception handler that allows an escalation of user privileges. To system administrators, a vulnerability may be the presence of unneeded services, or it may be an easily guessed password.

In general, a **network security vulnerability** is a defect in a network device, device configuration or implementation, or process or procedure that, if exploited, may result in a violation of security policy, which in turn may lead to a loss of revenue, a loss of information, or a loss of value to the organization.

Common Vulnerabilities

Network vulnerabilities fall into three major categories: defects in software or firmware, errors in configuration or implementation, and weaknesses in processes and procedures.

Defects in Software or Firmware

Defects in software or firmware (i.e., software that is embedded in a device such as a router or network switch) are common. In fact, an industry has grown up around researching, identifying, and fixing them, then deploying the fixes across an organization's infrastructure.

In their book, *24 Deadly Sins of Software Security*,[1] Michael Howard, David LeBlanc, and John Viega categorize the 24 types of programming flaws that create most vulnerabilities. As shown in the following list, some of the more frequently encountered of these are buffer overruns, command injection attacks, and information leakage.

- Web application sins
  - SQL injection
  - Web-server-related vulnerabilities
  - Web-client-related vulnerabilities
  - Use of magic URLs, predictable cookies, and hidden form fields
- Implementation Sins
  - Buffer overruns
  - Format string problems
  - Integer overflows
  - C++ catastrophes
  - Catching exceptions
  - Command injection
  - Failure to handle errors correctly
  - Information leakage
  - Race conditions
  - Poor usability
  - Not updating easily
  - Executing code with too much privilege
  - Failure to protect stored data
  - Weaknesses introduced with mobile code
- Cryptographic Sins
  - Use of weak password-based systems
  - Weak random numbers
  - Using cryptography incorrectly
- Networking Sins
  - Failing to protect network traffic
  - Improper use of PKI, especially SSL
  - Trusting network name resolution

9

The Web-application vulnerabilities listed previously were discussed in Chapter 8. The remaining vulnerabilities are discussed in the following sections.

Buffer Overruns Buffer overruns (also called buffer overflows) arise when a programmer does not ensure that the quantity of input data fits within the size of the available data area (buffer). The most innocuous outcomes of exploiting these vulnerabilities are the program or application crashing, but an attacker can craft instructions that are executed by the computer when the buffer overflows. Executing these instructions is referred to as arbitrary code execution, and this mini-program can insert a backdoor for later access, install malware, or provide a remote login to an attacker.

Format String Problems Format string vulnerability arises when a software program asks the user for input, does not validate that input, and then passes the input to a formatting function. For example, a contact database program might ask the user to input a phone number to search, but if the code has a vulnerability in it and the user's entered phone number hasn't yet been validated, an attacker could input memory location, commands, or other data to control program execution. The classic (yet oversimplified) example involves the printf command in C:

```
printf (user_input);
```

In this example, the user input is not assigned a particular data type by the printf command, which opens the door to a variety of inputs. The proper form of the command would restrict input to a string data type, as follows:

```
printf ("%s", user_input);
```

Integer Overflows In its broadest sense, the term "integer overflow" refers to a wide range of arithmetic overflows that occur when a programmer does not restrict data to the size boundaries of their data types. For example, in Windows, a "short int" data type has a defined length of 16 bits. An attacker could input a number that caused the arithmetic operation to overflow the 16 bits used to represent the integer, thus resulting in an integer overflow.

Integer overflows are more subtle than stack or heap overflows in that they don't typically allow an attack to overwrite memory or direct program execution. Instead, the intent is to store an erroneous value that can be exploited later in the code. However, in cases where the overflowed integer is allocating a buffer size, the attack could attempt more serious cases of direct memory manipulation.

C++ Catastrophes These vulnerabilities have to do with intrinsic properties of the C++ programming language. In particular, most of these vulnerabilities rely on uninitialized function pointers in a class. If an attacker is able to modify the contents of the class—through initializing, reinitializing, freeing, or double-freeing a pointer—he or she could take control of program execution. Although this category of vulnerabilities focuses on C++, there are a number of other object-oriented languages that can be vulnerable.

Catching Exceptions Many languages, applications, and operating systems have standard error-handling routines. In some cases, the programming team does not implement the error-handling routine correctly and inadvertently introduces a vulnerability in that portion of the code. An attacker who has uncovered this vulnerability can cause an error in the program. Knowing that the program will head to the error-handling routine, the attacker can then intercept the call in order to run his own malicious code.

Command Injection Injection attacks can occur when the programmer does not properly validate user input, which allows an attacker to include input that, when passed to a database, can give rise to SQL injection vulnerabilities. Consider this example of a Windows command script:

```
echo off
set /p newdir = "Directory to be created:"
mkdir %newdir%
```

This simple script requests that the user input a directory name and then creates that directory. However, if a malicious user types mynewdir&cmd at the script's prompt, the content beginning with "&" (the command chaining character) opens another command window, which can be used to execute the command of the attacker's choice. SQL injection works similarly, by appending the attacker's SQL command(s) to a programmer's intended user input of a simple query variable, allowing the attacker to execute SQL commands that are different than those the developer intended.

A related issue, the failure to validate how user input is handled, can result in vulnerability to a cross-site scripting attack. This is a type of injection attack in which maliciously formed scripts are injected into otherwise trusted Web sites. The cross-site scripting (XSS) attack occurs when the attacker leverages a poorly configured or designed Web-based application so that it executes a browser-side script within the browser of the Web site visitor. Server-side applications (including variants of widely used Web servers) can enable these attacks to succeed. Any Web application that uses user-generated input directly as an output without validating or encoding it may be susceptible.

The attacker will use the XSS attack to inject a script crafted with malicious intent and ensure that it is executed by the browser of an unsuspecting user. That end user's browser will not suspect the script because it trusts the Web server to deliver trustworthy code. The browser being attacked will execute the script. Because the script is trusted, the attacker will have full access to the session tokens, cookies, and any other sensitive data being handled by the browser or accessible to the browser via the Web site it is visiting. For example, the Web camera or microphone of the client computer may be activated; or, when privileged accounts are used, the attacker can rewrite HTML content to the server.

Failure to Handle Errors Correctly Similar to problems in error-handling routines, the failure to handle errors correctly can lead to vulnerabilities in code. Most of the time, failing to catch an error and recover the program simply leads to a denial of service or a program crash; however, a crash is an opportunity to exploit the program execution flow. In *24 Deadly Sins of Software Security*, the authors arrange the error-handling mistakes into the following categories.[2]

- Yielding too much information (i.e., giving an attacker enough details to reliably troubleshoot and further hone an attack)
- Ignoring errors

- Misinterpreting errors
- Using useless return values
- Using non-error return values

Information Leakage Information leakage is the release of sensitive data outside the intended organization, either inadvertently through a variety of other vulnerabilities or purposefully by users in the organization. As mentioned in the previous section, there are cases in which the error message returned for bad input values gives away too much information about the authentication system. For example, consider this error message:

The password you entered is incorrect. You must use a password that is 6-8 characters long. No numbers or special characters are allowed.

Other cases are more subtle. An example is when a programmer doesn't realize that the application's owner doesn't want certain information released. Another example is when the program releases information that the programmer didn't realize would help the attacker carry out further attacks.

Race Conditions "Race conditions" refers to situations in which two threads, processes, or applications are able to modify a resource (and therefore interfere with each other) and the programmer has not taken precautions to ensure that the desired sequence of events is completed in the proper order. From a security standpoint, an attacker is looking to exploit the condition whereby a legitimate thread or process is consumed passing a code check and the malicious code slips by unnoticed.

The *24 Deadly Sins* authors mention an example in which an application, when creating a temporary file, first checks to see if the file already exists. If it does exist, the application uses the existing file. If not, the application creates a new file. In this scenario, an attacker could guess the application's temp file-naming conventions and insert a file with malicious data.

Poor Usability The problem with achieving security in applications is that the process may not be easy for users. When users find an application—or the secure way of using the application—difficult to work with, they often find a way to bypass the security features. Therefore, programmers must make the security measures both effective and easy to use.

Not Updating Easily Before there was auto-updating, most applications and operating systems required CDs or disks in order to perform an update. And only the most vigilant users—or those who wanted the latest features—even applied security patches, version upgrades, or fixes. Microsoft led the way in 2000 by developing an easy-to-use, automated, and comprehensive updating via the Internet with Automatic Updates.[3] Since then, most developers have updated their applications remotely using a similar type of service. Those companies who don't employ easy-to-use updating methods or automatic patch checking or who don't allow users to roll back patch problems pay the price with insecure code.

Executing Code with Too Much Privilege Many applications mistakenly require administrative privileges in order to be installed or run on a system. What's dangerous about this is that all software should be assumed to fail someday—and when it fails, that failure can be exploited by an attacker. To minimize the impact of such a situation occurring, applications should never run with administrative privileges. That way, even if an application's vulnerability is exploited, the attacker still has to find a way to elevate his privileges.

Failure to Protect Stored Data For applications that handle sensitive data, it is important to protect that data both while it is moving among systems (in transit) and while it is stored on disk (at rest). When attempting to protect data that's at rest, here are some common mistakes:

- The application relies on a file system that does not have file permissions (e.g., FAT).
- There are no data access controls, or the data access controls are weak.
- Permissions to the data are not set properly (e.g., a user is given full read, write, and execute privileges when read-only would be sufficient).
- The data is not encrypted, or the algorithm used to encrypt it is weak.

Weaknesses Introduced with Mobile Code Mobile code is code that is downloaded and executed on a user's computer—for example, a Web page that contains an ActiveX control, Flash application, or Java applet. Vulnerabilities introduced by programmers can be exploited, or attackers could trick users into executing malicious mobile code. To prevent this, browsers must implement strict control over which sites can execute the code or ensure that the code requires user approval. (This latter control, by allowing users to decide which mobile code to run, can lead to its own problems.)

Use of Weak Password-Based Systems Passwords are the bane of most security professionals' work lives. To avoid cracking, complex passwords are required, but users tend to hate complex passwords and, therefore, attempt to circumvent the password requirements. Software developers have a responsibility as well. The software developed should require complex password systems. Requirements for a complex password system include using a salt value (explained in Chapter 3), implementing strong encryption, requiring periodic password changes, and generally implementing a system where guessing a password or its hash is very difficult.

Weak Random Numbers Although most operating systems have libraries that provide pseudo-random numbers, these numbers are not truly random. This can be a security concern, because the strength of the security of encryption, session keys, and other cryptographic functions relies on the use of the degree of randomness of the values used as inputs. To generate adequately random pseudo-random numbers, programmers should use seed values and cryptographic libraries that provide the necessary functions.

Using Cryptography Incorrectly A number of cryptographic algorithms and systems provide powerful protection against data leakage. Unfortunately, application developers often incorrectly implement the cryptographic functions, or they fail to follow the proper steps to encrypt data properly. Implementing cryptography requires a rigorous effort in implementing the function. This class of vulnerabilities covers those software errors that fail to implement cryptography correctly.

9

Failing to Protect Network Traffic Network traffic is vulnerable to eavesdropping because a network medium is essentially an open channel. Through active network taps and other attacks, wired networks are just as vulnerable to sniffing as wireless networks. Once an attacker has access to the medium, he or she can record (and later replay) traffic, modify it, or hijack a communications session.

Improper Use of PKI, Especially SSL Public-key infrastructures (PKIs) are difficult to manage. Although the cryptographic algorithms are sound (for now) and the keys are exchanged effectively, revoking keys, issuing new keys, establishing trust among keys and providers, and other factors create enough complexity to introduce weaknesses. Additionally, SSL is a powerful method for encrypting data in transit. However, like any security mechanism, the application developer must implement it correctly in order for it to be effective.

Trusting Network Name Resolution DNS and its Microsoft cousin, WINS, are ubiquitous network services. Users only have to remember domain names or system names, not IP addresses. (This is especially important for the 128-bit long IPv6 addresses!) However, these services were not developed with security in mind; thus, the information they render can be manipulated by attackers. It is important for developers to understand that the data provided by network name resolution services can fail and that it is, therefore, important that applications verify the true communication destination during execution.

Errors in Configuration or Implementation

It would be easy to blame most of the network vulnerabilities on software developers. We hear the same story over and over: Developers create software, the software has a bug, and the bug is exploited for malicious gain by an attacker. What is talked about less often is how software can be exploited because of the way it is configured or implemented.

As an example, the Apache Software Foundation created one of the most popular Web servers in use today: Apache HTTP Server. Like any other software product, Apache HTTP Server has software vulnerabilities, but the security problems most organizations face from using Apache HTTP Server is the way it is installed and/or configured within the network environment.

In Apache HTTP Server, the MaxClients configuration directive indicates to the system how many requests HTTP Server processes concurrently. By default, the value is 256, which means that the server should be able to handle 256 user requests at a time. The problem is that HTTP Server creates a new process for every request. If a system is to handle 256 processes, it must have the memory capacity to do so. If the server administrator does not get the hardware configuration correct or does not set the MaxClients value to match the hardware, the admin will cause a denial of service situation with the Web server.

Another configuration problem on HTTP Server installations is that, by default, if the Web software can access parts of the underlying operating system's file system through normal URL mappings, it will. This is referred to as a directory traversal attack and was a very popular vulnerability to exploit in early versions of various Web server applications.

The Apache Software Foundation offers the following advice in regard to configuration issues to prevent directory traversal vulnerabilities:[4]

Consider the following example:

 # cd /; ln -s / public_html
Accessing http://localhost/~root/

This would allow clients to walk through the entire filesystem. To work around this, add the following block to your server's configuration:

<Directory />
Order Deny,Allow
Deny from all
</Directory>

This will forbid default access to filesystem locations. Add appropriate Directory blocks to allow access only in those areas you wish. For example,

<Directory /usr/users/*/public_html>
Order Deny,Allow
Allow from all
</Directory>
<Directory /usr/local/httpd>
Order Deny,Allow
Allow from all
</Directory>

The point here is that there are no inherent bugs in the Apache HTTP Server software, at least in relation to these issues. Instead, security problems are caused because administrators do not follow Apache's advice or do not implement the software correctly.

Weaknesses in Processes and Procedures

Although they generate much less buzz than software vulnerabilities, weaknesses in processes and procedures are just as hazardous, and they are more difficult to detect and fix because they typically involve the weakest link in security defense: the human element. These "soft" vulnerabilities often arise when a policy is violated or when the processes and procedures that implement the policy are inadequate or fail.

For example, consider passwords. Almost all organizations have policies that specify a degree of password complexity (e.g., the password must be at least eight characters long and include at least one alphabetic character) as well as a schedule for changing passwords and restrictions on how often they can be reused. However, if these policies are not enforced through the appropriate processes and procedures, the organization is vulnerable to a dictionary attack on access credentials.

To ensure its security policies are implemented, an organization should hold regular security-awareness training sessions for its employees as well as contractors and business partners. However, training by itself is not sufficient and must be supplemented with a regular review of the policies and their implementation. These reviews have many names, but a common one is the policy compliance audit.

Audits verify that an organization's security policies are prudent (cover the right issues) and are being implemented correctly. For example, to verify the implementation of the password policy, an auditor would seek evidence that employees are required to change their passwords on a regular basis and that the complexity and reuse standards are enforced as part of that process.

The auditor typically looks at two things: the policy and the evidence that the policy is being implemented. If the compliance is not documented, you are not in compliance with the policy.

Security professionals view the process of implementing policy and auditing (verifying) compliance with that policy as integral parts of policy development. Resources on policy and compliance are offered by the Computer Security Resource Center at the U.S. National Institute of Standards and Technology (*http://csrc.nist.gov*) and by textbooks such as *Management of Information Security*, by Michael Whitman and Herb Mattord (CENGAGE/Course Technology).

Finding Vulnerabilities on the Network

The heart of any vulnerability management program is identifying the various vulnerabilities we've outlined. This section discusses various automated tools that perform a wide variety of network reconnaissance and vulnerability mapping. It also discusses the manual process of penetration testing.

Scanning and Analysis Tools

To truly assess the risk within a computing environment, you must deploy technical controls using a strategy of defense in depth, which is likely to include intrusion detection/prevention systems (IDPS), active vulnerability scanners, passive vulnerability scanners, security information and event management (SIEM), and protocol analyzers (commonly referred to as sniffers). The IDPS helps to secure networks by detecting intrusions; the scanners and analyzers help to discover vulnerabilities. More specifically, scanners and analysis tools can find vulnerabilities in systems, holes in security monitoring coverage, and unsecured aspects of the network.

Scanner and analysis tools are typically used as part of an attack methodology to collect information that an attacker would need to launch a successful attack. The **attack methodology,** or **attack protocol**, is a series of steps or processes used by an attacker, in a logical sequence, to launch an attack against a target system or network, as shown in Figure 9-1. Although this approach is more of a pedagogic tool, it offers security testers a roadmap to follow when scanning the network.

Reconnaisance, fingerprinting, and vulnerability analysis tools are invaluable because they enable administrators to see what weaknesses the attacker sees. Some of these tools are extremely complex; others are rather simple. Some are expensive commercial products, but some of the best scanning and analysis tools were developed by the security research community and are available free on the Web. Others have been created by the attack community and have become widely used.

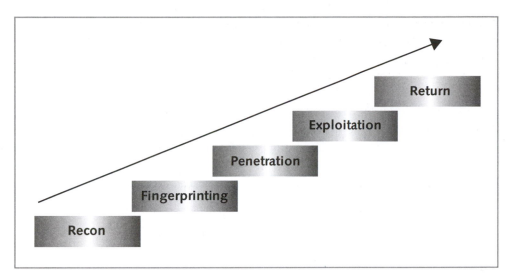

Figure 9-1 Standard attack methodology
© Cengage Learning 2013

There is nothing wrong with a security administrator using the tools that potential attackers use in order to examine network defenses and find areas that require additional attention. In the military, there is a long and distinguished history of generals inspecting the troops under their command before battle, walking down the line to inspect the equipment and mental preparedness of each soldier. In a similar way, the security administrator can use vulnerability analysis tools to inspect the units (host computers and network devices) under his or her command. A word of caution, though: Many of these scanning and analysis tools have distinct signatures, and some Internet service providers (ISPs) watch for these signatures and might pull the access privileges of those who use them. Administrators should establish a working relationship with their ISPs and notify them if planning to scan the external network.

Reconnaissance One of the preparatory parts of the attack methodology is the collection of publicly available information about a potential target, a process known as **reconnaissance** (often shortened to **recon** by Americans and to **recce** by the British). This process of exploring the Internet presence of a target is sometimes called **footprinting**. This could include information on the target's Web site, contact names and phone numbers, job posts issued by the target, Internet addresses owned or controlled by a target organization, and anything else that could provide valuable intelligence on the network, systems, and people associated with the target.

Target IP Addresses Imagine you're an attacker and your target is a Web site: fictitious.com. A great way to start conducting reconnaissance would be to identify the Web site's assigned address range, beginning with the IP address of the Web site itself. This is easily done using the `nslookup` command (note that these examples are contrived to use RFC1918 addresses rather than publicly routable addresses):

```
:nslookup www.ficticious.com
```

And its output might be:

```
Server: mynameserver.hackersrus.com
Address: 10.1.2.100
Non-authoritative answer:
Name: www.ficticious.com
Address: 192.168.3.100
```

The next step is to consult the responsible domain registrar to see what IP address ranges are registered to the organization. Assuming that ficticious.com is located in North America, you would use the ARIN database at *http://ws.arin.net/whois*.

A query on 192.168.3.100 reveals the following information about ficticious.com:

```
OrgName: Ficticious.com
OrgID: FC-7
Address: 126 Anywhere Lane
City: Somecity
StateProv: Somestate
PostalCode: 99999
Country: US

NetRange: 192.168.3.0 – 192.168.3.255
CIDR: 192.168.3.0/24
NetName: FC-8
NetHandle: NET-192-168-3-0-1
Parent: NET-192.168.0.0.0
NetType: Direct Assignment
NameServer: NS1.ficticious.com
NameServer: NS2.ficticious.com
NameServer: NS3.ficticious.com
NameServer: NS4.ficticious.com
Comment:
RegDate: 2007-12-20
Updated: 2011-12-23

RTechHandle: XV191-ARIN
RTechName: Doe, John
RTechPhone: +1-999-999-9999
RTechEmail: jdoe@ficticious.com
```

The most important information for recon purposes is the NetRange, which shows that ficticious.com has been assigned the addresses 192.168.3.0–192.168.3.255. All publicly accessible services will be offered on addresses in a valid NetRange, so when you begin the fingerprinting process, you will look at all those addresses.

Also useful is the name, phone number, and e-mail address of the technical contact. With this information, you might be able to launch a social-engineering attack on the organization. For this reason, it is a recommended practice to provide generic information rather than actual employee names (e.g., network operator, the phone number of the help desk, and an e-mail address such as *netops@ficticious.com*).

Target Web Site When attackers move to the next phase of their attack methodology they often look for more information about their targets. IP address information can be augmented by browsing the organization's Web pages because those pages usually contain information about internal systems, individuals developing Web pages, and other tidbits that can be used for social-engineering attacks. The `View Source` command, available on most popular Web browsers, allows users to see the source code behind the page. Details in this source code can provide attackers with clues and give them insights into an internal network's configuration, such as the locations of and directories for Common Gateway Interface (CGI) scripts and the names or addresses of computers and servers.

Business Research Another source of attack intelligence is the use of business-oriented Web sites, such as Hoovers, Forbes, Google Finance, and Yahoo! Business. These sites routinely provide data used for market research as well as more general information about a company. In doing so, they often reveal information that attackers can use, like: company mergers (i.e., two companies will be connecting networks), company divestitures (i.e., network will be divided), or information on company officers for social-engineering attacks.

Google Hacking Another type of security research is called Google hacking. The idea is to use the advanced search options provided by Google to locate more and more information about your target. Although advanced Google searches are not malicious in and of themselves, attackers are using the search to further their recon efforts. For example, a simple search might reveal any site that links to a proposed target. By doing more focused research into a company, however, an attacker can often find additional Internet locations that are not commonly associated with the company—such as business-to-business (B2B) partners and subsidiaries. Armed with this information, the attacker can find the weakest link into the target network.

Let's say Company X has a large datacenter located in Atlanta. The datacenter has been secured, making it very hard for an attacker to break into it via the Internet. However, the attacker has run a "link:companyx.com" query on Google and found a small Web server that links to Company X's main Web server. After further investigation, the attacker learns that the small Web server was set up by an administrator at a remote facility, and that the remote facility has, via its own leased lines, an unrestricted internal link into Company X's corporate datacenter. The attacker can now attack the weaker site at the remote facility and use this compromised network—which is an internal network—to attack the true target. If a company has a trusted network connection with 15 business partners, one weak business partner can compromise all 16 networks.

Here are some of the more complicated and elegant Google hacks catalogued on the Google Hacking Database (GHDB)[5] Web site:

- intitle:index.of.secret, intitle:index.of.private, intitle:index.of.password—returns Web sites that display indexes of files labeled with sensitive names
- indexof:cgi-binreturns—Web sites that allow indexing of scripts located in the cgi-bin directory
- inurl:j2ee/examples/jsp—returns Web sites that contain sample JavaScript or JSP scripts that come with the Java 2 Platform, Enterprise Edition application
- intitle:webeye inurl:login.ml—returns links to WebEye webcams available via the Internet

9

Fingerprinting After gathering publicly available information, the attacker will often communicate with the systems on the target network. This is the **fingerprinting** stage of the attack methodology, a systematic survey of the target organization's Internet addresses, conducted to identify the network services offered by the hosts in that range. Using the tools discussed in the next sections, fingerprinting reveals information about the internal structure and operational nature of the target system or network.

Sam Spade To assist in the recon process, the attacker will often use an enhanced Web scanner that, among other things, scans an entire Web site for valuable pieces of information, such as server names and e-mail addresses. One such scanner is called Sam Spade. The original developer's Web site, *samspade.org*, has not been operational for some time. However, a number of other Web sites also offer the Sam Spade scanner, such as *www.petri.co.il/sam_spade_tools.htm* and *www.pcworld.com/downloads/file/fid,4709-order,1-page,1/description.html*. A sample screenshot from Sam Spade is shown in Figure 9-2. This scanner can also do a host of other scans and probes, such as sending multiple ICMP information requests (pings), attempting to retrieve multiple and cross-zoned DNS queries, and performing network analysis queries (known, from the commonly used UNIX command for performing the analysis, as traceroutes). These are all powerful diagnostic and hacking activities. Sam Spade is not, however, considered hackerware (or hacker-oriented software); rather, it has become recognized as a utility that happens to be useful to network administrators and miscreants alike.

Figure 9-2 Fingerprinting with Sam Spade
Source: SamSpade

Wget UNIX or Linux systems support a tool called "wget" that allows a remote individual to "mirror" entire Web sites. With this tool, attackers can copy an entire Web site and then go through the source HTML, JavaScript, and Web-based forms at their leisure, collecting and collating all the data from the source code that will be useful to them for their attacks.

Port Scanners Port-scanning utilities (or **port scanners**) are tools used by both attackers and defenders to identify (or fingerprint) the computers that are active on a network as well as the ports and services active on those computers, the functions and roles the machines are fulfilling, and other useful information. These tools can scan for specific types of computers, protocols, or resources, or the scans can be more generalized. You need to understand the network environment you are using so that you can select the tool most suited to the data collection task at hand. For instance, if you are trying to identify a Windows computer in a typical network, a built-in feature of the operating system, nbtstat, may be able to get the answer you need very quickly, without the installation of a scanner. This tool does not work on other types of networks, however, so you must know your tools in order to make the best use of the features of each.

The more specific the scanner is, the more useful the information it provides to attackers and defenders. However, you should keep a generic, broad-based scanner in your toolbox as well, to help locate and identify rogue nodes on the network that administrators may be unaware of. Probably the most popular port scanner is Nmap, which runs on both UNIX and Windows systems. You can find out more about Nmap at *http://nmap.org*. As of 2007, Nmap includes the Zenmap GUI front end,[6] which simplifies the use of the tool.

A port is a network channel or connection point in a data communications system. Within TCP/IP, TCP, and User Datagram Protocol (UDP), port numbers differentiate the multiple communication channels that are used to connect to the network services being offered on the same network device. Each application within TCP/IP has a unique port number. Some have default ports but can also use other ports. Some of the well-known TCP port numbers are presented in Table 9-1. In all, there are 65,536 port numbers in use for TCP and another 65,536 port numbers for UDP. Services using the TCP/IP protocol can run on any port; however, the services with reserved ports (also called well-known ports) generally run on ports 1–1023. Port 0 is not used. Ports greater than 1023 are typically referred to as ephemeral ports and may be randomly allocated to server and client processes.

Why should you secure open ports? Because an open port is an open door and can be used by an attacker to send commands to a computer, potentially gain access to a server, and possibly exert control over a networking device. The general rule is to remove from service or at least secure any port not absolutely necessary to conducting business. For example, if a business doesn't host Web services, there is no need for port 80 to be available on its servers.

Firewall Analysis Tools Understanding exactly where an organization's firewall is located and what the existing rule sets on the firewall do are very important steps for an attacker or any security administrator. There are several tools that automate the remote discovery of firewall rules and assist the administrator (or the attacker) in analyzing the rules to determine exactly what they allow and what they reject.

The Nmap tool mentioned earlier has some advanced options that are useful for firewall analysis. The Nmap option called "Idle scanning" (which is run with the -sI switch) allows you to bounce your scan across a firewall by using one of the idle DMZ hosts as the initiator

TCP Port Numbers	TCP Service
20 and 21	FTP
22	SSH
23	Telnet
25	SMTP
53	DNS
67 and 68	DHCP or bootstrap
80	HTTP
110	POP3
161	SNMP
194	IRC
443	HTTPS
8080	Used for HTTP proxy services

Table 9-1 Commonly Used Port Numbers
© Cengage Learning 2013

of the scan. More specifically, given that most operating systems do not use truly random IP packet identification numbers (IP IDs), if there is more than one host in the DMZ and one host uses nonrandom IP IDs, then the attacker can query the server (server X) and obtain the currently used IP ID as well as the known algorithm for incrementing the IP IDs. The attacker can then spoof a packet that is allegedly from server X and destined for an internal IP address behind the firewall. If the port is open on the internal machine, the internal machine replies to server X with a SYN-ACK packet, which forces server X to respond with a TCP RESET packet. In responding with the TCP RESET, server X increments its IP ID number. The attacker can now query server X a second time to see if the IP ID has incremented. If it has, the attacker knows that the internal machine is alive and that the internal machine has the queried service port open. In a nutshell, running the Nmap Idle scan allows an attacker to scan an internal network as if he or she were physically located on a trusted machine inside the DMZ.

Another tool that can be used to analyze firewalls is Firewalk. Written by noted author and network security expert Mike Schiffman with David Goldsmith,[7] Firewalk uses incrementing Time-to-Live (TTL) packets to determine the path into a network as well as the default firewall policy. Running Firewalk against a target machine reveals where routers and firewalls are filtering traffic to the target host. More information on Firewalk can be obtained from *http://packetstormsecurity.org/UNIX/audit/firewalk/*.

Another firewall analysis tool is hping, which is a modified ping client. It supports multiple protocols, and you can use a command line to specify nearly any of the ping parameters. For instance, you can use hping with modified TTL values to determine the infrastructure of a DMZ. You can use hping with specific ICMP flags in order to bypass poorly configured

firewalls (i.e., firewalls that allow all ICMP traffic to pass through) and find internal systems. You can find hping at *www.hping.org*.

Administrators who are wary of using the same tools that attackers use should remember two important points: (1) Regardless of the nature of the tool used to validate or analyze a firewall's configuration, it is the intent of the user that dictates how the information gathered will be used, and (2) In order to defend a computer or network, it is necessary to understand the ways it can be attacked. Thus, a tool that can help close up an open or poorly configured firewall helps the network defender minimize the risk from attack.

Operating System Detection Tools Identifying vulnerabilities on a target computer is much easier once an attacker knows the operating system. As a system administrator or security tester, the same logic holds true. Once the OS is known, it is easy to determine all the vulnerabilities to which it is susceptible. There are many tools that use networking protocols to determine a remote computer's OS. One such tool is XProbe2, which uses ICMP to determine the remote OS. This tool can be found at *http://sourceforge.net/projects/xprobe/*. XProbe2 sends a lot of different ICMP queries against the target host. As reply packets are received, XProbe2 matches these responses from the target's TCP/IP stack with its own internal database of known responses. Because most OSs have a unique way of responding to ICMP requests, Xprobe2 is able to find matches and thus detect the operating systems of remote computers. System and network administrators should take note of this and restrict the use of ICMP through their organization's firewalls and (when possible) within their organization's internal networks.

The port scanner Nmap, described earlier, also includes a version detection engine, which attempts to identify the operating system version and version information for any running services, as shown in Figure 9-3.

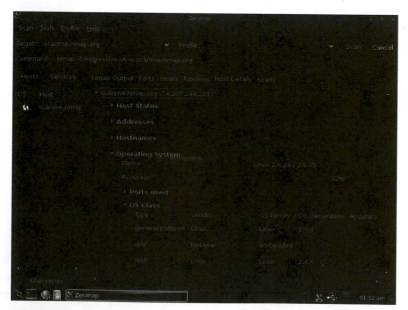

Figure 9-3 Version detection with Nmap

Source: Linux

9

Wireless Security Tools 802.11 wireless networks exist as subnets on nearly all large networks. A wireless connection, though convenient, has many potential security holes. An organization that spends all its time securing the wired network while neglecting its wireless networks is opening itself up for a security breach. As a security professional, you must assess the risk of wireless networks. The wireless security toolkit you choose should include the ability to sniff wireless traffic, scan wireless hosts, and assess the level of privacy or confidentiality afforded on the wireless network.

There are several tools that apply packet sniffing to wireless networks, including NetStumbler, which is offered as freeware and can be found at *www.netstumbler.org*. (For Windows Vista and Windows 7 support, a similar tool, called Vistumbler, is available at *www.vistumbler.net*.) Figure 9-4 shows NetStumbler running on a Windows XP machine. Another wireless tool is AirSnare, also free, which can be run on a low-end wireless workstation. AirSnare monitors the airwaves for any new devices or access points. When it finds one, it sounds an alarm alerting the administrators that a new, potentially dangerous wireless apparatus is attempting access on a closed wireless network. Figure 9-5 shows AirSnare in action.

Finally, Aircrack-ng (*http://www.aircrack-ng.org/doku.php*) is a tool designed to crack WEP and WPA-PSK keys to allow packet sniffing and wireless network auditing.

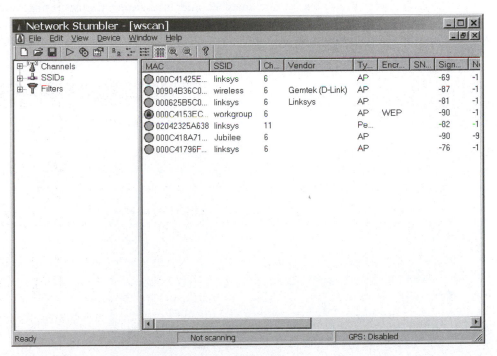

Figure 9-4   Wireless scanning with NetStumbler
Source: NetStumbler

Vulnerability Scanners Vulnerability scanners are tools designed to identify known system vulnerabilities. They fall into three types: active, passive, and fuzzers. Active scanners produce network traffic to actively probe systems for vulnerabilities. Passive scanners listen to network traffic to analyze traffic for vulnerabilities. Fuzzers produce a variety of user

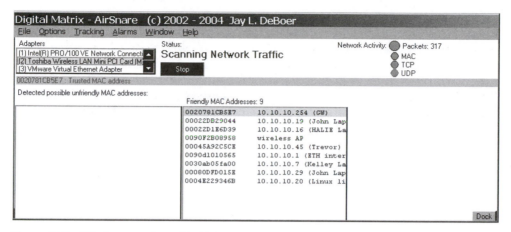

Figure 9-5 Wireless scanning with AirSnare
Source: AirSnare

inputs to monitor programs for unexpected crashes. Each type of scanner is discussed further in the upcoming sections. Table 9-2 lists the Top 10 vulnerability scanners, according to Security Tools *(sectools.org)*. The popularity of these tools was determined by surveys answered by the security community.[8]

Ranking	Product	Web Page
1	Nessus	*www.nessus.org* and *www.tenablesecurity.com*
2	OpenVAS	*www.openvas.org/*
3	Core Impact	*www.coresecurity.com/content/core-impact-overview*
4	Nexpose	*www.rapid7.com/products/vulnerability-management.jsp*
5	GFI LanGuard	*www.gfi.com/network-security-vulnerability-scanner*
6	QualsyGuard	*www.qualys.com/*
7	MBSA (Microsoft Baseline Security Analyzer)	*technet.microsoft.com/en-us/security/cc184923*
8	Retina	*www.eeye.com/Products/Retina.aspx*
9	Secunia PSI	*secunia.com/vulnerability_scanning/personal/*
10	Nipper	*nipper.titania.co.uk/*

Table 9-2 Top 10 Vulnerability Scanner Products[9]
Source: sectools.org
© Cengage Learning 2013

There are also support Web sites such as *http://www.vulnerabilityassessment.co.uk/index.htm*, which provide information on other products.

Active Vulnerability Scanners An **active vulnerability scanner** initiates traffic on the network in order to identify security holes. In doing so, it exposes usernames and groups, open network shares, and configuration problems as well as other vulnerabilities in servers. An example of a vulnerability scanner is GFI LanGuard, which is available as a 30-day evaluation download, then requires a paid registration. Another vulnerability scanner is Nessus, a professional freeware utility that uses IP packets to identify available hosts, the services (ports) each host is offering, the operating system and OS version they are running, the type of packet filters and firewalls in use, and dozens of other network characteristics. Figures 9-6 and 9-7 show sample LanGuard and Nessus result screens.

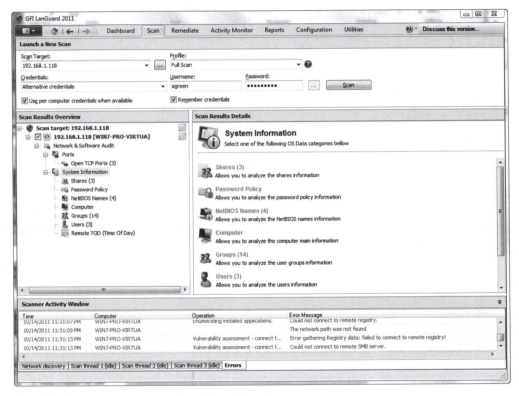

Figure 9-6   Vulnerability scanning with LanGuard
Source: LANGuard

Passive Vulnerability Scanners A **passive vulnerability scanner** listens in on the network and identifies vulnerable versions of both server and client software. There are currently two primary vendors offering this type of scanning solution: Tenable Network Security, which offers a product called Passive Vulnerability Scanner, and Sourcefire, which offers a product called RNA. Passive scanners are advantageous in that they do not require vulnerability analysts to get prior approval for testing. They simply monitor the network connections to and from a server to obtain a list of vulnerable applications. Furthermore, passive vulnerability scanners can find client-side vulnerabilities that are typically not found by active scanners. For instance, an active scanner operating without Windows Domain Admin rights would be unable to determine the version of Internet Explorer running on a desktop machine, but a passive scanner can observe the traffic to and from the client to make that determination.

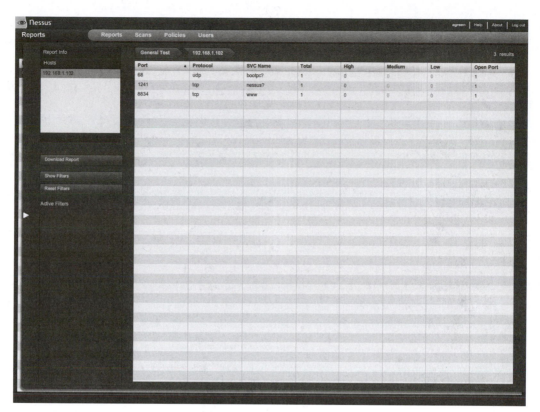

Figure 9-7   Vulnerability scanning with Nessus
Source: Nessus

Fuzzers Vulnerability scanners are proficient at finding known, documented holes, but what happens if the Web server is from a new vendor, or if the application was developed by an internal development team? That's where a class of vulnerability scanners called black-box scanners, or fuzzers, comes in. **Fuzz testing**, also known as "fuzzing," is a straight-forward technique that looks for vulnerabilities in a program or protocol by feeding random input into the program or the network running the protocol. Vulnerabilities can be detected by measuring the outcome of the random inputs.

Examples of fuzzers are shown in Table 9-3.[10] For a list of protocol-specific and other fuzz-testing tools, go to *http://blogold.chinaunix.net/u2/69926/showart_706962.html.*

One fuzz scanner, SPIKE, has two primary components. The first is the SPIKE Proxy, a full-blown proxy server. As Web site visitors use the proxy, SPIKE builds a database of each of the traversed pages, forms, and other Web-specific information. When the Web site's owner determines that enough history has been collected to fully characterize the Web sites, SPIKE can check the Web site for bugs—that is, administrators can use the usage history collected by SPIKE to traverse all known pages, forms, active programs (e.g., asp, cgi-bin) and can test the system by attempting overflows, SQL injection, cross-site scripting, and many other classes of Web attacks.

Fuzzer APIs and Frameworks	
Product	**Web Page**
SPIKE	*http://immunityinc.com/resources-freesoftware.shtml*
Scratch	*http://packetstormsecurity.org/UNIX/misc/scratch.rar*
LXAPI	*http://lxapi.sourceforge.net/*
PEACH	*http://peachfuzzer.com/*
antiparser	*http://antiparser.sourceforge.net/*
Autodafe	*http://autodafe.sourceforge.net/*

Web Application Fuzzing Tools	
Product	**Web Page**
MielieTool	*https://www.ee.oulu.fi/research/ouspg/MielieTools*
Wapiti	*http://wapiti.sourceforge.net/*
WebFuzzer	*http://gunzip.altervista.org/g.php?f=projects#webfuzzer*
HP WebInspect	*https://h10078.www1.hp.com/cda/hpms/display/main/hpms_content.jsp? zn=bto&cp=1-11-201-200^9570_4000_100__&jumpid=reg_R1002_USEN*

Browser Fuzzing Tools	
Product	**Web Page**
MangleMe	*http://lcamtuf.coredump.cx/soft/mangleme.tgz*
AxMan	*http://metasploit.com/users/hdm/tools/axman/*
COMRaider	*http://labs.idefense.com/software/fuzzing.php#more_comraider*
TagBruteForcer	*http://research.eeye.com/html/tools/*
Hamachi	*http://metasploit.com/users/hdm/tools/hamachi/hamachi.html*

Table 9-3 Fuzzing Tools
© Cengage Learning 2013

SPIKE can fuzz any protocol that utilizes TCP/IP. By sniffing a session and building a SPIKE script, or building a full-blown C program using the SPIKE API, a user can simulate and fuzz nearly any protocol. Figure 9-8 shows a sample SPIKE script being prepared to fuzz the ISAKMP protocol (which is used by VPNs). Figure 9-9 shows the SPIKE program generic_send_udp fuzzing an IKE server using the SPIKE script. As you can see, SPIKE can be used to quickly fuzz and find weaknesses in nearly any protocol.

Penetration Once an attacker has gained the necessary intelligence on the target, he can start penetrating the network. Typically, this is accomplished through a type of manual testing called penetration testing (more on that shortly). However, there are also tools that automatically attempt to exploit vulnerabilities on a system.

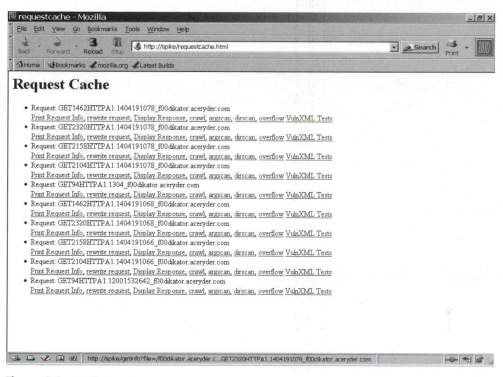

Figure 9-8   SPIKE in action
Source: BackTrack

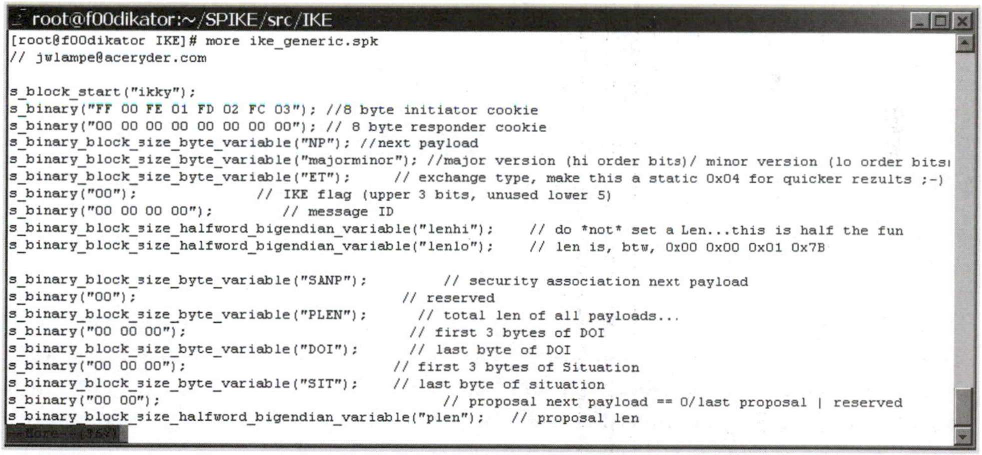

Figure 9-9   SPIKE vs. IKE
Source: BackTrack

The Nessus scanner has a class of attacks called "destructive." If these are enabled, Nessus attempts common overflow techniques against a target host. Along with fuzzers, Nessus in destructive mode can be a very dangerous tool and should only be used in a lab environment. In fact, these tools are so powerful that even system defenders who use them are not likely to employ the most aggressive modes on their own production networks.

There is a class of scanners that actually exploit the remote machine and allow the vulnerability analyst (sometimes called a penetration tester) to create an account, modify a Web page, or view data. These tools can be very dangerous and should be used only when absolutely necessary. This is usually when the applications or systems can be isolated in a test environment. Examples of testing tools include Core Impact, Immunity's CANVAS, and the Metasploit Framework.

Of these three, only the Metasploit Framework is available without a license fee (see *www.metasploit.com*). The Metasploit Framework is a collection of exploits coupled with an interface that allows you to customize exploitation of vulnerable systems. For instance, you can customize the overflow to exploit a Microsoft Exchange server and enable the specific attack script to insert a unique command (perhaps to create a new user and add that user to the administrators group). See Figure 9-10 for a screenshot of the Metasploit Framework in action.

Figure 9-10   Vulnerability exploitation with the Metasploit Framework
Source: Metasploit Framework

Tools can also be combined to form a quite effective penetration solution. For example, Nmap can identify open network ports and make a good guess as to the software versions running on the servers. This information can then be used with the Metasploit Framework to run all available exploits for that software and version. In Figure 9-11, this operation is shown as the "hack-o-matic." For this technique to succeed, there only has to be one server accessible to the attacker somewhere in the infrastructure.

Exploitation   When considered as part of the attack methodology, "exploitation" refers to the tools and techniques for breaking into more systems, gaining further network access, or gaining access to more resources. Other than netcat (see the next section), there are fewer legitimate security tools that fall into this category; however, sniffers can be incredibly

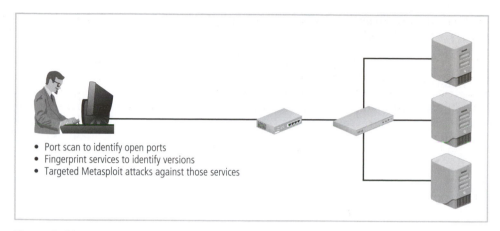

Figure 9-11 Hack-o-matic technique
© Cengage Learning 2013

powerful in gaining further access to networks during an attack or helping administrators detect further vulnerabilities.

Netcat Once the remote system has been subverted, many attackers use FTP, TFTP, and similar types of file transfer utilities to store the necessary attack tools in a data cache. These tools can then be transferred to other servers within the target environment and used later. One of the most useful utilities to accomplish this type of file transfer is netcat. Netcat is a full client and server environment that allows the transfer of data between netcat installations.

However, netcat also does a lot more: it can be used as a remote shell utility to allow control of a remote system, as shown in Figure 9-12. With this feature, attackers and testers alike can use netcat as a backdoor to allow future access to the exploited system. Netcat can also grab Web banners—and it can act as a port scanner. This tool offers a cornucopia of security testing features.

Figure 9-12 Netcat
Source: netcat

Packet Sniffers A **packet sniffer** (sometimes called a network protocol analyzer) is a network tool that collects copies of packets from the network and analyzes them or stores the packets for later analysis. As such, it can provide a network administrator with valuable information for diagnosing and resolving networking issues. In the wrong hands, however, a sniffer can be used to eavesdrop on network traffic.

Many administrators feel that they are safe from sniffer attacks when their computing environment is primarily a switched network environment. This couldn't be farther from the truth. There are a number of open-source sniffers that support alternative networking approaches that can, in turn, enable packet sniffing in a switched network environment. Two of these alternative networking approaches are ARP-spoofing and session hijacking, both of which use man-in-the-middle tools like ettercap. To secure data that's in transit across any network, organizations must use encryption.

Typically, to use these types of programs most effectively, the user must be connected to a network from a central location. Simply tapping into an Internet connection floods you with more data than can be readily processed and, technically, constitutes a violation of the Wiretap Act. In order to comply with legal requirements, an administrator using a packet sniffer must: (1) be on a network that the organization owns, (2) be under direct authorization of the owners of the network, and (3) have knowledge and consent of the content creators. If all three conditions are met, the administrator can selectively collect and analyze packets to identify and diagnose problems on the network. The first two conditions are self-explanatory. The third, consent, is usually handled by having all system users sign a release when they are issued a user ID and passwords. Incidentally, these three conditions are the same requirements for monitoring employee activities on the network. Unless consent from all users of a network has been acquired, packet sniffing should be construed as a form of employee monitoring.

There are both commercial and open-source sniffers. A free, client-based network protocol analyzer that happens to be free is Wireshark (*www.wireshark.com*), known as Ethereal until a trademark battle in 2006. Wireshark allows the administrator to examine data from both live network traffic and captured traffic. It also has several other features, including a language filter and a TCP session reconstruction utility. Figure 9-13 shows a sample screen from Wireshark.

Table 9-4 provides a list of the Top 10 Packet sniffers—again, according to survey results from the security community.

Return When considered as part of the attack methodology, "return" refers to actions an attacker takes to ensure she is able to return to the target unobstructed. This could entail installing backdoors, installing bots, creating user accounts, or other actions. There are no legitimate security tools administrators can use to mimic this stage, nor are such tools necessary. If the team can stop the attack in the first place, there will be no return.

Penetration Testing

Many organizations use a specialized service called a penetration test to assess their security posture on a regular basis. A penetration test uses all the techniques and tools available to an attacker in an attempt to compromise or penetrate an organization's defenses.

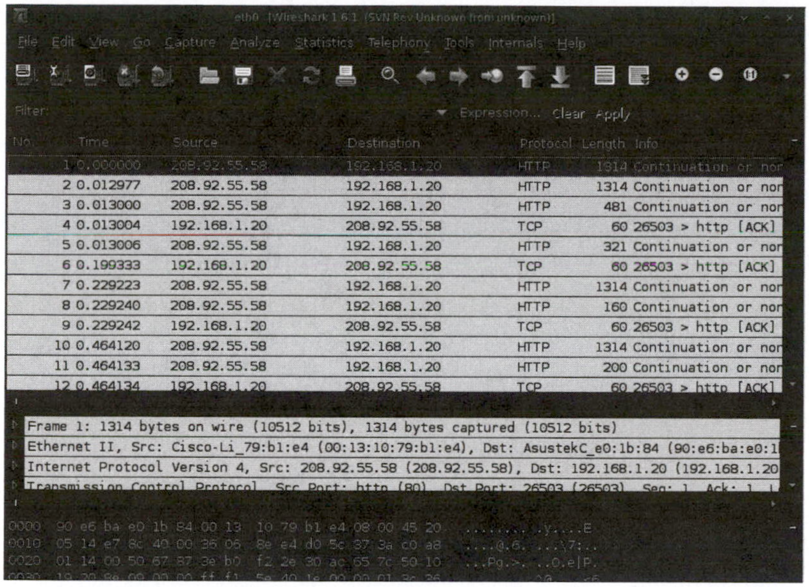

Figure 9-13 Wireshark

Source: Wireshark

Ranking	Product	Web Page
1	Wireshark	www.wireshark.org
2	Cain & Abel	www.oxid.it/cain.html
3	Tcpdump	www.tcpdump.org/
4	Kismet	www.kismetwireless.net/
5	Ettercap	ettercap.sourceforge.net/
6	NetStumbler	www.stumbler.net/
7	Dsniff	www.monkey.org/~dugsong/dsniff/
8	Ntop	www.ntop.org/
9	Ngrep	ngrep.sourceforge.net/
10	EtherApe	etherape.sourceforge.net/

Table 9-4 Top 10 Packet Sniffers[11]

© Cengage Learning 2013

Penetration tests can be performed in a variety of ways and with different scopes. For example, the organization might only wish to assess the quality of its network defenses and would, therefore, limit the scope of the test to its externally accessible network resources (Web sites, e-commerce sites, wireless networking infrastructure, etc.). For a more complete assessment, the scope may include all the organization's defenses, including physical security.

The scope will depend on the goal of the test—for example, whether the compromise will stop at identifying an exploitable vulnerability or whether the exploit should actually be carried out. There are advantages and disadvantages to either decision. For example, stopping at the identification phase has minimal impact on the organization, whereas carrying out a full exploit exercises the organization's incident detection and response plans.

Penetration testing can be performed by an internal group (so-called "red teams") or outsourced. Needless to say, when a penetration (or pen) test is outsourced, the agreement must carefully specify the scope and limitations of the test and ensure absolute confidentiality of the results.

One variable of the penetration test, whether it's performed internally or outsourced, is the amount of information provided to the red team. There are three categories of testing:

- *Black box*—The red team is given no information about the organization and approaches the organization as an external attacker. Although this is the most realistic type of test, it also requires the most work on the part of the red team and is, therefore, the most expensive. This is also the most difficult type of test for an organization to do internally, as its employees cannot really approach the organization as if they knew nothing about it.

- *Gray box*—The red team is given some general information about the organization, such as its general network architecture, its network address ranges, and the software versions it uses. This reduces the level of effort for the red team and reduces the cost of the exercise.

- *White box*—The red team is given full information about the organization and its structure, including detailed network maps, software documentation, details on alarm systems, and the like. This type of test is perhaps easiest to perform and can serve the very useful purpose of verifying that the controls in place are actually installed and operating correctly and, most importantly, do what they are supposed to.

The tools used in a penetration test are the same tools security professionals use to defend the organization (a fine example of dual-use technology). Whereas a defender uses the tools to identify potential weaknesses that can be remediated, the red team uses them as an attacker would, to identify portals and methods of entry.

Remember that not all attacks against an organization's assets are technical attacks. For example, an attacker, using the domain registration information for ficticious.com, could call the organization's help desk and claim he was the network's technical contact, then have the organization's password reset.

Recommended Vulnerability Assessment Methodology

Now that you understand the tools involved in conducting a vulnerability assessment, it's time to put them all together. An excellent reference in this area is the NIST Special Publication 800-115, which recommends using the set of review techniques shown in Table 9-5 and the Baseline reviewer skills shown in Table 9-6. Together, these provide a systematic approach to identifying and validating vulnerabilities in systems and networks.

Evaluating and validating vulnerabilities in an organization's systems falls into three stages, each stage including multiple steps:[14]

Technique	Capabilities
Documentation Review	• Evaluates policies and procedures for technical accuracy and completeness
Log Review	• Provides historical information on system use, configuration, and modification • Could reveal potential problems and policy deviations
Ruleset Review	• Reveals holes in ruleset-based security controls
System Configuration Review	• Evaluates the strength of system configuration • Validates that systems are configured in accordance with hardening policy
Network Sniffing	• Monitors network traffic on the local segment to capture information such as active systems, operating systems, communication protocols, services, and applications • Verifies encryption of communications
File Integrity Checking	• Identifies changes to important files; can also identify certain forms of unwanted files, such as well-known attacker tools

Table 9-5 NIST SP 800-115 Review Techniques[12]
© Cengage Learning 2013

9

Technique	Baseline Skill Set
Documentation Review	General knowledge of security from a policy perspective
Log Review	Knowledge of log formats and ability to interpret and analyze log data; ability to use automated log analysis and log correlation tools
Ruleset Review	Knowledge of ruleset formats and structures; ability to correlate and analyze rulesets from a variety of devices
System Configuration Review	Knowledge of secure system configuration, including OS hardening and security policy configuration for a variety of operating systems; ability to use automated security configuration testing tools

Table 9-6 NIST SP 800-115 Baseline Skill Sets for Review Techniques[13]
© Cengage Learning 2013

Stage I: Identify technical weaknesses in a system's security architecture and security configuration while minimizing risk from the assessment itself.

- *Step 1. Documentation Review. Identify policy and procedure weaknesses and security architecture flaws.*

- *Step 2. Ruleset and Security Configuration Review. Identify deviations from organizational security policies in the forms of the system's network security architecture and system security flaws.*

- *Step 3. Wireless Scanning. Identify rogue wireless devices within proximity of the system, and additional security architecture weaknesses related to the wireless networks used by the system.*

- *Step 4. Network Discovery and Vulnerability Scanning. Identify all active hosts within the system and their known vulnerabilities.*

Stage II. Identify and validate technical weaknesses in a system's security architecture and security configuration—validation will include attempts to exploit selected vulnerabilities.

- *Step 1. Ruleset and Security Configuration Review. Identify deviations from organizational security policies in the forms of the system's network security architecture and system security flaws.*

- *Step 2. Network Discovery and Vulnerability Scanning. Identify all active hosts within the system and their known vulnerabilities.*

- *Step 3. Penetration Test with Social Engineering. Validate vulnerabilities in the system.*

Stage III. Identify and validate technical weaknesses in a system's security architecture and security configuration from an external attacker's viewpoint—validation will include attempting to exploit some or all vulnerabilities. Evaluate the effectiveness of the organization's audit capabilities for attacks against the system.

- *Step 1. External Penetration Testing. Perform external network discovery, port scanning, vulnerability scanning, and attacks to identify and validate system vulnerabilities.*

- *Step 2. Log Review. Review security control audit logs for the system to determine their effectiveness in capturing information relating to external penetration testing activities.*

For more information on the implementation of this methodology, review SP 800-115 at *http://csrc.nist.gov/publications/nistpubs/800-115/SP800-115.pdf.*

Addressing Vulnerabilities

Understanding risks posed by a software vulnerability starts with the disclosure of the vulnerability by security researchers or by the software vendor. From there, the vulnerability assessment tools can start to look for the vulnerabilities and notify organizations when they exist. Once a system vulnerability has been discovered, either through testing or through being notified by the software vendor, the risk posed by the vulnerability must be assessed. After all, if there is minimal risk, there's no reason to do anything. In general, though, there are three ways to address a vulnerability:

- Fix it (e.g., apply a software patch)
- Mitigate it (e.g., provide IDPS to stop applicable attacks)
- Ignore it
- Remove the system, service, or process

Vulnerability Disclosure

Organizations must stay informed of vulnerabilities in the software products they deploy. There are two general sources of this type of information: software vendors and security researchers. These two sources employ very different philosophies on the kind of information that is shared with the general public. Vendors tend to take a long time to fix a vulnerability—if they admit the vulnerability exists at all, that is. (There's no additional revenue to be gained by diverting resources to fixing bugs.) However, most security researchers believe that everyone needs to know about vulnerabilities as soon as they are discovered. The idea is that, if attackers know about a vulnerability, so should administrators.

There are three philosophical approaches to handling the disclosure of vulnerabilities that encompass the views of both groups:

- Full disclosure—Announce to the public immediately upon discovery.

- Delayed disclosure—Disclose only after a fix is available.

- Responsible disclosure—Report the vulnerability to the vendor. Allow the vendor time to develop a fix. If too much time passes, report the vulnerability to the public.

The advantages and disadvantages of these approaches have been hotly debated since the early-1990s.[15] Well-known security experts such as Bruce Schneier advocate full disclosure[16] because it is likely that attackers already know about the vulnerabilities and public disclosure encourages vendors to provide fixes in a timely fashion, but others maintain that publicly disclosing the vulnerability only encourages the production of automated attack tools that "script kiddies" can use to mount attacks.

A successful example of a delayed disclosure was the Sendmail vulnerability that was discovered in 2003.[17] This vulnerability was quietly communicated to the affected vendors and only publicly disclosed when a fix was available. In fact, the first public exploit of the vulnerability appeared the day after its existence became public.

Full-disclosure adherents are quick to point out that there is really no way to ensure that a vulnerability has not been discovered in the hacker underground and that there are often measures that can prevent a successful exploit in advance of the fix.

A complicating factor is that the person who discovers a vulnerability is the one who decides whom to tell. Although many security researchers follow the "responsible disclosure" approach of communicating the vulnerability to the affected vendor and withholding public disclosure until a vendor fix is released (or a reasonable amount of time has passed), others may immediately disclose the vulnerability to the hacker underground, on public Web sites, or via full-disclosure mailing lists.

This debate shows no sign of resolving; wise security professionals carefully monitor both vendor security announcements and the full-disclosure mailing lists.

How can security professionals remain informed of all the vulnerabilities that are out there? First, they should know the following:

- Their organization's security policies—A vulnerability is not necessarily a cause for concern. The danger arises from the damage that the vulnerability, if exploited, could cause. Consider a Web server with a known vulnerability that operates only on a protected network and that provides data of limited value. That might not need to be

9

dealt with, but if that same vulnerability existed on an Internet-exposed e-commerce server, it would be essential to repair it immediately.

- What software and hardware devices the organization uses—If the organization does not use a vulnerable piece of software, then the risk is minimal. If a new vulnerability for Microsoft Internet Information Server is announced, this is of little concern to a company that uses only Apache Web servers.

Information security professionals should regularly consult the following types of public-disclosure lists:

- Vendor announcements
- Full-disclosure mailing lists
- The Common Vulnerabilities and Exposures database (CVE List) maintained by Mitre Corporation
- The National Vulnerability Database (NVD) sponsored by the Department of Homeland Security[18]

Vendor Announcements Most of the major vendors maintain mailing lists to announce vulnerabilities, fixes, or any compensating actions that can be taken (e.g., closing the network port associated with a vulnerable network service or disabling script execution in a vulnerable Web browser). Figure 9-14 shows a Microsoft security bulletin summary for January, 2011.[19] Figure 9-15 shows the exploitation index associated with the vulnerabilities mentioned in Figure 9-14. Figure 9-16 shows the Windows operating systems and components affected by these vulnerabilities.

Security professionals should subscribe to the relevant vendor mailing lists and conduct risk assessments on each new announcement to determine the appropriate actions to be taken.

Full-Disclosure Lists Vendors tend to delay announcing vulnerabilities until they've had time to research them and develop a fix or identify compensating actions, which can create a "window of vulnerability"[20] for organizations if the problem has been discovered elsewhere or disclosed to others.

The hacker community and some security researchers release details of vulnerabilities as soon as they are discovered on Web sites, blogs, IRC channels, chat rooms, or full-disclosure mailing lists such as Bugtraq or Full-Disclosure.

The Bugtraq mailing list is a widely known, major source of public vulnerability announcements. As a founding member of the "full disclosure" movement, Bugtraq disseminates vulnerability information as soon as it is discovered, regardless of whether vendors have been notified or a fix is available. Bugtraq has been alternately praised for improving software quality (by focusing public attention on the prevalence of security flaws) and castigated for informing potential attackers of methods for compromising systems.

A sample Bugtraq posting is shown in Figure 9-17.[21]

Internet Storm Center The SANS Institute, which hosts many respected network security conferences and offers various security certifications, also operates the Internet Storm Center (ISC). The ISC's mission is to provide detection and analysis of network

TechNet Home > TechNet Security > Bulletins

Microsoft Security Bulletin Summary for January 2011

Published: January 11, 2011

Version: 1.0

This bulletin summary lists security bulletins released for January 2011.

Bulletin Information

⊟
Executive Summaries

The following table summarizes the security bulletins for this month in order of severity.
For details on affected software, see the next section, **Affected Software and Download Locations**.

Bulletin ID	Bulletin Title and Executive Summary	Maximum Severity Rating and Vulnerability Impact	Restart Requirement	Affected Software
MS11-002	**Vulnerabilities in Microsoft Data Access Components Could Allow Remote Code Execution (2451910)** This security update resolves two privately reported vulnerabilities in Microsoft Data Access Components. The vulnerabilities could allow remote code execution if a user views a specially crafted Web page. An attacker who successfully exploited this vulnerability could gain the same user rights as the local user. Users whose accounts are configured to have fewer user rights on the system could be less impacted than users who operate with administrative user rights.	Critical Remote Code Execution	May require restart	Microsoft Windows
MS11-001	**Vulnerability in Windows Backup Manager Could Allow Remote Code Execution (2478935)**	Important Remote Code Execution	May require restart	Microsoft Windows

Figure 9-14 Example of Microsoft security bulletin summary

Source: http://technet.microsoft.com

threats, assessments of their severity, and advice on how to counter them. Perhaps the most useful feature of the site is the "handler's diary," a daily log written by volunteer intrusion analysts who staff the storm center. The handler's diary is available as an RSS feed (*http://isc.sans.edu/xml.html*), which includes the ability for forwarding the entries to a pager.

Because it accepts firewall and intrusion logs from many sources, the ISC is often one of the first organizations to spot network anomalies, and it often traces them to specific malware or vulnerability exploits. For example, an advisory issued on January 20, 2011 described a possible new Twitter worm, as shown in Figure 9-18.

First The Forum of Incident Response and Security Teams (FIRST) is another organization that facilitates information sharing on the latest cyber-threats and attacks. On its Web site (*www.first.org*), the organization describes its mission this way:

> *FIRST brings together a variety of computer security incident response teams from government, in incident prevention, to stimulate rapid reaction to incidents, and to promote information sharing among members and the community at large.*[22]

TechNet Home > TechNet Security > Bulletins

Microsoft Security Bulletin Summary for January 2011

Published: January 11, 2011

⊟
Exploitability Index

The following table provides an exploitability assessment of each of the vulnerabilities addressed this month. The vulnerabilities are listed in order of decreasing exploitability assessment level then CVE ID. Only vulnerabilities that have a severity rating of Critical or Important in the bulletins are included.

How do I use this table?

Use this table to learn about the likelihood of functioning exploit code being released within 30 days of security bulletin release, for each of the security updates that you may need to install. You should review each of the assessments below, in accordance with your specific configuration, in order to prioritize your deployment. For more information about what these ratings mean, and how they are determined, please see Microsoft Exploitability Index.

Bulletin ID	Vulnerability Title	CVE ID	Exploitability Index Assessment	Key Notes
MS11-001	Backup Manager Insecure Library Loading Vulnerability	CVE-2010-3145	1 - Consistent exploit code likely	**This vulnerability has been disclosed publicly**
MS11-002	DSN Overflow Vulnerability	CVE-2011-0026	1 - Consistent exploit code likely	(None)
MS11-002	ADO Record Memory Vulnerability	CVE-2011-0027	1 - Consistent exploit code likely	(None)

↑Top of section

Figure 9-15   Example of Microsoft security bulletin exploitability index

Source: http://technet.microsoft.com

TechNet Home > TechNet Security > Bulletins

Microsoft Security Bulletin Summary for January 2011

Published: January 11, 2011

⊟
Affected Software and Download Locations

The following tables list the bulletins in order of major software category and severity.

⊟
Windows Operating System and Components

Windows Vista		
Bulletin Identifier	**MS11-002**	**MS11-001**
Aggregate Severity Rating	**Critical**	**Important**
Windows Vista Service Pack 1 and Windows Vista Service Pack 2	Windows Data Access Components 6.0 (KB2419640) (Critical)	Windows Vista Service Pack 1 and Windows Vista Service Pack 2 (Important)
Windows Vista x64 Edition Service Pack 1 and Windows Vista x64 Edition Service Pack 2	Windows Data Access Components 6.0 (KB2419640) (Critical)	Windows Vista x64 Edition Service Pack 1 and Windows Vista x64 Edition Service Pack 2 (Important)
Windows Server 2008		
Bulletin Identifier	**MS11-002**	**MS11-001**
Aggregate Severity Rating	**Important**	None

Figure 9-16   Example of Microsoft security bulletin affected software

Source: http://technet.microsoft.com

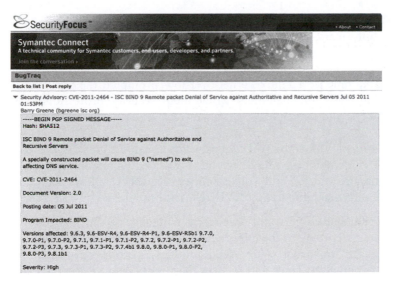

Figure 9-17   Example of a Bugtraq posting

Source: www.securityfocus.com

Diary

Possible new Twitter worm

Share |

Published: 2011-01-20,
Last Updated: 2011-01-20 16:41:39 UTC
by Manuel Humberto Santander Pelaez (Version: 1)
1 comment(s)
Looks like there is a new twitter worm out there. There are an increased number of messages like the following ones:
(see http://isc.sans.edu/diary.html?storyid=10297) for examples...
Those short URL points to the servers providing the malware. The following are some of the malicious URL I could gather (CAREFUL: THEY ARE
STILL ACTIVE):

- http://cainnoventa.it/m28sx.html
- http://servizialcittadino.it/m28sx.html
- http://aimos.fr/m28sx.html
- http://lowcostcoiffure.fr/m28sx.html
- http://s15248477.onlinehome-server.info/m28sx.html
- http://www.waseetstore.com/m28sx.html
- http://www.gemini.ee/m28sx.html

After clicking to the URL, you are sent to a faveAV web page.
The malware downloaded is named pack.exe, md5 264ebccca76bdb89f4ae9519c4cd267e, sha1
d16573ce7ce7710865b34bc1abeef699c20549ed. 2 of 43 AV from virustotal detect it as SecurityShieldFraud as of january 20 2011 16:19:58
UTC.
When the malware infects the machine, it copies itself to C:\Documents and Settings\<your username>\Local Settings\Application
Data\mbcjmhny.exe, ensures that cmd.exe exists, kill the malware, deletes the downloaded malware and starts it again from the location it
copied itself with the following instruction:
"C:\WINDOWS\system32\cmd.exe" /c taskkill /f /pid 1576 & ping -n 3 127.1 & del /f /q "C:\pack.exe" & start
C:\DOCUME~1\ADMINI~1\LOCALS~1\APPLIC~1\mbcjmhny.exe -f
We will keep analyzing the malware and post an update with more information.
-- Manuel Humberto Santander Peláez | http://twitter.com/manuelsantander | http://manuel.santander.name | msantand at isc dot sans dot
org

Figure 9-18   Example ISC alert

Source: http://isc.sans.edu

The CVE List @ Mitre Common Vulnerabilities and Exposures (CVE) is "a dictionary of publicly known information security vulnerabilities and exposures."[23] In addition to announcing vulnerabilities, the CVE List (*http://cve.mitre.org*) assigns unique identifiers to individual vulnerabilities. Thus, if two Microsoft Word buffer overflow vulnerabilities were announced at the same time or a Linux kernel overflow prompted the creation of fixes by Debian and Red Hat, the CVE identifiers would help security professionals distinguish among the vulnerabilities and their fixes.

The NVD The National Vulnerability Database (*http://nvd.nist.gov/*) is the U.S. governmental repository of vulnerabilities, which includes CVE identifiers and alerts from the US-CERT on current threats, attacks, and vulnerabilities. The NVD allows searches in either direction (from CVE reference numbers to NVD reference numbers and vice versa).

NVD employs the Open Vulnerability and Assessment Language (OVAL) to allow vulnerability information queries. According to the introduction to OVAL at *oval.mitre.org*, OVAL provides a common language "to encode system details and an assortment of content repositories held throughout the community. Tools and services that use OVAL for the three steps of system assessment—representing system information, expressing specific machine states, and reporting the results of an assessment—provide enterprises with accurate, consistent, and actionable information so they may improve their security. Use of OVAL also provides for reliable and reproducible information assurance metrics and enables interoperability and automation among security tools and services."[24]

OVAL can collect data directly from systems using XHTML and report it directly to the OVAL database.

US-CERT The United States Computer Emergency Response Team (*www.us-cert.gov*) is a centralized collection and reporting facility that focuses on the tracking and dissemination of information about current computer security threats. A US-CERT National Cyber Alert, which corresponds to the Microsoft Alerts illustrated in Figures 9-14 to 9-16, is shown in Figure 9-19.

According to the frequently asked questions at the US-CERT's Web site:

> *The National Cyber Alert System is America's first cohesive national cyber security system for identifying, analyzing, and prioritizing emerging vulnerabilities and threats. Managed by the US-CERT, the system relays computer security update and warning information to all users. It provides all citizens—from computer security professionals to home computer users with basic skills—with free, timely, actionable information to better secure their computer systems. The National Cyber Alert System provides valuable cyber security information in the form of Technical Cyber Security Alerts, Cyber Security Alerts, Cyber Security Tips, and Cyber Security Bulletins.[25]*

US-CERT also maintains several mailing lists to allow individual information security professionals, organizations, and government institutions to receive periodic and emergency updates.

ISACs The U.S. government's plan to protect the country's critical infrastructure relies heavily on the US-CERT. According to the U.S. Department of Homeland Security, critical infrastructure are "the assets, systems, and networks, whether physical or virtual, so vital

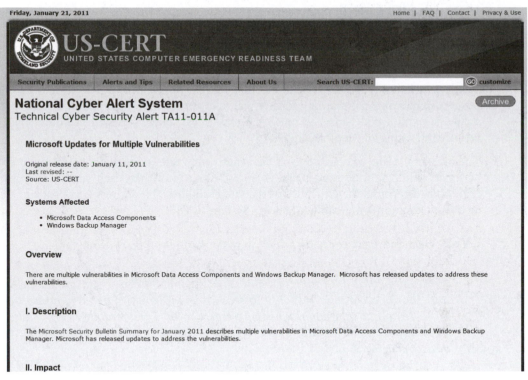

Figure 9-19   US-CERT National Cyber Alert

Source: www.us-cert/gov/cas

to the United States that their incapacitation or destruction would have a debilitating effect on security, national economic security, public health or safety, or any combination thereof."[26] However, another critical component is reaching out to key industries to collect and provide information about the latest cyber-threats. Many of these industry groups have Information Security and Analysis Centers (ISACs) to help provide these operational capabilities. For example, the IT and Telecom industry sectors have the IT-ISAC to provide this type of threat information to its member organizations.

Here is a description of IT-ISAC taken from its Web site (*www.it-isac.org*):

> *Founded in 2000 and achieving operational capability in 2001, the Information Technology - Information Sharing and Analysis Center (IT-ISAC) is a non-profit, limited liability corporation formed by members within the Information Technology sector as a unique and specialized forum for managing risks to their corporations and the IT infrastructure. Members participate in national and homeland security efforts to strengthen the IT infrastructure through cyber information sharing and analysis. As a result, members help their companies improve their incident response through trusted collaboration, analysis, coordination, and drive decision-making by policy makers on cybersecurity, incident response, and information sharing issues.[27]*

Vulnerability Risk Assessment

Once an organization knows about vulnerabilities, it must assess the risks they pose. Keep in mind that, although each vulnerability poses some risk, the remediation effort must be in proportion to the assessed risk.

Vendors commonly assign priorities to their fixes. For example, a fix for a vulnerability that poses a significant risk that an attacker will take control of a system and already has publicly available exploit code, may be rated "critical." Less dangerous vulnerabilities may receive a fix priority rating of "recommended."

The problem is one of consistency. One vendor may rate its most dangerous vulnerabilities as "critical" while another rates them as "high." On top of that, each vendor may use different criteria to determine the criticality of the vulnerabilities. To address this problem, FIRST created the Common Vulnerability Scoring System (CVSS).

CVSS Here is a brief overview of CVSS taken from the FIRST Web site:

> *CVSS is a vulnerability scoring system designed to provide an open and standardized method for rating IT vulnerabilities. CVSS helps organizations prioritize and coordinate a joint response to security vulnerabilities by communicating the base, temporal and environmental properties of a vulnerability. For additional information on CVSS v2, please see www.first.org/cvss and http://nvd.nist.gov/cvss.cfm?version=2.*[28]

CVSS consists of three groups of metrics: base, temporal, and environmental. These cascade down from one to the next to come up with an overall vulnerability score for a particular organization, as shown in Figure 9-20.

Base Score Generally speaking, software vendors (who participate in using the CVSS metrics) set the Base Score, which does not change. This score focuses on the characteristics of the vulnerability itself. Here are the factors that contribute to the Base Score:[29]

- Access vector—Measures the ability of the attacker to reach a target system with this vulnerability. Does the attacker need to be on the local network (e.g., SMB is generally only routed on internal networks)? Can she be on a connecting network? Or can she exploit the vulnerability over the Internet?

- Access complexity—Measures the difficulty level of exploiting the vulnerability.

- Authentication—Measures the number of times the attacker must successfully authenticate himself in order to exploit the vulnerability. The worst case is none.

- Confidentiality impact—Measures the extent to which the attacker can access unauthorized information as a result of exploiting the vulnerability.

- Integrity impact—Measures the extent to which the attacker can modify data on the target system as a result of exploiting the vulnerability.

- Availability impact—Measures the extent to which the attacker can prevent the availability of the information resources as a result of exploiting the vulnerability.

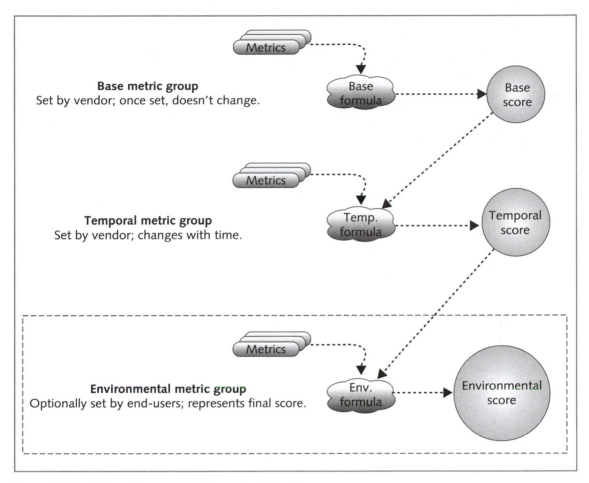

Figure 9-20 CVSS metric groups and how they interact

Source: www.first.org/cvss/faq/

© Cengage Learning 2013

Temporal Score The Temporal Score is also set by the software vendor but changes over time once exploits are discovered, fixes are released, or more reliable threat intelligence is received. Here are the factors that contribute to the Temporal Score:[30]

- Exploitability—Measures the availability of proven, reliable exploit code, simple proof-of-concept code, or whether any known exploits exist.

- Remediation level—Measures whether an official patch is available, only a temporary fix is available, a workaround exists, or there are no current fixes.

- Report confidence—Measures the reliability of the vulnerability report. Was it confirmed by the vendor? Is it a rumor on a mailing list? Is the source credible?

Environmental Score The Environmental Score is set by the organization using the software. This represents the overall score for the vulnerability, taking into account unique factors of the IT environment. Here are the factors that contribute to the Environmental Score:[31]

- Collateral damage potential—Measures loss of lives, physical assets, or financial well-being from the successful exploitation of the vulnerability.

- Target distribution—Measures the percentage of systems that could be affected by this vulnerability.

- Security requirements—The subjective analysis of the local security team to determine which aspect—confidentiality, integrity, or availability—would be most affected if the vulnerability is exploited.

Other Factors Additional factors that must be taken into account when conducting a risk assessment for a vulnerability include:

- Exposure—How susceptible is the organization to an exploit of the vulnerability? A critical defect in an Internet-facing router or firewall leads to much more exposure than one in a Web server that is only accessible from within the organization.

- Criticality of the affected assets—Patches are produced by the same developers who introduced the problem in the first place; therefore, the patches must be tested to ensure that they do not have undesirable side effects when installed. Loss of access to a critical asset is equally disruptive to an organization, whether the cause is a malicious attack or a bad software patch.

- Compensating factors—There may be other ways to prevent the vulnerability from being exploited before the fix can be tested and installed. For example, it might be possible to close the network port associated with a vulnerable network service or disable script execution in a vulnerable Web browser.

- Downtime requirements—Many patch installations require the server to be rebooted during installation. This restart will impact the availability of the services hosted by the server and may require special scheduling, failover to alternate servers, or other accommodations.

A risk assessment takes all these factors into account to determine what percentage of an organization's scarce IT resources should be dedicated to the deploying of a fix.

Chapter Summary

- To maintain secure networks, information security professionals must be prepared to systematically identify system vulnerabilities. This is often done by performing self-assessment using scanning and penetration testing.

- Many vulnerabilities have common underlying causes that stem from frequently encountered errors or shortcomings that developers create or overlook when deploying networks or systems.

- Common vulnerabilities fall into two broad classes: defects in software or firmware, and weaknesses in processes and procedures, which typically involve the weakest link in security defenses, the human element.

- To keep informed of emerging vulnerabilities, information security professionals should regularly consult vendor announcements, full-disclosure mailing lists, and

CVE, which is the common vulnerabilities and exposures database maintained by Mitre Corporation for the U.S. Department of Homeland Security.

- To assess the risk within a computing environment, network professionals must use tools such as intrusion detection/prevention systems (IDPS), active vulnerability scanners, passive vulnerability scanners, automated log analyzers, and protocol analyzers, commonly referred to as sniffers.

- Many organizations use a service called a penetration test to assess their security postures on a regular basis. A penetration test team, called a red team, uses all the techniques and tools available to attackers in order to attempt to compromise or penetrate an organization's defenses.

Review Questions

1. What is a vulnerability? How does it differ from a threat?

2. What are the major classes of vulnerability?

3. What is a buffer overflow? What can occur when software has a buffer overflow vulnerability?

4. What is an injection attack? What kind of vulnerability gives rise to this type of attack?

5. What kinds of vulnerabilities can occur when programmers assume all network connections are secure?

6. What is a cross-site scripting attack? How is it used to compromise a network service?

7. Why are an organization's security policies important to how it defends itself against network attacks?

8. What are the most significant sources of vulnerability information, and what do they provide?

9. What is an attack methodology, and how is it used to attack a network?

10. What is network footprinting? What is network fingerprinting? How are they related?

11. Why do many organizations ban port scanning activities on their internal networks? Why would ISPs ban outbound port scanning by their customers?

12. What is an open port? Why is it important to limit the number of open ports a system has to only those that are absolutely essential?

13. What is a vulnerability scanner? How is it used to improve security?

14. What is the difference between active and passive vulnerability scanners?

15. What is a fuzz testing? How is it used to find network vulnerabilities?

16. What is firewall analysis? What is it used for?

17. What kind of data and information can be found using a packet sniffer?

18. What capabilities should a wireless security toolkit include?

19. What is penetration testing, and how is it used in most organizations?

20. What are the categories of penetration testing? Describe each of them.

Real World Exercises

Exercise 9-1

Visit the Open Web Application Security Project (OWASP) at *www.owasp.org*. Find the OWASP chapter nearest to you. When and where is the next scheduled OWASP chapter meeting? If there is a meeting agenda, what will be covered?

Exercise 9-2

Use a Web search engine to find out more about Nessus. Use the search results to answer these questions:

1. Who started the Nessus Project?

2. When was it begun?

3. What does Nessus do?

Exercise 9-3

Visit the Web site of SecurityFocus (an organization that serves as an online portal for security information and security services) at *www.securityfocus.com/archive/1*. Answer the following questions:

1. What is the most recent announcement? When was it posted?

2. Looking at the Vulnerabilities section, what is the most recent vulnerability announcement? When was it posted?

Exercise 9-4

Visit the Web site of the Common Vulnerability and Exposures service at *cve.mitre.org/cve/index.html*. Answer the following questions:

1. What is a CVE?

2. When did the CVE process start?

3. Who owns a CVE?

Exercise 9-5

Search for "Internet Storm Center" using a Web search engine. Answer the following questions:

1. What is the ISC?

2. When was it established?

3. Which organization is the primary sponsor of the ISC?

Hands-On Projects

Project 9-1

For this project, you will need to download and set up the BackTrack suite of tools to run in a virtual environment. The ISO can be located at *www. backtrack-linux.org/downloads/*. Download and set up the appropriate ISO for your environment, then create a virtual image using the VM software package of your choice. Finally, we will need a "victim" system that we can scan against. There are numerous preconfigured virtual systems available for download that are designed to be used for just this type of exercise. For demonstration purposes, we have chosen to use the Metasploitable virtual system. Metasploitable is available for torrent download at *http://updates. metasploit.com/data/Metasploitable.zip.torrent*. IMPORTANT: You MUST have permission from the network owner to engage in this exercise. We will use Zenmap, an Nmap GUI that comes pre-installed on the BackTrack ISO.

1. Start the Metasploitable virtual system.

2. On the BackTrack system, start Zenmap by clicking the graphic in the lower-left side of the taskbar that looks like a dragon, then choosing **BackTrack -> Information Gathering -> Network Analysis -> Network Scanners -> zenmap**, as shown in Figure 9-21.

Figure 9-21   Starting Zenmap in BackTrack
Source: BackTrack

3. Enter the IP address of the Metasploitable system in the Target field.

4. Choose **Quick Scan** in the Profile field. Notice the Command field shows the actual command-line options you would type if you were not using the GUI.

5. Click **Scan** to begin the scan.

6. After the scan completes, Zenmap returns results, as shown in Figure 9-22.

Figure 9-22 Zenmap scan results
Source: Zenmap

These results show a system that has several open ports. However, the results are vague and not helpful in assessing potential vulnerabilities. We need to use additional options to get deeper details about the system.

7. In the Command field, manually add **-O** as an option, before the IP address, then click **Scan**. This option enables the Nmap operating system feature.

8. After the scan completes, Zenmap returns results. Scroll down to the bottom of the screen, and you will now see details regarding the operating system. This information can be used to help research vulnerabilities for the "victim" system. Your output should look similar to what is shown in Figure 9-23.

Having details about the operating system is an important step in conducting a vulnerability analysis. However, having details about the individual applications that actually answer requests on the open ports is important as well. To collect details about the installed applications, we will have to use yet another option.

9. In the Command field, remove the -O option and replace it with **-sV**, then click **Scan**. This option enables the Nmap service scanning feature.

10. After the scan completes, Zenmap returns results. Click the **Ports/Hosts** tab and review the results. As you see, you now have details regarding the application and version level operating on the "victim" system. This information can be used to help research vulnerabilities related to the "victim" system. Your output should look similar to what is shown in Figure 9-24.

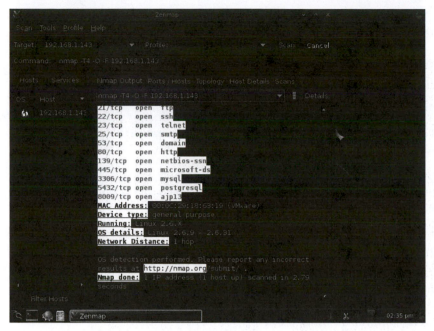

Figure 9-23   Zenmap operating system scan results
Source: Zenmap

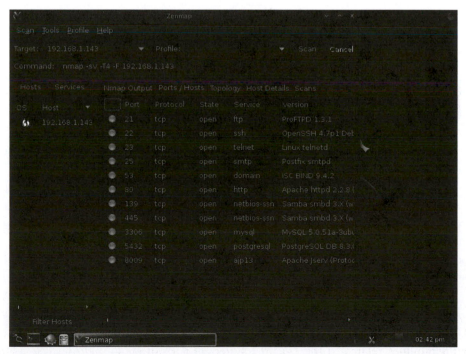

Figure 9-24   Zenmap service scan results
Source: Zenmap

Now that you are armed with details regarding the services being offered, you can conduct an even more detailed and thorough vulnerability assessment.

Endnotes

1. Howard, M., Leblanc, D., and Viega, J. *24 Deadly Sins of Software Security: Programming Flaws and How to Fix Them*. New York: McGraw-Hill, 2009.

2. Ibid..

3. Thurrott, P. "Introducing AutoUpdate, A Windows Me Technology Showcase." Accessed January 3, 2012 @ *www.winsupersite.com/article/windows-95/introducing-autoupdate-a-windows-me-technology-showcase-127980*.

4. Apache Software Foundation. "Apache HTTP Server 2.2 documentation: Security Tips." Accessed July 5, 2011 @ *http://httpd.apache.org/docs/current/misc/security_tips.html*.

5. Hackers for Charity. "Welcome to the Google Hacking Database (GHDB)!" Accessed July 7, 2011 @ *www.hackersforcharity.org/ghdb/*.

6. Nmap.org. "Zenmap Reference Guide." Accessed January 3, 2012 @ *http://nmap.org/zenmap/man.html#man-history*.

7. Goldsmith, D., and Schiffman, M. "Firewalking: A Traceroute-Like Analysis of IP Packet Responses to Determine Gateway Access Control Lists." Accessed January 4, 2012 @ *http://packetfactory.openwall.net/projects/firewalk/firewalk-final.pdf*.

8. Security Tools. "SecTools.org: Top Network Security Tools." Accessed 4 January 2012 @ *http://sectools.org/about/*.

9. Security Tools. "Top 10 Vulnerability Scanners." Accessed January 21, 2011 @ *http://sectools.org/vuln-scanners.html*.

10. zhao3stones. "What is Fuzz Testing (zt)." Accessed January 21, 2011 @ *http://blogold.chinaunix.net/u2/69926/showart_706962.html*.

11. Security Tools. "Top 11 Packet Sniffers." Accessed January 21, 2011 @ *http://sectools.org/sniffers.html*.

12. Scarfone, J., Souppaya, M., Cody, A., and Orebaugh, A. "NIST SP 800-115: Technical Guide to Information Security Testing and Assessment." Accessed January 21, 2011 @ *http://csrc.nist.gov/publications/nistpubs/800-115/SP800-115.pdf*.

13. Scarfone, J., Souppaya, M., Cody, A., and Orebaugh, A. "NIST SP 800-115: Technical Guide to Information Security Testing and Assessment." Accessed January 21, 2011 @ *http://csrc.nist.gov/publications/nistpubs/800-115/SP800-115.pdf*.

14. Scarfone, J., Souppaya, M., Cody, A., and Orebaugh, A. "NIST SP 800-115: Technical Guide to Information Security Testing and Assessment." Accessed January 21, 2011 @ *http://csrc.nist.gov/publications/nistpubs/800-115/SP800-115.pdf*.

15. "Full disclosure." Wikipedia. Accessed January 21, 2012 @ *http://en.wikipedia.org/wiki/Full_disclosure*.

16. Schneier, B. *Secrets & Lies: Digital Security in a Networked World*. New York: John Wiley & Sons, 2000.

17. Verton, D. (2003). "Major Internet vulnerability discovered in e-mail protocol." *Computerworld.com*. Accessed December 15, 2007 @ *www.computerworld.com/security topics/security/holes/story/0,10801,78991,00.html*.

18. National Institute of Standards and Technology. "National Vulnerability Database." Accessed January 4, 2012 @ *http://nvd.nist.gov/about.cfm*.

19. Microsoft. "Microsoft Security Bulletin Summary for January 2011." Accessed January 21, 2012 @ *www.microsoft.com/technet/security/bulletin/ms11-jan.mspx*.

20. Wikipedia. "Vulnerability." Accessed January 21, 2012 @ *http://en.wikipedia.org/wiki/ Window_of_vulnerability*.

21. SecurityFocus. "Gentoo Linux Security Advisory GLSA 201101-08."Accessed January 28, 2012 @ *www.securityfocus.com/archive/1/515869*.

22. FIRST. "FIRST is the global Forum for Incident Response and Security Teams." Accessed January 4, 2012 @ *www.first.org/*.

23. Mitre.org. "CVE." Accessed January 5, 2012 @ *http://cve.mitre.org/*.

24. Mitre.org. "Open Vulnerability and Assessment Language. (OVAL)" Accessed January 21, 2011 @ *http://oval.mitre.org/*.

25. US-CERT. "Frequently Asked Questions." Accessed January 21, 2011 @ *www.us-cert. gov/faq.html#ncas*.

26. Department of Homeland Security. "Critical Infrastructure." Accessed January 5, 2012 @ *www.dhs.gov/files/programs/gc_1189168948944.shtm*.

27. IT-ISAC. "Information Technology Information Sharing and Analysis Center." Accessed January 5, 2012 @ *www.it-isac.org/*.

28. FIRST. "New version of Common Vulnerability Scoring System released." Accessed July 7, 2011 @ *www.first.org/cvss/*.

29. FIRST. "CVSS: A Complete Guide to the Common Vulnerability Scoring System Version 2.0." Accessed January 5, 2012 @ *www.first.org/cvss/cvss-guide.html*.

30. FIRST. "CVSS: A Complete Guide to the Common Vulnerability Scoring System Version 2.0." Accessed January 5, 2012 @ *www.first.org/cvss/cvss-guide.html*.

31. FIRST. "CVSS: A Complete Guide to the Common Vulnerability Scoring System Version 2.0." Accessed January 5, 2012 @ *www.first.org/cvss/cvss-guide.html*.

9

chapter 10

Auditing, Monitoring, and Logging

The unexamined life is not worth living. — Socrates

Upon completion of this material, you should be able to:

- List the various events that should be monitored in network environments
- Describe the various network logs available for monitoring
- Discuss the various log management, SIEM, and monitoring technologies
- Explain the role that configuration and change management play in auditing the network environment
- Discuss formal audit programs and how they relate to network environments
- Describe Certification and Accreditation (C&A) programs implemented by the U.S. federal government and other international agencies

Finding the Needles in the Haystacks

EBS had come a long way in its preparation for the upcoming PCI audit. One area yet to be addressed was monitoring systems for security-related events. As the volume of attacks increase on computer systems, it is important that an organization monitor activities and respond quickly to attacks. Some of the critical technical requirements for this type of monitoring are contained in PCI DSS Section 10. In particular, Section 10 requires that organizations address the following issues related to their PCI systems: installing file integrity monitoring, retaining log files for one year, and reviewing the security logs daily. EBS had already spent a good deal of time centralizing logs via syslog and archiving them, as required. However, Paige Davis realized that the company was not reviewing, on a daily basis, the security logs for EBS systems that are used for PCI-governed credit card activity.

In order to meet the compliance requirements, Paige had to start doing some research on the people, processes, and technology needed to meet these requirements. First, she would need to understand what types of events were currently being tracked on PCI systems. Second, she would need to understand how (or if) the necessary logs were being collected. Third, she would have to determine how the necessary events could be reviewed daily. She had some serious log work to do.

Introduction

Auditing is a term used frequently in business and IT. It has a number of meanings, but the dominant information security and business definition states that auditing is a review of organizational processes for compliance to policies, standards, or regulations. This is often viewed by those being examined as an unpleasant event, with overtones of fear and dread. In this book, we focus on two additional meanings. First, audit is a procedure for recording and reviewing the variety of events that occur on a network or systems. Second, audit is a periodic self-review of a network environment required to safely operate any complex organization.

The first of our definitions is probably better termed *systems monitoring*, which refers to the continual self-examination of a system or a network of systems operations. This would encompass the use of its applications and the actions of those who access and use those systems. Thus, formally speaking, **systems monitoring** is the ongoing review of a system or network of systems to determine if the operational results and events are within the bounds established as proper functioning. This will include processes to detect potential incidents and ensure compliance with systems policies.

NOTE Systems monitoring is not to be confused with information security **program monitoring**, also known as **continuous monitoring**, which is defined by NIST Draft Special Publication 800-137 as "maintaining ongoing awareness of information security, vulnerabilities, and threats to support organizational risk management decisions." SP 800-137 goes on to say: "The objective is to conduct ongoing monitoring of the security of an organization's networks, information, and systems, and respond by accepting, avoiding/rejecting, transferring/sharing, or mitigating risk as situations change."[1]

Program monitoring is outside the scope of this text. For additional information on this topic, go to *http://csrc.nist.gov/publications/nistpubs/800-137/SP800-137-Final.pdf.*

The second meaning of auditing being examined in this chapter refers to review of the design and operational outcomes that come from the use of particular systems. In this context, an **audit** is a periodic or ad hoc review of program or system functions to determine compliance with a set of established standards. With regard to network security, this means looking at all the systems, policies, personnel, and operations associated with protecting the organization's information and networking devices and making sure they are operating and being used in accordance with the will or intent of management. In this text, we examine only those aspects of auditing that are of benefit to network security along with the standards that are used to audit network security operations. Keep in mind that *auditing* is also the term used for reviews of financial (accounting) systems and information systems. In fact, there are domains of knowledge for financial auditing and information systems auditing that will have characteristics that overlap those being discussed here.

10

Monitoring Network Systems

Monitoring a system involves keeping a close watch on the operations (internal) and usage (external) of that system—that is, tracking specific events that occur on the system and recording them in the logs. As a detective control (a security control that detects intrusions), logging is perhaps one of the best ways to get a picture of what is happening or has happened on a system.

The term *log* comes from the formal records kept by ships' captains as they traveled the open seas. The term was later adopted by aircraft (and spacecraft) captains as well. As for a **computer log,** it is a detailed chronological record of the operation of a computer system, including the use of that system and any modifications to it. Most modern operating systems have the ability to collect and store various types of data, including system events, user events, and security events. In addition, network devices—firewalls, proxies, VPN concentrators, and so forth—and their associated operating systems or firmware record events in logs.

The basic operation of a system logging facility is to collect information from the operating system or application whenever specific actions occur. For example, whenever the operating system receives a request for a user to log in, the OS should send this information to the logging facility, as shown in Figure 10-1. All the events that trigger entries in the system log are customizable, giving the administrator control over which events are watched.

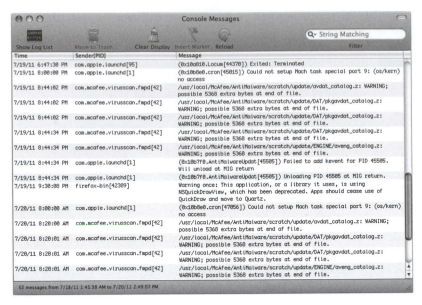

Figure 10-1 Mac OS X console log

Source: Mac OS X

What to Audit?

Although logging—or auditing—facilities differ from system to system and application to application, you have to decide exactly what you are going to monitor on a device. First, you need to understand that an **event** is any action that may be of interest to you on a device. For example, a **security event** is an occurrence that you think might affect the system's security. The following sections discuss various categories of security events that might be audited on a system.

Most advanced network devices and server systems give administrators the ability to modify the audit system in order to choose which events are logged (as shown in Figure 10-2) and how the log files are managed (as shown in Figure 10-3). From a security standpoint, we would like to capture all data possible to help us detect suspicious behavior or reconstruct the steps of an attack. However, from a practical standpoint, additional logging can tax system CPU cycles, memory usage, and storage needed. This tradeoff should be spelled out clearly in the system audit policy or log management policy. These policy decisions are discussed later in this chapter.

Process Events Part of being able to audit a computer or other networking device is having an awareness of the processes and services that are operating within the systems or network so that you can distinguish between those that should be running and those that should not. In the domain of information processing, a **process** is a task being performed by a computing system. This is often done at the same time that the computer system is processing other tasks. Therefore, many processes may be underway at the same time, each of them being handled by the systems processor in its turn. Processes

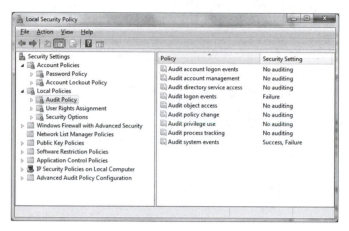

Figure 10-2   Windows 7 audit policy
Source: Microsoft Windows

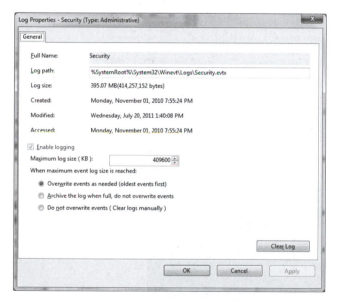

Figure 10-3   Windows 7 log settings
Source: Microsoft Windows

are often called *tasks* in embedded operating systems. The word *process* suggests something that takes time, as opposed to *memory*, which suggests something that takes up space.

In general, an operating system process consists of the following attributes:

- Memory—Contains executable code or task-specific data

- Operating system resources—File descriptors (in *nix) or handles (in Windows) as well as other resources allocated by the OS

- Security attributes—The process owner and the process's set of permissions
- Processor state—The content of registers, physical memory addresses, and other processor attributes[2]

Many of these attributes are recorded in the logs when the process is created or when it makes a significant change on the system. However, logs do not provide dynamic records of running processes. To investigate running processes, we would turn to the Task Manager in Windows (as shown in Figure 10-4) and the ps command in Linux (as shown in Figure 10-5).

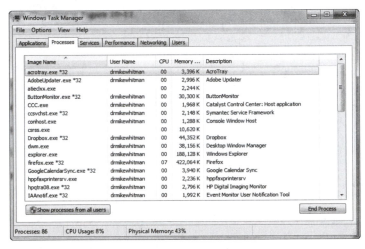

Figure 10-4 Windows processes

Source: Microsoft Windows

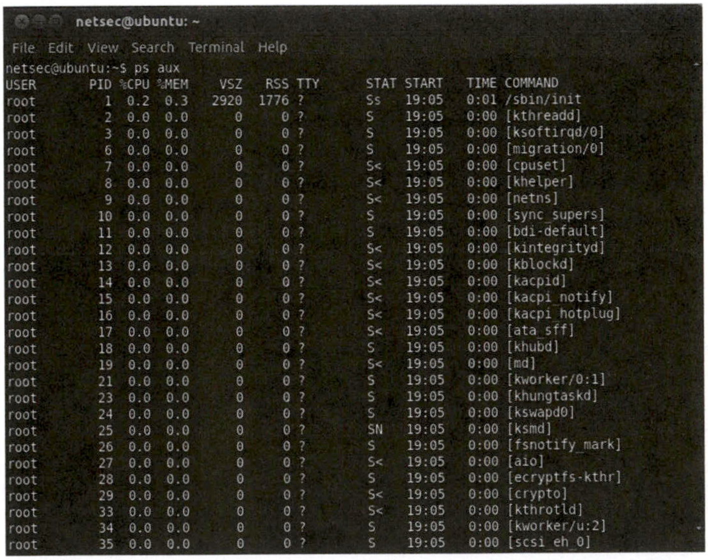

Figure 10-5 Linux processes

Source: Linux

Services are processes that are designed to operate without user interaction. In the Windows OS, services are usually initiated (loaded or started) at boot-up as dynamic-link libraries (DLLs), which consist of software code, data and/or other resources necessary to provide the service. You can view Windows Services in the Microsoft Management Console (MMC), as shown in Figure 10-6. In a Linux environment, this type of background service is known as a **daemon** and is loaded upon start-up in a variety of ways, depending on the Linux distribution. You can view Ubuntu Linux distribution daemons using the `service` command, as shown in Figure 10-7.

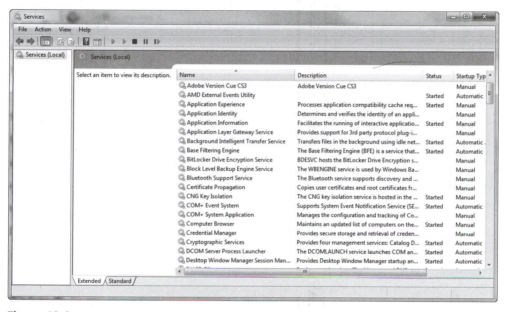

Figure 10-6 Windows services

Source: Microsoft Windows

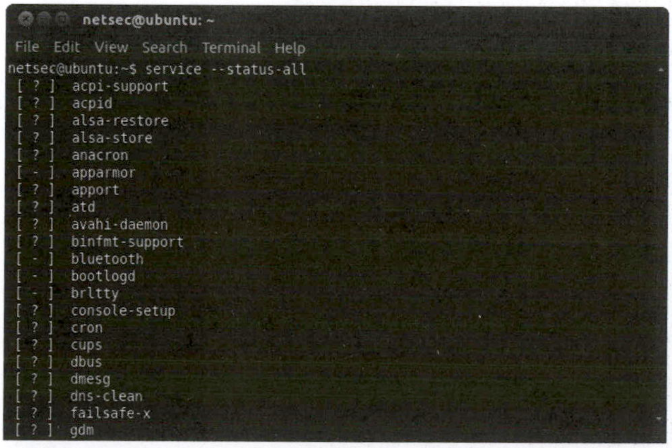

Figure 10-7 List of Ubuntu daemons

Source: Ubuntu Linux

Logon Events Although it is important to understand the various processes running on a system, it is equally important to understand what users are currently on the system. Tracking user-related activities helps to identify what actions are taking place, who is initiating those actions, and ultimately provide an overview of the user session. To this end, audit systems will usually log an event when:

- A user logs on or off
- An attempt to log on fails
- A user starts or stops a network session

Log files may not give you an accurate picture of what users are currently logged on to the system. To see this information in a Windows environment, use the PsLoggedOn tool, available free from Microsoft.[3] In a Linux environment, use the `last` command.

Group or Permission Change Events Once an attacker has gained access to a system through a normal user account (either by cracking a password or through social engineering), the next step in the attack is to elevate those privileges to those of an administrator. This is referred to as **privilege escalation**. Tracking events in which group membership has changed or rights have been elevated gives security professionals a warning that privilege escalation is occurring.

Resource Access Events Audit systems typically provide the ability to track when users or processes access files, directories, printers, and other system resources. This type of information is extremely valuable when trying to investigate an incident or track specific user activity. It provides granular information about what user performed what activity on what object and when.

However, auditing is not without costs, and the decision of what events to collect is one of tradeoffs. Recording every possible detail for auditing carries a heavy cost. By enabling a maximum degree of audit detail, you will capture all legitimate events not just those that are exceptions. The total number of these events can be astronomical. Table 10-1 identifies some of the types of events that can be captured by the Windows auditing system. In most cases, system administrators make the tradeoff decisions and limit this type of auditing either to certain types of events or to certain critical areas of a system, or both.

Object Access Event Number	Description
560	Access was granted to an already existing object.
562	A handle to an object was closed.
563	An attempt was made to open an object with the intent to delete it.
564	A protected object was deleted.
565	Access was granted to an already existing object type.
567	A permission associated with a handle was used.
568	An attempt was made to create a hard link to a file that is being audited.

Table 10-1 Partial List of Object Access Events That Can Be Captured by Windows Auditing

Object Access Event Number	Description
569	The resource manager in Authorization Manager attempted to create a client context.
570	A client attempted to access an object.
571	The client context was deleted by the Authorization Manager application.
572	The administrator manager initialized the application.

Table 10-1 Partial List of Object Access Events That Can Be Captured by Windows Auditing [4] (*continued*)
© Cengage Learning 2013

Network Connection Events Many of the security incidents that concern organizations the most have to do with the external connections the organization's systems make to Internet systems. By tracking the communication sessions that are initiated and torn down, administrators can detect any access to malicious IP addresses or URLs (provided they are able to correlate network activity with threat intelligence that lists malicious IP addresses and URLs).

These types of events can be tracked at a system level, but they can also be tracked at the firewalls (or other network egress points) to provide the most visibility on network activity. Administrators can track connections that are allowed and established, connections that are denied and fail, or other network activity that does not fall into the firewall's ruleset. Figure 10-8 shows a basic example of firewall connection logging using Ubuntu's Uncomplicated Firewall (ufw) application.

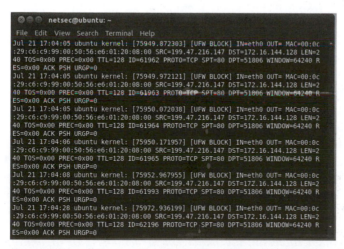

Figure 10-8 Network connection events in Ubuntu's ufw
Source: Ubuntu Linux

Network Data Transfer Events The exfiltration or unauthorized release of data, known as **data leakage**, is a top concern for most security professionals. Losing valuable company secrets, customers' personally identifiable information (PII), or other sensitive information has forced most organizations to focus on technology and programs that prevent this kind of data loss. Tracking the particular Web sessions and the amount of information transferred can help organizations identify data leakage as it is occurring and, hopefully, stop the activity before it is too late. Systems and network devices can do this type of monitoring; however, **data leakage prevention (DLP)** and network proxies provide a much more granular level of logging information. DLP is implemented as software or an appliance and is designed to crawl data at rest on hard drives, monitor data saved to removable media, and monitor communication systems like e-mail or instant messaging, looking for sensitive data leaving the network.[5]

System Restart and Shutdown Events Keeping systems available for use is an IT team's number one priority. Therefore, it is important that auditing systems keep track of when systems are booted, restarted, and shut down. From a security perspective, these types of events may also indicate that a system has been attacked, although the attack, instead of exploiting the system in some way, led to a crash.

Audit System or Log Events As mentioned earlier, log records are a valuable source of information, particularly when they are centralized for consolidation and analysis. In most cases, the auditing system reports when various activities have occurred to the logs—when the logs have reached their capacities, when they have been truncated, and so forth. This information can reveal that the logs have been manipulated by an attacker. Unfortunately, attackers are well aware of this and often delete or modify log records to conceal their activities. For this reason, unexplained gaps in records or modifications to records are definite indicators of an incident.

Log Management Policy

Auditing events for a single data source (e.g., a server) is extremely important to understand the health of that particular resource. However, looking at all the data sources within an IT environment in aggregate provides a more comprehensive picture of the overall health of the IT environment. To collect, review, and retain those aggregate logs requires a unifying standard in order to both provide a reliable source for incident management investigations and an accurate source to meet compliance requirements.

To be effective, logs must first be configured to record event data, as mentioned earlier. Some types of logging are enabled by default; others must specifically be activated. Log data is typically stored both locally and also at another recording location separate from the system being audited. Many organizations choose to create a central logging service (e.g., a central syslogd server). The central logging service must be configured to be suitably hardened to protect the information as well as large enough to handle the quantity of data that is usually collected.[6]

NIST's *Guide to Computer Security Log Management* advocates the following:

> *To establish and maintain successful log management activities, an organization should develop standard processes for performing log management. As part of the planning process, an organization should define its logging requirements and goals. Based on those, an organization should then develop policies that clearly define mandatory requirements and suggested recommendations for log management activities, including log generation, transmission, storage, analysis, and disposal. An organization should also ensure that related policies and procedures incorporate and support the log management requirements and recommendations. The organization's management should provide the necessary support for the efforts involving log management planning, policy, and procedures development.[7]*

To create effective log management practices within your organization, you must address the following:

- Storage—You must prepare the system to handle the amount of data generated by logging. Some systems create gigabytes of data that have to be stored or otherwise managed. Some systems overwrite older log entries with newer entries in order to comply with the space limitations of the system. You need to ensure that the rotation of log entries is acceptable rather than merely accept system defaults.

- Retention—Log systems can copy logs periodically to remote storage locations for long-term storage and later investigation. It is important to understand what regulatory requirements your organization may have in keeping log file information. For organizations that have no formal requirements, there is a debate among security administrators as to what the retention period should be for log files. **Retention** is the period of time that log files or log file data should be maintained. Some argue that log files may be subpoenaed during legal proceedings and, thus, should have short retention periods and must also then be routinely destroyed to prevent unwanted disclosure during this process. Others argue that the information to be gained from analyzing legacy and archival logs outweighs the risk. Still others take a middle ground and aggregate the log information, then destroy the individual entries. Regardless of the method employed, some plan must be in place to handle these files, and the legal environment is such that whatever policy is in place, it must be rigorously followed.

- Baseline—To recognize and react to abnormal operations and functions of a system, the administrator must be intimately familiar with the normal operations and functions of the system. This is done through establishing activity baselines. A **baseline** is a measurement of activity that represents the normal state or routine condition. The first baseline is logging all the activity while the server is detached from the network. This shows you what the system generates on its own. The second baseline is established by connecting the server to the network—without user activity—and logging several days' worth of events to examine the amount and types of activity. The third baseline is a snapshot of the server in production performing normal tasks as everyday users log on and operate the system.

- Encryption—If the organization decides to archive logs, the logs should be encrypted in storage. Should the log file system be compromised, this prevents unwanted disclosure.

- Disposal—When log files have outlived their usefulness, and have been retained as long as policy or procedure allows, they should be routinely and securely destroyed.[8]

Standard OS Logs

A comprehensive look at the logs produced by network devices and servers is beyond the scope of this book; however, it is important to look at some common systems to get a sense of the nature of the type of data that they can log and some of the kinds of information recorded. To provide such an overview, we will look at Windows and Linux systems.

Windows-Based Logging On most current versions of Microsoft Windows-based systems, logging is managed by the Event Viewer, which is accessible from the system control panel, as shown in Figure 10-9. The Event Viewer is actually a snap-in for the Microsoft Management Console (MMC), a utility designed to allow central management

10

and administration of a system. Note that you can also use the Wevtutil utility to manage event logs from the command line, as shown in Figure 10-10.

With the introduction of Windows 7, Microsoft divided logs into two categories: (1) Windows Logs and (2) Applications and Services Logs.

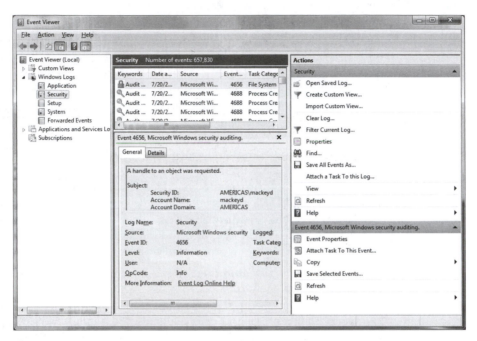

Figure 10-9 Windows Event Viewer

Source: Microsoft Windows

Figure 10-10 Command-line Wevtutil utility

Source: Microsoft Windows

Windows Logs The Microsoft Windows operating system has a number of data elements it can report. These are captured in logs, each of which captures the events associated with that category. In some cases, Windows programs use these logs to record specific program events as well. Microsoft Technet provides the following list, which outlines the standard logs and their main purposes:[9]

- Application log—This records events generated by specific applications or programs (see Figure 10-11). For example, a spreadsheet program might record an error for access to a file in the application log. Each program will have the locations of its logging activity determined by the associated development team.

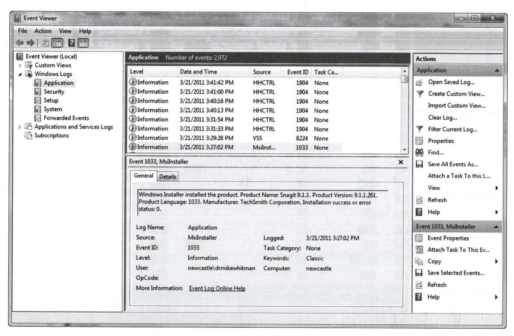

Figure 10-11   Application log
Source: Microsoft Windows

- Security log—This (see Figure 10-12) contains details about security-related events, such as logon attempts (whether valid or invalid), along with details about resource use (including creating, opening, or deleting files or other objects). Systems administrators have the option of specifying the events that are recorded in the security log. For example, if you have enabled file deletion auditing, each attempt to delete a file is recorded in the security log.

- Setup log—This is used to make a record of the various events that occur during Windows setup and other patches and/or application programs that are installed or reconfigured (see Figure 10-13).

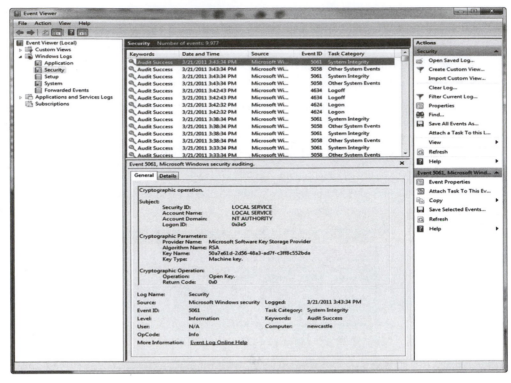

Figure 10-12   Security log
Source: Microsoft Windows

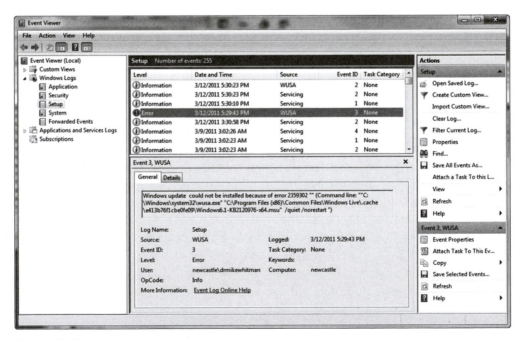

Figure 10-13   Setup log
Source: Microsoft Windows

- System log—This is used to record events logged by the various components that make up the Windows operating system (see Figure 10-14). When some system element fails (e.g., a software driver for a connected hardware device attempting to initiate itself during startup), the details of that failure are recorded in the system log. What is logged in the system log is predetermined by Windows.

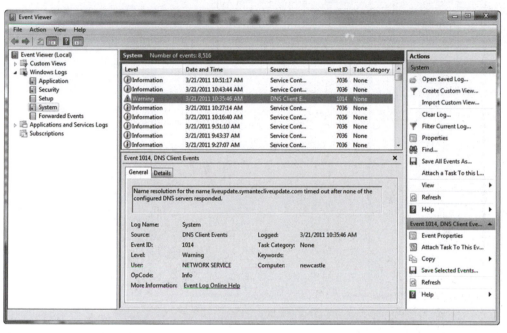

Figure 10-14   System log
Source: Microsoft Windows

- Forwarded Events log—This stores events that have been reported by remote computers. These events can only be recorded when systems administrators have established an event subscription.

- Applications and Services logs—This is made up of four subtypes of information: Admin, Operational, Analytic, and Debug. These logs are used to record functional data rather than trying to capture system-wide events. They are used to enable very specific types of activities, such as application debugging or tracing specific application activities, as shown in Figure 10-15.

  ○ Admin—This area of the log records events intended for end users, administrators, and support personnel. These events are usually from a problem that is well understood and has a readily accessible solution that can be acted upon. Figure 10-16 shows how an Admin/Operational log could be used to identify network issues—with a DHCP client configuration, for example—if a problem existed.

  ○ Operational—This area of the log records operational events that are used to analyze and diagnose certain issues. This area is often used when a specific action can be triggered by the log entry. For example, when a printer is added or removed from a system, an entry here may trigger the installation of a driver for that printer.

10

Figure 10-15 Applications and Services logs
Source: Microsoft Windows

- Analytic—This area of the log records events that happen frequently during routine use and is used to make after-action assessment of systems' performance. The events are usually the result of problems that cannot be handled by user action.

- Debug—This area of the log is used to record debugging events. These are generated by developers who may be troubleshooting issues with specific programs.[10]

From a network security perspective, the admin and operational logs are the most valuable to a systems and network administrator in identifying and resolving issues. Of particular value in the MMC/Event Viewer is the link at the bottom to Event Log Online Help, which can help diagnose Windows-specific issues. The link brings the admin to the Microsoft TechNet Events and Errors Message Center, where the database can be queried to determine if it is a known issue, as shown in Figure 10-17.

Linux-Based Logging In any operating system it is important to understand the logging capabilities. Without sufficient logging, it is impossible to tell when a system is misbehaving, has a security violation, or has been compromised. Linux has files used for logging various activities on the machine. Although the location depends on the Linux

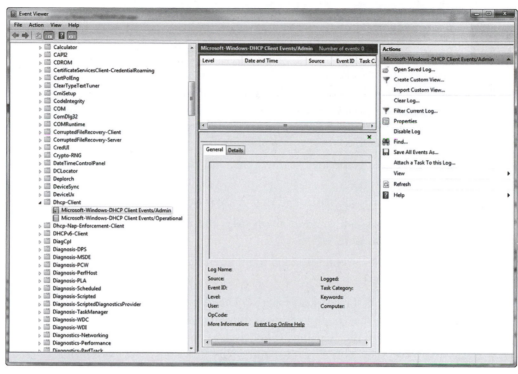

Figure 10-16 Admin/Operational log
Source: Microsoft Windows

10

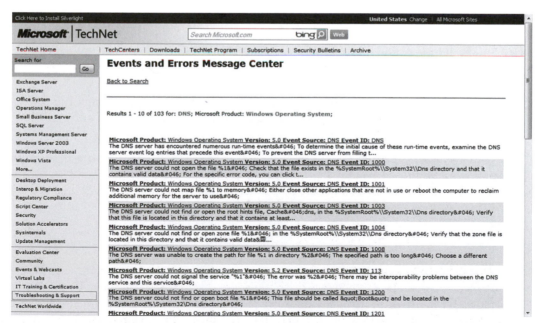

Figure 10-17 Microsoft's Events and Errors Message Center
Source: Internet Explorer view of Technet Web Site

distribution, these files are typically located in the /var/log/ directory. Here are short descriptions of each file:

- boot.log—Records events that occur during the boot sequence
- cron—Contains messages from the cron daemon which allows system administrators to schedule the execution of processes or application
- messages—Contains all the messages displayed on the console, which can be operating system messages or errors, networking messages or errors, or application messages or errors
- lastlog—Records the login name, time, and port of the last time each user logged on to the machine
- wtmp—Records all logins and logouts that occur on the system
- utmp—Records information about users that are currently using the system (e.g., login times, console, etc.)
- btmp—Shows a listing of failed login attempts

Syslog **Syslog** stands for "system logger." The idea behind syslog is to allow multiple system utilities to log using the same mechanism, thus alleviating the need for every operating system utility to implement its own logging facility. Syslog can be used to log messages from Linux applications and tools, such as Web servers and e-mail programs. From a security standpoint, syslog also allows organizations to store logs on a separate system altogether, thereby helping to keep the logs away from abusers who might tamper with their contents and hide their own tracks.

Syslog has its own daemon, syslogd, which runs as a background process. Syslogd uses a configuration file, /etc/syslog.conf, to determine the type and extent of logging to perform. The syslog.conf file can be configured to report on different levels in different ways. For example, the following entry logs all info messages to /var/log/messages:

```
*.info  /var/log/messages.
```

Figure 10-18 shows a simple example of the syslog.conf file.

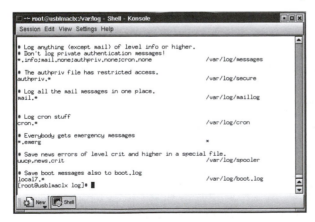

Figure 10-18   Contents of a simple syslog.conf file

Source: Linux

Log Management Technology

Most system logs are very difficult to collect, store, read, and understand. In cases where an administrator is looking for a specific event, the chore can be overwhelming. Luckily, a number of software manufacturers make tools that make log file analysis much easier.

Log Management A log management tool collects events from log files, processes the data, stores the results, and performs notification or alerting, as required. Based on the concept introduced by syslog of consolidating and centralizing all network and system logs, vendors like ArcSight (purchased by HP), Splunk, Q1 Labs (purchased by IBM), and LogLogic provide a number of log management tools and appliances to help organizations manage the mountain of logs. Here are some of the things that log management technologies are designed to do:

- Collect and centralize events in order to comply with various industry regulations

- Retain log information in accordance with company policies or regulations

- Normalize log information among a variety of endpoint technologies (e.g., Windows systems, Linux systems, Checkpoint firewalls, Juniper routers)

- Correlate events from the various event sources

- Provide searching mechanisms to find specific events

- Provide reporting mechanisms to help analyze the data

A typical log management architecture includes connectors or collectors that are able to capture events from the various endpoint technologies and systems. These collectors work to normalize and summarize events as the events are collected. From there, the normalized events are forwarded to the log management appliance or software for storage. Reports like those shown in Figure 10-19 can then be generated to help the organization meet compliance requirements or investigate incidents.

10

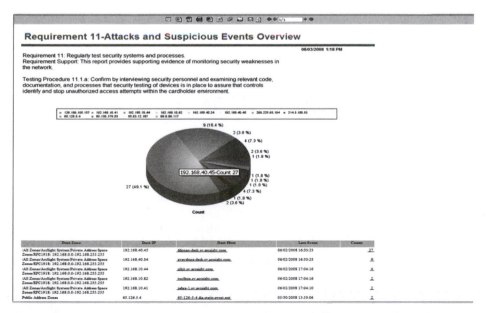

Figure 10-19 ArcSight Logger Report

Courtesy of HP Enterprise Security, Arc Sight

Security Information and Event Management (SIEM) Although log management is focused primarily on the collection, centralization, and storage of network event information, the next level of intelligence is provided by security information and event management (SIEM) technology. SIEM technology (also known as SEM technology) provides a layer of correlation that groups similar events from various technologies, locations, and environments. For example, if an attacker enters through a firewall, is detected by a network IDPS appliance, tries to log in to a system, and then launches malware, the SIEM technology should be able to correlate events from the firewall, IDPS, server, and antivirus logs in order to show a more complete picture of the overall attack.

As shown in Figure 10-20, SIEM technology applies more information to the events to show geographic location of attacks, correlate this with threat intelligence, and present the system events in human-readable format. Like the log management architecture, events are collected from endpoint systems; those events are then normalized and sent to a log management layer for long-term storage. Additionally, those events can be forwarded from the connectors or the logging systems to the SIEM database for correlation, alerting, and real-time monitoring.

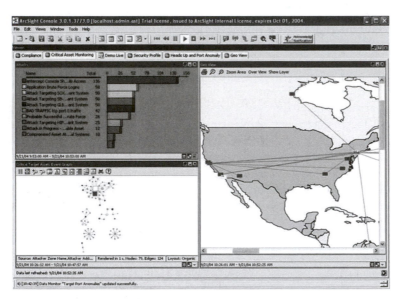

Figure 10-20   ArcSight ESM dashboard
Courtesy of HP Enterprise Security, Arc Sight

Security Operations Center (SOC) One of the needs that quickly becomes apparent with the deployment of log management and SIEM technologies is a talented pool of people to manage these technologies, watch these events as they occur, and then investigate and resolve them as needed. A security operations center (SOC) provides the operational infrastructure to detect attacks and prevent damage to the organization. It is staffed with talented information security professionals, has mature processes and procedures for repeatable investigations, and has a SIEM technology to bring all the intelligence to the team's fingertips. Most complex organizations have a SOC that serves as a command center for information security activities.

Configuration and Change Management (CCM)

The purpose of configuration and change management (CCM) is to manage the effects of changes or differences in configurations on an information system or network. Though not technically part of network monitoring or a formal audit program, this process is crucial in performing ongoing audits of the network systems and their associated configurations. In some organizations, **configuration management** is the identification, inventory, and documentation of the current information system's status—the hardware, software, and networking configurations. **Change management** is sometimes described as a separate function that only addresses the modifications to this base configuration.

Configuration Management

Just like documents, a system's technical components—its software, hardware, and firmware—should have version numbers, revision dates, and other features that allow the changes made to them to be monitored and administered.

Here are several terms used in CCM:

- Configuration item—A hardware or software item that is to be modified and revised throughout its life cycle.

- Version—The recorded state of a particular revision of a software or hardware configuration item. The version number is often noted in a specific format: "M.N.b." In this notation, "M" is the major release number, and "N.b" can represent various minor releases or builds within that major release.

- Major release—A significant revision of the version from its previous state

- Minor release (update or patch)—A minor revision of the version from its previous state

- Build—A snapshot of a particular version of software assembled (or linked) from its various component modules

- Build list—A list of the versions of components that make up a build

- Configuration—A collection of components that make up a configuration item

- Revision date—The date associated with a particular version or build

- Software library—A collection of configuration items that is usually controlled and that developers use to construct revisions and to issue new configuration items

To make these definitions more concrete, imagine there's a company named Security Solutions Corporation that develops "the ultimate security solution," a software application called Panacea. Here, Panacea is the configuration item, and the configuration consists of three major software components: See-All, Know-All, and Cure-All. Because this is the first major release of Panacea and its components, the build list consists of See-All 1.0, Know-All 1.0, and Cure-All 1.0. The revision date is the date associated with the first build.

To create Panacea, the programmers at Security Solutions Corporation pulled information from their software library. Suppose that while the application is being used in the field, the programmers discover a minor flaw in a subroutine. When they correct this flaw, they issue a minor release, Panacea 1.1. If at some point they need to make a major revision to the

10

software to meet changing market needs or to fix more substantial problems with the sub-components, they will issue a major release, Panacea 2.0.

The configuration management process helps avoid confusion, problems, and unnecessary spending, as shown in Figure 10-21. The additional resources required to correct a problem that could have been prevented through sound configuration management practices is likely to far exceed the amount of resources required to develop and implement an effective enterprise process.

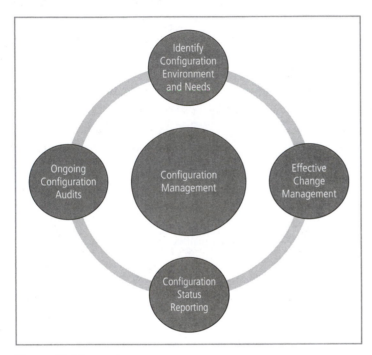

Figure 10-21   Configuration management process
© Cengage Learning 2013

NIST Special Publication 800-64, "Security Considerations in the Information System Development Life Cycle," outlines the need for configuration and change management:

> *Configuration management and control procedures are critical to establishing an initial baseline of hardware, software, and firmware components for the information system and subsequently to controlling and maintaining an accurate inventory of any changes to the system. Changes to the hardware, software, or firmware of a system can have a significant impact on the security of the system...[C]hanges should be documented, and their potential impact on security should be assessed regularly.*

NIST SP 800-53, R.1, "Recommended Security Controls for Federal Information Systems," defines seven CM controls that organizations are required to implement based on an information system's security categorization. These are:

- *CM-1 Configuration Management Policy and Procedures—The organization develops, disseminates, and periodically reviews and updates (1) a formal, documented CM policy that addresses purpose, scope, roles, responsibilities, and compliance; and (2) formal, documented procedures to facilitate the implementation of the CM policy and associated CM controls.*

- *CM-2 Baseline Configuration—The organization develops, documents, and maintains a current baseline configuration of the information system and an inventory of the system's constituent components.*

- *CM-3 Configuration Change Control—The organization documents and controls changes to the information system. Appropriate organization officials approve information system changes in accordance with organizational policies and procedures.*

- *CM-4 Monitoring Configuration Changes—The organization monitors changes to the information system and conducts security impact analyses to determine the effects of the changes.*

- *CM-5 Access Restrictions for Change—The organization enforces access restrictions associated with changes to the information system.*

- *CM-6 Configuration Settings—The organization configures the security settings of IT products to the most restrictive mode consistent with information system operational requirements.*

- *CM-7 Least Functionality—The organization configures the information system to provide only essential capabilities and specifically prohibits and/or restricts the use of the following functions; ports, protocols, and/or services: [Assignment: organization-defined list of prohibited and/or restricted functions, ports, protocols, and/or services]. Information systems are capable of providing a wide variety of functions and services. Some of the functions and services provided by default may not be necessary to support essential organizational operations (e.g., key missions, functions). The functions and services provided by information systems should be carefully reviewed to determine which functions and services are candidates for elimination (e.g., voice over Internet protocol, instant messaging, file transfer protocol, hypertext transfer protocol, file sharing).*

Change Management

Change management seeks to prevent changes that could detrimentally affect the security of a system. In its entirety, the CCM process reduces the risk that any changes made to a system (insertions, installations, deletions, uninstallations, or modifications) result in a compromise to system or data confidentiality, integrity, or availability. It does this by providing a repeatable mechanism that effects system modifications in a controlled environment. In accordance with the change management process, system changes must be tested prior to implementation to observe the effects of the change, thereby minimizing the risk of adverse results.

Each organization must take into account the costs, the planning and scheduling, and the training that will be needed for a thorough and effective change management process. However, because the general approach to change management is universal, organizations can structure and implement a repeatable process to save organizational resources on future projects.

The change management process also identifies the steps required to ensure that all changes are properly requested, evaluated, and authorized. Also, the process provides a detailed, step-by-step procedure for identifying, processing, tracking, and documenting changes. An example of a change management process is described in the following sections.

Step 1: Identify Change The change process begins with the identifying of a need for change. The change can be initiated by individuals, such as users or system owners, or it can be identified by audits or other reviews. It may consist of updating the database fields or records, or it may consist of upgrading the operating system using the latest security patches. After the need for a change has been identified, a **change request** is submitted to the appropriate decision-making body.

Step 2: Evaluate Change Request After a change request has been made, an analysis of the affects that the change management will have on the system or related systems is conducted using the following guidelines:

- Is the change viable? Does it improve the system's performance or its security?
- Is the change the correct one, technically? Is it necessary? Is it feasible, given the system's constraints?
- Will the system's security be affected by the change?
- Have the associated costs of implementing the change been considered?
- Will security components be affected by the change?

Step 3: Implementation Decision After the change has been reviewed and evaluated, one of the following actions is taken:

- Approve—Implementation is authorized and may occur at any time after the appropriate authorization signature has been documented.
- Deny—The request is denied, regardless of circumstances and information provided.
- Defer—The decision is postponed until further notice. In this situation, additional testing or analysis may be needed before a final decision can be made.

Step 4: Implement Approved Change Request If implementation is authorized, the change is moved from the test environment and into production. In general, the persons who are updating the production environment should be distinct from the persons who developed the change in order to provide greater assurance that unapproved changes do not get implemented.

Step 5: Continuous Monitoring The change process calls for continuous monitoring to ensure that the system is operating as intended and that implemented changes do not adversely affect either the performance or the security posture of the system. Organizations can achieve the goals of continuous system monitoring by performing configuration verification tests. These tests ensure that the selected configuration for a given system has not been altered outside the established change process. In addition to configuration verification tests, organizations can perform system audits.

Configuration verification tests and system audits entail an examination of characteristics of the system and supporting documentation to verify that the configuration meets user needs and ensure that the current configuration is the approved system configuration baseline.

Auditing (Formal Review)

In this section, we examine the other definition of *auditing*, which refers to the systematic review of an organization to ensure it meets regulations. Auditing must be performed by well-qualified individuals. In the United States, the Auditing Standards Board of American Institute of Certified Public Accountants has developed sets of standards referred to as Generally Accepted Auditing Standards (GAAS). Although they are designed for financial auditing, the principles outlined in these standards are applicable to technology auditing:

General Standards:

1. *The auditor must have adequate technical training and proficiency to perform the audit.*

2. *The auditor must maintain independence in mental attitude in all matters relating to the audit.*

3. *The auditor must exercise due professional care in the performance of the audit and the preparation of the report.*

Standards of Field Work

1. *The auditor must adequately plan the work and must properly supervise any assistants.*

2. *The auditor must obtain a sufficient understanding of the entity and its environment, including its internal control, to assess the risk of material misstatement of the financial statements whether due to error or fraud, and to design the nature, timing, and extent of further audit procedures.*

3. *The auditor must obtain sufficient appropriate audit evidence by performing audit procedures to afford a reasonable basis for an opinion regarding the financial statements under audit.*

Standards of Reporting

1. *The auditor must state in the auditor's report whether the financial statements are presented in accordance with generally accepted accounting principles.*

2. *The auditor must identify in the auditor's report those circumstances in which such principles have not been consistently observed in the current period in relation to the preceding period.*

3. *When the auditor determines that informative disclosures are not reasonably adequate, the auditor must so state in the auditor's report.*

4. *The auditor must either express an opinion regarding the financial statements, taken as a whole, or state that an opinion cannot be expressed, in the auditor's report. When the auditor cannot express an overall opinion, the auditor should state the reasons therefore in the auditor's report. In all cases where an auditor's name is associated with financial statements, the auditor should clearly indicate the character of the auditor's work, if any, and the degree of responsibility the auditor is taking, in the auditor's report.*[11]

IT Auditing

Most formal IT audits examine established control objectives and compare those to the organization's implementations. This can be done for a single system or for an entire IT infrastructure and program. One of the most prevalent standards for **IT auditing** was issued by the Information Systems Audit and Control Association (ISACA). This document, called "IT Standards, Guidelines, and Tools and Techniques for Audit and Assurance and Control Professionals"[12] provides a comprehensive set of standards and guidelines for the IT audit professional. In fact, ISACA provides a certification for auditors; one is declared a Certified Information Systems Auditor (CISA) after demonstrating five years of work experience as an auditor and passing an exam that covers the following five job-practice domain areas:

1. *The Process of Auditing Information Systems—Provide audit services in accordance with IT audit standards to assist the organization with protecting and controlling information systems.*

2. *Governance and Management of IT—Provide assurance that the necessary leadership and organizational structures and processes are in place to achieve objectives and to support the organization's strategy.*

3. *Information Systems Acquisition, Development and Implementation—Provide assurance that the practices for the acquisition, development, testing, and implementation of information systems meet the organization's strategies and objectives.*

4. *Information Systems Operations, Maintenance and Support—Provide assurance that the processes for information systems operations, maintenance and support meet the organization's strategies and objectives.*

5. *Protection of Information Assets—Provide assurance that the organization's security policies, standards, procedures and controls ensure the confidentiality, integrity and availability of information assets.*[13]

Although the specifics of an audit differ from organization to organization, most audits follow this approach:

Phase 1: Initiation and Planning

Phase 2: Fieldwork

Phase 3: Analysis and Review

Phase 4: Final Reporting

Phase 5: Follow-up

We will discuss these phases in the following sections.

Phase 1: Initiation and Planning In the initiation portion Phase 1, the auditing group is contacted by an organizational entity that requested an audit of a particular system, department, or organization. This could be a senior manager asking for an audit of one or more organizational components or an external regulatory entity requesting an independent audit of a third-party organization. Either way, the senior auditing manager contacts the organization to be audited (if the requester so desires) or makes it "a surprise." The senior auditing manager also begins to determine the scope and specifications of the audit, including how many systems will be audited and how deep the audit will reach. The standard to which the target will be audited is also determined.

It is customary for an **engagement letter** to be developed at this point, which serves as a service agreement between the auditing team and the requesting entity. This document includes information on the details of the audit as well as any contractual components, such as costs, time frames, etc.

The planning portion of Phase 1 typically includes the formulation and preparation of the auditing team. Details from the engagement letter are distributed to individual team members, and specific assignments are made. The logistics of the on-site visit (fieldwork) are developed, as are any other administrative tasks that will make the next phase more efficient. Should documentation be available beforehand, including organizational policies, procedures, and standards, this information is reviewed and incorporated into the audit plan.

Phase 2: Fieldwork

The second phase of the audit process involves the on-site visit. From the target organization's perspective, this *is* the audit. A group of auditors arrives on the site and is given access to systems, documentation, organizational policies, procedures and standards, and pretty much anything else they need to conduct the evaluation. The auditing team then begins looking at these documents (if they were not provided previously). If the auditors were expected, the organization has typically prepared for the on-site visit by setting up facilities to aid the auditors in their evaluation.

During the fieldwork phase, it is crucial that the target organization provide as much support for the auditing team as possible. The longer it takes to examine the systems and supporting documentation, the longer and more expensive the audit can become. It is especially crucial to make sure that key personnel are made available to answer any questions the auditors have. Note that the bulk of the audit involves interaction between an auditor and a key system administrator, network administrator, security professional, or IT manager. The primary focus of an audit is to determine if the standards and/or regulations the organization claims to comply with are in fact complied with. This means the organization is "practicing what it preaches" and not only has developed and disseminated its operational methodology but (as revealed by a physical investigation of the organization's systems) also has implemented that methodology. A security audit (and many IT audits) seeks to determine if critical controls are implemented and effective, for example.

Phase 3: Analysis and Review

The third phase involves taking the findings from the on-site visit and conducting detailed analyses of those findings. The reports developed by the various auditors are compiled and compared, and the overall findings are examined. This can include statistical analysis of surveys and other investigatory data. A category of support technology known as Computer-Assisted Auditing Techniques (CAATs) is commonly used to support the on-site investigation and subsequent analysis. CAATs include auditing software and hardware designed to improve the auditors' efficiency and effectiveness.

Phase 4: Final Reporting

After the analysis and review are complete, the auditing team makes a formal report to the target organization and/or requesting entity. This report summarizes the findings of the audit team. Note that the audit report typically will not specify how to resolve any identified deficiencies. That is not the purpose of an audit. The audit is designed to identify deficiencies in an organization's IT infrastructure and operational methodology. Resolution of these issues is typically the focus of the audited organization's employees and can involve consultants, either internal or external.

Phase 5: Follow-Up

At a predetermined interval after the final report has been delivered—hopefully, after the target organization has had a chance to resolve any issues—there is typically a follow-up audit. This follow-up is usually not nearly as in-depth or intensive, and it focuses exclusively on those areas identified as deficient. The results of the follow-up investigation are summarized in a report and provided to whoever requested the audit.

Systems Certification, Accreditation, and Authorization

In security management, **accreditation** is what authorizes an IT system to process, store, or transmit information. It is issued by a management official and serves as a means of ensuring that systems are of adequate quality. It also challenges managers and technical staff to find the best methods to ensure security, given technical constraints, operational constraints, and mission requirements. In the same vein, **certification** is "the comprehensive evaluation of the technical and nontechnical security controls of an IT system to support the accreditation process that establishes the extent to which a particular design and implementation meets a set of specified security requirements."[14] Organizations pursue accreditation or certification to gain a competitive advantage or to provide assurance to their customers. IT systems used by U.S. federal government agencies require accreditation under OMB Circular A-130 and the Computer Security Act of 1987. Accreditation demonstrates that management has identified an acceptable risk level and provided resources to control unacceptable risk levels.

Accreditation and certification are not permanent. Just as standards of due diligence and due care require an ongoing maintenance effort, most accreditation and certification processes require reaccreditation or recertification every few years (typically every three to five years).

At first glance, it may appear that only systems handling secret government data require certification or accreditation. However, organizations are increasingly finding that, in order to comply with all the new federal regulations involving the protection of personal privacy, they need formal mechanisms for verifying and validating their systems.

Auditing for Government and Classified Information Systems

Two documents provide guidance for the certification and accreditation of information system used by the U.S. federal government agencies:

- SP 800-37, Rev. 1: Guide for Applying the Risk Management Framework to Federal Information Systems: A Security Life Cycle Approach.
- NSTISSI No. 1000: National Information Assurance Certification and Accreditation Process (NIACAP).

Information processed by the federal government is grouped into three categories: national security information (NSI), non-NSI, and intelligence community (IC). National security information is processed on national security systems (NSSs). NSSs are managed and operated by the Committee for National Systems Security (CNSS), and non-NSSs are managed and operated by the National Institute of Standards and Technology (NIST). Intelligence community (IC) information is a separate category and is handled according to guidance from the Office of the Director of National Intelligence (DNI).

The Committee on National Security Systems (CNSS) defines an NSS as any information system (including any telecommunications system) used or operated by an agency or by a contractor of any agency, or other organization on behalf of an agency, the function, operation, or use of which:[15]

- Involves intelligence activities
- Involves cryptologic activities related to national security
- Involves command and control of military forces

- Involves equipment that is an integral part of a weapon or weapon system
- Is subject to subparagraph (B), is critical to the direct fulfillment of military or intelligence missions, or is protected at all times by procedures for information that have been specifically authorized under criteria established by an executive order or an act of Congress to be kept classified in the interest of national defense or foreign policy

However, the Federal Information Security Management Act states that this criterion "does not include a system that is to be used for routine administration and business applications (including payroll, finance, logistics, and personnel management applications.)"[16]

National security information must be processed on NSSs, which have more stringent requirements. NSSs (which process a mix of NSI and non-NSI) are accredited using CNSS guidance. Non-NSS systems follow NIST guidance. More than a score of major government agencies store, process, or transmit NSI, and many of them have both NSSs and systems that are not rated as NSSs. You can learn more about the CNSS community and how NSSs are managed and operated at *www.cnss.gov*.

In recent years, the U.S. government's Joint Task Force Transformation Initiative Working Group and NIST have transformed the formal certification and accreditation (C&A) program for non-NSI systems from a separate C&A process into an integrated risk management framework (RMF) that can be used for normal operations and yet still provide assurance that the systems are capable of reliably housing confidential information. NIST SP 800-37, Revision 1 provides a detailed description of the new RMF process (see *http://csrc.nist.gov/publications/nistpubs/ 800-37-rev1/sp800-37-rev1-final.pdf*).

NIST SP 800-37, Rev. 1 specifically cites NIST SP 800-39, "Integrated Enterprise-Wide Risk Management: Organization, Mission, and Information System View," as the reference for its RMF. The NIST RMF uses a three-tiered approach to risk management, as shown in Figure 10-22. The following text is taken from the recommendations of the Joint Task Force Transformation Initiative that prepared NIST Special Publication 800-37, Rev. 1:

10

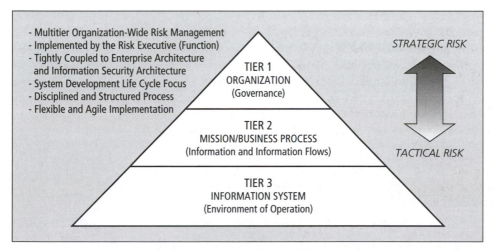

Figure 10-22 Three-tiered approach to risk management

Tier 1 addresses risk from an organizational perspective with the development of a comprehensive governance structure and organization-wide risk management strategy....

Tier 2 addresses risk from a mission and business process perspective and is guided by the risk decisions at Tier 1. Tier 2 activities are closely associated with enterprise architecture....

Tier 3 addresses risk from an information system perspective and is guided by the risk decisions at Tiers 1 and 2. Risk decisions at Tiers 1 and 2 impact the ultimate selection and deployment of needed safeguards and countermeasures (i.e., security controls) at the information system level. Information security requirements are satisfied by the selection of appropriate management, operational, and technical security controls from NIST Special Publication 800-53.

The Risk Management Framework (RMF) [shown in Figure 10-23] provides a disciplined and structured process that integrates information security and risk management activities into the system development life cycle. The RMF operates primarily at Tier 3 in the risk management hierarchy but can also have interactions at Tiers 1 and 2 (e.g., providing feedback from ongoing authorization decisions to the risk executive [function], dissemination of updated threat and risk information to authorizing officials and information system owners).

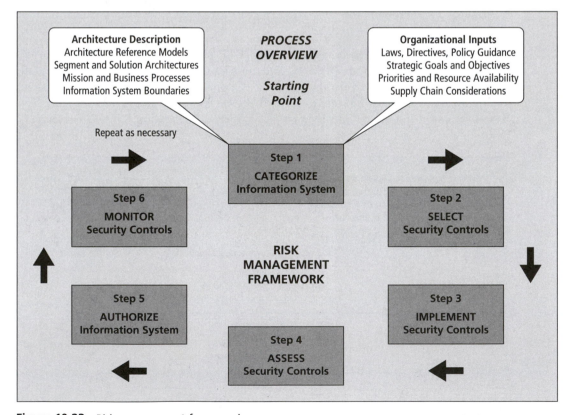

Figure 10-23   Risk management framework
© Cengage Learning 2013

The RMF steps include:

- *Categorize the information system and the information processed, stored, and transmitted by that system based on an impact analysis.*

- *Select an initial set of baseline security controls for the information system based on the security categorization; tailoring and supplementing the security control baseline as needed based on an organizational assessment of risk and local conditions.*

- *Implement the security controls and describe how the controls are employed within the information system and its environment of operation.*

- *Assess the security controls using appropriate assessment procedures to determine the extent to which the controls are implemented correctly, operating as intended, and producing the desired outcome with respect to meeting the security requirements for the system.*

- *Authorize information system operation based on a determination of the risk to organizational operations and assets, individuals, other organizations, and the nation resulting from the operation of the information system and the decision that this risk is acceptable.*

- *Monitor the security controls in the information system on an ongoing basis including assessing control effectiveness, documenting changes to the system or its environment of operation, conducting security impact analyses of the associated changes, and reporting the security state of the system to designated organizational officials.*[17]

The bottom line is that if your organization's systems are subject to these standards, they must be configured, operated, and audited accordingly.

10

Auditing and the ISO 27000 Series

Most commercial systems audit against a recognized standard. Currently, the most widely recognized one is called "Information Technology—Code of Practice for Information Security Management." Published in 2000 as British Standard BS7799, this document, now known as ISO/IEC 17799, was adopted as an international standard framework for information security by the International Organization for Standardization (ISO) and the International Electrotechnical Commission (IEC). It was revised in 2005 (as ISO 17799:2005) and then renamed ISO 27002 in 2007 when it was aligned with ISO 27001. Although the details of ISO/IEC 27002 are available to those who purchase the standard, here are the areas it covers:

1. Risk Assessment and Treatment
2. Security Policy
3. Organization of Information Security
4. Asset Management
5. Human Resource Security
6. Physical and Environmental Security
7. Communications and Operations
8. Access Control

9. Information Systems Acquisition, Development and Maintenance

10. Information Security Incident Management

11. Business Continuity Management

12. Compliance

For more details on these ISO/IEC sections, see *www.praxiom.com/iso-17799-2005.htm.*

The stated purpose of ISO/IEC 27002 is to provide recommendations for information security management for use by those who are responsible for initiating, implementing, or maintaining security in their organization. It is intended to provide a common basis for developing organizational security standards and effective security management practice and to provide confidence in interorganizational dealings. It is also designed to serve as a metric for the assessment of "good security management" within the organization, as defined in the ISO series.

Whereas ISO/IEC 27001 provides a broad overview—information on 127 controls divided into 10 areas—ISO/IEC 27002 provides information on how to implement ISO/IEC 27001 and how to set up an information security management system (ISMS). The major steps of this process are presented in Figure 10-24. In the United Kingdom, the correct implementation of these standards (as determined by a BS7799 certified evaluator) allows an organization to obtain ISMS certification and accreditation.

ISO/IEC 27001 provides implementation details using a step-by-step process that outlines how you should approach implementing change. This is known as the Plan-Do-Check-Act cycle:[18]

Plan:

1. Define the scope of the ISMS.

2. Define an ISMS policy.

3. Define the approach to risk assessment.

4. Identify the risks.

5. Assess the risks.

6. Identify and evaluate options for the treatment of risk.

7. Select control objectives and controls.

8. Prepare a statement of applicability (SOA).

Do:

9. Formulate a risk treatment plan.

10. Implement the risk treatment plan.

11. Implement controls.

12. Implement training and awareness programs.

13. Manage operations.

14. Manage resources.

15. Implement procedures to detect and respond to security incidents.

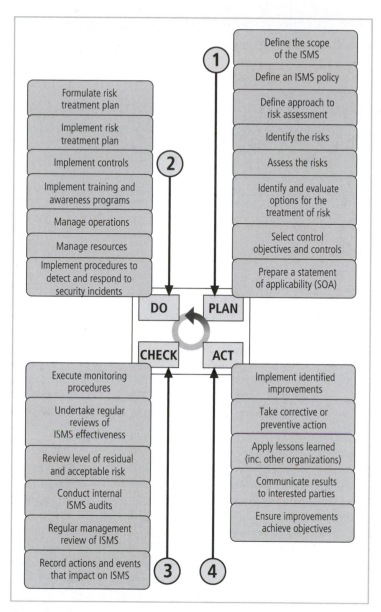

Figure 10-24   Setting up an information security management system
© Cengage Learning 2013

Check:

16. Execute monitoring procedures.

17. Undertake regular reviews of ISMS effectiveness.

18. Review the level of residual and acceptable risk.

19. Conduct internal ISMS audits.

20. Undertake regular management review of the ISMS.

21. Record actions and events that impact an ISMS.

Act:

22. Implement identified improvements.

23. Take corrective or preventive action.

24. Apply lessons learned.

25. Communicate results to interested parties.

26. Ensure improvements achieve objectives.

Although ISO/IEC 27001 provides some implementation information, it simply specifies what must be done—not how to do it. As stated earlier, its primary purpose is to enable organizations to obtain certification; thus, it serves more as an assessment tool than an implementation framework.

Auditing and COBIT

Control Objectives for Information and Related Technology (COBIT) provides advice about the implementation of sound controls and control objectives for information security. This document can be used not only as a planning tool for information security but also as an auditing framework controls model. COBIT was created in 1992 by the Information Systems Audit and Control Association (ISACA) and the IT Governance Institute (ITGI). Documentation on COBIT was first published in 1996 and then updated in 1998, 2000, 2003, 2005, and 2007 (May). ISACA has prepared the following introduction to the COBIT framework:

> COBIT is an IT governance framework and supporting toolset that allows managers to bridge the gap between control requirements, technical issues, and business risks. COBIT enables clear policy development and good practice for IT control throughout organizations. ITGI's latest version—COBIT 4.0—emphasizes regulatory compliance, helps organizations to increase the value attained from IT, enables alignment, and simplifies implementation of the COBIT framework. It does not invalidate work done based on earlier versions of COBIT but instead can be used to enhance work already done based upon those earlier versions. When major activities are planned for IT governance initiatives, or when an overhaul of the enterprise control framework is anticipated, it is recommended to start fresh with COBIT 4.0. COBIT 4.0 presents activities in a more streamlined and practical manner so continuous improvement in IT governance is easier than ever to achieve.[19]

COBIT presents 34 high-level objectives that cover 215 control objectives. The control objectives are categorized into four domains, which are discussed in the following sections. Those domains are: plan and organize, acquire and implement, deliver and support, and monitor and evaluate.

Although COBIT was designed to be an IT governance structure, it provides a framework to support information security requirements and assessment needs. Organizations that incorporate COBIT assessments into their IT governance are better prepared for general information security risk management operations.

Plan and Organize This domain focuses on the planning and organization of IT use, including recommendations for achieving goals and objectives. Part of this process is to examine the form IT takes in the organization to obtain the best possible results. The high-level controlling objectives for planning and organization are:

PO1—Define a Strategic IT Plan.

PO2—Define the Information Architecture.

PO3—Determine Technological Direction.

PO4—Define the IT Processes, Organization, and Relationships.

PO5—Manage the IT Investment.

PO6—Communicate Management Aims and Direction.

PO7—Manage IT Human Resources.

PO8—Manage Quality.

PO9—Assess and Manage IT Risks.

PO10—Manage Projects.

Acquire and Implement The acquisition and implementation domain focuses on the specification of requirements, the acquisition of needed components, and the integration of these components into the organization's systems. Ongoing maintenance and change requirements to extend the usability of the system are also focused on. The high-level controlling objectives for acquiring and implementing are:

AI1—Identify Automated Solutions.

AI2—Acquire and Maintain Application Software.

AI3—Acquire and Maintain Technology Infrastructure.

AI4—Enable Operation and Use.

AI5—Procure IT Resources.

AI6—Manage Changes.

AI7—Install and Accredit Solutions and Changes.

10

Delivery and Support The delivery and support domain focuses on the functionality of the system for the end user. It also focuses on the systems applications—including the input, processing, and output components. Efficiency and effectiveness of operations are critical to the system function, and therefore processes that support those operations are also examined. The high-level controlling objectives for delivery and support are:

DS1—Define and Manage Service Levels.

DS2—Manage Third-Party Services.

DS3—Manage Performance and Capacity.

DS4—Ensure Continuous Service.

DS5—Ensure Systems Security.

DS6—Identify and Allocate Costs.

DS7—Educate and Train Users.

DS8—Manage Service Desk and Incidents.

DS9—Manage the Configuration.

DS10—Manage Problems.

DS11—Manage Data.

DS12—Manage the Physical Environment.

DS13—Manage Operations.

Monitor and Evaluate The monitor and evaluate domain focuses on the alignment between IT systems usage and organizational strategy. This assessment identifies the regulatory requirements for which controls are needed. Another function of this domain is monitoring the effectiveness and efficiency of IT systems against the organizational control processes in the delivery and support domain. The high-level controlling objectives for monitoring and evaluating are:

ME1—Monitor and Evaluate IT Processes.

ME2—Monitor and Evaluate Internal Control.

ME3—Ensure Regulatory Compliance.

ME4—Provide IT Governance.

The latter sections are much more suited to systems auditing than the former. With an eye toward the objectives of an information system, the functions of it become much more critical. Auditing compares the functions to the objectives and identifies deficiencies.

Chapter Summary

- The term *auditing* has more than one meaning. It can refer to the ongoing review of a system's functional data to evaluate proper operation of the system, detect potential incidents, and ensure compliance with systems policies. Alternatively, it can refer to a periodic self-review of the network environment to evaluate it against policy requirements.

- The process of monitoring a system involves keeping a close watch on both the internal operations and the use of that system.

- A computer or network device log is a detailed chronological record of the operation of a computer system, including the use and modification of that system. The kinds of events to be recorded include process events, logon events, group or permission change events, resource access events, network connection events, network data transfer events, system restarts and shutdown events, and audit system or log events.

- Aggregated log files from network devices, servers, and even critical workstations must be well managed and should typically be stored off the entity that generates them, and this storage area must be suitably hardened to protect the information. Log management deals with storage, retention, baselining, encryption, and disposal.

- Key log sources include: Windows-based systems logs, such as Application, Security, Setup, Forwarded Events, and System logs, as well as the Windows-specific Admin, Operational, and Debug logs. Linux-based logging uses files for recording various activities on the system. These files, typically located in the /var/log/ directory, include boot.log, cron, messages, lastlog, wtmp, btmp, and utmp. Linux also has a centralized logging facility named syslog that allows multiple system utilities to log using the same mechanism.

- Given that system logs are often difficult to collect, store, read, and understand, log management solutions have been made available. These tools collect events from log files, process the data, store the results, and provide notifications or alerts, as required. The goals for log management technologies are to collect and centralize events, retain log information, normalize log information, correlate events, provide searching, and provide reporting.

- An advanced form of log management called security information and event management (SIEM) provides superior correlation and notification capabilities.

- Some organizations find the need for a Security Operations Center (SOC) to provide the operational infrastructure for detecting attacks, coordinating responses, and reducing damage to the organization.

- Change and Configuration Management (CMM) controls the effects of revisions to configurations on information systems and networks, a crucial aspect in performing ongoing audits of the network systems and their associated configurations. Configuration management seeks to monitor and perhaps control complex systems configuration in an organization. Change management seeks to prevent and/or control changes that could detrimentally affect the security posture of a system.

- Auditing should be performed by individuals who are well qualified using a set of Generally Accepted Auditing Standards. Auditors must have adequate technical training and proficiency to perform the audit and must maintain independence.

- The certification and accreditation of federal information systems is governed by two documents: SP 800-37, Rev. 1 ("Guide for Applying the Risk Management Framework to Federal Information Systems: A Security Life Cycle Approach") and the CNSS Instruction-1000 ("National Information Assurance Certification and Accreditation Process").

- Currently, the most widely recognized model for security assessment and practice, found in the ISO/IEC 27000 series of standards, is called "Information Technology—Code of Practice for Information Security Management."

- IT auditing examines established control objectives and compares them with the actual implementations of the organization. Control Objectives for Information and Related Technology (COBIT) provides advice about the implementation of sound controls and control objectives for information security.

Review Questions

1. What are the two meanings of *auditing* used in this chapter?

2. Systems monitoring involves observing which two types of activity?

3. What is a log file?

4. What kinds of events are recorded in logs?

5. What does log management entail?

6. What are the key log sources to be considered for network security?

7. What is Linux's centralized logging facility called? What does it do?

8. What does a log management tool do?

9. What advanced option is available if additional capabilities are needed for log management?

10. What facility dedicated to managing network security do some organizations create?

11. What is configuration management?

12. What is change management?

13. Which NIST publication sets the standard for a configuration management process?

14. What should an organization look for in the people who will be auditing its systems and networks?

15. What is IT auditing?

16. What documents govern the auditing needs of U.S. federal government information systems?

17. Information processed by the U.S. federal government is grouped into what three categories?

18. What is the ISO/IEC 27000 series of standards?

19. What is ISACA?

20. What is COBIT? What does it do?

Real World Exercises

Exercise 10-1

The Gartner Group makes recommendations for SIEM (Security Incident and Event Management) using something called the magic quadrant. You should be able to find a relatively recent magic quadrant for SIEM products by searching for it online. After looking it over, discuss which products seem to have the best vision and the best execution.

Exercise 10-2

Using an Internet browser, search for background material on firms that specialize in information systems auditing. What are some of the firms working in this area? What job skills would you need to have to work for a firm like this?

Exercise 10-3

Using an Internet browser, search for Web sites that offer open source solutions for systems log consolidation. Pick one Web site and describe the tools that are made available and the platforms for which those tools can collect and process log information.

Hands-On Projects

Project 10-1

This project examines ways to audit various processes and services in a typical Windows environment. To successfully complete this project, you need a functioning Windows 7 system.

There are several methods for auditing running processes and services in a typical Windows 7 environment. In this project, we use the Task Manager.

1. To open the Task Manager, click the **Windows Start** button and type `taskmgr.exe` in the Search Programs and Files box at the bottom of the menu. Make sure the file appears in the search results at the top of the search box, and then press **Enter**. The Windows Task Manager window appears.

2. There are several tabs across the window that allow you to examine various applications, processes, and services running on the system. Click the **Processes** tab to show a list of running processes. If you are logged in as a user with administrative privileges, you can click the **Show processes from all users** box to show processes for all users currently running; otherwise, you can only see processes spawned by your user account.

3. Right-click one of the entries in the window and select **Properties** from the menu. Here, you can see details about the file, such as size, location, and details regarding when the file was created, last modified, and last accessed. To see which users have permissions associated with this file, click the **Security** tab to see both the list of users or groups and the permissions given to each.

4. Scroll through the list, paying particular attention to the filenames listed in the Image Name column. If you logged in as an administrator and enabled the check box, as described in the previous step, pay attention to the names listed in the User Name column. If you see an image name you're not familiar with, use a search engine like Google or Bing to search for that image name. If, based on your research of the image name, you believe the process should not be running or could be malicious, you may want to stop the process from running. Do this by right-clicking the entry in the window and selecting **End Process** from the menu. This should be done with extreme care and only after thoroughly researching the process in question. Killing critical processes such as explorer.exe can make the system unstable and force you to reboot the system to make it usable again.

5. Click the **Services** tab to view the list of running services.

10

6. As you did earlier, examine the list of running service names to see if there are any unfamiliar services running. You may also right-click an unfamiliar service and select **Go to Process** to see the process this service is associated with. If, based on your research of the service, you believe the service should not be running, you may want to stop the service from running. To do this, right-click the service and choose **Go to Process** to be taken to the process responsible for this service, then right-click the service and select **End Process** from the menu. As discussed earlier, this should be done with extreme care and only after thoroughly researching the process in question.

Project 10-2

This project examines ways to audit various processes and services in a typical Linux environment. To successfully complete the project, you need a functioning Linux system. We used the BackTrack R1 application running in a virtual environment.

There are several methods for auditing running processes and services in a typical Linux environment. In this project, we use the ps command.

1. Open a terminal window.

2. Type **ps** and press **Enter**. A list of active jobs will appear.

3. For details about the active jobs, type **ps x** and press **Enter**. The x option displays information about the services and processes that are running in our X-windows session, as shown in Figure 10-25.

Figure 10-25   Command output

Source: Linux

4. Depending on circumstances, you may need to see a complete list of processes running system-wide. To do this, type **ps -AF** and press Enter. Note the addition of a new column that shows the user ID (UID) that the listed service or process is running under. The output should look similar to what is shown in Figure 10-26.

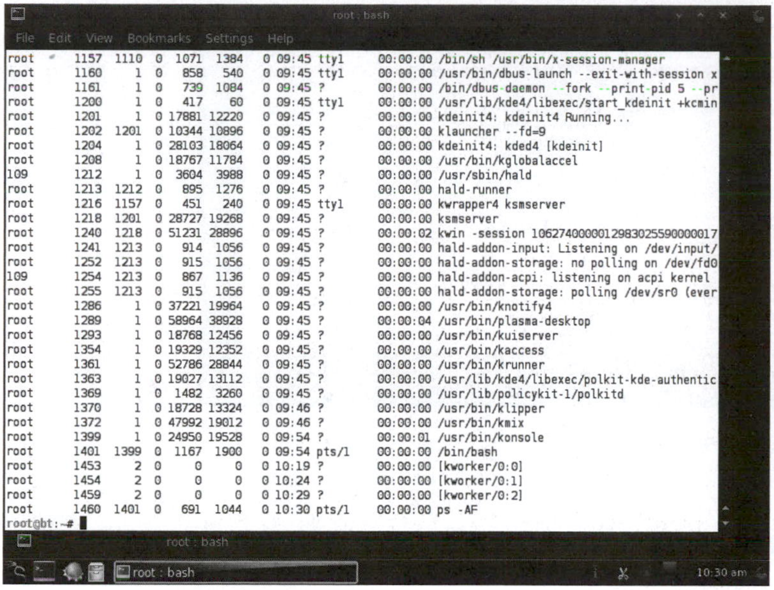

Figure 10-26 AF command output
Source: Linux

5. You can also audit running processes and services using the top command, which allows you to view processes running in real-time, with periodic updates. Open a terminal window.

6. Type **top** and press **Enter**. Your results should be similar to what is shown in Figure 10-27.

7. The default view displays, based on CPU usage. However, this sort option can be changed. To change the sort option, type **F** (note this is a capital letter).

8. You will now see a list of sortable options. Type **n** to sort by memory usage. Note that the Current Sort Field in the upper-left corner has changed from K to N, and that the menu item now has an asterisk to its left, as shown in Figure 10-28. Press **Enter** to return to the main display.

9. We will now examine the processes in the order they started on the system. Type **F**. When the sort menu appears, type **a** to sort by process ID (PID), then press **Enter** to return to the main display.

10. The order is inverted, with the display showing the largest PID first. To reverse this, type **R** (note that this is a capital letter). Notice the order has changed, and the lowest PIDs are now being displayed, as shown in Figure 10-29.

10

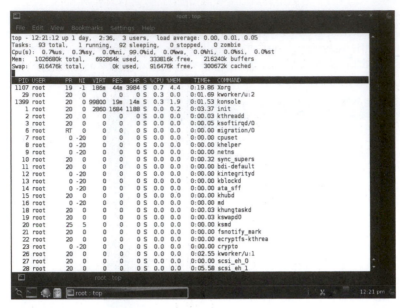

Figure 10-27 `top` command output

Source: Linux

Figure 10-28 Change `top` sort option

Source: Linux

11. We can stop (or "kill") processes that we don't want to run any longer. Sort the process list by PID, highest to lowest, using the steps discussed previously.

12. Locate the PID for the `top` command.

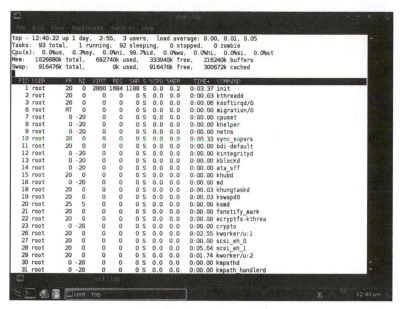

Figure 10-29   PID ordered listing

Source: Linux

13. Type **k** (note this is lower-case). Notice the prompt asking us for the PID to kill. Type the PID number for the `top` command and press **Enter**. Your display should look similar to what is shown in Figure 10-30.

10

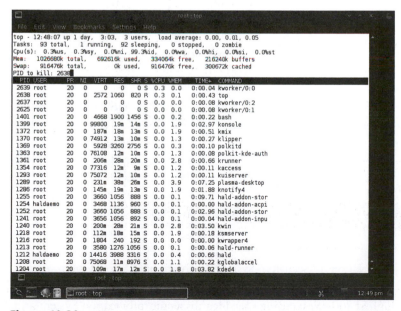

Figure 10-30   Killing a process

Source: Linux

14. You're now prompted for confirmation to kill the process using signal 15. Press y, then press **Enter**.

15. You've now killed the top process and have been returned to the command prompt.

Endnotes

1. Dempsey, K. et. al., NIST SP 800-137: *Information Security Continuous Monitoring for Federal Information Systems and Organizations.* Accessed January 15, 2012 @ *http://csrc.nist.gov/publications/nistpubs/800-137/SP800-137-Final.pdf.*

2. Wikipedia. "Process (computing)." Accessed January 15, 2012 @ *http://en.wikipedia.org/wiki/Process_%28computing%29.*

3. Russinovich, Mark. "PSLoggedOn v1.34." Accessed January 15, 2012 @ *http://technet.microsoft.com/en-us/sysinternals/bb897545.*

4. Microsoft Technet. "Audit object access." Accessed July 21, 2011 @ *http://technet.microsoft.com/en-us/library/cc776774%28WS.10%29.aspx.*

5. McAfee. "Solution Brief: McAfee Data Loss Prevention." Accessed January 15, 2012 @ *http://www.mcafee.com/us/resources/solution-briefs/sb-dlp.pdf.*

6. Kent, Karen and Murugiah Souppaya. NIST SP *800-92: Guide to Computer Security Log Management.*

7. Ibid.

8. Phillip Maier. *Audit and Trace Log Management,* (Boca Raton, FL: Auerbach, 2006).

9. Microsoft Technet. "Event Logs." Accessed January 15, 2012 @ *http://technet.microsoft.com/en-us/library/cc722404.aspx.*

10. "Microsoft Windows 7 Events Viewer Help File." Accessed March 19, 2011 @ embedded help system.

11. "AU Section 150 Generally Accepted Auditing Standards." Accessed April 21, 2011 @ *www.aicpa.org/Storage/Resources/Standards/DownloadableDocuments/AU-00150.PDF.*

12. ISACA. "IT Standards, Guidelines, and Tools and Techniques for Audit and Assurance and Control Professionals." Accessed April 25, 2011 @ *www.isaca.org/Knowledge-Center/Standards/Pages/default.aspx.*

13. ISACA. "Certified Information Systems Auditor® 2011 Bulletin of Information." Accessed April 25, 2011 @ *www.isaca.org/Certification/CISA-Certified-Information-Systems-Auditor/Pages/CISA-BOI.aspx.*

14. National Institute of Standards and Technology. "Detailed Overview: Background." Accessed May 27, 2003 @ *http://csrc.nist.gov/groups/SMA/fisma/overview.html#background.*

15. Committee on National Security Systems. "National Information Assurance (IA) Glossary." Accessed January 15, 2012 @ *http://www.cnss.gov/Assets/pdf/cnssi_4009.pdf.*

16. Barker, W. *NIST SP800-59:* Guideline for Identifying an Information System as a National Security System. Accessed January 15, 2012 @ *http://csrc.nist.gov/publications/nistpubs/800-59/SP800-59.pdf.*

17. Joint Task Force Transformation Initiative. *NIST Special Publication 800-37, Rev. 1: Guide for Applying the Risk Management Framework to Federal Information Systems: A Security Life Cycle Approach.* Accessed March 27, 2010 @ *http://csrc.nist.gov/publications/PubsSPs.html.*

18. Humphries. T. "The Newly Revised Part 2 of BS 7799." Accessed May 27, 2003 @ *www.gammassl.co.uk/bs7799/The%20Newly%20Revised%20Part%202%20of%20BS%207799ver3a.pdf.*

19. SOX-online. "COSO & COBIT Center." Accessed August 14, 2006 @ *www.sox-online.com/coso_cobit.html.*

10

chapter 11

Contingency Planning and Networking Incident Response

Subtle and insubstantial, the expert leaves no trace; divinely mysterious, he is inaudible. Thus he is master of his enemy's fate. — Sun Tzu

Upon completion of this material, you should be able to:

- Explain the need for contingency planning
- List the major components of contingency planning
- Create a simple set of contingency plans, using business impact analysis
- Prepare and execute a test of contingency plans
- Explain the network incident response process
- Explain the need for sound backup and recovery practices and what they consist of

Rusty Response

EBS had made great strides in preparing for the upcoming PCI audit. The IT team had remediated a number of issues with its firewalls and intrusion prevention devices, and it had audited a number of security program components that hadn't been scrutinized in years. It was determined to address its security problems so as not to affect PCI compliance.

Still, Scott McCaffrey, the IT operations manager, was nervous. He and his staff had made great strides since the EBS Web site had been hacked several years before. Because the company had been fortunate enough not to suffer another attack, there had been no real-world test of the incident management process that had been enacted at that time. The EBS IT staff felt confident, but they didn't want to slide back into the reactive security posture that had allowed the initial Web defacement.

Because Paige Davis was leading the PCI compliance effort, Scott entrusted her to lead the effort in updating the process. Paige enlisted some of the security folks to research and document threats, categorize the threats to help educate the rest of the IT staff, and analyze the EBS' security defenses in relation to these documented threats. These combined actions would help EBS understand its current IT "enemies" and develop the appropriate responses.

Introduction

In addition to deliberate attacks from hostile parties, networks are susceptible to outside events and internal failures. In fact, many network outages are the unintended consequences of actions taken by friendly parties. When the network is disrupted, business operations often come to a standstill. NIST Special Publication 800-34 Rev 1, "Contingency Planning Guide for Federal Information Systems," specifies the following:

> *Because information system resources are so essential to an organization's success, it is critical that identified services provided by these systems are able to operate effectively without excessive interruption. Contingency planning supports this requirement by establishing thorough plans, procedures, and technical measures that can enable a system to be recovered as quickly and effectively as possible following a service disruption. Contingency planning is unique to each system, providing preventive measures, recovery strategies, and technical considerations appropriate to the system's information confidentiality, integrity, and availability requirements and the system impact level.*[1]

Some organizations—such as federal and state governmental agencies, financial institutions, and healthcare providers—are required by law or other mandate to have such procedures in place at all times.

Organizations in both the public and private sectors should prepare for the unexpected. In general, an organization's ability to weather losses caused by an unexpected event depends on proper planning and execution of such a plan; without a workable plan, an unexpected event can cause severe damage to an organization's information resources and assets, from which it may never recover. "On average, over 40 percent of businesses that don't have a disaster plan go out of business after a major loss like a fire, a break-in, or a storm."[2]

What Is Contingency Planning?

Contingency planning (CP) is the process by which the information technology and information security teams position their organizations to prepare for, detect, react to, and recover from man-made or natural events that threaten the security of information resources and assets. The main goal of CP is to restore normal modes of operation, with minimal cost and disruption to business activities, after a disruptive event has occurred. Ideally, CP should ensure that information systems are continuously available to the organization.

CP consists of four integrated components:

- Business impact analysis (BIA)
- Incident response plan (IR plan)
- Disaster recovery plan (DR plan)
- Business continuity plan (BC plan)

Depending on the size and business philosophy of an organization, information technology and information security managers can either (1) create and develop these four components as one unified plan or (2) create the four components separately in conjunction with a set of interlocking procedures that assure continuity. Larger, more-complex organizations will typically create and develop the CP components separately, given that the functions of each component differ in scope, applicability, and design. Smaller organizations tend to adopt a one-plan method consisting of a straightforward set of recovery strategies. Even in those organizations that develop independent plans, however, there is usually a high degree of collaboration and cooperation (information sharing) among the various groups that develop and test the individual components.

In general, four teams of individuals are involved in contingency planning and contingency operations:

- The **CP Management Team (CPMT)**, also known as the CP Team, manages the overall CP process, performing the following functions:
  - Developing the master plan for all CP operations
  - Collecting information about information systems and the threats they face
  - Conducting the BIA

11

- ○ Organizing and staffing the leadership for the subordinate teams
- ○ Providing guidance to and integrating the work of the subordinate teams

The CPMT often consists of a coordinating manager, a few CPMT representatives from various business functions, and representatives from each of the subordinate teams.

- The **incident response (IR) team** develops, tests, manages, and executes the IR plan by detecting, evaluating, and responding to incidents.

  - The **disaster recovery (DR) team** develops, tests, manages, and executes the disaster recovery plan by detecting, evaluating, and responding to disasters and by reestablishing operations at the primary business site.

  - The **business continuity (BC) team** develops, tests, manages, and executes the business continuity plan by setting up and starting off-site operations in the event of an incident or disaster.

Incident response focuses on immediate response to small-scale events, such as hacking attempts, malware outbreaks, and misuse of corporate assets. However, if the incident escalates into a disaster, the IR plan may give way to the DR plan and BC plan, as shown in Figure 11-1. The DR plan typically focuses on restoring systems after disasters occur; therefore, it is closely associated with the BC plan. In some organizations, these two plans are considered one plan, which is known as the **Business Resumption Plan**. The BC plan occurs concurrently with the DR plan when the damage is major or long term, requiring more than simple restoration of information and information resources, as shown in Figure 11-2.

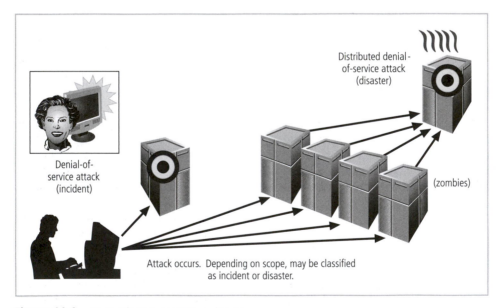

Distributed denial-of-service attack (disaster)

Denial-of-service attack (incident)

(zombies)

Attack occurs. Depending on scope, may be classified as incident or disaster.

Figure 11-1 An incident turns into a disaster
© Cengage Learning 2013

Some experts argue that the three plans contained within CP are so closely linked that they are indistinguishable. In fact, each has a distinct place, role, and planning requirements.

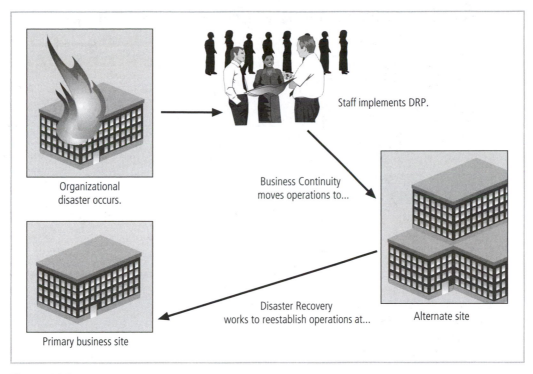

Organizational
disaster occurs.

Staff implements DRP.

Business Continuity
moves operations to...

Disaster Recovery
works to reestablish operations at...

Alternate site

Primary business site

Figure 11-2   Move from disaster recovery to business continuity
© Cengage Learning 2013

11

Furthermore, each plan (IR, DR, and BC) comes into play at a specific time in the life of an incident. Figure 11-3 shows this sequence and shows the overlap that may occur. How the plans interact and the ways in which they are brought into action are discussed in the sections that follow.

Stages and Components of Contingency Planning

According to the National Institute of Standards and Technology, as noted in NIST Special Publication 800-34 Rev.1: Contingency Planning Guide for Federal Information Systems, CP involves the following major steps:

1. *Form the CPMT. Assemble the management team that will guide CP planning and execution. This includes representatives from business management, operations and the projected subordinate teams.*

2. *Develop the contingency planning policy statement. The CP Policy is the formal policy that will guide the efforts of the subordinate teams in developing their plans, and the overall operations of the organization during contingency operations.*

3. *Conduct the BIA. The BIA, described later in this chapter, helps identify and prioritize organizational functions, and the information systems and components critical to supporting the organization's mission/business processes.*

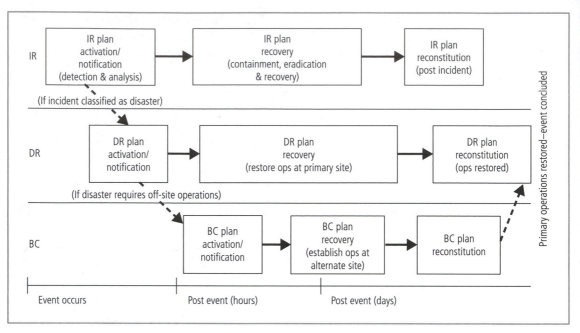

Figure 11-3 Incident response, disaster recovery, and business continuity workflow
© Cengage Learning 2013

4. *Form subordinate planning teams. For each of the subordinate areas, organize a team to develop the IR, DR and BC plans. These groups may or may not contain individuals responsible for implementing the plan.*

5. *Develop subordinate planning policies. Just as the CPMT developed an overall CP policy, the newly formed IR, DR and BC planning teams will begin by developing an IR, DR or BC planning policy, respectively.*

6. *Integrate the BIA. Each of the subordinate planning teams will independently review and incorporate aspects of the BIA of importance to their planning efforts. As different teams may need different components, the actions and assessments of each team may vary.*

7. *Identify preventive controls. Assess those countermeasures and safeguards that mitigate the risk and impact of events on organizational data, operations and personnel.*

8. *Organize Response Teams. Specify the skills needed on each subordinate response team (IR/DR/BC) and identify personnel needed. Ensure personnel rosters are exclusive (no personnel on two different teams) and that all needed skills are covered. These are the individuals who will be directly called up if a particular plan is activated in response to an actual incident or disaster.*

9. *Create contingency strategies. The CPMT, with input from the subordinate team leaders will evaluate and invest in strategies that will support the IR, DR and BC efforts should an event impact business operations. These include data backup and recovery plans, offsite data storage and alternate site occupancy strategies.*

10. *Develop subordinate plans. For each subordinate area develop a plan to handle the corresponding actions and activities necessary to a) respond to an incident, b) recover from a disaster and c) establish operations at an alternate site following a disruptive event.*

11. *Ensure plan testing, training, and exercises. Ensure each subordinate plan is tested and the corresponding personnel are trained to handle any event that escalates into an incident or a disaster.*

12. *Ensure plan maintenance. Manage the plan, ensuring periodic review, evaluation and update.*[3]

The flow of these steps integrates the efforts of the various tasks (BIA, IR planning, DR planning, and BC planning), as shown in Figure 11-4.

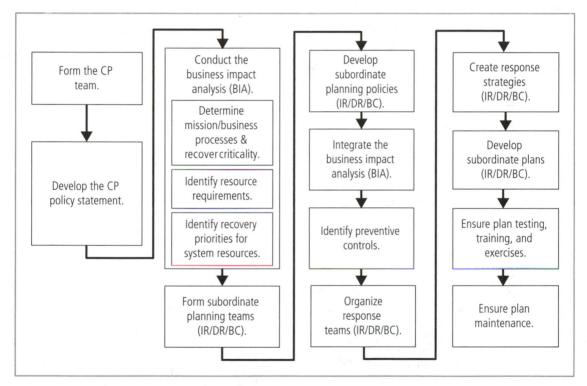

Figure 11-4   Contingency planning life cycle
© Cengage Learning 2013

Depending on the organization, the DR and BC planning could be integrated into a Business Resumption Plan, as mentioned earlier. In this event, the overall planning methodology would address the general contingency-planning strategies as well as the business resumption components. The IR planning would be developed and integrated into the overall CP planning process but would also require additional information, as described next.

Business Impact Analysis (BIA)   The business impact analysis (BIA), the first major component of the CP process, provides the CPMT with information about systems and the threats they face. It is a crucial component, given that it provides an assessment of the system operations that the organization absolutely needs to keep going during and after an event. According to NIST Special Publication 800-34, Rev.1, the BIA involves three major steps:

1. *Determine mission/business processes and recovery criticality. Mission/Business processes supported by the system are identified and the impact of a system disruption to those processes is determined along with outage impacts and estimated downtime. The downtime should reflect the maximum time that an organization can tolerate while still maintaining the mission.*[4]

2. *Identify resource requirements. Realistic recovery efforts require a thorough evaluation of the resources required to resume mission/business processes and related interdependencies as quickly as possible. Examples of resources that should be identified include facilities, personnel, equipment, software, data files, system components, and vital records.*[5]

3. *Identify recovery priorities for system resources. Based upon the results from the previous activities, system resources can be linked more clearly to critical mission/business processes and functions. Priority levels can be established for sequencing recovery activities and resources.*[6]

An example of the three stages of a BIA is shown in Figure 11-5.

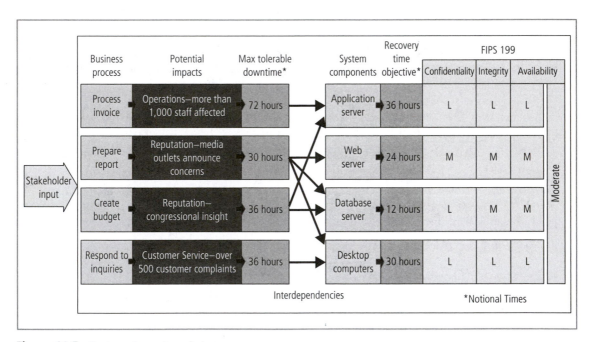

Figure 11-5 Business impact analysis process
© Cengage Learning 2013

Incident Response Plan According to the Carnegie Mellon Software Engineering Institute, "[Intruders] actively develop and use sophisticated programs to rapidly penetrate systems. As a result, intrusions and the damage they cause are often achieved in a matter of seconds."[7] The Institute also reports that organizations "will not know what to do in the event of an intrusion if the necessary procedures, roles, and responsibilities have not been defined and exercised in advance." The absence of systematic and well-defined procedures, it says, can lead to:

- *Extensive damage to data, systems, and networks due to not taking timely action to contain an intrusion. This can result in increased costs, loss of productivity, and loss of business.*

- *The possibility of an intrusion affecting multiple systems both inside and outside your organization because staff did not know who else to notify and what additional actions to take.*

- *Negative exposure in the news media that can damage your organization's stature and reputation with your shareholders, your customers, and the community at large.*

- *Possible legal liability and prosecution for failure to exercise an adequate standard of due care when your systems are inadvertently or intentionally used to attack others.*[8]

The actions an organization should take while an incident is in progress are defined in a document referred to as the **incident response (IR) plan**. You might care to note that NIST has begun using the term "Cyber Incident Response Plan" (CIRP) to differentiate computer incidents from physical incidents. An **incident** is any clearly identified attack on the organization's information assets that would threaten the assets' confidentiality, integrity, or availability. The IR plan deals with the identification, classification, response, and recovery from an incident and provides answers to questions that victims might pose in the midst of an incident, such as "What do I do now?" For example, a systems administrator may notice that someone is copying information from the server without authorization, signaling a policy violation by a potential hacker or an employee. What should the administrator do first? Whom should he or she contact? What should he or she document? The IR plan supplies the answers.

For example, in the event of a serious virus or worm outbreak, the IR plan may be used to assess the likelihood of imminent damage and to inform key decision makers in the various communities of interest (IT, information security, organization management, and users). The IR plan also enables the organization to take coordinated action that is either predefined and specific or ad hoc and reactive.

We will delve deeper into the aspects of the IR plan later in this chapter.

Disaster Recovery Plan The next vital part of contingency planning is the disaster recovery plan. The IT community of interest, under the leadership of the CIO, is often made responsible for disaster recovery planning, including aspects that are not necessarily technology based.

Disaster recovery planning (DRP) entails the preparation for and recovery from a disaster, whether natural or human-made. For example, if a malicious program evades containment actions and infects or disables most of an organization's systems and its ability to function, the DR plan is activated. Sometimes, incidents are, by their nature, immediately classified as disasters, such as an extensive fire, flood, damaging storm, or earthquake.

11

In general, a disaster has occurred when either of two criteria is met: (1) the organization is unable to contain or control the impact of an incident, or (2) the level of damage or destruction from an incident is so severe that the organization cannot quickly recover from it. The distinction between an incident and a disaster may be subtle. The CP team must document in the DR plan whether an event is classified as an incident or a disaster. This determination is critical because it determines which plan is activated. The key role of a DR plan is defining how to reestablish operations at the location where the organization usually operates.

Business Continuity Plan

Business continuity planning (BCP) ensures that critical business functions can continue if a disaster occurs. Unlike the DR plan, which is usually managed by the IT community of interest, the business continuity plan (BC plan) is most properly managed by the CEO of an organization. It is activated and executed concurrently with the DR plan when the disaster is major or long term and requires fuller and complex restoration of information and IT resources. If a disaster has rendered the current business location unusable, there must be a plan to allow the business to continue to function.

Although the BC plan reestablishes critical business functions at an alternate site, the DR plan focuses on the reestablishment of the technical infrastructure and business operations at the primary site. Not every business needs such a plan or such facilities. Some small companies or fiscally sound organizations may be able to simply cease operations until the primary facilities are restored. Manufacturing and retail organizations, however, depend on continued operations for revenue. Thus, these entities must have a BC plan in place so as to quickly relocate operations with minimal loss of revenue.

CP Disruption Phases

The CP Disruption Phases define the actions that actually occur when an event becomes an incident and/or disaster. According to NIST Special Publication 800-34 Rev.1, an organization goes through three distinct phases when reacting to an event that is determined to pose a threat to the organization:

1. *The Activation/Notification Phase describes the process of activating the plan based on outage impacts and notifying recovery personnel.*

2. *The Recovery Phase details a suggested course of action for recovery teams to restore system operations at an alternate site or using contingency capabilities.*

3. *The Reconstitution Phase includes activities to test and validate system capability and functionality and outlines actions that can be taken to return the system to normal operating conditions and prepare the system against future outages.*[9]

For evaluating IR life cycles, NIST's Computer Security Incident Handling Guide[10] suggests a four-step life cycle: (1) preparation, (2) detection and analysis, (3) containment, eradication, and recovery, and (4) postincident activity. These categories could be used as replacements for the CP stages, given that they address the same basic functions, as described in later sections. Whether the event is an incident or full-scale disaster, the progression through these phases is the same. What is different between incidents and disasters is the escalation component, whereby an event becomes an incident and then is escalated to a disaster, or goes straight from event to disaster. This determination is part of the CP Activation/Notification phase or the IR Detection and Analysis phase.

Data and Application Resumption

There are a number of data backup and management methods that aid in contingency planning and eventual recovery. The most commonly used varieties, disk backup and tape backup, are presented here. Backup methods must be based on an established policy that meets organizational needs. In general, data files and critical system files should be backed up daily, with nonessential files backed up weekly.

Equally important is the determination of how long data should be stored. Some data must, according to law, be stored for specific lengths of time. If data is not covered by law or regulation, it may be in the organization's best interest to destroy it quickly. Management should create a formal data retention plan that includes recommendations from legal counsel that conform to the applicable laws, regulations, and standards. For routine data backups of critical data, the organization only needs to retain the one or two most recent copies (daily backups) and at least one off-site copy. For full backups of entire systems, at least one copy should be stored in a secure location, such as a bank vault, security deposit box, remote branch office, or other secure data storage facility.

Disk-to-Disk-to-Tape

With the decrease in the costs of storage media, including hard drives and tape backups, more and more organizations are creating massive arrays of independent, large-capacity disk drives to store information, at least temporarily, in storage area networks (SANs). In fact, many home users are employing similar methods, adding external USB-mounted ATA drives, in the 200–300 GB range, and simply copying critical files to these external and portable devices as routine backup. The availability of these devices not only precludes the need for time-consuming tape backups, but it also avoids the costs and implementation challenges of employing tape at the user level. It also allows quick and easy recovery of individual files and directories, as opposed to making extractions from tape.

Individuals and organizations alike can build libraries of these devices or massively connected SANs to support larger-scale data backup and recovery. The problem with this technology is the lack of redundancy if both the online and backup versions fail, because of a virus or hacker intrusion. This is why the secondary data disk series should be periodically backed up to tape or other removable media.

Backup Strategies

There are three basic types of backups: full, differential, and incremental. A **full backup** is just that, a complete backup of the entire system, including all applications, operating systems components, and data. The advantage of a full backup is that it takes a comprehensive snapshot of the organization's system. The primary disadvantages are that it can require large amounts of media and can be time-consuming. A **differential backup** is the storage of all files that have changed or have been added since the last full backup. The differential backup is faster and uses less storage space than the full backup, but each daily differential backup is larger and slower than that of the day before. For example, if you conduct a full backup on Sunday, then Monday's backup contains all the files that have changed since Sunday, and Tuesday's backup contains all the files that have changed since Sunday, including Monday. By Friday, the quantity of data to back up has increased substantially. If one backup is corrupt, the previous day's backup contains almost all the same information. An **incremental backup** only archives the data that have been modified since the last backup (regardless of type), and thus requires less space and time than a differential backup. The disadvantage of incremental backups is that if an incident occurs, multiple backups are needed to restore the full system. In general, incremental backups are designed to complete the backup in the shortest elapsed time. An incremental backup also requires less storage space.

Regardless of the strategy employed, the following guidelines apply: (1) All on-site and off-site storage must be secured. It is common practice to use media-certified fireproof safes or filing cabinets to store backup media. The off-site storage in particular must be in a safe location, such as a safety deposit box in a bank or at a professional backup and recovery service. The trunk of the administrator's car is not secure off-site storage. (2) A conditioned environment must be provided for the media, preferably an airtight, humidity-controlled, static-free storage container. (3) Each media unit must be clearly labeled and write protected. (4) Because media wears out, it is important to retire media units before they reach the end of their useful life.

Tape Backup and Recovery There is still value in tape backups as a cost-effective method for organizations with large quantities of data. Traditionally, tape has been able to store larger quantities of data in smaller containers. The most common types of tape media include digital audio tapes (DATs), quarter-inch cartridge (QIC) drives, 8 mm tape, digital linear tape (DLT), and Linear Tape Open (LTO). The media types differ in their capacities, lifetimes, and performance characteristics, and a type will be chosen based on the capacity and performance requirements of the organization's backup processes.

The most common backup schedule is a daily on-site, incremental or differential backup, with a weekly off-site full backup. Most backups are conducted during twilight hours, when systems activity is lowest and the probability of user interruption is limited. There are three classic methods for selecting which files to back up: six-tape rotation, Grandfather-Father-Son, and the Towers of Hanoi.

Six-Tape Rotation Six-tape rotation, which rotates six sets of media, is perhaps the most simple and well-known backup method. It uses five media sets per week (plus one set for rotation off-site each week). Monday through Thursday, the organization performs a differential or incremental backup. On Friday, a full backup is performed and stored off-site. During the next week of backups, the organization uses the extra backup media set for the Friday full backup and retrieves the previous Friday set for the upcoming week.

The six-tape rotation method offers roughly two weeks of recovery capability in a five-step process. First, the organization attempts to recover the file(s) using the Monday through Thursday tapes, if they are on hand. If the file that needs to be restored is not contained within the backups that are on hand, the last full backup that was stored off site is retrieved and the file(s) are recovered from that media. For additional ease of use and for redundancy, an organization can make a copy of each full backup so that an on-site version can be kept in the data center and an off-site set of full backup (Friday) tapes can be sent to the secure storage location. This prevents the need to retrieve the off-site set.

Grandfather-Father-Son The **Grandfather-Father-Son (GFS)** method uses five media sets per week and allows recovery of data for the previous three weeks. Every second or third month, a group of media sets is taken out of the cycle for permanent storage, and a new set is brought in. This method equalizes the wear and tear on the tapes and helps to prevent tape failure.

The Towers of Hanoi The **Towers of Hanoi** is a more complex approach than the other two methods and uses statistical principles to optimize media wear. This 16-step strategy assumes that five media sets are used per week, with a backup each night.

Selecting a Rotation Method Which rotation method is best? Table 11-1 lists the advantages and disadvantages of each.

Rotation Method	Advantages	Disadvantages
Six-tape rotation	Requires only a few tapes, therefore an easy and cheap rotation method; ideal for small volumes of data (as much as one tape can hold)	Keeps only a week's worth of data unless you regularly archive the full backup tapes
Grandfather-Father-Son (GFS)	Provides the most secure data protection and implements monthly archival of tapes; a simple method that most software supports	Requires more tapes, which can become expensive
The Towers of Hanoi	Allows for easy full-system restorations (no shuffling through tapes with partial backups on them); ideal for small businesses that wish to do full restores; more cost effective than GFS (uses fewer tapes)	Requires a rotation strategy that is not as straightforward to implement as the other rotation methods; unless your backup software supports it, too complex to track tape rotation manually; requires a time-consuming full backup every session

Table 11-1 Selecting the Best Rotation Method[11]
© Cengage Learning 2013

11

Online Backups and the Cloud One of the newest forms of data backup is online backup to a third-party data storage vendor. Several backup software and service providers now offer multi-terabyte online data storage available to anywhere, from anywhere. Even for the home user, companies like Memeo (*www.memeo.com*), Dropbox (*www.dropbox.com*), and Microsoft (Live Mesh 2011, at *http://explore.live.com/windows-live-mesh*) offer data storage ranging from free 1 and 2 GB accounts to low-cost multi-gigabyte and multi-terabyte solutions.

For the corporate user, this online data storage is sometimes referred to as storing data "in the cloud"—as in "cloud computing," in which organizations lease computing resources from a third party. Many organizations also lease data storage from these cloud vendors. Cloud computing usually takes one of three forms:

- Software as a Service (SaaS)—Applications are provided at a fee but hosted on third-party systems and accessed over the Internet (and the Web).

- Platform as a Service (PaaS)—Development platforms are available to developers for a fee and similarly hosted by third parties.

- Infrastructure as a Service (IaaS)—Unofficially known as Everything as a Service, this provides hardware and operating systems resources to host whatever the organization desires to implement, again hosted by a third party for a fee.

Organizations can lease SaaS online backup services and receive data storage as part of the package. From an ownership perspective, clouds can be public, community, private, or some combination of the three:

- Public clouds—The most common implementation, in which a third party makes the services available to whoever needs them, over the Internet (and the Web).

- Community clouds—A collaboration between a few entities for the sole benefit of those entities.

- Private clouds—An extension of the intranet applied to cloud computing. Though technically negating the benefits of cloud computing (little or no capital investment), a theoretical implementation could exist in which a parent company creates a cloud for its own use and for its subordinate organizations' use.

From a security perspective, the leasing of third-party services is always a challenge. If you don't own the hardware, software, and infrastructure, you can't guarantee effective security, so you must "warranty" it by scrutinizing the service agreement and insisting on minimal standards of due care.

Threats to Stored Information

Most organizations understand the need to back up their information, but not all have recognized the risks of storing backups. Backup media hold copies of much, if not all, of an organization's information assets, and they are commonly moved around outside the secured confines of the data center—that is, transferred to a different data center, subsidiary, business partner, or offsite storage facility. If these media are misplaced, this may constitute unauthorized disclosure of the information and trigger notifications required by CA SB 1386 and other privacy legislation. Careful processes and the use of professional bonded couriers are among various techniques that organizations can use to avoid the accidental loss of backup media. New technologies, such as tape encryption, can also provide valuable protection for externalized data.

Another risk derives from the persistent nature of backup media—once written, the data remains until it is erased or overwritten with fresh data. Consider, for example, a magnetic tape containing the backup of a sensitive database. When the contents of the backup are replaced by newer backup data, it is a common practice to return the tape to the "scratch pool," where it is available for reuse. If the contents of the media are not erased before being returned to the pool, their contents are still available on the tape and can be accessed in violation of security policy. For this reason, it is a good practice to erase backup tapes before returning them to the scratch pool.

Backup and Recovery Elapsed Time One of the drawbacks of tape backups is the time required to store and retrieve information. Even differential or incremental backups to tape can take some time to complete. For planning purposes, remember that it typically requires at least twice as much time to restore information from backup media as it does to produce the backup. This additional time is required because disks usually take longer to write to than to read.

Redundancy-Based Protection Using RAID Another form of data protection, **redundant array of independent disks (RAID)** systems, provides another method to ensure that data is not lost. RAID is not a replacement for backup and recovery processes; instead, it serves as a valuable complement to provide high availability for data. It uses a number of hard drives to store information across multiple drive units. For operational redundancy, this can spread out data and, when coupled with checksums, eliminate or reduce the impact of a hard drive failure. There are many RAID configurations (called levels); the most commonly encountered ones are covered in the following sections.

The original title of Patterson, Gibson, and Katz's 1988 paper had the word "inexpensive" rather than "independent" to highlight the differences in cost between the expensive mainframe disks of the time and the much less expensive mass market disks used in their RAID implementation. Eventually, this was changed to "independent."

RAID Level 0 RAID 0 creates one larger logical volume across several available physical hard disk drives and stores the data in segments, called stripes, across all the disk drives in the array. This is often called **disk striping** without parity and is frequently used to combine smaller drive volumes into fewer, larger volumes to gain the advantages that larger volumes offer as well as increased I/O throughput. Unfortunately, the failure of one drive makes all data inaccessible. In fact, RAID 0 does not improve the risk situation when using disk drives; rather, it increases the risk of losing data from a single drive failure. Some RAID configurations combine RAID 0 with RAID 5 or RAID 1 to provide both data protection and improved I/O throughput.

RAID Level 1 Commonly called **disk mirroring**, RAID 1 uses two drives in which data is written to both drives simultaneously, providing a backup if the primary drive fails. It is a rather expensive and inefficient use of media. Mirroring is often used to create duplicate copies of operating system volumes for high-availability systems—for example, by splitting disk mirrors to create highly available copies of critical system drives.

RAID Level 2 This is a specialized form of disk striping with parity and is not widely used. (There are no commercial implementations.) It uses a specialized parity coding mechanism known as the Hamming code to store stripes of data on multiple data drives and corresponding redundant error correction on separate error-correcting drives. This approach allows the reconstruction of data in the event that some of the data or redundant parity information is lost.

RAID Levels 3 and 4 RAID 3 uses byte-level striping of data, and RAID 4 uses block-level striping of data. These approaches use a process in which the data is stored in segments on dedicated data drives and parity information is stored on a separate drive. As with RAID 0, one large volume is used for the data, but the parity drive operates independently to provide error recovery.

RAID Level 5 RAID 5 is most commonly used in organizations that balance safety and redundancy against the costs of acquiring and operating the systems. It is similar to RAID 3 and 4 in that it stripes the data across multiple drives, but there is no dedicated parity drive. Instead, segments of data are interleaved with parity data and are written across all the drives in the set.

RAID Level 6 RAID 6 is very similar to RAID 5; however, this level adds another layer of parity data striped across the drives. Having two blocks of parity data solves one problem with RAID 5 in that RAID 6 protects against situations where a second drive fails before the first drive has been recovered.

RAID Level 7 This is a proprietary variation on RAID 5 in which the array works as a single virtual drive. RAID 7 is sometimes performed by running special software over RAID 5 hardware.

RAID Level 10 There are a number of ways to combine the various RAID methods into a single hybrid system. One of the most popular is RAID 10 (also referred to as RAID 1+0), which combines the benefits of RAID 0 and RAID 1. The data is striped like RAID 0, but the striped set is mirrored, as in RAID 1. This hybrid system is really a mirror of a striped set.

Some of the more common implementations of RAID are shown in Figure 11-6.

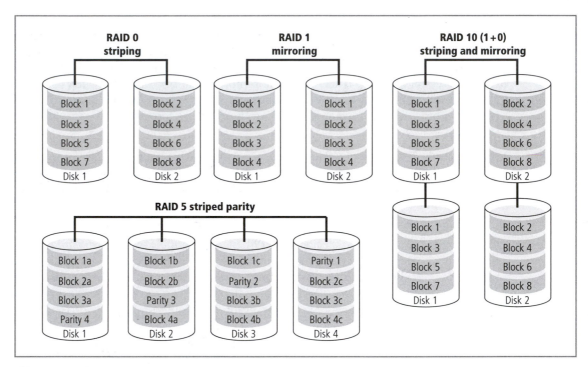

Figure 11-6   Samples of RAID implementations
© Cengage Learning 2013

Database Backups

Systems that make use of databases—whether that database uses a hierarchical, relational, or object-oriented technology—require special backup and recovery procedures. Depending on the type of database and the software vendor, you may or may not be able to back up the database with the utilities that are provided with the server operating systems. A further consideration is whether system backup procedures can be used without interrupting the use of the database. In most databases, a system backup can work correctly only if all user access to the database is stopped (or quiesced). Using these databases while they are being backed up requires additional backup tools. Administrators also need to know whether the database being safeguarded is using special journal file systems, such as run-unit journals or after-image journals that enable database concurrency functions. If these file systems and the files they are built upon are not backed up properly, the backup tapes or disk images may be unrecoverable when it comes time to restore the prior state of the system.

Application Backups

Some applications use file systems and databases in ways that invalidate the customary way of doing backup and recovery. In some cases, applications write large binary objects as files and manage pointers, and they handle internal data structures in ways that make routine backups unable to handle the concurrency or complexity of the application. Make sure that members of the application support and development teams are part of the planning process when these systems' backup plans are made, and that these team members are included in training, testing, and rehearsal activities.

Real-Time Protection, Server Recovery, and Application Recovery Some

data protection strategies seek to improve the robustness of a server or system in addition to or instead of performing data backups. One approach that provides real-time protection as well as data backup is the use of mirroring. Mirroring provides duplication of server data storage by using multiple hard drive volumes, as described earlier. RAID 1 can be achieved with software or hardware, writing data to other drives, even if they are located on other systems. This mirroring concept can be extended to vaulting and journaling, which are discussed later in this chapter.

One way to implement server recovery and redundancy through mirroring servers uses hot, warm, and cold servers. In this strategy, the online primary server is the hot server, which provides the services necessary to support operations. The warm server serves as an ancillary or secondary server that services requests when the primary server is busy or down. The cold server is the administrator's test platform, and it should be identically configured to the hot and warm servers.

Before a patch, upgrade, or new application is applied to the hot and warm servers, it is first tested on the cold server. Should the hot server go down, the warm server automatically takes over as the hot server, and the cold server can be used as the new warm server while the hot server is taken offline for repair.

Recent advances in server recovery have developed **bare metal recovery** technologies designed to replace operating systems and services when they fail. These applications allow you to reboot the affected system from a CD-ROM or other remote drive and quickly restore your operating system by providing images backed up from a known stable state. Linux and UNIX have been able to use boot CDs such as Knoppix or Helix for some time; Microsoft developed its Preinstallation Environment (Win PE) to provide similar capabilities. Use of bare metal recovery applications, in conjunction with routine backups, allows the recovery of entire servers quickly and easily.

Another option for online backup and application availability is **server clustering**. Clustering works similarly to the hot/warm server model described earlier. The simpler clustering model is active/passive clustering in which two identically configured servers share access to the application data storage. At any point in time, only the active server is controlling the storage

11

and responding to requests. If the active server crashes or hangs, the passive server takes control of the application storage and begins servicing requests.

Active/active clustering is a more complex model in which all members of a cluster simultaneously provide application services. As noted earlier, mirroring of data, whether through the use of RAID 1 or alternative technologies, can increase the reliability of primary systems and also enhance the effectiveness of business resumption strategies. Vaulting and journaling dramatically increase the level of protection. They are discussed in the sections that follow.

Electronic Vaulting The bulk transfer of data in batches to an off-site facility is called **electronic vaulting** (see Figure 11-7). It is usually conducted via dedicated network links or data communications services that are provided for a fee. The receiving server archives the data as it is received. Some disaster recovery companies specialize in electronic vaulting services. The primary criteria for selecting an electronic vaulting (or e-vaulting) solution are the cost of the service and the required bandwidth. If the organization does not currently have enough bandwidth to support e-vaulting, it must select a vendor to obtain the additional bandwidth needed.[12]

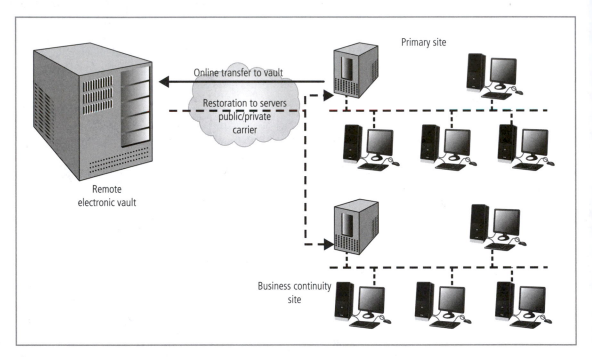

Figure 11-7   Electronic vaulting architecture
© Cengage Learning 2013

Electronic vaulting can be more expensive than tape backup and slower than data mirroring, so it should be used only for data that warrants the additional expense, such as critical transactional data and customer databases. Although e-vaulting can be performed over public infrastructure, the data must be encrypted while in transit, which can slow the data transfer rate.

For managed solutions from vendors, typically a software agent is installed on all servers to be included in the e-vaulting process. Once installed, the software initiates a full backup of data to the remote vault and then prepares to continuously copy data as it is created or modified. The vendor is then responsible for the maintenance and protection of the data. Data can be accessed via a Web interface or by using installed software to facilitate restoration or validation of transferred data. Different applications can facilitate the transfer among organizationally owned equipment over public or private communications links for an organization that wants to transfer data to its own vault.

Remote Journaling Remote journaling (RJ) is the transfer of live transactions to an off-site facility. RJ was developed by IBM in 1999 for its AS/400 V4R2 operating system. RJ differs from electronic vaulting in that only transaction data is transferred, not archived data, and the transfer is performed online and much closer to real time. Although electronic vaulting is much like a traditional backup, with a dump of data to the off-site storage, remote journaling involves online activities on a systems level, much like server fault tolerance, in which data is written to two locations simultaneously or asynchronously, as preferred. RJ facilitates the recovery of key transactions nearly in real time. Figure 11-8 shows an overview of the remote journaling process.

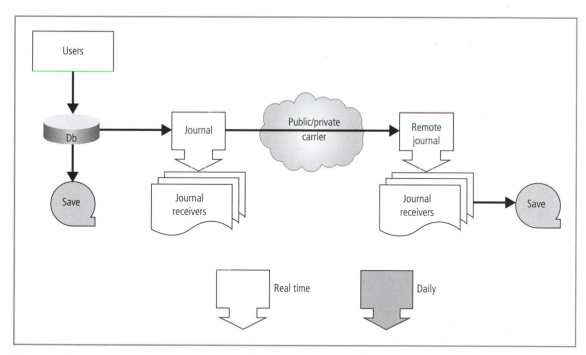

Figure 11-8   Remote Journaling Architecture[13]
© Cengage Learning 2013

When journaling is enabled, the operating system initiates a process that creates a record of changes to the object being journaled. These changes are recorded as a journal entry, which is stored in a journal receiver, similar to storing a record in a database file. Once the journal receiver is full or reaches a preset level, a new journal receiver is linked to the journal, and the full receiver is available for storage.

To recover data, the stored receivers can be pulled from tape and applied to the data in the production database, restoring the data to a known stable point. Remote journaling involves the transferring of journal entries to a remote journal, which in turn stores them to a remote journal receiver. This remote journal receiver is transferred to remote tape or other storage when full, creating a virtual real-time backup of the entries.[14]

Database Shadowing Database shadowing is the propagation of transactions to a remote copy of the database. It combines electronic vaulting with remote journaling, applying transactions to the database simultaneously in two separate locations. This technology can be used with multiple databases on a single drive in a single system or with databases in remote locations across a public or private carrier, as shown in Figure 11-9.

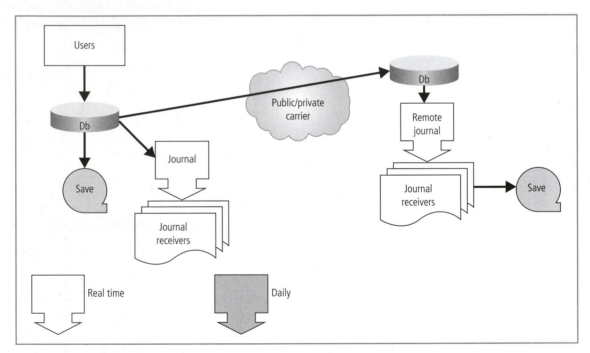

Figure 11-9 Database shadowing architecture
© Cengage Learning 2013

Shadowing techniques are generally used by organizations needing immediate data recovery after an incident or disaster. The "shadowed" database is available for reading as well as writing and thus serves as a dynamic off-site backup. According to E-Net, a company that provides mainframe software solutions for business continuity and disaster recovery, database shadowing also works well for read-only functions, such as the following:

- Data warehousing and mining
- Batch reporting cycles (for example, quarterly and year-end reports)
- Complex SQL queries
- Local online access at the shadow site
- Load balancing[15]

Network-Attached Storage and Storage Area Networks

Two other advances in data storage and recovery are **network-attached storage (NAS)** and **storage area networks (SANs)**. NAS is usually implemented via a single device or server that attaches to a network. It uses common communications methods—such as Windows file sharing, NFS, CIFS, HTTP directories, or FTP—to provide an online storage environment. Often used for additional storage, NAS is configured to allow users or groups of users to access data storage.

NAS does not work well with real-time applications because of the latency of the communication methods. For general file sharing or data backup, NAS provides a less expensive solution. For high-speed and higher-security solutions, SANs may be preferable.

SANs are similar in concept but differ in implementation. NAS uses TCP/IP-based protocols and communications methods; SANs use fibre-channel or iSCSI connections between the systems needing the additional storage and the storage devices themselves. This difference is shown in Figure 11-10 and described in Table 11-2.[16]

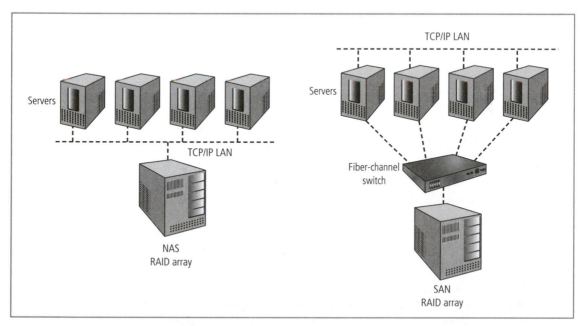

Figure 11-10 SAN and NAS architectures
© Cengage Learning 2013

Feature	NAS	SAN
Connectivity	Any machine that can connect to a LAN and use standard protocols (such as NSF, CIFS, or HTTP)	Only server-class devices with iSCSI or fibre channel; has a topology limit of 10 km
Addressing, identification, and file transfer	By filename with NAS handling security, including permissions, authentication, and file locking	By disk block number, with no individual security control

Table 11-2 NAS versus SAN
© Cengage Learning 2013

Service Level Agreements (SLAs)

When an organization is making arrangements for off-site IT support options, the terms and conditions of that site should be made known to all parties by negotiating and executing a service agreement. **Service level agreements (SLAs)** are the contractual documents guaranteeing certain minimum levels of service provided by vendors.

An effective service agreement should contain the following sections:

1. Definition of applicable parties—Identifies whom the document applies to

2. Services to be provided by the vendor—Specifies exactly what the client is to receive in exchange for the payments

3. Fees and payments for these services—Specifies what the vendor receives in exchange for the services rendered

4. Statements of indemnification—Declares that the vendor is not liable for actions taken by the client

5. Nondisclosure agreements and intellectual property assurances—Obligates the vendor to protect the confidentiality of the client's information from everyone except authorized law enforcement officials and parties that serve legal papers directing the vendor to provide such information

6. Noncompetitive agreements (covenant not to compete)—States that the client will not use the vendor's services to compete directly with the vendor and that the client will not use vendor information to gain a better deal with another vendor

Organizations strive for near-perfect availability. Availability is usually expressed as the percentage of time that systems are available over a specific period of time, after allowing for planned maintenance times. Perfect uptime is not realistically achievable. Errors and mistakes happen, and even when allowances are made for planned maintenance, most organizations rely on external vendors for Internet service, power, and other services, and these will have outages from time to time.

When service levels are measured, they are commonly reported as a series of nines. As a frame of reference, most organizations feel that uptime less than 99.9 percent for data (often called three nines availability) and 99.99 for voice communications (four nines availability) is unacceptable. That means that most organizations consider acceptable downtime (outside of planned maintenance times) for a data network to be 10.1 minutes or less per week. The voice network cannot be unavailable for more than 1 minute per week.

Incident Response Plan

Although DR and BC are equally important to an organization, your primary focus, with regard to networking, will be on IR planning and on operations to ensure the confidentiality, integrity, and availability of data both on the network and stored on networking devices. The remainder of this chapter examines the details of the IR plan.

As indicated earlier, unexpected activities occur periodically and are referred to as **events**. In CP, an event that indicates a threat to the security of the organization's information is called an incident. An **incident** occurs when an attack (natural or human-made) affects resources and/or assets, causing disclosure, damage, or other disruptions. **A computer incident** occurs when an attack affects information resources and/or assets, causing actual damage or other disruptions.

Incident response (IR), then, is a set of procedures that commences when an incident is detected. IR must be carefully planned and coordinated, because organizations heavily depend on the quick and efficient containment and resolution of incidents. As was noted earlier in this chapter, the IR plan comprises a detailed set of processes and procedures that anticipate, detect, and mitigate the effects of an unexpected situation that might compromise information resources and assets. Incident response planning (IRP), therefore, is the preparation for such a situation. The three-step model that NIST recommends for CP operations (described earlier) can also be used to describe IR functions. Figure 11-11 shows that NIST defines the IR execution process based on a different standard. As mentioned earlier, the two are similar in function, with the latter mostly focused on IR rather than general CP operations. Figure 11-12 provides a slightly broader perspective, showing how the Computer Emergency Response Team Coordinating Center (CERT/CC) approach to IR planning fits into its overall IR model.

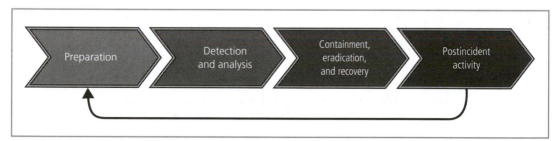

Figure 11-11   NIST incident response process[17]
© Cengage Learning 2013

When the CPMT completes the BIA, it begins to transfer the information gleaned from the organization to the various subordinate committees. To assist in their subordinate planning, the IR, DR, and BC committees are given some overlapping information on the attacks they could face. They must also extract information from the organization's periodic risk assessments, provided the organization conducts them on a regular basis. In addition, the subordinate planning committees get as much of the overall contingency plan as has been completed. Once subordinate team members have this information, they begin to formulate their subordinate

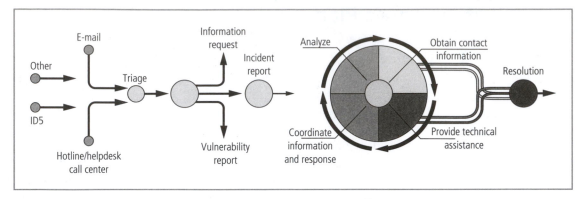

Figure 11-12   CERT/CC incident identification, analysis, and response[18]
© Cengage Learning 2013

plans. In the case of IR planning, the group conducts its portion of the overall CP methodology described in Figure 11-4, focusing on the following stages (described in the following sections):

- Form the IR planning teams.
- Develop IR planning policy.
- Integrate the BIA.
- Identify preventive controls unique to IR.
- Organize the Computer Incident Response Team (CIRT).
- Create IR contingency strategies.
- Develop the IR plan.
- Ensure plan testing, training, and exercises.
- Ensure plan maintenance.

Some of these stages involve work conducted exclusively by the IR team; other stages may involve other subordinate teams. The latter two stages, especially, may be conducted by the IR team by itself, but at some point the organization should invest in joint CP operations training and exercises.

Form IR Planning Team

The IRP process begins with staffing the IR planning team. Much of the preliminary organizing effort is done by the CPMT, but the IR team needs to be organized as a separate entity, and that begins by identifying and engaging a collection of stakeholders—that is, a representative collection of individuals with a stake in the successful and uninterrupted operation of the organization's information infrastructure. These stakeholders are used to collect vital information on the roles and responsibilities of the actual response team. Stakeholders include representatives from general management, IT management, information security management and operations, and other specialized groups such as legal affairs, public relations, and customer support.

Develop IR Planning Policy

One of the first projects to be undertaken by the IR planning committee should be the IRP policy, which defines the IR-related roles and responsibilities for the **Computer Security Incident Response Team (CSIRT)** and for others who will be mobilized in the activation of the plan. A CSIRT is the team—either dedicated staff or virtual team—responsible for incident response and handling. The following list from NIST's Computer Security Incident Handling Guide provides a structural overview of a typical IR policy:[19]

- Statement of management commitment
- Purpose and objectives of the policy
- Scope of the policy (to whom and what it applies and under what circumstances)
- Definition of information security incidents and their consequences within the context of the organization
- Organizational structure and delineation of roles, responsibilities, and levels of authority; should include the authority of the IR team to confiscate or disconnect equipment and to monitor suspicious activity, and the requirements for reporting certain types of incidents
- Prioritization or severity ratings of incidents
- Performance measures
- Reporting and contact forms

IR policy must gain the full support of top management and must be clearly understood by all affected parties. It is especially important to gain the support of those communities of interest that will be required to alter business practices or make changes to their information technology infrastructures.

The responsibility for creating an organization's IR plan usually falls to the chief information security officer (CISO). Planning for an incident and the responses to it requires a detailed understanding of the information systems and the threats they face. The IR planning team and CSIRT (defined later in this chapter) seek to develop a series of predefined responses that will guide the team and information security staff through the IR steps. Predefining IRs enables the organization to react to a detected incident quickly and effectively, without confusion or wasted time and effort.

Integrate the Business Impact Analysis (BIA)

To determine these predefined responses, the IR planning committee must first identify potentially successful attacks and understand the possible outcomes of these attacks. This is a three-stage process:

1. Threat Attack Identification and Prioritization—In this stage, organizations update the prioritized threat list created during the risk assessment process and add an **attack profile**, which is a detailed description of the activities that occur during an attack, including the preliminary indications of the attack as well as the actions taken and the outcome.

2. Attack Success Scenario Development—Next, the BIA team creates a series of scenarios depicting the effects of an occurrence of each threat on each prioritized functional area.

Attack success scenarios are added to the attack profile, including alternative outcomes: best, worst, and most likely to occur.

3. Potential Damage Assessment—From these detailed scenarios, the IRP team must estimate the cost of the best, worst, and most likely outcomes by preparing an attack scenario end case, which identifies the costs associated with recovering from each possible case. For every attack scenario end case, the IR team creates the incident plan, which is made up of three sets of incident-handling procedures to be deployed during, after, and before the incident.

Identify Preventive Controls Unique to IR

The next step is to identify (and evaluate) the preventive controls that are currently in place and protecting critical assets, from an IR perspective. An effective risk assessment involves an asset inventory and prioritization. This information, along with the information from the BIA, should give the team a head start in determining if the controls currently implemented are effective. If the risk management team is doing its job, this phase may simply consist of reviewing the most recent report and ensuring that it is current. Note that some assets protect the organization from both incidents and disaster. It's a matter of scale. A small fire is an incident; a large fire is a disaster. Good fire suppression equipment can protect against both. Thus, it is especially important for all subordinate teams to collaborate in this area, sharing information on preventive controls and safeguards.

Organize the Computer Security Incident Response Team (CSIRT)

The Computer Security Incident Response Team (CSIRT), which is also known as the Security Incident Response Team (SIRT), is the group of individuals who would be expected to respond to a detected incident. The selection of CIRT personnel should be based on the skills and access privileges needed to quickly and effectively react to a given situation. Different CSIRT subteams can be formed based on the type and scope of the incident. The organization may well have different teams to react to different incidents. Care should be taken to ensure that critical skills necessary for other CP activities, like DR or BC, are balanced between the IR, DR, and BC activities. It is conceivable that all three could be conducted concurrently.

Once the organization has staffed the CSIRT, training begins. Training computer IR team members can be conducted in various ways. There are several national training programs that focus on IR tools and techniques. The SANS Institute offers a number of classes and certifications designed to train the information security professional (see *www.sans.org*), including ones related to IR. SANS even has a set of conferences—SANS Forensics and Incident Response Education (SANSFIRE)—that specifically focuses on IR. In addition to formal external training, the organization can set up its own training program in which more experienced staff members share their knowledge with less-experienced employees. An ongoing training program should include this mentoring-type training to prevent a loss of organizational knowledge when certain employees depart.

Create IR Contingency Strategies

As the team moves its attention to the actual activities performed by organizational personnel, including CSIRT members, it needs to decide exactly how it plans to respond to various incidents. This is an area in which some of the work must be done by the CPMT, given that budgetary decisions could be very wide reaching. There are also strategies that benefit or impact more than one subordinate group. Contingency (or response) strategies vary greatly, both in their effectiveness in responding to an attack and in their impact upon the organization. If an organization automatically severs its Internet connection every time it is scanned by an outside entity, odds are it will not be in business long.

Some organizations may choose to have a single IR strategy in place for all incidents. Others may choose to have several optional plans to handle different circumstances. Here are a number of factors that influence the IR strategy that an organization decides to use:

- Are the affected systems impacting profitable operations?
- If information was stolen, what was the level of sensitivity or classification?
- Which business functions are being impacted, and at what level?
- Has the incident been contained, or is it continuing?
- What is the origin of the emergency? Is it internal or external to the organization?
- Is the incident public knowledge?
- What are the legal reporting requirements? Does the law require this matter to be reported immediately to authorities? Who are those authorities? Should this matter be handled as a human resources function? Should this matter be handled as a civil suit?
- What, if any, steps should be immediately taken to discover the identity of an outside-agency attacker?
- As of the moment the incident is contained, what are the financial losses?
- Should the organization involve law enforcement? [20]

Two general categories of strategic approaches are *protect and forget* strategies, which are the simplest, and *apprehend and prosecute*, which require a greater and more complex effort.[21] The response to the incident is the same regardless of which strategy is employed, but the data collection tasks differ dramatically.

Protect and forget strategies focus on the detection, logging, and analysis of events for the purpose of determining how they happened and preventing reoccurrence. Once the current incident is over, who caused it or why is immaterial except insofar as it is relevant to the prevention of future incidents. *Apprehend and prosecute* strategies focus on the identification and apprehension of the intruder (if a human threat-agent is involved), with additional attention given to the collection and preservation of potential evidentiary materials that might support administrative or criminal prosecution.

The key steps used in both strategies are shown in Table 11-3.

Develop the Incident Response (IR) Plan

Once the organization's IRP team has progressed to this point, it begins developing the actual IR plan. The IR plan can be broken into the following four general sections:

1. Identification
2. Response
3. Containment and Eradication
4. Recovery

Protect and Forget	Apprehend and Prosecute
1. Determine if the event is a real incident.	1. Determine if the event is a real incident.
2. If the event is an incident, terminate the current intrusion.	2. If the event is an incident and the circumstances warrant doing so, contact law enforcement.
3. Discover how access was obtained and how many systems were compromised.	3. Document each action taken, including the date and time as well as who was present when the action was taken.
4. Restore the compromised systems to their preincident configuration.	4. Isolate the compromised systems from the network.
5. Secure the method of unauthorized access by the intruder on all systems.	5. If the organization has the capability, it should entice the intruder into a safe system that seemingly contains valuable data.
6. Document steps taken to deal with the incident.	6. Discover the identity of the intruder while documenting his or her activity.
7. Develop lessons learned.	7. Discover how the intruder gained access to the compromised systems, and secure these access points on all uncompromised systems.
8. Conduct brief evaluation by upper management in the incident's aftermath.	8. As soon as sufficient evidence has been collected, or when vital information or vital systems are endangered, terminate the current intrusion.
	9. Document the current state of compromised systems.
	10. Restore the compromised systems to their pre-incident configuration.
	11. Secure the method of unauthorized access by the intruder on all compromised systems.
	12. Document in detail the time in man-hours as well as the cost of handling the incident.
	13. Secure all logs, audits, notes, documentation, and any other evidence gathered during the incident, and appropriately identify it to secure the "chain of custody" for future prosecution.
	14. Develop lessons learned.
	15. Conduct brief evaluation by upper management in the incident's aftermath.

Table 11-3 Key Steps in Reaction Strategies
© Cengage Learning 2013

Identification The identification of an incident begins with the **trigger**—that is, the circumstances that cause the IR team to be activated and the IR plan to be initiated. This trigger could be any of a number of situations or circumstances, including the following:

- A phone call from a user to the help desk about unusual computer or network behavior
- Notification from a systems administrator about unusual server or network behavior
- Notification from an intrusion detection device
- Review of system log files indicating unusual pattern of entries

- Loss of system connectivity
- Device malfunctions
- Other specific identifiable situations that result in the invocation of the IR plan

The IR team's lead person, also known as the IR duty officer, determines when the IR plan must be activated. A **duty officer** is a CSIRT team member, other than the team leader, who is on call for purposes of responding to an incident report.

Data Collection The routine collection and analysis of data is required to properly detect and declare incidents. Even if an incident is not detected in real time, the data collected by automatic recording systems assist the teams in better understanding the normal and routine operations of the systems that process, transmit, and store information. Understanding normal operations assists in detecting abnormal operations. The information that should normally be collected is presented in Table 11-4.

Data Category	Data to Be Collected
Network performance	• Total traffic load in and out over time (packet, byte, and connection counts) and by event (new product or service release) • Traffic load (percentage of packets, bytes, connections) in and out over time sorted by protocol, source address, destination address, other packet header data • Error counts on all network interfaces
Other network data	• Service initiation requests • Name of the user/host requesting the service • Network traffic (packet headers) • Successful connections and connection attempts (protocol, port, source, destination, time) • Connection duration • Connection flow (sequence of packets from initiation to termination) • States associated with network interfaces (up, down) • Network sockets currently open • Whether or not network interface card is in promiscuous mode • Network probes and scans • Results of administrator probes • Protocols in use
System performance	• Total resource use over time (CPU, memory (used, free), disk (used, free)) • Status and errors reported by systems and hardware devices • Changes in system status, including shutdowns and restarts • File system status (where mounted, free space by partition, open files, biggest file) over time and at specific times • File system warnings (low free space, too many open files, file exceeding allocated size) • Disk counters (input/output, queue lengths) over time and at specific times • Hardware availability (modems, network interface cards, memory)

Table 11-4 **Examples of Information to Collect During Incident Investigations** (*continues*)

Data Category	Data to Be Collected
Other system data	• Actions requiring special privileges • Successful and failed logins • Modem activities • Presence of new services and devices • Configuration of resources and devices
Process performance	• Resources used (CPU, memory, disk, time) by specific processes over time; top resource-consuming processes • System and user processes and services executing at any given time
Other process data	• User executing the process • Process start-up time, arguments, filenames • Process exit status, time, duration, resources consumed • The means by which each process is normally initiated (administrator, other users, other programs or processes), with what authorization and privileges • Devices used by specific processes • Files currently open by specific processes
Files and directories	• List of files, directories, attributes • Cryptographic checksums for all files and directories • Accesses (open, create, modify, execute, delete), time, date • Changes to sizes, contents, protections, types, locations • Changes to access control lists on system tools • Additions and deletions of files and directories • Results of virus scanners
Users	• Login/logout information (location, time): successful attempts, failed attempts, attempted logins to privileged accounts • Login/logout information on remote access servers that appears in modem logs • Changes in user identity • Changes in authentication status, such as enabling privileges • Failed attempts to access restricted information (such as password files) • Keystroke monitoring logs • Violations of user quotas

Applications	• Application- and service-specific information such as:
	
	   o Network device and system logs: sender IP address, receiver IP address, network ports, packet information
	   o IDS logs: intrusion alerts
	   o FTP logs: files transferred and connection statistics
	   o Web server logs: pages accessed, credentials of the requestor, connection statistics, user requests over time, which pages are most requested, and who is requesting them
	   o Mail logs: sender, receiver, size, and tracing information; for a mail server, number of messages over time, number of queued messages
	   o DNS logs: questions, answers, and zone transfers

Table 11-4   **Examples of Information to Collect During Incident Investigations**   (*continued*)

Data Category	Data to Be Collected
	○ File system logs: file transfers over time ○ Database server logs: transactions over time
Log files	• Results of scanning, filtering, and reducing log file contents • Checks for log file consistency (increasing file size over time, use of consecutive, increasing time stamps with no gaps)
Vulnerabilities	• Results of vulnerability scanners (presence of known vulnerabilities) • Vulnerability patch logging

Table 11-4 **Examples of Information to Collect During Incident Investigations** (*continued*)
© Cengage Learning 2013

Incident Response Plan Activation Among the earliest challenges IR planners face is determining how to classify events as they occur. Some events are the product of routine system activities, whereas others are indicators of situations that require an urgent response. **Incident classification** is the process of evaluating organizational events, determining which events are possible incidents, also called **incident candidates**, and then determining whether or not the incident candidate is an actual incident or a nonevent, also called a false positive incident candidate.

Designing the process used to make this judgment is the role of the IR design team; the process of actually classifying an event is the responsibility of the IR team. Some organizations have a single incident center where all incident candidates are sent as soon as they are recognized. Others have geographically separate review locations, perhaps based on time zones, wherein preliminary determinations about the status of an incident candidate can be assessed. Still other organizations handle incident candidate evaluation by business unit, product line, or some other criterion.[22]

Incident candidates can be detected and tracked via a variety of sources: end users, intrusion detection systems, virus management software, systems administrators, and so forth. Careful training in incident candidate reporting allows end users, the help desk staff, and security personnel to relay vital information to the IR team.

Classifying Incidents A number of different events can signal the presence of an incident candidate. Unfortunately, these same events may occur when a system becomes overloaded, encounters an error, or through a normal operation that mimics an incident candidate. To help make the detection of actual incidents more reliable, D. L. Pipkin has identified three broad categories of incident indicators: possible, probable, and definite.[23] This categorization enables an organization to expedite the decision-making process of incident classification and ensure that the proper IR plan is activated as early as possible.

Possible Indicators of an Incident The four types of possible actual incidents are:

• Presence of unfamiliar files—Users might discover unfamiliar files in their home directories or on their office computers. Administrators might find files that are not in a logical location or owned by an authorized user.

11

- Presence or execution of unknown programs or processes—Users or administrators might detect unfamiliar programs running, or processes executing, on office machines or network servers.

- Unusual consumption of computing resources—Memory consumption or hard disk usage might suddenly spike or fall. Many computer operating systems, including Windows, Mac OS, Linux, and many UNIX variants, allow users and administrators to monitor CPU and memory consumption. Most computers also have the ability to monitor hard drive space. In addition, servers maintain logs of file creation and storage.

- Unusual system crashes—Older operating systems running newer programs are notorious for locking up or spontaneously rebooting whenever the operating system is unable to execute a requested process or service. You are probably familiar with systems error messages such as "Unrecoverable Application Error," "General Protection Fault," and the infamous Windows Blue Screen of Death. However, if a computer system seems to be crashing, hanging, rebooting, or freezing more frequently than usual, the cause could be an incident candidate.

Probable Indicators of an Incident Pipkin identifies four types of probable indicators of actual incidents:

- Activities at unexpected times—If traffic levels on an organization's network exceed the baseline values, an incident candidate is probably present. If this activity surge occurs when few members of the organization are at work, the probability becomes much greater. Similarly, if systems are accessing drives, such as floppy and CD-ROM drives, in the absence of user actions, an incident may also be occurring.

- Presence of new accounts—The presence of an account (or accounts) that the administrator did not create or that are not logged in the administrator's journal signal an incident candidate. An unlogged new account with root or other special privileges has an even higher probability of being an actual incident.

- Reported attacks—If users of the system report a suspected attack, there is a high probability that an attack has occurred, which constitutes an incident. The technical sophistication of the person making the report should be considered.

- Notification from IDS—If the organization has installed and correctly configured a host- or network-based intrusion detection system (IDS), then notification from the IDS indicates that an incident might be in progress. However, IDSs are seldom configured optimally and, even when they are, tend to issue many false positives or false alarms. The administrator must determine whether the notification indicates an incident or is the result of a routine operation by a user or other administrator.

Definite Indicators of an Incident There are five types of definite indicators of an actual incident—that is, indicators that clearly and definitively signal that an incident is in progress or has occurred. In these cases, the IR plan must be activated immediately.

- Use of dormant accounts—Many network servers maintain default accounts, and quite often accounts exist from former employees, employees on a leave of absence or sabbatical without remote access privileges, or dummy accounts set up to support system testing. If any of these accounts begins accessing system resources, querying servers, or engaging in other activities, an incident is almost certain to have occurred.

- Modified or missing logs—Log records are a valuable source of information, particularly when centralized for purposes of consolidation and analysis. Unfortunately, attackers are well aware of this value and often delete or modify log records to conceal their activities. For this reason, unexplained gaps in records or modifications to records are definite indicators of an incident.

- Presence of hacker tools—Network administrators sometimes use system vulnerability and network evaluation tools to scan internal computers and networks to determine what a hacker can see. These tools are also used to support research into attack profiles. Too often the tools are used by employees, contractors, or outsiders with local network access to hack into systems. To combat this problem, many organizations explicitly prohibit the use of these tools without written permission from the CISO, making any unauthorized installation a policy violation. Therefore, if unauthorized hacker tools are detected on a system, an incident has occurred.

- Notifications by partner or peer—If a business partner or another connected organization reports an attack from your computing systems, then an incident has occurred.

- Notification by hacker—Some hackers enjoy taunting their victims. If an organization's Web pages are defaced, it is an incident. If an organization receives an extortion request for money in exchange for its customers' credit card files, an incident is in progress.

Additional Incident Indicators The following additional events indicate that an incident is underway:

- Loss of availability—Information or information systems become unavailable.

- Loss of integrity—Users report corrupt data files, garbage where data should be, or data that just looks wrong.

- Loss of confidentiality—You are notified of sensitive information leaks, or information you thought was protected has been disclosed.

- Violation of policy—If organizational policies addressing information or information security have been violated, an incident has occurred.

- Violation of law—If the law has been broken and the organization's information assets are involved, an incident has occurred.

Identification Triage An important role of the IR duty officer is to talk to the incident reporter and triage the information presented. Many organizations will design a script to help the duty officer triage the situation during the report and determine how best to respond. The script will include questions like:

- What symptoms or information did you witness?
- When did you detect the event?
- What was happening on the system when the event occurred?
- What actions were you performing on the system when the event occurred?
- Whom else did you notify, or with whom did you discuss the event?
- What actions did you take once the events were identified?

- What systems or network devices are affected by these events?
- Has anything changed recently with regard to the system in question?

Challenges in Incident Identification It should be painfully obvious by this point that the detection of incidents can be a tedious and technically demanding process. Only those with advanced technical skills in a certain set of hardware and software can manually detect signs of an intrusion through reviews of logs, system performance, user feedback, and system processes and tasks. This underscores the value of two key facets of incident detection: (1) effective use of technology to assist in detection, and (2) the necessity of cooperation between IR and information security professionals and the entire IT department. The former is discussed in detail in Chapter 6. As for the latter, the IT staff is best prepared to understand the day-to-day operations of the hardware, software, and networking components that support organizational operations on an ongoing basis. It can work with the CSIRT and information security teams to identify anomalies in the system's performance and administration. This should underscore the necessity to integrate IT systems and network administrators as part of CSIRT operations.

Response The next IR plan component is the determination of what must be done to react to a particular situation. An organization may have spent great effort in developing an IR Plan (IRP is IR Planning) yet still be unprepared when an incident occurs. It is not enough to simply prepare plans; it is necessary to alter the culture of the organization to make the organization more responsive and resilient when incidents occur. The best plans may not necessarily be the most thorough or most elaborate; the best plans are those that improve the outcome when an incident occurs. How and when to activate IR plans is determined by the IR strategy the organization chooses to pursue. Whether a one-size-fits-all IR strategy or a more complex and responsive multipart approach is chosen, the organization must make sure the outcome from the planned response meets the organization's strategic and tactical needs.

Notification As soon as the IR team determines that an incident is in progress, the right people must be immediately notified in the right order. Most response organizations, such as firefighters or the military, maintain an alert roster for all emergencies. An **alert roster** is a document containing contact information for the individuals that need to be notified in the event of an incident.

There are two ways to activate an alert roster: sequentially and hierarchically. A **sequential roster** requires that a contact person call each and every person on the roster. A **hierarchical roster** requires one person to call certain other people, who in turn call other people, and so on. Each approach has advantages and disadvantages. The hierarchical system is quicker, because more people are calling at the same time, but the message can become distorted as it is passed from person to person. The sequential system is more accurate, but it is also slower because a single contact person provides each responder with the message.

The **alert message** is a scripted description of the incident that consists of just enough information so that each CSIRT responder knows what portion of the IR plan to implement without impeding the notification process. It is important to recognize that not everyone is on the alert roster; only those individuals who must respond to a specific actual incident are on it. As with any part of the IR plan, the alert roster must be regularly maintained, tested, and rehearsed if it is to remain effective.

During this phase, other key personnel not on the alert roster, such as general management, must be notified of the incident as well. This notification should occur after the incident has been confirmed but before media or other external sources learn of it. In addition, some incidents are disclosed to the employees in general, as a lesson in security, and some are not, as a measure of security. Furthermore, other organizations may need to be notified if it is determined that the incident is not confined to internal information resources or if the incident is part of a larger-scale assault. For example, during Mafiaboy's distributed denial-of-service attack on multiple high-visibility Web-based vendors in late 1999, many of the target organizations reached out for help. In general, the IR planners should determine in advance whom to notify and when, and should offer guidance about additional notification steps to take as needed.

Documenting an Incident As soon as an incident has been confirmed and the notification process is under way, the team should begin to document it. The documentation should record the who, what, when, where, why, and how of each action taken while the incident is occurring. This documentation serves as a case study after the fact to determine whether the right actions were taken and if they were effective. It also proves, should it become necessary, that the organization did everything possible to prevent the spread of the incident. Legally, the standards of due care protect the organization should an incident adversely affect individuals inside and outside the organization or other organizations that use the target organization's systems. Incident documentation can also be used as a simulation in future training sessions on future versions of the IR plan.

Interviewing Individuals Involved in the Incident Part of determining the scale, scope, and impact of an incident is the collection of information from those reporting the incident and responsible for the systems impacted by the incident. This can be potentially dangerous when you consider that one of the individuals interviewed during IR may in fact be the cause of the incident.

Interviews involve three groups of stakeholders: end users, help desk personnel, and systems administrators. Each group can provide a different perspective on the incident as well as clues to its origin, cause, and impact. Interviews with end users require the CSIRT to collect information in a manner that does not intimidate them or overwhelm them with technical jargon and questions.

The interview should make the user feel that he or she is contributing to the IR effort. Interviews with the help desk tend to be more technical, intense, and often seek information beyond that gained from the one or two individual users who initially contacted the help desk. Interviewers frequently ask the help desk staff to review previous trouble tickets looking for signs of similar attacks that could indicate a previous incident or attempted incident by the same attacker. Interviews with systems administrators similarly seek additional information—specifically, logs from the affected systems and possibly online or offline forensic images to be analyzed in a lab.

Containment/Eradication One of the most critical components of the IR plan is stopping the incident or containing its impact. Incident containment strategies vary depending on the incident and on the amount of damage caused. Before an incident can be stopped or contained, however, the affected areas must be identified. During an incident is not the time to conduct a detailed analysis of the affected areas; those tasks are typically performed after the fact, in the forensics process. Instead, simple identification of

11

what information and systems are involved determines the containment actions to be taken. Incident containment strategies focus on two tasks: stopping the incident and recovering control of the affected systems.

The CSIRT team can attempt to stop the incident and try to recover control by means of several strategies. If the incident originates outside the organization, the simplest and most straightforward approach is to disconnect the affected communication circuits. Of course, if the organization's lifeblood runs through that circuit, this step may be too drastic; if the incident does not threaten critical functional areas, it may be more feasible to monitor the incident and contain it another way. One approach used by some organizations is to dynamically apply filtering rules to limit certain types of network access. For example, if a threat agent is attacking a network by exploiting a vulnerability in the Simple Network Management Protocol (SNMP), then applying a blocking filter for the commonly used IP ports for that vulnerability stops the attack without compromising other services on the network. Depending on the nature of the attack and the organization's technical capabilities, ad hoc controls can sometimes allow an organization to gain valuable time to devise a more permanent control strategy. Other containment strategies include the following:

- Disabling compromised user accounts
- Reconfiguring a firewall to block the problem traffic
- Temporarily disabling the compromised process or service
- Taking down the conduit application or server—for example, the e-mail server
- Stopping all computers and network devices

Obviously, that last strategy is used only when all system control has been lost and the only hope is to preserve the data stored on the computers so that operations can resume normally once the incident is resolved. The IR team, following the procedures outlined in the IR plan, determines the length of the interruption.

Recovery Once an incident has been contained and system control has been regained, incident recovery can begin. As in the Response phase, the first task is to inform the appropriate human resources. Almost simultaneously, the CSIRT must assess the full extent of the damage to determine what must be done to restore the systems. Each individual involved should begin recovery operations based on the appropriate incident recovery section of the IR plan.

The immediate determination of the scope of the breach of confidentiality, integrity, and availability of information and information assets is called *incident damage assessment*. Incident damage assessment can take days or weeks, depending on the extent of the damage. The damage can range from minor (a curious hacker snooped around) to severe (the infection of hundreds of computer systems by a worm or virus). System logs, intrusion detection logs, configuration logs, as well as the documentation from the IR provide information on the type, scope, and extent of damage. Using this information, the CSIRT assesses the current state of the information and systems and compares it to a known state. Individuals who document the damage from actual incidents must be trained to collect and preserve evidence in case the incident is part of a crime or results in a civil action.

The following sections detail the appropriate steps to be taken in the recovery process.

Identify and Resolve Vulnerabilities Although it may appear simple, identifying and resolving vulnerabilities could prove to be a major challenge in reestablishing operations. Forensics analysis, used both as a tool for intrusion analysis and evidentiary purposes, can also help organizations best assess how the incident occurred and what vulnerabilities were exploited. In some cases, such as disasters, computer forensics may not be necessary, but when hackers, worms, and other systems violations are involved, organizations can benefit greatly from better understanding exactly what occurred.

However, if the incident data is to be used in legal proceedings, it is imperative that the individuals performing the forensic collection and analysis be trained to recognize and handle the material in such a way that does not violate its value as evidence in civil or criminal proceedings.

After any incident, address the safeguards that failed to stop or limit the incident, or were missing from the system in the first place, and install, replace, or upgrade them. Whether the result of a faulty, malfunctioning, or misconfigured network security device (such as a firewall, router, or VPN connection) or a breach in policy or data protection procedures, the safeguards that were already in place must be examined to determine if they were part of the incident. If the incident was due to a missing safeguard, an assessment as to why the safeguard was not in place should be conducted. It may be determined that the incident occurred because a planned safeguard had not been procured yet, or it may be determined that a safeguard that could have prevented or limited the incident was assessed as being unnecessary.

Evaluate monitoring capabilities, if present. Improve detection and reporting methods, or install new monitoring capabilities. Many organizations do not have automated intrusion detection systems. Some feel that the performance does not justify the cost, especially when perceptions of "it can't happen to me" cloud the judgment of those responsible for the recommendation. Unfortunately, some decision makers must witness firsthand or secondhand the damage, destruction, or loss caused by an incident before they are willing to commit to the expenses of intrusion monitoring. This is especially unfortunate because in some cases, open-source software can provide many of the capabilities needed with little or no additional hardware or software expense (for example, Snort, found at *www.snort.org*). Although each set of circumstances needs to be carefully analyzed, in many cases the expense of training staff and providing support for open-source solutions is much less than replacing existing proprietary solutions.

If you don't have monitoring capabilities, get them. If you have them, review the implementation and configuration to determine if they failed to detect the incident. Network or host IDSs won't detect all incidents, especially attacks that are not network based. Burglar and fire alarm systems are also needed to detect physical forms of incidents.

Restore Data The CSIRT must understand the backup strategy used by the organization, restore the data contained in backups and then use the appropriate recovery processes from incremental backups or database journals to recreate any data that was created or modified since the last backup, as described previously.

Restore Services and Processes Compromised services and processes must be examined, verified, and then restored. If services or processes were interrupted in the course of regaining control of the systems, they need to be brought back online.

Continuously monitor the system. If an incident happened once, it could easily happen again. Hackers frequently boast of their exploits in chat rooms and dare their peers to match their efforts. If word gets out, others may be tempted to try the same or different attacks on your systems. It is, therefore, important to maintain vigilance during the entire IR process.

Restore Confidence across the Organization   The CSIRT may wish to issue a short memorandum outlining the incident and assuring all that the incident was handled and the damage was controlled. If the incident was minor, say so. If the incident was major or severely damaged systems or data, reassure the users that they can expect operations to return to normal as soon as possible. The objective of this communication is to prevent panic or confusion from causing additional disruption to the operations of the organization.

After Action Review (AAR)   Before returning to its routine duties, the CSIRT must conduct one last process, the after-action review (AAR). The **after-action review** entails a detailed examination of the events that occurred from first detection to final recovery. All key players review their notes and verify that the IR documentation is accurate and precise. All team members review the actions taken during the incident and identify areas where the IR plan worked, didn't work, or should improve. This exercise allows the team to update the IR plan. AARs are conducted with all role players in attendance. The CSIRT team leader presents a timeline of events and highlights who was involved at each stage, with a summary of their actions.

Ideally, each involved person relates what he or she discovered or did, and any discrepancies between documentation and the verbal case are noted. The entire AAR is recorded for use as a training case for future staff. All parties should treat the AAR not as an inquisition but as a discussion group. If properly structured and conducted, the AAR can have a positive effect on the organization's IR capacity and employee confidence in responding to incidents. If poorly handled, the AAR can actually reduce the organization's ability to react because individuals, especially users, may prefer to sweep potential incidents under the rug rather than risk improperly responding and having to face a punitive-seeming AAR.

The AAR serves as a review tool, allowing the team to examine how it responded to the incident. Examining the documentation of the incident should reveal the point at which the incident was first detected, the point at which the IR plan was enacted, and how the first responders and CSIRT reacted. This is to ensure that the best methods were employed and that any mistakes made during the process, whether from a failure to follow the IR plan or from errors in the IR plan, are not made again. The IR plan is continually reexamined during AARs to ensure the procedures are in fact the best method of responding to incidents. Should the AAR reveal that the incident represents a new type or variation of incident, additional material can be added to the IR plan to better prepare the team for future interactions.

An additional use of the AAR is a historical record of events. Such a record may or may not be a requirement for legal proceedings, depending on the laws that apply to your organization. In any case, it is useful to be able to establish a timeline of events, drawn from a number of different sources, to show the evolution of the incident, from first identification to final resolution. This timeline then serves other purposes, as described in the following sections.

One of the positive aspects of an incident is that it can improve an organization's ability to respond to future incidents; that is, "That which does not kill us, makes us stronger."[24] By examining previous attacks, students of information security and IR can learn from others' actions, whether correct or incorrect. You can learn as much from mistakes as from successes. As Thomas Edison is credited with saying "I have not failed. I've just found 10,000 ways that won't work."[25]

Honest effort in the pursuit of one's goals is not failure. By studying the AAR reports from an organization's past incidents, not only do the new information security professionals and CSIRT members become familiar with the system, plans, and responses of the organization, they get a lesson in how to deal with the challenges of incident response in general. Part of knowing yourself is knowing how you and your team handle victories as well as defeats. Even in defeat, however, as in the case of a successful and consequential attack, the organization must continue, recover, and rebuild its defenses.

One final quote on the AAR and its reports, this one from Yogi Berra: "It ain't over 'til it's over." People require closure, especially in the wake of traumatic events. The AAR serves as a closure to organizational incidents, although there may still be a great deal of systems data and recovery and training to be done.

Ensure Plan Testing, Training, and Exercises

An untested plan is no plan at all. Very few plans are executable as written; they must be tested to identify weaknesses, faults, and inefficient processes. Once problems are identified during the testing process, improvements can be made, and the resulting plan can be relied on in times of need. Five strategies that can be used to test contingency plans are:

- Desk check—Each member of the CSIRT performs a desk check by reviewing the IR plan and creating a list of correct and incorrect components. Although not a true test, it is a good way to review the perceived feasibility and effectiveness of the plan.

- Structured walk-through—All involved individuals walk through the steps they would take during an actual event. This can consist of an on-site walk-through, in which the team discusses its actions at each location and juncture, or it may be more of a "chalk talk," in which team members sit together and discuss in turn their responsibilities as the incident unfolds.

- Simulation—Each team member works separately, simulating the performance of each task. The simulation stops short of the physical tasks—installing the backup or disconnecting a communications circuit. The major difference between a walk-through and a simulation is that individuals work on their own tasks and are responsible for identifying the faults in their own procedures.

- Parallel testing—Team members act as if an incident occurred, performing their required tasks and executing the necessary procedures without interfering with the normal operations of the business. Great care must be taken to ensure that the procedures performed do not halt the operations of the business functions, creating an actual incident.

- Full interruption—Team members follow each and every procedure—interrupting service, restoring data from backups, and notifying appropriate individuals. This type of testing is often performed after normal business hours in organizations that cannot afford to disrupt business functions. Although full interruption testing is the most rigorous, it is unfortunately too risky for most businesses.

- War gaming—Team members act as defenders, using their own equipment or a duplicate environment, against realistic attacks executed by external information security professionals. This valid, effective training technique is so popular that there are national competitions at conferences like Black Hat (*http://blackhat.com*) and DEFCON (*www.defcon.org*). War gaming competition at the collegiate level is held at the West Point Military Training Academy (*itcf.cs.ucsb.edu*). A National Collegiate CyberDefense Competition has been held annually since 2005, and details can be found at *www.nationalccdc.org.*

While the authors emphatically denounce the actions of hackers and the criminal acts associated with hacking, these conferences are typically attended not only by hackers but by information security professionals and representatives of law enforcement and the military. In keeping with our philosophy of "know your enemy," one cannot pass up the opportunity to visit the enemy's camp and observe them preparing for battle, learning their strategies and tactics firsthand.

At a minimum, organizations should conduct periodic walk-throughs (or chalk talks) of each of the CP component plans. A failure to update each of these plans as the business and its information resources change can erode the team's ability to respond to an incident, and possibly cause greater damage than the incident itself.

Training the Users Training the end user to assist in IR is primarily the responsibility of those individuals who provide security education training and awareness (SETA) for the organization. As part of the ongoing employee-training program, SETA trainers should instruct end users on:

- What is expected of them as members of the organization's security team.

- How to recognize an attack; each user should be instructed on what to look for and be apprised of the key attack indicators.

- How to report a suspected incident and who to report it to—that is, the help desk and the information security hotline or e-mail address or some another designated mechanism.

- How to mitigate the damage of attacks on the desktop by disconnecting the system from the network if they suspect an attack in progress, and by reporting suspected incidents promptly.

- Good information security practices that prevent attacks on the desktop, such as:

  - Keeping antivirus software up to date

  - Using spyware detection software

  - Working with systems administrators to keep the operating system and applications up to date with patches and updates

  - Not opening suspect e-mail attachments

  - Avoiding social engineering attacks by not providing critical information over the phone or e-mail

  - Not downloading and installing unauthorized software or software from untrusted sources

  - Protecting passwords and classified information

IR Plan Maintenance

The final phase of the IR planning function is plan maintenance. The specific processes for maintaining the IR plan vary from one organization to another, but there are some commonly used maintenance techniques. When shortcomings are noted, the plan should be reviewed and revised to remediate the deficiency. Deficiencies may come to light based on AARs, when the plans are used for actual incidents, during rehearsals when the plan is used in simulated incidents, or by review during periodic maintenance. At periodic intervals, such as one year or less, an assigned member of management should undertake a review of the IR plan that addresses the following questions:

- Has the plan been used since the last review?
- Were any AAR meetings held, and have the minutes of any such meetings been reviewed to note deficiencies that may need attention?
- Have any other notices of deficiency been submitted to the plan owner, and have they been addressed?

Depending on the answer to these questions, the plan may need to be reviewed and amended by the CPMT. All changes proposed to the IR plan must be coordinated with the CPMT so that the plan remains aligned with the organization's other contingency planning documents.

Chapter Summary

- Contingency planning (CP) is the process of positioning an organization to prepare for, detect, react to, and recover from events that threaten the security of information resources and assets. The goal of CP is to restore normal operations after an unexpected event—in other words, to make sure things get back to the way they were within a reasonable period of time.

- CP has 12 stages:
  - Form the CPMT.
  - Develop the contingency planning policy statement.
  - Conduct the business impact analysis (BIA).
  - Form subordinate planning teams.
  - Develop subordinate planning policies.
  - Integrate the BIA.
  - Identify preventive controls.
  - Organize response teams.
  - Create contingency strategies.
  - Develop subordinate plans.
  - Ensure plan testing, training, and exercises.
  - Ensure plan maintenance.

11

■ The BIA provides the CP team with information about systems and the threats they face.

■ The actions an organization should take while the incident is in progress are defined in an incident response plan (IR plan).

■ Disaster recovery planning (DRP) entails the preparation for and recovery from a disaster, whether natural or human-made.

■ Business continuity planning (BCP) ensures that critical business functions can continue if a disaster occurs.

■ Incident classification is the process of determining which events are possible incidents. Three broad categories of incident indicators have been established: possible, probable, and definite. The routine collection and analysis of data is required to properly detect and declare incidents.

■ How and when to activate IR plans is determined by the IR strategy the organization chooses to pursue. The organization must make sure the outcome from the planned response meets the organization's strategic and tactical needs. Two general strategies govern how an organization responds to an incident: "protect and forget" or "apprehend and prosecute."

■ One of the most critical components of IR is stopping the incident or containing its scope or impact. Incident containment strategies vary depending on the incident and on the amount of damage caused.

■ Once an incident has been contained and system control has been regained, incident recovery can begin. The IR team must assess the full extent of the damage to determine what must be done to restore the systems.

■ The ongoing maintenance of the IR plan includes effective after-action reviews (AARs), planned review and maintenance, training staff that will be involved in incident response, and rehearsing the process that maintains readiness for all aspects of the incident plan.

■ There are a number of data backup and management methods that aid in the preparation for IR. The most commonly used varieties are disk backup and tape backup. Backup methods must be based on an established policy that meets organizational needs.

Review Questions

1. What are the components of contingency planning?

2. Who are the typical teams involved in contingency planning and contingency operations?

3. What are the major steps in the BIA?

4. What are the three types of backup? Describe each.

5. What is RAID? What does RAID 3 provide that RAID 0 does not?

6. What is remote journaling?

7. What is bare metal recovery?

8. What are SAN and NAS technologies? Describe them.

9. What is the Computer Security Incident Response Team (CSIRT)?

10. What is an incident candidate?

11. What are the three broad categories of incident indicators? What types of events are considered possible indicators of actual incidents? What types of events are considered probable indicators of actual incidents? What types of events are considered definite indicators of actual incidents?

12. What types of events indicate that an incident is in progress?

13. What are the components of an incident response plan (IRP)?

14. What are the key steps included in the "protect and forget" IR strategy? What are the key steps included in the "apprehend and prosecute" IR strategy?

15. What is the primary objective of recovery operations during an incident response?

16. What are the key steps used to accomplish recovery?

17. Why is the restoration of user confidence an important step in the recovery process?

18. What is an after-action review (AAR)? What are the primary reasons for undertaking one?

19. What are the primary techniques used for plan review and maintenance?

20. What purpose does rehearsal serve? Why should organizations continue to rehearse once a plan is known to work?

11

Real World Exercises

Exercise 11-1

Using a Web browser, go to *www.is.depaul.edu/_downloads/6_irtfwk.pdf*. Review the article entitled "A Framework for Incident Response." How does the approach in that article differ from the NIST approach presented in this chapter?

Exercise 11-2

Using a Web browser, go to *http://technet.microsoft.com/en-us/library/cc700825.aspx*. Review the Microsoft article entitled "Responding to IT Security Incidents." What does the article recommend that systems and network administrators do to minimize the number and severity of security incidents?

Exercise 11-3

Using a Web browser, go to *www.us-cert.gov/current*. Identify the top current incident threats. Categorize the incidents as either technical or behavioral (such as phishing). What is the largest group?

Exercise 11-4

Using a Web browser, go to *www.sans.org/rr*, the SANS Information Security Reading Room. What categories are available that would benefit someone preparing to organize and train an incident response team? Select one of these headings and then select a paper from within it. Summarize the paper and bring your summary to class to discuss.

Exercise 11-5

Using the list of possible, probable, and definite indicators of an incident, draft a recommendation to assist a typical end user in identifying these indicators. Alternatively, using a graphics package, such as PowerPoint, create a poster to make the user aware of the key indicators.

Hands-On Projects

Project 11-1

In this project, we examine ways for organizations to monitor their networks for signs of possible attack. This project was created using the "Security Onion" open-source project built for Intrusion Detection and Network Security Monitoring. You can find out more about the project and its creator, Doug Burks, at *http://securityonion.blogspot.com*.

To complete this project, it is recommended that you run Security Onion as a virtual machine. Configure the VM to allow 1 GB of memory, 20 GB of disk space, and a single NIC set to "bridged." Configuring virtual machines is outside the scope of this project, but there are numerous tutorials available on the Internet. You will also need to install the Nmap/Zenmap GUI network scanning application or have it available elsewhere on the network.

This project was written using VMWare and the 20111103 release of Security Onion.

1. Start the virtual machine. When prompted, choose the **live – boot the Live System** option. After a brief delay, Security Onion will start.
2. On the desktop, double-click the **Setup** icon, as highlighted in Figure 11-13, to start the setup process.
3. Click **Yes, Continue!**
4. Click **Yes, use Quick Setup!**
5. When prompted, enter a username for the Sguil setup, as shown in Figure 11-14. Note: Remember this username, as it will be needed later in the exercise.

Figure 11-13   Security Onion setup
Source: SecurityOnion

Figure 11-14   Sguil username setup
Source: SecurityOnion

6. When prompted, enter a password for the username you entered in the previous step. Note: Remember this password, as it will be needed later in the exercise.

7. When prompted, reenter the password for verification.

8. Click **Yes, proceed with the changes!**

9. After a brief delay, click **OK** to complete the setup process.

One of the many features built into Security Onion is SQueRT, a Web-based tool that allows monitoring of IDS/NSM events in real time. SQueRT can be accessed either within the VM by double-clicking the Squert icon on the desktop or by opening a Web browser on another system and pointing it to http://*IP address of the Security Onion system*/squert/squert.php—for example, http://192.168.1.114/squert/squert.php. Either method is acceptable for the steps going forward.

10. At the SQueRT login screen, enter the username and password you supplied during the initial setup, as shown in Figure 11-15, then click **submit**.

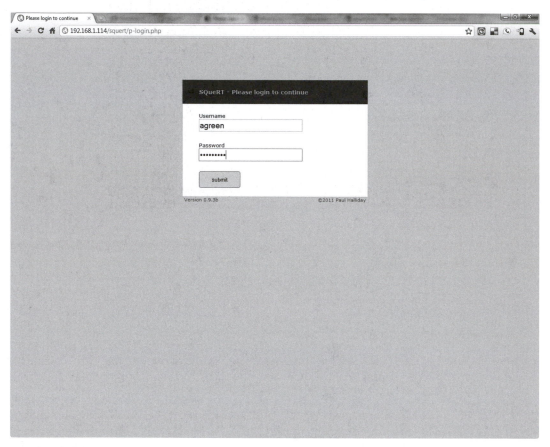

Figure 11-15   SqueRT login screen
Source: SecurityOnion

11. Depending on the level of network activity present, you may already see alerts already present. Disregard these, as we will be generating our own using the Nmap application. Note that at the top of the page there are several tabs to choose from. Click through all of them quickly to become aware of what each has to offer, then return to the Summary. Take note of the data presented at the top of the page, including "total events."

12. On the second system, start the Nmap/Zenmap GUI.

13. In the Target field, type the IP address of the Security Onion system and choose the **Intense scan** option in the Profile list, then click **Scan**. After a brief delay, Nmap/Zenmap should complete its scan and return a set of results, similar to what is shown in Figure 11-16.

Figure 11-16 Nmap/Zenmap results

Nmap/Zenmap

14. Go back to the SQueRT browser window and refresh the page. Note that the "total events" count has increased and has new information in the "Event Distribution" and "Top Signatures" sections. This is a lot of general information, but the details are sketchy. Click **Query** at the top of the page in order to get further details on the questionable traffic.

15. Change the View option from **signature** to **event detail**, and click **submit**. SQueRT will display details from the current day, which should look similar to what is shown in Figure 11-17.

16. We now examine one of the entries in greater detail. Look through the entries until you find one with the Signature value of "ET POLICY Suspicious inbound to MSSQL port 1433," then click the date/time stamp for that entry. A window will pop up that shows complete details on the traffic in question, as shown in Figure 11-18. Once these details are displayed, security professionals can make a further determination as to whether or not an incident is actually occurring and take appropriate steps based on that finding.

ST	Timestamp	Source	Src Port	CC	Destination	Dst Port	CC	Signature	SigID
NA	11-11-15 00:36:00	192.168.1.20	1768	LO	192.168.1.114	80	LO	URL 192.168.1.114	420042
NA	11-11-15 00:36:00	192.168.1.20	1767	LO	192.168.1.114	80	LO	URL 192.168.1.114	420042
NA	11-11-15 00:36:00	192.168.1.20	1767	LO	192.168.1.114	80	LO	URL 192.168.1.114	420042
NA	11-11-15 00:35:59	192.168.1.20	1767	LO	192.168.1.114	80	LO	URL 192.168.1.114	420042
NA	11-11-15 00:35:15	192.168.1.20	6568	LO	██████████	80	US	████████████	420042
NA	11-11-15 00:35:11	192.168.1.20	1760	LO	192.168.1.114	80	LO	URL 192.168.1.114	420042
NA	11-11-15 00:35:10	192.168.1.20	1760	LO	192.168.1.114	80	LO	URL 192.168.1.114	420042
NA	11-11-15 00:35:10	192.168.1.20	1761	LO	192.168.1.114	80	LO	URL 192.168.1.114	420042
NA	11-11-15 00:35:10	192.168.1.20	1760	LO	192.168.1.114	80	LO	URL 192.168.1.114	420042
NA	11-11-15 00:34:19	192.168.1.20	6568	LO	██████████	80	US	████████████	420042
NA	11-11-15 00:34:14	192.168.1.20	1742	LO	192.168.1.114	80	LO	URL 192.168.1.114	420042
NA	11-11-15 00:34:12	192.168.1.20	1742	LO	192.168.1.114	80	LO	URL 192.168.1.114	420042
NA	11-11-15 00:34:12	192.168.1.20	1743	LO	192.168.1.114	80	LO	URL 192.168.1.114	420042
NA	11-11-15 00:34:12	192.168.1.20	1742	LO	192.168.1.114	80	LO	URL 192.168.1.114	420042
UN	11-11-15 00:33:38	192.168.1.102	38232	LO	192.168.1.114	5804	LO	ET SCAN Potential VNC Scan 5800-5820	2002910
UN	11-11-15 00:33:36	192.168.1.102	38232	LO	192.168.1.114	5903	LO	ET SCAN Potential VNC Scan 5900-5920	2002911
UN	11-11-15 00:33:33	192.168.1.102	38231	LO	192.168.1.114	5805	LO	ET SCAN Potential VNC Scan 5800-5820	2002910
UN	11-11-15 00:33:28	192.168.1.102	38231	LO	192.168.1.114	5918	LO	ET SCAN Potential VNC Scan 5900-5920	2002911
NA	11-11-15 00:33:23	192.168.1.20	6568	LO	██████████	80	US	████████████	420042
UN	11-11-15 00:33:20	192.168.1.102	38232	LO	192.168.1.114	5817	LO	ET SCAN Potential VNC Scan 5800-5820	2002910
UN	11-11-15 00:33:09	192.168.1.102	38232	LO	192.168.1.114	5902	LO	ET SCAN Potential VNC Scan 5900-5920	2002911
UN	11-11-15 00:33:00	192.168.1.102	38231	LO	192.168.1.114	162	LO	GPL SNMP trap tcp	1420
UN	11-11-15 00:33:00	192.168.1.102	38232	LO	192.168.1.114	162	LO	GPL SNMP trap tcp	1420
UN	11-11-15 00:33:00	192.168.1.102	38231	LO	192.168.1.114	5920	LO	ET SCAN Potential VNC Scan 5900-5920	2002911
	11-11-15 00:32:59	192.168.1.102	38232	LO	192.168.1.114	1521	LO	ET POLICY Suspicious inbound to Oracle SQL port 1521	2010936
	11-11-15 00:32:59	192.168.1.102	38231	LO	192.168.1.114	1521	LO	ET POLICY Suspicious inbound to Oracle SQL port 1521	2010936

Figure 11-17   SqueRT query results
Source: SecurityOnion

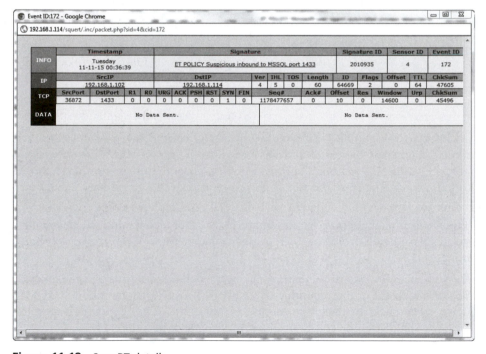

Figure 11-18   SqueRT details
Source: SecurityOnion

Endnotes

1. Swanson, M., Bowen, P., Phillips, A., Gallup, D., and Lynes, D. *NIST Special Publication 800-34 Rev.1: Contingency Planning Guide for Federal Information Systems.*

2. The Hartford Insurance Group. "Business Disaster Recovery Tips." Accessed February 4, 2012 @ *www.thehartford.com/cs/Satellite?c=Page&cid=1253718686264&pagename=HIG%2FPage%2FgeneralPage.*

3. Swanson, M., Bowen, P., Phillips, A., Gallup, D., and Lynes, D. *NIST Special Publication 800-34 Rev.1: Contingency Planning Guide for Federal Information Systems.*

4. Swanson, M., Bowen, P., Phillips, A., Gallup, D., and Lynes, D. *NIST Special Publication 800-34 Rev.1: Contingency Planning Guide for Federal Information Systems.*

5. Swanson, M., Bowen, P., Phillips, A., Gallup, D., and Lynes, D. *NIST Special Publication 800-34 Rev.1: Contingency Planning Guide for Federal Information Systems.*

6. Swanson, M., Bowen, P., Phillips, A., Gallup, D., and Lynes D. *NIST Special Publication 800-34 Rev.1: Contingency Planning Guide for Federal Information Systems.*

7. Firth, Robert, et. al. "Detecting Signs of Intrusion." *Carnegie Mellon University* 2000. Accessed February 4, 2012 from *www.sei.cmu.edu/reports/98sim001.pdf.*

8. Firth, Robert, et. al. "Detecting Signs of Intrusion." *Carnegie Mellon University* 2000. Accessed February 4, 2012 from *www.sei.cmu.edu/reports/98sim001.pdf.*

9. Swanson, M., Bowen, P., Phillips, A., Gallup, D., and Lynes, D. *NIST Special Publication 800-34 Rev.1: Contingency Planning Guide for Federal Information Systems.*

10. Scarfone, K., Grance, T., and Masone, K. *NIST Special Publication 800-61, Revision 1: Compute Security Incident Handling Guide*, March 2008.

11. Tandberg Data, *Guide to Data Protection Best Practices*. Accessed February 4, 2012 from *www.exabyte.com/support/online/documentation/whitepapers/basicbackup.pdf.*

12. Cook, Rick. "Deciding on electronic vaulting." *SearchStorage*. Accessed February 4, 2012 from *searchstorage.techtarget.com/tip/1,289483,sid5_gci797551,00.html?bucket=ETA.*

13. Based in part on graphics created by Chris Hird and Shield Advanced Solutions, "Remote Journaling and Data Recovery." Accessed July 8, 2005 from *www.shield.on.ca/download/Remote%20Journaling%20and%20Data%20Recovery.pdf.*

14. iTera, "The Benefits of Remote Journaling in iSeries High Availability Solutions." Accessed February 4, 2012 from *advgroup.com/NEWpdfs/Benefits%20of%20Remote%20Journaling%20-%20whitepaper.pdf.*

15. E-Net, "Data Recovery Without Data Loss." Accessed February 4, 2012 from *www.enet.com/pages/rrdf_recovery.html.*

16. NAS-SAN. "Technology Overview." Accessed February 4, 2012 from *www.nas-san.com/differ.html.*

17. Scarfone, K., Grance, T., and Masone, K. *NIST Special Publication 800-61, Revision 1: Compute Security Incident Handling Guide*, March 2008.

18. West-Brown, Moira, et. al. "Handbook for Computer Security Incident Response Teams (CCIRT)." *Carnegie Mellon University* 2003. Accessed February 4, 2012 @ *www.cert.org/archive/pdf/cCIRT-handbook.pdf.*

11

19. Scarfone, K., Grance, T., and Masone, K. *NIST Special Publication 800-61, Revision 1: Compute Security Incident Handling Guide*, March 2008.

20. Sterneckert, A. *Critical Incident Management*. Boca Raton, FL: Auerbach/CRC Press LLC, 2004.

21. Adler, David, and Kenneth Grossman. *Establishing a Computer Incident Response Plan*. Accessed July 17, 2004 from *www.fedcirc.gov/library/documents/82-02-70.pdf*.

22. Masurkar, V. "Responding to a Customer's Security Incidents—Part 2: Executing a Policy." *Sun Microsystems Web site*, March 2003. Accessed February 4, 2012 from *www.filibeto.org/sun/lib/blueprints/817-1796.pdf*.

23. Pipkin, Donald L. *Information Security: Protecting the Global Enterprise*. Upper Saddle River, NJ: Prentice Hall PTR, 2000: 256.

24. Nietzshe, Friedrich. "Friedrich Nietzsche Quotes." *Brainy Quote*. Accessed February 4, 2012 from *www.brainyquote.com/quotes/quotes/f/friedrichn101616.html*.

25. "Thomas Alva Edison Quotes." *Thinkexist.com*. Accessed January 23, 2012 from *thinkexist.com/quotation/i_haven-t_failed-i-ve_found-ways_that_don-t/346094.html*.

chapter 12

Digital Forensics

If the law has made you a witness, remain a man of science. You have no victim to avenge, no guilty or innocent person to convict or save—you must bear testimony within the limits of science. — Dr. P. C. H. Brouardel, nineteenth-century French medicolegalist

Upon completion of this material, you should be able to:

- Explain how U.S. law enforcement and the U.S. legal system affect digital forensics
- Describe the roles and responsibilities of digital forensic team members
- List the steps involved in collecting digital evidence
- Discuss the process used to analyze evidence
- Explain how encryption can thwart digital forensic analysis

Analyzing the Analyzers

With all the due diligence completed, the EBS team was finally able to take a breath. The PCI audit was next week, and most of the loose ends were tied up. Through several months, the team had looked at its vulnerability management program, hardening practices, security event monitoring, and incident response procedures. The effort was finally paying off.

One of the last items to address was EBS's digital forensics capability. In a typical business day, forensics was not part of the information security program. It was only in cases of compromised servers, zero-day vulnerability exploits, or unusual attacks that EBS enlisted the services of a third party in order to properly analyze the residual data on a system.

Despite the lack of in-house resources, this ability to perform digital forensics was critical and was going to be of interest to the auditors. Paige planned a last-minute trip to the third-party digital forensic consultancy that EBS used. The visit would help her evaluate the processes the agency used as well as the evidence-handling procedures.

Introduction

The word *forensics* comes from the Latin word *forensis*, which in ancient Rome referred to the forum—the precursor to today's courts of law.[1] When its information resources have been affected by an incident and an organization decides to apprehend and prosecute the offender(s), it must collect information in such a way that the information will be usable in a criminal or civil proceeding. This information is usually called "evidence," but in fact nothing is evidence until a judge admits it as evidence in court. During legal proceedings, opposing counsel can (and usually will) challenge this admission on every available ground. Even something as simple as just taking a look at a compromised computer may allow opposing counsel to challenge the information gathered from that computer on the grounds that it might have been modified or otherwise tainted.[2]

What we really mean by *evidence*, therefore, is *items of potential evidentiary value*.[3] **Computer forensics** is, thus, defined as the use of technical investigation and analysis techniques to identify, collect, preserve, and analyze electronic items of potential evidentiary value so that they may be admitted as evidence in a court of law, used to support administrative action, or simply used to further analyze suspicious data. This definition has been generally interpreted to apply almost exclusively to computers and computer-based media. The term **digital forensics**, which covers a broader area, applies to all modern electronic devices, including mobile phones, personal digital assistants (PDAs), portable music players, and other electronic devices capable of storing digital information.

In this chapter, you will learn the requirements for digital evidence, the processes involved in identifying and acquiring it, and the general process of analyzing digital evidence.

Legal Matters

Although the process of conducting digital forensics within an organization does not necessarily lead to prosecution, that is the most important outcome. Thus, it's important to understand various aspects of the U.S. legal system that have a bearing on the digital forensics process, including how to interact with law enforcement personnel.

Search and Seizure

The laws governing private sector search and seizure are somewhat more straightforward than the ones that govern public sector search and seizure. Certain conditions must be met in order to ensure that any evidentiary material found is admissible in any legal proceedings that follow, whether administrative or judicial. In the public sector, law enforcement agents generally must have a search warrant or the employer's consent to search for evidentiary materials. In the private sector, an organization wishing to search an employee's computer must generally meet the following conditions:

- The employee must have been made aware of the organizational policy establishing that such a search may occur.

- The search must be justified from its inception. There must be a legitimate business reason for the search—that is, it will be conducted by an authorized individual to locate legitimate evidence or to look for suspected misconduct involving organizational resources. If an organization routinely searches every employee's computer or if it conducts truly random searches and uncovers potential evidentiary material, then the findings are admissible.

- The search must be permissible in its scope—that is, it must have a specific focus and be constrained to that focus. This requirement does not prohibit the use of materials found during a normal, less focused business search, but it precludes a search of the organization's entire set of data if the identified area of interest has been confined to one or two folders or directories.

- The organization must have clear ownership of the container the material was discovered in. This precludes searches of the employee's person, personal belongings, and personal technologies but does not exclude those containers provided by the organization for the employee's use, such as a PDA, cell phone, laptop, and so on. Gray areas include employee-purchased briefcases, satchels, and backpacks used to transport work as well as personally owned computers, PDAs, and cell phones used by telecommuters.

- The search must be authorized by the responsible manager or administrator. For systems, the senior system administrator must authorize the search, unless of course that person is a suspect in an internal investigation. For most organizational equipment, a designated manager must provide authorization. Forward-thinking organizations designate a senior executive officer (e.g., the chief information officer) as a magistrate who authorizes organizational searches. Even then, the search should

12

be conducted by a designated, disinterested individual, such as the CISO or other individual recommended by legal counsel.

Once these conditions are met, an organization should have a reasonable degree of confidence in its right to search for and collect potentially evidentiary material. This does not mean that any administrative or judicial actions will go unchallenged; however, it does mean that the organization has much stronger grounds to refute any allegations of impropriety.

Interacting with Law Enforcement

When an incident violates civil or criminal law, it is the organization's responsibility to notify the proper authorities. Which is the appropriate law enforcement agency depends on the type of crime committed. The Federal Bureau of Investigation (FBI), for example, handles computer crimes that are categorized as felonies. The U.S. Secret Service investigates crimes involving U.S. currency, counterfeiting, and certain cases involving credit card fraud and identity theft. The U.S. Treasury Department has a bank fraud investigation unit, and the Securities and Exchange Commission has investigation and fraud control units as well. However, given these agencies' heavy caseloads, they typically give priority to those incidents that affect the country's critical infrastructure or that have significant economic impact. Gordon Snow, the assistant director of the FBI's Cyber Division, is on record as saying:

> Countering efforts by foreign countries to steal our nation's secrets, evaluating the capabilities of terrorists in a digital age, and fighting cyber crime are the FBI's highest priorities. It is difficult to overstate the potential impact these threats pose to our economy, our national security, and the critical infrastructure upon which our country relies…
>
> Cyber criminal threats to the U.S. result in significant economic losses. But the threat against financial institutions is only part of the problem. Also of serious concern are threats to critical infrastructure, the theft of intellectual property, and supply chain issues. U.S. critical infrastructure faces a growing cyber threat due to advancements in the availability and sophistication of malicious software tools and the fact that new technologies raise new security issues that cannot always be addressed prior to adoption. The increasing automation of our critical infrastructures provides more cyber access points for adversaries to exploit.[4]

In other words, if the crime doesn't affect the U.S. national infrastructure or is not an attempt to commit an interstate criminal act, the FBI may not be able to assist an organization as effectively as state or local agencies could. However, in general, if a crime crosses state lines, it becomes a federal matter. The FBI may also become involved at the request of a state agency.

Each state, county, and city in the United States has its own law enforcement agencies. These agencies enforce all local and state laws, handle suspects, and secure crime scenes for state and federal cases. Local law enforcement agencies rarely have computer-crime task forces, but the investigative (detective) units are quite capable of processing crime scenes and handling most common criminal violations, such as physical theft, trespassing, damage to property, and the apprehension and processing of suspects in computer-related crimes.

Involving law enforcement agencies has advantages and disadvantages. Such agencies are usually much better equipped for processing evidence than business organizations. Unless the security forces in the organization have been trained in processing evidence and computer forensics, they may do more harm than good when attempting to extract information that can lead to the legal conviction of a suspected criminal. Law enforcement agencies are also prepared to handle the warrants and subpoenas necessary when documenting a case. They are adept at obtaining statements from witnesses, affidavits, and other required documents. For all these reasons, law enforcement personnel can be a security administrator's greatest allies in prosecuting a computer crime.

It is, therefore, important to become familiar with the appropriate local and state agencies before you have to make a call announcing a suspected crime. Most state and federal agencies offer awareness programs, provide guest speakers at conferences, and offer programs such as the FBI's InfraGard program (*www.infragard.net*). These agents clearly understand the challenges facing security administrators.

The disadvantages of involving law enforcement include possible loss of control of the chain of events following an incident, including the collection of information and evidence and the prosecution of suspects. An organization that wishes to simply reprimand or dismiss an employee should not involve a law enforcement agency in the resolution of an incident. Additionally, the organization may not hear about the case for weeks or even months because of heavy caseloads or resource shortages.

A very real issue for commercial organizations when involving law enforcement agencies is the tagging as evidence of equipment vital to the organization's business. When this happens, organizational assets can be removed, stored, and preserved to prepare the criminal case. Despite these difficulties, if the organization detects a criminal act, it has the legal obligation to notify the appropriate law enforcement officials. Failure to do so can subject the organization and its officers to prosecution as accessories to the crime, or they can be charged with impeding the course of an investigation. It is up to the security administrator to find out when each law enforcement agency needs to be involved and which crimes it addresses.

Adversarial Legal System

Perhaps one of the most confusing things about the U.S. legal system is its adversarial nature. Two parties enter the proceeding holding opposing views on a question of fact and attempt to prove that their own views are correct either beyond a reasonable doubt (criminal proceeding) or with a preponderance of the evidence (civil proceeding).

Within the rules of the court, everything is open to challenge by opposing counsel. Consider a criminal case involving possession of child pornography. During her analysis, the prosecutor's forensic investigator found criminal images involving small children on the defendant's computer; the defense would likely challenge this finding on some of the following grounds:

- Was the prosecution's forensic expert properly trained and qualified?
- Did the evidence collection process follow established procedures to ensure that the evidence was not modified in any way during its collection and analysis?
- Was the evidence under proper controls at all times, and is the chain of custody complete?
- Were the images actually downloaded by the defendant, or were they downloaded by a hacker, virus, or other malware?

These types of issues are what laypeople think of as technicalities—the kinds of things that a sly attorney uses to get a guilty person off. However, the adversarial roles played by opposing counsel ensure that all parties "follow the rules." Thus, the wise forensic practitioner never thinks in terms of "if this is challenged" but in terms of "when this is challenged."

Digital Forensics Team

In their book, *Principles and Practice of Criminalistics*, Keith Inman and Norah Rudin argue that forensics is really about translating a real-world problem into one or more questions that can be answered by means of forensic analysis.[5] Therefore, the digital forensics team is a team of experts responsible for translating a real-world problem into one or more questions that can be answered by means of *digital* forensic analysis. For example, let's say Joe is suspected of having violated his organization's intellectual property policy by disclosing details of a new product to a competitor in hopes of gaining employment with that competitor. The challenge for the digital forensic analyst is to translate the question "Did Joe violate the IP policy by disclosing the product details to a competitor?" into a series of questions answerable by digital forensic investigation, such as:

- Did Joe access the new product information during the relevant time period?
- Are there indications of a quid pro quo agreement between Joe and the competitor?
- Did Joe send e-mails to the competitor containing that information?
- Did Joe transmit the information to the competitor over the network?

The answers to these questions might be found on the disk image of Joe's computer, network logs, access logs for a file server, data leakage protection (DLP) tools, or within other digital sources.

To tackle the task of digital forensics, many organizations divide the roles into two teams:

1. First response—This team will assess the location, identify sources of relevant digital information, collect evidence, and preserve the evidence for later analysis.

2. Analysis and presentation—This team will analyze the collected information to identify material facts relevant to the investigation, prepare the results of the investigation, and finally present the results of the analysis to management or support possible legal action.

First Response Team

The size and makeup of a first-response team will vary based on the size of the organization and other factors, but the team often includes the following roles and duties:

- Incident manager—Surveys the scene and identifies sources of relevant information; orchestrates the work of the other team members and usually produces any photographic documentation
- Scribe or recorder—Produces the written record of the team's activities and maintains control of the field evidence log and locker
- Imager—Collects copies or images of digital evidence

Consider a situation in which a digital forensics team has been given the assignment of performing on-site data collection at an employee's office. After securing the scene, the scribe begins the written record of the events taking place. The incident manager enters the scene to survey the situation, identify and photographically document the locations of evidence (computer, servers, disk arrays, etc.), and prioritize the collected evidence. Some considerations that guide this prioritization are:[6]

- Value—The likelihood that the information will be useful
- Volatility—The stability of the information over time. Some types of information are lost when the power is cut, and others are lost by default over time (e.g., log records overwritten with newer data).
- Effort required—The amount of time needed to acquire a copy of the information

After the sources of information have been prioritized, the incident manager photographs equipment that will be removed for imaging, identifies a safe area for the imager to set up equipment, and directs him or her in removing items to image. The scribe also documents the equipment removals within the written record.

As the imager finishes imaging an item, its integrity assurance (hash and other information) is documented in the written record, the image is logged into the field evidence locker, and the original item is returned for reinstallation.

When all the items have been imaged, the incident manager, as part of the exit process, compares the scene's appearance to the initial photographic survey to ensure that the team has left little trace of its presence.

Analysis Team

Whether performed in-house or outsourced to a third party, the analysis and presentation phase is performed by persons specially trained in the use of digital forensic tools to analyze the collected information and provide answers to the question(s) that gave rise to the investigation. These digital forensics tools help forensic analysts recover deleted files, reassemble file fragments, and interpret operating system artifacts.

The forensic analysis phase is sometimes further broken into two parts: examination and analysis. The examination phase involves the use of forensic tools to recover deleted files, retrieve and characterize operating system artifacts, and obtain other relevant material, whereas the analysis phase involves using those materials to answer the question(s) that gave rise to the investigation.

Larger organizations may delineate these two functions as separate job descriptions: forensic examiners, who are skilled in the operations of particular tools used to gather the information, and forensic analysts, who know operating systems and networks as well as how to interpret the information gleaned by the examiners. Additionally, an incident will sometimes require expertise in subject areas beyond the purview of the forensic analysis team—for example, analyzing data from a Lotus Notes server that has been compromised. In these cases, the team should draw upon a pool of resources that's already been set up to help with forensic analysis.

The presentation portion of the analysis and presentation phase encompasses reporting and presenting the investigation's findings. Forensic reports serve a variety of audiences, ranging from upper management to legal professionals and other forensic experts that may use the findings to build a case in court; therefore, the reports must clearly communicate highly technical matters without sacrificing critical details.

Effective communication becomes even more critical when the forensic analyst is called into court, where the audience includes a judge and jury (who likely have only a nodding acquaintance with computer technology) and an opposing counsel whose job is to undermine the analyst's findings and expertise.

 Presenting a forensic analysis to a nontechnical audience can be quite challenging. If the analyst's presentation is ineffective, the findings are likely to be regarded as technical gobbledygook; worse, members of the jury may perceive that the analyst is talking down to them.

Analogies play an important part in communication; a common analogy is using the library card catalog to illustrate how deleted files are recovered. A computer hard drive is rather like a large library in which books (files) are shelved according to the information in a card catalog (file system directory). Deleting a file is rather like removing the book's card from the card catalog. The pointer to the book is gone, but the book itself can still be found in the library stacks, although it might take some searching.

This analogy aptly illustrates how a technical process can be explained to a nontechnical audience. Sometimes the most challenging part of presenting the results of forensic analysis is finding a relevant analogy that helps the audience grasp the technical details.

Dedicated Team or Outsource?

Should an organization have a dedicated digital forensics team? That depends on the size and nature of the organization as well as the available resources. Sometimes, the need for a digital forensic unit is obvious, as in the case of large enterprises that are subject to frequent network attacks (government agencies or high-profile companies like Microsoft); but as digital information becomes more and more critical for business operations, organizations of all types and sizes may be required to engage in some form of digital forensic investigation. In the case of smaller companies, they may need to consult a third party for this type of expertise.

An organization should consider the following in deciding whether to employ in-house investigatory expertise:[7]

- Cost—This includes the tools, hardware, and other equipment used to collect and examine digital information as well as staffing and training.

- Response time—Although hiring an outside forensic consultant may seem less expensive because you only pay when the service is actually used, the interruption to normal business operations while the consultant gets up to speed may turn out to be more expensive than maintaining an in-house forensic capability.

- Data sensitivity—Providing outside consultants with access to the organization's information resources may prove complicated. Forensic data collection can expose highly sensitive information, such as personal health records, credit card information, business plans, and other sensitive information.

Forensic Field Kit

Most digital forensic teams have a prepacked field kit, also known as a jump bag, which has a set of all the portable equipment and tools needed for an investigation. This preplanning ensures that the team can leave at a moment's notice to perform the necessary response and analysis. The key is that the equipment in the kit should never be borrowed or used in order to keep the kit at the ready. The field kit is typically as personal as the individual investigator, but the one shown in Figure 12-1 is a fairly standard kit.

Figure 12-1   Example of a forensic field kit
© Cengage Learning 2013

12

A kit can include:

- Forensic laptops that have multiple operating systems and can be dedicated to the field kit. These ensure that no prior evidence contaminates the investigation by using the investigator's laptops.

- Call list with subject matter experts in various IT technologies, management, and other stakeholders in the incident management process

- Mobile phones with extra batteries and chargers for continuous communication during the investigation

- Hard drives, blank CDs, blank DVDs, and thumb drives to use for evidence collection (must be sanitized and free from previous evidence!)

- Imaging software or hardware with write blockers (more on these tools later in the chapter)

- Forensic software and tools to perform the forensic data collection and analysis (more on these tools later in the chapter)

- Ethernet tap to sniff network traffic. This can be a DIY project using a simple switch or prepackaged products sold by Barracuda Networks or Net Optics.

- Cables to provide access to other devices. These can be crossover cables for system-to-system communication, Ethernet cables, USB cables, or serial cables.

- Extension cords and power strips to power all the equipment in areas that have either few or hard-to-reach outlets

- Evidence bags, seals, and permanent markers for storing and labeling evidence. The bags should be anti-static and might need desiccants—or drying agents—to absorb any moisture.

- Digital camera with photographic markers and scales to take detailed photos of an investigation area—also tie-on labels (for identifying cables, etc.)

- Incident forms (if used), extra notebooks, and a generous supply of pens for detailed logging of the investigation

- Computer toolkit with computer screws, assortment of spare screws, anti-static mats and straps, mechanics' mirrors, telescoping lights and grabbers, and other tools that may come in handy for opening computer equipment.

Digital Forensics Methodology

Usually, a digital investigation begins with an allegation of wrongdoing—either a policy violation or the commission of a crime (see Figure 12-2). Based on that allegation, authorization is sought to begin the investigation by collecting relevant evidence. In the public sector, this authorization may take the form of a search warrant; in the private sector, it takes the form specified by the organization's policy. Many private sector organizations require a formal statement, called an affidavit, which furnishes much of the same information usually found in a public sector search warrant. In the private sector, it is more common to authorize collecting images of digital information; in the public sector, the warrant authorizes seizure of the relevant items that contain the information.

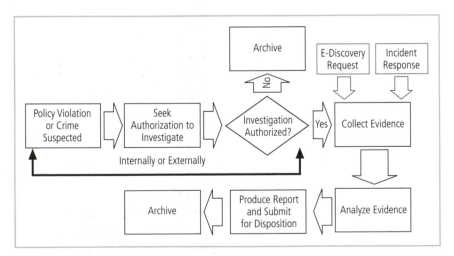

Figure 12-2 Flow of a digital investigation
© Cengage Learning 2013

Assessing the Scene

It is important to assess the scene and document its state before the forensics team moves in to collect evidence. This process typically involves interviewing the key contacts (the incident reporter, the relevant system owner, business unit manager, etc.) and documenting the scene as is. To do so, forensics teams typically use two methods: photography and field notes.

Photography Photographic evidence plays a major role in documenting evidence and its provenance. Like forensic analysis of computer systems, capturing the state of the scene can help investigators go back for reference during the analysis phase. For example, photographs can help answer questions like: Did the server have both network cables plugged in at the time of the incident, or was it only connected to one network? The best tool for photography is the digital camera, which offers much more convenience than a traditional field camera but does require some preparation and sound practices. When using a digital camera, one should:

- Sterilize the digital photographic media (memory card). Forensic sterilization can easily be performed by formatting the card to destroy the directory information and then using a tool such as SDelete from Sysinternals (*www.sysinternals.com*) to clear the card of any existing content.

- Set the camera's clock to ensure that the dates/times recorded for the digital photographs are accurate.

- Make the photographic media "self-documenting" by taking the first exposure of a "Begin Digital Photography" marker.

- Ensure that the :DPM (Digital Photographic Media) number—a tracking number assigned to the particular card—is identified in the digital photography log as each photograph is taken.

- At the conclusion of the on-site activities, make an "end of photography" exposure.

- Remove the card from the camera, package it in a static bag, and seal it in an evidence envelope, like any other piece of digital evidence. (There is more on evidence handling later in this chapter.)

- Do not make hashes of digital photographs until the first time the evidence envelope is opened.

Field Notes A valuable companion to the digital photographs is the collection of field notes. Field notes are any notes that help investigators remember key aspects of a scene and the evidence collected. These notes are normally assembled into a case file that travels with the investigation team and becomes a permanent part of the documentary record of the investigation.

A number of forms can help the team keep these notes, such as:

- Scene Sketch form—The scene sketch is the only item that can be done in pencil. Its purpose is to show the general locations of items. A sample is provided in Figure 12-3.

- Field Activity Log form—This documents the team's activities during evidence collection (see Figure 12-4).

12

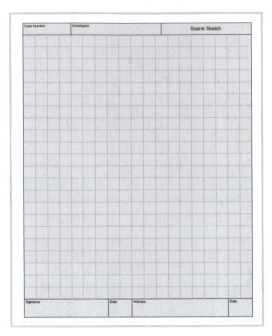

Figure 12-3 Scene sketch form
© Cengage Learning 2013

Figure 12-4 Field activity log form
© Cengage Learning 2013

- Field Evidence Log form—This identifies each item collected by filename number (see Figure 12-5).

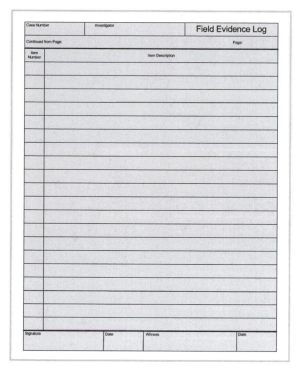

Figure 12-5   Field evidence log form
© Cengage Learning 2013

12

- Photography Log form—This tracks each picture taken and the context of the picture (see Figure 12-6).

Acquiring the Evidence

An organization's incident response (IR) policy must spell out the procedures for initiating the investigative process, including management approvals. This is particularly critical in the private sector, as private organizations do not enjoy the broad immunity accorded to law enforcement investigations. In general, a law enforcement organization cannot be sued for its conduct during an investigation; a private organization can become the target of a retaliatory lawsuit for damages arising from an investigation that proves to be groundless.

Once the authorization to conduct an investigation is obtained, the collection of evidence can begin. As shown earlier, this is also the point when IR begins to interface with the forensics process.

At heart, digital evidence collection is a four-step process:

1. Identifying sources of evidentiary material
2. Authenticating the evidentiary material

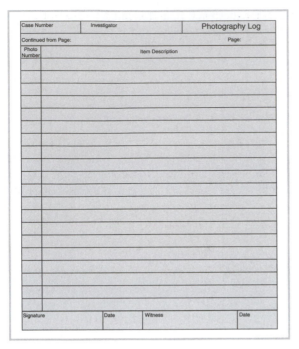

Figure 12-6 Photography log form
© Cengage Learning 2013

3. Collecting the evidentiary material

4. Maintaining a documented chain of custody

Upon completion of the collection process, the evidence awaits presentation and reporting in some formal proceedings.

Identifying Sources Identifying evidence sources is somewhat straightforward in the physical world of bloodstains and fingerprints, but it is much more complex in the digital world. In a suspect's corporate office, simple data collection may involve hundreds of gigabytes of information that resides on:

- Disks in a desktop or laptop computer (or both)
- Disks in external storage enclosures
- Memory sticks or cards
- PDA (possibly with additional removable memory cards installed)
- Cellular phone (including any memory cards installed in it)
- Storage devices such as MP3 players
- Optical storage such as CDs and DVDs
- Networked storage

When identifying evidence in a data center (perhaps as part of an intrusion or complex fraud investigation), the sources of potential evidence also include:

- Disks attached to servers
- Storage attached to a storage network, such as a fiber channel or iSCSI SAN
- Files on NAS (network-attached storage) devices
- Logs on servers, routers, firewalls, or centralized logging servers

One of the more perplexing problems in collecting digital data concerns so-called volatile information, such as the contents of a computer's memory. Traditional forensic practice calls for photographing a running computer's screen and then disconnecting the power, but this leads to loss of volatile information. Should investigators sacrifice the evidence stored on disk by running tools to collect the volatile information, or should they sacrifice the volatile information in favor of the information on disk? In time, better tools will make this less of a quandary, but currently it is a challenge.

Authenticating Evidentiary Material Unlike objects in the physical world, which have characteristics that set them apart from other objects, one binary digit looks pretty much like any other. This presents a significant challenge in the practice of digital forensics, as the legal system demands assurances that the information presented in court is authentic—for example, it is a genuine image of the disk in John Doe's workstation or a true copy of the log records from the RADIUS server collected on January 15. You must be able to demonstrate that the particular collection of bits being prepared is a true and accurate copy of the original.

One way to identify a particular digital item (which is represented as a collection of bits) is by means of a cryptographic hash. This involves collecting a file or data into evidence and then feeding that data through the hash function. (The hash tool is typically carried with the digital forensics teams so as not to rely on any cryptographic libraries on a compromised system.) As discussed in Chapter 3, hashes are mathematical functions that have the following properties that make them ideal for this purpose:

- Regardless of the size of their input, hash functions produce a fixed size output (128 bits for MD5 and 160 bits for SHA-1).
- It is computationally infeasible to determine a particular hash value based on a given input.
- It is computationally infeasible to find another input that could produce the same output value as a given input.

As the following example shows, simply changing the case of two letters generates very different hash values:

```
:echo hello there > test.txt

:md5sum test.txt
782a482a8ba848cec578e3006678860c *test.txt

:echo Hello There > test.txt

:md5sum test.txt
937e9f428b23c367247b2c29318093b0 *test.txt
```

When a piece of digital evidence is collected, its hash value is calculated and recorded. At any subsequent point, the hash value can be recalculated to show that the item has not been modified since its collection. This technique can also authenticate copies of the original item as true and accurate copies. Two commonly used hashes are MD-5 and SHA-1. Command line and GUI tools for calculating hashes are widely available, such as: md5sum, WinMD5-Free, and MD5Deep.

In the recent past, there have been a number of research studies aimed at validating the cryptographic strength of hash algorithms.[8] In Australia, this research was successfully used to challenge digital evidence,[9] but the general consensus is that hashes are still acceptable for demonstrating the integrity of digital evidence.[10] NIST is developing new hash algorithms that will be more resistant to the types of attack outlined in recent research.

Collecting Evidence When collecting digital evidence, an investigator must decide on the mode of acquisition: live or dead. **Live acquisition** is collecting evidence from a currently running system, whereas **dead acquisition** involves powering down the system to copy the data from the hard drives. The investigator must also decide how to package and image the collected material. All the activities she undertakes must be accurately and thoroughly documented. Most importantly, she must make no changes to the evidence.

The emphasis on making no changes to the evidence may seem overstated, but is justified by the potentially serious consequences. Digital forensic findings can cost an organization millions of dollars and deprive people of their jobs or (if used in criminal proceedings) their freedom or even their lives.

When a piece of digital information is altered, the question arises: What exactly was changed? Did an investigator inadvertently boot up a computer, or did the investigator plant evidence and cover the modification by booting up the computer? Although it is possible to minutely describe every change that occurred during the computer boot to verify that only those changes were made in the image, such an effort is not likely to be rewarded, given the time and expertise involved, the difficulty in explaining these changes to the judge and jury, and the possibility of lingering doubts that will cause the evidence to be discounted.

To prevent doubts regarding the handling of evidence, labels and seals are crucial. Although any secure package will serve, the use of packaging specifically designed for this purpose aids proper documentation and storage. The evidence envelope is preprinted with a form that collects the relevant information for establishing where, by whom, and when the information was collected. The evidence seal is designed for single use and is very difficult to remove without breaking it. Types of evidence labels and seals are shown in Figures 12-7 and 12-8.

Challenges can also come from alleged contamination—that the evidence came from somewhere else or was somehow tainted in the collection process. For this reason, media that is used to collect digital evidence must be forensically sterile, meaning that it contains no residue from previous use. There are various ways to prepare sterile media, but a common method is to write 0s to every block on the device to erase any previous contents and then, if needed, format the device with a file system.

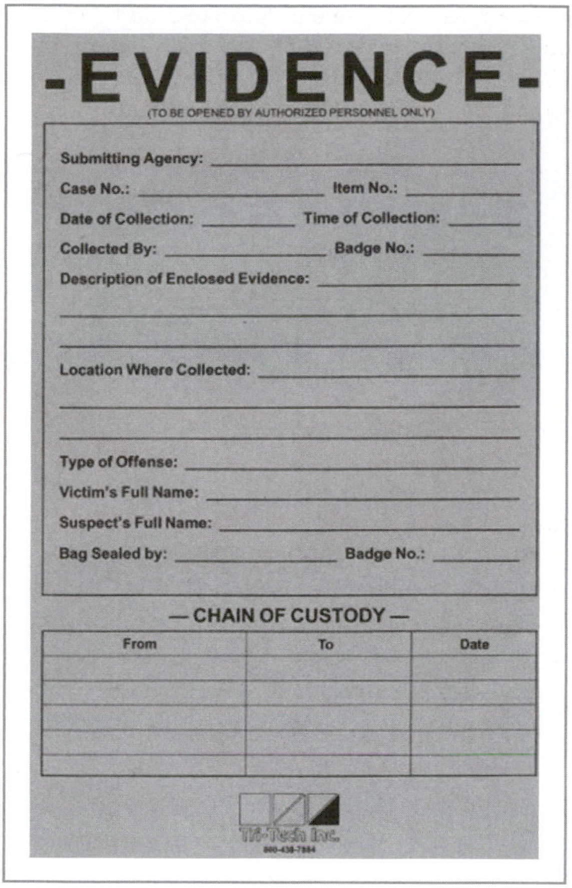

-EVIDENCE-
(TO BE OPENED BY AUTHORIZED PERSONNEL ONLY)

Submitting Agency: _____

Case No.: _____ Item No.: _____

Date of Collection: _____ Time of Collection: _____

Collected By: _____ Badge No.: _____

Description of Enclosed Evidence: _____

_____

_____

Location Where Collected: _____

_____

_____

Type of Offense: _____

Victim's Full Name: _____

Suspect's Full Name: _____

Bag Sealed by: _____ Badge No.: _____

— CHAIN OF CUSTODY —

From	To	Date

Tri-Tech Inc.
800-438-7884

Figure 12-7   Evidence label with chain of custody listing
© Cengage Learning 2013

12

Figure 12-8   Evidence seal
© Cengage Learning 2013

All sterilization procedures must be codified, and all media sterilization processes must be documented. Most forensic practices maintain an inventory of sterilized media that should be sealed and tagged to preclude the possibility of tampering (see Figure 12-9).

Live Acquisition   When an investigator is faced with a running system that may have been compromised, valuable information such as open network connections and other running processes may reveal the intentions and mode of entry of the attacker. The investigator may

Figure 12-9   Sample media packages sealed and tagged

conclude that this volatile information is important enough to warrant conducting a live acquisition, thus sacrificing the durable information that might be obtained by powering down the system. Note that the investigator can later shut the computer down and image its disk(s) to gather information that may be useful in identifying the mode of entry and other activities of the attacker. However, because the live response tools modified that state of the system, it is very unlikely that the information collected from the disks would be admissible in any legal proceeding.

In a live acquisition, the investigator has no idea what the attacker did to the system during the compromise. Common system tools may have been replaced with malicious versions, or various traps may have been put in place to destroy information if the system is disturbed. For these reasons, the investigator will typically use a trusted set of CD-based tools, such as BackTrack, Helix, KNOPPIX STD, or F.I.R.E. These Live CDs, or CDs with full bootable operating systems, contain a collection of tools and scripts that run a series of known-to-be-good executables, and preserve their outputs.

There are also many stand-alone tools that help investigators gather evidence from live acquisition. Examples include Windows Forensic Toolchest (WFT), which you can learn more about at *www.foolmoon.net/security/wft/*, SANS Investigative Forensic Toolkit (SIFT), which you can learn more about at *http://computer-forensics.sans.org/community/downloads*, and First Responder's Evidence Disk (FRED), which you can learn more about at *http://darkparticlelabs. com/portfolio.php*. These tools capture volatile information that might be useful in investigating a system compromise.

WFT is essentially a driver script for running a series of tools that identifies and lists running processes, active network connections, and other activity, then saves the output on an external medium such as a thumb drive. It is designed for forensics use and includes a number of integrity checks such as verifying the tools before they are run (see Figure 12-10).

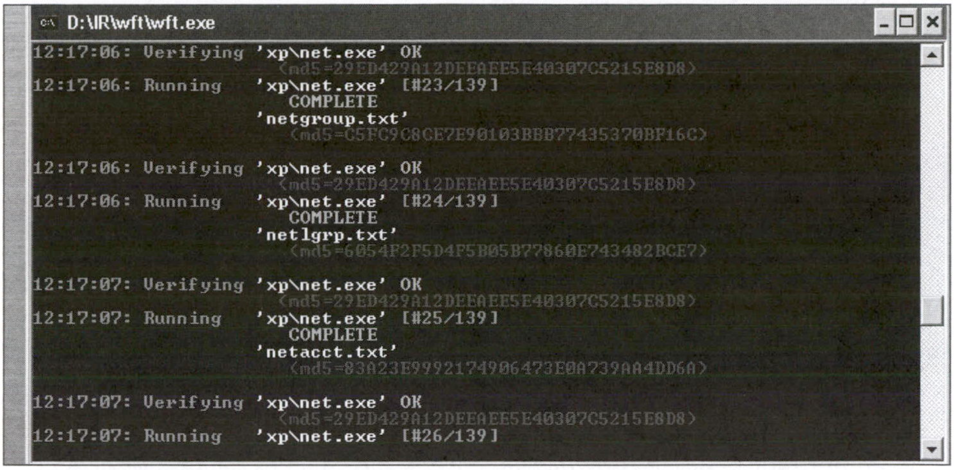

Figure 12-10   Integrity checks from WFT
Source: Windows Forensic Toolchest

At the completion of WFT, the files logging its execution are hashed and their values displayed in order to provide an integrity reference, as shown in Figure 12-11.

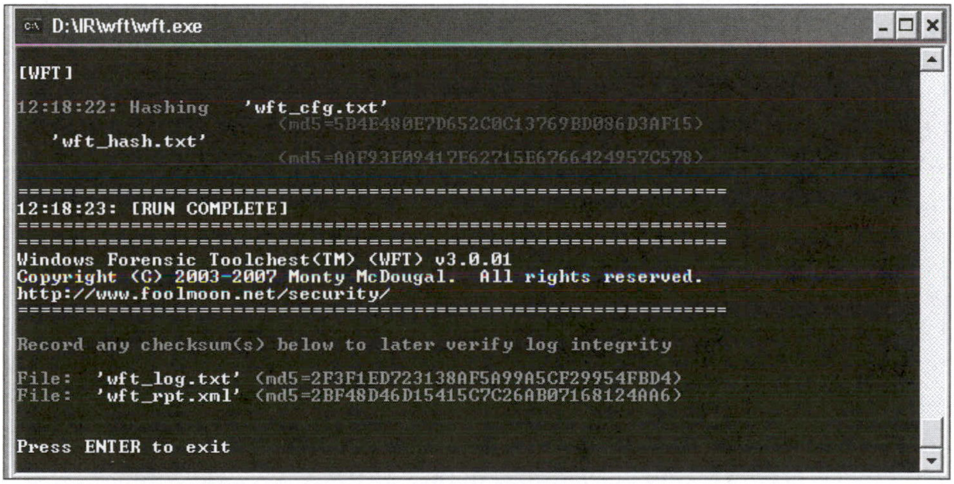

Figure 12-11   Hash generation of evidence from WFT
Source: Windows Forensic Toolchest

Although live acquisition is usually thought of in the context of a running server, the need to acquire the state of an active process arises in at least two other situations:

- Logs, the records for which are generated on a continuous basis, thus requiring a live acquisition to capture their state at a point in time
- Active devices such as PDAs and cellular phones

A continuously changing process presents challenges in acquisition, given that there is no "fixed" state that can be collected, hashed, and so forth. This has given rise to the idea of "snapshot forensics,"[11] which involves capturing a point-in-time picture of a process, much like a photograph that freezes the action of a running child.

Consider the log files on a centralized syslog server that is continually receiving log records from firewalls, intrusion detection systems, authentication servers, application servers, and other sources. Because log records are arriving on a more or less continual basis, there is no "fixed" state of the log file that can be collected and hashed. For this reason, a snapshot is taken of the active log file by copying it, perhaps using a normal filecopy. This copy is then acquired (perhaps by another copy) and hashed to verify that a true and accurate copy has indeed been acquired. The investigator should be prepared to produce good documentation and to fully justify the actions in testimony, perhaps using the analogy of extracting a single frame from a motion picture or of taking a still photo of a running child, the idea being that the copy operation does not "add" information to the item copied.

Often, an intrusion is detected by the end effect it has, such as the disk devices being deleted. In these cases, the investigator must work backward to identify the evidence sources, but the information in log records often provides critical evidence of how the situation developed over time. For example, logs from the VPN and authentication servers might show an intruder logging in from outside the corporate network, and records generated by management applications might reveal the exact operations performed in deleting the disks from the storage array.

Active devices such as PDAs and cellular phones present similar challenges.[12] As long as they have power, they are active (monitoring the status of tasks and appointments, checking for e-mail or instant messages, managing connections with the cellular network), so their internal state is continually changing. They also retain in memory a lot of volatile information that is lost if the batteries are removed.

These types of small wireless devices are increasingly critical to modern forensic investigations because almost everyone has at least one and they are increasingly used for a variety of business and personal communications, including e-mail and instant messaging. They are also fairly promiscuous—if there is a compatible network available, it will connect to it. A PDA seized from a suspect might be accessed wirelessly to modify or delete information, and a cellular phone could continue to receive calls, instant messages, and e-mails after its seizure.

For these reasons, it is critical to keep wireless devices from accessing (or being accessed through) the network after seizure and during analysis. Because turning off the device's power would cause the volatile information to be lost, a better solution is to block wireless access using a Faraday Cage. A Faraday Cage is an enclosure that ensures that electromagnetic waves are blocked so that a device cannot transmit or receive radio waves while in custody. For example, Paraben Corporation has developed the Wireless StrongHold Bag shown in Figure 12-12 to protect wireless devices from wireless access while being transported or stored.

This bag has a metallic coating that prevents the enclosed device from receiving or sending wireless signals. To provide similar protection while an investigator works with the device, Paraben designed the StrongHold Box, which is shown in Figure 12-13.

Figure 12-12   Paraben Corporation's Wireless StrongHold Bag
© Cengage Learning 2013

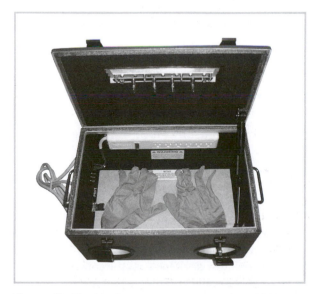

Figure 12-13   Paraben Corporation's StrongHold Box
© Cengage Learning 2013

This enclosure also uses a Faraday Cage to shield the device from network connectivity while enabling access by the investigator. It also includes shielded connections so that investigators can use external devices for imaging and analysis.

12

Equipping an organization to handle forensics with these types of devices can easily cost $10,000–$20,000 in specialized hardware and software alone. For that reason and because of the rapid change in the technology, forensic analysis using these devices is an excellent candidate for outsourcing to a specialist consultant.

Dead Acquisition   In a dead acquisition, the computer is typically powered off so that its disk drives can be removed for imaging; the information on the devices is static ("dead") and durable. Although dead acquisition was developed for computer disks, it applies equally well to disk-like devices such as thumb drives, memory cards, MP3 players, and others.

In dead acquisition, an investigator seeks to obtain a forensic image of the disk or device. This image must include active files and directories as well as deleted files and file fragments. Figure 12-14 shows a small snapshot of a portion of a file system.

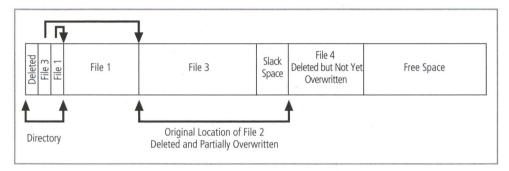

Figure 12-14   Small portion of a file system
© Cengage Learning 2013

A normal file system copy of the disk shown in Figure 12-14 would obtain File1 and File3, which are the only active files. However, there is more information on the device, including:

- The "Deleted" entry in the directory, which might contain useful information about the deleted file

- The remnant of File2 that was not overwritten by File3, which might contain useful file fragments

- File4, which has been deleted but not yet overwritten, so its contents should still be recoverable

- The free space, which might contain other files or fragments

To make sure this potentially valuable information is acquired, forensic investigators use bit-stream (also known as sector-by-sector) copying when making a forensic image of a device. Bit-stream copying reads a sector (or block, 512 bytes on most devices) from the source drive and writes it to the target drive; this process continues until all sectors on the suspect drive have been copied.

Forensic imaging can be accomplished using specialized hardware tools or software running on a laptop or other computer. The advantage of hardware tools specialized for the purpose of copying disks is that they are generally faster. When performing a large imaging task (e.g., imaging disks from 150 desktop computers involved in a complex fraud investigation), a hardware imaging solution will speed the process. A common type of hardware imaging solution is the ImageMaSSter Solo, which is shown in Figure 12-15.

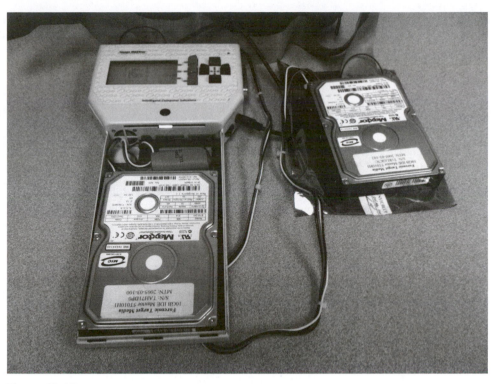

Figure 12-15   Intelligent Computer Solutions' ImageMaSSter
© Cengage Learning 2013

The disadvantages of hardware imaging platforms are cost and the fact that they support only certain interfaces. For example, an IDE imaging device might require an expensive upgrade to support SATA drives.

There are many software imaging and other forensic tools. Popular software tools include EnCase Forensic, UNIX/Linux's dd command, and Paraben's Forensic Replicator. These software packages run on a standard laptop or other system and support any disk interface supported by the host. A laptop-based imaging solution is shown in Figure 12-16.

Figure 12-16   Laptop-based imaging solution
© Cengage Learning 2013

In the figure, the suspect drive on the left (enclosed, for imaging, in a protective rubber "boot") is connected to the laptop through a forensic bridge, which serves two purposes:

- It bridges the IDE drive interface to the laptop USB interface.
- It blocks any write requests the laptop might generate.

It is critical that the information on the suspect media not be changed during the imaging process, because its value as evidentiary material may be compromised. Because Helix is specialized for forensic use, it does not mount file systems or create swap partitions on any of the attached disks; an experienced investigator following correct procedure should not need any additional write block protection.

However, investigators are human, and most will admit to having at least once confused the suspect and destination disks when performing imaging (say, at 4:00 AM, while imaging the 72nd of 83 disks). For this reason, and to preclude any grounds for challenging the image output, it is common practice to protect the suspect media using a **write blocker**.

Write blockers are devices that allow you to acquire the information on a drive without accidentally damaging the drive's contents. They do this by allowing read commands to pass while blocking write commands—hence, their name.[13] Write blockers are traditionally hardware devices, but software write blockers are beginning to emerge. Hardware write blockers have the advantage of having been vetted more often in legal cases. They're also better understood by the legal community, and they can perform the bridging function described earlier. For example, a write blocker kit (such as the UltraKit sold by Digital Intelligence) may contain bridges for IDE, SCSI, and SATA devices that both provide the write blocking function to protect the suspect media and "bridge" the connection to a USB or FireWire compatible with the laptop.

The Imaging Process Before imaging a piece of disk media, its origin and a description of it (vendor, model and serial number) are documented in both written and photographic form. This establishes the provenance of the disk image and helps to ensure its authenticity. Also, the media used as the target for forensic imaging should be forensically sterile, and that should be documented as well.

Once the suspect media is attached to the imaging setup, the general imaging process is as follows:

1. Calculate and record a baseline cryptographic hash of the suspect media.
2. Perform a bit-stream image of the suspect media.
3. Calculate and record a hash of the target (and, optionally, another hash of the suspect media to verify it was not modified by the imaging process).
4. Compare the hashes to verify that they match.
5. Package the target media for transport.

The screenshot shown in Figure 12-17 shows the imaging process using the UNIX/Linux dd command being carried out with the following simple naming convention for the files produced:

- The PI prefix indicates a pre-image hash.
- The DI prefix indicates the disk image.
- The AI prefix indicates a post-image hash.

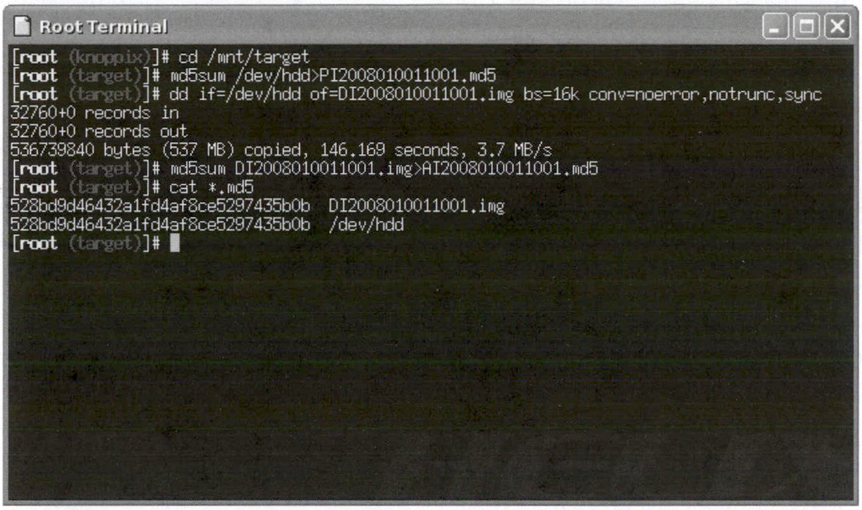

```
█ Root Terminal                                               _ □ ×
[root (knoppix)]# cd /mnt/target
[root (target)]# md5sum /dev/hdd>PI2008010011001.md5
[root (target)]# dd if=/dev/hdd of=DI2008010011001.img bs=16k conv=noerror,notrunc,sync
32760+0 records in
32760+0 records out
536739840 bytes (537 MB) copied, 146.169 seconds, 3.7 MB/s
[root (target)]# md5sum DI2008010011001.img>AI2008010011001.md5
[root (target)]# cat *.md5
528bd9d46432a1fd4af8ce5297435b0b  DI2008010011001.img
528bd9d46432a1fd4af8ce5297435b0b  /dev/hdd
[root (target)]# █
```

Figure 12-17   Imaging process using dd
Source: Linux

Case numbers are of the form YYYY-BK-PAGE, in which the case numbers are assigned from a standard record book of numbered pages. In the example, the case number assigned is for the year 2008, book 1, page 0011. The four-digit item number provides a reference number for this particular item of evidence and can be cross-referenced in the Field Evidence Log.

As you can see in Figure 12-17, the hash for the image file matches the hash for the device; thus, you can be confident that you have obtained a true and accurate image of the device. Once the imaging is completed, the target media must be securely packaged. It can then be sealed in an anti-static bag, sealed in an evidence envelope, and signed as shown in Figure 12-18.

12

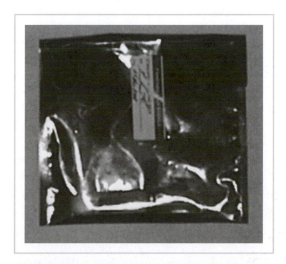

Figure 12-18   Target media packaged in an anti-static envelope, sealed, and signed
© Cengage Learning 2013

Note the practice of signing across the seals to assure that someone else doesn't break the seal and replace it.

Maintaining a Chain of Custody Documentation of processes and procedures, digital fingerprints, and secure packaging help demonstrate the authenticity of digital evidence, but there are additional requirements in order to demonstrate that the evidence has been protected from accidental or purposeful modification at every point from its collection through analysis to presentation in court. What is protected is called the **chain of custody**.

In principle, the chain of custody is quite simple; basically, it is a legal record of where the evidence was at each point in its lifetime as well as documentation of each and every access there was to it. An example of a chain of custody log is shown in Figure 12-19.

Figure 12-19   Sample chain of custody log
© Cengage Learning 2013

The usual process is that the field investigator maintains personal custody and control of the sealed item until it is logged into the chain of custody log at the evidence storage room. Each time the item is removed (for analysis, copying, etc.), it is logged out, forming a documented trail of who accessed the information and when that access occurred.

Collected evidence must be stored and handled appropriately to protect its value, especially because, in some cases, items may be stored for weeks or months before they are analyzed. In fact, if the investigation results in legal proceedings, the evidence may be stored for years before the matter is heard in court.

Proper storage requires a protected, controlled-access environment coupled with sound processes governing access to its contents (e.g., limiting access to specifically authorized personnel and documenting each access in the chain of custody log). The storage facility must also maintain the proper environment for holding digital information, which means:

- Controlled temperature and humidity
- Freedom from strong electrical and magnetic fields that might damage the items
- Protection from fire and other physical hazards

The evidence storage facility can be a specialized evidence room, a locked filing cabinet in an office, or something in between.

Analyzing Evidence

To settle an issue that originated in the physical world and triggered a digital investigation, an analyst must translate that issue into a series of questions that are answerable through forensic analysis. These "digital world" questions will set the analysis' scope and guide its progress.

The first step in the analysis process is to obtain the evidence from the storage area (signing it out in the chain of custody log) and performing a physical authentication. This involves verifying the written documentation (i.e., the manufacturer, serial number, and other identifying information) against the actual item of evidence. After successful completion of that step, a copy of the evidence is made for analysis, while the original returned to storage. (It is crucial that the analysis never take place on the original evidence.) The copy of the evidence can then be authenticated by recomputing its hash and comparing it to the written record.

Disk images must be loaded into the particular forensic tool used by the organization. This typically involves processing the image into the format used by the tool, performing preprocessing such as undeleting files, carving data (recovering files, images, and so forth from fragments in free space), and comparing to the hashes created by the digital forensics team at the time of disk imaging.

Two of the major tools used in digital forensic analysis are EnCase Forensic, from Guidance Software, and Forensic Toolkit (FTK), from AccessData. Although very similar in function, they take different approaches to the analysis task.

FTK does extensive preprocessing of the evidence items, as shown in Figure 12-20, and it organizes the various items into a tabbed display. It is common for an analyst to start this preprocessing late in the day and leave it running overnight, so that it will be completed at the beginning of the following workday.

EnCase Forensic takes a slightly different approach in that it presents an extensible forensic platform that makes it easy for trained investigators to carry out their tasks. For example, rather than finding all the deleted files and folders during lengthy preprocessing, EnCase provides a right-click menu function to conduct analysis on specific files.

EnCase also supports EnScripts, which are written in a C-like language and automate tasks not provided by the main program. There is a very active user community that develops and contributes these scripts, and some of the functionality has been incorporated into recent versions of EnCase. One type of EnScript is the "filter" that searches for particular types of information. Running the Deleted Files filter produces the list of deleted files.

12

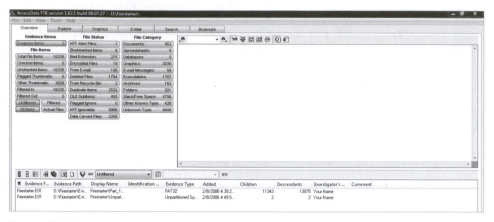

Figure 12-20 FTK's preprocessing step
Source: FTK

Searching for Evidence

With the increasing sizes of disk devices, identifying relevant information is one of the more important analysis tasks. For example, when investigating a computer image in a case involving widespread identity theft, credit and Social Security numbers are highly relevant.

As part of its preprocessing, FTK constructs an index of terms found in the image; the results are available under the Search tab. Figure 12-21 shows the occurrences of the word "arson" and the context of one of the search hits.

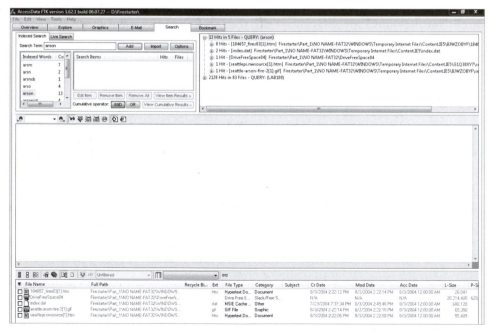

Figure 12-21 FTK's search for the term "arson"
Source: FTK

FTK also includes the Live Search tab, which allows searching on user-specified terms. Developing relevant search terms can be challenging. A technique from the legal profession called "cartwheeling," in which a term is extended via links to subsidiary terms, can help.[14] For example, the cartwheel diagram shown in Figure 12-22 shows how you can develop search terms when investigating the unauthorized use of a keylogger.

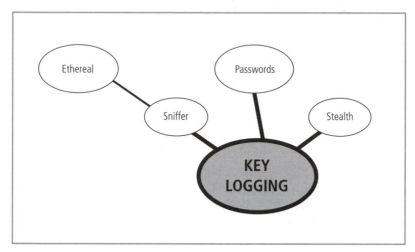

Figure 12-22   Cartwheel diagram from the term "key logging"
© Cengage Learning 2013

EnCase also offers a flexible search interface and includes predefined filters for common items such as e-mail and Web addresses as well as Social Security numbers. As relevant items are located, they are "bookmarked" for inclusion in the final report.

Reporting the Findings

Once the analysis is complete, the findings must be reported in a written presentation and (often) legal testimony. This report must clearly communicate the findings to the various audiences that will use the report, such as the following:

- Upper management, which is typically interested in the recommendations as to whether or not the allegations were correct, the scope of a data breach, and the impact and cost of that breach

- A forensic expert retained by the opposition, who is interested in the details of evidence collection and analysis so he can judge whether the analysis was done properly and identify weaknesses that could be used to challenge it in court

- Attorneys, judges, and juries, who are interested in compliance with the legal requirements and the real meaning of the evidence in deciding a question of fact

- Other professionals (e.g., auditors and human resources departments), who are interested in compliance with organizational policies and in identifying possible changes to those policies

It is tempting to prepare a series of reports, each tailored to a particular audience. However, if the investigation leads to legal proceedings, all these various reports are discoverable (i.e., must be disclosed) by the opposing side. Any differences among the various versions could cast doubt on the conclusions.

The safest approach is to prepare a single report, with an index to point the parties to their particular areas of interest. The report should identify what gave rise to the investigation, the sources of the evidence that was analyzed, the tools and processes that were used to analyze the evidence, the specific findings, and an interpretation of the findings (i.e., whether the evidence supports or disproves the allegation).

In general terms, the report summarizes the detailed records contained in the case file, the analyst's notebooks, and other documentation, which can be produced to address detailed questions.

Encryption Concerns

Forensic tools excel at retrieving information that has been deleted through normal means or hidden by the operating system. However, doing so can pose a significant threat to privacy and to the confidentiality of an organization's information assets.

Actions in the digital world leave many traces (such as records of Web sites visited or archived e-mail messages), and these can be easily retrieved from discarded or recycled computer equipment, causing data to leak outside the organization. This process is called data leakage, as discussed in Chapter 9. Simson Garfinkel did an empirical study in which he purchased used computers and drives from online merchants and analyzed what was left on the devices by their previous owners (either inadvertently or due to poor deletion processes).[15] He found medical and business records and many other types of confidential information.

NIST has documented recommended practices for removing data from storage media in Special Publication 800-88, *Guideline for Media Sanitization*. These practices range from overwriting disk media with 0s or random data to physical destruction.

Organizations must be aware that forensic tools are not just in the hands of honest professionals, they are available to everyone. Therefore, policies and procedures must be in place to assure that discarded digital information is destroyed beyond the reach of forensic recovery.

An increasing concern for privacy and availability of encryption products has led to the widespread use of encryption for individual files or entire devices. Although some encryption is poorly done and is easily broken, quality products are increasingly available that use good encryption algorithms beyond our current capability to use brute force in cracking the data.

Encrypted information can present challenges to forensic investigators. A fairly common encryption product accepts the encryption key when the user logs on and decrypts information on the fly. When the system goes into screen saver mode or is powered down, the encryption key is destroyed and must be reentered. Unfortunately, data collected by a forensic investigator is encrypted and will not be readable without the key.

Some forensic products offer brute-force attacks against the encrypted information by using dictionaries of common pass phrases. They are sometimes successful but can be defeated by a good pass phrase. Also, encrypted information may exist in unencrypted form in temporary "work files" or the paging file.

Chapter Summary

- Computer forensics is the use of computer investigation and analysis techniques to indentify, collect, preserve, and analyze electronic items of potential evidentiary value so that they may be admitted as evidence in a court of law or used to support administrative action. The term *digital forensics* refers to all modern electronic devices, including mobile phones, personal digital assistants (PDAs), and portable music players.

- A digital investigation begins with an allegation of wrongdoing—either a policy violation or the commission of a crime. Based on that allegation, authorization is sought to begin the investigation by collecting relevant evidence; once authorization has been obtained, the collection of evidence can begin.

- The first response digital forensics team secures and collects the devices, media, or media images that are potentially evidentiary. Later, analysis and reporting techniques are performed by persons specially trained in the use of forensic tools to analyze the collected information and provide answers to the question(s) that gave rise to the investigation.

- To settle the issue that prompted an investigation, the analyst must translate that issue into a series of specific questions that are answerable through forensic analysis, then use the proper tools to answer those specific questions.

- When an incident violates civil or criminal law, it is the organization's responsibility to notify the proper authorities and work with them throughout the investigation and resolution of the matter.

- Forensic tools can be used by investigators even to obtain information that has been deleted from digital media. These tools can also be used for nefarious purposes—that is, to illegitimately obtain private or proprietary information from discarded digital media.

12

Review Questions

1. What is the primary goal of digital forensics?

2. What factors guide an organization that is setting up a forensic capability?

3. How do organizations subdivide the practice of digital forensics?

4. What are the common roles and duties of a digital forensic first response team?

5. What factors determine the priority in collecting digital evidence?

6. What are the differences between examination and analysis when discussion forensic analysis?

7. What is a good analogy for explaining how deleted files can still be recovered?

8. What part does an affidavit play in obtaining authorization for a search?

9. In what main way does search and seizure differ in the public and the private sector?

10. What are the four steps in collecting digital evidence?

11. What two hash functions are commonly used as digital fingerprints?

12. What is the purpose of sterile media?

13. What type of forensics is used for devices that continue to function operations that continue to process during the acquisition of information?

14. What is a critical concern when seizing a device such as a cellular phone?

15. What types of information are missed by a normal copying process but included in a forensic image?

16. What are two required characteristics of an evidence storage facility?

17. What are the two best-known commercial tools used in forensic analysis?

18. What is the relationship between forensics and anti-forensics, and why is it important to the forensics investigator?

19. Why is cryptography a good thing for IT workers but a bad thing for forensic investigators?

20. When is the involvement of law enforcement optional in a forensics investigation? Who should make this determination?

Real World Exercises

Exercise 12-1

Using a Web search engine, look up "Trojan Defense." How can it be used to question the conclusions drawn from a forensic investigation?

Exercise 12-2

At the end of 2006, a new edition of the Federal Rules of Civil Procedure (FRCP) went into effect. Using a Web search tool, learn more about the FRCP. What likely effect will its emphasis on electronically stored information (ESI) have on an organization's need for a digital forensic capability?

Exercise 12-3

Using a Web search tool, identify some common certifications for digital forensic practitioners and determine whether the certifications are for practitioners at public sector organizations or private sector organizations.

Exercise 12-4

Using a Web search tool, identify cases in which private information was disclosed when computer equipment was discarded. Recent examples have included smartphones (like BlackBerry) that were sold without proper data cleansing and hard drives that have been sold without data cleansing after the computers they were originally used in were upgraded.

Hands-On Projects

Project 12-1

In this exercise, you learn more about various logs created by Linux systems as well as how to view their contents. We use the logs of the "Security Onion" virtual system created in Chapter 11.

1. Start the Security Onion virtual machine.

2. After logging in using the credentials created in Chapter 11, double-click the **Terminal** icon on the desktop to start a terminal session.

3. At the command prompt, type **cd /var/log** and press **Enter**.

4. To display the directory contents, type **ls** and press **Enter**. Note there are several logs present, but we will focus on the dmesg, messages, and lastlog files. The dmesg file contains kernel messages generated at system boot. This can include messages regarding hardware found and configured (or not) during boot, and it can also include messages from the kernel during system operation. The contents of this file can be read two different ways, as explained below.

5. At the command prompt, type **dmesg | more** and press **Enter**. This will display file output one page at a time. To advance a single line at a time, press **Enter**. Alternatively, we can advance forward a screen by pressing the **spacebar**.

6. If for some reason the dmesg command is not available, we can use the tail command to view file contents located at the bottom of the file, which are the most recent entries made. Type **tail dmesg** and press **Enter**. By default, the tail command returns the last 10 lines present. To change this to a different number, use the –n <*number*> *option*—for example, **tail –n 20 dmesg**. In general, dmesg file output should look similar to what is shown in Figure 12-23.

12

```
[   0.000000] BIOS-e820: 000000003feff000 - 000000003ff00000 (ACPI NVS)

agreen@green-virtual-onion:/var/logs tail dmesg
[  106.556261] type=1505 audit(1326257929.823:10):  operation="profile_replac
e" pid=967 name="/sbin/dhclient3"
[  106.556551] type=1505 audit(1326257929.823:11):  operation="profile_replac
e" pid=967 name="/usr/lib/NetworkManager/nm-dhcp-client.action"
[  106.556680] type=1505 audit(1326257929.823:12):  operation="profile_replac
e" pid=967 name="/usr/lib/connman/scripts/dhclient-script"
[  108.371790] type=1505 audit(1326257931.639:13):  operation="profile_load"
pid=968 name="/usr/bin/evince"
[  109.334910] type=1505 audit(1326257932.599:14):  operation="profile_load"
pid=968 name="/usr/bin/evince-previewer"
[  109.337668] type=1505 audit(1326257932.603:15):  operation="profile_load"
pid=968 name="/usr/bin/evince-thumbnailer"
[  109.347367] type=1505 audit(1326257932.611:16):  operation="profile_load"
pid=972 name="/usr/lib/cups/backend/cups-pdf"
[  109.363032] type=1505 audit(1326257932.630:17):  operation="profile_load"
pid=972 name="/usr/sbin/cupsd"
[  109.452580] type=1505 audit(1326257932.719:18):  operation="profile_load"
pid=975 name="/usr/sbin/mysqld"
[  109.459294] type=1505 audit(1326257932.723:19):  operation="profile_replac
e" pid=982 name="/usr/sbin/ntpd"
agreen@green-virtual-onion:/var/logs
```

Figure 12-23 dmesg log file output

Source: Linux

The messages file functions as a "catchall" log file, collecting messages from various applications and system log daemons. This is an important file to examine when trying to do any type of forensic analysis, as it can provide a great deal of data. We will examine this file's contents using the `tail` command in combination with the `grep` and `more` commands. The `grep` command provides a way to search a file or files for a text string. When combined with the `pipe` command (|), the `grep` command allows you to efficiently sift through many lines of text to display only what you are looking for.

7.   Type **tail messages | grep "Jan 11"** and press **Enter**. This will display all lines in the file that contain "Jan 11" anywhere in the text. If you find the output scrolls off the top of the screen, remember you can use the `more` command to control the display—for example, **tail messages | grep "Jan 11" | more**. Your output should look similar to what is shown in Figure 12-24.

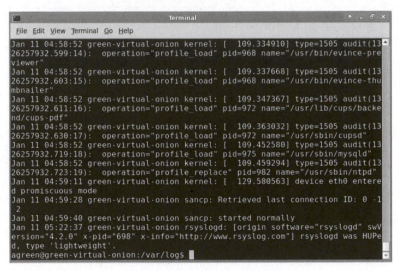

Figure 12-24   messages log file output

The lastlog file contains login times for all users. You would examine this file to help determine if any unusual or unauthorized logins have taken place on the system. Unlike the logs we discussed previously, you cannot use the `tail` command to view the contents, given that this is a binary file.

8.   To view the log file contents, type **lastlog |more** and press **Enter**. Note this command is available only to users with root privileges. Your output should look similar to what is shown in Figure 12-25.

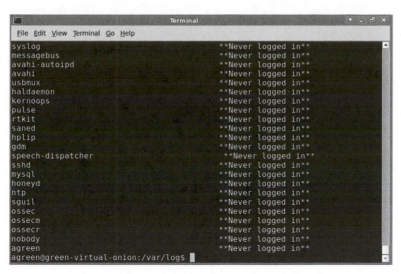

Figure 12-25 lastlog log file output

Source: Linux

Endnotes

1. Merriam-Webster's Collegiate Dictionary (10 ed), s.v.

2. Lewis, Paul G., "Curiosity May Kill the Case." *New Jersey Law Journal*, 182:11, 1030–1031.

3. Brown, Christopher L. T. (2006). *Computer Evidence Collection and Preservation*. Hingham, MA: Charles River Media.

4. Snow, Gordon M. (2011). "Cybersecurity: Responding to the Threat of Cyber Crime and Terrorism." *FBI.gov*. Accessed February 14, 2012 @ *www.fbi.gov/news/testimony/cybersecurity-responding-to-the-threat-of-cyber-crime-and-terrorism*.

5. Inman, Keith & Rudin, Norah (2001). *Principles and Practice of Criminalistics: The Profession of Forensic Science*. Boca Raton, FL: CRC Press.

6. Ibid.

7. Kent, K., Chevalier, S., Grance, T., and Dang, H. (2006). *Guide to Integrating Forensic Techniques into Incident Response*. Accessed February 15, 2012 @ http://csrc.nist.gov/publications/nistpubs/800-86/SP800-86.pdf

8. Schneier, B. (2005). "More Hash Function Attacks." Accessed February 15, 2012 @ *www.schneier.com/blog/archives/2005/03/more_hash_funct.html*.

9. McCullagh, D. (2005). "MD5 flaw pops up in Australian traffic court." Accessed February 15, 2012 @ *www.news.com/8301-10784_3-5829714-7.html*.

10. U.S. Department of Justice. (2004). "Forensic Examination of Digital Evidence: A Guide for Law Enforcement." Accessed February 15, 2012 @ *www.ncjrs.gov/pdffiles1/nij/199408.pdf*

11. Kipper, Gregory (2007). *Wireless Crime and Forensic Investigation*. Boca Raton, FL: Auerbach.

12

12. Cohen, Tyler & Schroader, Amber (2007). *Alternate Data Storage Forensics.* Burlington, MA: Elsevier.

13. ForensicsWiki. (2011). "Write Blockers." Accessed February 15, 2012 @ *www.forensicswiki. org/wiki/Write_Blockers.*

14. Slatsky, William P. (1982). *Legal Research and Writing.* West Publishing.

15. Garfinkel, S. (2006). *New Directions in Disk Forensics.* Accessed February 15, 2012 @ *www.blackhat.com/presentations/bh-federal-06/BH-Fed-06-Garfinkel.pdf*

Glossary

access The ability to use, manipulate, modify, or affect an asset or resource.

access control list (ACL) A list of authorization rights attached to an object—in other words, who can access that information asset and what they can do with it.

access control matrix A combination of access control list information, which specifies users' rights on an asset, and capability table information, which specifies asset rights for a particular user.

accreditation The authorization of an IT system to process, store, or transmit information. Accreditation is issued by a management official and serves as a means of ensuring that systems are of adequate quality.

accuracy A characteristic of information in which it is free from mistakes or errors and has the value that the end user expects it to have.

active vulnerability scanner A device or software program that initiates traffic on a network in order to identify security holes and expose usernames and groups, open network shares, and configuration problems as well as other vulnerabilities in servers.

Advanced Encryption Standard (AES) Federal standard that specifies a cryptographic algorithm to be used by the U.S. government; designed to replace DES and 3DES.

AJAX Short for "Asynchronous JavaScript and XML," AJAX does not refer to a new programming language but to the new use of JavaScript and XML to provide real-time communication between the Web client and the Web server.

alarm *See* "alert."

alert An indication that an IDPS has detected a possible attack. IDPS alerts take the form of audible signals, e-mail messages, pager notifications, or pop-up windows. Also referred to as an "alarm."

algorithm In cryptography, the programmatic steps to convert an unencrypted message into an encrypted message, and vice versa.

amplitude The height of the waveform in analog signal.

amplitude shift keying (ASK) A technique to embed digital information in an analog signal by modifying the amplitude of the signal waveform.

Application layer A layer in the OSI network model where users communicate using services to exchange information via application protocols.

application-level gateway A firewall that makes high-level application connections on behalf of the internal hosts and other systems.

Application Programming Interface(API) A set of routines, methods, and/or other specifications that allow software to communicate and/or interact with another software application.

application protocol verification Similar to protocol stack verification, this process verifies that a data packet meets the uses outlined within the higher-level application protocols (HTTP, FTP, SSH, etc.).

ARP poisoning Method of attack that sends out false Address Resolution Protocol (ARP) messages in an effort to direct network traffic toward an IP address controlled by an attacker.

asset An organizational resource that has value to the organization. In information security, this is often the resource that is being protected.

asymmetric encryption Encryption method that employs two different but mathematically related keys to encrypt/decrypt data.

attack An act or action that takes advantage of a vulnerability to compromise a controlled system using intentional or unintentional steps that can cause damage or loss.

attack profile Detailed description of the activities that occur during an attack, including the preliminary indications of the attack as well as the actions taken and the outcome.

attenuation The loss of signal strength as a signal moves across media.

audit A periodic or ad hoc review of program or system functions to determine compliance with a set of established standards.

authentication, authorization, and auditing (or accountability) (AAA) server A centralized server that maintains all the authorizations for users regardless of where a user is located and how the user connects to the network.

authenticity A characteristic of information in which it is in a quality or state of being genuine or original rather than a reproduction or fabrication.

autonomous system (AS) A system owned or managed by a single entity and generally consisting of analogous technologies.

availability A characteristic of information in which authorized users—persons or computer systems—have access to information without interference or obstruction and are able to receive it in the required format.

back door A hidden opening in a system that could allow viruses, Trojan horses, or hackers to access the system at will, bypassing standard forms of authentication.

basic service area Broadcast range of a basic service set (BSS).

basic service set Basic model of wireless clients within a defined network area.

baud rate In data communications and telecommunications, the number of symbols or pulses transmitted per second.

BCP *See* "business continuity planning."

Berkeley Internet Name Domain (BIND) Widely used DNS software.

bits per second (bps) In data and telecommunications, the number of bits processed or transmitted per second.

boot virus A form of computer virus that infects the key operating system files located in a computer's boot sector.

border gateway protocol (BGP) The dominant external routing protocol used for communication between autonomous systems (AS). These provide translation between the possibly different internal routing protocols.

bot Short for "robot," a malicious code capability in a virus or worm that implies that the computer is infested and is under another entity's control. *See also* "zombie."

bridging The process of connecting networks with the same DLL protocols (e.g., Ethernet) while maintaining the integrity of each network and only passing messages that need to be transmitted between the two.

brute force attack A form of password guessing attack that uses computing and network resources to try every possible combination of available characters, numbers, and symbols for a password.

BSA *See* "basic service area."

BSS *See* "basic service set."

buffer overflow An application error that occurs when more data is sent to a buffer than it can handle, possibly resulting in the targeted system executing unintended instructions or performing some other unauthorized action.

business continuity plan (BC Plan) The guiding document used by organizations to ensure that, if a disaster occurs, critical business functions can continue by establishing operations at a temporary site.

business continuity planning (BCP) Planning process to ensure that critical business functions can continue if a disaster occurs.

business continuity team The work team responsible for development, testing, management, and execution of the business continuity plan.

Business Resumption Plan (BRP) Combination of the Business Continuity and Disaster Recovery plans.

capability table A list of authorization rights associated with a user—in other words, what information assets the user can access and what the user can do with them.

CAPTCHA Short for "Completely Automated Public Turing Test to Tell Computers and Humans Apart," CAPTCHA is a challenge-response mechanism that allows a Web site to make sure an automated script or system is not making a Web request.

Cascading Style Sheets (CSS) A file or group of files that standardizes the HTML formatting for an entire Web site by allowing developers to customize fonts, tables, and other page elements.

centralized IDPS control strategy A control strategy in which all IDPS control functions are implemented and managed in a central location.

certificate revocation list (CRL) A list of revoked digital certificates, published by a certificate authority.

certification The comprehensive evaluation of the technical and nontechnical security controls of an IT system to support the accreditation process that establishes the extent to which a particular design and implementation meets a set of specified security requirements.

chain of custody A legal record of where the evidence was at each point in its lifetime as well as documentation of each and every access there was to it.

change management A managerial function designed to document and control changes to an organization's information assets. Change management is separate from but related to configuration management.

change request A formal request for modification to a system, submitted to the appropriate decision-making body, after the need for a change is identified.

channel One-way flow of information from a sender to a receiver.

chief information officer (CIO) The member of an organization's management team (often the senior technology officer) who is in charge of all information systems.

chief information security officer (CISO) The member of an organization's management team who is primarily responsible for the assessment, management, and implementation of information security.

C.I.A. triad An industry standard for computer security based on three characteristics of information that form the foundation for many security programs: confidentiality, integrity, and availability. Sometimes called the "C.I.A. triangle."

cipher Encryption method or process that encompasses the algorithm, key, and procedures to perform encryption or decryption.

ciphertext A message after encryption has been applied.

circuit Two-way flow of information between a sender and a receiver.

circuit-level gateway A firewall that operates at the Transport layer and prevents direct connections between one network and another by creating tunnels connecting specific processes or systems on each side of the firewall and then allowing only authorized traffic, such as a specific type of TCP connection for authorized users, in these tunnels.

clipping level With statistical-anomaly-based IDPS, this refers to the established baseline of normal network traffic. The IDPS periodically samples network activity and, using statistical methods, compares the sampled network activity to this baseline.

COBIT *See* "Control Objectives for Information and Related Technology."

code To translate components (words or phrases) of an unencrypted message into encrypted components.

collision A situation in which more than one network station attempts to transmit at a given time.

Common Gateway Interface (CGI) An API that allows external programs or scripts to interact with a Web server.

communications security The protection of an organization's communications media, technology, and content.

computer forensics The use of technical investigation and analysis techniques to identify, collect, preserve, and analyze electronic items of potential evidentiary value so that they may be admitted as evidence in a court of law, used to support administrative action, or simply used to further analyze suspicious data.

computer incident An attack that affects information resources and/or assets, causing actual damage or other disruptions.

computer log A detailed chronological record of a computer system's operation, including the use of that system and any modifications to it.

Computer Security Incident Response Team (CSIRT) A group of individuals who will be mobilized when a computer incident is detected and the incident response plan is activated.

computer viruses Segments of code that perform malicious actions, including macro viruses and boot viruses.

confidence A value placed on an IDPS's ability to correctly detect and identify certain types of attacks. The confidence value an organization places on the IDPS, IDPS signatures, or specific events is based on experience and past performance measurements.

confidentiality A characteristic of information in which it is limited or restricted to authorized individuals or systems and thus protected from disclosure or exposure.

configuration management The identification, inventory, and documentation of an information system's current status—the hardware, software, and networking configurations. *See* "change management."

configuration rule policies The specific instructions entered into a security system to regulate how it reacts to the data it receives.

connection-less model A network model in which individual packets are transmitted separately, without prior negotiation, each with its own addressing information.

connection-oriented model A network model in which a connection is established between two points, with all communications occurring over that dedicated end-to-end connection.

contention A media access control approach in which a station transmits data after listening to determine if the network is currently being used.

contingency planning The process by which the information technology and information security teams position their organizations to prepare for, detect, react to, and recover from man-made or natural events that threaten the security of information resources and assets.

continuous monitoring *See* "program monitoring."

control Security mechanisms, policies, or procedures that can successfully counterattack, reduce risk, resolve vulnerabilities, and otherwise improve the security within an organization.

Control Objectives for Information and Related Technology (COBIT) An IT governance framework and supporting toolset that allows managers to bridge the gap between control requirements, technical issues, and business risks.

correlation attack A collection of brute force methods that attempt to deduce statistical relationships between an unknown key and ciphertext.

countermeasure *See* "control."

country code second-level domain (ccSLD) Second-level domain under the country's top-level domain or ccTLD. For example, "*co*" in the FQDN of *mailserver1.mail.sampleorg. co.uk*.

CP *See* "contingency planning."

CP Management Team (CPMT) Also known as the CP team, the group of employees responsible for managing the overall CP process.

CPMT *See* "CP Management Team."

cracker An individual who "cracks" or removes software protection that is designed to prevent unauthorized duplication or use.

cracking Guessing, breaking, and/or removing software protection to gain access to a valid user account's password.

Cross-Site Request Forgery (CSRF) An attack that exploits a Web site's trust or previous authentication of a user.

cross-site scripting (XSS) An attack in which a legitimate Web site is exploited in order for the Web server to send unverified data to the Web client. The Web client, in turn, executes malicious code or is sent to a malicious Web site.

crosstalk The effect of one communications channel upon another.

cryptanalysis The process of obtaining the original message from an encrypted message.

cryptography The process of making and using codes to secure the transmission of information.

cryptology The science of encryption, which encompasses cryptography and cryptanalysis.

cryptovariable Information used in conjunction with an algorithm to either encrypt or decrypt a message.

CSIRT *See* "Computer Security Incident Response Team."

cyberactivist *See* "hacktivist."

cyberterrorist An individual or group that bypasses legitimate system controls so as to conduct terrorist (or, more often, terrorist-like) activities using technical or social engineering means.

data communications The exchange of computer-based or other digital messages across a medium.

data custodians Those who work directly with data owners and are responsible for the storage, maintenance, and protection of the information.

Data Encryption Standard (DES) A symmetric encryption system developed in the 1970s; now considered outdated.

datagram Packet organized into a header and data for transmission across a network.

data leakage The exfiltration or unauthorized release of an organization's data, which could include valuable company secrets, customers' personally identifiable information (PIIs), or other sensitive information.

data leakage prevention (DLP) Software or an appliance designed to crawl data at rest on hard drives, monitor data saved to removable media, and monitor communication systems like e-mail or instant messaging, looking for sensitive data leaving the network.

Data Link layer (DLL) A layer in the OSI network model that provides the addressing, packetizing, media access control, error control, and some flow control for networks.

data owners Those who are responsible for the security and use of a particular set of information.

data users The end users who work with the information to perform their daily jobs supporting the mission of the organization.

de facto standards Communication standards that have been widely adopted without having been formally reviewed.

de jure standards Communication standards that have been reviewed by a group of experts and endorsed by a standards body. Also referred to as "formal standards."

dead acquisition Powering down a system to copy the data (digital evidence) from the hard drives.

decipher *See* "decryption."

decryption The process of converting the ciphertext message back into plaintext.

deep packet inspection Detailed analysis that combines stateful packet filtering with the ability to analyze packet data used in communication to determine if there are any malware, inconsistencies, deviations, or malformed packets.

defense in depth A strategic approach to security in which multiple, concentric control options are implemented to ensure that the failure of one, or even several, control layers does not result in a loss to an asset.

denial-of-service (DoS) attack An attack against a network-based asset in which the attacker sends a large number of otherwise innocuous requests to a target, thus keeping it from being able to perform its primary function for legitimate users.

deterministic approach A media access control technique that outlines a controlled method of allowing clients to transmit data.

dictionary attack A form of password guessing attack that narrows the field for guesses by selecting specific target accounts and using a list of commonly used passwords (the dictionary) instead of random combinations.

differential backup A backup of all files that have changed or have been added since the last full backup.

Diffie-Hellman key exchange A method for exchanging temporary (session) private keys using public-key encryption.

digest *See* "hash function."

digital certificate A public-key container file that allows computer programs to validate the key and its owner's identity.

digital forensics The application of computer forensics to all modern electronic devices, including mobile phones, personal digital assistants (PDAs), portable music players, and other electronic devices capable of storing digital information.

digital signature Encrypted message that can be mathematically proven to be authentic.

Direct-Sequence Spread Spectrum A telecommunications modulation technique in which the original data stream is broken into smaller bits, then transmitted on different frequency channels simultaneously.

disaster recovery plan (DR Plan) The guiding document used by an organization to reestablish operations at the primary or new permanent site after a disaster.

disaster recovery planning (DRP) Planning process to ensure that critical business functions can continue if a disaster occurs, through specific steps to reestablish operations at the primary or new permanent site after the disaster.

disaster recovery (DR) team The group of employees responsible for development, testing, management, and execution of the DR plan.

discretionary access controls (DACs) An access control model in which the controls are implemented at the discretion of the data owner.

disk mirroring (RAID 1) An implementation of RAID data storage in which the system writes data to two drives simultaneously, providing a backup if the primary drive fails.

disk striping (RAID 0) An implementation of RAID data storage in which the system creates one larger logical volume across several available physical hard drives and stores the data in segments or stripes.

distortion The unintentional variation of a communication over a medium.

distributed denial-of-service (DdoS) attack A variant of the denial-of-service attack against a network-based asset in which multiple and geographically disbursed sources of attack (often bots being controlled by others) are used to deny service to legitimate users of a service or system by overloading the target with otherwise innocuous requests.

distributed system A method of interconnecting wireless access points to provide networking connectivity.

distributed system service A service provided by a distributed system to enable wireless access points (WAPs) to provide cross-domain connectivity for clients.

DNS cache DNS feature used to speed up communication by allowing the DNS server to provide translation results without having to look up frequent queries.

DNS open resolver A DNS server that provides address resolution but is configured so that anyone internal or external to the organization may query the zone's complete list of hosts and their translations to IP addresses.

DNS poisoning An attack in which incorrect translation information is inserted in the DNS server (or within the communication between the resolver and server) in order to take a legitimate domain name and point the resolver to a malicious server, thereby secretly subverting the session.

Domain Name System (DNS) Application protocol that translates an Internet domain name into an IP address for proper routing.

dotted decimal notation The typical network layer address scheme that, in IPv4, uses periods to separate octets, as in 192.168.1.114.

DRP *See* "disaster recovery planning."

DS *See* "distributed system."

DSS *See* "distributed system service."

DSSS *See* "direct-sequence spread spectrum."

dynamic addressing A method to manage a limited pool of addresses in which an address assignment server assigns an address from a pool to a network station, using a protocol like Dynamic Host Configuration Protocol (DHCP).

echo The reflection of a signal because of equipment malfunction or poor design.

encipher *See* "encryption."

encryption The process of converting an original message into a form that is unreadable by unauthorized individuals.

engagement letter A formal document that serves as a service agreement between the auditing team and the requesting entity.

enterprise information security policy (EISP) An executive-level document that sets the strategic direction, scope, and tone for all security efforts in guiding the development, implementation, and management of the security program.

enticement The process of attracting attention to a system by placing tantalizing information in key locations; considered legal and ethical.

entrapment The act of luring an individual into committing a crime to get a conviction; not considered legal or ethical.

ephemeral port Port numbers that are dynamically assigned as needed and have no special meaning outside the connection using them.

error control The process of handling problems with the transfer process, which results in modified or corrupted segments.

evasion The process by which an attacker changes the format of the network packets and/or timing of their activities to avoid being detected by the IDPS.

event Related to business continuity, an unexpected activity that might escalate or be later categorized as an incident or disaster. *See* "security event."

exclusive OR operation Function of a binary operation in which two bits are compared. If identical, the result is a binary zero (0); otherwise, the result is a binary one (1).

exploit A technique used to compromise a system.

exposure A condition or state of being exposed. In information security, exposure exists when a vulnerability known to an attacker is present.

Extensible Markup Language (XML) An extension to HTML that allows developers to define their own tags for structure. In other words, they can come up with their own dictionaries of tags—what each tag means and how the Web application or browser will handle the XML as it is passed to the client.

exterior gateway protocol (EGP) An obsolete routing protocol replaced by BGP.

extranet An extension of an organization's network using the Internet or other external network.

false negative The failure of an IDPS to react to an actual attack event. This is the most grievous failure because the purpose of an IDPS is to detect and respond to attacks.

false positive An alert or alarm that occurs in the absence of an actual attack, sometimes produced when an IDPS mistakes normal system activity for an attack. Also referred to as "noise."

FHSS *See* "Frequency Hopping Spread Spectrum."

File Transfer Protocol (FTP) Application protocol for transferring files between computer systems.

filtering The process of reducing events in order to increase confidence in the alerts that are received; the reducing occurs by restricting traffic using a criterion such as packet header or content information.

fingerprinting A systematic survey of a target organization's Internet addresses, conducted to identify the network services offered by the hosts in that range.

firewall Anything, whether hardware, software, or a combination of the two, that can filter the transmission of packets of digital information as they attempt to pass through a boundary of a network.

firewall rules Rules created and modified by firewall administrators that specify a protocol (such as ICMP, UDP, or HTTP), the IP address or address range, the TCP or UDP ports, and the desired firewall action.

footprinting *See* "reconnaissance."

frequency The length of the waveform of an analog signal, often measured in signals per second, or hertz.

frequency division multiplexing (FDM) A multiplexing technique used primarily to combine analog voice channels.

Frequency Hopping Spread Spectrum Method of transmitting radio signals by jumping (hopping) rapidly through a number of predefined frequencies.

Frequency Shift Keying (FSK) A technique used to embed digital information in an analog signal by manipulating the frequency of the signal.

full backup Complete backup of the entire system, including all applications, operating systems components, and data.

fully distributed IDPS control strategy An IDPS control strategy in which control functions are applied at the physical location of each IDPS component.

Fully-Qualified Domain Name (FQDN) Domain name that uniquely identifies a host by representing the host name, subdomain, second-level domain (SLD)—or possibly a country code second-level domain (ccSLD)—and top-level domain (TLD), separated by dots or periods (e.g., *mailserver1.mail.sampleorg.com*).

fuzz testing A technique that looks for vulnerabilities in a program or protocol by feeding random input into the program or the network running the protocol and then measuring the outcome of the random inputs to determine vulnerabilities.

general security policy *See* "enterprise information security policy."

go-ahead polling A deterministic media access control method in which the first client on the list transmits data if it needs to; if it doesn't, it notifies the next client that it may transmit data if needed.

grandfather-father-son backup Backup methodology that uses five media sets per week and allows recovery of data for the previous three weeks.

guessing attacking Attempt to bypass access controls by guessing passwords.

hackers Individuals who gain access, often illegally, to information or systems without explicit authorization.

hacktivist An individual (sometimes a group) who interferes with or disrupts systems to protest the operations, policies, or actions of an organization or government agency.

hash algorithm A mathematical equation that generates a message summary or digest that is used to confirm the identity of a message and to ensure the message's content has not been changed.

hash function *See* hash algorithm.

header That part of the network packet that is located at the beginning of the packet and consists of general information about the size of the packet, the protocol that was used to send it, and the IP addresses of the source computer and the destination. Also known as "IP header."

hertz A measure of signal frequency, typically one analog wave iteration or cycle per second; named after German physicist Heinrich Hertz.

HIDPS *See* "host IDPS."

honeynet A collection of honeypots connected on a subnet.

honeypot A decoy computer system designed to lure potential attackers away from critical systems as well as detect and monitor the attackers' activities.

host IDPS An IDPS that resides on a particular computer or server, known as the host, and monitors activity only on that system.

hub A device that provides a physical connection in order to link multiple systems. Hubs do little in the way of treating transmissions other than rebroadcasting them.

hub-and-spoke configuration A network topology in which any participant needs only to connect to the central server, not to any other machines.

Hypertext Markup Language (HTML) The primary markup language of the Web, which uses tags to tell Web browsers how to format the content displayed to the user.

Hypertext Transfer Protocol (HTTP) An application protocol that consists of requests and responses; it serves as the basis for the World Wide Web.

IDPS *See* "intrusion detection and prevention system."

IDS *See* "intrusion detection system."

impulse noise A sudden, short-lived increase in signal frequency or amplitude, also known as a spike.

incident An attack that affects resources and/or assets, potentially causing disclosure, damage, or other disruptions.

incident response (IR) The process that encompasses all the actions an organization takes when an intrusion is detected.

incident response plan (IR Plan) A set of defined actions taken by an organization when a suspicious event is detected or while an incident is in progress.

incident response planning (IRP) Planning process to ensure the organization can respond to an incident.

incident response team The group of employees responsible for development, testing, management, and execution of the IR plan.

incremental backup A data backup scheme in which all files that have been modified since the last backup are archived.

information security (InfoSec) The protection of information and its critical elements, including the systems and hardware that use, store, and transmit that information.

information security policy A set of rules that provides for the protection of the information assets of the organization. *See also* "enterprise information security policy."

integrity A characteristic of information when it is whole, complete, and uncorrupted.

intellectual property (IP) The product of creative thought and other activities of the mind, such as invention, literature, art, logos, names, symbols, and other creative works.

Interior Gateway Routing Protocol (IGRP) A distance-vector routing protocol that overcomes the limits of RIP to use other route metrics, such as bandwidth, delay, load, MTU, and reliability.

Intermediate System to Intermediate System (IS-IS) A link-state routing protocol that determines the best path for datagrams transmitted through a packet-switched network.

Internet Physical set of networks that supports a host of services to help users meet their information, entertainment, and communication needs.

Internet Assigned Numbers Authority (IANA) A department of ICANN responsible for coordinating domain names, the global pool of IP and AS resources, and protocol assignments.

Internet Message Access Protocol (IMAP) Application protocol used to allow an e-mail client access to e-mail located on a remote server.

Internet Protocol Security (IPSec) Open-source protocol framework for security development within the TCP/IP family of protocol standards.

intrusion An event characterized by the attempt of an attacker to gain entry or disrupt the normal operations of an information system, almost always with the intent to do harm.

intrusion detection The set of procedures and systems that identify system intrusions.

intrusion detection and prevention system A system designed to detect abnormal or malicious traffic on the network by using a network sniffer and then block that traffic using a firewall.

intrusion detection system Software designed to detect abnormal or malicious network traffic, which may indicate that a system or network has been compromised.

intrusion prevention A set of procedures and systems that deter or prevent an intrusion.

IPSec concentrators Routers that support IPSec set up at the perimeter of the LANs to be connected.

IP spoofing The falsification of the source IP address in a packet's header so that it appears to have come from a trusted or legitimate sender.

IR *See* "incident response."

IRP *See* "incident response planning."

issue-specific security policy (ISSP) A targeted policy that addresses specific areas of technology, stating the organization's position on each issue and how security in that area can be addressed.

IT auditing The formal review of a single system or entire IT infrastructure and program, which examines established control objectives and compares those to the organization's implementations.

IT security policy *See* "enterprise information security policy."

JavaScript A client-side Java scripting language developed to allow Web site authors to create interactive Web sites, primarily by interacting with HTML code to provide dynamic content.

jitter Signal modification caused by malfunctioning equipment, such as a faulty network interface card or hub.

jump rules A set of firewall rules that, when certain conditions are met, enables the firewall to execute a separate set of rules that examines the packet in question in much greater detail.

Kerberos An example of a centralized authentication and encryption service.

key *See* "cryptovariable."

keyspace Entire range of variables that can be used to construct an individual key.

Layer 2 Tunneling Protocol (L2TP) An extension of PPTP using IPSec rather than MPPE to encrypt data sent over PPP.

least privilege A principle by which members of the organization are allowed to access the minimal amount of information for the minimal amount of time necessary to perform their required duties.

LFM *See* "log file monitor."

Lightweight Directory Access Protocol (LDAP) Application protocol that provides a communication framework with centralized directories that hold a variety of useful data (e.g., user information).

link encryption Series of encryptions and decryptions among a number of systems, wherein each system in a network receives and decrypts a message, then re-encrypts it and sends it along to the next station in the system, the process being repeated until the message reaches its final destination.

live acquisition Collecting digital evidence from a currently running system.

local area network (LAN) A network that contains a dedicated server that provides services for connecting systems within or between a few buildings over a small geographic area.

log file monitor (LFM) A system that reviews the log files generated by servers, network devices, and even other security devices, looking for patterns and signatures that may indicate that an attack or intrusion is in process or has already occurred.

log files Computer files that record attempted intrusions and other suspicious activity, as well as mundane events such as legitimate file accesses, unsuccessful connection attempts, and the like.

loss The instance of an information asset suffering damage, unintended or unauthorized modification, or disclosure.

macro virus A form of computer virus that is embedded in the automatically executing macro code common in word processors, spread sheets, and database applications.

mail bomb A form of e-mail attack in which an attacker routes large quantities of e-mail to the target system to effect a denial of use for legitimate users.

maintenance hook *See* "back door."

malicious code (malcode) Software components or programs designed to damage, destroy, or deny service to the target systems; it includes viruses, worms, Trojan horses, and an expanding taxonomy of other malicious software.

malicious software (malware) *See* "malicious code."

man-in-the-middle (MITM) attack An attack technique used to gain unauthorized access to computers wherein an attacker monitors (or sniffs) packets from the network, modifies them using IP spoofing techniques, and inserts them back into the network, allowing the attacker to eavesdrop as well as to change, delete, reroute, add, forge, or divert data.

management information base (MIB) Instructions for an SNMP agent designed to gather information sent from a particular agent or class of agents.

managerial guidance SysSP A form of system-specific policy created by management to guide the implementation and configuration of technology as well as to regulate the behavior of people in the organization.

mandatory access control (MAC) A set of access controls in which the system enforces the controls without the input or intervention of the system or data owner.

McCumber cube A graphical description of the architectural approach widely used in computer and information security, consisting of a representation of a 3 x 3 x 3 cube in which the 27 cells represent areas that must be addressed to secure information systems.

medium The transmission channel used for data communications.

mesh configuration A network topology in which each participant has an approved relationship with every other participant.

message authentication code Key-dependent, one-way hash function that allows only specific recipients to access the message digest.

message summary *See* "hash function."

metropolitan area network (MAN) A network that covers a region the size of a municipality, county, or district.

mission A written statement of an organization's purpose.

mobile hotspot Service provided by a wireless telephony service provider to allow users to connect their wireless devices to a specific commercial wireless service.

modulation The process of modifying or manipulating the medium so that it can carry a message.

monitoring port A specially configured connection on a network device that is capable of viewing all the traffic that moves through the entire device; also known as a "switched port analysis (SPAN) port" or "mirror port."

monoalphabetic substitution Use of a single alphabet in cryptographic processes.

multifactor authentication The use of two or more authentication factors to authenticate remote users.

multiplexing The combination of multiple digital inputs onto a high-bandwidth stream to carry signals over long distances.

NAS *See* "network-attached storage."

NBA *See* "network behavior analysis."

need to know A principle that limits a user's access to the specific information required to perform the currently assigned task, not some category of data required for a general work function.

Network Access Control (NAC) An authentication technology that intercepts attempts to access the network and instead scans the system to determine the security of the system. If the system meets the internal security policy, it is allowed to connect to the network.

Network Address Translation (NAT) A method to manage a limited pool of addresses in which an internal network can use nonroutable addresses, but a device (e.g., router) provides translation between the internal address and the routable Internet address.

network-attached storage (NAS) Data storage via a single device or server that attaches to a network.

network behavior analysis (NBA) A method of evaluating network traffic, using a version of anomaly detection, to identify unusual actions or variations from normal operations.

network behavior analysis (NBA) system A system that examines network traffic in order to identify problems related to the flow of traffic.

network IDPS An IDPS that resides on a computer or appliance connected to a segment of an organization's network and monitors network traffic on that network segment looking for indications of ongoing or successful attacks.

network layer The layer in the OSI network model that is primarily responsible for communications between networks and has three key functions: packetizing, addressing, and routing.

Network News Transfer Protocol (NNTP) An application protocol designed to facilitate Usenet newsgroup communications.

network protocol analyzer An application or system that can intercept network traffic and decode it, allowing a network administrator to detect anomalous content or issues with the packet formation.

network security The protection of networking components, connections, and contents, which is the primary focus of this textbook.

network security vulnerability A defect in a network device, device configuration or implementation, or process or procedure that, if exploited, may result in a violation of security policy, which in turn may lead to a loss of revenue, a loss of information, or a loss of value to the organization.

networking The interconnection of groups or systems with the purpose of exchanging information.

noise (1) In communications, the various types of interference over a particular medium, including attenuation, crosstalk, distortion, echo, impulse noise, jitter, and white noise. (2) In IDPS, an alert or alarm that occurs in the absence of an actual attack, thereby rendering users insensitive to alarms and, thus, less likely to react to actual intrusion events; also referred to as "false positive."

nondiscretionary control An access control method in which the computer system implements controls as determined by a central authority and can be either role-based access controls (RBAC) or task-based controls.

nonrepudiation Verification that a message was sent by a particular sender and cannot be refuted.

object of attack A computer host, network entity, or other asset of value that is being attacked.

OFDM *See* "orthogonal frequency-division multiplexing."

one-time pad *See* "Vernam cipher."

open relay An SMTP server in which the administrator has not restricted who can use it to send e-mail.

open shortest path first (OSPF) Link-state routing protocol that, unlike RIP, does not transmit the entire router table, only information on the neighboring routers.

operations security The protection of the details of a particular operation or series of activities.

orthogonal frequency-division multiplexing (OFDM) A version of frequency-division multiplexing that carries multiple digital signals.

packet analysis Viewing a network packet to determine what type of traffic is being transmitted, who is sending, who is receiving, when the information is being sent, and even what applications may be involved.

Packet analyzer *See* "network protocol analyzer."

packet-filtering firewall A firewall that is installed on a TCP/IP-based network, typically functions at the IP level, and determines whether to alert the sender that a packet will not be delivered (reject), ignore a packet (drop), or forward it to the next network connection (allow) based on the rules programmed into the firewall.

packet monkeys A class of script kiddie hackers who use automated tools to inundate a Web site with a barrage of network traffic, usually resulting in a denial of service.

packet sniffer *See* "network protocol analyzer."

partially distributed IDPS control strategy An IDPS deployment method in which the individual IDPS agents analyze and respond to local threats but report to a central facility upon detecting enterprise-wide attacks.

passive vulnerability scanner A device or software program that listens in on the network without initiating traffic to identify vulnerable versions of both server and client software.

password attack An attempt to bypass password controls.

password cracking An attempt to bypass access controls by guessing passwords.

perimeter A boundary between two zones of trust, such as the organization's internal network and the Internet.

Perl One of the first programming languages used for its CGI capability, Perl was developed in 1987 by Larry Wall as an interpreted language (based on C syntax) that helped provide a more robust scripting capability for UNIX.

personal security The protection of those who are authorized to access an organization and its operations.

phase The period of time it takes for a wave to pass through a reference point twice.

phase shift keying (PSK) A technique for embedding digital information in an analog signal by manipulating the phase of the analog signal waveform.

PHP Hypertext Processor (PHP) A programming language that allows developers to create dynamically generated HTML content.

phreaker A class of hackers who attack the public telephone network to make free calls or disrupt services.

Physical layer The layer in the OSI network model that describes the placement of the transmission signal carrying the message onto the communications media.

physical security The protection of the physical items or areas of an organization from unauthorized access and misuse.

plaintext The original message, before any encryption is applied.

Point-to-Point Protocol (PPP) over Secure Shell (SSH) A UNIX-based method for creating a VPN.

Point-to-Point Tunneling Protocol (PPTP) A protocol used in VPNs to connect remote users to a network using a dial-in modem connection. PPTP most commonly uses Microsoft

Point-to-Point Encryption (MPPE) to encrypt data that passes between the remote computer and the remote access server.

policy (1) Guidance or instructions that an organization's senior management implements to regulate the activities of the organization members who make decisions, take actions, and perform other duties. (2) Specific instructions or configurations in a computer system that define the actions permissible by users of that system.

polyalphabetic substitution Use of two or more alphabets in cryptographic processes.

port scanners Tools used by both attackers and defenders to identify (or fingerprint) the computers that are active on a network as well as the ports and services active on those computers, the functions and roles the machines are fulfilling, and other useful information.

possession The ownership or control of some object or item.

Post Office Protocol 3 (POP3) An application protocol used to receive e-mail.

Presentation layer The layer in the OSI network model that is responsible for data translation and encryption functions.

private key encryption *See* "symmetric encryption."

privacy A characteristic of information that is used in accordance with the legal requirements mandated for employees, partners, and customers.

process A task being performed by a computing system.

program monitoring The process of maintaining ongoing awareness of information security, vulnerabilities, and threats to support organizational risk management decisions.

promiscuous mode Configuration mode for network interfaces that allows the device not only to see traffic destined for it but also to see all network traffic traversing the same network segment.

protection profile The entire set of controls and safeguards (including policy, education, training and awareness, and technology) that the organization implements (or fails to implement) to protect the asset.

protocol stack verification The process of verifying packets that are not malformed under the rules of the TCP/IP protocol. A data packet is verified when its configuration matches that defined by the various Internet protocols.

protocols The message formats and rules developed for communications, including syntax, semantics, and synchronization.

proxy server *See* "application-level gateway."

public-key encryption *See* "asymmetric encryption."

Public Key Infrastructure (PKI) Integrated system of software, encryption methodologies, protocols, legal agreements, and third-party services that enables users to communicate securely.

pulse amplitude modulation (PAM) A digital modulation technique that uses analog frequencies to encode one or more bits by measuring the height of the analog signal and converting that value to a digital binary code.

pulse code modulation (PCM) A common pulse amplitude modulation (PAM) version that uses an 8-bit sample size.

RAID 0 *See* "disk striping."

RAID 1 *See* "disk mirroring."

rainbow attack A form of password guessing attack that uses a database of precomputed hashes (or rainbow tables) derived from sequentially calculated passwords to look up the hashed password and derive the plaintext version.

rainbow cracking *See* "rainbow attack."

rainbow table A database of precomputed hashes derived from sequentially calculated passwords to look up the hashed password and read out the text version.

real-time blacklisting (RBL) The process of maintaining and making publicly available to e-mail providers a list of IP addresses known to promulgate spam or malware.

reconnaissance The process of collecting publicly available information about a potential target.

redundancy The process of planning for duplicate service capabilities, usually to improve availability in the event of a failure of a device or service.

redundant array of independent disks (RAID) Method of data protection with multiple levels.

Remote Authentication Dial-In User Service (RADIUS) A common protocol used to provide dial-in authentication.

remote journaling Transfer of live transactions to an off-site facility.

retention The period of time that log files or log file data should be maintained.

risk The probability that something unwanted will happen.

Rivest-Shamir-Adleman (RSA) algorithm First asymmetric encryption developed and published for commercial use, in 1977.

Robust Security Network Wireless network that, as a way of protecting against WLAN security threats, only allows connections that provide encryption.

Robust Security Network Association A wireless connection that provides encryption to protect against WLAN security threats.

rogue access point An unauthorized wireless access point.

roll-call polling A deterministic media access control method in which the central control unit polls each client to determine if it has traffic to transmit.

rootkit A form of malicious software designed to operate with administrative access while hiding itself from the operating system and monitoring tools.

routing The process of moving a Network layer packet across multiple networks.

Routing Information Protocol (RIP) A distance-vector routing protocol that uses hop count as its route metric; it limits the number of hops to 15.

RSN *See* "Robust Security Network."

RSNA *See* "Robust Security Network Association."

safeguard *See* "control."

SAN *See* "storage area network."

script kiddies A class of hackers of limited skill who use expertly written software to attack a system.

second-level domain (SLD) Domain below the top-level domain (TLD)—for example, "*sampleorg*" in the FQDN of *mailserver1.mail.sampleorg.com*.

security association (SA) A defined relationship between two network participants.

security blueprint The basis for the design, selection, and implementation of all security program elements; it is a detailed version of the security framework.

security domains Areas of trust within which users can freely communicate without the need to authenticate repeatedly.

security event An occurrence that might affect the system's security.

security framework An outline of the overall information security strategy and a roadmap for planned changes to the organization's information security environment.

security perimeter The boundary between the outer limit of an organization's security and the beginning of the outside world.

security policy *See* "policy."

security posture *See* "protection profile."

separation of duties A principle that requires that tasks be split up in such a way that more than one individual is responsible for their completion.

server clustering Multiple servers identically configured and placed online in an effort to ensure redundancy.

service level agreement (SLA) Contractual documents guaranteeing certain minimum levels of service provided by vendors.

session authentication An authentication approach that requires authentication whenever a client system attempts to connect to a network resource and establish a session (a period when communications are exchanged).

session key Generally, an encryption key that is valid for only the duration of one communication session between two host computers.

Session layer The layer in the OSI network model that is responsible for establishing, maintaining, and terminating communications sessions between two systems.

Shannon-NyQuist theorem A theorem that states that if a signal is sampled at a rate at least twice the highest frequency and at regular intervals, the sample will contain all the relevant information of the original signal.

shoulder surfing A process of observing others' passwords by watching system login activities.

signature Preconfigured, predetermined attack patterns used by signature-based IDPSs.

signature-based IDPS An IDPS that examines network traffic in search of patterns that match known signatures—that is, preconfigured, predetermined attack patterns.

Simple Mail Transfer Protocol (SMTP) An application protocol used to send e-mail.

Simple Network Management Protocol (SNMP) An application protocol used to monitor the status and performance of network devices and systems.

six-tape rotation Backup methodology that rotates six sets of media.

SLA *See* "service level agreement."

sniffer A program or device that monitors data traveling over a network. Sniffers can be used both for legitimate network management functions and for stealing information from a network.

SOA The first record in a DNS zone, called the Start of Authority, or SOA, for the zone.

social engineering A process of using social skills to convince system users to reveal access credentials or other valuable information to the attacker, which enables an attack or loss to the system.

socket The combination of Network layer address and port, which uniquely identifies the service requested by the user.

software piracy The unlawful use or duplication of software-based intellectual property.

spam Unsolicited commercial e-mail that is sometimes used as a means of making malicious code attacks more effective.

specific sign-on An access control method in which the client must authenticate each time it accesses a server or uses a service on the protected network.

split tunneling A configuration option in VPN systems in which two connections are allowed over a single VPN connection.

spoofing An attack technique used to gain unauthorized access to computers, wherein the intruder sends messages whose IP addresses indicate to the recipient that the messages are coming from a trusted host.

SQL injection An attack in which SQL instructions sent from a Web server to a database are modified from what was originally intended to be sent via URL or HTML form.

STA Abbreviation for "station," used to denote individual stations that are authorized as members of a particular BSS.

Standard Generalized Markup Language (SGML) A system for "marking up" documents by representing structural, presentational, and semantic information alongside content.

standard sign-on An access control method in which the client, after being authenticated, is allowed to access whatever resources the user needs to perform any desired functions, such as transferring files or viewing Web pages.

standards Detailed descriptions of what must be done to comply with policy.

state table A table that tracks the state and context of each packet in the conversation by recording which station sent what packet and when.

stateful inspection *See* "stateful packet filtering."

stateful packet filtering An examination of the data contained in a packet as well as the state of the connection between internal and external computers.

stateful protocol analysis The process of comparing predetermined profiles of generally accepted definitions of benign activity for each protocol state against observed events to identify deviations.

stateful protocol analysis IDPS An IDPS that employs stateful protocol analysis in order to detect malicious events.

stateless inspection *See* "stateless packet filtering."

stateless packet filtering Firewall packet inspection that blocks or allows a packet through based solely on the information in the header.

statistical anomaly–based IDPS An IDPS that collects statistical summaries by observing traffic that is known to be normal and alerting about events that exceed the clipping level; also known as "behavior-based IDPS."

statistical time division multiplexing (STDM) A time division multiplexing (TDM) technique that adds header information to each packet, allowing any station with traffic to transmit on an as-needed basis.

steganography Hiding messages in such a way that no one but the sender and intended recipient(s) know(s) the message exists.

storage area network (SAN) Data storage similar to a NAS that provides higher speed and higher security.

strategic planning A process of moving the organization towards its vision by identifying means and methods to accomplish change.

subject of attack A computer host or network entity used to conduct an attack on another asset.

subnet mask A notation that tells the network what parts of the address are subnet and what parts are host.

subnetting The process of internally dividing a block of addresses into smaller logical groups for ease of organization.

substitution cipher An encryption method that works by replacing plaintext values with other values to form ciphertext.

symmetric encryption Encryption method that employs a single key between sender and receiver.

syslog (system logger) A utility that allows multiple system utilities to log information using the same mechanism, thus alleviating the need for every operating system utility to implement its own logging facility.

system integrity verification Technology that benchmarks and monitors the status of key system files and detects when an intruder creates, modifies, or deletes monitored files. Usually integrated with a host IDPS.

systems monitoring The ongoing review of a system or network of systems to determine if the operational results and events are within the bounds established as proper functioning.

tcpdump A network sniffer that allows packet analysis. Because of its ubiquity in UNIX/Linux systems, tcpdump has become the de facto standard in network sniffing.

Technical Specification SysSP A form of system-specific policy designed to guide the technical configuration of a control; these are often access control lists or configuration rule policies.

telnet An application protocol used to connect to a remote computer and issue commands.

threat A category of objects, persons, or other entities that presents a danger to an asset.

threat agent The specific instance of a threat or a particular component of a threat.

TIA 568 A/B Data communications standards issued by TIA that ensures that both ends of a twisted pair cable are connected correctly between endpoints by specifying the color code sequence for wires crimped in a data jack.

time division multiplexing (TDM) A multiplexing technique used predominantly in digital communications that assigns a time block to each client, then polls each client in succession to transmit a set of information (predefined byte or block).

time-memory trade-off attack *See* "rainbow cracking."

timing attack A means of attack that uses a measure of elapsed time to deduce useful information about what is happening out of site. An attack method whereby the attacker eavesdrops on the victim's session and uses statistical analysis of patterns and inter-keystroke timings to discern sensitive session information.

top-level domain (TLD) Highest level domain for DNS on the Internet—for example, "*com*" in the FQDN of *mailserver1.mail.sampleorg.com.*

topology A physical or logical pattern of associations among network components.

Towers of Hanoi backup Complex backup methodology that uses statistical principles to optimize media wear.

trailer (a.k.a. footer) That part of the network packet that is located at the end of the packet and can contain error-checking data.

Transport layer The layer in the OSI network model that provides reliable end-to-end transfer of data between user applications.

transposition The process of rearranging plaintext values to form ciphertext.

trap A simple SNMP message providing status information about the monitored device.

trap-and-trace system A honeypot system that uses a combination of techniques to detect an intrusion and trace it back to its source.

trap door *See* "backdoor."

Triple DES (3DES) A data encryption protocol that improves upon DES by replicating the encryption process a total of three times.

Trivial File Transfer Protocol (TFTP) An application protocol similar to FTP that is designed to transfer files between computer systems over UDP.

Trojan horses Software programs that reveal their designed behavior only when activated, often appearing benign until that time.

tuning The process of adjusting an IDPS to maximize its efficiency in detecting true positives while minimizing both false positives and false negatives or grouping almost identical alarms that happen at close to the same time into a single higher-level alarm.

utility A characteristic of information that describes the information as having value for some purpose or end.

Vernam cipher A cipher that uses a set of characters only one time for each encryption process.

virtual circuit A technique that allows higher-level communications to occur without the overhead of packet reassembly.

virtual private network (VPN) A means of secure point-to-point communications over a public network.

vision A written statement of an organization's long-term goals.

VPN appliance A hardware device specially designed to implement VPNs and connect multiple LANs.

vulnerability Weaknesses or faults in a system or protection mechanism that open it to the possibility of attack or damage.

WAP *See* "wireless access point."

war dialer An automatic phone-dialing program that dials every phone number in a configured range (e.g., from 555–1000 to 555–2000) and checks to see if a person, answering machine, or modem answers. If a modem answers, the war dialer program makes a note of the number and then moves to the next target number.

wardriving The practice of driving around looking for and mapping insecure WLANs.

wave division multiplexing (WDM) A multiplexing technique found exclusively in fiber-optic communications that uses different colors of light to allow multiple light-based signals to travel on the same fiber-optic channel.

well-known ports Port numbers that are defined for most common services—the Web (port 80), SSH (port 22), Simple Mail Transport Protocol (port 25), POP Mail (port 110), and many others.

white noise Unwanted noise from a signal coming across the media at multiple frequencies; also referred to as "static noise."

wide area network (WAN) A very large network that covers a vast geographic region like a state, a country, or even the planet.

wireless access point A device that allows systems with wireless network cards to attach to a wired network.

wireless IDPS An IDPS that monitors and analyzes wireless network traffic, looking for potential problems with the wireless protocols (Layers 2 and 3 of the OSI model).

wireless local area network (WLAN) A group of interconnected networking nodes operating within a limited geographic area that offers network access by the use of broadcast rather than physical media.

WLAN *See* "wireless local area network."

work factor The amount of effort required to decode an encrypted message when the key and/or algorithm is unknown.

World Wide Web (WWW) A set of documents on the Internet linked via Hypertext Transfer Protocol (HTTP).

worms Malicious programs that replicate themselves without requiring another program to provide a safe environment for replication.

write blockers Devices that allow an investigator to acquire the information on a drive without accidentally damaging the drive's contents.

XML *See* "Extensible Markup Language."

XOR *See* "exclusive OR operation."

XSS *See* "cross-site scripting."

zombie *See* "bot."

Index

A

AAR (after-action review), 478, 481

access

  balancing information security and, 8–9

  described, *3*

  restricting to networks, 137

  spoofing, 15

access control

  categories of, 174

  discretionary, nondiscretionary, 176–177

  failure to restrict URL access, 334

  introduction to, 173–174

  mandatory (MAC), 174–176

  matrix (fig.), 177

  other forms of, 178

access control lists (ACLs), *24, 144, 183–184*

access control matrix, *24*

accountability, *173*

accounts, access control, 178–179

accreditation, *422*

accuracy, *6*

ACLs (access control lists), *24*

active intrusion prevention, 253

active vulnerability scanners, *366*

Adaptive Differential PCM (ADPCM), 43

addresses, Web, 74

addressing

  at DLL, 61

  dynamic, 66

  at Network layer, 65–67

Advance Fee Fraud (AFF), 17

Advanced Encryption Standard (AES), *103–104, 271*

after-action review (AAR), 478, 481

Aircrack tool, 364

AirSnare tool, 364

AJAX programming language, 326–327

alarms

  described, *220*

  IDPS response, 235

alert messages, *474*

alert rosters, *474*

alerts

  described, *220*

  IDPS terminology, 249–250

algorithms

  cryptography, *89*

  hash functions, 99–100

  S/MIME (table), 115

Almes, Guy, 37

American National Standards Institute (ANSI), 49

amplitude, *40*

amplitude shift keying (ASK), *43*

analog signals, 41

analog to analog modulation, 40–41

analog to digital modulation, 42–43

analysis tools, 356–372

antivirus programs with e-mail attachment alerts, 136

Apache Software Foundation, 354–355

API (application programming interface), *324*

application and services logs, 409–410

application backups, 457–461

Application Firewall, 159

Application layer, OSI Reference Model, 75–78, 80–82

application logs, 407–408

application protocol verification, *226*

application resumption, 451–462

application-level gateways, *148–150*

applications, and Application layer, 75

architectures

  electronic vaulting (fig.), 458

  firewall, 159–162

remote journaling (fig.), 459

virtual private network, 199–201

Web client/server, 319

wireless, 278–280

WLAN (fig.), 56

archiving, IDPS response, 236

ArcSight Logger report (fig.), 413

ARP poisoning, *287*

ARP-spoofing, 372

Art of War (Sun Tzu), 10

ASCII (American Standard Code for Information Interchange), 74

assets

  described, *3*

  safeguarding technology in organizations, 10

asymmetric encryption, *104–105*

Asynchronous JavaScript and XML (AJAX), 326

Asynchronous Transfer Mode (ATM), 60

attack methodology, *356, 357*

attack profiles, *465*

attack protocol, *356*

attack success scenarios, *466*

attacks

  See also specific attack

  on cryptosystems, 124–126

  described, *3–4*

  on DNS, 317–319

  on e-mail, 306–307

  on FTP, TFTP, 309–310

  on information security, 12–18

  on LDAP, 313–314

  malcode vectors (table), 12–13

  on NNTP, 315

  on SNMP, 313

attenuation, *46*

audit trails, enabling, 140

auditing